CIVILIZATION

A New History of the Western World

CIVILIZATION
A New History of the Western World

ROGER OSBORNE

PEGASUS BOOKS

NEW YORK

CIVILIZATION

Pegasus Books LLC
80 Broad Street
Fifth Floor
New York, NY 10004

First Pegasus Books cloth edition 2006
First Pegasus Books trade paperback edition 2008

Library of Congress Cataloging-in-Publication Data is available.

ISBN: 978-1-933648-76-7

10 9 8 7 8 6

Printed in the United States of America
Distributed by W. W. Norton & Company, Inc.

CONTENTS

ILLUSTRATIONS

Stone circle at Avebury, Wiltshire, *c.* 1800 BC (*The Ancient Art and Architecture Collection*).

The standing stones of Callanish, Isle of Lewis, Outer Hebrides (*The Ancient Art and Architecture Collection*).

Silbury Hill, Wiltshire (*The Ancient Art and Architecture Collection*).

The Greek Temple of Ceres, Paestum, Italy, sixth century BC (*Bridgeman Art Library*).

The Pantheon and the Egyptian Obelisk in Rome, second century AD (*Alinari/Bridgeman Art Gallery*).

West Front portals of the Cathedral of Notre Dame, Reims, begun in 1231 and completed in 1430 (*Bridgeman Art Library*).

'The Bishop's Eye', Lincoln Cathedral, fourteenth century (*Bridgeman Art Library*).

The Basilica of St Denis, Paris: view of the columns and vaulting in the ambulatory (*Peter Willi/Bridgeman Art Library*).

Rock painting showing a horse and a cow, *c.* 17000 BC, caves of Lascaux, Dordogne, France (*Bridgeman Art Library*).

Prehistoric rock paintings of horses in the Black Room, Grotte de Niaux, Ariege, Midi-Pyrenees, France (*Index/Bridgeman Art Library*).

The battle of Lapiths and Centaurs, from the south side of the Parthenon, 447–32 BC (*British Museum/Bridgeman Art Library*).

The Book of Kells: MS 58 fol. 104r, page of majuscule script with zoomorphic initials, by Scribe D, Irish (vellum), no date (© *The Board of Trinity College, Dublin, Ireland/Bridgeman Art Library*).

Viking animal head carving, from a sledge found with the Oseberg ship, ninth century (*Viking Ship Museum, Oslo/Bridgeman Art Library*).

Detail from the façade of San Pietro, depicting scenes from 'Le Roman de Lenart', twelfth century, Spoleto, Umbria, Italy (*Bridgeman Art Library*).

Palazzo Ducale, Piazza San Marco, Venice, begun c. 1340 (*Giraudon/ Bridgeman Art Library*).

The main square at Cesté Budejovice, Bohemia (*Martin Jones/ www.arcaid.co.uk*).

Palazzo Strozzi, Florence, begun in 1489 by Benedetto da Maiano and continued by Cronaca (*Guido Mannucci/Bridgeman Art Library*).

Palazzo Cattedrale di San Calisto, Rome (*Bridgeman Art Library*).

Courtyard of the Palazzo Pitti, Florence, fifteenth century (*Alinari/ Bridgeman Art Library*).

Trinity Episcopal Church at Broadway and Wall Street, New York (*Leonard McCombe/Time Life Pictures/Getty Images*).

Bronze statue of Poseidon, c. 460–450 BC (*National Archaeological Museum, Athens/Bridgeman Art Library*).

Venus de Milo, Hellenistic period, c. 100 BC (*Louvre, Paris/Peter Willi/ Bridgeman Art Library*).

Discobulus, marble copy of a bronze originial, after Myron (fl. c. 450 BC) (*Vatican Museum and Galleries/Alinari/Bridgeman Art Library*).

Bust of Pericles, fifth century BC (*Vatican Museum and Galleries/Alinari/ Bridgeman Art Library*).

Emperor Augustus holding a sceptre and thunderbolt, Herculaneum, first century AD (*Museo Archeologico Nazionale, Naples/Alinari/Bridgeman Art Library*).

Statue of Hercules and Cacus, by Baccio Bandinelli, 1534, Piazza della Signoria, Florence (*Alinari/Bridgeman Art Library*).

St Clement, Byzantine tempera on panel, fourteenth or fifteenth century (*Church of Sveti Kliment, Ohrid, Macedonia, Greece/Lauros Giraudon/ Bridgeman Art Gallery*).

St Michael, Byzantine tempera on panel, fourteenth century (*Byzantine Museum, Athens/Bridgeman Art Library*).

Madonna and Child, with St Jerome and St Francis, by Mirabello Cavalori (1510/20–72) (*Galleria degli Uffizi, Florence/Bridgeman Art Gallery*).

Detail from *The Last Judgement* by Fra Angelico (*c.* 1387–1455) (*Museo di San Marco dell'Angelico, Florence/Bridgeman Art Library*).

The Coronation of the Virgin, attributed to Bicci di Lorenzo (1375–1452) (*Santa Maria Assunta, Pescia/Bridgeman Art Library*).

Calvary, by Giovanni Bellini, *c.* 1465–70 (*Louvre, Paris/Giraudon/Bridgeman Art Library*).

Lamentation over the Dead Christ, by Fra Angelico, 1436–41 (*Museo di San Marco dell'Angelico, Florence/Bridgeman Art Library*).

Apache chief Geronimo, photographed in captivity in 1898 (*F. A. Rinehart/Hulton Archive/Getty Images*).

Native American girl carrying her sister, 1973 (*Keystone/Getty Images*).

Young man standing in the doorway of a store marked 'White only', *c.* 1950 (*Hulton Archive/Getty Images*).

Jesse Owens starting for the 200-metre final race at the Olympic Games in Berlin, 1936 (*akg-images*).

Persecution of the Jews: after the *Kristallnacht*, Jewish women have their hair shaved off and are forced to wear a sign reading 'I have been ostracised from the national community', Linz, November 1938 (*akg-images*).

French collaborators are led through the streets to be sentenced after the liberation of Paris, August 1944 (*akg-images*).

Gustav Mahler in 1892 (*akg-images*).

Igor Stravinsky, *c.* 1925 (*akg-images*).

The fifteen-year-old Pablo Picasso, 1896 (*akg-images*).

Bessie Smith, *c.* 1935 (*Three Lions/Getty Images*).

Aretha Franklin during her first recording session, 1961 (*Frank Driggs/Getty Images*).

Harold Pinter (*akg-images/Ullsteinbild*).

Tennessee Williams, *c.* 1950 (*akg-images*).

Huddy 'Leadbelly' Ledbetter, *c.* 1935 (*Hulton Archive/Getty Images*).

LIST OF MAPS

PROLOGUE

ON 21 September 2001, President George W. Bush said of America's response to the attack on the World Trade Center, 'This is civilization's fight.' On 5 December 2001, he declared, 'I'm not moving on because we're in a fight for civilization itself.' And nearly two years later, speaking about continuing attacks on US troops in Iraq, the President said, 'the choice is between civilization and chaos'. Other western leaders had already adopted the same theme: on 12 September 2001 Gerhard Schroeder, Chancellor of Germany, described the previous day's attacks as 'a declaration of war against the entire civilized world'; and on 8 October the leader of the British Conservative Party described al-Qa'eda as 'dedicated to the destruction of civilization'.

The events of 11 September 2001 shocked the world. They also focused our attention on what was being attacked – not only the lives of innocent office workers, not only some glass and metal buildings, but something less tangible and more difficult to define. In such a grave situation our political leaders needed to invoke something grand and noble, something strong and enduring to stand in opposition to the enormity of the offence that had been committed. Whatever we put up against the forces of terror needed to embody both the values of our society and its traditions; its current state of being and its history. The word that carries these meanings is 'civilization', so civilization became and has remained the entity that we wish to protect, and the concept for which we believe we must fight.

For most of the last 50 years we have allowed the concept of civilization to lie comfortably undisturbed, tucked away somewhere at the back of our minds. But the events of 11 September 2001 and its aftermath have brought this vague notion suddenly into the foreground.

Catastrophic events tend to focus minds. By invoking civilization at such a tragic and dangerous time, our political leaders have tapped into a latent but powerful belief and shown how central it is to our sense of ourselves. Our civilization is a reflection of who we are and what we value, but we are not used to thinking about what civilization really means to us. Now that the idea of civilization has been hauled out into the light, it must inevitably be subjected to closer examination: if the war *against* terror is a war *for* civilization then we need a strong sense of what civilization is.

The following chapters comprise an investigation of western civilization by re-examining the events and legacy of our history. Before we embark on that history, this brief Prologue will set out our past and current understanding of the concept of civilization, the reasons why we need a re-appraisal, and the arguments in favour of a historical approach. If we are to investigate the real meaning of civilization, then we need to understand from the outset that civilization and western civilization are quite different things. Though political leaders may like to pretend that one stands for the other, it is clear that the values that westerners hold are quite different from those of others – indeed the whole idea of 'values' can be seen as a western invention. The civilization that was invoked in the aftermath of 11 September 2001 was not Aztec or Chinese or Polynesian, but specifically western. The civilization that we must seek to understand is our own and no one else's.

We like to believe that western civilization is something we have inherited from the ancient Greeks, the Romans and the Christian Church via the Renaissance, the scientific revolution and the Enlightenment. Its spirit is embodied in beautiful buildings – Ionian temples, Gothic cathedrals, Art Deco skyscrapers – and in wonderful paintings, in the plays of Sophocles and Shakespeare, the novels of Cervantes and Tolstoy and the work of Galileo and Einstein. We sense that civilization is not *Hamlet* or Mont St Victoire or the Chrysler Building, it is not even Shakespeare or Cézanne or William van Alen; it is something to do with the spirit that inspired them and the society that allowed this spirit to manifest itself. This spirit is hard to pin down, but we believe there is some relationship between the cultural icons of the west and the values of western society, so that together they embody western civilization.

We nod in agreement when the leader of the western world tells us that our civilization has always stood for 'openness, tolerance, freedom and justice', but at the same time we recognize a potential difficulty.

The inclusiveness that makes civilization useful to political leaders is, of course, selective; they want us to think of civilization as tolerance, freedom of expression and democracy; not poverty, family breakdown, inequality, crime and drug dependency. If civilization stands simply for everything good, then we can happily fight wars on its behalf, but we can only accept this if we are prepared to divorce the theoretical values that we hold from the practical effects of western society over its history.

Here we have a choice to make. If we look at civilization purely in conceptual terms, then we can happily accord it every virtue, while giving its opposite every vice. But when we talk of defending our civilization, we do not just mean our present way of life, we mean the values that we have gratefully inherited. Civilization is not simply a collection of virtuous concepts, it is the historical effects that those concepts have generated. But we are only too aware that the history of the western world contains an almost unbearable amount of suffering and misery, of injustice and cruelty to ourselves and to others. Do we include war and torture, slavery and genocide in our concept of civilization? And if we simply place them outside our definition of civilization, are we not in danger of misunderstanding the real meaning of our past? If we seek a real understanding of civilization, we need to ask whether the glories and disasters of our past that accompany each other through the pages of history form a necessary conjunction. Does freedom always means the freedom to exploit others, is tolerance always matched by exclusion, is opportunity always partnered by selfishness and greed? The quest for the meaning of civilization must begin with the untangling of the threads of our history.

The word civilization was first used in eighteenth-century France, but the western idea of a civilized society dates back to ancient Greece and Rome. During the classical period, Greeks began to see themselves as not just different from, but better than, other peoples. When Herodotus, writing in the mid-fifth century BC, referred to 'the barbarians', this was really a shorthand term for non-Greeks; but by the time of Aristotle, a hundred years later, barbarians and barbarous nations could be defined by certain types of behaviour – their treatment of slaves, a barter rather than money economy – that were frowned on by the civilized Greeks. Barbarians had, through their cultural habits, become lesser people than the Greeks, who were seen by themselves, and later Europeans, as the epitome of civilization.

Civilization derives from *civis*, the Latin word for citizen. Although the Romans used the word *cultura* or 'culture', rather than civilization, to describe their spiritual, intellectual, social and artistic life, to be a citizen was to be part of this culture. The Romans, like the Greeks on whom they modelled much of their behaviour, believed themselves to be uniquely cultured. The two concepts of culture and civilization became, in retrospect, synonymous. Romans, surrounded by barbarians, also felt impelled to bring civilization to others; as Virgil wrote: 'Romans, be it your duty to rule the nations with imperial sway . . . to impose the rule of peace, to spare the humbled and crush the proud.'

The definition of civilization in the west was revived by the Christian scholars of the seventh and eighth centuries, such as Gregory of Tours and Bede, whose histories of the previous centuries showed Christianity under severe threat, before triumphing over the pagans. The organization of the church, its literacy and its alliance with the likes of Charlemagne allowed Latin Christendom to become self-consciously synonymous with western civilization.

The revival of interest in the classical world before and during the Renaissance re-ignited the idea of a distinctly European civilization reaching back beyond, and existing parallel to, Christianity. Western Europeans gave themselves a noble tradition by adopting Sophocles, Plato, Virgil and Seneca, as well as Christ and St Paul, as their cultural ancestors. The discovery of a New World across the Atlantic, and of multitudes of seemingly primitive peoples in all parts of the world, encouraged sixteenth-century Europeans to identify even more strongly with the ancient Greeks and Romans – civilized people surrounded by barbarians.

By the eighteenth century, when the word civilization was coined, European intellectuals were in a state of optimism about the essential goodness of the world, the grace of God, and the ability of the rational mind to categorize all knowledge and solve humanity's problems. The notion of civilized behaviour took hold as French-inspired *politesse* converted landowners, merchants and traders (previously possessed of bad habits such as living and eating with their workers) into refined gentlefolk with correct, if not exquisite, manners. Eighteenth-century gentlemanly culture seemed a welcome revival of the spirit of Athens and Rome and, while the optimism of the French Enlightenment wilted beneath the blade of the guillotine and the carnage of the Napoleonic wars, it blossomed again in the gentlemen's clubs of nineteenth-century

Britain. During the Age of Progress and the growth of the British empire, Macaulay, Carlyle and Buckle showed how the wonders of ancient Greece and Rome, of Venice and Florence, were of a piece with each other and with the marvels of industrial Britain. The Victorian historian Henry Thomas Buckle showed, in 1857, how civilization could be understood as a great chain of history whose first link, the civilization of ancient Egypt, 'forms a striking contrast to the barbarism of the other nations of Africa'. From Egypt the chain links led to Greece and on through Rome, the Renaissance, Reformation and Enlightenment, up to the present glories of British society. Those who lay outside this sacred line were discounted as barbarian – and those within as civilized. The civilized world of Buckle's time was not only self-defining, it had a mission 'to suppress, to convert and to civilise' the rest of humanity, justifying the European colonization of the world as a beneficial mixture of evangelism and moral superiority. The boundary between civilization and the uncivilized was easily drawn, even if it involved some sleight of hand when dealing with Moghul maharajas, and Chinese and Japanese emperors: civilization was white and Christian and everything else was barbarian.

The concept of western civilization as a continuous (if occasionally interrupted) chain of history was strengthened by renewed interest in both the classical and Renaissance worlds. Eighteenth- and nineteenth-century British, French, Dutch and German gentleman-scholars toured the Continent and went south to unearth for themselves the wonders of the past. Pieces of pottery, statues, carved stones, paintings and mosaics were transported north in huge quantities, and in hundreds of north European towns museums were built to accommodate finds brought from Egypt, Greece, Rome and Florence. Eminent Europeans took to having their portraits painted or sculpted wearing Roman togas and laurels, their houses imitated Greek temples, and their clubs and regiments all bore Latin mottoes. Political thinkers revived Greek words like democracy, and J. S. Mill even declared that 'The battle of Marathon was more important to English history than the Battle of Hastings.' The forging of the chain of history continued, as the fifteenth-century innovations in Italian art were named as the Renaissance, or rebirth, of European culture; a description confirmed by Jacob Burckhardt's magisterial 1869 book, *The Civilization of the Renaissance in Italy*. In the 1890s European colonization expanded dramatically and it seemed likely that the whole world would soon feel the benefits of western civilization.

This comfortable way of thinking about civilization came to a rude end in the Great War of 1914–18, when the deaths of 10 million soldiers, and the maiming and blinding of uncounted others, exposed it as a grand illusion. The 1914–18 war was either a conflict between groups of civilized nations, or a fight between the civilized nations (France, Britain, America) and those who had, quite suddenly, become uncivilized (Germany and Austria). Either way it was unarguably as much the product of western civilization as steam trains and Michelangelo's *David*.

How could civilization have come to this? How could so many millions have died so unnecessarily? The most persuasive answer came not from historians or philosophers, but from an entirely unexpected quarter. Sigmund Freud, whose views of human psychology were beginning to spread across Europe, had a startling and pessimistic message for humanity. Freud said of the First World War, 'It is not that we sank so low, but that we never came so high as we thought.'

Human beings, Freud argued, are prey to the base and brutal instincts that we inherit from our animal and primitive human ancestors. Civilization tames the brutal savagery that lies within all of us, but it cannot rid us of our instincts. Occasionally these break through the fragile veneer and we commit extraordinary acts of violence. Freud's explanation of the carnage of the Great War forged a relationship between individual psychology and the nature of civilization, and made psychoanalysis the dominant method for exploring that relationship. The boundaries of civilization were no longer drawn on a map around western Europe and North America, or in a historical space around ancient Egypt, Greece and Rome, but in ourselves. We became both the barbarians and the civilized.

Freud's theories overturned the nineteenth-century idea of civilization as a benign force and demolished the idea of human progress. His ideas were controversial and apparently novel, but they were actually a throwback to the radical pessimism of St Augustine, the fifth-century father of Christian theology. Catholic doctrine asserts that we are born bearing the sins we inherit from Adam and Eve. While baptism washes these away, humans are ready to sin at any opportunity. St Augustine's words: 'Take away the barriers created by laws, men's brazen capacity to do harm, their urge to self-indulgence, would rage to the full' could have been written by Freud, whose Augustinian ideas about civilization focused attention away from society and on to the individual. Ever

since then, the first place we have looked to find answers to the great
questions of war, cruelty, progress, hatred, creativity and destruction
has been the individual human mind.

More conventional historians tried to explain the upheavals in Europe
by mapping the rise and decline of the world's civilizations. Oswald
Spengler's *Decline of the West*, published in 1918, was followed in
1934 by the first part of Arnold Toynbee's multi-volume *A Study of
History*. Both were inspired by the nineteenth-century belief that history
was guided by universal laws. The historian's task was to show how
those laws applied to all civilizations.

By the early twentieth century a new barbarian force had arrived to
confront western civilization – mass culture. In the 1920s and 1930s,
European intellectuals spoke and wrote despairingly of the end of civi-
ization being brought about by the sheer numbers of the urban masses,
and their execrable cultural tastes and habits. Civilization could only
be preserved by a small elite producing and appreciating works of art
that were beyond the reach of the majority. Civilization became, in
some eyes, the preserve of the few.

We might have expected that the Second World War, the Holocaust
and the Stalinist Terror would have finished, once and for all, any idea
of human progress and of the benign effects of civilization. In fact the
opposite happened. The horrors of the Nazi era, while they made us
ask what it meant to be human, gave a new impetus to the belief that
humans could and must find their way to a better world. For a decade
or two, desperate to believe in a world of good things and buoyed by
the defeat of Nazism, westerners fell back on the old prescriptions.
While careful to avoid banal declarations of progress, cultural historians were able to share their pleasure in the 'greatness' of artists and
philosophers and the beauty of paintings, ornaments and great houses,
without feeling the need to ask whether these had been bought at a
price that was too heavy to bear. In choosing *Civilisation* as the title
for his 1969 television series about European art, Kenneth Clark deliberately pointed attention away from war and genocide, and towards
great artists and beautiful objects, as the true products of civilization.

The meaning of civilization for the now-dominant culture of the
western world has, through all these changes, remained ambiguous.
The writers of the United States Constitution were men of the
Enlightenment, utterly embedded in the classical tradition, while
European settlers used the idea of a 'civilizing mission' to justify their

takeover of the American continent and the destruction of its indigenous population. But America was founded in opposition to established European values and, particularly after the mass migrations of the late nineteenth century, became a different kind of society. The civilization of which Europeans spoke was in many ways an affront to American ideals – elitist and nostalgic where Americans were populist and forward-looking. And the mass culture and popular art forms that European intellectuals so derided in the nineteenth and twentieth centuries were, after all, mainly American creations. Only after the Second World War, when America assumed political leadership of the western world, did the potential arise for these contradictions to be resolved. Civilization became a more democratic, less elitist concept (a shift reinforced by the Nazi leaders' love of 'high culture'), and its meaning became both vague and inclusive – the whole of society, rather than a few elite art forms, was the basis of western civilization. This vague inclusiveness brings us back to where we started, with the revival of a concept that, while seeming to have lost some of its clarity, has clearly retained an extraordinary political and emotional power.

The two dominant ideas of civilization, the nineteenth-century 'great tradition', and the Freudian calming of the beast within, with its echoes of Christian theology, have remained with us at the beginning of a new century. The image of a golden thread of civilization, carrying the shining light through the barbarian darkness that surrounds it, has proved a powerful and enduring symbol for historians. In 1999 Christian Meier wrote that the narrow channel in which the Athenians defeated the Persian fleet at Salamis was 'the eye of the needle through which world history had to pass', while Kenneth Clark referred to the period when Christianity 'survived by clinging on to places like Skellig Michael, a pinnacle of rock eighteen miles from the Irish coast' as civilization getting through by 'the skin of our teeth'. At times like these the golden thread stretched alarmingly but it did not break. Our link with the great tradition was thereby both preserved and exemplified.

Historians also call on Freud's theories to explain brutal behaviour as a beast lying within us, occasionally breaking through the fragile restraint that civilization offers. Discussing the 1917 Russian Revolution and the subsequent civil war, Orlando Figes recently wrote: 'It was as if all the violence of the previous few years had stripped away the thin veneer of civilization covering human relations and exposed the primitive zoological instincts of man. People began to like the smell of blood.'

It is not only historians who make use of the notion of the beast within. Artists, film-makers and, in particular, crime writers are enamoured of Freud's vision of brutal humanity held in check by civilizing forces. As P. D. James has commented, crime writers are 'demonstrating how fragile are the bridges which we construct over the abyss of social and psychological chaos'.

In the last few decades these concepts, and the beliefs that sustain them, have looked increasingly shaky. Our ways of studying the past have radically altered, and traditional ways of learning history, so brilliantly lampooned as long ago as 1930 by Sellar and Yeatman in *1066 and All That*, have given way to a much more varied and richer approach to the past. We consume history with ever-increasing enthusiasm in books and films and on television and radio. But we do not want to be summarily told that Napoleon was good for France but bad for Europe, or that Stalin was a monster, or that Elizabeth I was a 'great' queen. We want to be given information, stories, documents, eye-witness accounts from the past and then make up our own minds. We know that events are never seen with an innocent eye, and that the historian's preconceptions are the dominant influence on the way that history is told. Historians have responded by abandoning their pretence at objective dispassion; instead of just giving us the results, they are showing us how they work and are sharing their methods, their difficulties, their uncertainties and their enthusiasms. In this atmosphere, Kenneth Clark's renewal of the tradition of 'great men' has lost credibility. What seemed a bold innovation in 1969 now looks like the last gasp of a patrician elite.

If new and more transparent treatments of traditional subjects are popular, then so are explorations of the previously obscure and the downright peculiar. Histories of cod, the spice trade, the Dutch tulip obsession, the search for a way of measuring longitude, eating fish in ancient Athens, and a thousand other stories have all found enthusiastic audiences. We now eagerly consume histories of cultures outside the great tradition: of India, of China, of Native American societies, of Polynesia and of Aboriginal Australia.

We have also developed a taste for the archaeology of the historic and prehistoric past, putting us in touch with the rich, and previously disregarded, culture of our ancestors. Studies of such things as mitochondrial DNA, ancient climate and vegetation patterns, isotopes preserved in human teeth and geophysical anomalies have opened up new and fascinating aspects of our history.

When we demand that historians show us the evidence of their work, and when our desire for knowledge of the past takes us into such byways of history, then the golden thread begins to look more like a river of time with a multitude of tributaries and backwaters and slow pools and sudden rapids. Or perhaps it is like a vast rope net rolled up into a ball, with connections made in every direction. The notion that European civilization, or indeed the very existence of civilization itself, has depended on the continuation of a particular, narrowly defined tradition begins, in the face of the multiplicity of the past, to look a little absurd.

One response has been to write and talk about civilizations in the plural. Authors such as Fernand Braudel (*A History of Civilizations*) and Felipe Fernández-Armesto (*Civilizations*) have written histories of different civilizations that avoid the traditional obsession with underlying patterns; while books like Robert Tignor et al.'s 2002 *Worlds Together, Worlds Apart* are aimed at the growing number of American college courses on world history that deliberately avoid the prejudices of Euro-centrism. Samuel Huntingdon's *The Clash of Civilizations and the Remaking of the World Order* (1996) depicted a world of several distinct and potentially powerful civilizations. In *Europe: A History*, also published in 1996, Norman Davies has given a new perspective on the history of Europe itself by showing, just a decade after the collapse of the Iron Curtain, how the stories of eastern and western Europe can and should be unified.

The fading of the old belief in the moral and intellectual superiority of Europeans has been given intellectual force by the emergence of what we might call environmental history. The American scientist and historian Jared Diamond has persuasively argued that geography, topography, climate, ocean currents and coastlines affect the development of different societies – not in some vague sense, but in ways that are open to investigation and measurement. In this analysis Europeans simply happened to live in a place that made them likely to develop technologies with which they could conquer the world.

*   *   *

If the idea of the great tradition has been pushed aside, what about Freud's revival of Augustine's belief that civilization tames the beast that lies within the human psyche? Freud's use of the behaviour of primitive man in support of his theories has proved a two-edged sword – impressive in the short term but vulnerable to hard-headed investigation thereafter. That investigation has shown that most of Freud's pick'n'mix anthropology was misdirected. Freud's promotion of the unconscious suffered not because the concept was wrong, but because he used his own idea of the content of the unconscious to explain every aspect of human life. And while psychoanalysis proved popular among mildly neurotic, or even apparently quite normal, if well-heeled, people, its failure to cure serious mental disorders has inevitably dented the credibility of Freud's theories of the mind.

But if we distrust Freudian ideas about civilization, then how do we account for the brutality of the twentieth-century wars that Freud explained with such apparent success? The theory of the 'beast within' gained great credence from the carnage of the First World War, but recent historians have developed a different approach to the psychology of warfare. John Keegan has argued that between the defeat of Napoleon in 1815 and the outbreak of war in 1914, Europe came increasingly to resemble a vast military camp. There was no geopolitical reason for this, since in 1815 Europe looked forward to a long period of relative peace. However, nearly a century later: '. . . on the eve of the First World War, almost every fit European male of military age carried a soldier's identity card among his personal papers telling him when and where to report for duty in the event of general mobilisation . . . At the beginning of July 1914 there were some four million Europeans actually in uniform; at the end of August there were twenty million, and many tens of thousands had already been killed.'

The military culture, which existed in parallel to civil society, had become ever more powerful and warfare had become an automatic response to political difficulties. Once the Great Powers went to war in 1914, the availability of millions of men, and the development of new forms of artillery and small arms based on high-quality steel, meant that massive loss of life was certain to follow. Keegan also shows that the ethos of glorious combat, of a noble death in war and the desire to destroy your enemy are elements of a peculiarly western idea of warfare – such murderous conflict would simply not have arisen in other cultures. From the historian's viewpoint, the world wars were not the reversion of European humanity to a primitive state of barbarism, but were born of a culture that had been deliberately promoted and fostered over the previous century.

These new ways of looking at history reflect our changed understanding of the world. But not only do they bypass the question 'What is civilization?', they make it increasingly difficult to answer. Our changed outlook on the world presents us with some stark difficulties. We have come to believe, for example, that so-called primitive societies have the right to continue their existence undisturbed. How then do we view a civilization that has routinely destroyed such societies and has justified such destruction on moral, religious and historical grounds? If our civilization includes our history and is an expression of our enduring values, then when these two are in such obvious conflict, what remains?

We can begin to answer these questions by looking at how we, the present generation, differ from our predecessors, and why our view of the world is so different from theirs. I have described how civilization has been viewed in the past, and given some of the reasons why those views have fallen away, but what are the particular characteristics of the present that influence our view of our civilization?

In the 1930s and 1940s it was quite clear what western society and western civilization stood for. Whether you were a socialist or conservative, civilization was everything that Hitler, Mussolini and imperial Japan were trying to destroy, and the task of civilization was to preserve itself. Belief in a Christian God had given way to belief in progress before being replaced by the urgent need to defeat fascism. Those who fought on 'the wrong side' saw this clearly too, once the war was over. The immediate task of the post-war years was not to rebuild the society that existed before – it was to make a fresh beginning. Nevertheless, the war took an enormous toll of the emotional and cultural energies of those who went through it, and after a brief flirtation with radicalism, the west subsided in the 1950s into a politically and culturally conservative society, eager to cling to what it had, static and frightened of change.

The 1960s were, in part, a reaction against the atrophying of society that followed the Second World War. The wartime generation was simply relieved to have survived and be given the chance to build a peaceful and prosperous world; their sons and daughters, then approaching adulthood, wanted something else. The previous sense of fighting to preserve civilization was transformed into a new belief that it was precisely the existing society with its hierarchies, its rigidity, its deference to authority, its 'doctor-knows-best' mentality that had been to blame for Europe's slide into conflict. At Nuremburg, when the world asked how citizens of a civilized country like Germany could have committed such horrors, the continual refrain was 'I was only obeying orders.' This harrowing phrase became the reverse shibboleth of the new generation – from now on, no one was to give and no one obey orders. Europe was ridding itself of the militarism that had haunted the continent for more than 150 years.

It is difficult in retrospect to appreciate the utter faith that most people had in the pillars of society in the immediate post-war period, and the palpable sense of personal and collective shock as one institution after another was exposed as hypocritical, self-serving and corrupt. In Britain the Suez crisis, Profumo, Poulson, Thalidomide, the demand for Catholic civil rights in Ulster and a series of miscarriages of justice ended our illusions and dealt immense blows to our previously rose-coloured view of the established order.

In America the disillusionment was just as profound and potentially more disturbing. The Vietnam war projected the futile brutality of the government into every living room, while the civil rights movement exposed America's dirty secret – legalized segregation and dehumanization of its black population – to the world. My Lai, the murder of Martin Luther King, the shooting dead of peaceful demonstrators at Kent State University, the sight of white cops beating black protestors in Alabama; all this and more repelled the generation that came to adulthood as it was all unfolding. In France, Germany and Italy the effects were the same, while the Russian suppression of the Prague Spring in 1968 destroyed any vestiges of admiration for the Soviet alternative to western society.

While members of the post-war generation were disgusted by the sight of the old order trying to hold the world still, the previous generation must have been dismayed at the antics of its children – their disregard for its struggles, their easy assumption of the wealth that came their way, and their joyous desecration of its icons. One of the central props in Joe Orton's play *What the Butler Saw*, which packed in London audiences in 1969, was a jar containing the preserved penis of Winston Churchill. This iconoclasm extended to anything and everything old and venerable – art, buildings, politicians, generals, education, culture. It was as if the sins of the past had been so great that only a total cleansing and fumigation of society would suffice. Everything must be thrown out so that everything could be built anew.

This social revolution happened at the same time as a sudden increase in affluence, particularly in western Europe (the United States had felt the effects in the 1950s). The disdain for authority and the desire for instant gratification were spurred on by the sheer amount of new, cheap stuff that was suddenly available to almost everyone – records, cars, clothes, transistor radios, cameras, telephones, colour magazines, tabloid newspapers and, above all, television.

In the 1960s, technology not only offered a better, more colourful, more interesting set of experiences, it also offered an escape from a communal, conforming, collaborative society. There was no longer any need for the family to sit round the fire in the evening 'making their own entertainment' or listening to little Annie murdering a succession of songs on the piano. Central heating and portable record-players and radios meant that every room in the house became a potential private entertainment centre. Teenagers' bedrooms were transformed from freezing dormitories entered only in the hours of darkness to warm dens full of gadgets beaming in music, photographs and sheer excitement from across the world. The communality of family life was abandoned in the pursuit of individual gratification and the novelties of remote shared experiences. More technology fostered more production and more spending power, which made new stuff ever cheaper and more disposable.

By the mid-sixties the excited enthusiasm for making and spending money began to pall among some members of the newly liberated young. The counterculture that formed in opposition to the Vietnam war began to turn its back on consumerism and individualism in the search for a new kind of communality and spirituality. It is this movement that is often taken to embody the spirit of the 1960s, though it was really an attempt to reach back to a time that the materialism of the 1960s was destroying. As it turned out, the counterculture stood little chance against the battalions of the commercial world and the more immediate joys of buying and having. The hippy movement's call for a new spirituality in the face of mindless consumerism fell on deaf ears. We chose to shop and have done so ever since. In this analysis we have gone on spending, not in spite of the changes that took place in the 1960s, but because of them.

The combination of consumerism, material prosperity and distrust of established authority has given us a troubling relationship with our past. It is as if we have simultaneously been gifted the keys to the treasure house and the knowledge of where the loot has come from. We want to enjoy our wealth, but we want to know how our world was built – and we are uncomfortable with many of the answers. Stories of the murderous exploitation of the rest of humanity, the crushing of other cultures, the genocide of natives of those lands we deemed desirable have all been absorbed by a generation whose distrust of the established order prepared them for the worst. This process has continued unabated; the genocide of native Quebecois Indians, the funding of the British Industrial Revolution by the slave trade, the torture of Algerian prisoners by the French army, abuse of Iraqis in Abu Ghraib prison; every week seems to bring a new revelation to add to what we already know, and to confirm our worst suspicions. We sometimes seem to have reached a stage of compulsive self-flagellation, where we positively welcome bad news that locks us further into our conviction of the ills that western civilization has brought on the world. There are individual stories of goodness and salvation in our past but these only emphasize the moral bleakness of the world in which they are set. Indeed, every heroic act engenders the suspicion of ulterior dark motives – a suspicion that is then confirmed by ardent research. Kennedy was a philanderer, Churchill a bully, Newton an insufferable egotist, Jefferson an adulterer, Hardy a cheat, Larkin a pervert; the list goes on and on. Even the saint-like Albert Schweitzer was culpable for his dismissal of modern medicines, while Mother Teresa is accused of doing more harm than good to the poor and sick of Calcutta.

What may have the greatest influence on our changing view of civilization is our growing disillusion with the most powerful of all western beliefs, the idea of progress. For the past 60 years the countries of the west have been at peace with each other, their citizens have enjoyed continuous and growing prosperity; scientific and technological developments have delivered ease of communication, convenience and longer life spans free of debilitating disease, while progressive legislation has encouraged and reflected an increasing tolerance of different races, genders and ways of living. And yet, while our lives are technically more comfortable and convenient, we are beginning to understand some of the illusory nature of our gains. The degradation of the natural environment, the destruction of family and community networks, the emergence of new diseases such as AIDS, growing obesity and mental illness among the young, the intractable increase in serious drug abuse, the growth in disparity between rich and poor, both within the west and between the west and the rest, the uncertainties brought on by a globalized economy; all are stark reminders that talk of progress must be heavily qualified. But there are more insidious aspects of economic prosperity that affect our daily lives. The last few decades have seen economics and business management applied to every part of life. Not only are governments, schools, colleges, public housing and hospitals subjected to a kind of techno-managerialism (with its accompanying meaningless jargon), we are constantly told to think of our lives as an individual long-term financial investment. We must put money and effort into our education in order to earn more later (and contribute more to our national economy), and while working we must continually think of saving for our old age. It has taken decades of economic prosperity for us to realize the costs of ever-greater efficiency. We see a life of unremitting work stretching ahead of our children, without the compensations of community life and connection with the natural world that we ourselves enjoyed.

The attacks of 11 September 2001 and their aftermath have put new strains on the comfortable idea that, for western citizens, life could just go on getting better. The danger of more attacks, immediate restrictions on civil liberties, arguments for the use of torture, the immense military power of one nation over all others, the contemplation of the use of battlefield nuclear weapons and the rift between and within western nations over issues like 'pre-emptive war' have provoked concern at the apparent fragility of the institutions that are supposed to uphold western values. Those who know their history recall how easily democratic values disintegrated in the 1920s and 30s in all but a few nations. We are beginning to wonder whether the peace and prosperity of the six decades since 1945 have resulted from the determined application of liberal values, or whether these are an indulgence that only continuous prosperity allows. Is the fading of memory of the Second World War allowing the re-emergence of war as an instrument of policy?

And where, in this shifting view of the world, do we place art, the jewel in the crown of our civilization? If we no longer believe in Kenneth

Clark's easy assurance that 'great' art is the ultimate manifestation of civilization, then what do we think about it? Has the predominance and ubiquity of popular art forms like pop music, film and television made so-called 'high art' redundant; and if painting, sculpture and literature often seem bent on criticizing, mocking or turning away from society's predominant values, then in what sense are they, and have they ever been, a celebration of civilization?

So, we have some difficult problems to resolve before we can say that we understand what our civilization really means to us. The mismatch between values and events; our persistent belief in progress versus the catastrophe of mechanized war and environmental degradation; our growing disdain for established authority against our belief in a noble tradition; appreciation of other cultures sitting uncomfortably with our desire to bring western liberal values to the whole world; our view of art as a vital critique of society, living alongside our historical view of fine art as the pinnacle of our civilization – all these contradictions make any use of the word or concept of 'civilization' dangerous and partial. Nevertheless, as I began by saying, civilization is the word that stands for what we most value about our society. We cannot simply dismiss it as being so full of contradictions as to be meaningless, so we must make some attempt to understand it. This, I suggest, can only be done by looking at the whole of western history in the spirit of the present: seeing how values and events are connected, investigating the context in which ideas that we take for granted arose, bringing cultural, philosophical, social and political history together, and viewing received wisdom and venerable authority with healthy scepticism. Before we embark on that history, I want first to say some things about the ways in which we look at the past.

History, the evidence-based investigation and interpretation of the past, is another of those concepts that is peculiar to the west – indeed, the invention of history will be one of the first subjects we have to deal with. I have already argued that history depends on the outlook of both historian and audience, and that each of them has interests that drive the direction of their research or their consumption of history. But history, despite the recent expansion of interests and approaches, is still written by the winners. Anyone who has the educational, financial and social wherewithal to have a book or article or paper published or to front a TV series has done well out of western society, and his or her viewpoint must reflect that benefit. A history of the west written by a confused drug addict facing 40 years' imprisonment in California for his third offence of stealing chocolate bars, or by a farmhand who has never left his Galician village, would look very different from any that we have ever read. Such a document will never be produced and we cannot will it into existence, but we should be aware of its absence.

The same applies to the timing of history. Wordsworth said that poetry 'takes its origin from emotion recollected in tranquillity'. History too is written after the din of battle. Again, we do not have an account of western civilization written from Oradour-sur-Glane or Auschwitz in 1944, or from Kolyma labour camp. What would history look like if the point of reference – the present – were a living hell? We can never know because, although we have the personal accounts of survivors, history is not written at such times and in such places.

History is also, as Harold Wilson said of politics, 'the art of the possible'. Everything that is written or said by historians depends, ultimately, on evidence and mostly on written evidence. Societies and cultures that had no written language are almost beyond our reach, while great epochs and many aspects of western civilization are a blank page to us because documents have not survived, or because many of the things our ancestors did were not recorded. (The great task of recent and current European history is, as I have already hinted, the construction of the history of these neglected epochs from archaeological and other non-written evidence.) Conversely, as we come nearer to the present, there is such an abundance of written material that the historian is in danger of being overwhelmed by the evidence.

It has been suggested that bird-watching is popular in Europe because the number of species is small enough to enliven the interest of the moderately dedicated, while being large enough to present a life-long challenge to the obsessive. There is something of this in the selection of historical subjects. We are endlessly fascinated by the sixteenth to eighteenth centuries, which is the period following the spread across Europe and beyond of printing based on movable type. In these centuries there are official documents, personal letters and county records to be unearthed, as well as political pamphlets and newspapers. Much of the documentation is familiar, but there is always the chance of turning up something important in an uninspected ledger or letter. By the nineteenth century the romance of the search for those hidden gems wears off; the industrialization of printing and manufacturing methods means there is simply so much stuff that the historian becomes a selector rather than a discoverer. In the fifteenth and earlier centuries documentation is much harder to come by and largely restricted to official matters; the nature of the lives of the general population has to be divined by clever interpolations of whatever material exists, and here the chance of new discoveries is close to zero.

History is selective in the standpoint, background and social status of the historian, in the time it is written, in the availability of documents, in its connection to the great themes of the past, and in the possibility of new revelations and discoveries. If there is not much we can do to alter the course of our journey through the past, we should at least be aware of the invisible forces that guide our footsteps.

I

IN THE BEGINNING

Prehistory and Illiterate Societies

MODERN humans first came to the lands of the west around 40,000 years ago. At this boundary between geological time and human prehistory Europe was undergoing a succession of Ice Ages that profoundly affected the landscape and habitat. Humans arrived not as the ice retreated, but during an interglacial period; the story of the earliest people of the west is one of adaptation to an ever-changing world. These first modern humans came from north-east Africa and the Near East, where finds have been dated to around 90,000 years ago. They probably lived alongside Neanderthal humans for a short period before the latter died out, around 40,000 years ago, leaving *Homo sapiens sapiens* as the last surviving human species.

Europe was then, as now, a series of zones of vegetation. The ice sheets to the north (and around the Alps) were succeeded to the south by a vast belt of open tundra and steppe, with forests pushed back to the rim of the Mediterranean. Sea levels were around 120 metres below present levels, giving huge coastal plains in the southern North Sea and western France, forming continuous land out to, and beyond, Britain and Ireland. Though winters on the tundra and steppe were harsh, these open spaces were home to large herds of grazing animals, particularly reindeer, but also bison, wild horses, aurochs, and, in the earliest times, mammoths and other 'Ice Age' mammals.

It is likely that the earliest 'archaic' humans in Europe lived off finds of dead animals, but Neanderthals and modern humans developed methods of killing large mammals. Hunting is a task that must not be underestimated – the human animal (a feeble clawless ape) cannot kill even the most sedentary grazing animal without the use of tools and a degree of organization. With the influx of modern humans, blade forms of stone tools proliferated – scrapers, chisels, spear blades, knives, awls – with early Europeans showing consummate creativity, as well as practical ingenuity, in tool-making. From as early as 33,000 years ago there are examples of bone and ivory being carved, sawn, ground and polished with extraordinary skill.

Cold conditions meant that humans, like the animals they hunted, were seasonal migrants, going north in the summer and retreating south in the winter. To begin with they were probably opportunist hunters, but they soon developed more apparently reliable methods, which in turn affected the social organization of human groups. From as early as 30,000 years ago, hunter-foragers were drawn to the major migration routes of grazing animals. Vézère and the Dordogne valley, for example, were on the route of reindeer migration from the summer grazing on the Massif Central to winter habitats on the Atlantic Plain. The bone remains found at these sites are predominantly of one animal at each site, usually reindeer, indicating the systematic exploitation of a single species. The human communities became larger – tens or even hundreds of people lived at Laugerie Haute and Laussel in southern France and at Dolní Vestonice, Willendorf and Kostenski in central and eastern Europe. Such expansion was possible because the communities were more settled – instead of following herds, people could wait for them to arrive. This change allowed settlements to be established in cave systems but also on open ground, with substantial houses made of bone, stone and wooden posts. Although Europe was still largely unpopulated, population densities and bigger settlements increased significantly in those regions where the supply of animals was good.

On 12 September 1940 four French teenagers stumbled into a cave at Lascaux in southern France, and found the famous 'painted gallery'. The upper reaches of the chamber, together with much of the vault, were entirely covered in naturalistic paintings of aurochs, horses, buffalo, ibex and other creatures; further galleries showed carvings and paintings of yet more animals, all dating from around 17,000 years ago. The cave complex at Altamira in northern Spain, where excavations began in 1879, had already revealed tools and other artefacts, as well as paintings, created by humans who inhabited the caves from 18,000 to 14,000 years ago.

While their beauty and sophistication are clear to all, the discoveries at Lascaux and Altamira provoked a long and inconclusive debate on the function of art in prehistoric societies. The paintings are deep within the cave systems, they are almost exclusively of hunted animals (human depictions are rare and generally non-naturalistic) and, strangest of all, they are often painted on top of one another. We can only speculate that the painting of these animals was part of a ritual, and that the depiction of a bison, for example, was some attempt to connect with the animal or acquire power over it through spiritual means. We might dismiss these ideas as too functional, but we should be aware that all humans were, until recently, utterly embedded in the natural world – their source of food and sustenance, and a dangerous and a magical place.

The occurrence of artistic activity so early in human history is presumably connected to some small but significant difference between humans and other animals, while the subject of their art shows the degree of connection between early humans and their fellow creatures. All animal species are unique; the genetic mutations that produced humans simply provided the world with another member of the ape family. This ape seems to have a conscious faculty that allows it to think and plan and conceive in certain ways that other apes do not (combined with the unconscious mind, brain and basic anatomy that make it share such primate characteristics as affection, greed, sexual desire, social inter-course, companionship and violence). We need to tread carefully here since recent studies have shown that primates and other animals are capable of language-based communication together with a host of other activities (including deception and drug-taking) that were long thought to be uniquely human. Nevertheless, humans have always had an impulse to represent the world around them in pictures and images that is, so far as we know, unique. It is a fair assumption that this is connected to, and presumably a by-product of, our consciousness. The ability to conceptualize and plan and think ahead gave humans distinct advantages in tool-making, organizing food collection and hunting, and building shelters – all of which offered them a vastly greater potential range of habitation and diet than their primate cousins. But the same consciousness, as we know from our own experience, has led humans to look for and require meaning from the world around them. The ability to make a spear that will enable a clawless ape to kill a rein-deer is part of the same mental equipment that asks whether, for example, the phases of the moon are connected to the weather or to good hunting or to sickness. While most animals seem to deal with the vagaries of the world in a pragmatic, perceptual way, human consciousness rebels against meaninglessness. And so humans have constructed symbols, invented stories and engaged in rituals that bring meaning, that help them to understand the variations in weather, changes in fortune, health, hunting and harvest. Art, culture, religion and, latterly, science, have all been part of this process, which has been with us, it seems, from the beginning.

The occupation of caves like Lascaux and Altamira came to an end as the European climate began a rapid change. The peak of the last glaciation occurred about 18,000 years ago, and from 13,000 to 10,000 years ago the rapidly warming climate began to have a dramatic effect on the European landscape and its small human population. This transition marks the end of what is known as the Palaeolithic and the beginning of the Mesolithic period. By 10,000 to 8,000 years ago dense forest had spread across much of the continent, sea levels had risen, drowning coastal plains and cutting off land bridges, and open tundra was pushed ever further north. The human population moved north too, staying ahead of the encroaching forest rather than following the retreating ice. The human population in southern Europe (previously the area of heaviest population) dropped dramatically as the food supply diminished. The diet of reindeer was replaced by forest species, such as red deer and wild boar, while mammoth and giant deer became extinct. The size of human groups declined, while the artefacts that have been found show less concern with quality of craftsmanship and naturalism in art than previously. Tools made of wood, bone and antler replaced ivory and were more plentiful and varied. Archaeological finds of flint arrow heads (some found embedded in animals), axe and adze heads, scrapers and borers from the Mesolithic period are common, while antler mattocks and fish traps made from wickerwork have been discovered.

All of this indicates that humans struggled at first to cope with the dense forests of the south, while northern Europe and the Atlantic fringe became favoured regions for human habitation, with inland and coastal waterways providing a good source of food and transport. At Tybrind Vig, a submerged site off the Danish coast, fish-hooks with twine and 'textile' pieces made from a yarn spun out of plant fibres have been found, together with a decorated boat paddle. Pottery vessels (once thought to have been introduced by the later Neolithic farmers) were also in use in Scandinavia around 5,600 years ago, as were huts with

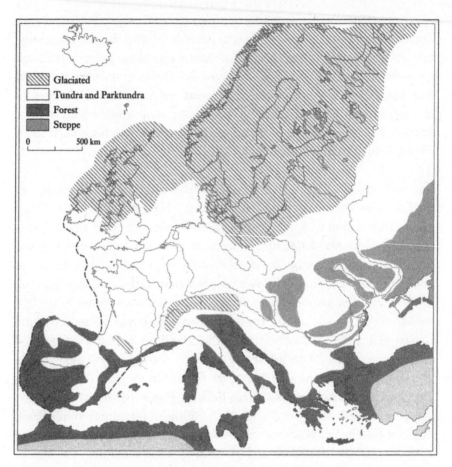

predominantly a vast area of open tundra, including the present-day seas off western France and the southern North Sea.

post holes and wooden floors made of split logs of birch and pine, interleaved with sheets of bark. Star Carr, a Mesolithic site near the east coast of Yorkshire, was almost certainly a summer outpost of the Mesolithic culture of Scandinavia. Finds at this lakeside settlement include antler headdresses, a wooden canoe paddle, antler harpoons and barbed arrow heads. The summer visitors ranged over about 200 square miles of forest and lived off red deer, roe deer, boar, fish, ducks and other aquatic birds (it is estimated that there would have been as many as 3,000 red deer living within their hunting area).

These northern Europeans had adapted to life on the edge of a forest moving ever north, but their environment continued to change. Studies of peat deposits at Star Carr have shown that around 11,000 years ago

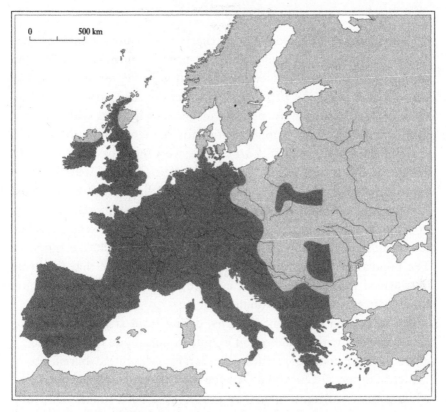

Eight thousand years ago, after a rapid rise in temperature, the same area was dominated by dense forest, to which our ancestors were forced to adapt.

willow and aspen began to encroach on the shallow lake, slowly draining its receding waters. The inhabitants cleared trees and scrub from the lakeside by fire, but changing vegetation defeated them, as, by around 10,500 years ago, dense hazel growth turned the lake into a bog and Star Carr was abandoned. Adaptation meant moving on.

The best-preserved dwellings of Mesolithic Europe are at Lepenski Vir on the Danube, which was occupied from 7,750 to 6,250 years ago. In this fishing village, hunters had settled into a sedentary lifestyle. Their houses were trapezoidal in plan and up to 30 metres square, built on terraces cut into the banks of the river. Sculptures depicted humans with fish heads, while the dead were buried with their heads pointing downstream, in order, it is thought, for their spirits to be carried away by the river. The river also embodied renewal as each spring beluga sturgeon, measuring up to nine metres in length and thought to represent the returning dead, came upstream to spawn.

Human groups adapted to the encroaching forests by inhabiting river plains, coastal sites, lakesides and the surviving northern tundra, but as time went on, they learned how to deal with the forest in inventive ways. The topography of Europe, with its unusual pattern of mountains, valleys, rolling hills, plains and plateaux packed within a relatively small space, gave opportunities for human groups to establish seasonal bases, as at Star Carr. These were not the fully nomadic people of the earliest times, but groups who made regular journeys from lower ground in winter, where the woodland, without its dense summer undergrowth, allowed easier movement for hunting, to uplands in summer. Europe in the later Mesolithic (from 6,000 years ago) had fewer but larger settlements, each with a series of satellites or outposts. The population as a whole recovered from the decline that the dense post-glacial forests first brought as Europeans learned how to exploit the variations in their environment.

The change in settlement patterns, dating from around 6,500 years ago, coincided with an alteration in human burial practices from single grave sites to communal sites. The largest Mesolithic burial site in western Europe, at Carbeço da Arruda in Portugal, has over 170 graves, while others with more than 100 graves have been found. This indicates settled societies and a greater interest in the fate of the dead. Late Mesolithic cemeteries give another clue to the changes in human society – remains from larger settled groups (e.g. Skateholm, Vedbaek) show a noticeably wider range of diseases, principally arthritis and caries, but also hyperostosis and rickets, than those from more mobile groups (Grotta dell'Uzzo, Arene Candide), which demonstrate evidence of caries but not much else. It seems that large permanent settlements carried increased exposure to both parasites and infectious disease.

Ornaments made from parts of hunted animals, like tooth pendants, were placed in Mesolithic graves, as well as effigies of animals and humans, harpoons, combs, spears and axes – as many as 400 items have been found in some graves. There was a noticeable change from the earlier art of the Palaeolithic, with its naturalistic depictions of animals, towards symbolic imagery, including depictions of humans, that is equally impressive in execution and effect. While the figures are non-naturalistic, the use of simple line and form to convey movement and drama is astonishing.

Many of the most developed Mesolithic sites have been found on Europe's Atlantic fringe – from the coast of Portugal to Brittany, the

British Isles and southern Scandinavia – leading to speculation about a distinct Atlantic culture. Certainly the variety and volume of food resources was immense and was fully exploited. At Mesolithic sites on the island of Risga off Argyll in Scotland, remains of every kind of shellfish have been found, together with tope, dogfish, skate, ray, conger eel, mullet, haddock, sea bream, great auk, gull, goose, cormorant, razor bill and guillemot, as well as both common and grey seals. Millions of discarded seashells have been found at Ertebølle in Denmark, a site that was probably occupied for 700 to 800 years.

Though early sea-going boats have not been preserved, it is clear from catches of bottom-feeders like cod, haddock and skate that boats made of hide stretched over wooden frames (similar to the traditional curragh boats of western Ireland) were in use in the Mesolithic. River boats made of single logs and of oak planks bound by yew and willow have been found at North Ferriby on the Humber. The earliest organized cemeteries in western Europe are also near the Atlantic coast, providing an argument for a separate sea-facing culture existing in a zone where food was plentiful.

The end of the Mesolithic period in Europe is marked by the coming of agriculture – the effect of the so-called 'Neolithic Revolution'. For 30,000 of the last 36,000 years, central, western and northern Europe was inhabited exclusively by hunter-foragers. During that time the natural environment of the continent changed out of all recognition. Climate, vegetation, even the shape and extent of the land altered dramatically and the survival of the human population depended on adapting to the changing world. In contrast the last 6,000 years have seen little natural change, while the environment has been drastically altered by human intervention.

Around 9,000 years ago, the practice of keeping domesticated animals and rearing crops began to appear in south-eastern Europe. Over the next 3,500 or so years these practices spread north and west across the continent, reaching central and western Europe by 7,500 years ago and the far north and west around 2,000 years later. But the spread of agriculture was a fitful process that revealed the underlying complexities of the existing European society.

European hunter-foragers learned to exploit small-scale variations in habitat, but the overall geography of Europe was also crucially important to its human history. A vast low-lying plain stretches from the

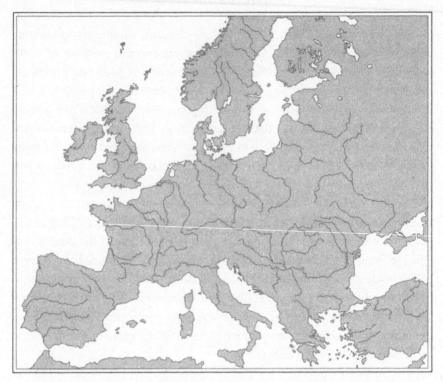

Modern maps show land features with the seas blank, but to our ancestors the seas and rivers of the west were highways, defences and an inexhaustible source of food.

Atlantic to the Urals, interrupted by rivers flowing north and south, which offer both natural boundaries and easy transport. The mountain ranges are high enough to give defensible sanctuaries, but none are so extensive that they are impossible for humans to cross. The European coast, with its vast quantity of sheltered coves, estuaries, inlets and offshore islands (over 10,000), and with relatively short distances between safe landings, makes for easy sea-borne travel and trade but also allows independent communities to grow up facing the sea, while protected from incursion by land. Italy, Greece, Scandinavia, Portugal, Spain, France, Britain and Ireland contain a multitude of islands and valleys that are close to impregnable from the land, while giving easy access to the sea.

It is almost certain that agriculture was brought into Europe by small groups of migrants, either overland from the south-east, or travelling west along the Mediterranean coast and then north. These were not indigenous hunters learning new techniques, but outsiders bringing their own culture, together with imported domestic animals and crops. The types of wheat, barley and millet grown in Europe were, for thousands of years, derived from Near Eastern varieties, as were the domesticated breeds of sheep and goat. In the heavily forested regions of central and western Europe these incomers encountered few groups of hunters, and were able (once they cleared forests by burning undergrowth and felling trees) to feed animals and grow crops on the rich loess soil of the flood plains of the Danube, Vistula, Oder, Elbe, Rhine, Garonne and Rhône and their multitude of tributaries. The farmers built large longhouses, mostly 15 to 30 metres long by 6 to 7 metres wide, sometimes arranged in groups and mostly without any defensive palisade. The early agricultural settlements were clustered together, for example in the Merzbach valley near Cologne in Germany. These people also brought a type of pottery known as bell beaker (one type, linear pottery, came via central Europe; another, impressed pottery, came via the western Mediterranean); pottery has been found in hunter-forager sites, but was much more commonly used by farmers.

The spread of agriculture was comparatively rapid across central Europe (c. 7,500 to 7,000 years ago), but when the farmers arrived in the north and west an interesting change took place. Firstly, on the northern fringe of Europe, they found the sand and gravel soil not conducive to crops – the inhabitants of a coastal zone from the Netherlands to Poland remained as fishers and hunters for around another thousand years. Secondly, on the Atlantic fringe they encountered a settled, well-developed group of hunter-fisher communities that had no urgent need of agricultural techniques. The coming together of the incoming farmers, either by migration or cultural diffusion, with the established Atlantic culture seems to have been responsible for an astonishing phenomenon that is without parallel in European history.

Across the landscape of north-western Europe looms a massive and deeply mysterious series of stone monuments whose scale, variety and meticulous construction have challenged our understanding of the world that our ancestors occupied and created. Neither the indigenous hunter-fishers nor the incoming pastoralists had produced anything of this scale or type before, nor do they appear elsewhere on the continent of Europe – the monuments are the products of a uniquely western European culture. From about 6,800 years ago megalithic tombs, often in the form of passage graves, began to appear on the Iberian coast and in Brittany, usually accompanied by massive standing stones, many decorated with carvings. The passage graves were designed for continuous use, with grave sites set along a central corridor. As farming spread west between 6,500 and 5,500 years ago, megalithic monuments were built on the Atlantic coasts of Britain and Ireland, with long barrow graves appearing in Wessex. The most impressive examples include passage graves at Newgrange and Knowth in Ireland, stone circles at Callanish on Lewis, the tumulus at Maes Howe, stone houses at Skara Brae, and standing stones at Howe, Brogdar and Stenness on Orkney, all constructed between 6,000 and 4,000 years ago.

The amount of work and ingenuity involved in building these monuments was prodigious. The so-called Grand Menhir standing stone from Brittany weighs 348 tonnes and would have needed 2,000 people to drag it from its source, while the passage grave at Newgrange is covered in 200,000 tonnes of rubble and turf. Above the capstone over the entrance to Newgrange a small opening has been left such that at dawn on the midwinter solstice 5,000 years ago, a beam of sunlight would have shone along the passage and illuminated a triple spiral carved into the wall of the main burial chamber. The chamber at Maes Howe (c. 4,800 years old) is constructed from slabs of stone fitted with extraordinary precision and topped by a corbelled roof. Like Newgrange, it is aligned with the sun at the winter solstice.

The Wessex area of England underwent an era of monument building after Orkney, with five complexes (Avebury is the best known) being erected around a central henge. Several huge barrows and the enormous Silbury Hill were all made around this time. An early construction at Stonehenge dates from about 5,000 years ago. The blue stones were transported from west Wales and erected around 1,000 years later. The trilithons were then added and the stones re-arranged in a circle and horseshoe, completing Stonehenge as the focus of a ritual complex reaching from the Channel coast to the Chilterns, and unequalled anywhere in prehistoric Europe. The bringing of stone from west Wales, and common patterns of spirals, squares and chevrons marked on entranceways, show strong connections between different groups over considerable distances. The presence of grooved pottery in locations as far apart as Orkney and Wessex demonstrates the extent of the cultural network of this society, while the locations themselves show that, for our ancestors, the 'far' north and west of Europe was not a remote region, but a territory with its own rich and sophisticated culture.

The sophistication of Neolithic society is confirmed by evidence of long-distance trading. A collection of stone axes found in the Pennines of northern England, for example, contains samples from established axe 'factories' in the north of Ireland, North Wales, Cumbria, the Scottish borders, south-west England, the Midlands, East Anglia and possibly Sussex. At the Pike of Stickle in Cumbria 450 tonnes of waste flakes lie on the hill-side, as debris from the manufacture of 45,000 to 75,000 axe-heads.

The Neolithic monuments of the Atlantic fringe were a central part of the lives of our ancestors, and the process of building, as well as their continued existence, undoubtedly carried great significance. Their astronomical elements demonstrate a continuous sophisticated culture, while the monuments themselves are a profound declaration of connection to a piece of territory and to the dead. Although monument building came to a halt around 4,400 years ago, the great mounds and henges remained a dominant feature of the landscape for millennia, and are likely to have held a spiritual meaning for generations of descendants of those who built them.

The introduction of farming into Europe was rapidly followed by a significant technological innovation – the smelting of metal. Smelting used the intense heating techniques needed for baking pottery and was probably developed independently in the Near East, south-east Europe and Iberia some time between 7,000 and 6,000 years ago. To begin with, worked metals, mainly copper and gold, were used for decoration and ornament. A 6,000-year-old cemetery found at Varna on the Black Sea coast of Bulgaria contained six kilograms of gold and even more copper, while copper dating back 6,500 years has been found in Almeria in Spain.

While metallurgy may have originated independently, around 5,000 years ago the development of urban societies in Mesopotamia began to affect Europe through their demand for goods and spread of techniques. Two-piece moulds and copper-arsenic alloys, wheeled vehicles, light ploughs and wool-bearing sheep, the domesticated horse and more substantial timber houses all arrived in Europe in this period. Different regions took these on according to their needs, but after 3000 BC shared burial practices show that Europe had become a more unified culture. Slash-and-burn techniques replaced small-scale horticulture, and flint was quarried for axes for more forest clearance.

Forest clearance, crop planting and the herding of domestic animals intensified and accelerated the human-made changes to the landscape. Local effects could be profound and long-lasting. As one example, the open landscape of the North York Moors in north-east England (and just a few miles north of Star Carr) was, before the advent of agriculture, a mixed forest. Early farmers began to fell and burn the trees to make clearings for penning wild deer and domestic animals and to create open land for planting. The effect, over a few hundred years, was to deprive the thin, fragile soil of its nutrients and its structural base. Useless for crops, grass or its original tree cover, its 200 square miles was abandoned by humans and became, and has remained, an open heather moorland on which hundreds of Neolithic tumuli have been preserved. (Ironically, the practice that ruined the land for cultivation made a wilderness whose beauty is now highly valued.) The conversion of Europe to a continent of intensive farmers absorbed the megalith and monument builders, and only in western Britain and Ireland did the old monumental culture continue. But the picture in the west showed significant differences from central Europe.

Archaeologists now stress the need to see the adoption of agriculture by indigenous hunters and foragers as a series of choices about producing food. These were particularly complex in a region like the Atlantic seaboard. Was it more productive to put out to sea in search of fish, to forage on the shoreline, to place fish traps, to clear forest and sow corn, to hunt in the forest for deer and boar, or to acquire domesticated animals? The answers would have been different in different times and places, and would not have inevitably flowed towards the adoption of agriculture. It has also been argued that the adoption of agriculture was disadvantageous for many people. A life of intermittent hunting and rest was exchanged for one of unremitting toil, which enabled more people to live together but benefited only those with power over these larger groups. This was perhaps less true of early western European farmers, who had some control over their own food production within small groups. Nevertheless, as game for hunting became less numerous, the choices available were reduced, and by 5,000 years ago, Europe had become overwhelmingly a food-producing rather than a hunting region.

Around 4,000 years ago the introduction of bronze smelting made metalwork more common. European metal-workers probably learned the basic technique of combining the copper of the Harz Mountains with the tin of Bohemia from contact with the Near East, but they developed their

own highly sophisticated ways of working bronze into daggers, orna-
mental cups, jewellery and axes, combining beauty and practicality. Great
hoards of highly sophisticated bronze and gold objects have been found
in spectacular burial sites in central Germany, which remained the heartland of bronze production in Europe for centuries, instigating a trading
network that reached across the Continent. Tin and copper ores were
imported from Cornwall, north Wales, Ireland, Brittany and Iberia, while
bronze objects were traded for amber, furs and leather goods from
Scandinavia and the west. The people of central Europe were also trading
directly with the eastern Mediterranean.

The increasing use of intensive agriculture, the spread of bronze and
other metallurgy and the opening-up of long-distance trade routes
implies a unified culture with a central controlling power. But it seems
that small sub-regional groups found that making alliances gave them
security, while none of them was strong enough to impose their will
on the others. The spread of the 'beaker' culture (so called because of
the beaker pottery found in graves) across Europe led to an assumption that some form of mass migration, or conquest, took place around
5,000 years ago. But archaeologists now believe that the trading
networks of Europe were sufficiently developed to allow the spread of
pottery techniques and of exotic new burial practices, and that these
were often adopted by elites as a way of distinguishing themselves from
the rest of their group. The emergence of wealthy elites is shown in
the later Bronze Age by spectacular single burials in Wessex (which had
become the crossroads of England), Brittany, Ireland and western Iberia,
as well as central Germany.

By 3,000 years ago Europe had become a mosaic of small settlements.
Work revolved around field agriculture – both animals and crops – and
workshop crafts, including metalwork. Trading networks were extensive and well established – a ship in the eastern Mediterranean might
carry ivory from Africa, amber from the Baltic, glass from Phoenicia,
copper from Iberia and tin from Cornwall (brought to the Mediterranean
through the river systems of the Loire, Garonne, Rhine and Danube).
The links between the Near Eastern and east Mediterranean urban
cultures and Europe were still tentative, but the collapse of the Minoan
and Mycenean civilizations around 3,300 years ago (see Chapter Two)
made the east and west Mediterranean into a complete trading system
that was, in its turn, to affect the west of Europe.

The movement of peoples, cultures and technologies that followed the collapse of Mycenae and the overthrow of the Hittite empire have proved difficult to untangle. There are theories that a mass of people came west from Anatolia, some diverting into the Aegean to build a new Hellenic culture on the ruins of the Mycenean civilization, while others pushed west to found the Celtic culture of central Europe. In the light of what we have already said about the beaker culture, these ideas must be viewed with caution. What we can say is that, from 3,300 years ago, new technologies and cultural practices began to be taken up across a wide area of continental Europe.

There was a surge in the amount of bronze being produced, while the introduction of the lost wax method allowed exquisite detail (as on the sun chariot found at Trundholm), and disposable clay moulds made the process of casting much easier. Cultivation of wheat and barley was supplemented by peas and lentils, and new crops like broad beans, millet, flax and poppy (used for oil). Honey and yoghurt, as a way of preserving milk, were brought into widespread use. Different groups and regions specialized in different domestic animals – cattle, pigs or goats – and horses became much more common, with bronze and later iron harnesses beginning to be seen as status items.

The change that is most apparent to archaeologists was the introduction, around 3,300 years ago, of cremation of the dead and the placing of their ashes in urns. This so-called Urnfield culture spread rapidly across Europe, again probably by a mixture of limited migration and cultural diffusion. The late Bronze Age Urnfield culture is closely linked with the apparent emergence of a people, or at any rate a culture, that we have come to know as the Celts. The survival of Celtic culture into recorded history (and of its remnants into our own times) gives us a dramatic link with the prehistoric past, but it now seems likely that the Celts themselves, particularly those in the west, were the descendants and inheritors of an even older culture.

Celtic history highlights the old problem of migration and diffusion. Did the Celts come west from a 'heartland' in the Caucasus, and spread across the whole continent before being pushed into the far west by other migrating groups? Or were certain cultural practices taken up by existing societies? The latter explanation has gained strength in recent years, opening up the fascinating prospect of a settled west European culture and people (albeit one that absorbed a succession of influences) stretching back into the Mesolithic and beyond. Our culture is a historical mixture, but its origins may well lie further back than we have previously thought.

Around 3,000 to 2,700 years ago the smelting of iron and trade in iron objects became more common throughout Europe – this was the beginning of the Iron Age. Celtic culture and innovation was then firmly established in southern Germany. By 2,450 years ago (the start of a period known as La Tène), the Celts were trading with Greek colonies in the western Mediterranean and with the Etruscans of Italy. Celtic culture spread out from southern Germany and Bohemia, and Celtic art showed the beginnings of its distinctive curved, flowing style. Craftsmen across central Europe and beyond began to show extraordinary skill, innovation and originality in iron-working.

In the fourth century BC (i.e. 2,400 to 2,300 years ago) there were definite migrations of Celtic communities across the Alps into the Po valley, and east and south into Macedonia and southern Greece; and as far as Asia Minor. At the same time the Celtic culture spread west to the Atlantic seaboard but it seems doubtful that this was also due to migration of Celtic people. The Celts of the west have traditionally been grouped together with those of central Europe on the basis of archaeological finds. But the continuity of local traditions, in Brittany and Britain for example, was much more dominant than the imports of La Tène culture. It seems the Celtic culture of the far west of Europe was a distinct variation on a continental culture and may not even have shared the same language. The Celts of the west are more likely to be descendants of the Atlantic people of Mesolithic and earlier times than of Iron Age incomers; and when we look at Celtic culture we may be seeing elements of customs that originated in the Palaeolithic era.

Celtic society was essentially agricultural. Early settlements comprised one or more longhouses, each shared by an extended family with their animals, and space for leather- and wood- and metal-working, all under one roof. The longhouse was superseded over time by individual family dwellings with separate buildings for animals and for grain storage and crafts. By the first century BC, there were separate rooms within the houses for cooking and sleeping. Agriculture became more intensive as experience was handed on from one generation to the next. Specialization of labour increased so that individuals and families could trade their goods and services. The population grew as agricultural productivity increased and land began to be divided by formal field boundaries. Villages, where trade and community could thrive, and land could be apportioned by agreement, became more common, and the field systems of Europe became ever more deeply established.

There were fortified settlements too; some were used as refuges, others as places of permanent residence, while a few may have been reserved for particular elite groups. The hill-forts that appeared across a swathe of north-central and western Europe, including southern Britain and northern France, were mostly abandoned after about 400 BC, though some remained inhabited until the first century BC. A number of sites dating from between 200 and 50 BC have uncovered craft villages where intense and large-scale manufacture of cloth, iron nails, glassware, bone, ceramics, metal brooches and coins took place. But the most impressive Celtic sites are the *oppida* – large settlements in defensive enclosures. Typically the enclosed area was 20 to 30 hectares, though some range up to 600 hectares and one, at Heidengraben in the Jura, was 1,500 hectares. (As compared, for example, with medieval Paris, which in AD 1210 covered 250 hectares.) Inside, some of the *oppida* houses were surrounded by their own fences and laid out in streets.

Celtic culture in continental Europe was severely affected by the Roman conquest and by the adoption of Germanic culture. But in the far west of Europe the Celtic culture (adopted and transformed by the indigenous people) remained intact into the era of written history and even, in some aspects at least, to the present day. Ireland, in particular, retained strong Celtic customs even in its adoption of Christianity. Historical accounts of Irish society therefore tell us something of the prehistoric culture of the west. Society was essentially loosely divided into a hierarchy of social groups, and was bound together by complex networks of kinship. At the top of the hierarchy was the extended family from which the monarchs were chosen. The custom of fostering favoured and talented individuals (also followed among the Roman elite) meant that the 'royal family' included many from outside its bloodlines. Allowing fostered children to be candidates for succession, with no rule of primogeniture, was a clever way of ensuring a high quality of leadership. Women were often leaders of households and were sometimes selected as rulers – for example Maeve in Ireland, Cartimandua of the Brigantes and Boudicca of the Iceni. Beneath the monarchs in the social hierarchy were clan leaders, similar in status to the class of druids, bards and skilled craftsmen and artists. Most of the population were commoners – small-scale farmers and craftspeople –

often described as 'freemen', whose rights and obligations were clearly laid down in customary law.

Customary laws, which are in effect rules for governing and regulating society, are present in every society, and many European customs are likely to date from the earliest Neolithic times, if not before. In some parts of Europe (particularly Ireland, Wales and England) they have survived as common law, though in others they have been brought into a formal set of constitutional laws. The crucial foundation of these customary laws was that the individual must be seen within the context of society and, more specifically, the intricate network of the extended family. If a crime was committed it was the family (in the broadest sense, the kinship group) that made reparation, and so it was up to the family to guide its own members in obedience to the customary laws, and to mete out punishment to them. The kindred shared rights and responsibilities, paid each other's fines, had a claim on each other's inheritance and stood or fell together. Disputes between family groups were generally settled by custom, but when conflict did break out, it was carefully managed, once again according to custom. Two groups of men would face each other across a field; the leaders or champions would come forward, shout abuse at each other, then engage in single combat. At the end the forces would disperse or there might be a general mêlée. This careful choreography kept destructive violence to a minimum, while satisfying the grievances of both parties, and was, as we shall see, quite different from the Greek and Roman method of making war.

While the vibrant mythology of the western Celts and the legends of their kings survived into the age of literacy, the druidic tradition of secrecy has meant that Celtic rituals and belief systems are difficult to penetrate. Nevertheless we know that belief in the afterlife was strong, while the voyage to the underworld, made through fabulous landscapes and strange adventures, was a major theme of Celtic legend. The content of these legends bears a strong relationship to the fluidity of Celtic art, full of ambiguity and paradox, where animals change shape and form and are interwoven in intricate patterns that elude and confuse the eye. Celtic literature is often taken up with riddles, and people and gods pass between the natural and supernatural worlds with such ease that there seems no barrier between these two spheres. For the Celts the world was an utterly enchanted place.

The place you went after death was called *Tir inna beo*, 'the land of the living'; a paradise where old age and sickness never happened, where music issued from the ground and food and drink appeared in magic vessels. This land was everywhere and anywhere – in the sea, under the ground, in caves, forests and lakes. Celtic gods inhabited places that evoked spiritual experience – groves in sacred woods, hidden lakes, springs, rivers and their sources. Offerings have been recovered from sacred sites at such places as Sequana (the source of the Seine), Llyn Cerrig Bach in Anglesey, the spring at Carrawburgh near Hadrian's Wall, which was a shrine to the Celtic goddess Coventina, and the well of Segais at the source of the Boyne in Ireland. The Roman writer Strabo relates that great treasures were plundered from sacred sites by the Romans, and Lucan tells that Caesar felled a sacred wood near Marseilles.

Each Celtic community probably had its own gods, whose attributes were changeable (there are over 400 known names of Celtic gods), and occasionally, one god would stand for everything sacred. Certain animals were sacred, including bulls (sometimes shown with three horns), deer, boars, horses, hares and geese, while human heads figure prominently in Celtic myth and carvings, and held deep spiritual significance. We associate all this with the Celts, but if western Celtic culture is, as it seems, continuous with the Bronze Age and the monumental cultures that preceded it, and thereby with the earliest inhabitants of the west, then these beliefs are the legacy of tens of thousands of years of cultural understanding.

The Celtic La Tène culture that spread across the west of Europe did not penetrate that strip of coastal territory that today comprises the north Netherlands and Germany, Denmark and Poland. Here the culture of the indigenous people, intricately bound up with their aquatic environment, seemed resistant to outside influence. These were, to later Roman writers, the Germanic people. In 320 BC the Greek traveller Pythaeus, who sailed around the island of Britain, distinguished the 'Germanoi' of northern and central Europe from the 'Keltoi' of the west, showing that the culture of the former was already superseding the Celts in the heart of the continent. It was the culture of the Germanic people, rather than Celts (or Greeks or Romans), that was to dominate the subsequent history of Europe.

The western Germanic people included the Angles, Saxons, Franks, Frisians and Alemanni; their language gave rise to English, German and Dutch. An eastern group, which included the Ostrogoths and Visigoths, Vandals and Burgundians, ended up in different parts of western Europe, but their languages have not survived. A northern group were the ancestors of today's Scandinavian people and their languages. The early history of these peoples is difficult to trace and once again we need to appreciate the complexities of migration and cultural diffusion. It seems that by 300 BC, the Gothic tribes had migrated south to an area stretching from the Danube to the Don – the traditional grazing and hunting lands of nomadic peoples of the east – while the western German people spread southwards into present-day central Germany (the Alemanni) and west into the Low Countries (the Franks).

Most of our impressions of these German peoples come from the writings of their Roman adversaries – though some, like Tacitus, praised these barbarians in order to make political points about Rome's own failings. Tacitus wrote *Germania* in AD 98, when Rome ruled the provinces of Upper and Lower Germania on the west side of the Rhine. He was impressed by the conduct of the regular assemblies: 'On matters of minor importance only the chiefs debate; on major affairs, the whole community. But even where the commons have the decision, the subject is considered in advance by the chiefs . . . If a proposal displeases them, the people shout their dissent; if they approve they clash their spears . . . The Assembly is competent also to hear criminal charges, especially those involving the risk of capital punishment . . . These same assemblies elect, among other officials, the magistrates who administer justice in the districts and villages.' Tacitus also approved of traditions of hospitality in Germania: 'It is accounted a sin to turn any man away from your door. The host welcomes his guest with the best meal that his means allow.' Julius Caesar noted that German magistrates or headmen allocated land to farmers to work on an annual basis so that there would be no accumulation of wealth, which was seen as a threat to the cohesion of society.

An insight into Germanic life has emerged from archaeological excavation of a site known as Fedderson Wierde. The remains of a Saxon village that existed from around 50 BC to AD 450, it shows cultivation of oats and rye on seasonally flooded fields, together with manuring and crop rotation. Germanic peoples knew about Roman towns and Celtic *oppida*, but preferred to live in small villages – settlements of 100 to 500 people with at least one communal meeting place or hall.

The Germans did not build temples to their gods, believing it would be absurd to contain them within any structure; instead, like the Celts, they held certain woodland groves to be sacred since these were places where the presence of Wodan, leader of the gods, could be most keenly felt. The intricate stories of Germanic and Norse gods, with their incursions into the world of humanity and their changes of form and substance, have survived. Most interestingly, in the light of what came later, these stories are set within an overall drama which begins with the creation of the natural world and ends with Gotterdämmerung or Ragnorak, the twilight of idols, the final battle in which the heroes and gods are slain.

Later Germanic culture flourished across much of Europe, particularly after the dissolution of the western Roman empire. The Frankish culture of much of western Europe and the Anglo-Saxon culture of England had their roots in Germany, but the transformation of England from a Celtic to a west Saxon culture is a good example of how myth and history became entangled. Generations of schoolchildren have been taught that waves of invaders from Jutland and west Saxony swept into the east and south of Britain as the Romans withdrew. The Celtic inhabitants of the lowlands were then forced back to the far west and north – Cornwall, Wales and Scotland – and England (or Angle-land) was occupied by people who became known as Anglo-Saxons. This story, which is almost entirely untrue, was largely created in the seventh century (i.e. 300 years later) by Bede. It seems likely that Bede's depiction, in the *Ecclesiastical History of England*, of a proud pagan people, settling in England and converting to Christianity, was intended to promote the idea of England as a single kingdom. The mass invasion of southern and eastern Britain by Angles and Saxons never took place, and there is some doubt about whether the Anglo-Saxon inhabitants of Britain ever existed. Villages from the British Anglo-Saxon period have been discovered on sites dating back to the Bronze Age – for example at West Heslerton in Yorkshire and at Lakenheath and West Stow in Suffolk – showing a continuation of custom, rather than a radical change. The Anglo-Saxon cemetery at West Heslerton was placed among Bronze Age burial mounds, and more than 80 per cent of the 200 human remains discovered were of people of Celtic, or old British, ancestry – and none suffered violent deaths or major injuries. This seems to have been a peaceful, stable community of around 100 people making a reasonably good living off the surrounding lands.

It had been thought that the incomers to Britain were attracted to ancient rather than Roman sites, but there is good evidence for continuous settlement of these sites right through the Roman occupation and withdrawal. Archaeologists now believe that the people of southern Britain retained the structure of their society through the Roman occupation and, from the fifth century onwards, adopted the culture of a relatively small number of Germanic incomers and migrants. The result was a combination of British and Germanic cultures – the resulting language, for instance, was Germanic in vocabulary, but Celtic in construction. The same process may have happened in the area of the Low Countries and northern France where the Franks, an originally west Germanic people, spread across the old Celtic lands of Gaul.

Perhaps the most important physical aspect of these non-literate western European cultures, and one that is easily overlooked by modern land-bound humans, is their intimate relationship with water. When you look at a map of western Europe try, instead of focusing on the land, to see the spaces in between. For the people of the west, the sea, rivers and lakes were their highways, the beaches, shoals and pools their food sources. Coastlines, river mouths and estuaries were seen from boats, not from clifftops or river banks.

The western people were highly skilled workers of wood, constructing buildings as weatherproof as any Roman villa, and boats whose design has never been bettered. Finds of buried ships, for example at Nydam in south Denmark, dating from 320 BC, have shown designs as well developed and executed as the Viking boats of a thousand years later. The famous ship buried at Sutton Hoo in Suffolk could have reached river settlements like York, or the south coast of England, within a day or so, and the French coast within two days. Roman roads are famous relics of European history, but for the indigenous people, both before and after the Roman occupation, they were a vastly inferior alternative to the Rhine, Maas, Scheldt, Seine, Loire, Garonne, Rhône, Douro, Tagus, Guadalquivir, Thames, Trent, Humber and a thousand smaller rivers, together with the coastal waters of the Baltic and North seas and the Atlantic.

The great ship burials, including Sutton Hoo, which contained more than 250 pieces of jewellery showing extraordinary craftsmanship, dating from about AD 625, show the centrality of the sea. The jewellery at Sutton Hoo displays the same shifting of shapes seen in Celtic art and Saxon brooches, jewellery and carvings and in illuminated manuscripts – the Lindisfarne gospels (inscribed about a century after the last Sutton Hoo burial) are a combination of Celtic and Anglo-Saxon imagery overlaid on a Latin Christian text. *Beowulf*, the best-known relic of Anglo-Saxon oral culture, has direct resonance with Sutton Hoo, since it begins with the funeral in which a king's body is set adrift in a ship piled with treasure, and ends with the burial of Beowulf's ashes on a headland overlooking the sea. These were seafaring people, linked by thousands of years of culture that pre-dated and survived the incursions of Rome.

Archaeology and anthropology (the study of humanity as a species) became serious disciplines in the late nineteenth century, a time when Europeans believed utterly in the progress of humankind, with themselves and their society at its leading edge. The history of humanity was fitted into a mindset where distance from western Europe matched distance in historical time, so that people in Tasmania, southern Africa, Alaska and Patagonia were remnants of the early days of humanity, and were the equivalent of the earliest Europeans. Progress could be traced on a map, as well as through time. In the early twentieth century, scientific illustrators invented the visual image of the cave man, complete with wooden club and fur loincloth (neither of which had or have ever been discovered by archaeologists). The archaeological divisions of the period were originally based on finds of tools, and so technological improvements became an obvious guide to the overall improvement, or progress, of early Europeans over time. It has taken painstaking work by thousands of archaeologists and anthropologists to overturn this simple fiction and present a more complex, nuanced and, it must be said, interesting view of our early history.

Contrasting European habitats enabled hunter-foragers to adapt to changing conditions. It has become clear that the systems of settlements of the early hominid, Neanderthal and Palaeolithic peoples was infinitely more complex than was thought as recently as 50 years ago. The range of environments that early Europeans inhabited has severely undermined the notion of technological progress; instead, archaeologists believe, we should think about differing peoples adapting themselves to changing environmental and social conditions. They look for evidence of survival behaviour by studying variations in the materials that have been preserved. One group of people adapted in quite different ways from another, not because they were backward but because their situation made different demands. This becomes clear when we study the same groups of people operating under varying conditions – mobile groups operating in different climatic regions used different 'tool-kits' for different tasks in different places. It is now apparent that you cannot date an artefact by its appearance, nor the 'advancement' of a group by the nature of its tools; a realization that makes technological progress through time a questionable concept.

Changes in social arrangements and types of artefacts have also been traditionally viewed as evidence of progress. But here too the evidence points to a complex series of variations and an unintended rather than a progressive improvement. The hunters of Europe realized they might have an easier time if they settled on the migration routes of the animals they hunted. But the consequent reliance on a single species and on a consistent migration pattern was potentially catastrophic if the single food source failed – particularly with a large settlement to support. This danger did not exist for smaller hunter-forager groups. Large, sedentary settlements also brought increased risk of disease – an unintentional trade-off between a life of healthy, but physically tough, continual movement and one that was less strenuous but with more risk of sudden food shortage and disease. Notions of territory to defend and attack become stronger too in settled rather than migratory communities.

The art produced by early Europeans also challenges our notions of linear progress. Is the naturalistic art of the Upper Paleolithic period more sophisticated, or somehow better, than the symbolic art of the later Mesolithic? Was the introduction of vibrancy and movement made at the expense of realism, and if so does this present a step forward, or back? These questions show that a much more fruitful relationship with the past (including the history of art) awaits us, so long as we are prepared to abandon the notions of progression that we have always been taught.

This chapter has pushed on from the hunter-foragers, the megalith builders and the farmers of the west, into and past the Roman conquest. What these people have in common is their lack of a written language and, as seems more and more likely, the existence of a continuous history. This continuity is obscured by the ways in which the people of the west absorbed and adapted and originated a huge range of cultural changes. These seem so extraordinary that we have long believed they must have been caused by migration or conquest, or at the instigation of some more advanced group of outsiders. But recent interpretations emphasize continuity and change, rather than interruption and progress. A western culture, diverse and ever-changing, existed in prehistory and survived into historical times.

When we mention the lack of a written language in this culture we are making one of the most significant yet unnoticed value judgements of history. The arrival of alphabetic writing has had an enormous impact on every aspect of western life. This is something I will look at in the next chapter, but it is worth considering the loss entailed when an oral culture disappears. The art of verbal story-telling is only one small aspect of this. The communal, local, interpersonal, instinctive, extemporary and impressionistic aspects of life become degraded in favour of the individual, distanced, considered and well ordered. Customary laws give way to written rules, experience to abstraction. The tension between these two ways of living has, as we shall see, become a central aspect of western life.

The story of the people of western Europe who lie outside written history gives us some interesting insights into the practice of history itself. Our tendency to mould the past into a comforting prelude to the present is most obvious when the past is so little known. An enthusiasm for archaeology, combined with a few chronicles and histories of doubtful value, enabled our predecessors to make a plausible story. The people of the west and north did not write documents, their monuments are inconvenient for putting in museums and remain mysterious to our modern minds. Our forefathers first placed them outside serious history and then romanticized them into an alternative culture to the European mainstream. The primitive Stone Age cave man, the wise druid, the advanced farmer, the ignorant pagan, together with stories of invasions and migrations (so easily inscribed on maps with a single stroke of the pen), were all in their different ways designed to dovetail into a particular vision of the world. But history is not simply guided by the political ideology of the time in which it is conceived; it is always a radical simplification of the past – and the 30,000 years of European prehistory are particularly vulnerable to our need to categorize, shape, conceptualize and explain. The absence of any individual voice, or name, or human face makes our ancestors seem like anonymous members of a sub-species, simply living out its destiny under the forces of history. But the adaptation of early Europeans to the dramatically changing environmental and social landscape should show us, not that this is some simply understood inevitable zoological process, but, conversely, that the multitude of choices involved in such adaptations are complex, contradictory, unconscious and blind, and their consequences unknowable and unforeseen.

When we analyse the past we smooth out complexity. The prehistoric past is divided into periods that give us a mental model but risk providing explanation instead of understanding. The technological development from Stone to Bronze to Iron Age looks like inevitable progress; the change from individual to communal and back to individual burial seems to indicate a changing relationship to land and property; the presence of common artefacts across the Continent shows a shared culture, maybe brought by migration; an ancient document, even if written centuries later, is a useful guide to historical events. Archaeologists and historians have learned to be wary of all these things, and to emphasize complexity and contingency. But we should be aware that new techniques and new evidence are, and always will be, just as vulnerable to categorization as was the Stone Age cave man of the nineteenth century. For all our technical ingenuity we will never be able to *explain* the building of such awe-inspiring structures as Maes Howe or Newgrange or Callanish or Stonehenge or Silbury Hill, and any understanding we have will always be based on our current view of the world. But what then should we 'do' with these remnants of the past; what use are they, what impact or influence can they have on our lives? Perhaps we derive most from these giants of human creation when we forget their place in some grand scheme, and simply look on them in a spirit of humility.

The past is a place of discovery, but it is also a setting for the stories we tell. Our desire for narrative and development and completion provides us with a past that, while often complex and contradictory, must be made ultimately comprehensible. As, through new techniques and discoveries, the prehistoric past becomes part of our history, it also becomes part of our civilization, linking itself to the present through geography, culture and connection to the natural world. But here is the paradox that history always presents – are we giving order to a past that, in reality, had none? Are we looking to the past for reassurance in the present; is belief that the world will unfold before us in an orderly fashion more comforting than the reality that we are faced with an unforeseeable future?

A TORRENT OF WORDS

Change and Custom in Classical Greece

WHILE the previous chapter related a history that offers no written evidence, we now turn to a part of European history that is overflowing with writing. The near-miraculous preservation of so many documents (as well as buildings, sculptures and artefacts) from ancient Greece completely changes the nature of our investigation of the past. The hopes, desires and motivations of Europeans need no longer be guessed at, while their myths, religious beliefs, laws, systems of government, discoveries and arguments are all available to us through the simple act of reading.

The use of an alphabetic written language did more for ancient Greece than preserve its history for future generations; it helped to give birth to astonishing changes in art, architecture, politics and humanity's view of itself, its history and the world around it. Historians and philosophers have struggled for centuries to explain the sudden appearance of such a range of cultural innovations in one place. Were the Greeks more intelligent, sensitive and artistic than anyone before or since, or did they have a rare inclination towards beauty, contemplation and rational thought? The absurdity of these questions (which were taken seriously until the last few decades) has been replaced by an analysis of historical, social and geographical factors, and one element that is receiving more attention is the impact of alphabetic writing. Much of the story of ancient Greece, which came to a climax in Athens in the fifth and early fourth centuries BC, can be seen as the struggles of a rural society based on ancient customs to adjust to prosperity, urbanization and the written word.

We have been taught to view classical Greece as a leap forward, out of the darkness of tribal life into the light of rational thought, democracy and aesthetic sensitivity. But the last chapter showed that so-called tribal existence should no longer be viewed as a collective life of blank ignorance: 'barbarian' prehistoric society was built on customs that distributed power and put restraints on crime and warfare in highly effective ways, adapted effectively to changing conditions and was capable of producing art and cultural artefacts that are beyond our comprehension. If we are to understand our past we need to see the relationship between these different European cultures in a less prejudiced and more productive way.

From 1899 to 1907, while working on the island of Crete, the British archaeologist Arthur Evans made a series of astonishing discoveries that revealed a previously unknown civilization. For over a thousand years, from about 2500 to 1400 BC, the Cretan city of Knossos had been the centre of a society that developed a sophisticated form of writing, used advanced techniques in working bronze and copper, and built great palaces for its kings. The Minoan civilization (named after King Minos) was destroyed around the middle of the second millennium, possibly weakened by a volcanic eruption and then attacked by invaders. Around 1200 BC the mainland city of Mycenae, successor to the Minoan culture, and the Hittite empire, which dominated Anatolia and the Near East, both collapsed. The causes and consequences of this collapse are little known, but it has been suggested that refugees from Anatolia came west, forcing those living around the mouth of the Danube to migrate south and east into the Greek peninsula and islands. The 500 years that followed the fall of Mycenae have yielded little archaeological or other evidence (they have been called the Greek Dark Ages), but it seems that the valleys and narrow coastal plains around the Aegean became inhabited by Greek or Hellenic people. The Greeks themselves believed they were the descendants of two tribes of immigrants, the Ionians and Dorians, who came into Greece from elsewhere, and many of their legends seem to derive from the great disruptions of the thirteenth and twelfth centuries (the fall of Troy is traditionally dated at 1184 BC).

The dominant cultural, economic, political and military powers of this region had for thousands of years lain to the east of the Mediterranean – in Mesopotamia and Anatolia. The Assyrian empire that succeeded the Hittites stretched from the Persian Gulf to the Mediterranean and, for a short period, to the Nile delta. But in the seventh

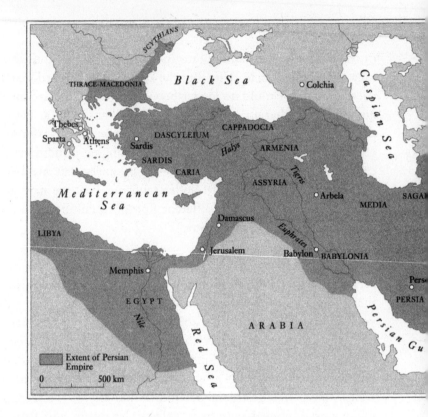

century BC, Assyria came under attack: in 625 BC Babylon was captured, and by 612 BC Nineveh, the Assyrian capital, was taken by a tribe known as the Medes. The Medes ruled the northern reaches of the Assyrian empire, while in the south the Persian people, originating on the Iranian plateau, came to dominate the Tigris–Euphrates basin. In 550 BC, Cyrus, the Persian Great King, defeated the Medes and established an empire that reached from the banks of the Indus to the eastern shores of the Mediterranean.

Successive empires had built their power on the agricultural production of the Fertile Crescent. But the move from the early agricultural settlements in the hills on to the vast plains of Mesopotamia involved risk. Exploitation of the fertile soil required sophisticated methods of irrigation and cultivation, lack of raw materials meant that extended, and therefore vulnerable, trading networks had to be established; and the open landscape forced the building of towns with defensive walls. In contrast to much of Europe, where small settlements were a response to the varied topography, the development of an urban society in Mesopotamia emerged from the dangers of the open landscape.

For the Hellenic people dotted around the Aegean Sea there were two important aspects to these developments. First, the imperial

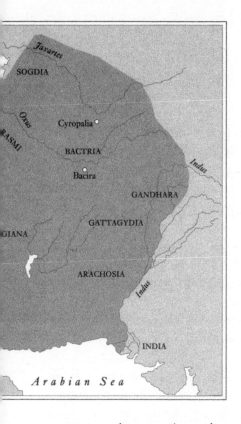

In 500 BC Greece was perched on the western edge of the vast Persian empire.

powers to the east were a huge mixing pot of cultures and traditions from a vast historical and geographical span. Cultural influences from as far afield as India and China, the Kirghiz Steppe, central Asia, the Hindu Kush, the Iranian Plateau, the Caucasus, southern Mesopotamia, Palestine and Syria, Anatolia, Lydia and Egypt had all been sucked into the Babylonian, Hittite, Assyrian and Persian empires, and all of this was available to the Hellenic people. Second, the Aegean area was irrelevant in the power struggles over the Fertile Crescent and so was left alone – the Greeks were left to go about their business unmolested.

Their business was fishing, agriculture, crafts and trade, and here geography and history were in their favour. Goods came to the Mediterranean coast from the empires to the east and were shipped onwards by merchant traders. This trade was dominated by the Syrians and Phoenicians of the Levant, whose territory lay on the most direct trade route, but as the empires spread north into Anatolia, the Aegean became more important. The Hellenic world was sea-based – Socrates aptly described the Greeks as 'frogs, squatting round a pond' – and settlements were located in the steep river valleys that cut through the mountainous interior of the Greek peninsula and islands. The mountains were difficult to cross but sea travel between the settlements was simple. The result was a plethora of small independent communities, sharing a language and culture but remaining physically separate and independent.

To the west of Greece was the Ionian Sea, southern Italy and, beyond Sicily, the opening into the western Mediterranean. From the eighth century BC, Greeks set up satellite colonies around the shores of the Mediterranean, spreading west to present-day Italy, Sicily, France and Spain. Southern Italy was so peppered with Greek colonies that it was later known to the Romans as Magna Graecia. The same myths, gods, rituals and poems were known in cities as far apart as Miletus on the coast of Asia Minor, and Saguntum in southern Spain. Opinions and ideas on all subjects were freely exchanged and transmitted across the Hellenic world without the interference of any central authority. Nevertheless the history of relations between the independent Greek cities presents a catalogue of wars in which betrayals, massacres and enslavement were commonplace.

Of all the cities of the Hellenic world the one we know most about is Athens, simply because the writings of Athenians, both contemporary citizens and later historians, have been preserved (itself a sign of the high regard in which they were held). In the seventh century BC the territory of Attica, with its principal settlement at Athens, began a transition from a loose collection of fishing and farming settlements to a single political entity. Historians suggest that before the seventh century there was little competition for political power, since society was simply an affinity of villages and families who came together to protect and promote their common interests, and who thereby felt an allegiance to one another.

Increasing trade with the east, and the discovery of silver at Mount Laurium, brought more prosperity to the Hellenic world and to Athens through the eighth and seventh centuries BC. The populations of the settlements grew and societies began to separate into a small wealthy core and a majority of ordinary farmers, fishers and artisans. Prosperity also necessitated a more formal organization of society, so that resources could be allocated, assets protected and disputes settled. Settlements turned into city-states as the urban life of the east began to be established in the valleys of Greece.

In communities and city-states across the Hellenic world certain families and individuals marshalled enough support to take political power for themselves. A string of single rulers, or tyrants, emerged; while in other places groups of families, or oligarchies, shared power between them. Herodotus records that in 632 BC, a man named Cylon attempted to take power in Athens: 'This man began to plume himself on his chances of becoming tyrant of Athens, and, with that end in view, collected a band of friends and tried to seize the Acropolis.' The attempt failed, but it shows that Athens had become a coherent political entity, so that a central hold on power was at least theoretically possible. In practice Athens was too big a state to be taken by a single would-be ruler, and instead became an oligarchy ruled by a council of wealthy families known as the Aeropagus.

According to Aristotle (writing 250 years later) in the period 650–600 BC serious social tensions began to arise in Athens and other Greek city-states. The principal grievance was debt-bondage, but the real cause was the growing divisions of wealth and power. Security for any debt rested on the person of the debtor, even children could be seized in lieu of payment, and this led to a situation in which, as Aristotle wrote, 'the majority were slaves of the few'. The custom of debt-bondage may have worked as a restraint in a rural community with networks of kinship and custom; in seventh-century Athens it began to have disastrous consequences. Indebtedness got out of control because powerful families began to annex common land and then either charged farmers rent, or excluded them. Farmers got into debt, which then led to slavery. And if they took their complaints to the Aeropagus, they were inevitably rejected by other wealthy landowners.

By 600 BC Athens was in real danger of civil war. The tension between 'the people and the rulers of the state' (who were also the wealthiest families) had reached breaking point. Many citizens had literally become slaves in their own country, while others had fled into exile. But it was the condition of the farmers that most threatened the ruling group. Though individually unable to resist the oppression of the ruling group, the Attican farmers were not without power. The villages supplied the men who fought in the Athenian army and navy, and though each wealthy family may have had its private set of guards, the farmers en masse were potentially stronger.

To avoid a bloody conflict, both sides agreed to give responsibility for solving the problems of the city-state, or *polis*, to one man, Solon, who was neither a member of the nobility, nor a village farmer – Aristotle describes him as 'middle class in wealth and position'. Why did they do this? It seems that Athens was caught in a difficult position – the rulers were plundering their own people but were restrained from gaining absolute control by the number of factions within their ranks, while the people and particularly the farmers were demanding changes to the system which no one in the ruling group was willing to give. Athens was becoming an urban society, with an increasing risk of authoritarian rule, but the farmers were powerful enough to insist that the custom of shared power be maintained.

Solon sought what the Greeks called *eunomia*, or 'good order', a central notion not only in the governance of cities but also in the ordering of life, in everyday behaviour and in the workings of the natural world. In governance as in many other things there was a right way of doing things. The challenge for Solon was not to find a model for an ideal society, nor to negotiate a solution between the two parties, but to discover the way that things should be. Once this was revealed and disseminated it would inevitably be agreeable to everyone. Solon would not have to enforce the *eunomia* on his fellow Athenians; the right order in society was simply good in itself and needed no struggle to implement.

Solon's reforms were not only a political episode but the beginnings of a philosophical change. The farmers were not seeking some pie in the sky; they wanted their land restored and their debt-bondage struck out. In order to give this to them Solon could not simply turn the clock back, but he could introduce a set of laws that re-created the harmony that, he believed, had previously existed. But 'good order', for all its practical implications, was an abstract concept that could be uncovered by contemplation rather than experience; while its effects were felt in the real world, it existed only as a disembodied idea or ideal. The invention of such ideals became a feature of classical Athens, and this may well be connected to the introduction of alphabetic writing, which arrived in the Greek world from the Phoenicians between 800 and 750 BC.

Writing was first used for stone memorial plaques and to write letters using pieces of pottery or wax tablets. Nestor's cup from southern Italy and the Diplon vase from Athens both date from around 740 to 730 BC and both carry long inscriptions. People scraped messages to the gods on pieces of broken pottery and left them at shrines, showing that writing had a symbolic and magical force as well as a prosaic value. For the Greeks, as for us, different forms of writing conveyed different subtleties of meaning.

The writing down of laws was a particularly interesting development – Solon's laws (*c.* 600 BC) were probably first inscribed on wood. One view is that laws were inscribed in order to make them incorruptible, but it has become clear that written laws formed a small and controversial part of the Greek legal system. Citizens' behaviour was still guided by customary unwritten laws, just as in other oral societies. The written laws may have been inscribed precisely because they were not customary and therefore not universally accepted. Most importantly, they changed the execution of justice from an interpersonal affair negotiated between people to the interpretation of a set of disembodied rules. This was a significant stage in the growth of the impersonal state and of abstract thinking.

Solon blamed the oligarchs for the majority of Athens' problems. Of the wealthy, he wrote: 'satisfy your pride with what is moderate, for we shall not tolerate excess, nor will everything turn out as you wish'. He outlawed debt-bondage, cancelled all such existing debts and recalled those who had fled Athens to escape its effects. Land confiscated for non-payment of debts was returned to the farmers. But, having settled the narrow point of the dispute, Solon understood that more was needed in order to bring about *eunomia*. He drew up a new constitution for the *polis*, which divided the population into four classes according to the property they owned. Each class was then allocated certain official posts – the archons and treasurers were to be drawn from the highest class; magistrates, prison officials, bailiffs and so on from the top three. The lowest class of citizen had the right to sit in a popular assembly and to be selected for a jury court.

As well as being divided horizontally by social status and wealth, Athenian society was divided vertically by order or *phyle*. Solon decided that the four *phylae* should propose candidates for the different posts and that the successful candidate should be chosen by lot. This helped to break the factionalism of the oligarchy. He also introduced a Council of 400, comprising 100 men from each *phyle*, in order to give the middle classes a political voice. Lastly, the popular assembly, which consisted of the whole citizenry (i.e. the free men) of the polis, and the jury courts were given a new role in overseeing officials, as well as judging disputes between citizens.

The most remarkable aspect of Solon's measures, apart from their boldness, was that they were agreed by all parties. Nevertheless, 50 years later, Athens had developed a more centralized political structure that made it vulnerable to takeover, and in 546 BC, a man called Pisistratus managed, after three attempts, to seize control of the city. Pisistratus ruled Athens for 20 years, during which he maintained the constitution, simply taking the main offices for himself, instituted public works and did not tax the people overmuch. He understood that if he kept the farmers happy they would stay out of the city and leave him to get on with running the administration.

When Pisistratus died, in 527 BC, his two sons Hippias and Hipparchus, who were widely feared, took over. Hipparchus was murdered and Hippias ruled for another 17 years. Aristotle writes that in avenging his brother, Hippias 'killed or exiled many people, and was distrusted and hated by all'. The exiles eventually persuaded Cleomenes, the ruler of Sparta, to help them to free their city. Hippias and his supporters were driven out of Athens in 510 BC.

For all their apparent virtues, Solon's laws had not protected the people from misuse of those laws. When the tyrants were deposed, the skeleton of Solon's constitution still survived, but the Athenians needed to find a way to prevent another seizure of power. Cleisthenes, head of one of Athens' most powerful families, had lived in exile during the reign of Hippias, and when he returned he proposed a set of political reforms based on a radical reorganization of Athenian society. Like Solon, Cleisthenes was trying to hold back the centralization of power, and he recognized that this could only be achieved by recreating the diffusion of power that had existed in small, customary communities.

Cleisthenes' crucial reform, recognized by Aristotle as the most important innovation in Greek political thinking, was to dissolve the four orders, or *phylae*, of Athenian society, each dominated by a group of wealthy families, and set up a system of ten new *phylae*. At a stroke this cut away the root of the families' power. The old Athenian *phylae* had been dominated by geographical location, making it easier for a tyrant to seize power by winning the support of people from a particular region – the city, the coastal settlements or the inland villages. The ten new *phylae* avoided this danger by each being made up of a set of villages from each of the three elements of the *polis* – each *phyle* had a base in the city of Athens, another in the hill country and another on the coast. The inhabitants of different parts of the polis were forced into contact and cooperation, and the dominance of one family over any *phyle* was made near impossible. Each *phyle* had to distribute its 50 seats on the ruling Council of 500 evenly among its *demes*, or village-sized units, and the councilmen were elected or chosen by lot and served for one year. They could not be chosen again until every eligible citizen in their *deme* had served their turn. In addition, ten *strategoi*, or generals, were selected – one from each *phyle*. Along with a few other technical posts such as engineers and shipbuilders, the *strategoi* were allowed to be re-elected to the same post for an unlimited number of years.

Given the value placed on Greek democracy, it is surprising that Cleisthenes' name is not better known. His reforms were detailed and far-reaching and laid the basis for Athenian society during its 'golden age' in the fifth century BC. But these measures were not a leap in the dark. Cleisthenes had seen other systems of government during his exile and had obviously thought carefully about what he was trying to achieve. He set out consciously to prevent the concentration of power in a few hands; but unconsciously he did this by recreating an egalitarian tribal structure within a hierarchical semi-urban state. The *phylae* that existed before Cleisthenes were loose social networks; a cross between kinship clans and neighbourhood associations – in other words, they were like elements of a customary rural society. But in Athens these had become the routes to power for ambitious men, and so they had to be destroyed and re-made in order to preserve their proper customary functions. Societies can only operate if they have ways of distributing power, or agreeing to the accumulation of power in exchange for other benefits – protection or prosperity, for example. The Athenian people wanted to reinstate their customary wide distribution of power and so Cleisthenes had to artificially construct, or reconstruct, what humans had been doing for thousands of years.

The system that Cleisthenes devised stayed in place, with brief interruptions, throughout the fifth century BC – the age of classical Greece. In the middle of the century Pericles revised the constitution by depriving the Aeropagus, the council of nobles, of its powers, so that the popular assembly came to be the seat of all power. Athens was the largest city in the Hellenic world, and its increasing wealth and military power began, by the 440s BC, to bring about the situation that Greece had previously avoided – the dominance of one state over all the others.

As if to prove that no system is perfect, in 433 BC the popular assembly followed Pericles' advice and voted Athens into a disastrous war with Sparta, turned down a series of peace offers and elected to restart the war after a period without conflict. These democratic decisions not only brought Athens' independence to a sudden end; they encouraged a savage civil war throughout the Hellenic world that, as Thucydides wrote, caused 'a general deterioration of character throughout the Greek world . . . Society had become divided into two ideologically hostile camps, and each side viewed the other with suspicion.'

Athenian democracy, with all its faults, is now held to be an ideal system of government, not just for a small city in the ancient Mediterranean world but for every size and type of society in any and every part of the world. How has this come to be? One reason is that the Athenians themselves promoted the idea that their city was uniquely free. In his famous funeral speech of 431 BC Pericles told the Athenians that their forefathers had, 'by their courage and their virtues, handed on to us a free country. Athens is open to the world and its institutions make its people free.' According to Pericles, Athenians were uniquely tolerant of their neighbours, law-abiding, in love with beauty but not extravagance, brave, and each was 'able to show himself the rightful lord and owner of his own person, and to do this, moreover, with exceptional grace and versatility'. No other people in Greece or anywhere else had these qualities, which had, it seems, developed from living in a democracy.

Pericles was speaking in the early stages of a war; his task was to rally the troops by linking democracy, individual freedom, bravery, civic virtue, polite behaviour and aesthetic appreciation in an irresistible combination – he might have said that Athens was fighting for civilization itself. The speech was a dazzling piece of propaganda; nevertheless, Pericles was justified in comparing certain qualities of Athens with, for example, Sparta; and the Peloponnesian war did become an ideological war between oligarchs and democrats that engulfed the entire Hellenic world. It would be wrong though to extrapolate too broadly. Democracy gave Athens and other Greek cities some advantages over their neighbours; but it did not transform their citizens into uniquely tolerant and virtuous people (there was political censorship in Athens, and the citizens voted to execute military leaders who had performed heroically, as well as condemning the philosopher Socrates to death). More importantly for the future, Pericles is the first notable example of a politician holding one method of government to be superior to another *in principle*. His encouragement to the Athenians to fight for their values, in a war they were actually fighting for purely strategic reasons, was to be a strong influence on later western leaders.

While Athenian democracy can be seen as a practical response to a changing society, almost every way in which Greeks viewed the world around them was undergoing rapid change. The influence of alphabetic writing, though difficult to assess directly, seems to have been a crucial factor, and the transition from an oral to a literate culture is best shown in two of the great innovations of classical Greece – history and tragedy.

People have always told stories about the beginnings of the world, the birth of humanity and the adventures of the gods and heroes. These tales were born of the impulse to understand the place of humanity in the world; they were not literally true, but they filled a more important function than simply depicting actual events. Gods, demi-gods and heroes were brought into being because, over time, empirical truth gives way to moral truth – actual events become less important than the symbolic value they hold for those who come after. Almost all belief systems place human existence within a much greater story of creation, burgeoning, decline and death, and in this way myths, like other forms of art, make a bridge between the human search for meaning and the essential meaninglessness of the world. The writing of history, in our modern sense of the word, came from the same impulse, and in time documentary history replaced the telling of myths as the way of understanding the past.

Herodotus, the 'Father of History', and Thucydides, author of the history of the Peloponnesian war, were the two founders of written history. They did not believe that human events and actions should be understood as acts of the gods; their work is not concerned with temperamental Zeus or wise Athena or jealous Hera; instead, they wanted to preserve the deeds of men and women, to record important events and to give the real reasons (as they saw them) for the events and conflicts they recorded. This profound step that was ushered in by the coming of war, and by the change from an oral to a written culture.

Herodotus began his work some time in the 450s BC. Until then it appears that the Greeks of the classical period had no desire to pin down the past. History was not something that stretched behind and in front of them like an endless road; it was a living, dynamic entity that infected every morsel of the present. This was something the ancient Greeks held in common with almost every other culture except our own – it is our view of the past that is peculiar. The beginnings of a different vision of the past was provoked by the occurrence in Greece of a series of cataclysmic events – in which the present and recent past suddenly became as dramatic as anything that the gods had attempted or Homer described.

In 500 BC the Persian empire covered a vast area, using its base in the Tigris valley to control the richest part of the Eurasian world. Greece was on the periphery of this world and of little interest to the Persians – according to Aristagoras, the Aegean coast was a three-month overland journey from the Persian capital at Susa. Nevertheless, as Persian power waxed, the trade routes of the west came to their attention. Shortly before 500 BC Persian forces defeated the rulers of Lydia and took control of the sea route from the Black Sea into the Aegean. They then considered those Greek cities on the east, or Ionian, coast of the Aegean to be within their empire. These cities rebelled and fought a six-year war with the Persians before being defeated and occupied in 494 BC.

The other Greek cities watched nervously as the Ionian rebellion crumbled and their fellow Greeks were carried off to captivity. The Persians, on the other hand, had been surprised and impressed by the Ionians' prosperity and military expertise, and the equipment of their armies and fleets. Remote though it might be, the Aegean was clearly an interesting part of the world. Darius, the Persian king, saw that he had much to gain by bringing the whole of the Greek peninsula within his empire.

In 491 BC Darius sent envoys to all the independent Greek cities demanding gifts of earth and water as tokens of submission. Among those that refused were Athens, Eretria and Sparta. The following year a Persian fleet of 600 ships, carrying 90,000 men, crossed the Aegean from Ionia. The Persians met fierce resistance at Eretria on the west coast of the island of Euboea, but took the city after a six-day siege. They were then within sight of the mainland and the territory of Athens.

The Persian fleet sailed on from Eretria and landed near a place called Marathon on the east coast of the peninsula of Attica, within 40 kilometres of the city of Athens. The Athenian assembly sent to Sparta for help, knowing that this was unlikely to arrive in time. (The legend of the Marathon messenger may be based on the journey of Phidippides, a specially trained courier who ran over 250 kilometres to reach Sparta from Athens.) Rather than trying to defend a siege of the city walls, the Athenian council decided to send their army of 9,000 men out to Marathon to confront and delay the enemy. Seeing the danger of fighting on an open plain, the Athenian infantry tried to draw the Persian cavalry into the narrow inland passes around Marathon. But then, under cover of night, the Persians withdrew most of their cavalry on to their ships. Fearing that the Persian cavalry was being taken down the coast to approach the unguarded city behind their backs, the ten *strategoi*, led by Militiades, decided they must attack immediately and then withdraw towards the city. The attack was devastatingly successful: the Persian army was driven back to the ships with huge losses, the cavalry was unable to disembark and the Persian fleet was forced to sail away.

The significance of the victory at Marathon was immense. It was an Athenian victory, won without the help of the Spartans and won, moreover, by an army of citizens. Marathon gave the Athenians a new generation of heroes who were not legendary figures from a time beyond human memory, but the friends and neighbours and husbands and fathers and sons and uncles of the people of the *polis*. Drawn from every walk of life and from every village and district in Athens and its surrounding territory of Attica, they were real people, to be celebrated alongside Achilles and Hector and Odysseus.

The Athenians appreciated the help of the gods, and they had attacked only after offering sacrifices and reading signs. Nevertheless, everyone knew their decision to send an army in the first place, and then to attack, had been based on open discussion in the council and agreement between the generals. Marathon fostered the communal spirit of the Athenian people; when Militiades asked to be honoured for his leadership, the assembly refused, asserting that the victory had been won by all the soldiers and that none should be honoured above another.

Marathon ended one campaign but it did not end Persian interest in the Greek world. The Persians faced a rebellion in Egypt and the death of Darius, the Great King. But ten years after Marathon, Xerxes, son and successor of Darius, returned to Greece with an army of 100,000 troops. While the Persian army marched overland through Thrace and Macedonia and south towards Athens and Sparta, Xerxes also mustered a huge fleet at Ephesus on the Ionian coast. A contingent of Spartans was sent north to hold the Persian army in the narrow pass at Thermopylae, while a Greek naval force held its own against the huge Persian fleet off Artemisium. The battle at Thermopylae delayed the Persians (this was vital for the Spartans, who were feverishly building a defensive wall at Corinth to prevent the Persians from entering the Peloponnesian peninsula) but could not hold them; they pushed south. Apparent catastrophe faced the Greeks: the city of Athens was open to attack by land, while the Persian fleet threatened to sail around any defensive wall and attack Sparta and the Peloponnese from the sea.

The territory and city of Athens were evacuated, with most of the refugees being taken to the island of Salamis. The commanders of the fleet of the Greek allies, led by the Spartan Eurybiades, debated what action to take, as news arrived of Xerxes burning the city of Athens to the ground. Some of the allies wanted to sail west to the

narrow isthmus at Corinth and stop the Persians entering the
Peloponnesian peninsula. But the Athenian Themistocles persuaded
Eurybiades to take on the Persian fleet in the narrow strait between
Salamis and the mainland.

In late September 480 BC, the Persian fleet, now carrying much of
the Persian army, entered the strait of Salamis where the Greeks were
lying in wait. The ships' decks were used as fighting platforms, crowded
with men and ready to be manoeuvred into position with oars – the
most effective technique was to ram an enemy ship, and take it out of
the battle. Greek ships were better suited to ramming and their crews
more experienced in naval warfare. Losses were heavy on both sides,
but the Persian losses were such that they could no longer sustain a
military campaign in hostile territory; Salamis brought their campaign
to an end. Xerxes, who watched the battle from a nearby hilltop, left
for home immediately fearing that news of the defeat might provoke
a rebellion in Susa. His remaining troops marched back overland and
wintered in Thessaly. The next summer the Greek allies defeated them
at the land battle of Plataea and the Persian forces withdrew from the
Greek peninsula.

Greece had been devastated by the war, yet by their success, the
Greeks had altered the strategic geography of the Eurasian world. Their
victory was a symptom of something deeper than superior military
tactics. Not the moral or intellectual superiority of the (European)
Greeks over the (Asian) Persians, as our forebears were taught, but a
shift in economic power from the Fertile Crescent to the Mediterranean.
An ever-warmer climate, influxes of population from the east, discoveries of minerals, adaptation of farming practices, the exploitation of
the Mediterranean itself as a vast trading highway; all contributed to
the growing prosperity and economic power of those peoples who lived
around its shores. Athens and its allies could not yet compare in strength
and riches with the Persian empire, but their victory was a sign that
the Mediterranean could face the powers of Mesopotamia, Anatolia
and the Levant on equal terms.

The second Persian war ended in 479 BC, about 20 years before
Herodotus the historian began his work. Herodotus was born c. 484
BC at Halicarnassus, an Ionian city subject to the Persians. Not much
is known about his life, but he undoubtedly travelled throughout the
Mediterranean, while his upbringing on the eastern side of the Aegean
seems to have given him a sympathetic view of the Persians and other

non-Greek peoples. He probably began writing and reciting his works in the 450s and carried on until his death in the 420s BC. These were times of turmoil as war between Athens and Sparta loomed and then erupted, drawing in the whole of Greece; in a deliberate contrast, Herodotus' work looked back to a time when the Greeks were united. Herodotus had no template to use when he began his work, so he followed his own instincts; his *Histories* contain everything from fables to folklore to travelogue to high-class gossip and he reads like a great raconteur – a useful quality when facing a live audience. Nevertheless it is as a historian that he is known; it is Herodotus who first tells us what history is about.

We can be in no doubt about the effect of the Persian wars on Herodotus. The first words of *The Histories* are: 'Herodotus of Halicarnassus here displays his inquiry, so that human achievements may not become forgotten in time, and great and marvellous deeds – some displayed by Greeks, some by barbarians [for barbarians read Persians, though in general the term meant non-Greeks] – may not be without their glory; and especially to show why the two peoples fought with each other.' This is an extraordinarily revealing opening. First, Herodotus did not intend to relate deeds of the mythical past involving demi-gods and heroes; he wanted to record the events that had gone on in his own lifetime concerning the parents and grandparents of those around him. Second, he wanted 'especially to show why the two peoples fought with each other'. In customary stories of the past the question 'why?' did not arise. The fate or destiny of a man developed through a relationship with the gods, and though the working out of this destiny might be complex and subtle, there was no question of why an event should happen, or why a person should live or die in a certain way – something happened because the gods decreed it.

Herodotus begins his search for reasons by relating various kidnappings of kings' daughters by Phoenicians, Cretans and Greeks, each avenging the previous crime, and eventually culminating in the abduction of Helen by Paris, and the consequent Trojan war. 'Such then', Herodotus writes, 'is the Persian story. In their view it was the capture of Troy that first made them enemies of the Greeks.' The Phoenicians beg to differ and say that the first kidnapping of all, that of Io, was not really a kidnapping, but that Io fell for the ship's captain and fled to escape her repressive parents. Neither of these explanations impresses Herodotus, who prefers, he says, to rely on his own knowledge.

Once he has set all of this out, we might expect Herodotus to give us a rational, evidence-based analysis; but he does not. He sets out to find why the Greeks and the barbarians came to fight each other without ever really getting to the point. Instead he tells stories; marvellous, entertaining, fascinating and informative stories. So, for example, the first few pages of his first book tell of the war between Croesus, king of Lydia, and the Persians, but Herodotus feels bound to break off from his narrative to say of Periander, a minor player in the conflict: 'The Corinthians tell of an extraordinary thing that happened during his life, and the Lesbians confirm the truth of it.' He then proceeds to relate the wondrous story of Arion the musician, diving overboard from a Corinthian ship and being carried back to Greece on the back of a dolphin. The story, like many of the stories in Herodotus' *Histories*, does not serve any purpose. But along with these stories Herodotus gives detailed accounts of the birth of the Persian empire, the Ionian revolt and the life of Darius, as well as the wars between the Greeks and Persians.

Herodotus' mixture of story-telling, travel-writing, gossip and serious history seems puzzling to our modern minds, but it shows Herodotus as a man of his time. His task was to attract audiences by telling enter-taining stories, but also by relating the events of the great wars in which their grandfathers had fought, and by telling of his travels in foreign lands. He might have done all this from memory, but it became more common for performers – poets, dramatists and story-tellers – to inscribe their work. To start with, this may have been an aide-memoire, but the distribution of written works for individual or communal reading became more common. Herodotus is therefore a bridge between an oral and a written culture; a position that becomes clearer when we compare him with his younger contemporary Thucydides.

Thucydides wrote on only one subject: the long war through which he lived and in which he served, that brought about the end of Athens' supremacy. His work is the only surviving source of information about the Peloponnesian war and is the first history that was written to be read, rather than performed. By the time Thucydides' work was published, shortly after his death in 400 BC, the golden age of Athens was at an end.

First, the conflict itself. The Peloponnesian war was fought between Athens and Sparta (and dragged in most of the other cities of Greece) over a period of 27 years from 431 BC, with an interval of uneasy peace from 421 to 414 BC. The war began when the rulers of Corcyra (Corfu) sought Athens' help in a dispute with Corinth. Both Corinth and Sparta interpreted Athens' interference as an attempt by the dominant power in the Aegean to extend its power into the Ionian and Adriatic seas. A traumatic 10-year war was brought to a halt in 421 BC, but Athens rekindled hostilities in 414 by sending an expeditionary fleet to take over the Greek cities on the island of Sicily.

Though voices (including that of Nicias, the fleet commander) were raised against the expedition, the Athenian assembly voted to go back to war. The charismatic Alcibiades told his fellow citizens to 'make it your endeavour to raise this city to even greater heights'. The expedition failed, the remnants of the defeated army were stranded in Sicily, captured and sold into slavery, and the fleet, the source and symbol of Athens' power, was abandoned. Sparta re-entered the war on the side of the Sicilian Greeks. The war ebbed and flowed for the next decade, but finally the Spartans under their new leader Lysander, and with Persian backing, captured the rebuilt Athenian fleet at Aegospotami in 404 BC. The Athenians were forced to surrender on humiliating terms.

During the war the cities of Greece lined up behind the two major adversaries. This was partly to do with old loyalties and current strategies, but there was, according to Thucydides, an ideological element to the conflict, which provoked civil war in almost every city. Internal disputes were fanned into violent conflict by the availability of outside force – 'democratic leaders trying to bring in the Athenians, and oligarchs trying to bring in the Spartans'. In the civil conflict on the island of Corfu, 50 people were herded into a temple, given a summary trial and sentenced to death. To spare themselves from execution they killed each other or hanged themselves. But this did not stop the violence: 'And, as usually happens in such situations, people went to every extreme and beyond it. There were fathers who killed their sons; men were dragged from the temples or butchered on the very altars; some were actually walled up in the temple of Dionysus and left to die there.' The killing went on for a week, and all this Thucydides recorded in inglorious detail.

Thucydides also showed how, on at least three separate occasions, the Athenians were offered reasonable peace treaties and, after open debate in the assembly, refused them all. There was nothing inevitable about these decisions. Athens did not have to go to war to protect herself and could have halted the war while retaining her power and prestige. The citizens believed that Athens was too great to contemplate defeat or an equable peace. But just as important was the history of the war itself – when so many men had died, the city could not agree to a peace that simply restored the pre-war position. This dilemma could not be broken, and Athens was left with a choice between glorious victory and total defeat.

Thucydides was the first historian in our modern sense. He was impatient with explanations that call on the supernatural and, unlike Herodotus, he was uninterested in anecdotes that did not bear on his theme. Neither was he interested in tradition as a basis for understanding the past. He dismissed the old legend of Helen's suitors, for example – in which those who sought her hand, and were refused, agreed to stand by her chosen husband – and wrote that the heroes joined Agamemnon because he had the biggest army in Greece and would not take no for an answer. He is keen to tell his readers that he has not been content to give a general view or to repeat gossip: '. . . I have made it a principle not to write down the first story that came my way, and not even to be guided by my own general impressions; either I was present myself at the events which I have described or else I heard of them from eye-witnesses whose reports I have checked with as much thoroughness as possible.'

Educated Athenians were becoming less interested in the supernatural forces that controlled the world, or the coalescence of fate; they wanted reliable information that would be, as Thucydides writes, 'judged useful by those who want to understand clearly the events that happened in the past'. Evidence-based history was brought into being by the Persian and Peloponnesian wars, but also by the spread of alphabetic writing. Thucydides was able to abandon Herodotus' anecdotal style because he had no need to perform in front of a crowd. The oral culture of Athens lived on but Thucydides had his mind on a different kind of audience, as this resounding claim shows: 'My work is not a piece of writing designed to meet the taste of an immediate public, but was made to last for ever.'

The Greeks were well aware that writing makes thoughts, ideas and accounts permanent, and the desire for god-like immortality appealed not just to the writers, but to the participants of history. Great events provoked the writing of history, but the recording of events infected the motives of those taking part. Athenians became fond of telling the world just how great they were, and how their deeds would live for ever. A place in history became a motive in human affairs; posterity, rather than the present, became the hunting ground of great men.

Writing also enabled and encouraged a conscious effort to explain –

both Herodotus and Thucydides are keen to tell us that explanation (*why* these events took place) is their aim, and this is achieved by setting up a network, or string, of causes and effects. The Athenians attacked Sicily in order to help their allies, but also because they were ignorant of its size, and were persuaded by Alcibiades. We can see how different this is from the previous view of the past. In the *Iliad*, for example, the Acheans besiege Troy to win Helen back, but also to fulfil a host of prophecies – that Achilles will die beneath the walls of a foreign city, that Troy will fall if Paris returns, and so on. These mythic tales, like all good stories, were not intended to explain the past events they described, but to bring the listener to an understanding about the present. Stories have narratives and plots because the conscious human mind has a hunger for the apparent meaning they bring to the world, but real stories transcend the form they occupy. They use a plot to contain something that, while specific in its setting, says something of universal significance. The *Iliad*, the *Oresteia*, *Beowulf*, *Hamlet* and *Anna Karenina* are not endlessly performed or re-read because of their narratives, but because they each use a particular narrative to convey universal insights.

Through the work of Herodotus and Thucydides the mythic story-based view of the past, which was the possession of an oral culture, gave way to history and literature, which are the twin instruments of a literary culture. Thucydides' aim was to present the past as a framework of objective facts so that later readers would know exactly what had happened. But Thucydides, like all historians who have followed him, was bound to be selective in his choice of material, and was bound to shape his material into a coherent narrative. Once Thucydides abandoned Herodotus' instinctive rambling approach in favour of focus and precision, he gave history its purpose. But removing the gods from the stage did not make the record of the past into the rational series of causes and effects that Thucydides hoped for. The change from an oral to a literate culture simply substituted one kind of interpretation for another.

While the birth of history has an obvious connection to the advent of writing, the link between the emergence of tragic drama and the beginnings of a literate culture is less straightforward. Nevertheless, both the birth and death of tragedy were only possible in a culture that was in transition from the spoken to the written word.

Tradition has it that in the year 534 BC, the organizer of an Athenian poetry festival named Thespis arranged for a single member of the chorus to step forward to recite a distinct piece of verse. This person adopted the persona of one of the characters within the poem and so the essential basis of dramatic theatre – a player standing for a character – was born. Fifty years later, in 484 BC, Aeschylus won his first dramatic contest and the age of Greek tragic theatre began. Of the hundreds of plays that were written and performed over the next century, only just over 30 complete tragedies survive. Though we have only a fragment of what was produced and though the Greek drama that has survived was essentially the work of just four men – the three tragedians Aeschylus, Sophocles and Euripides, and Aristophanes the writer of comedies – the plays provide a resource of incalculable richness in any attempt to understand a world that is otherwise beyond our reach. Greek theatre describes a world at the moment of its passing. Its themes are not simply stirring dramas; they are, for us, the last breath of one world and the intimation of another.

In oral cultures story-telling is not only an art form, it is a history lesson, a moral instruction, a communal event and a celebration and promotion of shared understanding. Stories are told in verse because this is a good way for the human voice to impart meaning, and for the audience to retain both specific passages and the sense of the whole piece. The story-telling of Celtic, Norse, Assyrian, Persian, Polynesian, Amazonian and Greek cultures all gave rise to epic poetry, and those oral epics that survived into the written age – the legends of Beowulf and Gilgamesh, the *Mabinogion* and the *Iliad* – demonstrate the power and subtlety of the form. Poetry festivals, in which poets would tell of the great deeds of the gods of Olympus, of the founding of cities, and of the race of heroes, were part of Greek cultural life from the earliest times. Some of these celebrations became song festivals and some involved a chorus of citizens singing or reciting verses in unison. The poems and songs were part of religious ceremonies involving sacrifices and supplications alongside games, wrestling contests and animal shows.

In the fifth century BC, as Greek society became more affluent, the festivals became ever grander. In Athens there were two major festivals (and many more minor feast-days) each year: the Lenaia and, most spectacular of all Greek festivals, the Dionysia, held in honour of Dionysus, god of the harvest, of wine, intoxication and fertility. The Dionysia brought the countryside into the city and united the population of the *polis* of Athens in a celebration of the fertility of the earth, the power of their city and the skill of their poets and athletes. The festivals were organized to maximize participation – at least 1,000 men and boys from all parts of the *polis* took part in the singing, and more than 300 people were involved as actors at any one Dionysia. Everyone in the audience would have known at least one of the performers.

The sense of mass participation was heightened by the size of the audiences. The Theatre of Dionysus on the southern slope of the Acropolis had seating for an audience of 17,000, all with a perfect view of the stage. The themes of the songs and plays were designed to involve and connect with the audience by combining familiar legends with recent events such as wars, plagues and natural disasters.

A series of festivals in which entertainment went alongside religious celebration, a tradition of poetic performance, a spirit of participation and an audience eager to immerse itself in drama: all of this existed within a strictly oral culture; the emergence of dramatic theatre as an offshoot of poetic performance required another ingredient, the development of written language. Dramatic theatre combines an oral with a literate culture, the words are written and spoken, carefully honed by the playwright, but then performed as if they were spontaneous. While poets like Pindar kept a written version of their work, around which they built a performance, drama depended on an agreed text. In epic poetry, the performers were the key; interpreting and embellishing stories was at the centre of their craft. But writing allowed the dramatist to become the creative force, and enabled the traditional tales that were at the root of all Greek drama to be manipulated in novel ways. The birth of tragedy needed writing as much as it needed epic poetry.

The best-known of Greek tragedies is *Oedipus the King* by Sophocles, first performed around 430 BC. In common with almost all Greek drama, *Oedipus* retells a traditional story, and, like other tragedies, the underlying theme is the collision of human will and destiny. Sophocles' audience knew that the house of Oedipus was cursed, and that his parents had been told that he would murder his father and marry his mother; the dramatist's task was to use this ancient and disturbing story to reflect a profound contemporary reality.

Throughout the play Oedipus is shown to be a clever and wise ruler and a man of action. He declares the need to think rationally and meet whatever life has in store with equanimity, and in this he is the model of the fifth-century Athenian. In effect Sophocles has transplanted him from ancient Thebes to contemporary Athens. By the time the play was produced, Athens was at the peak of its prestige and power, and the construction of the Parthenon and other great public works were transforming the city into the most beautiful in Greece.

Some Athenians began to see their prosperity as the reward for their political freedoms and for their intelligent and rational approach to life, and this attitude affected their relations with the gods. Fifty years earlier, belief in the omnipotence and omnipresence of the Olympian gods was universal, but by 430 BC, educated Greeks were inclined to agree with Protagoras that 'Man is the measure of all things.' Nevertheless although some Athenians (and some characters in *Oedipus the King*) denied the power of the gods, they did not question the central role of fate in human life. Even if they began to lose faith in Zeus and Hera and Apollo, the Athenians did not believe they were free to construct their own destinies.

How could this paradox be resolved? How could people be in apparent control of their lives through rational thought and decisions, and at the same time be subject to the forces of fate? Sophocles approached this question by devising a startlingly radical treatment of the traditional Oedipus story. When the play begins, the prophecy that the oracle has given to Oedipus' father has already come to pass, but because no one, least of all Oedipus, knows this, no one suffers. Oedipus is happily married to his mother, Jocasta, in blissful ignorance of the prophecy; Jocasta, who knows about the prophecy, has dismissed it from her mind because she says she does not believe in such things.

The tragedy of the piece is based not on Oedipus' fulfilment of the prophecy, but in his own discovery of the truth about his life. His relentless search for the truth about himself is continually discouraged by others, particularly those who either know the truth or who fear it. But Oedipus will not be put off, saying, 'I must know it all, I must see the truth at last' and 'I am at the edge of hearing horrors, yes, but I must hear!' When he discovers the truth, his wife and mother Jocasta kills herself and Oedipus puts out his own eyes with the pins from her dress. Having blinded himself so that he will not look on a human face, he leaves the city of Thebes to find a place where he can hear no human voice. All of this has come about not because of the prophecy itself, but because of Oedipus' desire to know the truth and because of the rational, intelligent and purposeful way he has gone about discovering it.

In our modern misinterpretation Oedipus has come to be seen as a kind of monster, or as an actor-out of universal psychological forces. But by depicting him as a reasonable and intelligent man, Sophocles was showing his fellow Athenians the dangers that lay before them. The belief in humanity as the rational author of its own destiny was, Sophocles understood, an arrogant and dangerous delusion. The finest achievement of Greek literature was an argument against what we believe to be the spirit of its times. In *Oedipus the King*, tragedy arises from the delusion that a rational approach to life will give you mastery over fate; instead, Sophocles shows, it simply leads you back to your destiny.

Sophocles' ability to envisage and bring about the revolutionary structure of *Oedipus the King* was undoubtedly made possible by written language. The complexities of Greek tragic theatre and the skilful handling of dramatic and conceptual structures depended on the use of written scripts. But as well as providing an essential tool for dramatists, the development of written language ushered in new ways of thinking. Tragic theatre was the last fling of the long tradition of epic poetry. The technological change that transformed it from an oral into a combined written and oral form also brought about its demise. Sophocles' *Oedipus* was a cry of anguish, a warning against the elevation of rationalism. But once rationalism arrived, people stopped believing in the monumental collision of will and destiny; instead they thought that reason would allow humans to take control of their own fate, and tragic theatre lost its central place in Greek culture.

The development of writing was crucial in this process. A man's life, if recorded, might seem like a meaningful story, instead of a tragic-comic attempt to deal with fate. Indeed, man might begin to look like the author of his own life story. And if this was so, then behaviour was no longer linked to fate or destiny but to freely made choices. The ways that those choices should be made became a subject not for tragedy, but for a new area of human endeavour, moral philosophy.

While tragedy, in the hands of Sophocles, is clearly ambivalent about the growing belief in rationalism, we are often told that other art forms in classical Greece are evidence of its acceptance. The structure of the Parthenon, the revival of naturalistic sculpture and painting and the depiction of the human form are cited in support of a hunger for rationalism among classical Greek artists. This view was encouraged by the condition and context in which many Greek works of art were discovered by modern western Europeans – picturesque silent ruins without the colour, clamour and spirituality of the original temples, sculptures stripped of their painted coatings, poor copies that echo only the form and not the content of the originals: all this, combined with the rationalist spirit of the Enlightenment, led to a misunderstanding of Greek art. But when sculptures from the Parthenon, taken by Lord Elgin, first arrived in London in 1808, an English artist described the depiction of Theseus: 'every form was altered by action or repose . . . the two sides of his back varied, one side stretched from the shoulder blade being pulled forward, and the other side compressed from the shoulder blade being pushed close to the spine as he rested on his elbow, with the belly flat because the bowels fell into the pelvis as he sat . . .' Anyone seeing the friezes today is immediately struck by the same impression – the sense of movement and power captured in stone. The Greek artists unconsciously combined the traditions of naturalism and movement we saw in Chapter One; but the result had less to do with rationality than with the depiction of humans as physical animals, complete with musculature, bones, joints, tendons and sinews. The rationalists may have wanted depictions of humans as elevated thinkers; the artists (at least the best of them) responded like Sophocles, by reminding them of their animal nature.

The age of classical Athens lasted from Cleisthenes' reforms of around 500 BC to the defeat at Aegospotami in 404 BC. This golden age was brief because Athens, like the whole of Greece, was in rapid transition. An egalitarian society based on an oral culture and customary laws was faced with increased prosperity, and with the introduction of alphabetic writing, which brought profound changes in humanity's vision of itself. The effects of the transition to a written culture are clearly seen in the demise of myths, the birth of evidence-based history, and the growing interest in rationalism. The birth and death of tragedy, in particular, shows how writing gave rise to an art form, and also to the changes that killed it.

The remnants of classical Athens – the architecture, sculpture, writings, myths and dramas – are, quite simply, dazzling. In comparison, the legacy of western Europe in the Iron Age seems crude and limited. But this should not confuse us into believing that western Europe somehow owes everything to classical Greece. As Chapter One showed, societies adapt to changes that are forced on them. The freedoms that Athenians valued so highly were, and remained, a core aspect of life in western Europe from Mesolithic to late medieval times – interrupted only by the conquests of Rome. Farming societies were based on small groups working in cooperation and holding land in common. Western European society was largely organized on the basis of extended families, with leading members of those families meeting together in a council, or assembly – a mixture of public meeting, legislature, parliament and court of law; some assemblies even had the power to elect kings. This participation was what the Greeks were so keen to preserve.

These societies were not perfect ways of living, they were adaptations to particular circumstances and they too were vulnerable to sudden change or takeover or destruction. But they were not the groups of enslaved, ignorant brutes that we have for so long been told about, who without the incursions of Rome and Greece would still be living in an age of darkness and violence. We should also remember that the connection to the natural world that Greek artists felt impelled to display was at the centre of European life from Palaeolithic times. The Athenians were not trying to shed the embedded customs of their society; they were desperately torn between the need to preserve them and the need to adapt to change.

The change that was to have the greatest influence on later western society was something we have already touched on. The idea that rational deliberation and debate was a surer way to understanding the world than experience, or the oracle, or customary practice, or exchanging tales of heroes, was increasingly taken up by groups of educated Athenians. This tendency formed the basis for the founding not only of western philosophy, but of the western view of the world.

THE BIRTH OF ABSTRACTION

Plato, Aristotle and the Rational Mind

THERE were complex processes at work in Greece, and particularly in Athens, in the fifth century BC. The birth and death of tragic theatre and the replacement of mythology by history were consequences of the use of alphabetic writing, but this was no simple relationship. The epitome of tragic theatre was an anguished, terrifying warning against the elevation of humankind above its customary relation with the natural and supernatural world, while history in Thucydides' hands became an instrument of that elevation. And if written history tried to give rational explanations for human actions, other scholars were applying the same way of thinking to other fields.

As early as the sixth century, Greeks had begun to ask what the world was made of, how it was organized and how it changed. These were dramatic and revealing questions that arose from the same impulse to find a natural order that drove the work of Solon and Cleisthenes. Others made explicit attempts to link the order underlying the natural world with the way that humans lived, or ought to live. The work of all these thinkers survives only in fragments, and is often expressed in paradoxes, riddles or verse. In contrast, large portions of the work of Plato and Aristotle, who taught in Athens in the decades after 400 BC, has survived. In the following centuries the works of the classical era and these new ways of thinking about the world were disseminated and preserved by the creation of a new Greek empire, as the Mediterranean accrued enough power to dominate the ancient heartlands of Mesopotamia, Anatolia and beyond.

A casual remark in Herodotus' *Histories* gives us a beginning for what we call natural philosophy. A drawn-out war had been going on between the Ionian states of Lydia and Media. 'But then, after five years of indecisive warfare, a battle took place in which the armies had already engaged when day was suddenly turned into night. This change from daylight to darkness had been foretold to the Ionians by Thales of Miletus, who fixed the date for it in the year in which it did, in fact, take place.' The date of the eclipse has since been calculated as 28 May 585 BC, and its prediction is evidence of a sophisticated level of astronomical knowledge. Historians of science believe that Thales would not have been able to predict the eclipse, but Herodotus' story shows that such feats could at least be contemplated.

A number of natural philosophers were at work in the region of Ionia in the sixth century BC – Thales, Anaximander and Anaximenes came from the city of Miletus; Heraclitus from Ephesus, and Pythagoras from the island of Samos. These scholars were all concerned with the essential nature of the universe – its origins, its constituent parts, the basis of its composition. These ideas may well have circulated in the Persian empire, and by the beginning of the fifth century, men like Parmenides and Zeno were putting forward their own interpretations of the universe from Greek cities in southern Italy (Pythagoras had settled in Italy in the sixth century). Empedocles, who lived in the first half of the fifth century, came from Acragas in Sicily, Anaxagoras from Asia Minor and Democritus from Abdera in the north of Greece. All over the Greek world it seems that men had been considering the natural world, not just as the creation of the gods but as the expression of some natural order, or as the result of a combination of incorruptible elements, or as the corrupt shadow of a perfect universe beyond the reach of our senses.

The idea that the universe exists as a physical order, open to exploration by humans engaging in rational thought, was a dramatic step. Written fragments of the work of Thales and Anaximander provide the earliest evidence of this step, but it is debatable whether they are seen as innovators because we know little of how people thought before alphabetic writing preserved those thoughts, or because writing itself influenced the way that people thought. It has certainly been argued that writing produced the same effect on contemplation of the natural world as it did on the study of the past.

Many of the early natural philosophers were active in the governments of their cities. The way that Greek cities were planned and governed showed, in common with Solon's laws in Athens, a belief in a 'right way' or *eunomia* in the affairs of humankind. The early philosophers applied this search for order to the natural world. This began to happen within a few decades of the adaptation of the Phoenician alphabet to the Greek language, and the development of the written language gives strong clues to the way these thoughts emerged. The Greek word for order, for example, is *kosmos*, which is also the word for world and for universe; the real world is the order that underlies the world, and this order can be discovered by the rational mind.

From the fragments that survive, we know that the composition of the world was at the centre of strong disagreement. Thales thought that the earth rested on water, and that everything was ultimately made of water. He also taught that the soul was 'mixed in the whole universe' – a belief that ties early Greek thinkers to the traditions of the east. He is also thought to have made significant discoveries in geometry, including the technique of triangulation to measure distances. Anaximander proposed that the earth is a cylinder, that the first animals were born in moisture, but that the first humans were born from other animals, perhaps fish. Heraclitus proposed that everything is always in a state of flux (he said that we cannot step into the same river twice), while Parmenides said there is neither time nor motion, and Pythagoras that everything recurs. Pythagoras believed that numbers were the basis for understanding the universe. These men made pronouncements on the origins of matter, on fossils, rainbows and all manner of natural phenomena.

The search for the underlying order of human society was made more urgent by the changes that took place in the late fifth century BC. As belief in the omnipotent gods and the power of customary laws fell away, acute problems began to emerge: the apparent contradiction between good order and freedom, principles of law versus the fickleness of jury courts, the power of the majority to cajole a minority, and so on. These changes were felt most acutely in Athens which, in the closing decade of the fifth century, became an ever more turbulent city.

At the end of the long war, which was finally concluded in 404 BC, the Corinthians and Thebans wanted Athens utterly destroyed. The defeated Athenians had themselves expected to be deported and their city razed to the ground, but the Spartan leader Lysander decided that Athens had, in the past, contributed so much to the protection of Greece that it should be spared. The surrender terms were, in view of the Athenians' treatment of enemy cities, surprisingly light. The city walls were to be demolished, together with the defences around the harbour at Piraeus; the Athenian fleet was to be reduced to twelve vessels; and Athens was to give up any independent foreign policy. All exiles were allowed to return to the city. It was said that the ending of the war lifted a great burden from the Athenians and that the people sang as they pulled down the walls of their city. Although their political dominance was at an end, they believed that a time of peace and harmony was beginning for the cities of Greece.

But how was this new Athens to be governed? Lysander supported the rule of an oligarchy, known as the Thirty, but these aristocrats soon began to inflict terror on the city, murdering 1,500 of their political rivals. Civil war ensued as a man called Thrasybulus mustered an army that defeated the Thirty's forces. Nevertheless, the oligarchy kept control of the city and intensified the terror, drawing up a list of 3,000 favoured citizens; anyone not on the list knew they were liable to be persecuted and possibly executed. Once again Sparta was asked to intervene, and this time their king, Pausanias, oversaw the restoration of democracy. So, by 400 BC, Athens was once more a democracy and, for the first time in 30 years, at peace with its neighbours.

Among the philosophers we know were active at this time were Diogenes of Appollonia, Leucippus, Democritus of Abdera, and Socrates the Athenian. The latter two are crucial to our understanding of how later western thinking developed, but whereas we know little of the life of Democritus, details of Socrates' life and work have been preserved. So, we begin with him.

Socrates, who was born around 469 BC, served with honour in the war against Sparta. He became a familiar figure in the streets of Athens and in the assembly, asking awkward and piercing questions, obdurately sticking to the law, and generally lacking a proper regard for self-appointed authority. Though we have nothing that was directly written by Socrates, it is apparent that he was a mesmerizing talker who inspired enormous loyalty and affection among his band of followers. Although he dressed simply, Socrates liked a good feast with plenty of wine and good conversation. He also infused his followers with his approach to life and to the questions that life provokes. Chief among these was a deep and enquiring scepticism and an adherence to rational thought and discussion as the source of human knowledge. The desire for humans to increase their knowledge was deeply felt by Socrates because he believed that knowledge brought virtue and that men acted badly only out of ignorance. Conversely Socrates asserted that no harm can come to you if you do good, because the only real harm a person can suffer is to his or her soul. A just life will not harm your soul.

Socrates was not an isolated seeker after truth, but a product of his time and place. In the last decades of the fifth century BC, scholars in Athens and elsewhere began to tire of the restrictions of the old myths. Tragic theatre seemed to have exhausted all the possible answers that these legends could offer; new areas of thinking were needed to cope with the questions that the changing society was provoking.

Among those asking these questions were the sophists. They were educated men who saw that success in Athenian society required skill in argument and oratory. They therefore set themselves up as teachers of debate and rhetoric to the sons of the upper classes. There was much more to sophistry than its modern negative connotation implies. The development of debating skills was not just a matter of effect; in order to win an argument, a speaker must be able to show logical inconsistencies in his opponents' approaches, to think through and clarify his own reasoning in order to avoid being ensnared by others, to look for fault and rectitude in particular statements and arguments and to seek out evidence to support any assertions he might make. All of these were the tools of the sophist's trade that Socrates avidly applied. By tradition Socrates differed from the sophists because of his moral outlook. While they taught rhetoric for money, he debated for love of argument and went shoeless; while they paraded their knowledge for professional gain, he asserted his own profound ignorance.

Socrates was a sceptic but he was not a cynic. He believed that the laws that the Athenians had arrived at through rational debate were morally just, because he believed in the identity of knowledge and moral virtue. Informed detailed debate had elicited a set of laws that carried moral authority because of their origins. But things were not so simple in practice. Convictions in Athenian courts were made on the basis of jury votes. There were no police to enforce the law or to investigate evidence; there were simply the courts, where each side must present its case. In some cases the popular assembly worked as a court, and had the power of life and death over those elected or appointed to serve the city. While this may appear preferable to tyrannical justice, it created its own difficulties. The jurors and assembly members were responsible citizens, but they were not experts on the law. They listened to what was said, made up their minds about who was right, and then voted accordingly. They could be swayed (hence the teachers of rhetoric) and they could be inconsistent. In the popular assembly the inconsistencies became magnified in the tense and recriminatory atmosphere of war. When things went well, the Athenians stuck together; when the war against Sparta went badly, they did not hesitate to blame their leaders and generals.

For a rational thinker this system was unsatisfactory and inconsistent, and to Socrates it seemed that both society and individuals could only fulfil their functions if they understood the concepts that underlay their decisions. Ideas such as 'truth' and 'justice' had been used by Athenians like Solon and Aeschylus and were employed by sophists in their arguments in the jury courts and assembly. Socrates subjected these concepts to rational analysis that went beyond the casually assumed knowledge of other philosophers. Rather than using them as weapons in argument, he saw truth, justice and goodness as the highest goals of human endeavour. Goodness, in Socrates' mind, was something beyond, and superior to, pleasure or companionship or beauty, or even life itself.

This was the birth of human morality – the idea that there is some essential goodness to which we can all aspire. Socrates believed we could reach goodness through rational debate and the acquisition of knowledge, others have felt it would come through spiritual contemplation, or through political action, or through the forces of history, or through scientific progress. Whatever the means of reaching it, the concept of human morality is Socrates' gift to the world. It is an invention, born of a particular time and place, not a 'natural' phenomenon; and it is arguably the single concept that marks out western society from all others that have ever existed.

While Socrates asked 'What is justice?' 'What is truth?' and 'What is good?' he did not offer answers to these questions. Instead he argued that the real meaning of these concepts could be discovered by rational consideration and debate. This had the effect of installing the belief that these concepts actually existed independently of time, place and circumstance, as well as the notion that they were only available to those who could engage in rational discussion. Socrates may have wished to rescue ideas of truth and justice from the devious wiles of the sophists, but he ended up promoting the concept of morality, and making it a preserve of the educated.

Democracy was restored to Athens in 403 BC; four years later Socrates, who was then 70 years old, was brought before the assembly on charges of impiety and of corrupting the young. The first charge was used to rouse the assembly against him; the second was based on Socrates' friendship with, and tutelage of, a number of discredited young aristocrats who had been part of the Thirty. They had been granted an amnesty, and in a sense, Socrates became a scapegoat for their crimes. He was brought before an assembly of 501 citizens who, after hearing speeches from an accuser and then from the defendant, found him guilty by 280 votes to 221. His accusers asked for the death penalty. It was then up to Socrates to propose a lesser penalty and argue for it, but he refused to suggest any alternative. His supporters offered to pay a fine, but this was refused and he was sentenced to death. His final speech to the 501 people who had decided he must die was unrepentant and scornful: 'I suggest, gentlemen, that the difficulty is not so much to escape death; the real difficulty is to escape from doing wrong, which is far more fleet of foot.' His last words to the court were, 'Now it is time that we were going, I to die and you to live; but which of us has the happier prospect is unknown to anyone but God.' Socrates chose not to wait for execution, but took poison.

Because Socrates' work was preserved and expanded so effectively by his pupil Plato, his ideas appear to be the intellectual culmination of the classical age of Greece. The unrelenting application of reason and knowledge seems, in Socrates' hands, to promise great things. Moral failure, bad behaviour, misjudgement, evil can all, in theory, be corrected or eliminated by intellectual effort. This seductive vision fits with the modern view of the classical world, but just as copies of white marble statues and picturesque ruins are a pale and distorting shadow of Greek culture, so too is Socrates' belief in the supremacy of rationality as the route to truth and goodness. Democritus (c. 460–385 BC) was a younger contemporary of Socrates, who lived most of his life in the northern Greek city of Abdera. He was the author of a substantial number of works on physics, cosmology, geology, medicine, ethics and politics, all of which have been lost – only 300 or so fragments of his writings survive, some of which are paraphrasings of his work by later compilers. Nevertheless we know that Democritus was a substantial figure in Greece, and the work that survives shows an entirely different way of thinking about the world to that promoted by Socrates.

While Socrates believed that all real knowledge is knowledge of the truth, Democritus wrote, 'A man must learn on this principle, that he is far removed from the truth.' This scepticism about absolute truth, or absolute anything, underpinned all of his thinking. He did not believe in the Socratic notion that people would be good if they were in possession of knowledge, nor the idea that a society could be constructed to bring this about: 'There is no device in the present state of society to stop the wrongdoing of officials, however thoroughly good they may be.' In other words people could be both good and capable of doing wrong. Democritus also wrote, 'Poverty in a democracy is preferable to so-called prosperity among dictators, just as freedom is to slavery.' For him, 'the well-managed polis is the greatest source of success, and all depends on this'. This management involved hard work on the part of officials and generosity from civic leaders: 'When those in power venture to provide funds for the poor and to do them services and be kind to them, the result is compassion, an end to isolation, the formation of comradeships, mutual assistance and concord among the citizens . . .'

Democritus saw the political process as a practical endeavour that needed continual work, revision, mutual help and generosity, not theoretical constructs. There was no system that would guarantee this, though in the Greek *polis*, democracy was certainly preferable to dictatorship. But in his views of the natural world and human behaviour Democritus also considered that the search for absolutes was illusory: 'We know nothing truly about anything, but for each of us our opinions are a rearrangement of the elements of our soul.' This tradition grew out of the practical ways in which Greek cities had responded to the threats of tyranny, wealth and invasion, but its emphasis on relativism, pragmatism and experience was to be swept away by the dominant figure of Plato.

The trial, conviction and consequent suicide of Socrates was recorded by his most able disciple, and it is through Plato's work that Socrates became a figure of universal, rather than local, significance. Plato was born in Athens in about 427 BC to an aristocratic family. The first 30 years of his life encompassed some of the most turbulent, exhilarating and depressing in the city's history. Athens was at war with Sparta and the conflict was the background to a constantly shifting political scene. Plato served in the Athenian forces in 408 BC, and his family was intimately connected with the oligarchy of the Thirty that came to power after Athens' defeat in 404 BC – his great-uncle Critias and uncle Charmides were both members of that regime.

For Plato, who was then 30 years old, the death of Socrates was a bitter experience. Like many aristocratic Athenians he had been dismayed by the antics of the assembly during the war and blamed the defeat on the city's dissolution and incompetence as compared to the self-discipline and military professionalism of the Spartans. The conviction of his mentor by a citizens' jury court must have reinforced his feelings against the rule of the people. Plato left Athens immediately after Socrates' death and returned in 388 BC to set up the Academy – a type of advanced school that was the prototype of the modern university. At the Academy he wrote a series of works almost all of which have survived to the present day.

Plato's works take the form of a series of conversations enacted between two or more people. In almost every case one of the protagonists is Socrates, while the other is a well-known sophist. Plato's earliest works are about the trial and death of Socrates, and it is generally assumed that these dialogues offer a faithful representation of Socrates' views. Thereafter Plato begins, perhaps gaining in confidence, to put forward his own ideas and arguments while still using a character named Socrates as his vehicle.

During the course of each dialogue Socrates asks simple, but loaded, questions, such as 'What is justice?' or 'What is oratory?' or 'Are laws granted by the gods or constructed by man?' and proceeds to tie his unfortunate opponent in knots. More importantly they allow Plato to expound his views on a variety of subjects, under the guise of rational debate. Plato's method of investigating a subject, inherited from the sophists and from Socrates, was to wear away at it by continually asking questions that would reveal inconsistencies and illogic in the casually held views of the other participants. The intellectual thoroughness of Plato's work, the brilliance and utter clarity of his writing and the fact that the dialogues survived intact made him not simply the dominant thinker of his time but the founding father of western philosophy.

So much for Plato's methods; what were the ideas he expounded? Rather than asking, as natural philosophers like Anaximander and Heraclitus had, 'What are all these things *made of*?' Plato saw that our actual experience of the world is to ask more fundamentally 'What *are* all these things?' and to try to find answers. In other words, the way that we apprehend the world is not simply based on figuring out its physical attributes, but on a conceptual understanding. But what is our conceptual understanding of the world? How do we make sense of the world around us? Plato's answer to this question, the Theory of Forms, is his most enduring and influential idea. When we name particular animals as 'cats' or 'dogs' or particular plants as 'trees' or 'ferns', or particular objects as 'tables' or 'chairs', we are categorizing them. We do this easily and instinctively because we perceive that those within each category share certain characteristics. If we analyse a particular category, say, dog, we can arrive at a group of characteristics that tell us what 'dogness' is. So far so good. Why, though, do we make these particular categories? Why, for example, do we not group white cats and white dogs together in a group called 'whities' and brown dogs and brown cats in another group called 'brownies'? And how, even when we are very young, do we recognize a dog without going through some kind of checklist of features to see whether each beast meets the minimum requirements? Plato believed that this must be because we carry around within our minds an ideal form of a dog (and cat and tree and table) that informs our sense.

Not only do these ideal forms exist in our minds, they actually exist in another world. This ideal world is beyond the reach of our ordinary senses but is available to our minds through rational thought. The real world that is available to our sense is therefore a corrupted shadow of the ideal. In a famous passage in *The Republic,* Plato compared the life of the senses to living in a cave. Shut off from the light, all that the cave-dwellers see are the shadows of what is going on outside, in the gorgeous sunlight of the ideal world, projected on to the wall of their cave. This striking image shows Plato's distrust of the senses and his belief in the rational mind as the way of understanding the true, ideal world.

Plato believed that a natural order underlay all things, whether physical or moral. Greek natural philosophers had sought universal answers to questions about the physical world; the revolutionary nature of their work was to try to discover rules or causes or ingredients that applied *everywhere and at all times.* Plato took this 'universalist' way of thinking and applied it to conceptual understanding, but also to questions of justice, goodness, politics and governance. His work was designed to discover ideals that existed free of the world, but that could be sought out and applied anywhere, regardless of place, time, custom or experience. Plato's most influential work, *The Republic*, starts by asking 'What is justice?' and leads, via the Theory of Forms, to the depiction of an ideal society. The structure of the society is carefully worked out, right down to governance, jurisprudence, marriage, family life, education and military training – all arrived at through rational debate.

The first-time reader, knowing something of the reputation of ancient Greece and its great philosopher, might expect Plato's ideal society to be open and democratic, with a free exchange of ideas and information and a flourishing culture of art and poetry. In fact, the opposite is the case. Plato's republic is ruled by an oligarchy of philosophers selected from the class of Rulers, family life in the two upper classes (Rulers and Auxiliaries) is abolished in favour of eugenic breeding of children, and poetry, drama and representational art are forbidden. Truth comes through knowledge, so paintings and stories that pretend to be true depictions must not be allowed. *The Republic* shows how his own method of rational abstract debate led Plato to propose a fixed ideal society that was the opposite of Democritus' pragmatic, changing *polis*, and of the free and open city eulogized just 50 years earlier by Pericles.

A devastating attack on Plato's political work was mounted in 1945 by the philosopher Karl Popper, then a refugee from Hitler's Austria, in his book *The Open Society and its Enemies*. Popper argued that the introduction of idealism into politics and the search for an ideal society were disastrous precedents that led directly to totalitarianism. Any fixed society will, by definition, be hostile to criticism or to change; and preservation of the society itself becomes more important than the welfare of its people. Popper considered Plato's work to be an attack on the open society of Athens and a betrayal of those who had brought it about. He mentioned Democritus and Pericles, but really the openness of Athens owed more to the citizens who made Solon's and Cleisthenes' reforms necessary.

While abstract rationalism apparently led Plato to construct an ideal society, we must question the objectivity of his work. He was the son of an aristocratic family heavily implicated in the terror of 404 BC and his father-figure Socrates was sentenced to death by democrats. While Democritus argued that order and liberty could co-exist, Plato swept liberty aside in favour of control, which, combined with his belief in Socrates' legacy, led him to propose a society in which poets could not write for fear of offending authority, where only philosophers would have the right to rule, and where the future ruling class would be bred on demand and trained for their elevated role.

Plato showed that the path to the truth was to isolate key concepts like knowledge or justice by stripping away local variations and the impurities that come from everyday practice, and abstracting their underlying 'ideal' essence. This process did not need research into different methods of justice, nor was there any need to go out into the world to see how different people acquired and used knowledge. The whole point was to see through the corruption and messiness of the world to the ideal world beyond. This could only be done by men of good intelligence withdrawing from the world and rationally considering and debating these great issues. Western philosophy has followed the same path ever since: teasing out the universals, the constants, the invariables from among the clamour and noise of the real world; firmly believing that abstraction is the way to clarity of thought and thereby towards greater understanding of the human predicament.

Plato's rarefied view of the path to truth was adopted and amended by his pupil Aristotle. Born in Stagira in northern Greece in 384 BC, Aristotle was the son of the physician to the king of Macedon. Sent to Athens for his education, he entered Plato's Academy at the age of 17 and remained there for 20 years, until Plato died in 347 BC. He travelled for the next 12 years, including a short spell as tutor to Philip of Macedon's son Alexander. Aristotle returned to Athens in 335 BC and set up his own school, the Lyceum, where he taught for 12 years until he was forced to leave Athens in 323 BC, just a year before his death.

The period that Aristotle lived through is, in contrast to the century before, remarkably thinly documented. The decades between the end of the Peloponnesian war in 404 BC and the astonishing empire-building of Philip and Alexander are covered by only one complete history that has survived – Xenophon's *Hellenica* – and that is notoriously unreliable. Historians believe that during the fourth century BC, the city-states of central and southern Greece fought between themselves to a point where none could properly defend its borders. Thebes became the dominant state at this time, successfully invading the territory of Sparta, while Corinth and Athens became involved in major conflicts. All they achieved was to become too weak to resist the new power from the north. Philip of Macedon defeated the Athenians at Chaeronea in 338

BC to become master of the Greek mainland, and was succeeded in 336 by his son Alexander.

Aristotle, a Macedonian, was a follower of Plato, but the differences between them have sustained discussion among philosophers for centuries. Although Aristotle argued against some of Plato's central ideas, he followed him in holding rational enquiry to be the path to discovering the truth about the world and about humanity. Aristotle agreed that there was some sort of essence inhabiting each object in the world, but he did not believe that these essences existed independently – there is no such thing as catness or dogness that could exist outside of objects that are cats or dogs. Aristotle also saw that while this idea of an essence could be applied to static objects, the world, as earlier philosophers had pointed out, is full of growth and movement. He argued that each object contains not just a static essence, but the essence of what it can become, which he termed its natural end or *telos*. So an acorn contains the essence of an oak tree, a human child contains the essence of its adult self. The acorn and the baby grow because they have a natural cause to do so, in order to move from the potential that lies within them to its realization as an oak tree or adult human. Movement too involves the fulfilment or actualization of the potential within objects.

The fulfilment of a natural end or *telos* is a unifying principle in Aristotle's thinking about a whole range of subjects. He sees the aim of a good life to be the fulfilment of its *telos*, which is to engage in excellent activity such as intellectual contemplation or virtuous actions. In politics the city-state or *polis* is the fulfilment of the potential of good men to combine together, and the *polis* in turn has the potential to fulfil its goal of providing a society in which every citizen can find well-being.

The other major principle in Aristotle, which relates to the fulfilment of *telos*, is the existence of causes. While objects contain the potential to move, they are actually set in motion by some force outside themselves. This force is then the cause of their motion. Aristotle believed that even where such causes of movement and growth are invisible, such as in the growth of plants and animals, they nevertheless exist. Every movement, every growth must have a cause, and each cause is itself brought about by another movement, which has its own cause. By a long series of deductions Aristotle was able to show how all causes can be traced back through a chain of consequence to a First

Cause or Prime Mover. This First Cause is then the originator or creator of the universe.

By the time Aristotle died in 322 BC the Greek world had been transformed by the astonishing career of his one-time pupil Alexander of Macedon. The Eurasian heartland – the territories once controlled by the Sumerians, Hittites, Babylonians, Assyrians, Egyptians and Persians – was, in just 15 years, conquered by Alexander and made part of a new and vast Greek empire. The Hellenistic world created by Alexander and his successors preserved the culture of classical Greece but applied its lessons in a situation whose physical, social and political dimensions had utterly changed. The particular became the universal, as the locus of Greek intellectual enquiry changed from the city-state to the world empire. Practical and theoretical questions about how to be a good citizen of a *polis* gave way to enquiries into the universal nature of morality and justice. It was the writings of Plato and Aristotle, with their emphasis on universal phenomena, that were revered. Plato's seductive message that the power of reason could secure the truth and transform the human condition overcame Democritus' acceptance of the subjectiveness and contingency of human existence.

In 356 BC, when Philip acceded to the throne of Macedon, it was a small, relatively poor state in the north of Greece, on the edge of the Hellenic world. Thirty years later his son Alexander was ruler of an empire stretching from Italy to India and from Egypt to the Caspian Sea. This conquest was achieved with an army of just 30,000 men. The textbooks tell us that Philip's greatest ambition was to overthrow the Persian empire – a task so comprehensively completed by his son Alexander. But where did this impulse come from?

Macedon's northern borders contained valuable grasslands vulnerable to incursions from nomadic tribes travelling between the steppes of the north Caucasus and the Hungarian plain. Philip raised an army in order to protect his territory, which gave him access to continual supplies of horses and grazing. Once he had an army and a cavalry, Philip became a desirable ally for others and was soon drawn into a conflict between the cities of Thebes and Phocis, which ended with him in control of more territory. Soon the leader of an organization of northeastern Greek states, Philip was seen as a threat by Athens and Thebes, who declared war against him. Once he had defeated them, he found himself in control of virtually the whole of Greece.

For centuries Greece had been a collection of independent city-states, bickering, befriending, warring and making alliances. Under Philip most were suddenly part of one entity and that entity was an old-fashioned monarchy. The age of the *polis* was over, to be replaced by a kingdom and an empire. Why did Philip then take on the Persian empire? It may be that he wanted to liberate those Greek cities that still paid tribute to Persia, or that he wanted to remove the threat of a Persian invasion of Greece for good. But it is clear that Philip was a soldier king and all his power had been won for him by his army. Once he was in control of Greece, there was nowhere else for him and his highly motivated, experienced, battle-hardened troops to go. It seems that it was impossible for him to stop and go home to Macedon, and to send his troops back to their homes, to their farms and their fields. Philip may also have felt that his new power simply made him more likely to come under attack from Persia. For him and his son Alexander, the ultimate goal was not a good society or a well-governed *polis* or a secure confederation of bickering states, it was an empire that controlled the world. The only way to achieve that was to overthrow the Persian empire and set up your own in its place.

When Philip of Macedon died in 336 BC his 19-year-old son Alexander became king of Macedon and leader of the Greek federation. The path of Alexander's reign was already set; his armies were in Asia Minor, marching towards Issus and a confrontation with Darius III. Over the next 12 years Alexander remained at the head of an army that crossed and re-crossed the Persian empire, conquering and capturing Syria, Phoenicia, Egypt, Babylon, Susa and Persepolis. He defeated Darius on three separate occasions in battle and became ruler of every territory that his army could reach.

We see Alexander as a glamorous and romantic figure, perhaps the greatest soldier that ever lived. But it has been argued that he is an early example of a distinctively western culture of war-making. The traditional horse warrior of the Asian steppes relied on indirect attacks and evasion, using missiles, tactical withdrawals and stamina to wear down an enemy, rather than attempting to destroy him in pitched battle. When these peoples moved into the lowlands to establish agricultural and urban societies, they retained this method of indirect war-making and combined it with diplomacy and the absorption of enemies into their own culture. This belief in military restraint was the philosophy of Asian societies from the Chinese to the Islamic Arabs, and including the Persians.

Alexander's troops, in contrast, believed in the concept of honour in war, and were fighting for a cause rather than for a piece of territory. This belief was based on a sense of superiority over their enemies, which came from their understanding that they were uniquely free. In battle, the Greek infantry would stand and fight to the death, and would die with honour, since the outcome of the battle mattered more than survival, and a good death was to be welcomed not feared. Darius and his armies simply could not understand Alexander's lust for battle, and at the final confrontation Darius' entourage murdered their own leader and left his body for Alexander, in the hope that this would satisfy him – which, of course, it did not. The Persians went to war cautiously, in order to gain advantage; the Greeks went joyously, to find honour, and they did not know how to stop fighting.

Alexander conquered the Persian heartland, pushed north-east to Samarkand and Bukhara, then turned south-east, over the Hindu Kush and across the Afghan plateau, before crossing the Indus river and marching on across the Punjab. His aim was to push his line of defence eastward, to eliminate any threats from the people of central and southern Asia, but Alexander was chasing an illusion. Following the custom of thousands of years, the people of the steppes and plateaux of central Asia withdrew in the face of threat, only to re-emerge when the Greeks had passed by. Alexander could not build a wall around half the world and keep the other half out.

In 325 BC Alexander marched back to Persia from India and died in Babylon two years later, probably of typhus. He was just 33 years old. Though his futile push to the east had a strategic purpose, Alexander and his troops knew little else besides the military life. They carried on fighting because they knew no other way of living. In the end his troops rebelled and asked to be allowed home, but only when they had reached the end of the earth.

After Alexander's death his family, generals, governors and courtiers fought over the territory they had conquered. By around 280 BC the extent of each of their realms became more or less settled and the three great Hellenistic dynasties were founded.* The Seleucids controlled a vast region from Syria through Babylonia and east to the Indus; the

---

* The empire Alexander created is known as the Hellenistic world to distinguish it from the Hellenic world centred on the Aegean that preceded it.

Ptolemies ruled as kings in Egypt; and the Antigonids ruled over Macedon, whose territory included much, but not all, of mainland Greece. Smaller territories remained as independent kingdoms within this vast area. The Macedonians had not taken over the whole of the Hellenic world, for example, and many states in the 'old' Greek world remained independent. Many of these cities kept faith with their democratic institutions and participatory government, but the world around them had changed and no city could make external policy without reference to its large and powerful neighbours.

The old Greek cities had changed internally too. One of Alexander's most important innovations was the introduction of a single currency throughout his empire. This stimulated trade across a massive area, with the cities of the Mediterranean having direct access to the wheatfields of Egypt and the Levant. The transportation of grain across the Mediterranean became the vital engine of Greek prosperity, but this new way of trading based on money produced a polarization in society. The rich were able to accumulate wealth more easily, while the poor were largely unable to break into the world of money-making. Wealth and poverty had existed before, of course, but when the differences became so great, the cycle of political participation, military service, widespread education and civic identity that had driven the democracies of the fifth century was broken.

Nevertheless, small city-states did survive and flourish in third- and second-century Greece, but only by combining together in federations. The Aetolian and Achaean leagues both became regional powers in southern Greece. In the cities of the leagues all free men of military age met in a primary assembly twice a year; they elected an annual chief magistrate who served as the general of the combined armies; and they sent representatives both to a general council and to a committee, the *apokletoi*, which looked after the league's day-to-day business. The historian Polybius, writing around 150 BC, stated: 'One could not find a political system and principle more favourable to equality, free speech and in short genuine democracy than that existing among the Achaeans . . . the League quickly reached the goal it had set itself, being aided by two powerful factors, equality and humanity' (quoted in Walbank). The open cooperation of the leagues might have prospered, and federalism could have spread as a model of government that used the best aspects of the *polis* and the empire, if not for the growing power of Rome.

The internal make-up of the eastern kingdoms of the Hellenistic world was quite different. Alexander wanted Greeks to join with the ruling classes of the old Persian empire to form a new political and cultural elite, but his successors formed ruling groups that were exclusively Greek. Macedonian and other Greek soldiers put down roots in this brave new world, while Greek emigrants who flooded out from their homelands found that, whatever their background, they were socially superior to the native Persians, Mesopotamians, Egyptians and Phoenicians in whose cities they settled. Greek culture became the social standard, and the Greek language the lingua franca, of a huge part of the world. (Most Europeans still have only the vaguest idea of the geography of this area. The westernmost Greek cities on the coast of Spain were 1,500 miles from Athens and a further 3,000 miles from eastern settlements on the river Oxus. The total distance across the Hellenistic world was therefore around 4,500 miles, the same distance as Edinburgh to Kathmandu.)

The Hellenistic world was a model for future cultural entities, particularly in Europe. A well-defined ruling class imported its culture on the back of its conquests, and made that culture the defining motif of its civilization. To be civilized in the Hellenistic world you had to be immersed in Greek culture, the culture of your conquerors. Greeks paid for their sons to be educated in the poetry of Homer and Euripides, in music, in physical training and in arithmetic. The gymnasium became, in effect, a secondary school, giving further instruction to older boys who had acquired an elementary education. Scholars travelled between cities to learn from each other and to teach. Greek teaching and learning spread the ideas and impulses and texts of the classical period to a thousand towns and cities across the world. Athens, though a minor military power, was revered as the home of philosophy and of the famous triumvirate of Socrates, Plato and Aristotle. But other cities in the east became famous as centres of learning. Pergamum in Asia Minor and Ptolemy's capital Alexandria, home to a famous library and museum, were particular magnets for scholars, but eminent Hellenistic philosophers came from an enormous geographical range, including Samos, Cyprus, Athens, Rhodes, Syria, Asia Minor, Sicily and Thessaly.

The Hellenistic world preserved and spread the culture of classical Greece. But, as we have seen, that culture was itself contradictory. As well as that, the new generations of Greek thinkers found themselves

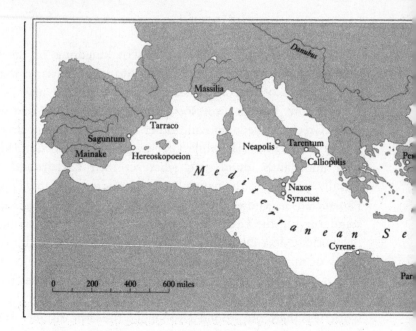

By 250 BC the Greek world encompassed the Hellenistic kingdoms of the east, and the old Greek cities and colonies in the west, stretching from the Atlantic seaboard to the Hindu Kush.

in a different situation from their illustrious forebears. Socrates and Plato had wondered how a good man should order his life, how a city should be governed, and how a man should be a good citizen. But the cities the Hellenists inhabited were self-governing in name only; the idea of seeing the *polis* and the human individual as identical, autonomous entities no longer held. Instead, the individual existed in a world whose boundaries had receded beyond the horizon.

The consequence of this physical and political change was a new focus on the life of the individual subject within a universal culture. Plato and Aristotle's belief in reasoning as the route to abstract knowledge became and remained the reference point for all serious thinkers, but circumstances altered its application. Philosophy polarized into those, like the followers of Epicurus, who viewed the individual in isolation, and those, like the stoics, who were concerned with the place of humans in society, and with the universality of humanity. The Hellenistic world also saw the development of a school of thought known as Neoplatonism, which interpreted Plato's depiction of ideal forms as being a religious or mystical philosophy. The ideal of goodness, of justice and of truth, was, for Neoplatonists, the One – that

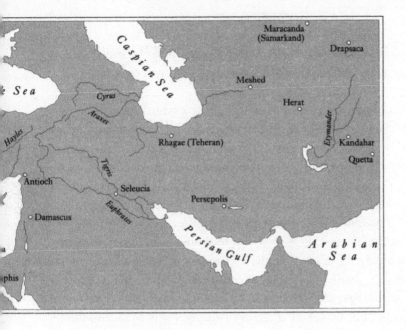

is, the divine source of everything – and truth could come through revelation as well as reason. These three philosophies were, several centuries later, to feed into different strands of Christian theology (see Chapter Five).

Hellenistic scholarship was not restricted to philosophers. People working as engineers, architects and physicians felt the impulse to look into the theoretical side of their work, and science began to flex its muscles as a quite separate activity from philosophy. Euclid's *Elements*, published around 300 BC, was a summary of previous mathematical knowledge showing how mathematical proofs are derived from a particular set of axioms. Archimedes, who lived in the Greek city of Syracuse in Sicily in the third century BC, worked on geometry, optics, astronomy, engineering and hydrostatics. Archimedes was close to being a practical scientist, using his theoretical knowledge to devise levers, pulleys, irrigators and machines for repelling besiegers. Appollonius, Eratosthenes, Hipparchus and a host of others made significant innovations in mathematics, geometry and astronomy.

Despite this theoretical interest in the natural world, the Hellenistic approach to practical matters was quite different to our own. Greek gentlemen shunned physical labour, and status in society was gained by written not practical works, and by teaching wealthy and influential pupils. Almost all scientists at this time were, in effect, observers rather than experimenters. Practical intervention in the world in order to get it to give up its secrets had to wait another 17 centuries.

While Greek culture swept across a vast area of Eurasia, two other powers were rising in the west. The Phoenician city of Carthage was, by the third century BC, powerful enough to control the western Mediterranean, while Rome began its entanglement in Greek affairs in 281 BC, with a war against King Pyrrhus of Epirus. Roman troops first crossed the Adriatic to mainland Greece in 229 BC, and in 217 BC Agelaus told a gathering of delegates from different Greek cities: 'If once you wait for these clouds that are looming in the west to settle on Greece, we may all of us find these truces and wars and games at which we play . . . [will be] rudely interrupted' (quoted in Walbank). He went unheeded and the Romans kept coming. They withdrew from Greece in 194 BC, but in 148 BC a change of policy saw Macedon made a province of Rome. In 146 BC Roman power over the Mediterranean, east and west, was asserted with violence rather than diplomacy when the cities of Carthage and Corinth were destroyed. Over the next century the Romans pushed east, taking over the whole of the Hellenistic world, apart from Egypt. Cleopatra, last queen of Egypt, tried to save the independence of her kingdom by seducing first Julius Caesar, and then Mark Antony, ruler of the eastern Roman empire. Her attempts ended when Octavian defeated Antony and the Egyptian forces at Actium in 31 BC. Cleopatra's death in 30 BC marked the formal end of the Hellenistic world.

Hellenistic culture did not disappear with the coming of the Romans. Instead, the Roman empire became a vehicle for the perpetuation of Greek, or Graeco-Roman, culture; and for its transmission to central and western Europe. The eastern part of the Roman empire remained a Greek cultural zone, at least for the ruling elite, for seven centuries after Cleopatra. But when Arab armies swept across the Near East in the eighth century, Islamic scholars found Greek texts from the fifth and fourth centuries BC intact and already translated into Aramaic and Persian. The works of Plato and Aristotle became part of the canon of the Arab world, and it was Arab scholars who were to reintroduce the culture of classical Greece into western Europe in the twelfth century. The legacy of classical Greece never did die out, only to be rediscovered in Renaissance Europe; it endured in the Hellenistic, Roman, Byzantine and Arab worlds. From Alexandria and Byzantium and from

Córdoba and Grenada the legacy of the innovations that had taken place in Athens was eventually, and gradually, transmitted to the people of western and northern Europe.

In our historical memory, classical Greece is a place of extraordinary innovation and achievement. Science, philosophy, democracy, theatre, mythology, epic poetry, architecture and sculpture were brought into being or given new life in just a few generations. All of these seem somehow connected to a new belief in rationality and in humans as the authors of their own destinies. But when we look closer we see that these connections are often contradictory. The work of Plato and Aristotle is seen as the summation and culmination of classical Greek thought, but Plato's promotion of abstract rationality as the route to truth and justice was a contentious and, in many ways, extreme vision. Plato, we should remember, came after the fact. Greek democracy, tragedy and art were created not by abstract rationalists, but by practical pragmatists handling the transformation of their societies with great courage, determination and imagination. Nevertheless, it is Plato's work that has survived, and it is his vision that has come to dominate the cultural assumptions of western civilization.

THE UNIVERSAL CIVILIZATION

Rome and the Barbarians

THE Greek and Hellenistic worlds described in the previous chapters brushed against the Iron Age societies of central, northern and western Europe; but between them there was only a small amount of trade and limited exchanges of technology. It was the Roman empire that, from the second century BC, brought the culture and civilization of the eastern Mediterranean to the north and west. The influence of Roman rule on Europe was, and remains, immense; but despite our interest in the classical world, we seldom discuss the impact of Rome on western Europe in its historical context. The later adoption of Greece and Rome as our cultural ancestors has obscured the story of what actually happened when Rome came to Iberia, Gaul, western Germania and Britain. Yet the meeting of these different cultures – the Mediterranean, the Germanic and the western Celtic – through trade, conquest, occupation and withdrawal was central to the development of western civilization.

Rome was a Mediterranean power. The republic was founded around 510 BC, after throwing off the controlling power of the Etruscans. As it expanded its territory in central Italy Rome became, like others before and since, drawn into more and more external conflicts. By the time it had conquered, absorbed or become allied with the central Italian peoples, Rome found itself in competition and conflict with the other major powers of the Mediterranean – Carthage in the west, and the kingdoms of Macedon, Epirus and the smaller Hellenistic powers in the east. The most rapid period of Roman expansion came between

250 and 140 BC, during which Carthage, Macedon and other Greek powers were defeated, and their territories annexed. Though more conquests were made later, Rome was, by 150 BC, master of the Mediterranean world.

For the peoples of central and western Europe, Roman expansion meant the replacement of several neighbours and trading partners by one dominant military and economic power. The Greek cities that dotted the southern Spanish, French and Italian coasts, the Carthaginian lands of north Africa and western Iberia, and the Etruscan territories in northern Italy were all absorbed into the Roman empire; from 140 BC onwards it was Rome that controlled trade between the Mediterranean and the north. The climax of Mediterranean conquest coincided with the rebellion led by the Gracchi brothers, which resulted in a long period of internal conflict in Rome. This halted further conquest in the west for nearly a century; but the pause in conquest did not prevent the development of trade between Romans and the western 'barbarians'.

Once Rome had control of the Mediterranean coast of Gaul in the second century BC, huge quantities of wine and other goods were shipped from Italy to Masillia (Marseilles) and Narbo (Narbonne) for onward transport. Thanks to the virtual indestructibility and distinctive provenance of the transportable wine flasks, or amphorae, the trade in wine has been extensively traced. Second-century amphorae have been found in large quantities throughout southern Gaul, along the Rhône–Rhine and Garonne–Aude river routes, along the Seine, on the Brittany coast, and around the Solent and north of the Thames estuary in southern England. While trade in wine and luxury goods extended as far north as southern Britain, Roman merchants were eager to acquire metals, furs, leather, woollen cloth, honey, grain and, from Iberia, olive oil.

The other major import into the empire was slaves. Taking and owning slaves had been a feature of the Mediterranean world for centuries, but developments in the heart of the Roman empire vastly increased the level of demand. To see how this happened, we need to understand how the Romans raised their armies and made their alliances, and how this in turn led to a continuing need for conquest.

Between 500 and 250 BC the Romans came to dominate the centre of the Italian peninsula – a fertile and heavily populated agricultural region – by a combination of conquest and alliance. The populations of subject states were made full citizens of Rome, citizens without suffrage rights (*sine suffragio*), or remained as allies. But all fell within the Roman confederation and all provided men for the Roman army. The grouping of states controlled by Rome had huge reserves of military manpower, and the empire quickly became self-propelling – more conquests gave more troops, which gave more ability to conquer. By 264 BC Rome had 150 treaties with defeated or allied cities or communities, all of which undertook to provide troops for the Roman army. Wars became an effective way of tying existing allies into the Roman commonwealth, and could be conducted at relatively little risk to Rome itself.

Military conquest and expansion might be advantageous for Rome, but why did her allies go along with it? Roman treaties gave a share of all war gains to her allies, including land as well as movable spoils – Italians were given grants of land in Gaul, Spain and elsewhere. The expansionism of Rome and her allies has been likened to a criminal gang – as long as the gang keeps stealing, everyone gets a share in the takings; but stop and the gang falls apart. The allies got security and protection and a chance for war gains, in return for contributing to the conquests.

This self-perpetuating system enabled Rome to defeat Carthage and the Hellenistic powers of the east, but the strains eventually began to show. The land-owning citizens of Italy were obliged to serve in the army in a series of seemingly never-ending overseas campaigns. The prolonged absence of peasant farmers led to smallholdings being taken into big estates, where, due to shortages of men, the labour was carried out by slaves – estimates vary between one million slaves out of a total Italian population of four million, to two million slaves out of six million, by the time of Augustus. In the first century BC, agricultural production in Italy was highly lucrative, with farmers and merchants pressing for more slaves and markets – the barbarian lands were an ideal source of both. Diodorus Siculus explained the connection between the market in slaves and the wine trade: 'Many Italian merchants look on the Gallic craving for wine as their treasure. They . . . receive in return an incredibly high price, for one amphora of wine they get in return a slave – a servant in return for a drink.'

Trade between the Romans and the west of Europe was strong enough for Roman merchants to take up residence in some of the larger *oppida* in Gaul, where wool, grain and slaves could be traded for cloth, wine and luxury goods. But the apparently comfortable relations between Rome and her western neighbours were to be transformed by the ambitions of Julius Caesar, and by the lure of greater riches than trade alone could bring. In the aftermath of civil conflict in Italy (known as the Social Wars) in 88 BC, Rome was split into factions supporting one of two powerful generals – Marius and Sulla. First one then the other took control of Rome and inflicted brutal revenge on the other's supporters. Sulla, who prevailed in the end, had 6,000 men executed while he made a speech to the senate. The institutions of the republic were swept aside, as the dictator (his official title) encouraged denunciations and revenge murders, provided they were committed in his name. In a chilling echo of the Thirty in Athens, Sulla posted lists of those who were enemies of the state, promising rewards for anyone who murdered them.

Julius Caesar, along with many prominent Romans, went into exile during Sulla's rule, returning to Rome in 78 BC. In 60 BC he formed a triumvirate of rulers with Pompey and Crassus. But what Caesar needed, in an empire that was increasingly run by its army commanders, was control of the legions. He persuaded the Roman senate that Germanic tribes west of the Rhine and the Helvetii of Switzerland were moving west, and that Gaul would fall to the Germanic barbarians unless Rome itself took control of the territory. At the time many Romans were sceptical, believing the apparent danger to be a convenient pretext for Caesar to acquire more power. However, in 59 BC the senate gave him control of Cisalpine Gaul and Illyricum and the following year ordered the invasion of Gaul.

The Roman conquest of Gaul took seven years of bitter fighting, during which all who offered resistance were destroyed. In 56 BC Caesar had all the elders of the Veneti put to death and the rest of the tribe sold into slavery; only 500 Belgica from a force of 60,000 survived a battle against the Romans, with the tribal council of 600 reduced to three; the *oppidum* of the Aduatuci was taken with 4,000 deaths, the remaining 53,000 people being sold into slavery; the Carnutes, who had murdered their Roman traders, were themselves murdered en masse, only 800 surviving out of a total population of 40,000. Plutarch estimates that during the campaign, one million Gauls were killed and another million sold into slavery. While other provinces had been captured for economic gain, the economy and social structure of Gaul were destroyed and were no use to Rome for another two generations.

Caesar won the loyalty of his army, but in order to win absolute power in Rome, he had to fight a civil war during which (and during the terror that followed Caesar's murder in 44 BC) further conquest

Provinces of the Roman empire. The conquest of Gaul, northern Iberia and Britannia brought the culture of the east and the Mediterranean to the west.

was once again postponed. In 12 BC Augustus, Caesar's successor, attempted to push the Roman frontier east to the Elbe. But unlike the Gauls, who were settled farmers, the Germanic peoples were mobile and much better prepared for war. The border of the empire was, after attempts to push north and east, stabilized at the Rhine and the Danube.

During the Gallic wars, Caesar had twice mounted expeditions to Britain – in 55 and 54 BC. He made alliances with southern and eastern tribes, for whom the Roman conquest of Gaul brought huge economic benefits. Roman goods and merchants travelled up the Rhine and across the Channel to the Thames estuary, establishing trade with the Trinovantes and Iceni of Essex and East Anglia. Roads built across

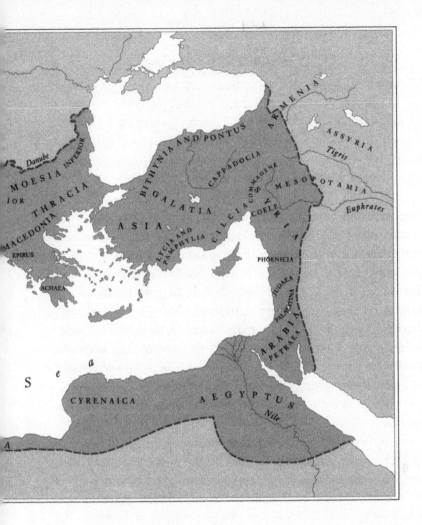

Gaul made the overland route ever easier and Atlantic shipping consequently declined. But this trade and transport infrastructure also made
Britain an attractive proposition for any Roman leader wanting to
enhance his prestige. In 43 BC the emperor Claudius ordered the invasion of Britain and the island was rapidly occupied as far north as the
Humber, and west to the Severn. Local rebellions by the Welsh and the
Iceni convinced Agricola to extend Roman conquest to the whole island,
though the far north always remained outside Roman control.

Roman conquest was driven by ambition, the system of rewards for
allies and, increasingly, by monetary gain. By the Augustan age (27 BC
to AD 14) the city of Rome had a population of nearly one million,
and the most urgent task of the empire was feeding the people of this
vast city. This was not some theoretical aspiration but a matter of

political and physical survival. The emperor and the senators lived among the people of Rome, and gave them huge hand-outs of bread and corn; if the people went hungry there would be civil unrest, riots or worse. Grain was shipped to Rome from every corner of the empire in a trade that made some Romans very wealthy. Cicero claimed that Rome went to war for her merchants, but these were often members of the senate – those who ordered the wars also profited by them.

This was the timetable and motivation of the Roman conquest of the west, but what effect did Rome have on the people and culture and civilization of the west of Europe? The answer, not surprisingly, is immensely complicated, and a far cry from the traditional view that the Romans brought civilization to an uncivilized part of the world and left it in dark chaos when they withdrew. One way to deal with the complexity is to look first at Romans' view of themselves – what did they think about Rome and its place in the world? The accounts we have were all written by patricians, the upper ruling class of Roman society; naturally their writings do not reflect the views of all Romans, but they nevertheless give us an insight into the people who ruled the republic and the empire.

By the time of Augustus, Rome was commander of the Mediterranean world, but that world was still informed by the dynamism and intellectual energy of classical and Hellenistic Greece. The Romans were in awe of the culture of their eastern neighbour – wealthy Romans sent their sons to be educated in Alexandria or Pergamum or Ephesus, the republic used Greek philosophers to draw up their table of laws, the principal gods of Rome were shadows of their Greek equivalents, and Romans even traced their ancestry to the mythic centrepiece of Greek culture, the siege of Troy. Augustus, along with other patrician Romans, sensed that Rome needed a stronger culture of its own, something that would unite its people and give meaning to the extraordinary situation in which they found themselves. The masters of the world needed to tell themselves not just how, but *why* they were destined to rule.

Romans had always believed that their city was founded by a combination of the two legendary figures of Aeneas and Romulus. Aeneas was a prince of Troy who escaped the siege and made his way to found a second Troy on the banks of the Tiber; while Romulus was an *enfant sauvage* who led a band of brigands. The Romans were the heirs of the race of heroes, descendants of a demigod, and also the offspring of a conniving and murdering bandit. Here, in a potent mix of nobility and aggression, is the origin of the Roman idea of Rome.

In the Augustan age Virgil turned these stories into an epic poem, the *Aeneid*, that showed Romans how Jupiter, Father of Gods and Men, had personally decreed the founding of Rome and even the reign of Augustus' revered predecessor: 'From this noble stock there will be born a Trojan Caesar to bound his empire by the Oceanus at the limits of the world, and his fame by the stars. He will be called Julius . . .' The *Aeneid* gave Romans a coherent myth and a literature to stand alongside the epics of Greece. The Romans felt they must be special people and Virgil confirmed this belief. Livy's early history of Rome began to be studied alongside Virgil's myths, and the Latin poetry of Ovid and Horace.

Educated Romans were eager to build on the Socratic tradition of rational enquiry; they too wanted to know what a good man's life should consist of. The teaching that most attracted Roman scholars and patricians was the school of philosophy known as stoicism. Stoics believed reason to be paramount in both the natural world and human affairs, but they emphasized the role of active conduct. They believed that each person, whatever their status, should do the best they could in any circumstance. A man should not to try to alter his luck through prayer or ritual, but make what he could of the situation in which he found himself. The stoic could then live not only a virtuous life, but a life apparently free from the vagaries of fate and the idiosyncrasies of the gods; if you could thrive under any circumstance, then circumstance need not affect you.

Stoics also believed that the highest virtue was gained through the attainment of wisdom. Knowledge of when and how to act, as well as a greater understanding of the world, were important elements of the stoical education. But stoicism was not simply a code of learning and behaviour, it contained, as did all ancient philosophy, a spiritual element. Stoics paid homage to the traditional gods of Rome, but Cicero, for instance, felt it was his patriotic, rather than his sacred, duty to worship Jupiter and Mars. He and his fellow stoics believed in one god, or spirit, that existed throughout the physical world and in every person, but was not a separate entity. Each person carried a piece of this god within them, and so each was an offspring of God and had some spark of divinity within their person.

These different elements of stoicism provided a way of living that was available to all people, and a theology that united humanity as the offspring and embodiment of God. Just as the Roman empire seemed to embrace the whole world, so came the belief that all men were brothers, and that every person had the chance to live a good and virtuous life. This may seem a far cry from the reality of life for most people in the Roman empire; but that was not the point – stoicism, along with most religions and philosophies of the ancient world, was not a moral code but an attempt to understand how to live. The writings of Seneca and Cicero and Pliny are filled with gossip and advice and intrigue, but mostly they are concerned with the central question – how should a good man live? And while Virgil's recreation of Homer seems a little forced and made-to-order, Seneca and Cicero are immediate and of-the-moment; politicians revelling in the cut and thrust of public affairs, and in the use and development of a language that suddenly seemed able to carry the monumental declarations of an imperial power, the poetics of Ovid and Horace, and the wavering inquisitive rationalism of the Roman nobility.

Romans were endlessly fascinated by themselves and profoundly occupied by questions of right and wrong. They wondered how they could have taken over the world, and they asked themselves how Rome and the world should properly be governed. They argued about whether virtue was in-born or achievable only through instruction; they held a man's reputation to be more important than his wealth; and they debated the practical contradictions of friendship, loyalty, justice and public service.

Stoicism reflected the ethos of the Roman empire. First, the good life should be lived in the world, not in contemplation of some abstract ideal; the virtuous man was an active man, albeit one who also studied to increase his knowledge of the world. Second, a man should seek universal answers to universal questions. The Romans, while conquering half the world, had a sense of a common humanity – in theory anyone within the empire could become a Roman citizen. This belief in a brotherhood of humanity as the offspring of a universal god also lent weight to the idea of Rome as an indefinable entity that must be defended and preserved at all costs. If Romans had simply been out to grasp whatever they could, then it is likely that Rome would have been either a small kingdom, or a short-lived empire. The empire endured because most Romans believed that Rome was an expression of common humanity and was therefore a force for good.

Romans believed that conflicts with other states were provoked by others, and that when Romans were forced to take over another territory, they brought with them the benefits of Roman civilization. This belief was codified in the fetial law, which disallowed aggressive war between states and introduced the concept of a just war. The Roman historian Livy was keen to show that Rome had adhered strictly to this law, which provoked Gibbon's sardonic comment that 'the Romans had conquered the world in self defence'. The belief that underlay the fetial law was the Roman notion of *fides*, the use of strength in a fair and conscientious way. The philosopher Panaetius and others flattered the Roman rulers by praising their unique possession of a sublime combination of stoicism and *fides*. By doing so they instilled and encouraged a sense among Romans that they were a superior, chosen people. Just as the Greeks' belief in their own virtues led them to wage a different kind of war to their pragmatic enemies, so the Romans fought for honour and the glory of Rome, in the firm belief that Roman victory was good for humanity.

There is a fascinating contrast between the ideal of Rome and the city itself. By the Augustan age nearly one million people were living in an area, squeezed between the hills and the Tiber, of 146 hectares. The great forum and its adjoining basilica and curia, where the administration, business and legal workings of the city were carried out, were hopelessly crowded almost as soon as they were built. This was partially solved by creating more magnificent public spaces and amphitheatres like the Colosseum; but behind the stunning grandeur of these public buildings, life for all but a tiny minority of Rome's inhabitants was squalid and dangerous. While the wealthy could live in villas on the Quirinal hill, with easy access to estates in the countryside, most people lived in four- or five-storey tenements – cold, dark, rat-infested slums. The risk of fire or collapse was high in these timber-framed buildings, more than 40,000 of which were recorded in Rome in the fourth century AD.

Rome was unlike other Roman towns in its chaotic growth, its enormous population and its apartment-living. The nature of the population was different too. Rome made itself an urban centre but there was little urban industry, apart from construction. The city survived on the tributes paid by the provinces and colonies, and successive rulers were forced to give rations of bread to the huge numbers of unemployed.

'Bread and circuses' was not a glib description of how to placate the masses, but a real and essential policy. Rome needed between 200,000 and 400,000 tonnes of wheat from its colonies per year; and Augustus gave hand-outs of grain to 350,000 male citizens of the city. The essential emptiness of Rome eventually showed when its political role was superseded by Constantine's new capital in AD 330. Its population declined rapidly, and when the empire finally collapsed, its meaning disappeared – by the ninth century its population was less than 20,000.

The aspect of Roman life that resists easy categorization is the relationship between the ruling patrician class, and the commoners or plebeians. The patricians managed to retain control of the republic, and of imperial Rome, but they relied on the consent of the plebeians. Early in the history of the republic the plebeians had flexed their muscles by banding together and threatening to secede from Rome. This major revolt was settled by granting the plebeians an assembly, the *concilium*, from which they could elect tribunes. The political structure that developed held the possibility of democratic rule by the people, and yet this never quite happened. This is a crucial matter in political history, since at the beginning of the republic in 510 BC, democracy was a serious option for any Mediterranean state, with working role models in existence, whereas by the end of the Roman republic democracies had vanished beneath Rome's imperial ambitions – and did not reappear for nearly 18 centuries. In fact, while the *concilium* had theoretical power to pass laws, and the tribunes had special protection, the patrician senate always managed to keep the upper hand. Wealthy plebeians and powerful tribunes were quietly admitted to the senate, while bribery and patronage were used to sway the voting in the *concilium*. During the imperial period, plebeian influence was limited to the legions, where it was assiduously courted and used by the succession of emperors.

While political cunning contributed to the dominance of the patricians, the element of Roman life that welded the patricians and the plebeians together was warfare. From the beginning, the plebeians' authority was confined to the civic realm, whereas the patrician senate and consuls controlled the field of war. The Punic wars against Carthage in the late third century BC ranged over a vast territory including Spain, southern France, Italy, Sicily and north Africa, and plunged Rome into a fight for survival – 50,000 Roman soldiers were killed in one battle at Cannae in 216 BC. The war required enormous administrative effort, military strategy, financial acumen and diplomatic manoeuvring. It became essential to have people with expertise in all these areas in the executive arm of the government; and so the senate became the government of the republic, and senators became the framers and executors of its foreign policies. In modern terms they were the ministers of defence and foreign affairs, the defence staff, the diplomats and the generals. The politicians were also linked to the military by service – in order to stand for political office young men had to serve as a legion tribune for a prescribed number of campaigns, usually over a period of 10 years. The ability to command in the field was an essential part of the legitimacy of a ruler.

Roman patricians may have contemplated how a good man should live, and how Roman victories must be tempered by a civilizing ethos; but it was the Roman army that carried Roman culture to the surrounding world, and it was the Roman military machine that built the empire. The Roman army began as a citizen army of heavy infantry (or hoplites), on the same lines as those of Athens and Sparta (which were in turn inherited from an older communal tradition). The small-scale landowners who made up the citizenry would volunteer for service without payment and supply their own weaponry. But by the fourth century BC Rome needed to pay its soldiers, who were campaigning further and further from home, and so instituted the largest professional organization the world had ever seen. It is these two words – professional and organization – that sum up the guiding ethos of the Roman army and the reasons for its success. Over nine centuries millions of men from nearly every corner of Europe, the Near East and north Africa became immersed in this vast organization. The military ethos was particularly expressed through the professional centurions and through soldiers who had no ambitions beyond the military life. But the military mindset pervaded every level of Roman society, including its art and technology. Triumphal arches were built in commemoration of victories and leaders, roads and magnificent aqueducts linked garrison towns, and amphitheatres were built to stage victory parades, recreate famous battles and mount spectacles of violent physical combat.

Rome was almost continually at war for 900 years, and as long as these wars were successful, the senate and emperors remained in control and democracy was kept at bay. The Roman army conquered the Hellenistic and Carthaginian empires, it meted out extreme violence to anyone who stood in its way, it built roads and aqueducts straight across hostile lands, ignoring the inconveniences of natural topography, and it imposed its will on the people, landscape and cultures of its neighbours. What then happened when this self-confident, militaristic, semi-urban, literate and phenomenally well-organized civilization met the small-scale communally based farming, fishing and trading communities of western Europe?

Conquest, trade and roads drew most of Europe, including the territories outside the empire, into a single economic system; while within the empire a single code of law, enforced by one authority, prevailed. Occupation of the west went hand-in-hand with urbanization. A number of *oppida* – large craft-manufacturing and trading settlements – had developed in the Celtic communities of the west, but the Romans brought a different type of urban life. Roman towns were built or designated in a hierarchical structure. The most important were the *coloniae* – such as Lugdunum (Lyons), Camulodunum (Colchester) and Lindum (Lincoln) – built for Roman citizens, especially retired legionaries who often married into the surrounding community. Second in rank were the *municipia*, such as Verulanium (St Albans), whose inhabitants enjoyed certain privileges without being full citizens. In return for paying taxes, administering their own affairs and generally cooperating with the Romans, they were given grants towards public buildings and other municipal functions. Local leaders would be elected as magistrates (becoming Roman citizens on taking office) and would deal with all minor criminal and civil cases, as well as the upkeep of public buildings. Any dispute involving two Roman citizens, as well as serious criminal cases, would be sent to the Roman courts in the *coloniae*. The lowest-ranked towns were the *civitas*, which were the centres of tribes who had fully accepted Roman rule. Despite their degree of local autonomy, both *municipia* and *civitas* centres were often built on new sites – the Romans having found the customary *oppida* unsuitable for their purposes. Defensive walls were built around many towns, but local people were allocated space to live within the walls.

How could such an urban system be transplanted with success into a largely rural culture? The answer lay in the function and funding of the towns. These were administrative, military and residential centres. Roman officials and, in particular, Roman legionaries (both active and pensioned) created a huge demand for local services and had enormous resources to give in exchange. Many towns survived on the pay and pensions of legionaries, with locals being drawn in to provide food, equipment, labour and entertainment – all needed by men who were paid good wages, and therefore had money to spend.

However, within this unified system, there was local variation in the adoption and acceptance of Roman culture – excavations in Iberia, Gaul and Britain have shown a complex but revealing pattern. Romans and Latins settled in the fertile south and east of Iberia, for example, where they built or remodelled towns to their own tastes. But in the rugged north and west, where physical and social resistance remained strong, the towns and social structures were largely unaffected by Roman occupation.

At Vipasca (Aljustrel) in southern Portugal, the organization of the local silver and copper mines was recorded on bronze plaques. The mines were owned by the Roman state, but local people could obtain a licence to work them, thereby continuing their traditional occupations. The state also owned the rights to commercial activities in the mines and the town, and so local people wanting to run bathhouses, trade in goods or process ore had to apply for a licence or concession. Roman law and administration therefore touched almost every aspect of life, but as long as taxes were paid, the people of the west and north were left to their own devices. From the patterns of building and town layout, the names of civic leaders and the persistence of ancient customs, it seems that these people remained largely untouched by Roman culture.

A similar picture is seen in Britain, which was conquered 200 years after Iberia. The south and east of the island was quickly taken over, while the north and west was made into a militarized zone, with the far north remaining totally outside Roman control. The first phase of conquest occupied the area south of the Humber and east of the Severn. In the late first century AD the Romans pushed into Wales and as far north as the Clyde–Forth valley, later retreating to the line of Hadrian's Wall. Forts and garrison towns were built in a broad zone (for example at Chester and York), with roads leading to the frontiers. Where these towns, and those in the civil zone, were built for Roman troops or as administrative centres they were modelled on Roman lines, but many British settlements remained untouched and unchanged by Roman occupation. In the militarized zone, north of the Humber and west of the Severn and Exe, there was little or no Romanization and local customs were unaffected. Archaeologists have noticed a stark contrast, for example, between the Dumnoni people of south-west England and

their immediate eastern neighbours the Durotriges. The settlements of
the Dumnoni were unchanged despite the presence of a Roman fortress
at Exeter and hardly any Roman coins have been found in their territory. The Durotriges were more Romanized, building rectilinear instead
of round houses and using Roman coinage and cultural habits. The
difference is thought to spring from a deliberate rejection of Roman
ways by the Dumnoni, which is probably a sign of the strength of
their own culture, something that might in turn be traced to the
economic and social independence of the Atlantic seafaring communities described in Chapter One.

In areas that were more receptive to Roman culture, the occupiers
deliberately encouraged local leaders to become immersed in the ways
of their masters. Tacitus is biting about the response of some Britons:
'Agricola gave private encouragement and official assistance to the
building of temples, public squares and private mansions . . . in place
of distaste for the Latin language came a passion to command it . . .
our national dress came into favour and the toga was everywhere to
be seen. And so the Britons were gradually led on to the amenities that
make vice agreeable – arcades, baths and sumptuous banquets. They
spoke of such novelties as "civilization" when really they were only a
feature of their enslavement.' Members of the local elite were often
brought into the Roman system by having their sons adopted, and taken
to Rome for their education, by notable Roman families. The countryside within the civil zone was dotted with Roman, or Romano-British,
villas. These were working, profitable farms rather than country resi-
dences, and were mainly built by Britons adopting the Roman style,
including mosaics and bathhouses – though some Roman soldiers and
officials undoubtedly retired to villas in the British countryside.

The adoption of Roman culture is seen more extensively in Gaul,
where many more Romans came to settle. Rome had been a strong
presence in Gaul for more than a century before Caesar's conquest.
The occupation of the south and trading links through the Rhône,
Loire, Aude and Garonne had all brought Roman culture and goods
to the Gallic tribes. Once Gaul was conquered the province was divided
along ethnic lines, and a series of roads built out from Lugdunum
(Lyons), north to Boulogne, west to the Atlantic, north-east to Cologne
and the Rhine. The Romans built new *municipia* and *civitas* towns
at the centre of each tribal territory, while the increasing trade saw
new ports springing up along rivers and coastlines. Gaul was a spring-

board for invasion and trade with Britain and Germania, and so vast quantities of goods were brought through its trading and transport system.

All of the western provinces supplied Rome with metals, furs, woollen cloth and grain, as well as soldiers and slaves. The army was supplied from every part of the empire, while slaves worked in their own provinces, and were transported south to feed the endless appetite of Rome. Slaves were used as labourers, construction workers, farmers and domestic servants. It is estimated that 40,000 slaves worked in the silver mines of Cartegena in Spain, while around 250,000 slaves were traded annually on the open market (a small proportion of the total trade); according to Strabo, the slave market at Delos processed 10,000 slaves per day.

This brief sketch can do no more than suggest that the interaction between the Roman and indigenous cultures of the west was highly complex. Occupation brought urbanization, new technologies and architectural grandeur, along with luxury goods and large-scale social organization. Local people were given a degree of autonomy and some at least took up Roman ways and the outward expressions of Roman culture. But this was by and large an occupation, not an invasion and settlement. The system of administration, enlightened though it may be, was held in place by force of arms. When the wealthy King Prasutagus of the Iceni died in AD 59 half his kingdom was bequeathed to Rome, and the other half divided between his two daughters. The details are unclear, but the wholesale takeover of the Iceni kingdom overrode agreements with local leaders, and may have involved the humiliation and rape of the king's two daughters. Prasutagus' widow Boudicca led a rebellion that was eventually crushed by the Roman army. Such rebellions were rare, but showed that local customs were tolerated only when they did not trouble Rome's interest. The religious customs of locals were similarly allowed only so long as they did not become the focus of resistance. Druidic communities on Anglesey were destroyed and their sacred groves and sites despoiled, just as sacred woods were deliberately felled in Gaul and elsewhere.

The real test of the interpenetration of the Roman and western cultures came when the Roman occupation ended in the fourth century. The withdrawal of Rome's protection gave rise to an interesting situation, far removed from the simple descent into chaos that we have traditionally been taught. Rome as an entity was both exclusive and inclusive. Access to the higher reaches of power was closely guarded, yet exceptional outsiders (non-Romans and non-patricians) were invited in to become senators, consuls and even emperors; Roman law was uniform and unbending, yet it was openly debated and was administered by locals; the Roman army was the guardian and expression of a distant state, but its soldiers came from every corner of the empire.

The barbarian tribes that pounded at the gates of the empire, before breaking them down and pouring through, were often, in reality, trading partners, allies, mercenaries and recruiting agents for the Roman state. By the time the western empire dissolved in the late fourth century, there were more Goth warriors than Roman legionaries in the service of the emperor. In northern England a concerted invasion by Saxons, Picts and Scots in AD 367 was repelled but led to the takeover of the Roman forts on Hadrian's Wall by local farmer-soldiers. Border tribes were given, or assumed, more autonomy, forming treaty states, and members of the Scotti and Atecotti tribes, who were nominally hostile to Rome, formed regiments in the army of the emperor Honorius (395–423). The east coast of England was vulnerable to raids by tribes from the north and from across the North Sea; but Roman authorities invited Saxons to settle in east Yorkshire, giving land in exchange for military service and thereby turning the enemies of the empire into its defenders.

Roman withdrawal was therefore a patchy affair, affecting different territories in different ways. It is clear that in Britain, Roman culture did not persist after the withdrawal and that, in the old civil realm, the Germanic culture of the Saxons rapidly became dominant (see page 40). In the militarized zone and the unconquered territories of Scotland, Wales and Cornwall, the strong Atlantic culture of the Bronze and Iron Ages persisted and proved resistant to the Saxon influence. Why then did the people of the south-east of Britain shed their Roman past so easily, and take up the new Saxon ways with such apparent alacrity? Why did the Latin language, building in stone, the Roman legal system and the physical fabric of the empire disappear?

We can only speculate that Rome remained an alien culture to the people of Britain, northern and western Gaul and Iberia, western Germania and the other places that were occupied but then so rapidly 'de-Romanized'. The system of Roman towns was artificially imposed and sustained by civil and military spending emanating from Rome. The towns were not natural settlements springing out of a need for trading, access to crafts, meetings and communal defence; they were elements in an organizing framework, there to defend an occupation and administer an empire. When the troops and the officials went, their purpose dissolved.

For all their wooing and assimilating of conquered elites, Roman culture seems not to have penetrated the lives of the common people of the western empire. One reason, apart from the sheer difference in cultural outlook between the Mediterranean and the Atlantic west, may have been the patrician nature of Roman culture. The people of Rome certainly had their own cultural identity, their household gods and their familiar customs; but these had been overlaid by a culture that was in part imported from the Hellenistic world, and in part deliberately developed by the Roman elite. Classical Greek culture had burst out of the tensions of everyday life in fifth-century Athens, but the Roman culture of the Augustan age was a much more considered and deliberate construction, an attempt to give Rome a 'classic' culture. The result lacked a real grounding in the experiences of the Roman people, and consequently failed to grip the imagination of the ordinary people of the west. While their leaders took to learning Latin and commissioning mosaics, the people tolerated Roman ways while they had to, and shed them as soon as they could.

The exceptions to this pattern were, naturally enough, those regions that were most akin to, and nearest, the Roman heartland. The Mediterranean coasts of Gaul and Iberia, with their hinterland, reaching intermittently as far north as the Loire, had been part of the Mediterranean trading and cultural system for a thousand years by the time the western empire fell. Greeks, Romans, Latins, Italians and others had traded and settled this region over hundreds of years. When the empire collapsed this region, more than any other part of the west, remained Roman in its outlook.

Earlier in this chapter I mentioned the stoics' belief in a universal humanity, their sense that peoples of all kinds possessed a common fragment of divinity, and that therefore certain principles of behaviour could be applied to a people. The Roman empire displayed both sides of this universality. Anyone could, in theory, become a citizen, a magistrate, a senator, a consul, or even an emperor (Diocletian was the son of a freed slave from Dalmatia), but to do so meant adopting the values of the Roman patricians. And universality engendered the belief that a

system of urbanization that worked in Italy would work in Iberia and
Gaul and Britain; and if this involved placing towns in geographically
awkward places, and building roads and aqueducts in defiance of
nature, instead of in sympathy with the landscape, then so be it. A
system of laws, debated and inscribed in a Mediterranean city, was
used to administer a host of different cultures. The empire promoted
the belief in universality, and this in turn brought about the organization that made the empire possible.

Add to universality the stoical belief that access to culture and civilization came only through education and the acquisition of a prescribed
corpus of knowledge, and we begin to see the Roman view of the world,
and the nature of its legacy. A relatively small group of people, drawn
in theory from every corner of the world, educated in the same body
of knowledge and holding to the same values, had a unique and incon-
testable right to call themselves civilized. Only they had a real appreciation of the arts, the wisdom to govern and wage wars properly, the
understanding and knowledge truly to understand human existence.
This enabled them not only to rule over others, but to do so from a
position of self-defined superiority. They were civilized because they
were the rulers, and they ruled because they were civilized.

To her western subjects, the legacy of classical Rome was a sense
that civilization was elsewhere. Real civilization was not embedded in
their own customs, languages, religions and laws, but in those of
another, more sophisticated culture. And access to this civilization was
available only through formal education, training in the art of rational
analysis, and the acquisition of a prescribed body of knowledge. Being
able to quote Plato, Virgil and Horace was civilized; knowing how to
enter the sacred grove of the Celtic god Dragda was not. This was a
universal civilization, able to be applied across the entire empire, but
available only to those who could afford it. The majority of western
Europeans therefore (both in Roman times and after the 'rediscovery'
of the classical world) were encouraged to believe that civilization was
both alien and beyond reach.

AUGUSTINE'S VISION OF CHRISTIANITY

From Rebel Sect to Universal Faith

THE Roman empire, which stretched from Mesopotamia to Iberia and from the Sahara to Northumbria, carried its imperial civilization to every part of its territory. Freedom of movement gave the potential for cultures to be transmitted and adopted across this vast area, though most people who lived within the empire remained attached to their local ways and customs, rather than the universal Roman culture. But an exception to this 'localness' emerged as the Christian faith became the official religion of the Roman empire and then, during the long slow dissolution of the western empire, became the central focus, the dominant cultural force in the lives of the people of the west. In three centuries Christianity grew from a small sect of Judaism into Rome's adopted religion, but unlike the Roman culture that was swept aside once the legions withdrew, Christianity penetrated into the lives of the people of western Europe and became the foundation of their culture and civilization.

The spread and eventual adoption of Christianity as the official religion of the empire happened over three centuries of intermittent persecution, martyrdom and extraordinary courage, alongside the vision and political skills of Christian leaders. But the Christian religion that was finally established in the west emerged from struggles within the faith, as well as from resistance to persecution. Christianity was able to become the universal religion of medieval Europe because its guiding principles were inclusive. Everyone, whether saint or sinner, monk or milkmaid, could and should be a Christian. This inclusiveness was made into the central tenet of western Christianity by St Augustine; but in order to show

that this was God's will, Augustine had to overcome the host of interpretations and contradictions that had existed within Christianity from
the beginning. The triumph of Augustine's theology gave western
Christianity, and western civilization, a solid orthodoxy that lasted for a
thousand years. Apart from the Bible, Augustine's *City of God* was the
most widely read book in medieval Europe, and just as the scholars of
the Hellenistic world had looked for practical ways to apply the principles laid out by Plato and Aristotle, so the Latin medieval church tried
to build structures, write rules and give instructions that would reflect
Augustine's vision of Christianity. To see how that vision was formed, we
need to look at the development of the Christian faith before Augustine.

In the late spring of AD 27, or perhaps 33, a young Jew from the northern
district of Galilee was put to death outside the walls of Jerusalem by
crucifixion – an execution used by the Romans for slaves and criminals
who were not Roman citizens. The ministry of Jesus, an itinerant charismatic preacher and, some said, miracle-worker, had attracted a small,
dedicated band of followers around Galilee, and when he came to
Jerusalem excited crowds gathered to see him for themselves. But the
message Jesus brought was not triumphal; in his teachings he had urged
compassion and forgiveness, love of the poor and the weak, and he had
come to Jerusalem to be betrayed, humiliated, whipped and executed.

The message that Jesus brought was wholly in keeping with Jewish
faith and history. Five hundred years earlier Isaiah had prophesied that
the Messiah (the Lord's anointed) would be 'despised, and rejected of
men' and be 'as a lamb that is led to the slaughter' (Isaiah 53). But
when Jesus was crucified, the authorities – the Roman governor, the
client king of Judea, the leaders of the Jewish faith – were relieved to
be rid of a potential troublemaker. Once he had been put to death,
most Jewish people seemed to disregard, if not dismiss, any idea that
Jesus was the Messiah – but it was only among Jews that such an idea
could even have been contemplated.

The Roman empire encompassed a vast number of religions, almost
all of which contained a multiplicity of gods. The Romans mostly tolerated other gods, and appropriated a few for themselves – the Greek gods
of Mount Olympus were borrowed wholesale, and there was widespread
worship of the Egyptian god Isis, Cybele from Asia Minor, and the Persian
Mithras, throughout the empire. Subject peoples were simply required to
respect the Roman gods through animal sacrifice and, in particular, to

regard the emperor as a deity. But Judaism was different to other religions. Jews believed in one god, and their religion would not permit them to praise another. The Roman authorities gave them special dispensation as a *religio licita*, excusing them from praising the emperor.

Although Jews lived in many cities of the Hellenistic and Roman worlds, they were notably insular, shunning marriage with people from other faiths or racial groups. At the centre of their faith were the sacred writings that intertwined the history of their sufferings with their uniquely monotheistic and moralistic religion, while also giving strict rules on diet, family life, circumcision and the Sabbath. Their faith, rather than their locality, was the foundation of their community – those in Ephesus or Antioch or Carthage remained as Jewish as their counterparts in Jerusalem and Lydda. The central place of faith in their lives meant that those Jews who believed Jesus to be the Messiah were utterly committed to the survival of Christianity.

The divinity of Jesus became clear to his followers when, days after his crucifixion, he appeared before them. The resurrection became the central act of the Christian faith. After his ascension to heaven it was the turn of this small band of disciples to spread the teachings of Christ (*christos* means 'the anointed one' in Greek) among the Jewish people. But the authorities and many ordinary Jews regarded the disciples' message as a grave insult to the Jewish faith; the Christians were driven out of towns, beaten and executed. One of the most ardent of the persecutors was a man named Saul, who witnessed the martyrdom of Stephen, the first disciple to be stoned to death for blasphemy, and organized the investigation of those accused of Christian sympathies. Saul's father was eminent enough to be a Roman citizen, though the family were devout followers of Judaism. They spoke Hebrew at home but were fluent in Aramaic and Greek, the lingua franca of the Hellenistic world. Saul's background was both intensely local and universal.

Saul became a Christian after hearing Christ's voice on the road to Damascus, and was thereafter known as Paul. The energy that he had shown in persecution was turned towards the promotion of Christianity and the building of a Christian church. Paul travelled through the Levant, Asia Minor and Greece, visiting Christian communities, preaching and writing letters of admonition and encouragement. In AD 58 he was arrested by Roman soldiers in Jerusalem, where he was in danger of being killed, and taken, eventually, to Rome for trial. In AD 64 the emperor Nero found it convenient to blame the city's

Christians for the destruction of much of Rome by fire. By tradition both Paul and Peter, the disciple ordained by Christ to be the founder of the Church, were murdered in the persecutions that followed.

The presence of a noticeable Christian community in Nero's Rome (there were probably a couple of hundred) showed that in the space of just three decades, this radical Jewish sect had spread out of the Judaic community and become embedded in cities across the empire. Paul's mission was central in this process, but before we look at his work, we need to understand why so many people took up a religion that sprang from an alien culture. Why did people with no connection to Judaism – Syrians in Damascus, Greeks in Corinth, Egyptians in Alexandria – come to believe that Jesus Christ was a messiah sent by God? And that this god was not simply the god of the Jews, and therefore one more among the many deities on offer, but was both the universal god of all humanity, and the one god who allowed no others?

From the earliest times, and in all cultures, religion has served different human needs. The desire to find meaning through belief in supernatural forces is combined with an innate sense of connection with some indefinable dimension of the natural world. This sense is difficult to describe, since it is a purely emotional response to place and circumstance, but this does not diminish its importance. Most religions have envisaged gods that controlled all aspects of the natural world, including human destiny. The gods are fickle, and the function of religion, and of priests, is to assuage the deities in order to bring good fortune. In ancient Greece this relationship began to founder; people still believed in the gods, they took part in feast-days and made sacrifices, hoping to curry favour, but the original connection between the gods and human spirituality was no longer felt. In the succeeding centuries the Graeco-Roman world became more urban, the connection to the natural world was felt less strongly, and the link between spiritual emotion and religious worship was further disrupted. Nevertheless, for our ancestors, the skies overhead were not the beginnings of empty infinite space, they were full of gods competing for their attention. Everyone believed in supernatural forces, but the nature of those forces began to change.

The Roman empire tolerated local worship only where it was no threat to their rule, but they did not hesitate to crush religious customs that strengthened the communal identity of their more troublesome subjects. By the middle of the first century AD, local religions (Judaism apart) had become largely emasculated, with sacred days turning into drunken festivals and entertainments, while the supposed deities of imperial Rome (including the emperors Caligula and Nero) offered a sorry and tragic spectacle to the world. Sacrifices to the Roman gods were regarded as routine demands, rather than meaningful experiences, while educated Romans had long been taught Socrates' dictum that a good life was the highest aspiration. Stoics believed, in Seneca's words, that you should 'Live among men as if God beheld you.' But religion and the actual experience of life, spirituality and belief seemed to have become fatally separated.

Into all this came a faith that reconnected spirituality, belief and experience, and presented a profound and meaningful alternative to the chaotic spiritual emptiness of the Roman world. The contrast could hardly have been greater. Christianity offered salvation through inner contemplation, but Jesus had also taught his followers to give to the poor, to honour the downtrodden and to pray for their enemies. The new faith presented a strong attraction to the spiritual heirs of Socrates, living at a time of moral confusion, and to the people of Rome, who were deprived of meaningful religious experience. But Christianity also offered a strong and supportive network of like-minded people. The artisan classes in particular were effectively closed off from the ruling elite by their lack of citizenship, but the Church offered an alternative spiritual empire in which they had full membership.

Paul, the great architect of the Christian church, never knew Jesus, and the written gospels did not emerge until shortly after Paul's death. But Paul believed, like many who came after him, that he was doing God's work, and that God was guiding his thoughts and deeds. Because of this he felt free to promote his own ideas about the Christian church and its faith, even when these were not directly derived from the teachings of Christ. Paul's overriding belief was in a universal and unified church. This meant the admission of non-Jews into the faith, something that was vigorously opposed by other Christians, and the creation of a single church with a universal doctrine. There was no obvious reason why Christian communities should not practise their religion in their own way, but Paul was determined that this should not happen. The Church was the mystical body of Christ, which had been granted divine power, and must therefore exist as a unity. Paul advocated that faith, not power or status or deeds, was the basis of salvation, and that through faith a Christian could attain God's grace and become one of God's elect.

He also held that belief in Christ's resurrection and the resurrection of all humanity at the Day of Judgement – something that many would-be converts and early Christians found difficult to accept – was an absolute requirement of the faith. Paul also wrote about the nature of Christ, both divine and human, Son of God and part of God, beginning a debate that would occupy the Christian community for centuries.

It was when he tried to satisfy aspects of both Judaism and Christianity that Paul's teachings appeared contradictory. All Christians were held to be equal before God – slaves and wealthy citizens worshipped together, and women were given the same status as men. In the gospels Jesus treats women with respect and interest, and the earliest Christians followed his example. Women had status in the Hellenistic and Roman worlds; they became the heads of households by outliving their husbands, and worked in almost every known profession from lawyers to physicians and teachers. Early Christian women were ministers, preachers and prophets. But in his letters, Paul, following Jewish custom, wrote that women had been created for men, and that they should not speak in church and should be modest and quiet at all times. Sexual relations were a difficult area; Paul asserted that the Church should accept the need for procreation but that sexual thoughts, fornication, adultery and the 'bondage of the flesh' were all deeply troubling and should be punished. This in turn would lead to the denigration of women as tempters of men (with Eve as the prime example) and the promotion of the Immaculate Conception and Mary's status as a virgin. Marriage was necessary but chastity was ideal.

Paul's commitment to a single church was shown by his ruthless anger with any who broke its rules – heretical thoughts or deeds which varied in any way from his own prescriptions must be punished by expulsion from the Church and eternal damnation. But Paul also advocated and practised charity, help for the poor and sick, and emphasized that material poverty led to spiritual richness.

In all his contradictions, his anger, humility, energy, faith, arrogance, certainty and dedication, Paul set out the stall of the Christian church and its faith. As an educated Jew living in the Graeco-Roman world, he invested Christianity with its unique combination of Greek rational universality and Hebrew moral fervour. The influence of Judaism on Paul's beliefs, and thereby on the Church, was considerable. Like the Jews, early Christians found themselves members of a community defined by shared beliefs rather than attachment to a particular place. The

Hebrew scriptures comprise the story of a people surviving in exile, through epic travels and under persecution. For most of their history the Jewish people existed as a discrete entity, separated from their oppressors and from the natural world, with their homeland as a disembodied ideal. This separation was made plain in the creation story: 'And God said, Let us make man in our image, after our likeness; and let them have dominion over the fish of the sea, and over the fowl of the air, and over the cattle, and over all the earth, and over every creeping thing that creepeth upon the earth' (Genesis 1:26). Humanity as a uniquely privileged creature – made by God in his image, and given power over all others – was a distinctively Judaic idea that fitted well with the Greek philosophers' promotion of distinctly *human* rationality; Christianity adopted these ways of thinking, and then took them a stage further by stating that God had sent his son in the form of a man. While most other religions – Egyptian, Celtic, Germanic, Greek, Persian, Hindu – saw gods woven into the natural fabric of the world, appearing as bulls, swans, griffins, rams, elephants or horses, Christianity was utterly based on the unspoken belief that human beings were not only the centre of the natural world, but were the reason for its existence.

Soon after Paul's death, anonymous accounts of the life of Jesus began to appear, and by the early second century, a core of sacred writings (comprising the four Gospels, the Acts and the Epistles, all written in Greek) was established. The Christian community had scriptures to define and reinforce their faith, but the world remained hostile to their message. Once it was clear that Christianity was not an element of Judaism, it was designated by Rome as an illegal sect. It was unlawful for Christians to meet, and if challenged, they must disavow their faith. For the next 250 years Christians endured continual harassment, interspersed with periods of intense persecution. Popes and bishops were executed along with many of their followers. Jesus had predicted persecution but had never urged others to be martyrs: 'But when they persecute you in this city, flee ye into another' (Matthew 10:23); and Paul had escaped from Damascus rather than stay to meet his death. Nevertheless, some church leaders advocated martyrdom as a way of understanding the experience of Jesus and in order to glorify Christ. The effect of public executions was to reinforce the faith within the Christian community, and to stimulate curiosity and admiration among pagan onlookers. For Christians a few hours of torture were nothing compared to the prospect of eternal damnation; they accepted painful, lingering deaths rather than renounce their faith. But their extraordinary courage was not born simply out of fear. They believed they were earning the love that God had granted them, but they were also echoing, or reviving, the old Greek belief in a good death. The Greeks were the first people to go to war, and to willingly die, for a principle, or an ideal. The Christian martyrs showed the Hellenistic influence on their faith by dying for a religious belief.

In AD 111 Pliny wrote to the emperor Trajan from the province of Bithynia and Pontus (on the southern shore of the Black Sea) about the adherents of the new faith: 'I have asked them in person if they are Christians and, if they admit it, I repeat the question a second and a third time, with a warning of the punishment waiting them. If they persist, I order them to be led away for execution . . .' But in the same letter, Pliny also said that 'the charges [against Christians] are becoming more widespread', and that his measures (including the torture of two slave-women who were deaconesses) were inadequate and unhelpful in stamping out this 'wretched cult'.

Pliny's view that Christianity was growing, and that persecutions simply drew attention to its message, was accurate. Slowly but surely, Christian communities were expanding and becoming bolder. The stability of the empire in the second century (the time of the Antonine emperors) saw a rise in the numbers of urban middle classes and gave them opportunities to travel. Small-time merchants and artisans, the backbone of Christian communities, suddenly found themselves citizens of the world. Nevertheless, until the middle of the third century, Christianity remained a cult – albeit a determined and enduring one – present in many towns, but not in large numbers, and based principally in the eastern part of the empire.

This steady, if halting, expansion of Christianity was transformed in the middle of the third century by the deepest crisis the Roman empire had yet experienced. In the four decades after AD 240 the frontiers of the empire suffered a series of dramatic and humiliating collapses. Not only were the legions outfought at every point of the compass, but the emperors themselves, the embodiment of the stability of the empire, became victims of Rome's enemies.

In 251 the forces of a Gothic confederacy trapped the emperor Decius and his army in the marshes of Dobrudja, and destroyed both. In 260 Shapur, emperor of a newly resurgent Persian empire, defeated and captured the emperor Valerian. At the same time tribes along the lower

Rhine began to attack Roman forces, and seafarers from north Germany raided the coasts of Britain and Gaul. In the 260s Goth raiders found their way to the Aegean and to the poorly defended and wealthy towns of the eastern Mediterranean. Emperors came and went with bewildering rapidity and the sense of crisis was such that, in 271, work began on a new defensive wall around the city of Rome itself.

The Roman empire was saved from collapse by a new generation of military leaders. These professional soldiers, mostly from the outer provinces, owed little to the political ruling class, and once they were in effective control, they forced a revolution in the way that Rome was governed. In 260 the new emperor, Gallienus, excluded the senatorial aristocracy from military command; the legions were broken into smaller, more mobile forces and a new heavy cavalry strike force introduced; and the number of men in arms was increased to 600,000, the largest regular force ever seen. In 268 Gallienus defeated invaders in northern Italy, and the following year Claudius II regained the Danube as the frontier of the empire. In 273 Galerian reclaimed the eastern provinces and in 296 the Persian threat was eliminated by Galerius, acting under the emperor Diocletian.

The generals and soldiers who brought about this remarkable turnaround were the antithesis of the patrician senate – Diocletian was the son of a freed slave, Galerius an ex-cattle herder from Carpathia – and they remade the empire in their own image. Diocletian divided the empire in two and appointed two men to rule each half; he instituted a formal system of recruitment and taxation to support the army – sons of soldiers and servants of landowners were required to serve, and a land tax was introduced throughout the empire. Diocletian cleared out the political establishment of venerable patrician families and put his trusted military colleagues in positions of power.

The empire might have been restored, but for 50 years almost the whole of it (with the exceptions of Britain and Gaul) had been in danger. As the empire became a fragile and dangerous place, the old ways of living and believing came into question. In the frontier provinces the stability that nurtured public grandeur and ritual was destroyed by the invasions. Public homage to the gods of Rome declined as people turned to a religion in which private contemplation brought spiritual fulfilment, together with a way of living a good life in an increasingly wicked world. In the midst of uncertainty the Christian church offered membership of a distinctive group with a clear message of redemption and salvation. The crisis emphasized the customary compassion and courage of Christians, in sharp contrast to the traditional Roman stoical disregard of one's own and others' difficulties. Christianity displayed an interesting and fruitful paradox – while holding to the idea of personal salvation and inner contemplation, Christians believed in the utter moral necessity of loving and helping your neighbour. St Paul, in the most resonant passage in all his writings, had told the Christian community, 'Though I speak with the tongues of men and of angels, and have not charity, I am become as sounding brass, or a tinkling cymbal' (1 Corinthians 13:1–3). As Roman society recovered from its worst crisis in two hundred years Christianity presented itself as a real alternative to the old ways. For many subjects and citizens of the empire, the crisis had shown that the conflict between the empire and Christianity was insignificant compared to the threat presented by the invaders. The world was no longer divided between pagans and Christians, but between the empire and the barbarians. This was a subtle but profound alteration – rather than being an 'enemy within', Christianity began to appear to many to be a fundamental weapon in the battle to preserve the empire.

While the practical impact of Christianity was increasing, its theology was also bringing the faith into the mainstream of Roman life. This was a gradual and controversial process, but there was a serious strand of Christian thinking that saw the building of the empire as the necessary precursor to Christ's arrival on earth – Christianity began to absorb the history of the empire into its own story. Origen of Alexandria, for example, writing in the middle of the third century, reinterpreted classical history as the forerunner to Christianity and described men like Socrates and Aristotle, who had sincerely enquired after such things as the nature of the soul, as 'Christians before Christ'. Plato's ideal was now understood to have been a reference to the Christian creator-God. The Christian theologian Eusebius, writing early in the fourth century, argued that, 'the power of the Romans came to its zenith at precisely the moment of Jesus' unexpected sojourn among men, at the time when Augustus first acquired power over all nations' (Eusebius, *Demonstratio Evangelica*, 3.7.30). Christians advanced the idea that Christ's mission was to unite all previous philosophies and religions and resolve all their differences, and that Christ's role in the world was not to overthrow the empire but to be a teacher and healer. This was a new and brighter and more outgoing path for Christianity to follow, which, as a consequence, ensured that the ideas of Plato and Aristotle did not disappear with the triumph of Christianity, but lived on through the Christian church.

At the same time as Christian theology began adopting Greek and Roman history as its own, the philosophers of the Graeco-Roman world began a journey in the opposite direction. In the middle of the third century the Alexandrian philosopher Plotinus opened an academy in Rome to teach his highly influential interpretation of Plato. Plotinus' work was an amalgam of Plato, Aristotle and stoicism that has since become known as Neoplatonism. He believed that everything must flow from one divine being, and that, in the end, everything must return to the same state of unity. This one being was supernatural and absolutely good, and extended its goodness into beings at lower levels of existence. Plato's ideals, for example, were creations of this ultimate being. Although Plotinus was ostensibly devising a philosophical system, this was, like Christianity, a spiritual response to a world undergoing immense change. Plotinus rejected Christian theology but his work laid the groundwork for the fusion of Christianity with Greek philosophy.

This rising power and influence of the Christian church in the late third century was not universally welcomed. Christianity was overwhelmingly a religion of the eastern, Greek-speaking part of the empire, while Diocletian and most of his army were Latin speakers from the west. When Diocletian built himself a palace at Nicomedia in 287 he found a Christian basilica already established on the opposite hill, and by the time he returned from the wars in 302, Christianity was a well-founded alternative power structure within the empire.

Diocletian decided that Christianity must be eradicated. This was a deeply shocking turn of events, even for those who were used to the low-level persecution of some Roman authorities. Most people considered Christians no longer as members of a dangerous sect but as respectable citizens in the mainstream of Roman life. Nevertheless, Christians in the army were stripped of their positions, churches were burned down and those who did not recant were sold into slavery; bishops were imprisoned and forced to make offerings to Rome's traditional gods. The persecution was patchy, with many officials reluctant to pursue the orders with vigour, but popes, bishops and their flocks were put to death and many other Christians were imprisoned and tortured. Once Diocletian retired in 305 the repressive measures were quietly dropped, but the Christian church leaders understood that without political power they were vulnerable to the whims of emperors.

By legend it was during the battle at Milvian Bridge on the River Tiber in 312, in which he defeated his rival Maxentius, that Constantine, Diocletian's eventual successor, was called to Christianity. His friend and biographer Eusebius described how he saw a vision of a cross of light in the heavens bearing the inscription, BY THIS SIGN THOU SHALT CONQUER, and immediately swore to worship no other God. But Constantine's was a political as well as a spiritual decision. He understood that the Christian church, with its network of bishops and dedicated adherents, could be a powerful ally to the emperor. It is also likely that, unlike Diocletian, he did not fear the strangeness of Christianity because his mother Helena had become a Christian, probably in Constantine's youth.

Diocletian had divided the empire into east and west, and Christianity was still (and remained until the eighth century) an overwhelmingly eastern faith. In 324 Constantine, who was emperor in the west, defeated his co-emperor Licinius in battle at Chrysopolis and became sole ruler of the entire empire. He then extended the empire by conquering the eastern provinces of Asia Minor and in doing so brought the heartlands of Christianity in the Levant and Anatolia under his personal control. In 325 Constantine chose the port of Byzantium as the new capital of the Roman empire, and in 330 the city was renamed Constantinople in his honour. It would soon become not just a centre of Christian learning but the focus for the preservation and transmission of 2,000 years of eastern Mediterranean culture.

Constantine used the Christian church to help him gain and use political power – the Church supported him against his rival Licinius, and he used bishops and the Christian community as an information network, reporting to him on political events and undercurrents in all the towns of the empire. In return Constantine tried, as Paul had done before, to unite the Christian faith in a single institution. He made ordinary people sympathetic to Christianity by making the Christian sabbath into a holiday and integrating pagan festivals into a Christian calendar. Crucifixion, gladiatorial contests and animal sacrifices were all banned throughout the empire.

By the fourth century Christianity had spread throughout Egypt and south as far as Ethiopia, to the eastern edge of the Black Sea, throughout Asia Minor, Syria, Phoenicia, Palestine and into Arabia. In the west, there were Christian communities in every Roman province, including Gaul, Iberia and distant Britannia. Alexandria and Antioch were the eastern centres of the Church and, while the Bishop of Rome's nominal leadership of the Church (based on apostolic succession from St Peter) had been grudgingly acknowledged in the third century, the early popes were all Greek rather than Latin speakers.

Constantine's elevation of his new city on the Bosphorus threw all of this into confusion. Rome, always a western outpost of the Church, was no longer even the centre of the political empire, while the bishops of Antioch and Alexandria resented the promotion of Constantinople as a Christian centre of equivalent importance. As well as political rivalry within the Church, there were profound differences in theology, centring on the nature of Christ and his place in the Trinity, the Second Coming, the Immaculate Conception, predestination and the status of the Elect. Constantine, who was immensely irritated by dissension and splits within the Church, sent envoys all over the empire to resolve differences and held a series of councils to force his quarrelsome bishops into agreement.

The most urgent crisis in the Christian church was brought on by the followers of Arius, an Egyptian priest who believed Christ subordinate to God and not fully divine. The excommunication of Arius in 321 was followed by the Council of Nicea in 325 at which Arian bishops were forced to agree to a statement of faith that gave Christ equal status, or be expelled. But Arianism continued to have followers, and was taken north to the Gothic peoples, whose different vision of Christianity was a major challenge to the Church in later centuries.

Arianism was only one of a number of sects with different interpretations of the Christian faith and doctrine. In the second century Marcion had preached that the Jewish god of the Old Testament was the creator of a wicked corrupt world and was not the true, higher god of Christianity. Gnostics similarly believed that Christ was a catalyst in a continuing struggle between a good and an evil god, and that the incarnation was an illusion. There were apocalyptic movements whose members believed the Second Coming was upon them, and visionaries who believed they spoke directly to God. Most seriously perhaps there were those sects who believed in purity. The Donatists believed that any who had recanted in the Diocletian persecutions should not be re-admitted to the Church; the Cathari, or pure ones, believed themselves to be the Elect spoken of in Mark's Gospel and in the Book of Revelation; the Manicheans believed the world to be divided into good and evil, ruled by a god of light and a god of darkness – the purpose of the *electi*, or priesthood, was to bring light into darkness. The belief that Christ had given an example of how a Christian life should be lived also led many Christians to give up worldly goods and live off the earth. The ascetic movement, which gave birth to monasticism, remained a powerful strand of Christianity, but how was it to be integrated into a church doctrine, and how were the many rival interpretations to be resolved?

Despite Constantine's authority as emperor, and his energetic attempts at unity, the decades after his death in 337 saw the growth of dissent within the Church. Councils held at Ephesus in 431 and Chalcedon in 451 were taken as opportunities for the bishops to lay down the law to each other, rather than search for common ground. The consequence was that the Church, Christ's single body on earth, so assiduously promoted by Paul and held together by Constantine, split into its cultural constituencies.

The doctrinal differences centred on the nature of Christ and Mary. Was Christ wholly divine, or part divine and part human, in which case were these separate elements brought together in his person, or did they always co-exist? And was it possible for Mary, as a human, to give birth to a divine being, and if it was, then was Mary somehow something more than human? These debating points became fatally tied up with the politics of the Church, as each group sought to be the single permissible orthodoxy. In the end bishops and their flocks in many of the eastern churches, where Christianity was still concentrated, found it preferable to break away rather than give up their own vision of the faith. The Copts of Egypt and Ethiopia, the Syrian Jacobites, the Armenians and the Nestorians all went their separate ways. The bishops of Rome looked on as the eastern church splintered and the primates of Constantinople, with the backing of the emperors, overtook them in status. From the fifth century, with the western empire collapsing around it, western Christianity, centred on Rome, was left to find its own way.

Christianity had come to prominence in the crisis of the late third century and flourished in the relative tranquillity of the fourth century. But from about 380 onwards the western empire began to disintegrate into smaller realms, vulnerable to incursions by non-Christian peoples and cultures. Christianity had to find a way of dealing with an unpredictable and potentially hostile world, and this time the western or Latin church had to find its own way of dealing with crisis, unaided by the political and military power of Rome. The schisms and dissensions had left Latin Christianity out on a limb, while the disintegration of the western empire apparently threatened its survival. The effects of the end of the empire have been overdramatized, as we shall see, but the decline of Rome's political apparatus left the Latin church as the sole institution with an extensive network of power. The dissensions that were splitting the eastern churches were equally felt in the west, but the western church did not divide in the same way. This was partly because the west was economically and politically undeveloped compared to the east, and therefore power lay in the hands of fewer people. But it was also because Augustine of Hippo managed to develop a coherent and inclusive theology that allowed the Latin church to live in peace with itself for a thousand years.

Augustine is an imposing figure because his huge output of writings has survived and been immensely influential, and because his candid autobiography – one of the first ever written – means that we know more about him than any other person of his time. Augustine was born into a Christian family in 354 in the Roman town of Tagaste (now Souk Ahras) in north Africa. From there he went to Carthage for his education in the classics of Latin literature. Augustine lived a dissolute life in Carthage, eventually taking a servant girl as his permanent mistress. His intention in Carthage was to become a lawyer in the service of the empire, but he was diverted from his planned career, and from the faith of his family, by encounters with dissenting groups of Christians.

The official Latin church held that the Bible was the source of true wisdom, and belief in its words was an inflexible law. But to young Roman scholars this seemed absurd. The Old Testament was full of peculiar stories and simple old folk-tales translated into bad Latin prose. Having been brought up on the sublime works of Cicero and Virgil, many were, despite their interest in Christianity, puzzled and even repelled by the form and content of the Old Testament.

Augustine, along with other educated Romans, was attracted by Manicheism, a sect that attempted to unite the religions of the world. The Manichees believed in Christ as a great teacher who had no need of support from Hebrew prophets. Their central belief was that the world was made of two distinct parts, good and evil, and that these were mingled in all things, including humans. A person could live through the good in his soul and mind and let the evil in him – evil thoughts, deeds and desires of the flesh – remain separate and inert. This was tremendously appealing for men like Augustine who, though they had sinned in the world, wanted to preserve the good part of themselves untarnished. The god who had created the corrupt physical world was evil, while the god who informed the spirit was good.

After teaching philosophy in Carthage, Augustine moved to Rome and then Milan, where he was appointed professor of rhetoric in 384. This was an extraordinary time in the dying decades of the western empire. The emperors had given grants of land within the empire to Gothic tribes being driven into their territory from the east and north, in return for military service. This was a very uneasy relationship whose disintegration led to the gradual dissolution of the empire. In the 380s the fragile arrangements between the emperor, the senate, the army and the forces of the Goths and Huns still held. Since the days of Diocletian the importance of the city of Rome had been diminishing. Emperors spent much of their time travelling, they built palaces in other places, and the empire itself was divided into separate realms. While the senate still sat in Rome, both city and patricians were increasingly irrelevant to the politics of the empire. The emperor Theodosius (ruled 379–95) based his court in Milan, a city inhabited by Romans, Ligurians, Milanese as well as hosts of foreigners; some were Catholic, others Arian or pagan, Manichees or gnostics. The frontier provinces of the empire had always been a mix of Roman and external cultures and peoples; in the late fourth century the frontiers shifted south and the whole western empire became a mosaic of different groups and interests.

In Milan Augustine became fascinated by the views of Ambrose, Catholic bishop of Milan and the leading political figure in the western church. Ambrose saw Christianity as a spiritual religion, in which souls existed as non-physical entities within the tattered shreds of the flesh. This non-material view of the religion and the world was utterly new to Augustine – he had always assumed, along with most others, that God must be an actual material presence. Ambrose's interpretation shows the growing influence of Plotinus and the other Neoplatonists. Plato's world of ideals seemed to represent the time-less, perfect realm of the spirit, while the real world represented a corruption that became increasingly degraded through time. Whereas Plato believed the ideal world was available to the human mind through rational thought, Plotinus, and subsequently Augustine, understood that it placed 'the One' or God utterly beyond the comprehension of humanity. As Augustine later wrote of God: 'I realised I was far away from You.' Ambrose's interpretation of Plotinus appealed to Augustine's scholarly instincts and induced him to abandon Manicheism and embrace the Catholic faith. In 386 he was baptized, and after five years in Sicily and Thagaste, he was appointed bishop of the seaport of Hippo on the north African coast, where he would remain until his death in 430.

Before we look at Augustine's work in Hippo, we should see the context in which he was writing. After the death of the emperor Theodosius in 395, agreements between the Gothic settlers and the Roman imperial authorities broke down. Alaric, leader of the Visigoths, felt aggrieved at the lack of payment for his services, and in 410 his forces took and sacked the city of Rome. This was a huge symbolic event, but it was symptomatic of a general decline of central political and ecclesiastical authority. The 'barbarians' were not always invaders, and they did not always bring destruction, but their growing dominance changed the face of western Europe. The Visigoths withdrew from Italy, only for another Germanic tribe, the Vandals, to cross into Africa in the west and make their way along the coast towards Hippo and Carthage.

From his position in Hippo, Augustine saw the authority of the Catholic church disintegrating, along with its protector and promoter, the western emperor. The Visigoths, Ostrogoths and Vandals were adherents of Arianism, the heretical sect banished at the Council of Nicea. And with no central authority, the direction of western Christianity, both within and outside the official church, was uncertain, undecided and unenforceable. Rival Christian sects felt free to brand anyone as a heretic, and Augustine earnestly believed he might end his life as a martyr. He viewed his writings not as a theoretical exercise, but as a desperate fight for the soul of Christianity in a disintegrating world.

Augustine saw the central task of a Christian scholar as confronting the question 'Where does evil come from?' If God was both good and all-powerful, then how did evil come into the world? Augustine's question shows the inheritance of the abstractions of Socrates and Plato. The idea that there is an abstract entity called 'evil' that is the opposite of an entity called 'good' had not occurred to other peoples at other times; it was a historical invention of post-classical Greece. But having come to believe in it, Augustine needed to solve the question of its provenance. The Manichees had provided one answer – that an evil god co-exists with a good god – but Augustine felt repelled by their 'enlightened fatalism'. He believed that evil must be confronted, not simply avoided.

By abandoning Manicheism, Augustine was again faced with the peculiarity of the Old Testament. How could the folk history of the Jewish people, with its vengeful Hebrew God, be assimilated with a Platonic disembodied ideal divinity, and a forgiving Christ? Augustine's answer was that a fierce imposition of strict laws had been necessary in order to keep the Jewish people on the right path; but humans were just as wicked and wayward as they had ever been and still needed strict laws to control them. 'Take away the barriers created by the laws! Men's brazen capacity to do harm, their urge to self-indulgence would rage to the full.' The Old Testament was a guide for all time, not just for the Jews of the past. But where did this innate human wickedness come from? Augustine's answer lay in a doctrine that had become common currency among people of different faiths in the late Roman empire – Original Sin.

Augustine saw that Adam and Eve had been created in perfection but had brought evil into the world by their own actions. Their descendants might live virtuous lives but they all carried within them the possibility of a reversion to evil and to sin. Augustine was particularly troubled by the potency of inappropriate sexual desire, a concern that may have sprung from his own youthful indiscretions. The belief that humans carried some ineluctable stain, or damage, or corruption helped to explain the degree of suffering and uncertainty in a troubled period of history.

There was another, equally challenging difficulty for Augustine. If the world was full of evil, and each human was stained by evil, then how should a Christian live? This question was at the heart of profound disagreements within the Latin church that remained unresolved. While the eastern church had divided over arguments about the divine nature of Christ and Mary, the western church was potentially split over the nature of a Christian life.

Augustine's most famous work, *City of God*, describes how humanity is divided into those who dwell in Babylon, the City of Evil, and those who dwell in Jerusalem, the City of God. Babylon will be destroyed at the Day of Judgement and Jerusalem preserved. Most Christian scholars agreed with this division of the flock, but how were the small numbers of the 'saved' to be chosen? A sect known as the Donatists answered this by affirming themselves as the Elect. They believed that by being morally pure and following the rules of the Christian faith they could separate themselves from the rest of humanity and gain entry to the city of God. Here was a model, they implied, for true Christians to follow. This assumption infuriated Augustine: 'Wherein has the Christian world offended you, from which you insanely and wickedly cut yourselves off? . . . Wherein has the peace of Christ offended you, that you resist it by separating yourselves from those whom you condemn?' Augustine believed that God alone could decide who would be saved and He, the remote, omnipotent God, would not be affected by the self-judging morality of any particular group or individual. It was heresy to suggest otherwise.

Pelagius, a theologian from the British Isles living in Rome in the early fifth century, wrote in the same vein as the Donatists. His view was that human nature was capable of improvement and even perfection through adherence to the Christian faith, and to strive for perfection was obligatory for the true Christian. Every Christian should aim to live the life of a monk or an ascetic. When Augustine's *Confessions* was circulated, after 412, Pelagius declared his opposition to the idea of Original Sin. He could not accept that human improvement was nullified by something from the distant past and that humans were condemned by Adam's first act of sin to be sinners for evermore. His follower, Julian of Eclanum, wrote to Augustine: 'You ask me why I would not consent to the idea that there is a sin that is part of human nature? I answer: it is improbable, it is untrue; it is unjust and impious; it makes it seem as if the Devil were the maker of men. It violates and destroys the freedom of the will . . . by saying that men are so incapable of virtue, that in the very wombs of their mothers they are filled with bygone sins' (quoted in Brown, 1967, p. 387).

To rational Christians like Pelagius and Julian the idea that the sin of Adam and Eve had indelibly stained all humans was both nonsensical and dangerous. This argument, put forward by a man who was his intellectual equal, provoked Augustine into offering *his* vision of the life of a true Christian. Augustine was not interested in the purity of a narrow sect, neither the Elect of the Donatists, nor the monkish perfectionists of Pelagius. He wanted a theology that could be lived by the whole Christian community – by the woman bearing more children than she wants, by the husband who has adulterous thoughts, by the rich man who feels a modicum of guilt and the poor woman who wants an easier life. This was Augustine's great contribution to Christianity – he constructed a theology in which a religion based on recognition of an omnipotent, vengeful God could be followed by people who were not worthy of His love. In this immense paradox Augustine, who had the harshest view of human nature, became the flag-bearer of moral tolerance. Nevertheless, the price was a heavy one. If Christianity were to embrace everyone – saint and sinner, monk and merchant, saved and damned alike – then what was the Christian life?

For the answer, Augustine turned to the Platonists' belief in a distant God, for whom humanity was a near-to-irrelevant part of His creation. The result was shuddering in its pessimism: the role of the true Christian was to fear God, to suffer and to await His judgement. Christians should live good lives for their own sake, because by freeing themselves from the enslavement of evil desires, they could appreciate the vision and love of God. This, though, would have no effect on God's final judgement because, and here was the most pessimistic message of all, their fate had already been decided. How else could it be? Everything that happened came about because God willed it. But the distant God did not wait to judge humans on their merits, because it was He who dictated their every thought and action – it would be absurd for Him to judge His own works. Instead, as Augustine explained in *On the Predestination of the Saints*, He sent certain people into the world to do great works. It was these saints who would inhabit the City of God at the Day of Judgement, while all others would perish in the City of Evil.

This theology apparently dealt with Augustine's question of 'Whence comes evil?' and explained the presence of human suffering in a world created by a good God. While humans were God's favourite creation, their lives, their fates, their sufferings, were of little interest to him. But this seemed to leave Christians in a state of passive helplessness, their every action predetermined, their free will an illusion. To suffer, to await God's judgement, was that really all that Christianity could offer? Augustine wrote that his theology did not deny freedom but simply urged Christians to make their actions more effective. They should study the scriptures and understand what was good and act on this: 'Thou shalt remember the Lord thy God, for He it is Who gives the strength to do great deeds.' They must be prepared to give up the idea of individual initiative in return for belonging to an active force that made sense of a seemingly meaningless world. While they may be sinners beyond salvation, they could be agents of God whose achievements would add to His glory.

Augustine managed to construct a world in which God has determined everything in advance, but where humans still have the free will to choose to do good. As an abstract philosophical argument, it does not hold water – but as a practical invocation for Christians to do good in a wicked world it succeeded beyond all measure. In the last year of his life Augustine wrote *On the Gift of Perseverance*, which articulated his belief that it was a Christian's duty to persevere in the world, to endure and to thereby enable the true Catholic church to endure.

In the course of answering the Manichees, the Donatists and the Pelagians, Augustine constructed a coherent theology of Catholic Christianity. Intensely gloomy and pessimistic about human nature, yet inclusive of all sinners; denying the possibility of human improvement or salvation through good deeds, but nevertheless a rallying call for Christians to do good, Augustine's theology was a dark, complex and paradoxical vision that was to stand as the basis of western Christian theology.

After the calamity of 410, the western empire dragged on in name only. By 476, when the last western emperor, Romulus Augustus, was pushed aside, the imperial throne had become a pawn in the power games between the various Gothic kings. When Odoacer, a German chief who controlled the largest force in Italy, forced Romulus out, and proclaimed himself king, not emperor, the empire in the west was officially dead. The last emperor's departure went mostly unnoticed and the empire slowly dissolved into its constituent parts.

Attempts were made by Christian emperors in the east, above all by Justinian in the seventh century, to reclaim the western empire, but this only weakened them at home. There were by then too many independent forces to subdue. Rome became an irrelevance and the popes, leaders of the Catholic church isolated in the capital of the old empire, were forced to do the bidding of either the Byzantine emperors or the local Gothic kings. The Roman Christian church survived the empire but its future was then in the hands of others. That future was to depend on the abilities of its leaders to make alliances with the new rulers of the west, in order to build a universal civilization based on Augustine's gloomy, pessimistic, inspirational and, above all, inclusive vision.

RELIGION AS CIVILIZATION

The Establishment of Western Christendom

THE phases of history that offer least evidence are open to the widest interpretations, offering ample opportunities for the present to impose its own views on the past. The centuries that followed the collapse of the western Roman empire have long been seen as the Dark Ages, a term that reflected the views of our predecessors, and served as a discouragement to other investigators – what ambitious young historian would want to specialize in such a gloomy and unrewarding period? But in the last decade there has been a sea change in attitudes. The period now known as late antiquity, or the early Middle Ages, has seen a torrent of new and interesting work that throws into question almost all of our previous assumptions. The image of centuries of dark chaos falling between the Roman empire and the 'awakening' of the late medieval world has long been viewed with scepticism, but there has been precious little to offer in its place. Only in the last few years have historians been able to combine archaeological and documentary evidence to construct a different story of a crucial period in the history of western civilization.

In AD 400 most of western European society comprised small groups of people, tied together by extended clan networks and using a multitude of languages and dialects. Some were directly ruled over by Rome, others were part of the trading network dominated by Roman taxation and wealth. Five hundred years later the geography of modern western Europe had begun to emerge; the territories of nations, often defined by a shared language, were roughly established, as was a complete ecclesiastical network of dioceses and parishes governing a continent of believers through a detailed system of rules, regulations and church law. By the end of the Dark Ages, European monarchs ruled in agreement with a court of nobles, whose power was based on their control of regions within each realm. The potential conflict between the secular power of kings and the spiritual power of bishops and popes had turned into a mutually beneficial relationship in which the monarch was given ecclesiastical status by being protector of the faith, while remaining apart from the Church. The peasantry even enjoyed a period of acknowledgement as freemen, unhindered by the previous punitive Roman taxation (which reduced most to paupers), or by the yet-to-come feudal system.

This fundamental construction of European civilization all happened in the so-called Dark Ages, but detailed evidence of how it came about is frustratingly slender. We can blame the prosperity of later times for some of this obscurity – medieval church builders pulled down, then built over, Saxon or Merovingian churches, and the expansion of industrial cities destroyed much of the fabric of those times (the remains of Bede's monasteries at Wearmouth and Jarrow are buried beneath modern Tyneside). The intricate system of 'monk's trods', pannier roads and trackways has mostly been covered over by later roads. Documentary evidence is scant and, worse still, frequently misleading – often written by monks eager to show Christianity triumphing over the dark forces of paganism, or of national salvation coming through conversion to the true faith. Nevertheless, enough evidence has recently emerged to allow historians to present a view of this period in which many of the landmarks of the history of our civilization have simply melted away.

The accepted view of the early Middle Ages has been dominated by the idea that unity is, or was, the ideal of European civilization. The Roman empire and Charlemagne brought political unity, while the Catholic church and the Frankish expansion from around AD 900 brought spiritual and cultural unity. Deviations from these 'ideal' unities signified chaos, anarchy and destruction. The barbarian invasions after AD 400 destroyed the unifying structures of Roman civilization, but Christianity managed to hang on in isolated communities, so that after AD 600 missionaries could go out into the barbarian lands of England, north Gaul, the Netherlands and Germany and convert the pagans. A Christian culture was born but even Charlemagne, the great unifier, was unable to impose enduring political unity on a continent of barbarian kings and, as a result, the individual nations of Europe emerged.

We have been taught that the collapse of the Roman empire was brought on by, and itself encouraged, great influxes of barbarian peoples. However, the temptation to draw impressively thick lines on maps leads us to overstate the migrations or invasions of discrete 'tribes'. Movement of people and cultures is likely to have been a more piecemeal affair; a continual drift born out of never-ending changes in circumstance. A recent interpretation (see Cunliffe) suggests that the boundaries of the empire were a barrier to the natural migration of people from east to west and later from north to south. This migration, associated with climate change and increased levels of farming, had been going on for centuries, slowly moving small groups of people from east to west across the map of Europe. The Roman conquest of Gaul, western Germania, Dacia, Britannia and other border provinces and the setting-up of customs posts and border patrols stopped this migration, leading to a build-up of population on the outside. This population pressure, rather than weakness at the centre, was most important in undermining Roman authority at the margins of the empire. These outsiders were not excluded from the Roman world; they were part of the Roman trading system, they absorbed Roman cultural habits and their leaders negotiated with Roman authorities. Barbarians were invited to fight for the empire, and even to form legions within the army, in exchange for grants of land or money – an implicit acknowledgement of both the barbarians' need for land and its availability within the empire. The number of barbarians fighting for the empire grew ever greater, power became diffused, and the discord between the various groups led not so much to the collapse of the empire, as to the irrelevance of central authority.

Some sense of the implosion of the empire is caught by the tortuous tale of Alaric's dealings with the imperial authorities. In the late fourth century, Alaric, the Visigoth leader, was invited into the western empire by Theodosius and given command of Goth auxiliaries in the imperial army. But after the emperor's death he went south to Greece and was then paid by the eastern emperor Arcadius to invade Italy. After a defeat by the forces of the new western emperor Honorius, he was paid to change sides again, but when the promised gold did not appear in 410, he took and sacked the city of Rome. By that time, though, the court of the emperor was in Ravenna, and Rome was a political irrelevance. The capture of Rome was a dramatic symbolic event, but the barbarians generally had little interest in destroying the empire; they had come south in search of land and security, not violence and uncertainty. The

movement of their peoples, which seems dramatic in historical hindsight, was, in reality, mainly gradual and peaceful.

As the central authority of Rome dissolved, local people assumed
more control, but this was not a simple transfer of power. The economy
of the western empire had been utterly geared towards its own survival.
Although different provinces enjoyed different levels of prosperity
through time, the economic system worked by circulating money raised
in taxes through the army and civil administration, which in turn spent
money on public buildings, equipment, food and so on. In this system
the local inhabitants within the western empire were kept in a state of
near poverty – with disease and malnutrition widespread – and were
therefore unable to contribute much to the economy besides taxation.
(This was quite different to the more heavily urbanized east.) When
the Roman administration withdrew, this system completely collapsed,
and it was this, rather than barbarian destruction, that changed the
social geography of western Europe so spectacularly.

The pattern for what happened after this collapse had been set, at
least in some provinces, by the earlier third-century crisis. Order had
been restored and the fourth century was a time of stability and prosperity – particularly in the western provinces of Gaul and Britain – but
the empire began to be both politically and culturally more fragmented.
The local *patronus,* the governor or magistrate nominally appointed by
Rome, became ever more powerful and autonomous. As contact with
Rome dwindled to nothing, the *patronus* became the man who medi-
ated between the citizens and subjects on the one hand, and the law
and the taxman on the other. The *patronus* aided stability by raising
revenue and troops for Rome, while keeping the citizens and peasants
under control. (This was the model for the later feudal system.)

In the late western empire local needs, customs and leaders emerged
as important alternatives to the central controlling culture of Rome.
The art and decoration of third- and fourth-century Roman buildings
show subtle 'native' variations on the classical Roman style as local
traditions of art and architecture were rediscovered. The wealthy built
grand estates and palaces in the country or suburbs, rather than in
town. These villas had spectacular mosaics, marble walls, curtained
arcades and, most noticeably, private not public bathing – private pleasures were in favour rather than public display. One effect of this local
autonomy was, paradoxically, to make locals more Roman. Having
more control over their own affairs gave the middle classes of Italy,

Spain, Gaul and elsewhere a liking for the culture of the empire. They began to speak local forms of Latin – laying the foundations of the Romance languages – and Celtic language and culture faded away even in rural Gaul. Locals built country villas and wore Roman clothing and brooches, and even the barbarians of southern Germany adopted Roman ways. The empire took on an abstract quality for these self-sufficient provincials and was embodied more by the person of the emperor than by the city of Rome itself or its institutions.

The culture of the empire changed in other ways during its declining decades, showing, in particular, the growing influence of Christian culture. Fourth-century mosaics from Ostia, the port at the mouth of the Tiber, point back to classical art but also forward to medieval depictions of human faces and figures. For nearly a thousand years the ideal life of the mind had been personified by the classical scholar, surrounded by books and by pupils looking enquiringly at the world. During the fourth and fifth centuries this picture altered and the ideal human became the Christian saint. Statues recovered from Ostia have immobile features and raised eyes, looking inwards to the soul and upwards to the heavens. The classical idealization of the human figure was abandoned. Portraits of saints and holy men were for inspiration and spirituality, and were made impressionistic and schematic; human flesh was corrupt, leading to a focus on the inner life through formalism and symbols. Nevertheless the developing Christian art of the Mediterranean, unlike most pagan faiths, put humanity at the centre of creation. Though each portrayed the human in different ways, classical and Christian art both depicted humanity as a special creature.

The collapse of the long-distance physical and economic structure of the western empire led to a different kind of Europe. The empire remained as a kind of ghostly echo, but the towns were largely abandoned, except where they were ecclesiastical centres, and the west became a rural economy, based on a purely regional infrastructure. Much has been made of the reduction of urban life – Rome's population declined from a peak of one million to around 20,000 by the seventh century, and a third of the towns of Italy were totally abandoned – but the Roman towns had been built for a purpose that no longer existed. It was necessary for Europe to return to its pre-empire structure in order to rebuild its prosperity. But we should not mistake regionalism, or a more rural existence, as a sign of ignorance or chaos. While the overall production of the economy reduced, rural life in the early Middle Ages had the advantages of lack of interference from outside, a strong and sustained communal existence, protection from large-scale famine, and relative security. The story of a peaceful empire followed by centuries of tempestuous conflict would have rung hollow in countless rural settlements that found themselves free of Roman authority and taxation.

Rather than viewing the end of the western empire as the sign of decline, recent historians (see Horden and Purcell) suggest that, while the rise of the empire was marked by the 'intensification' of activity in certain centres, its decline was a sign of 'abatement' or dispersal. Rome itself shrank in importance and population, but Constantinople grew into the largest city in Eurasia. Cultural, economic and political life in the west shifted from the towns to the countryside, and Christianity went with it; monasteries became centres of rural, not urban, living, and kings and nobles were found in hunting lodges and country houses. The first monasteries in western Europe were founded in 415 near Marseilles, and around 540 St Benedict established a set of rules for his small community on the high crags of Monte Cassino. Some of the monastic communities that followed were not content simply to live in a rural setting; they believed they could be closer to God if they sought the most tranquil and apparently remote places of the earth. Communities were founded on islands off Ireland, and eventually on almost every island off the west of Scotland, including Columba's famous community on Iona, from where similarly isolated communities were established at places like Lindisfarne, or Holy Island, off north-east England. The monks were not trying to escape pagan persecution, but were seeking to exist in places that seemed 'halfway between heaven and earth'. They were approaching God by embedding themselves in the natural world – a profoundly Celtic instinct.

The old Roman roads, built for heavy traffic between towns, were augmented by a rural network of trackways, linking a network of Christian as well as secular communities. And though the formal system of Roman communications had disappeared, this network stretched across a whole continent. Even the island communities were well served by transport networks; such was the traffic across the Irish Sea in the seventh and eighth centuries, and so numerous the settlements around its shores, that it is seen by historians as a Mediterranean of the west. Clearly we need to rid ourselves of the idea that Christians of the far west were somehow isolated. They certainly believed that

God existed everywhere, and that Christianity could be practised wherever there was a heaven above and a hell beneath. The universality of
their faith made it possible to found a Christian community anywhere,
while their desire to communicate with each other and to belong to a
universal faith meant that the same scriptures were being studied in
Iona and Antioch, in Armagh and Alexandria.

Even in Roman times, around 90 per cent of western Europeans lived
in the countryside. Rural dispersal gave Christianity the opportunity to
become the religion of these ordinary peasant people; but in doing so the
faith had to adapt to the needs of its new adherents. This process was
subtle and unconscious, but there is plenty of evidence that western
Christianity took on many aspects of the old Celtic and Germanic pagan
cultures. Eastern Christianity, with its Jewish inheritance and urban background, was utterly concerned with humanity and its relation to God, but
the western faith showed signs of a greater interest in the natural world.
The state of the harvest, the magical nature of 'sacred' plants and animals,
the tangible spirituality of the great forests, as well as festivals of spring,
midsummer and midwinter, and specific beliefs such as the magic nature
of threefold objects, were all brought within the Christian orbit.

If Christianity had become so well established in the Roman empire,
and the disruption of the empire's collapse had been less dramatic than
we previously thought, then what was the role of the second pillar of
the traditional Dark Age narrative, the conversion of the barbarians?
Here the tradition of the missionary saint is another illusion, or more
accurately, a mythological creation. For men such as Bede, writing up
to a century later, the stories of the missionary saints, like the Irish saints
Columba, Aidan and Columbanus, and Augustine, sent to England from
Rome, talking gently and persuasively to bemused but interested warrior
kings about the life of Jesus and the apostles, were an essential part of
Christian history. The oral culture of the Atlantic peoples was put fully
to use in creating legends, some of which made their way into print.
Adamnán's *Life of St Columba* and St Muirchú's *Life of St Patrick* were
followed by lives of Columbanus, St Brigid and St Cuthbert, as the saint
became the legendary hero of Christendom. But these stories under-
valued the extensive network of Christian communities that remained
when the empire dissolved. This was stronger in some places than others
but there is little evidence (apart from the imaginings of later Christian
writers) of pagan hordes sweeping away the Christian faithful.

Nevertheless the empire had been concentrated in the towns of the west, and when urban life contracted, Christian communities did too. The alacrity with which the Britons of the old civil zone (present-day England) took up the culture of Saxon incomers (see page 110) may show how their own culture had been degraded by Roman occupation but, while Germanic culture may have presented a challenge to Christians, that does not mean that Christianity had disappeared from England and Gaul. In post-Roman Gaul, the incomers found a well-established system of bishoprics, with church leaders acting as de facto provincial governors. In England the Saxons met a weaker church organization, which had to adapt to the new culture. Nevertheless the English Saxons, like the Franks and Goths who found their way into Gaul, were familiar with Christianity, viewing it as one of a number of religious tendencies.

Bede tells us that on his journey from Rome to Kent in 597, Augustine and his retinue 'began to contemplate returning home rather than going to a barbarous, fierce and unbelieving nation whose language they did not even understand'. But excavations of places like West Heslerton in east Yorkshire and West Stow in Suffolk have shown us that the pagan Anglo-Saxons inhabited a world that was no more dangerous or warlike than any other. Their lives were relatively peaceful, their communities stable; their cultural values were tied to the natural world in which they lived, their artistic skills were consummate, their oral culture profound and deeply woven. Some Anglo-Saxon leaders were hostile to the emissaries because they believed that Christianity threatened these values – Augustine was, after all, sent to convert the English from Rome, a city synonymous with external power and control.

If the English part of Britain adopted the Germanic culture of Saxon incomers, then the west of the island, together with Ireland, developed a Christianity that acknowledged Rome as the centre of the Church without ever being part of the empire. These 'Atlantic' communities paradoxically adopted Christianity (perhaps because it accorded strongly with their own customs), while remaining immune to both Roman and Saxon culture.

A network of Christian communities survived the withdrawal of Roman administration, but was left in a world, and in a church, without a governing centre. The idea of Rome was strongly felt, and each church gained strength from its connection to this near-mythic city, but for centuries there was no sense of the Church being led by Rome. The legendary journeys of missionaries and, eventually, popes northwards across the Alps, symbolic as they later became, were largely irrelevant to the Christian communities of the north. Instead the surviving Christian communities began, gradually and fitfully, to build a new kind of relationship with the rulers of the north and west. As the kingdoms of the west each emerged from the grouping of nobles around a single court, so Christian scholars, monks, bishops and lay people presented an attractive retinue for the new monarchs. The celebrated conversion of King Edwin of Northumbria in 627 was described by Bede as the result of long debate on the merits of this new religion by the king and his wise counsellors. In reality Edwin's wife, sister of the king of Kent, was already a Christian, and it is likely that other courtiers were too. Edwin's baptism in York may, like Constantine's three centuries earlier, have been an acknowledgement of the growing dominance of the faith among his people.

The earlier conversion of Clovis, king of the Franks, in 496 was portrayed by Gregory of Tours, writing a century later, as a great victory for the Catholic church. The Franks had occupied north-west Germany and the Low Countries, and had, with the removal of the Roman frontier, extended their influence into northern Gaul. By the late fifth century they occupied most of the key trading routes, as well as the richest farmland, of northern Europe. In much of Gaul local governors and bishops had stayed in place while the empire disintegrated around them. In the south, Ostrogoths had temporarily settled in some parts, and brought others under their control. They were Arian Christians, but there is little evidence of religious clashes between them and the existing Catholic Christians. The Franks, according to Gregory, were untouched by Christianity, but this is unlikely to be true. Remegius, Bishop of Reims and residual governor of part of Gaul, persuaded Clovis that he had much to gain from the support of the Catholic Christian network. His conversion certainly won him the cooperation of the local people of Gaul, and the Catholic bishops conferred on Clovis the secular leadership of Christianity, allowing him to 'liberate' true Christians from their Arian conquerors with the full authority of the Church. It seems that Clovis was taking on the predominant faith of his adopted countrymen; his conversion was, like Constantine's and Edwin's, a politically astute decision. Gregory of Tours' depiction of the king's baptism, on Christmas Day of the year 500, in the city of Reims, shows that churches were already well established: 'The streets were overshadowed with coloured hangings, the churches adorned with white hangings, the baptistery was set in order, smoke of incense appeared in clouds, perfumed tapers gleamed, the whole church about the place of baptism was filled with the divine fragrance.'

The spectacular description gives a romantic aura to the Christian story, but it detracts from the growing sense of a common purpose between the Christian communities and the landowners, nobles and monarchs of the west. As well as political expediency, people expected practical results and guidance from their religion. The Christian faith was associated with judgement and reckoning rather than forgiveness. Christian bishops were soon able to point to the success of the Franks as proof that God would protect other leaders from their enemies and give victory to their armies. Christianity also brought the extremely impressive skill of literacy; having literate priests and bishops as courtiers conferred prestige on princes, in the eyes of both their own people and other leaders.

The early Middle Ages, in contrast to the Roman past and the high medieval period to come, has left us few monuments apart from its monasteries. But the culture of these centuries was less concerned with stone buildings as symbols of power and patronage than with the custom of gifts. The donation of gold ornaments, chalices, tapestries, books, relics and even sons to the Church tied the nobility into a mutually beneficial relationship. In return the donors received blessings and masses for the souls of their departed relatives, but they did not feel the need to build great stone basilicas or cathedrals. Gifts to religious orders enabled them to extend their work in the secular world, eventually founding hospitals where the sick were asked to pray for the souls of those who had given money and gifts.

While western Christianity embraced many of the cultural beliefs of the western people, illiteracy brought a concentration on image, spectacle and ritual rather than words; the form of the faith took precedence over its content. The Catholic service became theatrical and the cross was made into a devotional symbol; the words of the service and of the psalms were chanted not spoken; and visual representations of holy figures in the form of icons became ever more prevalent. Reading the words of Christ was less important than feeling the sense of them in a dramatic setting. Icons and relics imbued with miraculous properties flooded the Mediterranean and western world as Christianity became a magical religion and the bishops and clerics direct agents of this new deity. This was the atmosphere in which the mythology of the saints was constructed and association with a saint was of great value to a monastery or abbey, increasing its spiritual power, and the number and values of gifts it received.

The early medieval church has been disdained by intellectual historians. Coming between the Latin church fathers – Jerome, Ambrose and Augustine – of the fourth and fifth centuries and the philosophers of the high medieval period – Abelard, Aquinas and Ockham – it seems to have had little to offer. But the immense task that the Church fulfilled in these centuries was a practical one. As well as bringing western Europeans, their nobility and their monarchs into the faith, and building a system of cooperation and exchange between the secular and spiritual worlds, Christians worked out, step by step, an intricate set of rules for Christian life – what one historian has called 'applied Christianity' (see Brown, 2003). Augustine had set out his vision of the Christian life, but what did this mean in practice? Benedict, founder abbot of Monte Cassino, and father of western monasticism, wrote his *Regula Monachorum*, the set of rules that monks should follow, in the mid-sixth century; while soon after, Gregory the Great, Benedictine monk and pope, issued his own *Regula Pastoralis*, rules for the pastoral care of souls, as a spiritual instruction manual for bishops and priests. These works set the tone for a Christian community that, while it must live alongside and offer guidance to the secular, must never be seduced into adopting its trappings of wealth and power. And from these works descended a multitude of advice and guidance for ordinary Christians: when was it right to kill in defiance of the sixth commandment; were there different levels of sin; was sin different from crime, and who should decide on punishment; was it possible for deceitful means to produce honest ends; was lending money for interest always a sin; were statues of Christ 'graven images' or aids to worship; and a thousand other practical questions. The Christian God was vengeful, and it was important to understand the rules of behaviour that might help to avoid eternal damnation.

From the eighth century onwards the kingdoms of the west began to combine, breaking out from the old Roman-defined territories to encompass ever-larger realms. By then England comprised six kingdoms – Cornwall, Wessex, Mercia, Kent, East Anglia and Northumbria – but the west of the continent was dominated by the kingdom of the Franks, which stretched from the Rhineland to the Atlantic, encompassing all of present-day France, except the province of Aquitaine. This vast area was ruled by the successors of Clovis, the Merovingian kings, whose kingdom was an alliance of clan leaders given prestige and influence in return for supplying the king with warriors. These nobles were presented with gifts of land, which in turn meant the need for more conquest and a further weakening of the power of the centre. On his death each Merovingian king divided his kingdom between all his surviving sons so that over time yet more power leached away from the kings. The result was a diversity and dispersal of power within an overall Frankish kingdom.

Until the eighth century the political geography of western Europe was fluid; kings held sway over some territories, but often regional or local leaders were more dominant, though even they had only nominal control over lands whose main focus of existence was the food-producing village. Each monarch ruled over a court of nobles rather than a definite territory, or even a discrete people, while the boundaries between territories were ill-defined and often irrelevant, and ethnic differences seem to have mattered little. We need to understand that when we talk about Franks or Saxons or Visigoths, we are using a convenient shorthand for the people who lived in a particular place, rather than a definable ethnic group. The great borders of the Roman empire – on the Rhine, at Hadrian's Wall and on the Danube – had dissolved to be replaced by the customary free movement of people and goods. This situation began to change in the eighth century, and the resulting conflicts give us a clearer understanding of the relation between the system of kingdoms and the Latin or Catholic church.

The Merovingian kings ruled much of western Europe from their heartland in the Low Countries, but in name only. The towns, estates, regions and counties of the west were autonomous to different degrees, with little connection to any kind of centre. In the late eighth century Merovingian influence petered out in south-west Gaul, while east of the Rhineland were the heartlands of the Frisians and Saxons, and further east still, the Poles, Lithuanians, Alemanni and Avars. Borders were virtually nonexistent, with continual trade and movement between these different peoples. The Frisian and Saxon people were, though, distinct from their Frankish neighbours in their rejection of Christianity and in their social and political arrangements, which derived from their situation on the margins of the North Sea, and among its islands and rivers (see Chapter One). From the fifth century, and perhaps earlier,

Saxon and Frisian people crossed the sea to settle in eastern England, which became part of a thriving trading network. Settlements on the Ouse, the Humber and the Thames looked to each other and to their cousins on the Ems, Weser and Elbe rivers. All were reachable in a few days' sailing, and for the Northumbrians and East Anglians, the region of Frisia and north Saxony, with its connection to rivers running inland, was the gateway to Europe. In the eighth century Saxony was still run by a collection of nobles who elected a king only in times of war and, unlike the English Saxon kings, remained wedded to their old religious customs. But the Saxons had become prosperous on their trade through Frisia; their farmers and merchants were as wealthy as any Frankish noble and the ports of the North Sea coast were bigger and busier than the Frankish towns. The prosperity of these leaderless pagans defies the later assumption that civilization came only through Christianity and kings.

Soon after 700 the Merovingian court was taken over by a family who were effectively chiefs of staff to the kings. Charles Martel, head of this family, persuaded the aristocracy of the two most important Frankish regions, Neustria and Austrasia (northern France, Belgium and the north Rhineland) that, by combining together, they could win greater power and wealth. The diverse, localized nature of European trade, and the diffusion of power since the withdrawal of Roman authority, had decreased the power of the aristocracy in their own lands. They did not have the power or authority to control, and more importantly to tax, a population of farmers and traders who saw themselves as essentially freemen. Charles Martel changed this situation by making the Frankish aristocracy into a formidable army, willing and able to use terrifying force to bring their own population, and those of surrounding territories, to heel. Over the next five centuries most of Europe came under Frankish control, as we shall see, but the immediate effect was on the Frankish people and their neighbours.

Under Charles Martel's rule the landowners, including monasteries and bishops, began to impose more control on the peasant farmers, instituting and enforcing systems of 'seigneurial' and feudal obligations. A particular type of society evolved, in which duty and land were bound up with military and political power. The peasantry were tied to the land and gave service to their master, who in turn gave service to the king. The rich farmland of Neustria and Austrasia produced enough surplus for the Frankish nobility to become extremely wealthy.

The success of this new system led the Franks to look for other lands to exploit. Charles took most of southern France after defeating the Arab armies at Poitiers, and then turned his attention to the east. The borderlands between Austrasia and Saxony were brought into the Frankish system, but Saxony itself resisted. For the first time since the Roman empire, a new frontier with a well-defined border arose. To the west were the Frankish lands, closely tied into a political system of service, tax and submission, ruled by a Christian, literate, central-ized court; to the east lay the lands of the Frisians and Saxons, a fluid society of farmers, traders and regional leaders, with a pagan, oral culture. The dividing line between the civilized and the barbarian was, after three centuries, re-established. For us who study the past, it is significant that the writers of history were all on one side of this border; the price of entering written history was to become a civi-lized, Frankish Christian.

After the death of Charles Martel, who had remained the 'mayor of the king's palace', the Frankish nobles and bishops chose Charles's son Pepin as king and in 751 sought the sanction of the pope to remove one Christian king and replace him with another. This was a curious request since, despite its nominal leadership of the western church, the Roman papacy was of little account in western European affairs. Having returned from Byzantium with a request to annul his debts refused, Pope Stephen faced the prospect that the Roman church was bankrupt. The city of Rome was itself a pale reflection of Augustan times, though it remained an impressive sight. Irish, English and Frankish Christians who travelled to the eternal city in expectation of a vast semi-ruin were not disappointed. Huge churches squatted inside the ghosts of imperial walls, squares and roadways, with the pope, impoverished, but clinging to the grandeur of his office, at the centre. To compound Rome's diffi-culties, while the Byzantines were occupied in holding off Arab attacks in the east, the Lombards had taken over their possessions in north Italy, leaving Rome surrounded by hostile powers.

In 753 Pope Stephen journeyed north from Rome to meet Aistulf, king of the Lombards, at Pavia in northern Italy. His requests for relief from unpayable taxes, and for a role in the Lombard church, were rejected. So from Pavia Stephen made his historic journey to meet Pepin, now king of the Franks. This was the first time that a pope had crossed the Alps, turning away from the Mediterranean in search of new allies in the north. This turned out to be a mutually beneficial journey. The new rulers of the Franks had little to gain strategically from the pope's presence, but Pepin had a grand vision of a Christian empire, ruled by his family and sanctioned by God's representative on earth. Pope Stephen, rejected by Byzantium and the Lombards, was fortunate in his next choice of ally, but his determination paid off, and the journey across the Alps symbolized a shift in European power – away from the Mediterranean and towards the west and north.

Pepin was anointed king by Stephen in a deliberate echo of Old Testament ritual, and in return drove Aistulf and his followers from Italy. The Franks were able to give the pope a swathe of territory across central Italy, including the Byzantine enclave of Ravenna, and Byzantine influence in the west came to an end. The pope became, thanks to Stephen's alliance with Pepin, lord of his own territory and undisputed head of the western Catholic church. The riches, and the land, that the Franks gained in Lombardy were distributed among their own aristocracy, with a large slice donated to the Roman church.

The alliance between the papacy and the Franks affected Charlemagne, Pepin's son and successor, profoundly. Charlemagne, who reigned for 46 years from 768, set out to conquer the territory of his neighbours and to convert them to Catholic Christianity 'with a tongue of iron'. In 772 he invaded Saxony along the same roads as Augustus 800 years earlier, and met with the same resistance. His armies destroyed the sacred places of Saxon worship, but because the Saxons had many leaders, they were almost impossible to defeat. Visits to Rome reinforced Charlemagne's ambition to build an empire, and provided him with a sense of epic and brutal power. The campaign against the Saxons grew more bitter as villages were forcibly relocated and hill-forts besieged and destroyed. Elements of the Saxon nobility were persuaded, by the prospect of more power over their own peasants, to betray their people to the Franks, and at Verden in 782, 4,500 Saxon prisoners were beheaded on the orders of Charlemagne.

In the peace that was finally agreed, as Charlemagne's secretary and biographer Einhard wrote: 'The Saxons were to put away their heathen worship and the religious ceremonies of their fathers; were to accept the articles of the Christian faith and practice; and, being united to the Franks, were to form with them one people.' The same conditions were applied to most of the peoples of the western European mainland as Charlemagne's armies took the Germanic heartlands and pushed east as far as the Avar Khanate of Hungary, while also forcing the Arab armies in Spain back as far as the Ebro. Local traditions of worship, either pagan or Christian, were abolished and any diversion from the Catholic faith was strictly punished, as Charlemagne's 'Capitulary Concerning Saxony' states: 'If anyone follows pagan rites [or] . . . is shown to be unfaithful to our lord the king, let him suffer the penalty of death.'

At its height, Charlemagne's kingdom extended from the Pyrenees to the River Oder and from the North Sea to south of Rome. Western Europe, excluding only Britain and Iberia, was under one ruler, its boundaries were strictly drawn, and its frontiers were closed. Charlemagne took a strongly Frankish view of how this society should be organized. In the time of his grandfather, monks had come to the Frankish kings from Ireland and England, eager to preach to the pagans of Frisia and Saxony – both Willibrord and Boniface followed a tradition of wandering or *peregrino* Christians. But Charlemagne's conquests and his strict enforcement of Christianity changed the nature of their travels. Instead of converting pagans, clerics were engaged in the education and 'correction' of the population, to ensure that they followed Catholic ways. This was not simply an authoritarian process; there was a widespread belief that God was waiting to punish humanity for its sins, which must therefore be eradicated.

Charlemagne felt his own need of instruction and looked once more to the now-celebrated Christian school of north-east England. Alcuin of York, inheritor of the scholarly reputation of Bede, travelled to the new palace complex at Aachen (characteristically built in the country-side) to be Charlemagne's spiritual adviser. And while his subjects must be shown the correct ways to be good Christians, they should also be good Franks. Subjection to the Lord God was matched by subjection, loyalty and deference to one's secular lord. Charlemagne was a master at creating an atmosphere of utter loyalty at his court combined with a system of formal friendship which served as a model for his aristocrats. But in this rigidly hierarchical Frankish society, any attempt to form communal organizations – guilds or brotherhood leagues, for example – was ruthlessly suppressed. The increased use of written instruction also allowed the imposition, just as in ancient Greece and Rome, of codified laws. Roman law was reintroduced either alongside, or in place of, the customary laws of local populations.

Charlemagne was declared Caesar, or emperor, on Christmas Day 800 by Pope Leo. This was less an anointment of a subject king than

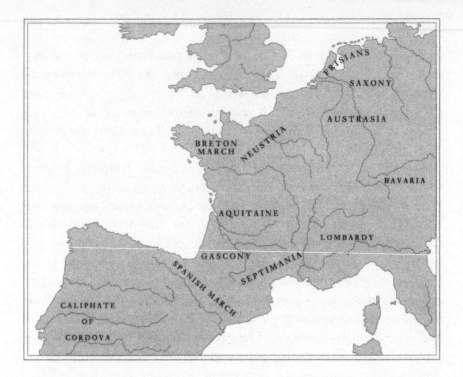

Charlemagne and his father turned the loose territories of the eighth century into a controlled and centralised empire.

a desperate attempt by the pope to endear himself to the most powerful man in Europe, and to gain some influence over the direction of Christendom. Despite Stephen's efforts of 50 years earlier, western Christianity was firmly in the hands of northerners – principally Charlemagne and whichever scholars he chose to come to his court. The pope needed entry into this charmed circle. The learned monks at Aachen were charged with giving spiritual direction to Charlemagne's kingdom, but they also helped to create a mythic history of western Christianity, with Charlemagne as its apogee. This was entirely understandable; it was important for the Aachen court to create a 'civilization story' that explained their own place in history. Alcuin, in particular, was aware of Viking raids on the coast of his homeland and took these as a sign of God's displeasure with his flock. Einhard, Charlemagne's contemporary biographer, understood that the emperor had been granted great power precisely in order to bring the faithful to heel.

These writers followed Bede's lead in seeing pagan darkness both in the past and all around. They described the Merovingian centuries as an age of darkness, barbarism and ignorance, allowing later writers to

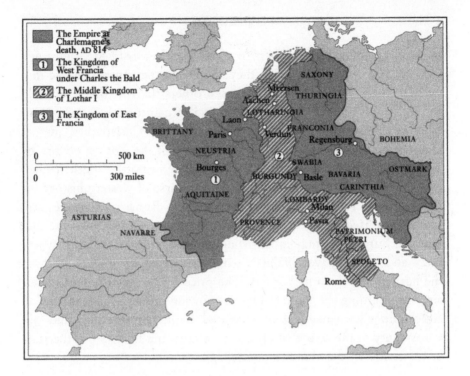

Charlemagne's son Louis divided the empire between his three sons, giving the basis for the later development of France, Burgundy and Germany.

speak of a 'Carolingian renaissance' in the eighth century. Both were a travesty of the truth, but fuelled the Franks' self-importance and gave justification to the severe brutality they had handed out. Even the Carolingian minuscules, the lower case Roman alphabet attributed to Charlemagne's court, emerged from the labours of generations of scribes who worked at the courts of 'barbarian' kings, while the development or reinstatement of 'correct' Latin by Alcuin and others (who came from regions where Latin had not been spoken for centuries) presented a new barrier between intellectual and ordinary life. People in Francia (and in Italy and Spain) in the early ninth century assumed they were speaking Latin which they had inherited from the Romans. But their Latin was an early form of French, and unintelligible to Latin scholars; Alcuin dismissed it as barbarous. Church Latin therefore became a language that was spoken by no ordinary people, but was the universal language of an educated elite and the required language of the Catholic liturgy – it was the language in which man spoke to God.

While Charlemagne wanted to create a Christian society in the form of a Holy Empire, Christian monks and bishops had begun to think about new political structures. In particular they read St Augustine's *City of God*, which told them they should not be content to live in a wicked world, but should aim to teach others the way that the world should be governed. The Christian church began to seek the establishment of a state governed by the doctrines of Christianity, just as Charlemagne wanted to recreate the majesty of the Roman empire by uniting the see of Rome with his own empire in the north. Charlemagne's power and ambition gave direction to the course of western history for the next 500 years by making the church in Rome part of western, rather than Mediterranean, Europe. Charlemagne created the state that many in Europe desired – a Christian empire centred on a court where piety and learning were valued, while converting or making war on the heathen tribes on its borders. The price was the quashing of diversity and granting the church an ever-growing influence in politics and education. Charlemagne had recreated Latin Christendom and put Christianity at the centre of the state's affairs, but he also put the state at the centre of the church's affairs.

The reign of Charlemagne marks the end of the first phase of the Middle Ages, but his empire did not last. In 843 Charlemagne's son Louis the Pious divided his empire between his own three sons – the Franks were effectively divided into a western (French) kingdom, an eastern (German) kingdom, and a middle kingdom. The resulting conflicts were exacerbated by the increasing raids of Scandinavian northmen or Vikings and by incursions by Magyars and Slavs. But the power of the German element of the Franks was reasserted by the emperor Otto I, who was king of the Germans from 936, and emperor from 962 until his death in 973. Otto's armies defeated the invading Magyars, pushed the Slavs back to the Balkans and took over most of Italy. The Germanic people became, and remained, the dominant force in central Europe. By 1000, the Scandinavian raiders and people had become integrated into the Christian culture of western Europe.

The power of the Franks was centred on the belt of rich farmland that runs through Normandy, Champagne, Savoy, Flanders, Brabant, Burgundy, the Rhineland, Swabia and Bavaria. The landowning families of this region were, in the late Middle Ages, to become the lords of Europe. We are used to thinking of the Middle Ages as a time of stagnation, waiting for the Italian Renaissance to give Europe its leg-up into modernity. But the central core of European prosperity was established by the year 1000, and for the next 300 years this core developed and fed the expansionary ambitions of its aristocracy. The first beneficiaries were the great Frankish families, the Joinvilles, the Grandmesnils, the Guiscards and the rest, whose vast estates and benefices brought them tax and trading income and, as trade and manufacture increased, income from the sale of goods into towns. But land remained the key to their wealth, and in the Frankish heartland, there was only so much land to go round.

The landowners were the knights of the emperor's court, whose holdings had come from inheritance and from military service. The Frankish knights acquired iron armour and weaponry that their poorer enemies could not match, forming squadrons of heavy cavalry in which both rider and horse were clad in an impenetrable wall of armour. For 300 years, from roughly 930 to 1250, they carried all before them. Having regained control of France and western Germany, they swept across Europe invading and conquering, and to varying degrees settling, England, parts of Wales and Ireland, Sicily, Greece, southern Italy, Bohemia, Moravia, Estonia, Finland, Austria, Hungary, Silesia, Castile and Aragon. The Norman conquest of England beginning in 1066 is thought by the English to be an event of enormous historical significance, but it was part of a much larger pattern of Norman-Frankish expansion – the Normans were, by origin, Scandinavians who settled in northern France and became integrated into the Frankish system. Sometimes the Franks fought pagans, sometimes Muslims and sometimes fellow Christians. By 1300, through conquest, marriage and colonization, Frankish nobles were established as the lords and power-brokers of practically every kingdom in Europe. They married into the upper ranks of local society and the resulting aristocracy formed the national nobilities of western Europe.

As well as Catholic Christianity, the Franks took their highly-developed system of feudalism and implanted it in societies that had lived by different means. Feudalism grew up in Francia by gradual assertion of aristocratic power; in countries that were conquered, England for example, it was brutally imposed as the fulfilment of deals made between monarchs and nobles in advance of conquest. After 1066 Norman nobles were given bishoprics, duchies and estates by William I in return for service and in recognition of feudal ties established in their homeland. The Domesday Book records the principal landowners for each English county and these are, invariably, Norman nobles. These new enfeoffed estates marked a change in the arrangement of the lands of Europe, marginalizing small independent farmers in favour of large-scale landlords. The domain, an estate or series of estates large enough to provide supplies in years of bad harvest and to defend its land against outsiders, became the social unit of Frankish Europe.

Local customs survived within the feudal system, at least in some places. The village of Laxton in Nottinghamshire still holds an annual communal meeting or court where boundaries are marked out and land allocated for the following year. This is often described as a feudal court, but it is really the preservation of an Anglo-Saxon pre-feudal system. Similarly the villagers in many places elected their own reeve or manager, and the lord simply let them get on with running their own affairs.

The administration of much of Frankish Europe was run by local officials called counts. The position of count was a an echo of the *patronus* of the Roman empire, a local noble or governor who collected taxes on behalf of himself and the monarch, presided over a county court a few times a year, and led the local troops in battle. Through the counts and the lesser nobles the military and civil parts of society became ever more closely entwined, and the king's generals effectively became the civil administrators of western Europe.

This fusion between the military and the civil was the bedrock of feudal society. The complex system of benefices, agreements, enfeoffments, charters and indentures linked not just the serf to his master but the lowest slave to the highest noble and on to the king. Agreements went on through layer after layer of society, binding the whole population into a net of legal, political, social, military and economic relations. Laws passed in Frankish realms, including England, decreed that all a father's land should pass to his eldest son. This immediately created the phenomenon of landless younger sons. Quite apart from needing an estate for status, no noble-born woman would marry a man without land. The only answer was more and more conquest.

The most significant resistance to the relentless expansion of the Latin church and Frankish nobility came from the Islamic people of the eastern Mediterranean. The eighth century had seen the sudden appearance of a new cultural force as Islamic armies swept out of the Arabian peninsula and, in a remarkably short time, conquered large swathes of the eastern Mediterranean, taking Damascus in 635, Jerusalem in 638, Alexandria in 646, before veering east to capture Basra in 656, Kabul in 664 and Samarkand in 710. Arab armies also pushed west across north Africa, taking the Byzantine cities that

Justinian had claimed back from the Vandals, and crossing into Spain in 711. By 730 they had taken over the Iberian peninsula and reached as far north as Poitiers. Meanwhile Arab forces crossed Asia Minor and, in 673, arrived at the walls of Byzantium itself. The city survived a five-year siege; it was besieged again in 717–18 and again survived.

The effect of Arab Islamic expansion on the eastern Christian church was devastating. Christianity had been a dominant religion in Syria, Persia, Egypt and Palestine for centuries, and was making inroads in Arabia. All of this was lost and Byzantium was no longer an empire but a city with a hinterland surrounded by hostile forces. It was forced into the splendid isolation that it maintained for the next 700 years.

The caliphs of the Arab Muslim world established a new court at Damascus in the late seventh century, but in the middle of the eighth century, the Muslims of Persia rebelled against the Umayyadd Caliphate of Damascus and set up the 'Abbassid Caliphate that ruled the Islamic world for the next 500 years. The 'Abbassids abandoned Damascus and set up a new court in the newly founded city of Baghdad far to the east. Although Arab families reigned in Baghdad, this was once again a Persian-dominated empire. Haroun al-Rashid, who became caliph in 786, and his successors turned away from the eastern Mediterranean and towards the old Mesopotamian and Persian interests. Trade with China via the Persian Gulf and the Silk Road was of prime importance, and while Charlemagne sent gifts to Haroun al-Rashid and travellers from Europe brought back tales of opulence beyond compare, Persians and Arabs did not trouble to come to Europe. The great port cities of the Eastern Mediterranean like Ephesus, Antioch, Byblos, Sidon, Tyre, Caesarea, Joppa and Gaza, for so long the crossroads of the Eurasian world, slowly declined. Europe had been saved from the Arab conquest by Byzantium's impregnable walls, but the price it paid was to be cut off from the east, the source of its cultural, political, mythic and technological ideas for more than a millennium. Europe had been the beneficiary of the astonishing array of ideas and innovations that came out of the inter-relations between the peoples of the Near East, and after 750 this was no longer available to them.

The Crusades, which began in 1095 and ended in 1205, were instigated by the papacy as a holy war, but they fit into the pattern of Latin-Frankish expansion. On their way to the Holy Land, the younger sons of northern nobles established fiefdoms across the Christian Mediterranean world – while hoping to do the same in Syria and Palestine. But in the Saracens the northern knights met a different type of enemy with much more sophisticated defences. In the eastern Mediterranean, stone castles and defensive walls had been in use for thousands of years, siege tactics were well developed and the use of cavalry was commonplace. The local people were not likely to convert to Latin Christianity, so conquest would mean driving the population out – an all but impossible ambition. Latin Christianity got a foothold in the Levant but it never managed a lasting presence.

Europe's eastern boundary was determined by the failure of the Crusades, but the whole adventure helped to define western Europe in other ways. Since the great disputes of the fifth century, the eastern church had pointedly refused to accept the primacy of Rome, while doctrinal disputes over the use of leavened bread in communion drove the two churches further apart. Once free of dependence on the eastern empire's overwhelming power, the western church and its adherents became disdainful of the eastern Christians. The Greek and Latin churches competed to acquire the newly converted pagans of eastern Europe, while Norman knights drove the Byzantines out of their last western outposts in southern Italy and Sicily. As the power of the Byzantine empire declined and the western Europeans grew more confident, the Latin church outgrew its Greek sister and one-time protector. Relations reached their nadir in 1204 when Crusaders, who thought of themselves as Latin Christians, were drawn into an internal conflict, and took temporary control of Byzantium. They went on an orgy of looting and slaughter and placed one of their own, Count Baldwin of Flanders, on the imperial throne. The Greek church was seen by then as an enemy of western Catholic Christendom, and though the Greeks recaptured the city, the separation was irreparable.

Just as important, the Crusades entwined the religious identity of the western Europeans with their racial background. In the twelfth century Europeans and Muslims began to write about 'the Christian people' and 'the Christian race'. The Crusader armies were a polyglot of nationalities and languages (though all led by families descended from Frankish nobility), but they began to think of themselves as one people unified in blood and religion.

The political influence and social status of the western nobility depended on continual warfare. These leaders did not stand on a hill and direct their men into battle; they strapped on their armour and led the charge. They believed in the glory of war and they fought as a matter of personal, family and tribal honour. The Franks integrated into local societies but brought their own culture with them. Across western and central Europe children of even the lowest in society were given Frankish names, as Saxon names like Ethelred and Alfred were replaced by William and Henry and Robert.

The continual aggressive warfare of the westerners was an alien concept to some of the people they encountered. Just as the Greeks had fought for freedom and the Romans for civilization, each being prepared to butcher and die for their cause, so the armies of the west fought for Christ. The people of the eastern Mediterranean viewed them with alarm. Crusader armies passing through Constantinople were regarded, even before the catastrophe of 1204, as avaricious and reckless, happy only when they were at war or enjoying the spoils of conflict. The Franks were expert at using terror to intimidate local populations, and when they met organized resistance or rebellion, as William did in the north of England, they simply destroyed everything. They brought the cult of the warrior to every corner of Europe. Brutal but honourable, greedy but loyal to one's family, avaricious but Christian – these were the characteristics of the new masters of Europe, together with a cultural addiction to the idea of war and a social structure that reflected the needs of a military society.

Charlemagne's successors failed to maintain a unified Christian empire in western Europe. This might have been a problem for the Roman church, which had tied itself so closely to the Carolingian cause. The Frankish takeover, however, allowed the papacy to assert itself as the universal spiritual power in a world of politically distinct realms – the one voice that could speak for the whole of Christendom. But they had to fight hard for this right. By the eleventh century the Church's authority was endangered by the feudal system, which gave lords and kings the right to appoint bishops and priests. Pope Gregory VII responded by issuing the *Dictatus Papae* or 'Papal Dictates' asserting the primacy of the Church in all matters – religious and secular. Although Gregory's dictates were taken from old church law, they had never been used for such an openly political purpose. The 27 clauses include the following:

> That the Roman church was founded by God alone.
> That the Roman pontiff alone can by right be called universal.
> That he alone can depose and reinstate bishops.
> That he alone may use the imperial insignia.

That all princes should kiss the feet of the pope alone.
That his name is unique in the world.
That he ought to be allowed to depose emperors.
That the Roman church has never erred, nor, as Scripture
    proclaims, will it ever err, through all eternity.

Gregory soon had the opportunity to use the power he had assumed. The Holy Roman Emperor Henry IV conquered lands in Italy in the 1070s and quarrelled with Gregory over their jurisdiction. Henry declared Gregory to be deposed, and in return Gregory excommunicated the emperor: 'I absolve all Christians from the bond of any oath which they have sworn or will swear unto him and I forbid anyone to serve him as king.' This extraordinary action led to one of the most symbolic acts in the tortuous history of emperor and Church. In 1077 Henry travelled to a church council at Canossa to seek readmission to the Church. Gregory himself described what happened: 'there, in a pathetic manner, having cast aside all his royal apparel, unshod and clothed in wool, he [Henry] remained before the gate of the town for three days . . . At last, having been overcome by the sincerity of his compunction . . . [we] received him back into the grace of communion and the bosom of Holy Mother Church.'

The reconciliation did not last long, though, and Henry was again excommunicated, declaring the pope a 'false monk' and questioning his right to represent God on earth: 'As if the kingdom and empire were in thine and not in God's hands!' Henry marched on Rome and deposed Gregory by force, placing his own pope in office. The result was civil war throughout Germany and eventual death in exile for both Gregory and Henry. After that catastrophe the papacy put a primacy on quiet strength and diplomacy rather than confrontation. But the tensions between spiritual and secular leaders continued throughout the Middle Ages. The emperors and kings were vulnerable to spiritual criticism, while the popes could be physically deposed; but by becoming a secular power and involving itself in the politics of kingdoms, the Church risked losing the respect of its followers.

For centuries the northern Christians had viewed the pope as a distant, almost historical figure. But from the tenth century the liturgy, laws, creeds and appointments of the Church were all decreed by a single organization with its head in Rome. Diversity of worship was quashed. The Spanish Mozarabic rite disappeared in the eleventh century and the Slavonic ritual was suppressed in those parts of the east that became Latin. Ireland had a more distinguished tradition of Christianity than any other north European country, but the church authorities in continental Europe and England viewed its church and society as an aberration. The Irish church was not funded by tithes and its bishoprics had no definite boundaries or lines of authority over priests. There was no unifying monarch, and certain practices, such as matrimonial services, were highly individual. The twelfth-century theologian St Bernard called the Irish barbarians and 'Christians in name only, pagans in fact'. The Latin church did not simply want the Irish church brought into line, it wanted Irish society completely revised so that it resembled the template of European society that the Franks were giving to the world. The Anglo-Normans were only too happy to oblige and duly invaded Ireland in the twelfth century, in order, as they said, 'to expand the boundaries of the church'.

In the previous century the Latin church's militant drive for uniformity and control had led to one of the bloodiest episodes in western Christianity. The Cathars or Albigensians of Languedoc in southern France were a throwback to the 'pure' sects of the fifth century. Their doctrine of a separate creation of good and evil, together with a select group of leaders known as the *perfecti* or *parfaits*, became deeply embedded in the region around Carcassonne. The Cathars (the name comes from *katharos*, the Greek word for pure) rejected the materialism and worldly power of the Church and wanted a return to the simple Christianity of the Sermon on the Mount. Among their number – which never rose above 10 per cent or so of the population – were members of the nobility who were given protection by the local counts, but there was little sign of conflict between Cathars and Catholics.

In 1209 Pope Innocent III launched a crusade against the Cathars with promises of land and riches for the participants. Northern French armies rounded up Cathars and burned them to death in groups of a hundred or more. The persecution united the people of the Languedoc – Cathar and Catholic alike – against the invaders, but the French king intervened and the region was won for the Latin church and for the northern Franks.

Modern European civilization was formed out of this inheritance of the Franco-Germanic, the Roman and the Christian. For the first time in centuries great monuments of stone were constructed to this new orthodoxy. Northern European cities, towns, villages and strategic hill-tops were, from the eleventh to the fourteenth century, inundated with a frenzy of building – cathedrals, churches, monasteries and castles covered the landscape. Normans built their castles right in the middle of English towns such as London, York, Warwick, Canterbury and Winchester, for the sole purpose of intimidating and suppressing the local population, while along their borders, at Harlech, Conwy, Carlisle and elsewhere, they built garrison forts. The French kings fortified the Loire valley at Angers, Loches and Tours, while in the east, castles at Prague and Karlstein, for example, were remodelled for Frankish needs. Alongside the castles came the great Romanesque and Gothic cathedrals. These were the first monuments, 'arguments in stone', to place alongside illuminated manuscripts, jewellery and metalwork of the early medieval northern culture.

The surviving stone cathedrals and churches preserve the dramatic tension between an autocratic church and state, dictating from above, and the artistic and cultural sensibilities of thousands of stonemasons, architects, wood-carvers, goldsmiths, glass-workers and painters, arising anonymously from below. Built on the plan of the old Roman basilica or meeting hall, these enormous buildings shook off their classical heritage and became expressions of a distinctly north European culture. The revolutionary use of a rib-vaulted roof at Durham Cathedral, begun in 1093, allowed church-builders to abandon the old Roman semi-circular barrel-vaulted ceilings in favour of pointed arches and soaring internal spaces. The new technique allowed more weight to be carried, so naves and aisles could be wider, supported, almost miraculously, by an intricate web of delicate stone ribs. This Gothic style was first fully realized at St Denis near Paris, begun in 1144, and spread rapidly across western Europe. The use of animal carvings, intricate stone tracery, trefoils and quatrefoils, the combination of carved pillars leading to radiating ribs and labyrinth patterns (such as the pavement maze at Chartres) all served to lend a sense of organic spirituality to inorganic stone. Although historians have struggled to define Gothic style, most agree it is based on a sense of open sequences that lead the viewer onwards, rather than a representation of reality from a single view-point. The cathedrals soared from the earth like great forest groves, or monoliths; the craftsmen of the north had taken the Roman basilica and remodelled it to recreate the sacred landscape of their culture.

*   *   *

The history of the Middle Ages that is emerging from recent scholarship challenges our deepest assumptions about the nature of western civilization. The fall of the Roman empire, the gloom and chaos of the ˙ Dark Ages, Charlemagne's renaissance and the triumph of Latin Christianity have all been shown to be suffused with distortion and myth-making. The early Middle Ages begin to seem like a period of diversity and mutual tolerance in which local culture, craftsmanship and scholarship could thrive within a continent-wide network, with few boundaries between nations, kingdoms, ethnic and religious orthodoxies, and little central control.

Charlemagne's grandfather, Charles Martel, began the reimposition of control by showing the Frankish nobles how to profit from their peasant farmers. The production of the rich farmlands of Neustria and Austrasia was organized into a social system that enabled wealth to make its way upwards. The acquisition and centralization of wealth through a system of control was the hallmark of the Carolingian empire, just as it was for the Romans. Although Charlemagne's empire disintegrated into separate realms, his imposition of Christianity and the parallel emergence of kingship as the only allowable method of government both survived to become the bedrock of western society and civilization. Pagan societies, including the Saxons and later the Vikings, were not just made Christian, they became societies modelled on hierarchical lines, and ruled by kings. The expansion of Latin Christendom in the tenth and subsequent centuries finally brought the whole of Europe into the Christian church. The most enduring resistance was among the west Slav peoples of Poland and the eastern Baltic; they had never converted in Charlemagne's time and remained a polytheistic society until the fourteenth century. The Lithuanian monarchy finally converted in 1386, in exchange for the Polish crown. The Latin Catholic Christendom of the late Middle Ages was the product of the colonization of Europe; a little over a century after the conversion of the Lithuanians, the same process of colonization began to be extended to the rest of the world.

ANOTHER WAY OF LIVING

The Medieval Town and Communal Life

IN the centuries of the Frankish expansion and conquest, the lands of Europe were divided up into great estates, and the lives of most people – their work, movements and even marriages – fell under the control of their feudal masters. But the growing prosperity of Europe led to the creation of another phenomenon, which allowed people to follow a different kind of life within the world of medieval Latin Christendom. Rural and village life may have been subject to arbitrary control by the nobility, but the medieval town became a refuge from feudalism, a place where communal life and individual needs could be met, and where the population had a say in the governance, and a stake in the protection and prosperity, of their community.

Until just a few decades ago, the medieval town, with its narrow twisting streets, its jumble of shops, houses, churches and workshops, its marketplaces, walls and gateways, its snickets, alleyways and gothroughs, all apparently unplanned and accidental, was derided as unhealthy, inefficient, illogical and downright primitive. Now we see the medieval town as both a historical treasure and the best hope for a life that bridges individual aspiration and communal identity. We have belatedly understood that the human interactions and accidental meetings that did, and still do, take place in these streets, lanes, pubs and shops are a profoundly important element in human existence. As Lewis Mumford wrote: 'We have tardily begun to realise that our hard-earned discoveries in the art of laying out towns . . . merely recapitulate, in terms of our own social needs, the commonplaces of sound medieval practice.' The medieval town gave the possibility of infinite variety without our later obsession with spatial progression; the streets wound and dipped and turned and opened and closed for no other reason than their own existence, and they existed as places for people to meet and work and trade and eat, and to be entertained.

Our view of the towns of the Middle Ages was in part an invention of the Romanticists and Gothic revivalists of the late eighteenth century. They wanted to invoke a sense of spiritual mystery about the pre-scientific past by making it a time of dark unfathomable fears and incipient madness, in which religious 'enthusiasts', lepers, plague victims and apocalyptic preachers paraded through desultory streets in a never-ending display of ecstasy and misery. In contrast, the rationalists of the Enlightenment wanted to sweep away superstition and replace it with universal truths – to them, the medieval town with its dark illogical streets was symbolic of the obscurity of the unenlightened human mind. But to us, the lack of planned purpose and indefinable organic structure is precious; the medieval town is not a period piece but an accidental creation whose qualities are continually enriching. How did this peculiar construction come about?

The Roman empire comprised around 2,000 cities funded by taxes (mainly on agricultural produce) and each containing a forum, baths, amphitheatre, governor's house, public meeting hall and, latterly, a Christian basilica, all supplied through an empire-wide trading network. While the small Celtic towns of central and western Europe had grown out of manufacturing villages where various trades thrived in proximity, Roman towns were quite different. Established for the governing of the empire and the billeting of troops, they were centres of consumption not production, and had no autonomous reason for existence – when there were no taxes to collect or imperial subjects to administer, the meaning of the Roman towns disappeared and they went into steep decline.

In some cases the picture is a stark one. In AD 400, just before its sacking by Alaric, Rome had around half a million inhabitants; by the 600s this had reduced to less than 50,000. The city became fragmented into different communities separated by derelict areas, while the public buildings decayed and were plundered for stone. The multi-storeyed concrete Roman apartment houses stood like skeletons in a wasteland. Of the 372 Roman cities in Italy mentioned by Pliny, one third disappeared, but urban life in Italy survived better than in Gaul and

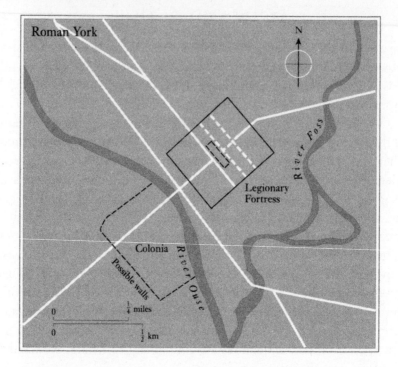

Roman York

N

River Foss

Legionary
Fortress

Colonia

River Ouse

Possible walls

0   ¼ miles

0   ½ km

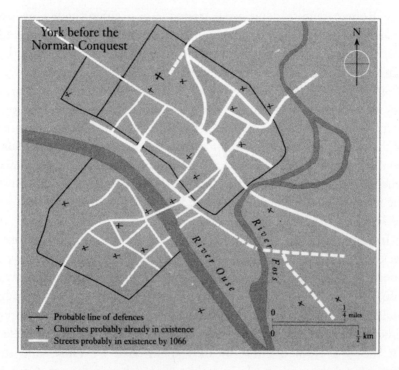

York before the
Norman Conquest

N

River Foss

River Ouse

Probable line of defences
+   Churches probably already in existence
Streets probably in existence by 1066

0   ¼ miles

0   ½ km

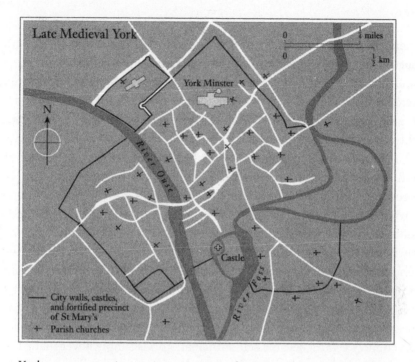

York was a strategic crossing point over the River Ouse at the confluence of the River Foss. It was a garrison town for the military zone of Roman Britain, a Saxon and then Viking settlement, a Christian centre and, in 1189, a medieval chartered town.

Britain. Here the Roman cities became like ghost towns, with small populations living inside decaying walls and between ruined buildings in houses made of wood and recovered stone.

In the late empire wealthy Romans had already left the towns to live on country estates, leaving magistrates and tax-gatherers, together with a few dealers in corn or oil. But once the western empire dissolved, the transport system that kept Roman towns supplied fell into immediate disrepair. Roman roads were usually built on a concrete base that deteriorated quickly if not regularly maintained, while aqueducts and bridges were simply not needed. There is no evidence of any attempt at similar road-building, or repair of existing Roman roads, after the fifth century. As one example, the city of York, founded as a major Roman settlement (Eboracum) at the lowest crossing point of the Ouse, continued as a Briton and then Saxon town. But the Roman walls and buildings fell into disrepair and the Roman bridge eventually collapsed. The city was split in two and the course of the Roman road was altered to allow traffic to ford the river at low water. York was, according to

Bede and Alcuin, a major town in Saxon times, yet almost no artefacts survive from this period. There are no remains of buildings and, as one archaeologist put it, 'all the middle Saxon pottery from York could readily be accommodated in one bag' (P. V. Addyman, quoted in Hutchinson and Palliser). The same is true of towns and cities throughout western Europe.

The irrelevance of Roman towns hastened their decline, but so too did the culture of those who had lived under Roman occupation. The people of the north and west of Europe had no tradition of town-dwelling, which they viewed as a facet and symbol of Roman oppression. Even the Frankish kings preferred to live in the countryside, moving their court from place to place while indulging their passion for hunting. The Merovingian kings and nobles kept certain places, such as Orléans, Soissons and Arles, as fortress towns, but they made no attempt to stimulate urban trade – only one market, at St Denis, is known to have been established in the whole Merovingian period from 470 to 800. As country estates became self-sufficient, goods simply never made their way to the urban centres, which added to their decline. The only major stone buildings being erected in western Europe in the early Middle Ages were monasteries – and these were almost always built in the countryside or on uninhabited islands, where monks could withdraw from the world. The astonishing growth of monasteries in the sixth and seventh centuries did not contribute to urban life.

This decline of urban life has been taken as a sign of the collapse of civilization. But cultural, economic and social activity had not disappeared, it simply moved elsewhere; into hamlets, villages, monasteries, estates and country houses. Urban life did continue, albeit in a reduced form, and those settlements that persisted became, in the late medieval period, the foundations of the network of European towns. The shape of this network was therefore another product of the so-called Dark Ages.

In the Frankish lands the overwhelming reason for the continuation of old urban centres was the Church. As the Roman empire dissolved, the bishops, who were often the principal citizens in their towns, stayed put and the Church based its administrative centres on the old Roman structure. Evidence for the importance of the Church lies in the towns that lost their bishoprics. The town of Tongres in Belgium, capital of its Roman district, lost its bishop to Maastricht and then Liège – both of which subsequently prospered while Tongres has remained a minor town. Aps in the Ardèche lost its bishop to Viviers, while other Roman centres at Boiorum and Diablintum disappeared entirely because they failed to hold on to their bishoprics.

In Britain the situation was different. The number of bishoprics was far fewer and towns survived only if they were used as Briton or Anglo-Saxon settlements. So while many, like York, Chester, Colchester and St Albans, continued, others were abandoned. The deserted Roman town of Viroconium is just to the north of Shrewsbury, while Hereford is at a fording point over the Wye near to an abandoned Roman town at Kentchester. In fact Chester is the only town on the Welsh borders that is sited on a Roman settlement. The long-term effect was the same in Britain as in Gaul, since the Church appointed bishops to the new Anglo-Saxon (and old Roman) settlements and the ones it chose became the most prosperous.

There is evidence of a revival of urban living in the early ninth century, in the time of Charlemagne, though it took another hundred years or so to begin to gather pace. New stone buildings were erected in Reims under Bishop Ebbo (817–41) and churches at Lyons and Orléans were extensively restored. Charlemagne had a palace and basilica built at Aachen (Aix-la-Chapelle) (though this was then a country setting, it was at least a permanent imperial court) and palaces at Ingelheim and Nijmegen, as well as a magnificent bridge over the Rhine at Mainz. In 822 Louis the Pious commissioned new court buildings at Frankfurt; ten years later a new aqueduct was built at Le Mans on the orders of the bishop. Looking retrospectively, these seem like straws in the wind.

The essential requirement for urban life is a surplus of agricultural production that allows some people to live by other means than farming. This began to appear in the ninth century, and as trade in agricultural surpluses (including the all-important wool) increased, a rash of new settlements grew up along estuaries, rivers and coastlines, particularly in north-east Gaul and southern England, where virtually every important settlement lay on a navigable river. The Flanders cloth trade was advanced enough for Charlemagne to send Haroun al-Rashid fine Flemish cloth as a gift, but Charlemagne's outlawing of usury made it difficult for trade to expand. He allowed the establishment of markets, effectively as occasional sites for monasteries to sell their surplus produce, but there was a lack of permanent locations for trade.

It had been thought that this fragile revival of town life in the ninth century was cut short by the Viking raids that terrorized northern and western Europe. But in the areas where the Vikings settled – in eastern England and Normandy – they founded new settlements, for example at Scarborough, or revived existing ones, such as Ipswich and York and Rouen. The Viking trading network reached from Novgorod to Dublin, and on to Iceland, Greenland and North America, but the volume and value of goods, and the size of the settlements, remained relatively small.

The real change came with the establishment of a single, extensive political authority in the heartland of Europe. At Augsburg in 955, King Otto of Saxony decisively defeated the Magyars, who had been terrorizing Europe for more than 60 years, and began the long period of Frankish and Norman expansion described in the last chapter. As the Franks brought stability, and agricultural production expanded, the population of Europe began to increase dramatically – historians have estimated that between 1000 and 1340 the population of central and western Europe trebled, from around 12 million to 35.5 million; the population of the entire continent roughly doubled, from 38.5 to 73.5 million in the same period.

In the late tenth and eleventh centuries, merchants who had traditionally travelled from one market to another began to settle in one place; bishops and counts with the rights to hold markets began to build warehouses in towns for the storage of goods; permanent market stalls appeared in certain places, followed by workshops and shops; industries emerged in these workshops, and the character of the small urban populations changed from a dominance of clerics, nobles and peasants to include artisans and merchants. Around the same time production loans, or *commenda*, which were previously unknown in the west, were introduced, as Charlemagne's old restrictions on usury were quietly put aside. The towns that incorporated these changes were radically different from the city-states of antiquity and from the Roman administrative centres. The medieval emphasis was on commerce, with markets, merchant quarters, workshops and warehouses built alongside religious houses and barracks.

The right to hold a market in England, France or the Holy Roman Empire was granted by the king or emperor, usually to a bishop or abbot or count. Markets began as portable affairs, with perishable goods sold off ox wagons and cloth and hardware from stalls. By the early eleventh century the variety of goods on sale was impressive. The fair held at Arras in Picardy in 1036 under the auspices of the *abbé* of St Vaast had cloth as its prime item, but there was also sturgeon, salmon, herring, shad and whalemeat; butcher's meat, bacon, dripping, salt meat; salt, honey, oil, butter, English and Flemish cheese, fruit and wine; raw and tanned hides, furs; iron, steel, wool, thread, dyes; leather footwear, knives, sickles, spades, spade handles, ropes, wooden vessels. Most of the goods were grown or caught or made in rural areas and brought to the town fairs, as artisans produced work for their feudal masters who then sold what they did not use. But later in the eleventh century artisans found they could afford to live in the towns alongside their customers. Shopkeepers then emerged to act as intermediaries between the producer and customer and as specialist buyers and sellers.

Documents from the tenth century show licences for the actual construction, rather than hosting, of markets. Towns that held these permanent markets began to build wharves and lodgings for merchants and their goods. These merchants' quarters were known as *wiks* in German, which became 'wich' in English, hence Ipswich, Harwich, Greenwich, Sandwich, all port towns trading with mainland Europe. By the eleventh century, what had been an innovation became a set of rules. The *seigneur* who held the market was permitted to mint coins and to take levies on goods sold, and in return he had to provide anchorages and warehouses and maintain law and order. Merchants came to those market towns where they would find accommodation, secure warehousing, safety, real currency and customers.

The region where this urban regeneration first took hold was, unsurprisingly, in the heart of the Frankish empire. The provinces of Flanders and Brabant and the area around the river systems of the Meuse and the Rhine were the forcing beds of this new type of distinctively medieval town. The vast network of navigable rivers, the huge reach of the Rhine and the Meuse, the rich agricultural land, the sea access to Britain and beyond, the tradition of the cloth industry and the prestige of the imperial homeland gave this region a head start. Almost as soon as Otto began to push the Magyars east and to establish a solid eastern frontier, towns began to spring up across the Germanic lands. In the ninth century large parts of Germany had been semi-wilderness, with vast forests and little cultivated land, but in the four centuries from Otto's victory in 950, 2,500 towns were founded and huge areas of land put into cultivation. These were territories that had never been conquered by Rome, and the origins of many German towns were in small settlements at the centre of old tribal districts. The rapid flowering of towns across the centre of the continent was a decisive step in the urbanization of Europe.

The rich trading core of Europe, comprising the Frankish heartland of northern and eastern France, the Rhineland, the Mediterranean ports of northern Italy, and the south and east of Britain, was the obvious location for commercial and trading centres. But people outside this core – monarchs as well as regionally powerful barons, abbots and bishops – needed defensible towns in all parts of their realms. After Henry II's marriage to Eleanor of Aquitaine in 1152, her vast possessions in south-west France were, for 300 years, a disputed English province. More than 300 so-called *bastides* or country towns were built in Aquitaine by the English and French between 1220 and 1350. There were 99 castles in England in the eleventh century, half of them belonging to the king. These were often located in existing towns, giving a strong boost to the local economy as well as enhancing the town's prestige. The relations between the European civil town and the garrisoned castle were complex and shifting. The castles were often built in towns to pacify the local population. But this assertion of central power altered as the castle became a guarantor of the town's security. The characteristic medieval stone walls were built to include both the town and castle, and the garrison was made up of a local militia drawn from the inhabitants of the town.

Long-distance trade was slowly re-established in the eleventh century with textiles, principally wool and woollen cloth, by far the most important manufactured product. Flanders and Tuscany led the way in production of cloth, but this was a continental industry, with wool traded from England and Spain to the Baltic and Bohemia. Regions that began as wool suppliers, such as the West Riding of Yorkshire, turned into manufacturing centres. Court records from 1201 show a dyer named Simon working in Leeds, and in 1258 a weaver named William Webster (a corruption of 'weaver') appeared in the records, while in 1275 a man named Simon Fuller was charged with selling cloths that were too narrow. By the sixteenth century, when reasonably reliable records are available, wool and woollen cloth represented 80 per cent of English exports by value.

In addition to the textile trade, furs and metals were shipped from the Baltic region; silks, spices, gold, dyes, jewellery and leather goods were brought from the east into the heart of Europe by Venetian and Genoese merchants, and in the twelfth century, silver and gold were being mined in great quantities in Bohemia and Hungary. All of these goods were exchanged at great trade fairs held firstly in Champagne and Burgundy, and then all over mainland Europe. These fairs were made secure by local rulers, who offered safe passage to merchants in return for levies on their goods. Military control had previously brought only short-term plunder and taxes on agricultural produce, but in the eleventh and twelfth centuries it led to instant levies on goods in exchange for safety. Europe was becoming an economic and commercial, rather than a military and geographic, entity.

Increasing trade prompted the demand for more goods, but the growth in trade and in urban populations remained dependent on agricultural surpluses. The dramatic increase in the rural population in the eleventh century had two immediate effects. First, more cultivated land was needed to feed and provide work for the extra millions. Drainage work started on the vast marshes of Flanders, Brabant and Gelderland, while forest clearance began in earnest across Europe. The other effect was that the traditional domain feudal system was unable to cope with the vastly greater numbers of people. The rigid restrictions of earlier times gave way to more independence; the lure of the town, and the law allowing a serf his freedom after one year and a day, meant that landlords had to entice their workers to stay. Large estates were forced by the increased cost of labour to use technology, some of which had been available, but unneeded and unused, for centuries. The introduction of water-power, horse collars and the increased use of draught animals gave a huge boost to agricultural productivity. Europe's farmland could feed the increased numbers of peasants and still produce enough surplus to feed the towns. Nevertheless, during the course of the twelfth and thirteenth centuries the growth of industry, population and consumption in many towns outstripped the capacity of their local countryside. Raw materials had to be fetched longer distances giving ever more impetus to trade on a continental scale. Even the most basic foodstuffs such as grain were brought from the Black Sea to feed northern Italy and from the Baltic to London, Paris and Flanders.

The use of gold and silver in coinage of recognized value turned Europe from a network of bartering into a money economy, and acted as another incentive to urban trade. From about 1100 onwards landowners began to collect rents in the form of money rather than goods or services. This meant that they no longer had to live on their estates in order to consume their wealth, but could move into towns and cities where their money could be brought to them. Cash became concentrated in urban centres rather than remaining as goods out in the country, and nobles needed to be near the centres of power, which were increasingly in cities rather than country estates. Once they had surplus cash, the nobility began to spend – on building town houses, on equipping themselves and their servants, and on luxury items like furs, jewels, silks and tapestries. This process was much more gradual in the north of Europe, where the nobility tended to remain in the country, than, for example, in northern Italy. Indeed the north of Italy became a special case of medieval urban development (see Chapter 8) because of its political situation and its economic growth. By 1200 or so, trade through Venice, Genoa, Florence and other northern Italian cities reached such a volume that merchants no longer travelled with their goods; instead they employed agents as buyers and sellers in the Levant and in the growing commercial centres of the north – in London, Reims, Paris, Bruges and elsewhere – and paid shippers to move their goods for them.

As early as 829 the will of the Venetian merchant Giustiniano Partecipazio showed that he had increased a sum by investment in a shipping venture, while a deed from 1073 shows an investor putting up two thirds and a shipper one third of the price of a cargo, in return for a similar split of the sale price. Venice led the way in this embryonic capitalist system because its access to the Orient gave it an economy based on gold coin before anywhere else; Genoa and Pisa quickly caught up, but elsewhere in Europe wealth remained tied to land until at least the twelfth century.

These were the external reasons for the resurgence of European town life, but what were the distinguishing characteristics of the medieval town? Because these were not formal administrative centres, in the way that Roman towns had been, they were able to develop a curiously autonomous status within the realms of emperors, kings, dukes, counts and prince-bishops. While political power lay with regional control of the land, its produce and the rural population (who also supplied the nobles with their foot soldiers), the towns were largely left to their own affairs. And if, as in Italy, the old aristocracy came into town, they found there was competition for municipal power from bishops, abbots, merchants, artisans and levy-payers, who all felt they had a right to a voice in civic administration. Citizens formed associations to protect and promote their interests as communes of nobles and guilds of merchants and craftsmen sprang up in every town in Europe. In some places they banded together to seek special privileges from the sovereign authority, while in others, particularly northern Italy, they grabbed power in the absence of external authority.

An acknowledgement of the special nature of towns, and their growing economic success, came with the granting of royal charters. Monarchs learned that the dispersal of power to towns was not necessarily a threat, and could enhance their own interests. Medieval towns became legal entities, granted special privileges that helped to promote economic activity, while townspeople were de facto more free to pursue their own trades than those in the country. The charter granted to Dublin by Prince (later King) John in 1192, for example, gives a series of special economic and legal privileges to the citizens within and outside their town. They were exempted from certain offences and any fines were strictly limited; they could build on land and collectively control the free space within the city; they could form guilds and had the right to marry their daughters to whomsoever they wished without the interference of any lord – a right denied to rural dwellers; citizens were also exempted from road tolls, and from being pursued for another man's debt; foreign merchants were forbidden from buying certain goods except from local traders and were forbidden from spending more than 40 days trading in the town.

The chartered medieval town was not just a bigger version of the ancient craft village; it was a legal and commercial entity separated from, and culturally different to, the surrounding countryside. The development of the network of trading towns across Latin Christendom had significant effects. Until the eleventh century, education in western Europe meant either a monastic training, or in a few cases training for feudal administration. But from around 1050, non-monastic church schools developed in the shadows of the urban cathedrals and parish churches. Education was still concerned mainly with theology, but the pupils were no longer novice monks, they were trainees for the clergy who lived within the secular community. Among their future tasks would be the administration and financial upkeep of their church, so they needed to be literate, and literacy brought more learning within their horizons. The use of paper (introduced into Europe in the late twelfth century) became widespread, and new books on logic began to appear – Peter Abelard became famous as a teacher of philosophical logic in Paris in the twelfth century and was followed by scholars like Peter Lombard and Gratian, who applied logical techniques to theological topics. Through fragmentary translations of Aristotle, the west began to be familiar with the language of Greece and Rome. Pupils flocked to hear these teachers at the cathedral schools of northern France and then took this new kind of learning back to their own schools, while scholars trained in monasteries, such as Thomas Aquinas, Roger Bacon and William of Ockham, produced work that argued about the relationship between faith and logic, between the spiritual and the rational.

Increasing literacy did not only mean the production of philosophical works. In 1130–36 Geoffrey of Monmouth assembled his *History of the Kings of Britain,* containing stories of King Arthur based on Celtic legend. A few decades later Chrétien de Troyes used the same material to tell the story of Perceval, which linked the Arthurian romances to the search for the Holy Grail. These stories captured and helped to create the culture of chivalry, of courtly love and Christian romance that became the ideal self-image of European nobility and gentry for centuries to come. The key elements of this literature were bravery as an ideal end in itself (the knights were not fighting to defend their homelands, but were going out to seek adventure), and the idealization of love between a man and a woman. In a clear urban alternative to the boorishness of rural warrior barons, and the restrictions of church literature, love became exquisitely refined, and was often adulterous – Lancelot, the principal hero of the Round Table, was created in order to give the Queen an illicit object of idealized love. Although this code of love was a highly artificial cultural creation, largely inspired by Iberian Arabic tradition, it was taken to be a natural phenomenon in the west for the next 800 or so years.

We know something of the atmosphere of medieval towns because so many have survived. These were semi-enclosed communal societies with the walls themselves lending a sense of togetherness, which was exemplified every night when the gates were closed and the drawbridges pulled up. Citizenship of a town implied a range of duties to be fulfilled – the burghers must be available for military service, while police duties were served in rotation (Rembrandt's *The Nightwatch* is a celebration of this communality). In return for being allowed to arm their citizens, town authorities could hold markets and mint coins. These shared duties fostered a sense of civic responsibility as well as an intimate knowledge of one's town.

Communal identity was strengthened by belonging to a group with its own traditions, rules and identity. The medieval guilds sprang from the need for association and developed into bodies offering insurance for health and old age, education, protection of rights, friendship, identity and status. People in particular occupations tended to gravitate to the same streets, so the guilds were neighbourhood societies too. They were the dominant institution of the communal medieval city. Communal life extended to the family home – the house of a burgher served as a workshop, storage depot, domestic space, counting house, while artisans and shopkeepers had no separation between work and labour. Their households were made up of apprentices, relatives from the countryside, workers and the central family, all of whom would work and eat together and sleep in large dormitories.

Construction was one of the biggest industries of the medieval age. Castles, houses, city walls, churches, hospitals, seminaries and cathedrals were put up in a frenzy of building activity, much of it paid for by the Church and religious orders. In York, for example, there were at least 57 religious houses established by the year 1300, to serve a population of 10–15,000, and Breslau, a town of 30,000, had 15 hospitals run by holy orders. Money for building also came from taxes and the sale of licences for tolls at bridges and gates, and on customs imports.

Our old ideas of the darkness and squalor of medieval urban life are a long way from reality. Streets were undoubtedly crowded at certain times of day, but religious houses and churches offered escape from the density of urban life. The dark interiors of churches allowed quiet, uninterrupted contemplation and, while the great cathedrals were built to glorify God, most architecture was on a human scale. Though the streets were narrow, they were often backed by open green spaces; the scale of the towns gave easy access to the countryside and there were plenty of gardens and orchards within the walls.

Medieval towns had bath-houses, both private and municipal – they are mentioned in Riga in the thirteenth century and by the fifteenth century there were, for example, 11 in Ulm, 12 in Nürnberg, 15 in Frankfurt, 17 in Augsburg and 29 in Vienna. These were social, medical and hygienic places, much as they had been in Roman times, where people met, ate, talked and were treated for ailments – and there are records of complaints about children running shamelessly naked through the streets on their way to the bath-houses.

Towns were also more colourful than their remnants sometimes suggest. Whitewashed shops and houses, churches decorated with carvings and with wall paintings (most of which did not survive later restorations), goods displayed in the open markets and sumptuous clothes brought out on festival days all contributed to a visual feast. The town also provided a stage on which the great civic and religious ceremonies were played out. At the centre of all ceremonials was the main parish church or the cathedral, whose construction was itself a communal affair, with craftsmen and women often giving their labour free. The pride in these glorious buildings was deeply felt, their presence always sensed and their function as the centre and destination of the numerous processions that wound around the narrow streets always appreciated.

The German artist Albrecht Dürer described a scene in early sixteenth-century Antwerp: 'I saw the procession pass along the street, the people being arranged in rows, each man some distance from his neighbour, but the rows close behind the other. There were the Goldsmiths, the Painters, the Masons, the Broderers, the Sculptors, the Joiners, the Carpenters, the Sailors, the Fishermen, the Butchers, the Leatherers, the Clothmakers, the Bakers, the Tailors, the Cordwainers . . . Likewise the shopkeepers and merchants and their assistants of all kinds were there. After these came the shooters with guns, bows and crossbows, and the horsemen and foot soldiers. Then followed the watch of the Lord Magistrates. Then came a fine troop all in red, nobly and splendidly clad. Before them went all the religious orders and the members of some foundations, very devoutly, all in their different robes . . . From the beginning to end the procession lasted two hours before it was gone past our house.'

Medieval towns were intimately linked to their topography because of the primary need for defence; they occupied hilltop sites, bends of rivers and peninsulas and they huddled around castle keeps. The streets were not laid out for buildings to follow, as they were in later urban planning. Instead buildings grouped around churches, monasteries, marketplaces, merchant quarters, quaysides, housing schemes and groups of traders; and then footways connected these 'islands' together, marking the routes where people came and went. There was no need for vehicle traffic in most parts of the town; everything was carried or barrowed or brought on the back of a horse. The streets wound to get around existing buildings, but narrow winding streets also offered shelter from the weather. Ground-floor shop fronts had no glass, so were half open to the elements; a narrow street and an overhanging upper storey gave protection.

Towns were limited in size by internal transport and by water supply and the availability of fresh produce from the surrounding area. The exceptional size of medieval Venice is partly explained by transport – getting goods around on water was much easier than getting them through narrow streets, a lesson that Amsterdam, St Petersburg and others learned later. Cities expanded – Florence, for example, rebuilt her walls three times – but could only reach a certain limit without losing the cohesion that was their principal reason for existence. Most remained less than a mile across and varied in population from 300 or 400 to the 40,000 of London – Paris and Venice with 100,000 each were highly exceptional. Around 1450 Louvain and Brussels, cities in the middle of Europe's most prosperous region outside Italy, had between 25,000 and 40,000, while no German city had more than 35,000 inhabitants. When towns needed to expand, they built another satellite town nearby rather than continually extending their own area, thereby maintaining the advantages of manageable size.

The chartered medieval town, with its strong element of communal life, self-determination and common identity, was the keystone of European culture. The revival of urban life is usually characterized as the emergence, or re-emergence, of civilized life from the blank misery of the Dark Ages. But a much more interesting story is beginning to emerge. The dispersal of economic and cultural life into the countryside that followed the collapse of the Roman empire allowed a localized culture to re-assert itself, free from the controlling and centralizing hand of Rome. But, in a centuries-long process beginning with the rule of Charles Martel in the eighth century, control over the countryside was re-imposed in almost every part of western and central Europe. In contrast to their rural cousins, citizens of towns were able to live and work independently and to group together to defend their interests. In this sense, medieval towns were a continuation of the independent communities that had existed in western Europe since prehistory.

Although medieval towns provided both an escape from the strictures of feudal estates and an alternative way of living a communal life, we should not assume that the people of the countryside were left in a helpless state of submission, obedience and ignorance. Despite the increase in urban living, medieval Europe remained an overwhelmingly rural society. But when we try to understand the lives of our medieval ancestors we are hampered not by their ignorance, but by our own. We are separated from the Middle Ages by the later creation of the self-governing individual – in whom we see ourselves – which distorts every conscious thought we have. The medieval acceptance of fate, the common belief in predestination and the imminent end of the world seem to us to offer only a suffocation of the spirit and a denial of all human initiative. But the lives of the great majority of the population, illiterate, uneducated peasants who hardly feature in written history, were imbued with a dense spirituality whose effects we struggle to understand.

The beliefs of their Celtic, Gothic, Viking and Slav forebears had been mutated by Christianity but not displaced. The rhythms of the seasons, the cycle of birth, life and death, the emotional dominance of family life were of overwhelming importance in a world where time was measured by the progress of the sun, and by the memories of the human community, and where geography was a matter of human experience, not abstract mapping. Identity started with family and extended to the village, domain or town (but not to country or nation) within a common framework of belief and experience. And the principal human experience was of the natural world, which remained a difficult and dangerous place but also a source of wonder, best understood through a spirituality that imbued nature with supernatural properties. The boundaries between the real and the unreal, the imaginary and the true, had no meaning in a world where sickness could strike without apparent cause, where cures were always miraculous, where good harvests came only if the correct, often pagan, rituals were observed. This was not some simple-minded, light-hearted superstition but a profound understanding that adherence to custom was a matter of life and death.

In this world, the symbols, miracles and rituals of the Christian church were just one more set of tools in the never-ending task of coming to terms with the perversities, cycles, fickleness and wonders of nature. Belief in the Christian God as the provider and arbiter of all things was universal, and the drama of the faith (which echoed the pagan belief systems of the west) provided the framework in which life could be understood; but the authority of the Latin church was felt more in the vestry and the castle than it was in the peasant's hut or tavern, or in the town apothecary.

Medieval peasants and tenant farmers and artisans may have been illiterate but they were not ignorant. They knew that observance of custom was vitally important for profound social reasons rather than simply as a way to gain good harvests. Simple equations of cause and effect appeal to our modern minds, but in this respect our ancestors were far more perceptive. They lived with and through the intricate and subtle complexities of their relations with each other and the natural world; they knew that prayer and ritual must go alongside good husbandry of land and animals, and be combined with careful crafts-manship. These things were not in opposition but continually feeding off one another. Christianity was accepted and adopted by the common people of the west not because it overturned their customary beliefs, but because it fitted into the eternal process of learning to live with the natural world. This process was never static, and the medieval world shows the same combination of eternal necessities and continual change as any other part of history. It was brought to an end, in a long and painful process, by its own success, as wealth and individual self-regard ushered in the modern world.

ART AS CIVILIZATION

Wealth, Power and Innovation in the Italian Renaissance

In Italy for thirty years under the Borgias they had warfare, terror, murder and bloodshed, but they produced Michelangelo, Leonardo da Vinci and the Renaissance. In Switzerland, they had brotherly love; they had five hundred years of democracy and peace – and what did that produce? The cuckoo clock.

Orson Welles, *The Third Man**

THE Renaissance is not so much a period of history as the repository of the myths we have created about western civilization. Its uniqueness as a historical idea comes from the way that it welds together two concepts – art and civilization – and makes them stand for each other. In histories of art, western painting, sculpture and architecture reach their perfection in the Renaissance and subsequently endure a long decline in the shadow of the great masters. When we look at a painting by Raphael, a Michelangelo sculpture or a building designed by Brunelleschi, we feel that these works embody the highest values of western, and indeed all, civilization; we even believe that the combined sense of awe and elevation that enfolds us when we stare at Botticelli's *Birth of Venus is* civilization at its most inexpressible and rarefied. But this intertwining of art and civilization in the Renaissance has had an odd effect on how we think about the past. Any period or place that has produced sublime art must, we believe, have possessed social, polit-

* This short speech was added to Graham Greene's screenplay by Welles, who played Harry Lime, the character who declaimed it.

ical and cultural qualities that were somehow out of the ordinary. Conversely, any period that produces no important art (only cuckoo clocks!) is beneath serious consideration.

The Renaissance is a difficult concept for historians because the history of Europe quite suddenly turns into a history of Italian painting, sculpture and architecture. It becomes more important to know who commissioned which painting and why than whose army won which battle, or which king passed which laws. The absence of art from any story of the fifteenth century is like a wedding without a bride, while the presence of art dominates and diminishes everything around it. The art becomes not just the centrepiece of the period but *the* phenomenon that has to be explained, and so history becomes subservient to this need.

Ever since the term Renaissance was coined in the 1840s, historians of Italian art have dominated the study of Europe in the fourteenth and fifteenth centuries. The Swiss historian Jacob Burckhardt set the agenda and tone for all who followed. His 1869 book *The Civilisation of the Renaissance in Italy* made the Italian Renaissance the apogee of European civilization and 'the beginning of the modern world'. Burckhardt showed that the great Renaissance paintings were produced in a world of political deception, violence and intrigue, and so, after Burckhardt, everyone wanted to know about the Medici, the Borgias, Machiavelli and the Sforzas, as well as Brunelleschi, Leonardo and Michelangelo. He also demonstrated how the rediscovery of antiquity, voyages of discovery and changing views of religion all fed into the innovations that Renaissance artists showed in their work. However, this admirably wide-ranging approach is undermined by the major premise of Burckhardt's work – he freely admitted that he believed in the idea of a rebirth or renaissance of civilization in fifteenth-century Italy and then sought evidence for it in every sphere. Rather than telling the history of Italy, he was looking for the signs of something that he already knew was there.

Nevertheless, Burckhardt seemed to open up the possibility of looking at art, politics, religion, economics, social movements and philosophy in late medieval Italy in the round, allowing others to adopt the same approach while offering critiques of his central thesis. But this opportunity was not taken up; instead Burckhardt's successors followed his lead and the Italian Renaissance attained an almost mythic position in the history of western civilization. In the late nineteenth and almost the whole of the twentieth century the art of the Italian Renaissance gained in value and status, while the time and place in which it was created was seen as a fabulous world where wealth, intrigue and the love of beauty went hand in hand. Historians of culture took the lead in promoting this view, and it is instructive to see how two leading art historians of the mid-twentieth century dealt with the peculiarities and superlatives of the Renaissance.

For Kenneth Clark, the story of Renaissance art was of ever-greater geniuses producing ever-greater masterpieces. The process began with Giotto's frescos of 1304–06, moved on to the sculptures of Donatello and the architecture of Brunelleschi in the early 1400s, finally reaching 'the dazzling summit of human achievement represented by Michelangelo, Raphael and Leonardo da Vinci' in the 1520s. Though considered ground-breaking at the time, Clark's 1969 television series *Civilisation* and its accompanying book now look like an elegy for a passing world-view. Meticulously humanist in his attitudes, Clark is nevertheless entranced by the notion of greatness, particularly of the artists of the past, and appalled by the inadequacy of the present. He tells us that Michelangelo 'belongs to every epoch, and most of all, perhaps, to the epoch of the great Romantics of which we are still the almost bankrupt heirs'. Clark's adulation of the Renaissance artists makes their works seem like miraculous gifts granted to us by super-human men of indefinable genius. They are awesome and remote and, most problematic of all, they are ahistorical. The legacy of the Renaissance was the invention of the artist as a gifted individual, and the concept of genius was devised to place certain individuals beyond analysis and beyond history – demigods existing outside the bounds of society and of time and place. Despite ostensibly telling the story of civilization, and its culmination in the Italian Renaissance, Clark essentially lifts his subject out of history and makes it a miraculous time in which people were, for some reason, suddenly more energetic, curious and loving of beauty. This is the history of art without real history.

Ernst Gombrich saw the changes wrought in the Italian Renaissance somewhat differently to Clark. He argued that the freedoms granted to artists by changes in society gave them immense opportunities, but that they also presented difficulties which they struggled to overcome. Each generation of artists both solved existing problems and created new difficulties – of representation, theme, spatial composition, harmony and so on – until these were all effectively solved by, once again, the great triumvirate of Raphael, Leonardo and Michelangelo.

In view of our current scepticism of the idea of progress, it is worth noting that Gombrich argued against the dominant view of birth, maturity and decline in art history: 'It is the naïve misinterpretation of the constant change in art as a continuous progress . . . we must realise that each gain or progress in one direction entails a loss in another, and that this subjective progress, in spite of its importance, does not correspond to an objective increase in artistic value.' Even the 'realist' art of the Renaissance, where a scene may be captured in the instant of its happening, does not represent progress from the 'idealism' of medieval art where the image of a saint is eternal – art simply gained immediacy at the price of eternity.

Gombrich's approach deals with the inherent absurdity in Clark's story – that Renaissance art got better and better because the artists that happened to come along were superior to their predecessors – but it tends to divorce the problem-solving of the artist from developments and currents in the society in which these artists lived. Gombrich argued that changes in art are not brought about by some group psyche shift, but by one individual finding a new way of doing something and then others being able to learn from that. While this provides a welcome alternative to the usual catalogue of facile connections between Renaissance art and society (in which humanism in politics leads to humanism in paint), it tends to make art into an isolated activity. Gombrich notes the alterations in society that provoked revolutionary changes in art, but he does not place the artists in the real political, economic, social or even philosophical history of their times. You can read both Clark and Gombrich without discovering, for instance, that from 1494 onwards Charles VIII and his successor Louis XII led French armies over the Alps and effectively destroyed the independence of all the Italian city-states except Venice – the one place where innovative art continued to be produced after about 1520. Clark and Gombrich perhaps understood that giving a nod to political and social history can compound any misinterpretation of the past. Building on an 'accepted' view of the past is the very opposite of doing history, which demands that we continually seek and question and re-interpret the evidence – otherwise, like Burckhardt, we go looking for what we already know is there. Too often there is a temptation to build the story of art on to the 'known' history of the west, and call the result western civilization.

Where does all of this leave us? We have long been taught that somewhere in the pictorial art of the Italian Renaissance lie the meaning, the
spirit, and the highest achievement of western civilization. But this raises
more questions than it answers. In what sense does art signify civilization? And if the story of art is one of change rather than progression,
as Gombrich convincingly argued, then is the Renaissance just a particularly interesting and intense period of change rather than a culmination? What do we think about living in peace with our cuckoo clocks
as opposed to living in turmoil amidst Raphaels and Botticellis? Is the
aim of civilization to produce men of genius, as Clark asserts, or is it
to provide a meaningful and secure life for as many people as possible?
Are the paintings and sculpture of the Italian Renaissance peripheral to
the history of the west while being central to its civilization?

Fortunately, in the last few decades, historians have begun to show
which of these questions are meaningful, and how they might be
approached. Art historians thinking of new things to say about
Michelangelo's *David* or Raphael's *School of Athens* have given way
to detailed investigations of the political, economic and social changes
flowing through late medieval Italy. The preceding centuries have begun
to appear not as preludes to the 'flowering' of the Renaissance, but as
fascinating times in which different ways of living were explored,
disputed and abandoned, and the fifteenth-century Renaissance appears
as a bittersweet ending to an astonishing period of Italian history. We
now understand that any investigation of the birth-pangs of modern
Europe must begin in medieval Italy.

From the time of Charlemagne to the mid-twelfth century, northern Italy
was a pawn in the power struggles between the papacy and the Holy
Roman emperors. Ignored for decades and then suddenly invaded and
besieged, with no king of Italy to ride to their rescue, Italian cities had
to organize their own defences and, by necessity, their own governments.
In 962 the emperor Otto followed tradition by crossing the Alps to be
declared 'Italic' king at Pavia, the ancient capital of the Lombards, before
travelling on to Rome to be crowned emperor by the pope. But after
Otto, the Germanic emperors began to find their Italian territories an
unwelcome distraction from difficulties at home, and rarely made the
journey south across the Alps. The Italic kingdom was mostly left alone.

In the eleventh century there was a significant increase in trade,
agricultural production and population in central and western Europe

(see Chapter Seven). Northern Italy lay at the southern end of the golden core of medieval Latin Christendom, with trading links to the wealthy towns of southern Germany, Burgundy, northern France, the Low Countries and England. Italy was the gateway from this axis to the Mediterranean and the Muslim east. The silk road across central Asia to northern China; the caravan roads to Persia, India and southern China; the ancient trading route from Egypt north across Palestine to Syria and Asia Minor; Byzantium and the Black Sea ports trading with Muscovy – goods from all these routes and places were brought into the heart of Europe through Venice and Genoa to begin with, and then later through other Italian cities.

As trade increased, peasants, traders, rural merchants and landowners moved into Italian towns, transforming obscure river ports like Florence, Pisa and Genoa into urban trading and manufacturing centres. Old cities like Milan, Verona, Padua, Pavia, Cremona, Piacenza and Mantua were reinvigorated, but the new wealth served to highlight the lack of central power in the north of Italy. Local bishops and imperial viscounts had some powers, but it was never clear who had authority over what; different sets of laws were contradictory and were not equipped to cope with the newly emerging trading and social arrangements. Who had the right to gather tax on whose behalf? Who would supply troops to defend the towns and give protection to peasants in the countryside? What laws should be used to settle commercial disputes? These questions were increasingly difficult to answer.

As agricultural land began to increase in value, the Church, which was the major landowner in Italy, began to enfeoff tracts of land in return for services. From the eleventh century vast areas of church lands were turned over to small landowners who became minor nobles, and who found they could move into town and live off their rents. This was a peculiarly Italian phenomenon; in Italy the new nobility, which had no tradition of feudal power, moved into the cities and took their power bases with them, whereas in the north and west of Europe they tended to remain in the country.

Inevitably the powerful men in the growing cities despaired at the lack of authority and moved to take control of events. Between 1081 and 1138 major cities in the Italic kingdom including Pisa, Lucca, Milan, Parma, Rome, Genoa, Verona, Bologna, Siena and Florence were taken over by regimes known as communes; associations of powerful men who swore to uphold and support the association and their fellow members. These were wealthy aristocrats whose aim was to govern their cities, provide security and stability and maintain their independence. The communes had no sanction from the emperor or the pope; they simply assumed de facto control by absorbing the existing authorities. The first task of each commune was to establish and defend the boundaries of its city, which they did by taking the surrounding countryside by force or persuading any feudal lords who were outside the commune to join them. Northern Italy became a patchwork of small, prosperous city-states.

By 1150 the cities of north Italy were riding high on the rush of economic and population growth and the self-confidence of running their own affairs. In generating trade and wealth, they caught up with and overtook many northern cities, such as Antwerp, Bruges, Mainz, Cologne and London. Milan, the biggest city, had a population of around 80,000, of whom 20,000 worked as artisans and labourers in textiles, building, metalwork and other trades. The Italian cities were manufacturing their own goods, as well as trading with others.

Into this self-organizing and increasingly prosperous world came the imposing figure of Frederick Barbarossa, Holy Roman Emperor and legitimate ruler of the Italic kingdom. When Frederick crossed the Alps to be crowned emperor in 1154, he was greeted by an unwelcome sight. The wealth and military power of his subject cities were a danger and a temptation to him, and he returned four years later with an army of German troops, determined to impose his authority. Frederick's army quickly occupied Milan, but an alliance of northern cities, led by Venice (which had always been outside the empire), formed a league against him. In 1176, after a series of campaigns, the league of cities defeated Frederick at Legnano. Under the Peace of Constance of 1183 the emperor granted the cities the right to govern, make laws and elect consuls in return for paying an imperial levy, which they soon ignored. After 1183 they were free to rule their own affairs – an arrangement that persisted for the next 300 years. Though north European towns enjoyed some freedom from interference, only the Italian (and latterly the Hanseatic and Dutch) cities were truly autonomous.

In the late twelfth century the communes were at the height of their power, ruling at least 40 major cities in Italy – most of them in the north. The typical commune comprised a general assembly from which between 4 and 20 consuls were elected to run the city's administration and judiciary. Following the Roman model, consuls held post for one year, returning to office only after a two-year interval. The election of consuls fell away, though, and increasingly they were simply chosen by the retiring consuls. Small groups of families emerged in all cities as the dominant or exclusive holders of power. By the late twelfth century the general assemblies gave way to smaller councils and power became ever more concentrated.

The commune was founded on a spirit and oath of cooperation, but competition between members was intense. The break-up of church lands had been followed by the dismemberment of feudal estates, so more families became land-holding gentry. In the 150 years before 1200 the Italian nobility was transformed from a small rural-based aristocracy, dependent on land and ancient lineage, into a far more numerous commercial-minded, urban group interested in political power, and in acquiring wealth through trade. The prospect of wealth and extraordinary power that flowed from the Peace of Constance turned the commune members of all the cities, without exception, against each other. For a few decades in the late twelfth century, Italian city streets became the setting for widespread gang warfare. The leading families had effectively acquired areas within each city by building houses for their relatives and employees, so that neighbourhoods became controlled by armed men representing family factions. The cities promised wealth and opportunity but they were menacing and dangerous places.

The most bizarre manifestation of this troubled time was the building of defensive towers. From around 1160 in Milan, Pisa, Verona, Parma, Florence, Bologna and elsewhere, family associations erected towers of astonishing heights (up to 97 metres in Bologna) and numbers (by 1180 there were 100 towers in Florence alone, reaching up to 75 metres in height). The towers were not habitable, they were purely for defence and refuge in times of trouble. Flyovers linking the towers over the warrens of narrow streets made this a fantastical scene but one that was deadly serious in its intent. The family controlled the neighbourhood, including the streets, the piazzas and the churches, and the towers were visible evidence of their dominance. The communes had fractured into their constituent parts, with each commune member scrambling to hold on to as much power as possible.

Out of this strange and menacing urban scene came a profound and enduring revolution. While the expanding nobility had been gaining power and wealth, the middle ranks of society had themselves become more organized. By 1200 the artisans and merchants of Italian cities, in common with those elsewhere in Europe, had formed themselves into sworn associations of members involved in the same trade, known as guilds. Butchers, builders, notaries, saddlers, metalsmiths, merchants, bakers, weavers and dyers set up trade guilds to protect and advance their common interests, but the increasing urban violence robbed the guild members of their most fundamental interest – safety of life and limb. In most cities a member of the nobility could murder a commoner without risk of punishment, while hired thugs would intimidate anyone who interfered in the affairs or territory of their employer.

The guilds responded to this threat by organizing themselves into armed neighbourhood companies. Members of the companies kept their weapons ready by day and night, prepared to answer the call of their captain; they were tightly disciplined and well organized and they developed a formidable *esprit de corps* – each carried their own banner bearing their emblem of a horse, lion, serpent or dragon. In the early thirteenth century Bologna had 24 companies, Florence 20, Milan, exceptionally, just one, the Credenza of St Ambrose, covering the whole city.

However, as well as force of arms, the nobility had special privileges in taxation and law, and had rights to use parts of the city that were forbidden to commoners. The guilds were powerless to change this situation without political representation. But the rule of the communes was founded on a hierarchy of power and wisdom; those with nobility and wealth were naturally thought to be the best rulers. The fact that the guild members wanted their share of civic power shows us that medieval people were not quite so rigidly fatalist as we have been taught. The demands of the *popolo*, as the organization of the guilds became known, were out of the ordinary, but they had no alternative if they were to defend their interests in a chaotic and violent situation.

But why should the communes of the nobility give political rights to groups of traders and artisans? The answer was simple – the *popolo* reached the point, in one city after another, where they had more men in arms, better organized and motivated, than the nobility. The *popolo* could argue their case for more political representation, but in the end they seized power through force, usually when their city had suffered a military defeat. Between 1200 and 1250 the *popolo* began to take control in Lucca, Piacenza, Lodi, Verona, Bologna, Modena, Bergamo, Siena, Pistoia, Parma, Florence and Genoa. From roughly 1250 to 1300, all the major cities of northern Italy, apart from the Venetian republic, were under the influence of, if not actually governed by, the *popolo*.

The rise and subsequent rule of the *popolo* was not a one-off rebellion but a sustained movement against established and self-serving authority. The political effects were important but the social, psychological and cultural effects were enormous and enduring. Firstly the whole notion of what cities and towns were, what they were for, how they should be lived in, was set out by the *popolo*. Down came the towers and out went the defendable neighbourhoods. From now on the urban space – the streets, the piazzas, the assembly rooms, the churches – was open to everyone. The city was not to be a collection of private fiefdoms, echoing in miniature the geography of the feudal countryside, but an entirely new conception in human living. This conception recreated the diffusion of power that existed in customary societies, and raised the status of the 'common man' – the artisan baker or saddler or notary – to that of a fully realized citizen. The life of the ordinary man or woman became as valuable as that of the noble or the prelate. Everyday urban life was now intensely interesting for a large part of the population, who no longer concerned themselves simply with working to feed their families, but were involved in the administration of their cities, in the passing of laws, in planning, in arrangements for caring for the sick, in looking after members of their guild and in soldiering.

Neither the communes nor the *popolo* revolutions happened in other European cities to the same degree, simply because everywhere else there was some outside controlling authority. Towns and cities in the Germanic empire, France, Burgundy and England were granted charters by monarchs rather than taking powers themselves, and while they were encouraged to organize their own town's defence, noble families would not have been able to take over sections of cities, nor would the guilds have been permitted to seize power. Personal family wealth and the power of guilds were both features of northern European cities, but in Italy these were much more extreme and more politicized.

The time of the *popolo* in the thirteenth century saw the biggest growth in both population and economic activity in Italian cities. There was a surge of interest and activity in education, public finance, citizens' armies, politics, vernacular architecture and in the visual and literary arts. By 1300 literacy was higher and education more widespread in Italian cities than anywhere else in Europe. Education in arithmetic, bookkeeping, common Latin for commerce and law burgeoned while governments expanded both their reach and the numbers of people they employed. The sense of a larger political community was firmly established. By 1300 there were around 300 cities in Italy acting as virtually independent states.

The second half of the thirteenth and the early fourteenth century provided artistic as well as political and social innovations. Sudden increases in wealth, in population and in the size of cities, the injection of politics into everyday life, more people reading and writing, violent tensions between aristocrats and artisans, the febrile energy of the townscapes all contributed to a sense of uncertainty and dislocation, combined with the thrilling taste of power. It was at this time that the craft work of the medieval artisans – church architects, fresco painters, balladeers and story-tellers – first began to be turned into artistic creations. The poet Dante Alighieri (1265–1321) served on the Supreme Council of Florence before being forced into exile by his political enemies in 1302. Dante is a notable example of an artist as a creation of his time, who nevertheless disdained many of its most characteristic features. His poetry was infused with a distaste for the growing materialist culture of late medieval Florence and its insular 'patriotism'. He craved a return to the ideal of a single empire on earth under one ruler answerable to God. But Dante wrote in vernacular Tuscan, and attempted to create a common Italian language, so that the poetry and writings of his time could be understood by everyone. It was his fusion of the eternal and the everyday in written verse that re-established European literature as an art form, and made the poet into a celebrity.

In 1303 Enrico Scrovegni, a Paduan merchant, commissioned Dante's near-contemporary Giotto di Bondone (1266–1337) to paint a series of frescos to commemorate his father's death. The paintings, on the life and passion of Christ, were full of bold innovations. Not only were they biblical scenes filled with ordinary Italian people in quite ordinary landscapes – *The Mourning of Christ*, for example, could have been happening at a roadside outside Padua – but both the people and scenes looked real. This depiction of the 'real' relied on Giotto's knowledge of Byzantine art but it catapulted western painting into an entirely new area of endeavour. His ability to give the illusion of three dimensions was a radical departure for Italian art – so radical that it took another 70 years for any other artist to adopt it successfully.

Giotto's work for the Scrovegni family showed other interesting innovations. The combination of a wealthy merchant seeking cultural status (Scrovegni's father had been found guilty of usury and denied a Christian burial) and an artist wanting to depict the real, everyday life of the people around him was to be the catalyst for much of the art that would follow. And Giotto's astonishing skill made him, like Dante, a celebrity, winning commissions in cities across northern Italy.

The rediscovery of the classical world is reckoned to be a key characteristic of the Renaissance. Dante used the Roman poet Virgil as his guide through purgatory and hell, and the poet Petrarch (1304–74) was an avid reviver of texts from classical Rome. These works, along with disused pillars, aqueducts and Roman amphitheatres, had always existed in Italy, but they seemed part of an alien and undesirable world. The artists who began to re-use them were not trying to recreate the past; they were looking around for tools and equipment that would help them to cope with the difficulties of the present. Members of the ranks of the educated minor nobility, and of the artisans brought up in the era of *popolo* government, looked for ways of dealing with a world that was shifting beneath their feet.

The writings of Giovanni Boccaccio (1313–75) perfectly capture the dilemma of this educated class. Boccaccio's *Decameron* contains stories about ordinary people, ostensibly being told by Florentines sheltering in the countryside from the plague of 1348. He is not much bothered by religious themes, or stories of saints, or the doings of great heroes, or even romantic love, but instead is occupied by the kinds of stories people tell to amuse and entertain each other. The titles of two tales from the *Decameron* give an idea of its tone and content: 'Masetto of Lamporecchio pretends to be dumb, and becomes a gardener at a convent, where all the nuns combine forces to take him off to bed with them' and 'Friar Cipolla promises a crowd of country folk that he will show them a feather of the Angel Gabriel, and on finding that some bits of coal have been put in its place, he proclaims that these were left over from the roasting of St Lawrence'. People had always told these kinds of bawdy and irreverent tales, of course, but before Boccaccio no one had taken the trouble, or felt the need, to write them down. Boccaccio was filling a need, not for the peasant tavern-drinkers of the countryside, who remained part of an oral tradition, but for the educated, literate Florentines, who had been pulled away from their roots and felt adrift in a world where communal security and cohesion was giving way to individual ambition.

Innovations in painting and literature were matched by developments in architecture. New ideas about urban space that arose in the time of the *popolo* encouraged the emergence of Italian vernacular urban architecture, particularly in the use of open spaces and public buildings. The Doge's Palace in Venice, begun in 1309, carries a fine example of an open arcade or loggia on the ground floor, while the church of Orsanmichele in Florence was built as a vast open-sided trade hall in 1304, before being walled in several decades later. This open style, which originated in the *popolo* regimes, was used in combination with piazzas by Italian architects over the next seven centuries – from Brunelleschi's Ospedale degli Innocenti in Florence to the endless colonnades of central Bologna and countless guild-halls, colleges and bridges – to reinforce the sense of the city as a communal space. We habitually associate northern Italy with the Renaissance, but the fabric of its cities, including many of their finest buildings, was a product of the *popolo* period, when control of the cities was taken from the nobility and given back to the citizens.

The rule of the *popolo* regimes came to an end because they could not adjust to the rapid changes that continued to surge through Italian cities. The *popolo* electorate, though more inclusive than the aristocratic communes, was restricted to those with five years' residence, membership of a guild, ownership of property or payment of taxes. These conditions excluded unskilled workers and the mass of new immigrants who continued to flood into the cities, and when political unrest erupted, the *popolo* could not call on those they had deliberately excluded from power.

In addition, the membership of the *popolo* itself became divided under the strains of increasing prosperity. The guilds of merchants and bankers had been enthusiastic members of a collective movement when their interests were under threat from the bullying aristocracy. But as their affluence and social status increased, they found more in common with the excluded nobility than with guilds of butchers and stonemasons. In the fourteenth century there was money to be made, and while poets wrote verses satirizing avarice, wealth became the passport to social respectability. People wrote about the coming of 'new people' and about there being nothing worse than having no money.

Under the torrent of individualistic materialism, the collective *popolo* regimes gradually crumbled. In the course of the fourteenth century, wealth was concentrated in fewer hands and in small groups of extremely rich merchants ambitious for political power. The *popolo* fought them off for a while and in some cities (Florence in 1378, for example) the lower orders managed to stage revolutions to seize power back from the new nobility. In the turmoil of the fourteenth century one citizen might see four or five changes of method of government in a lifetime. But on a broad time scale the century saw the decline of the *popolo* and its replacement by either a single ruler or an oligarchy of wealthy families.

The new plutocratic regimes were driven by the desire for power rather than by civic pride or duty – in the early fourteenth century exiled nobles from Genoa, Florence and Milan all made war on their own cities with the help of foreigners. While some cities – Milan, Ferrara, Mantua – fell under the rule of single families, several adopted a collective form of republican government. Venice (which had been a republic since the ninth century), Florence, Siena and Lucca were republics throughout most of the later fourteenth and the fifteenth centuries, while Genoa, Bologna and Perugia had intermittent periods of single-family and republican rule. Given all these variations, city rule in the fifteenth century was most often conducted either by a single prince and his successors, or by a group representing the 'new nobility'.

During the fourteenth century, bigger Italian cities also swallowed up smaller ones, either by agreement or by annexation, and the north of the peninsula became controlled by eight large states – Venice, Milan, Genoa, Ferrara, Modena, Florence, Mantua and Siena. The diffusion of power within and between cities that was such a feature of the thirteenth century was gradually but inexorably reversed until by the late fifteenth century the whole of northern Italy was controlled by just a few families. The power of a small elite over the rest of the nobility and over the city became the central fact of every Italian city as the fifteenth century unfolded. Milan was ruled by the Visconti and Sforza families, Mantua by the Gonzagas, Ferrara by the Este family, Florence by the Medici and Genoa by the Spinola and Doria families. But this was a fitful process, and to understand its relationship to the artistic innovations of the time more clearly we need to focus on Florence, the city where those innovations were most strongly expressed.

A late starter compared to Venice and Genoa because of its isolation from the sea, Florence caught up with and overtook its rivals by engaging in manufacture and commerce, as well as trade. All the cities of Europe were becoming manufacturing centres but Florence did it better than most. The industry was textiles: cleaning, carding, sorting, combing, spinning, weaving, fulling, dyeing, all carried out in small workshops combining together in a complex collective organization. Master-craftsmen controlled the manufacturing, while the buying and selling was carried on by merchants. This medieval system was transformed in two ways, and Florence took a decisive lead in both. Firstly, the master-craftsmen and merchants were replaced by a new breed of capitalist entrepreneur who controlled both the trading and manufacturing of textiles. From the thirteenth century Florentine merchants set up offices in cities all over Europe from Edinburgh to Constantinople – the archive of the Datini family shows letters from customers and suppliers in 200 different European towns – while they also bought up workshops in Florence, and employed managers to run them.

The second commercial innovation was the development of banking. To support their network of trade, the new entrepreneurs needed a sophisticated method of making money available and moving it around. Florentines got into this role sooner than anyone else, acting as guarantors and providing credit and financial and accounting services to the new merchants. The banker, someone who did not make or trade in goods or services, but only in money, was a new and powerful commercial phenomenon. At the height of its power Florence was controlled by about a hundred families, all of whom were involved in banking.

These commercial innovations may seem mundane, but improvements in organization were to have a revolutionary effect on European commerce. In part these depended on technological advances. By the thirteenth century paper was being manufactured in Italy, while the use of Arabic numerals was also spreading. Mechanical clocks became widespread in the fourteenth and fifteenth centuries, giving a new dimension to levels of organization and productivity. Techniques like double-entry bookkeeping were first introduced in Florence, while Florentine bankers organized the exchange of currency (a potential barrier to trade when every city-state was minting its own coinage), advancing credit, overdrafts, deposits and withdrawals. By 1355 the Peruzzi family had offices in Florence, Palermo, Naples, Avignon, Bruges and London, with agents running local banks in other major European cities, while the rival Bardi family had agents in Constantinople,

Jerusalem, Cyprus, Majorca, Barcelona, Nice, Marseilles, Paris, Avignon, Lyons and Bruges. The Florentines were not just bankers to the merchants of Florence, they were the bankers of Europe – and its richest merchants.

The education system of medieval Florence was, despite its lack of a university (which was probably the result of deliberate policy), highly developed. Around 10,000 young people, out of a total population of 90,000, were enrolled in schools in the mid-fourteenth century, with 1,500 of these in advanced schools of mathematics, Latin and logic. With further professional training for those entering law or banking, this was a formidable group of educated, literate and numerate people.

Despite the wealth of its merchant and banking families, Florence had a strong tradition of *popolo* and republican government. Granted nominal independent status in 1115 by the Countess of Tuscia, the Republic of Florence became the political battleground of factions favouring the pope (the Guelphs) and the emperor (the Ghibellines). The Guelphs held the upper hand through most of the subsequent centuries, and control was disputed between the Primo Popolo, headed by the merchants, and the Secondo Popolo, run by the craft guilds. In 1378 discontent among textile workers led to a brief seizure of power in the revolution of the *ciompi* (the workers with no property or political rights), but the merchant class quickly regained control. Until the elevation of Cosimo de' Medici in 1434, no one individual or family had gained control of Florence for 300 years. Coinciding with Florence's most prosperous period, the rule of the Medici was the beginning of the end of the city's hard-won tradition of civic republicanism.

While every city was filled with different kinds of crafts and trades, each was also known for a particular speciality – Venice for printing and her trade with the east, Padua for its university and intellectual tradition, Siena for its wool industry, Lucca for olive oil and silk, and Florence for its textiles, bankers and artists. For centuries boys from artisan families had been placed in apprenticeships. A family would pay a fee to a master in return for teaching his craft, and sometimes providing board and lodging, to their son. At the end of his apprenticeship, at the age of 21, he could apply for membership of the guild and become a master-craftsman. In the fifteenth century Florence had 270 textile, 84 wood-carving, 54 stonemason, 83 silk and 74 goldsmith workshops, the latter turning their hand to engraving, setting stones, designing jewellery, and sculpting in gold, silver, bronze and copper.

At the end of the fourteenth century it was the workshops of Florentine goldsmiths, the most prestigious of the craft trades, that attracted, trained and inspired a series of innovative artists. In 1391 the 15–year-old Filippo Brunelleschi told his prosperous father that rather than following his designated career as a notary, he wanted to be apprenticed to a goldsmith named Benincasa Lotti. The decision of the young Brunelleschi, who was to be the most influential artist in Florentine history, was also made by Ghiberti (whose stepfather was a goldsmith), Orcagna, della Robbia, Donatello, Uccello, Verrocchio, Botticelli, Leonardo and Gozzoli, all Florentine sculptors and painters who were apprenticed to goldsmiths in what had become general craftsmen's workshops. This was an intensely practical life, with the slow accumulation of hand skills and no education in, for example, reading and writing, let alone theology or classical literature. These were mechanical arts, physically tough, dirty and demanding.

While some apprentices may have been seeking an outlet for artistic expression, most were encouraged by the huge demand for craft skills, both in Florence and in other Italian cities. New churches, guild-halls, hospitals and private palazzi were being built, needing architects and craftsmen of all kinds; while private families were getting a taste for luxury objects such as jewellery, clothes embroidered with gold thread, tapestries, furniture and paintings. But why did the demand for these skills and objects bring about such an irreversible change in the nature of artistic expression?

The Florentine creative tradition and the still-echoing fame of Giotto were clearly attractions for young men of energy, vision and ambition, but the politics of Florence also had a significant impact on their work. In the first decades of the fifteenth century Florence was a strange mix of civic pride, communal identity and inordinate private wealth. The republican tradition of the city meant more than just the lack of a monarch or duke; republicanism was a living relationship between the city and its inhabitants and the source of a strong communal identity. In 1400 the centre of Florence was a flurry of activity – work on the cathedral of Santa Maria del Fiore had resumed, the Piazza dell'Opera was being laid out, with a new building for the Opera del Duomo under construction. But in the same year a plague epidemic carried off 12,000 of the city's 50,000 inhabitants, a disaster commemorated by the commissioning of a set of doors for the city's baptistery by the guild of cloth merchants. But before the competition for the doors (traditionally seen as a milestone in European art) could be settled, a new threat faced the city. In the summer of 1402 the armies of the tyrannical ruler of Milan, Giangaleazzo Visconti, blockaded and laid siege to Florence, threatening both its independence and its republican government. But in early September 1402, in the heat of the summer, Giangaleazzo died of a fever. The Milanese withdrew and the Florentines were left to celebrate their victory, and the triumph of republican freedom over tyranny. This was an opportunity for adventurous artists to display their skills and to explore new methods. The cloth merchant guilds controlled the public money allocated for the upkeep of the baptistery and the completion of the unfinished cathedral, while the Arti Maggiori, the Great Guilds, were given responsibility for decorating the exterior of the Orsanmichele with sculpture. Ghiberti, Verrocchio, di Banco, Tedesco and Donatello all won commissions from the guilds, while in 1420 Brunelleschi, after building several cupolas for the wool guilds, won the commission to build the dome of Santa Maria del Fiore, again from a committee of guilds.

The response of artists to these commissions was to make a decisive break with the past. Medieval and Byzantine painting and relief work was created to produce a sense of spiritual contemplation and awe, and to assist in the act of worship. Its principal subject was the saint, or saviour, at prayer. The best of these works were deeply moving, but over the centuries and through repeated copying they had become formulaic and uninspiring. In the same way that Marathon had provoked Herodotus into focusing the attention of his audience on his own time, so the defeat of the Milanese changed the focus of the Florentine artist. Rather than depicting saints at prayer, both they and their patrons wanted to celebrate the Florentine citizen, the guild member and republican who had stood firm against the forces of tyranny. When Florentine artists sought ways of achieving this celebration through their art, there were two obvious places to look – Giotto's paintings, which were all around them, and the remnants of Roman art. Much has been made of the rediscovery of the classical world, but we need to understand that this was not a straightforward adoption of the past. Artists like Brunelleschi and Donatello plundered the classical past – its sculptures, mosaics, ruined buildings and architectural treatises – not to recreate a bygone world, but because the existing ways of making buildings, paintings and statues no longer answered the needs of their audience. Rather than wanting to recreate the culture of the

Roman republic, the Renaissance artists just grabbed whatever they could use.

The change from medieval art is clearly seen in Donatello's 1415 sculpture of St George, commissioned by the Florentine guild of armourers. While remaining a religious figure, the saint has lost piety and contemplation in favour of action and solidity. He was not intended to induce a sense of sublime spirituality, but to make the viewer admire him *as a man*. Nevertheless, he is not a classical, but a distinctly modern figure, and although we think of Renaissance art as being of captivating beauty, Donatello, Masaccio, Mantegna and other early Renaissance artists were consciously downplaying customary medieval beauty in favour of honesty, clarity and straightforwardness.

Although knowledge of the classical world had never gone away, in the early fifteenth century there was a sudden enthusiasm for everything Roman. The language and literature of ancient Rome and the discovery of ancient manuscripts became an obsession. Cicero's house was found and excavated, as were his manuscripts, along with the poems of writers like Lucretius and Quintilian, while the bones of the historian Livy were disinterred and enshrined in the town hall of his birthplace of Padua amid scenes of almost religious excitement. According to some historians Brunelleschi and Donatello spent years digging among the ruins of Rome, making measurements and taking copious coded notes, before returning, reinvigorated, to Florence. These ruins had not been simply ignored by their predecessors, they were tainted with the blood of Christian martyrs. Brunelleschi's interest was not mere curiosity; it was an alteration in the European view of the past.

Interest in classical Rome led inevitably to interest in ancient Greece. In the mid-fourteenth century Boccaccio had complained that there was no one in Italy who could teach him Greek; but by 1400 teachers from Byzantium found there was a good living to be made in Italy, teaching Greek language, literature and philosophy to the sons of merchants and bankers. Just as wealthy Romans had travelled to the Hellenistic world to further their learning, so Florentines, Venetians and Milanese queued up to learn from Byzantine teachers. When, in 1452, the city of Byzantium fell to the armies of Mehmet II, Italy was flooded with Greek-speaking refugees and Greek manuscripts.

Brunelleschi returned to Florence where in 1420, and after much wrangling, he won the commission from the guild of masons to build the

dome of Santa Maria del Fiore. Brunelleschi's solution to the problem
of spanning the vast area of the Florentine cathedral brilliantly combined
the rib-vaulting techniques from Gothic cathedrals with the domes of
classical Rome, and in future commissions he continued to use elements
of classical Roman and Greek architecture in a radically eclectic way.
This master plunderer used arches, pillars, capitals, pilasters and pedi-
ments in buildings (the extraordinarily original Cappella Pazzi, for
example) that were unlike Roman and Greek temples or Gothic cathedrals.

In the search for honesty and naturalism in art, painters and sculptors edged closer to depicting the world as they saw it. In 1425 Masaccio
demonstrated the use of mathematical perspective in *The Holy Trinity*,
a fresco in the church of Santa Maria Novella, showing how painting
could depict a three-dimensional reality. He also introduced the idea
of tonal perspective, using colours to invoke a sense of distance, and
shunned the growing idealism of other painters in favour of harshly
realist depictions. Though undoubtedly an influence on later artists (and
now seen as a key figure in Renaissance art), Masaccio's crude direct-
ness did not thrive in affluent, plutocratic Florence and he left in 1427.

For the early Renaissance artists of Florence there were, therefore,
different impulses and influences at work. Their patrons, the guilds of
the city, wanted a celebration of Florence's republican ethos and had
the resources to fund the artists' endeavours. The artists, trained as
artisans and working to commissions, were able to adapt the medieval
crafts of fresco, carving and building to their needs by calling on the
pioneering work of Giotto and the growing fashion (which they helped
to inspire) for objects from the classical past. Since Giotto's time people
had praised an artist by saying that his work was as good as the ancients.
Ghiberti, Masaccio, Donatello and Brunelleschi were clearly aware of
mosaics, sculptures and images from Roman times, and along with
other artisans, they were keen to incorporate some of these classical
ideas in their work.

But even as Brunelleschi was giving European architecture a new
direction with the classical façade of the Ospedale degli Innocenti, the
political, social and cultural life of Florence was changing. The economy
of the city had foundered in the second half of the fourteenth century;
banking failures brought down the old Bardi and Peruzzi financial
empires, and plague halved the population and the level of economic
activity. The revolution of textile workers in 1378 was led by a demand

for orders of cloth at just half the levels of 50 years previously. But the stagnation allowed new merchant families to acquire a larger share of the city's industry, commerce and wealth – the Rucellai, Strozzi, Pitti and Medici muscled in. By the time of his death in 1429 Giovanni de' Medici had accumulated a vast fortune, which passed to his son Cosimo. Though the Florentine republic continued in name, Cosimo de' Medici took control of the council and effectively ruled the city from 1434 until his death 30 years later. The Medici rule was symptomatic of the growing influence of individual, rather than collective, power. The 1427 census of the Florentine state shows that 27 per cent of the city's wealth was held by 100 families, and half the city's borrowings (an important source of income for investors) were from 200 households, while one in seven of the population was officially destitute. Rents from the Florentine countryside flowed into the city and into the pockets of the wealthy elite. While artists continued to work for commissions granted by institutions – principally churches or guilds – and while their subjects were overwhelmingly religious in content, individual patronage began to make itself felt. So, while the decoration of a new chapel might be commissioned by the wool merchants' guild, one or two families would be the principal funders, and increasingly they expected their generosity to be acknowledged.

The next stage, which can be traced in fifteenth-century Florentine churches, was for communal patronage to be overtaken by individuals and families. Plutocrats became the patrons of their guild, and paid for lavish family chapels and tombs, their names appearing on altarpieces and on church façades. At the same time, around the middle of the century, architecture and sculpture, which had dominated the early Renaissance, began to be matched by a revival of painting as the location for displays of art moved from the public church to the private palazzo. The 1440s saw the building of palaces for the Medici, Rucellai and Pitti families, followed by 100 more Florentine palazzi before 1500, all of which needed beautiful objects to adorn their rooms and gardens.

In the 1430s Jan van Eyck had begun to use oil as a base for paints with stunning effects. Italian artists quickly discovered that oil paint could be applied in transparent layers, and with extreme delicacy, to give both depth and dazzling surfaces, imitating reality with almost magical effect. The oil painting was a transportable luxury, ideally suited to the new palazzi, but by making a piece of art a private rather than a public object, it divided the elite from the masses. Patrons also discovered that oil painters like Uccello, Ghirlandaio, Mantegna, Veneziano and Castagno could render extraordinary (and flattering) likenesses of their subjects; and so portraits, which were almost unknown before 1450, became increasingly popular.

As well as commissioning new works, art pieces from the past were sought by the wealthy; and so an art market sprang up, in which professional agents and advisers worked on behalf of collectors – the Duke of Milan had his own art-buying agent in Florence – and where artists touted for commissions. By the end of the fifteenth century a few leading artists – Lippi, Perugino, Leonardo, Michelangelo – by now the intellectual soulmates of their patrons, were able to use their status to move away from the guilds, to earn large sums, and to form, albeit unconsciously, a new artistic elite.

The huge increase in private patronage in Florence was not simply a result of greater personal wealth. Instead it seems as if the fashion for the classical world, the deep inculcation of secular education, an era of political stability and rapid artistic innovation combined with personal wealth to give Florentines a new vision of themselves. Classical texts by Seneca and Cicero seemed to speak much more clearly to these worldly plutocrats than the parables of the Bible or the gloomy restrictions of theological instruction. The old views of what was virtuous broke down, firstly because renouncing worldly wealth (as the Bible and the solemn edicts of Pope Gregory demanded) was simply not possible, and secondly because the classical authors and their contemporary interpreters offered an alternative set of morals. Men no longer wished to apologize for their wealth or their ambition; the Renaissance merchants wanted to spend their money on beautiful objects, and feel the same sense of virtue their predecessors experienced when they had given to the church and monastery and hospital. The answer was at hand in the doctrine of civic humanism.

This new ideal of citizenship was promoted by Florentine scholars such as Leonardo Bruni and Coluccio Salutati, and avidly taken up by the merchant classes. The humanist scholars taught their students that wealth and social position were not enough to give a person 'nobility'; they must demonstrate discernment in their appreciation of painting and architecture and show virtue by developing a moral dimension to their lives. The guidance of the Church was replaced by a sensibility based on classical literature, which embodied a noble tradition of republicanism, self-awareness and improvement. The ruler, the noble, the

prince should be a sage – wise and virtuous, with a refined appreciation of social and cultural arts. This was the ideal that the fifteenth-
century rulers of Italian cities adopted for themselves. Hypocritical and
vainglorious they may have been, but their lives were supposedly shaped
by the need to conform to this new social mode.

It is possible to be highly cynical about the whole exercise – civic
humanism seemed to use intellectual sleight of hand to transform political ambitions and money-grabbing into a doctrine of active citizenship
and enlightened patronage. And in any case, active citizenship had been
a feature of medieval urban life throughout Europe, and particularly
in Italy, since the twelfth century. But it was exactly this paradoxical
and contradictory nature of Florentine society that provided the catalyst for such rapid change. It is clear from Leonardo Bruni's work, for
example, that he was an ardent republican, who inveighed against the
acquisition of political power through wealth. Bruni was a seminal
figure in the promotion of civic humanism, using rediscovered classics
to support his case, but also trying to protect the medieval Florentine
tradition of republicanism against the emerging oligarchy. And while
they might be as arrogant as any medieval baron, the new plutocrats
and princes, their families and friends were the heirs of a sophisticated
urban culture that had developed over several centuries. The nature of
that culture had gradually changed to suit the needs of the money
economy, and in fifteenth-century Florence, some kind of tipping point
was reached that made that alteration irreversible.

Opportunities for social advancement and acquisition of wealth were
matched by a growing necessity for each person (and particularly each
family) to look after his or her own interests. As power became concentrated in a few hands, or in one family, others worked hard to be as near
as possible to that power by acquiring the wealth which in turn brought
social status. People began to see their lives in a different way. The
Augustinian and Gregorian orthodoxy of renunciation of pleasure and
concentration on prayer and charity gave way to a continual seeking after
activity and achievement. The medieval world had measured time by the
passing of the sun, and felt little need to cram activity into the passing
hours. But the Renaissance period is marked above all by the way that
individual achievement became central, and time became a commodity to
be used, with total and ruthless dedication, to acquire knowledge, for
social advancement, and to gain wealth. Cosimo de' Medici was said by
Marsilio Ficino to have 'spent his days parsimoniously, carefully counting

every hour, and avariciously saving every second', while mathematics gave a world that was like a giant puzzle, where everything was measurable and calculation became the key to a good life.

The princes were fabulously wealthy, and showing off their riches became a major part of their lives. The competition for public esteem was intense, leading to ever greater displays of patronage and extravagance. When the Duke of Milan made a state visit to Florence in 1471 he took 2,000 horses, 200 pack mules, 5,000 pairs of hounds, 12 carriages and several thousand courtiers. Everything was clothed in velvet embroidered with gold and silver and the total cost was around 200,000 ducats (a labourer's wages were around 15 ducats per annum). Lucrezia Borgia's bridal journey from Rome to Ferrara in 1502 was accompanied by 700 courtiers bringing a dowry of 100,000 ducats. Federigo da Montefeltro spent 200,000 ducats just on construction costs for his palace in Urbino, and then built another at Gubbio. These lavish displays of personal wealth were a new phenomenon and were accompanied by other types of self-glorification. The great families hired painters and sculptors to depict themselves, their relatives and children, even their dogs. Each was determined to outdo their rivals by hiring the best artists and by holding ever more lavish processions, marriages and investitures.

In this context we can see the real achievement of civic humanism. The Renaissance cult of the individual threatened to fragment society into a multitude of competing interests. The task of Bruni and his fellow humanists was to remind the plutocrats and their children of the noble traditions of their city, to give them a moral framework based on an even older tradition of knowledge and artistic sensibility, and to keep the wealthy, powerful individual culturally tied to the communal society of the city. This attempt ultimately failed, but while it lasted, the opposing tensions of individuality and communality gave rise to continuing artistic innovation.

So, how were the artists of Florence to respond to the needs of their new patrons and to the changing world around them? Firstly their subject matter changed. Although paintings remained overwhelmingly religious, secular images were brought into biblical scenes, while classical subjects also became legitimate – Botticelli's *The Birth of Venus*, for example, was commissioned by the Medici family in 1485. Princes and their families wanted to appear in the paintings they commissioned, but to begin with many portraits appeared within the traditional settings of biblical scenes – Mantegna painted the Gonzagas as the Holy Family, the young Lorenzo de' Medici is one of the kings in Gozzoli's *Procession of the Magi*, while Titian later showed members of the Pesaro family with the Madonna attended by saints. But the way that these subjects were portrayed also altered; the tough realism of Donatello and Masaccio was softened, through the use of oils, and by the need for a luxurious appearance. The symbolic message of the medieval fresco or sculpture was turned into a narrative painting in which a story was told; paintings became depictions of a particular moment in an event that was known to the viewer. This narrative style demanded ever greater approximation to reality, both in the naturalness of the scene and the imitation of real objects – people, animals, drapery, landscapes and so on. Patrons were astonished and delighted at the extraordinary skill of artists in producing the illusion of depth, surface and the sensuous quality of luxury objects. They saw paintings as a way of showing off their possessions, and so the central depiction of a worthy subject matter, for example a biblical scene, was often surrounded by sumptuous detail of luxury objects. John Berger and, more recently, Lisa Jardine have shown how artists fed the needs of their patrons by depicting their luxurious possessions, and how oil paintings themselves became luxury items that could be possessed and traded.

All of this tells us something about the art of the high Renaissance, but leaves out its most important quality. Art critics and historians have for centuries been eager to show how the architecture, sculpture and paintings are evidence of a great revival in classical rational humanism: art of the Renaissance is above all 'humanist' art. The connection is easy to make – paintings and sculptures became more apparently real, the figures in them were more and more like people in the street, the subjects were more secular – but that does not mean that it gives a true understanding. The merely very skilled artists of the Renaissance, like Pollaiuolo and Gozzoli, were perhaps content to show their subjects as 'new' rational men, in control of themselves and all they surveyed; but if that was all there was to Renaissance art it would have grown stale and dull long before now. The achievement of Mantegna and Michelangelo and Bellini and Titian was to use the opportunities that the new wealth and the intense climate of innovation provided in order to produce art that transcended their subjects. Mantegna's *Holy Family*, Michelangelo's *David*, the boy in Titian's *Pesaro* family, the nymph in Ghirlandaio's *Nativity of St John*, the expression of Leonardo's self-portrait are not depictions of rational humanism but reminders that, while they may be dressed in golden cloth and surrounded by clocks and books and jewelled caskets, humans are, in the end, a natural phenomenon. Renaissance art has been called the return of paganism, but historians have struggled to see how this might fit with the new cult of the individual and the ideal of the rational humanist. The answer may be that it does not. Renaissance artists were one product of the individualistic culture, but that does not mean that their art was a frank celebration of their own status, nor of the idealized rational humanist.

In the early fourteenth century Brunelleschi and Donatello had wanted to escape from the restrictions of medieval style, but the pace of change meant that their successors saw painting in danger of being transformed from a medium of spiritual expression to a luxury commodity. But if painting could no longer be used simply to evoke religious experience, as it had been in the previous century, then what should it do? The best Renaissance artists reasserted the meaning of pictorial art that had stood for thousands of years. Like their pagan forebears, they saw the human animal – its physical forms, its emotions, its immense subtleties, arrogance and weaknesses – as part of, and not above, the physical world. Michelangelo's *David* is not a rational object, but a physical animal, and the *Dying Slave* the embodiment of sexual emotion. Like the carvers of the Parthenon friezes 2,000 years earlier, Michelangelo reminded his viewers that they were, above all, physical, sensual and emotional beings.

The world of Italian princes, nobles and merchants operating against a background of independent wealth and political power was brought to a sudden and unwelcome close in 1494 when Charles VIII of France swept over the Alps with an army of 30,000 men and, allied with the Sforza dukes of Milan, made his way through Italy to claim the throne of Naples. This aggressive incursion threw the carefully constructed balance of power between the Italian city-states into confusion. Venice joined forces with the papacy, the Holy Roman Empire (now controlled by the Austrian Habsburg family) and Spain to expel the French, but the result was the end of the independent cities of northern Italy. For the next 50 years Italy, a glittering treasure house open to plunder, became once again the proxy battleground of outside powers. France, Spain and the Habsburg empire all poured armies into the peninsula; the city-state died under the ambitions of the national monarchies, and the dukes and princes of Italy became the puppets of Europe's great

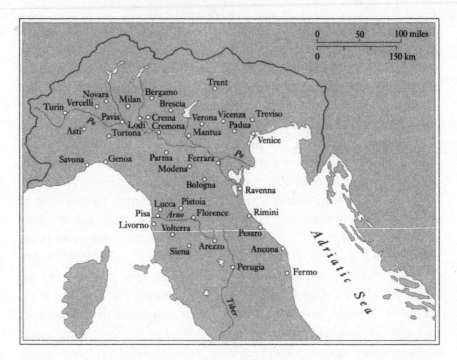

*The numerous communes within the nominal Italian kingdom in 1200 (above)
had, by the 1490s, been reduced to a small number of city-states (right).*

powers. Two of these monarchs – Charles V, Habsburg emperor, as well as ruler of Spain, Burgundy and the Netherlands, and Francis I of France – fought four wars in northern Italy between 1520 and 1544. The mad confusion of the wars, where changes in territory, switching of sides, treachery, diplomacy and rebellion were rife, completely destroyed the illusion of humans, particularly cultured princes, as noble beings. This was the atmosphere in which Niccolò Machiavelli wrote his bitter masterpiece *The Prince*. Machiavelli's career, more perhaps than any other, embodied the contradictions and delusions of late Renaissance Italy.

The Medici fled Florence in 1494 in anticipation of the French invasion and, after a four-year period in which the city was ruled by the ascetic monk Savonarola, a new republican regime emerged under Piero Soderini. Niccolò Machiavelli became the Florentine republic's ambassador to the courts of Europe before returning to organize the capture of Pisa by a Florentine 'citizens' army' in 1509. But the participatory government ended in 1512 when the Medici family was forcibly restored to power, against the wishes of the citizens of Florence, by the joint armies of Pope Julius II and the Spanish king. Machiavelli

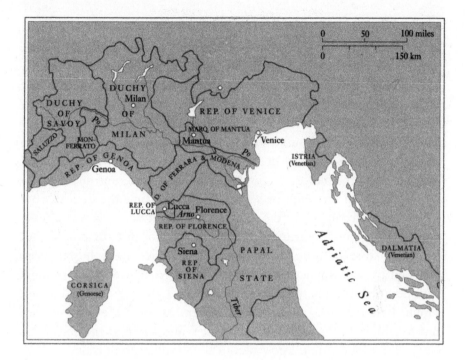

was briefly imprisoned and then forced to withdraw from public office.

An ardent republican who had been thrown out of office, tortured and imprisoned by a tyrannical authority, Machiavelli then wrote *The Prince*, an astonishingly frank commentary on the qualities required for political success. Centuries of debate have not settled whether *The Prince* was written as a bitter satire or a straight piece of advice for potential rulers. More importantly, as a vastly experienced politician and political observer, Machiavelli was probably the first writer to articulate the argument that good government could not be brought about by following abstract rational rules. The revival of interest in Roman authors such as Cicero, Livy and Seneca had been matched in the mid-fifteenth century by a growing interest in the works of Plato and Aristotle – in 1438 an academy for the study of Plato's works was set up in Florence. Scholars had absorbed the idea that rational thinking would reveal the principles of good governance in everything from individual life to the running of a city. The wealthy students of the humanist scholars took all this on board but, as Machiavelli was to show, its relation to practical politics was illusory. In previous centuries the *popolo* and other regimes had known well enough how to govern; they had not needed abstract theses by philosophers with no practical experience, and civic humanism had meant nothing in a time when a foreign army could simply impose a leader on a city. Machiavelli argued that politicians should not look to principles or rationality to guide them, but should learn to understand the situations that continually arose, and try to make them work to their advantage. Crucially he also understood that abstract qualities could not be identified in the same way in every situation. One day you might need to send your enemies greetings and gifts; the next you might go to war. Neither action could be seen as 'good' in some theoretical sense – everything depended on the needs of the situation. This was a revolutionary and much misunderstood message, not just for politics but for every area of human activity. Before Machiavelli it had been assumed by philosophers and political thinkers that abstract rational consideration and analysis would reveal the right way in which a city should be governed, or a war undertaken, or one's life planned out. But Machiavelli, through real experience, and living at the end of his city's glittering century, knew this to be a foolhardy illusion.

After the French had been expelled from southern Italy in 1503, a succession of popes fell under the protection of Spain and the Habsburg empire. While this alliance held, Rome was, for a decade or two, the centre of the Italian world, with popes dictating to the princes of Milan, Mantua and Ferrara, and installing their chosen favourites in Florence and Parma. This was the time of Pope Alexander VI (Rodrigo Borgia, father of Cesare and Lucrezia, ruled 1492–1503), Julius II (Giuliano della Rovere, ruled 1503–13) and Leo X (Giovanni de' Medici, ruled 1513–21), all northern plutocrats who used their position to set up new secular dynasties (the Borgias) or to revive them (the Medici). The College of Cardinals was stuffed with the noble families of Italy, who traded the papacy between them like a golden calf, and once elected, the popes paraded their nepotism and extravagance as if it was their duty to show that Rome could compete with Milan or Venice or Florence.

Leonardo, Michelangelo and Raphael were all called to Rome to glorify the papacy (a German friar named Martin Luther also happened to visit the Holy City at this time). But now the link between the subject matter of art and the real world was broken. With their cities in the hands of outsiders and their religion led by despots, Italian princes, artists and ordinary people felt they were no longer in control of their lives. With no meaningful civic society to commemorate, the artists of the high Renaissance turned away from reality towards idealization. Out went depictions of the everyday, or of religious scenes being played out in urban Italian settings, and in came idealizations of beauty. This was a revival of the Platonic ideal – the notion that the 'ideal' world was more real than the corrupted world of the senses. Artists went in search of perfect beauty, poets in search of perfect love. For a short time this idealization produced sumptuous pictures of extraordinary luminosity from the likes of Giovanni Bellini, Raphael and Michelangelo. But the detachment from reality was unsustainable, and painting entered the derivative period known pejoratively as mannerism. Art historians assert that because Raphael, Michelangelo and Leonardo had solved the problems that Giotto had set, there were no avenues of innovation left; but the subject and style of painting turned away from reality, and struggled to sustain its vitality.

After Rome itself was brought down by its own overblown grandiosity (it was sacked by a dissolute imperial army of Germans and Spaniards in 1527), Venice, the last remaining independent republic, became the centre of innovative Italian art. The pupils of Giovanni Bellini, notably Titian, followed his lead in making light and colour the focus of their works. But after training in Bellini's Venetian workshop and spending his early life in Italy, Titian left in 1530 to become the portraitist to Charles V and then to his son Philip II of Spain. Leonardo had left Italy in 1516 to live his final years under the protection of Francis, the French king. The most innovative Italian painters of their day, and the most venerated, were no longer patronized by Italian princes but by the most powerful men in Europe, the kings of the west.

If the invasions sounded the death knell of the Renaissance, the Counter-Reformation slammed the coffin lid. By 1519 Protestant pamphlets had reached Italy, and by 1542, with German states in open rebellion against the Church, all dissent in Catholic Italy was ruthlessly quashed, ushering in an era of rigid social divides and strict religious orthodoxy. The ageing Michelangelo was censured for painting nudes, and in 1563, following the Council of Trent, a list of forbidden books was published including works by the seminal names of Italian culture – Dante, Boccaccio, Machiavelli, Castiglione and Pietro Bembo. The Italian Renaissance had come to an end.

*   *   *

I began this chapter with Welles's bold statement of the contradictions of the Renaissance. The apparent mismatch between sublime painting and avaricious society in fifteenth-century Italy can never be resolved, but by using history to see how it came about, we can perhaps understand the relation of art and society – and therefore civilization – a little better. Recent historians have, if anything, found Renaissance society even more distasteful and contradictory than their predecessors. Lisa Jardine finished her survey of the Renaissance by describing its legacy: 'The world we inhabit today, with its ruthless competitiveness, fierce consumerism, restless desire for ever wider horizons, for travel, discovery and innovation, a world hemmed in by the small-mindedness of petty nationalism and religious bigotry but refusing to bow to it, is a world which was made in the Renaissance.'

At the same time, the art of the Renaissance has retained its place at the summit of western cultural achievement – the contradictions are as stark as ever. I have tried to show how, in the fourteenth and fifteenth centuries, Italian society was disintegrating and re-forming at bewildering speed. The artists who excelled in the new media of oil paint and stone sculpture were engaged not in a celebration of this change (though their patrons may have wished it) but in reminding their audience and themselves of the eternal verities of the human situation. When we look at Mantegna's *Holy Family* or Leonardo's *Madonna of the Rocks,* what captivates us is not the artist's ability, remarkable though it is, to render a human form or face or piece of drapery exactly as it appears, but the way he has been able to use this language of painting to communicate something that is otherwise inexpressible. In that sense art can never properly be described as the expression of civilization; instead artists use the techniques and the technology and the fashions that any society makes available to them in order to communicate. And often what they communicate is a deep aversion to the mood of the times in which they live.

This view of art working against the grain of history becomes clearer when we look at Renaissance literature. As the effects of greater material wealth and individual ambition swept across Europe in the sixteenth century, the whole continent experienced dramatic social change. Writers like Rabelais, Cervantes and Shakespeare were concerned not with demonstrating the theoretical abstract virtue of the rational Renaissance man, but with showing the vagaries, viciousness and absurdities of human behaviour, including the rationalist illusion that their actions could somehow make the world a better place. Shakespeare was living in a dangerous time and had to be extremely careful about criticizing any aspect of the English regime. Nevertheless he managed to show his distaste for the money-grubbing merchants of Venice (while giving them a romantic subplot to disguise their blatant avarice) and, by inference, the merchants parading their wealth through Elizabethan London. In *King Lear*, he showed the catastrophic results of treating a kingdom as if it were a map, and of constricting human diversity by rejecting 'outsiders'. *King Lear* is, like *Oedipus the King*, a warning against the abstraction and standardization that accompanied the commercialization of European life.

One legacy of the Renaissance has been hinted at in this chapter, but needs a final comment. During the course of the fifteenth and sixteenth centuries the painters, sculptors and architects of Italy became international celebrities. Their renown was so great that powerful rulers commissioned works in order to gain a form of immortality through association. The Sforza family, rulers of Milan, commissioned an immense sculpture of Francesco Sforza from Leonardo, knowing that Leonardo's work would live for ever (it was later destroyed by the family's enemies); and Pope Julius II sought eternity not through prayer, but by commissioning Michelangelo to build his tomb. These were the most celebrated, but the view that all artists were special individuals is taken to be a step forward in the development of western civilization. The separation and social elevation of the artist has certainly had a profound effect on European society. While those artists who attract the plaudits of society may feel the benefit, as do their cultured and socially powerful patrons, the overall effect has been ultimately divisive. Once the artist was lifted above the artisan then in every sphere of creative life a distinction between high and low art was introduced. The visual portrayal of saints and Bible stories had been a way of reaching the illiterate and uneducated, and so religious icons and church frescos had been available to everyone. The Renaissance took painting out of the church and into the private palazzo, and at the same time it made the appreciation of fine art a hallmark of the educated elite. The same process happened in music and, eventually, in theatre, poetry and prose fiction. The common songs and church music of medieval times were transformed into refined pieces for the cultured few; while mystery plays were plundered and mutated into more enlightened entertainment. In all these art forms the period of transition brought immense possibilities for artists who were both steeped in their tradition and saw ways to extend its potential, but the price was high.

Once the artistic element has been separated out from any area of human activity, whatever remains risks being devalued as mechanical and even contemptible. Once religious paintings were made into works of art, then any church decoration that did not bear the mark of a master was of little interest; any building not designed by a known architect was 'vernacular'; any anonymous folk song might be charming but could only become real art when arranged by a serious composer. Low art disappeared below the horizon of history until its rediscovery by social (but not art) historians.

This legacy has not simply divided 'low art' from 'high art', but has decreased the possibility of artistic achievement in everyday life. Once the decoration of churches or the painting of icons or the design of cathedrals and guild-halls was taken out of the hands of wood-carvers and masons and journeymen and given to artists, then the role of the artisan was decisively degraded. Artisans may take pride in their work but they must know that it is always somehow second-rate. When the artist is removed from society and made into a special person, then the artist within each of us begins to die.

Religious structures from western prehistory. Stone circles at Avebury, Wiltshire (*above*) and Callanish, Isle of Lewis (*left*); Silbury Hill, Wiltshire (*below*).

Sacred architecture and proportion in the Mediterranean classical world.
The Greek temple of Ceres, Paestum (*above*); the Pantheon in Rome (*below*).

Sacred architecture
and organic empathy in
north-west Europe.
(*Above*) The West Front
portals of the cathedral
of Notre Dame, Reims;
(*left*) the Bishop's Eye
window, Lincoln Cathedral;
(*below left*) the ambulatory
at St Denis, Paris.

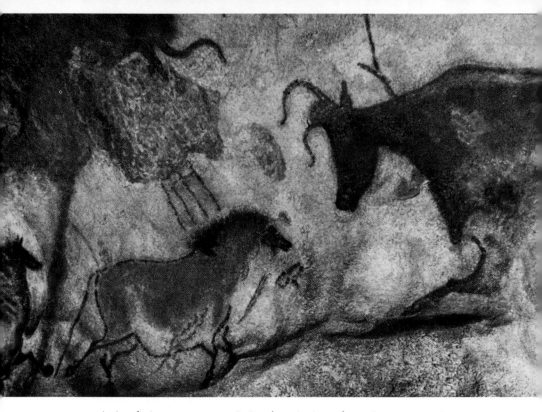

Animals in western art, I. Rock paintings from Lascaux caves, Dordogne (*above*) and from Niaux caves, Midi-Pyrenees (*below*).

Animals in western art, II. The battle of the Lapiths and Centaurs from the Parthenon (*above left*); the Book of Kells (*above right*); Viking carving (*below*); façade of the church of San Pietro, Spoleto, Umbria (*right*).

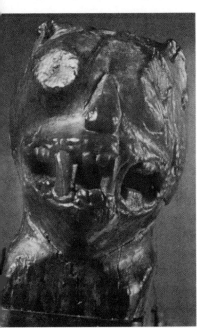

Open urban architecture. Palazzo Ducale, centre of the Venetian
republic with its loggia opening onto Piazza San Marco (*above*); the square
at Cesté Budejovice, Bohemia (*below*).

Closed architecture. Urban
Renaissance palaces: the
Palazzo Strozzi, Florence
(*above right*) and Palazzo
Cattedrale di San Callisto,
Rome (*right*) show forbidding exterior walls; the
Palazzo Pitti in Florence
(*below right*) keeps its
open arcade for the
private interior courtyard.

The sacred and the secular. Trinity Church, New York, surrounded by the skyscrapers of the financial district.

THE SEARCH FOR THE CHRISTIAN LIFE

The European Reformation as a New Beginning

THE Reformation, an apparently simple act of rebellion against the Catholic church, was in reality a complex series of events that appear to contradict the rules of historical cause and effect. The most obvious legacy of the Reformation was a period of intolerance, bitterness and religious conflict; yet the standing of the Christian faith was immeasurably enhanced. The Reformation was a protest against modern rationalist theology, and in support of a return to medieval piety; but its effect was to give the modern world the new kind of religion it needed. It was born out of anger at the extravagances of the Italian Renaissance popes; but the Protestant churches embodied the combination of religious faith, personal ambition and public duty that characterized the new Italian citizen. And while its adherents wanted to return to the communal piety of the early church, the most profound legacy of the Reformation was the creation of the individual conscience – the magnificent drama of the medieval church, culminating in the damnation and salvation of multitudes on the Day of Judgement, was replaced by the devout Christian standing alone before God.

This paradox can only be understood by looking at the different forces that were at work in late medieval Europe – the power and the potential weakness of the Catholic church, the growth of commerce and urban living, increasing nationalism, and the intellectual fashion for, and the reaction against, rational humanism. These forces pulled in different directions but their combined effect was to fatally fracture the apparent unity of the medieval world and its central institution, the Catholic church. In just 40 years, between 1520 and 1560, an alternative system of Christian worship was firmly established throughout northern Europe, including many of the German states, the Swiss cantons, the Netherlands, Scandinavia, England, Scotland and parts of France. How did the apparently unshakeable structure and power of the medieval Catholic church crumble so easily, and why did millions of devout Catholics turn away from their church so readily and so rapidly? Some of the answers lie in the ordinary medieval Christian's experience of the faith.

For the medieval citizen the Church was the centre of a life in which the physical and spiritual were inextricably entwined. What towered over this world of rugged practicality and mysticism, and over the faith and the practice of medieval Christianity, was the meaning of death. Christians felt themselves to be part of a great centuries-long drama, which began with the Creation, was punctuated by the Incarnation and Resurrection of Christ, and would end with the Day of Judgement, at which some would be granted eternal bliss and others damnation. The practices of the faith gave people a sense of being part of this extraordinary drama, and a degree of control over the consequences of death. The Mass was the focus of the drama; the priest was watched in awe by the spectators as he consecrated the bread and wine, converting it into the blood and body of Christ, in a re-enactment of the Last Supper. People felt closer to the sacred at Mass, and they also made pilgrimages to holy places, prayed intensely to the saints and, if they were fortunate, saw the bones or preserved blood of the celebrated martyrs. All this made them spectators and participants in the great unfolding story.

Control over the consequences of death was the other side of medieval Christian ritual. Prayers were said, Masses held and chapels consecrated for the dead, to help them in the afterlife. Strict Augustinian theology did not allow for influence over the salvation of souls, and so in the twelfth century the concept of purgatory as an anteroom to heaven emerged. Prayers and gifts might not save a soul who was to be damned, but they might shorten his time in this agonizing limbo. Purgatory became a major industry, with chantries, guilds, confraternities, monasteries and churches organizing Masses and consecrations in order to help the dead – generally in exchange for gifts and favours. Poor and wealthy alike would leave money and goods to churches, hospitals and chantries in their wills to fund the saying of Masses and prayers – and monks, priests and invalids were urged to remember their deceased benefactors in their prayers.

The vast pyramid of Latin Christianity comprised ranks of clergy, but was based on the structure of the early church, where bishops were responsible for their flock. The clergy were special people; literate and (after 1139) celibate men who were intermediaries between God and the common people, they were used by the central church authorities to regulate both the Church and the rest of society. The priests were professionals, paid by parish tithes. As the wealth of western Europe increased, more churches were built, and by the fifteenth century even the humblest parish churches had pulpits from where the priests spoke about the content of the Bible (which most of the congregation could not read), stories of the saints and the meaning of their faith. Bishops ruled over scores of such parishes, but were also great landowners, often holding as much secular power as a count or duke. The cathedral at the centre of a diocese was an immensely powerful commercial, political and spiritual institution.

Outside this episcopal structure lay a multitude of individuals who had dedicated their lives to God. Reforms introduced in the twelfth century brought monks and nuns within an organized set of orders, which were tied in more closely to the structure of the Church. The system of orders – Benedictines, Franciscans, Dominicans, Carthusians – became truly international, matching the international system of church or canon law.

At the centre and head of this vast network of priests, bishops and holy orders, providing the focus and cement of the western Christian church, was the pope. Descended from St Peter by divinely granted apostolic succession, the pope was a holy figure, a law-giver and God's representative on earth. Though physically remote from most of his spiritual subjects, he was the symbol of their faith.

The unity of this impressive institution was, despite its dominating place in the lives of medieval Europeans, something of a paradox. When we look at the medieval church for signs of weakness or intimations of collapse, we can be led astray by the scathing mockery of fat friars and libidinous nuns by Langland, Boccaccio and Chaucer, the occasional outbreaks of ascetic fervour, and the open questioning of the Church's authority. But much of the strength of orthodox medieval Christianity came from a judicious mix of tolerance and authority, of diversity and uniformity, and it is more likely that robust challenges demonstrate the underlying stability, rather than weakness, of the Catholic church. Nevertheless, there were certain events and tendencies that took root in medieval times, which became the foundations of the post-Reformation, modern western world.

In 1305 Clement V, a Frenchman, was elected pope and decided to reside in Avignon, then a semi-independent French protectorate, rather than Rome. A further five popes also took up residence in Avignon, where, perhaps because of their tranquil situation, they managed to bring the administration of the Church to previously unknown levels of efficiency. Tax-gathering from the various church benefices spread all over Latin Europe brought the Church huge income, while their control of local churches brought a new centralization. But the benefits of church efficiency were offset by other factors. The English, who were at war with France, and the Italians, who traditionally held the papacy, resented the French popes; monarchs and counts across Europe were disgruntled at the amount of tax that was going out of their realms and into the coffers of the Church (and its Florentine bankers); and local prelates and bishops disliked the loss of their autonomy. In England and the German states in particular local authorities, both secular and clerical, simply refused to comply with papal directives. In the early fourteenth century the emperor Lewis of Bavaria was excommunicated by Pope John XXII (who preferred his rival for the throne of emperor, and whose statements on doctrine drew accusations of heresy from eminent theologians), but most of his bishops stayed loyal to the emperor rather than the pope. With Germany, England and the Low Countries hostile to the Avignon papacy, and France and Italy generally in favour, the lines of future religious conflict were already drawn.

In 1376 Pope Gregory VI left Avignon to return to Rome. When he died two years later a huge crowd gathered outside the conclave to ensure that an Italian pope was elected. The man who was chosen, though Italian, proved to be a liability, and within a few months all but three cardinals withdrew from Rome and elected another pope, Clement VII, who promptly took himself off, once again, to Avignon. The situation remained in stalemate until in 1409 the Council of Pisa dethroned both popes and elected another. But the two existing popes refused to step down – there were now three popes and the Church was in a disastrous mess. This was eventually sorted out (though not entirely satisfactorily) at the Council of Constance in 1415, where the secular authorities dictated to the Church rather than vice versa. In a historic decision, the church council, made up of national delegates, was declared to have divine authority, and could therefore dictate to the papacy. During the fifteenth century the papacy gradually recovered its authority, and the council was pushed to one side, but national churches had shown their potential for power, and the divine aura of the papacy never recovered from the farce of the Avignon schism.

The growing power of national monarchs began to dominate late medieval Europe, but the micro-politics of towns, cities and regions also fostered disillusionment with the medieval church. Medieval towns were often enclaves within a countryside controlled by the nobility (see Chapter Seven), but in many dioceses senior church appointments remained the preserve of ancient noble families. Even wealthy urban merchants were excluded from this process, and with the Church as a major physical, political and economic (as well as spiritual) presence in every medieval town and city – in Mainz, for example, nearly one quarter of the population were clerics – the preservation of noble privilege was increasingly resented by ordinary citizens and civic leaders alike. Bishops, deans and priests began to be seen as outsiders and representatives of unwelcome authority.

The fourteenth-century schism took place against a background of war and plague that contributed to a further weakening of official church authority. The apparent helplessness of the Church in the face of the Black Death, which arrived in Europe in 1348 (between one third and a half of Europe's population died in the recurrent epidemics of bubonic, septicaemic and pulmonary plague between 1348 and 1390), lowered its status in the eyes of ordinary people and encouraged a revival of mysticism among Christian scholars, including Walter Hilton, author of *The Cloud of Unknowing*, Julian of Norwich, Catherine of Siena, Angela da Foligno, Johann Tauler and Thomas à Kempis. These believers, and their followers in movements like the *devotio moderna*, approached the mystery of God through personal contemplation and an intimate relation with their own spirituality, rather than through the vast superstructure of the Church. The Hundred Years War (1337–1453) between England and France reinforced the growing sense of national identity in western Europe, and hastened the transformation from the medieval world of Frankish overlords and Latin Christendom to a region dominated by national kings exercising control over their national churches.

The inclusiveness of medieval Christianity allowed a variety of interpretations of Christianity, so long as they did not challenge the authority of the Church. Visionaries, street-corner prophets and seers were largely left alone, provided they remained powerless. But Christianity had always contained a large number of adherents who believed a Christian life should be lived in imitation of Christ's life on earth – without worldly goods, in poverty and purity. The medieval monastic tradition brought this radical tendency within the Catholic establishment, but every so often it burst into the open.

The extraordinary fame of St Francis was both evidence of the desire for simple spirituality and an inspiration for those who sought a different kind of Christianity. Francis was the son of a twelfth-century Italian merchant, who turned his back on wealth and spent his life caring for the sick and preaching a message of charity and devotion. He came close to being excommunicated but he had no desire to challenge the authority of the Church; instead he founded an order of monks who, rather than shutting themselves away from the world, would work among the people.

Stories of the life of St Francis were retold throughout western Christendom, where his conscious re-creation of the life of Christ on earth, including the appearance of stigmata (marks on his body depicting the wounds that Christ suffered on the cross) and paintings of the infant saint in a manger, helped to shift the emphasis of Christian devotion. The influence of Francis and of the *popolani* citizens of northern Italy was felt as traditional depictions of Christ in heaven, ruling at the right hand of God, gradually gave way to images of the suffering Christ. By the fifteenth century an altarpiece painting like Rogier van der Weyden's *Descent from the Cross* showed Christ to be more like the man in the street or field than the pope on his throne.

While the example of St Francis was an emotional inspiration to ordinary Christians, intellectual inspiration, and a different challenge to the medieval church, came from another quarter. Western Christendom built its intellectual and spiritual foundation on the work of the fifth-century church father, St Augustine. But much of the practice of the medieval church flew in the face of Augustinian theology. While Augustine had shown how a Christian life of humility and fear could unite all believers, saints and sinners alike, neither the late medieval church nor many of its adherents could quite accept their own powerlessness in the face of God. Although it was never openly stated, prayers were said in order to change the mind of God, either directly or by asking saints in heaven to petition Him on someone's behalf. And while the invention of purgatory skipped round Augustine's assertion that human behaviour was irrelevant to God's plans for the salvation and damnation of human souls, everyone understood that they were trying, through Masses, gifts and prayers, to alter the fate of the dead by influencing God. The Church's role in this was central, since it was only through priests that Masses could be said, chapels consecrated, gifts accepted and indulgences bought. While the practice of western Christianity diverged from Augustine's principles, so too did its intellectual basis. In the twelfth century the Bible, the works of St Augustine, and the newly discovered Justinian Code, together with those few works by Aristotle, Plato and later Platonist philosophers that were available in Latin, formed the basis of the new university schools of logic, theology and law. The first univer-sities were established in the twelfth century in Italy, France and England, from where, by 1500, they had spread across Europe. The universities outside the original French-Italian-English core were modelled on the institutions that their founders had attended, and so European higher education evolved as a uniform international system. The study of law was of particular concern to clerical scholars, as the Church was trying to extend its legal jurisdiction into the secular world – against the wishes of kings, princes and emperors.

The universities were church institutions whose teachers and students were clerics, training either for pastoral ministry or for further study in monasteries. The rules were strict: Cardinal Robert de Courçon decreed that at Paris University, 'We decide concerning the theologians, that no one shall lecture at Paris before he is thirty-five years old, and not unless he has studied at least eight years and has heard the books faithfully in the schools.' The church authorities kept a strict watch on the teachings, particularly of theology. In 1241 Odo, the chancellor of Paris University, wrote a list of the 'errors' being taught there, including such things as 'That the bad angel [i.e. the Devil] was bad from his very creation, and never was anything but bad. We condemn this error, for we firmly believe that he was created good, and afterward through sinning he became bad.' But a contemporary account shows that the atmosphere among the students was anything but reverential: 'Almost all the students at Paris, foreigners and natives, did absolutely nothing except learn or hear something new . . . Very few studied for their own edification or that of others. They wrangled and disputed not merely about the various sects or about some discussions; but the differences between countries also caused dissensions, hatreds and virulent animosi-ties among them' (Odo and Jacques de Vitry, quoted in Cantor).

In France, William of Champeaux (c. 1100) and his pupil Peter Abelard (1079–1142) had begun to explore ways in which classical systems of logic could be integrated into the Christian theology. By 1200 university studies of law and logic, including the ancient philosophers, were well established and growing in importance, and were given a new urgency by the arrival in Europe of the whole of Aristotle's surviving works in newly made Latin translations. The texts came not from Greek sources, but from Arabic scholars working in Spain. Just as the Latin Christian schoolmen were grappling with questions of morality and universality, of goodness and reason, came an entirely worked-out philosophical system covering everything from politics and government to the physical make-up of the world, from the arrangement of the cosmos to the meaning of justice, and from the essence of life to the constitution of ancient Athens. The challenge of understanding how Aristotle's work might be read in a Christian context was compounded by the fact that Arab scholars such as Ibn Sina (known in the west as Avicenna) (980–1037) and Ibn Rushd al-Qurtubi (Averroes) (1126–98) had already written learned commentaries on subjects like the separation of faith and reason, some of which accompanied the new texts. Averroes, who lived in Córdoba and Seville, showed how such concepts as the eternity of the world, the mortality of the soul and a common intellect shared by all men were derivable from Aristotle, and he also created potential heresies within Islam by arguing for the primacy of philosophy over religion in determining such matters. Not only was the fabled Aristotle, a pagan philosopher whose system had no need of an omnipotent God, suddenly present in all his glory; his most cogent and intellectually interesting interpreter was a Muslim.

The man who answered the challenge of Aristotle and Averroes most successfully was Thomas Aquinas. Like many late medieval scholars he was a truly European figure. Born in 1224 or 1225 near Naples, Thomas studied at a local university founded by the German emperor, became a member of a monastic order founded by a Spaniard and then moved to Paris and Cologne to study Greek texts with a German tutor. He later lived at Orvieto and Rome, studying Arabic texts with a Flemish scholar, before returning to Paris and then finally to his home city of Naples.

Thomas devoted his life to the establishment of a philosophy and theology that would reconcile the works of Aristotle with Christian theology, while taking account of the works of Plato and the church fathers. This was an enormous task that was to involve the production of over a hundred philosophical and theological works, including the *Summa Theologiae*. Thomas Aquinas's crucial objective was to reinstate reason as a legitimate and worthy element in human nature. St Augustine, writing in the fifth century, had thought of human nature as essentially malign and in need of constant control by human laws and civilizing customs; he did not believe that human reason had the capacity to discern the difference between good and evil, or the ability to do good; and that therefore the only route to salvation was through God's grace, which was given in ways that were beyond human comprehension.

Thomas Aquinas overturned Augustine's pessimistic views by replacing them with a comprehensive analysis of the relations between human nature, religion, reason, society and the natural world. He revived the central belief of the ancient Greek philosophers that the universe is imbued with the quality of order, and that this order has both justice and purpose to it. In this order it is possible to find reasons for the way that the universe is arranged, why society is as it is and why humans behave in particular ways. Aquinas asserted that the central order and justice in the universe was the gift of the Christian God, who was a rational, just and loving creator (and the real embodiment of Aristotle's Prime Mover, or First Cause; see Chapter Three).

What did this mean for Christians in practical terms? Aquinas said, 'The things that reason is fitted by nature to know are most clearly true.' Since both order in the universe and reason in the human mind were deliberate creations of God, it was a legitimate enterprise, indeed a Christian duty, to use the gift of reason to explore the meaning of God's creation. Aquinas did just this by explaining the order and harmony that underlay human society, politics and morality. He argued that there were limits to the powers of human reason and that the ultimate truths about, for example, the nature of God might only be attained through faith. Nevertheless his argument for the use of human reason revealed a great change in Christian theology, which he reinforced by showing that the truths attained by faith and those attained by reason are in harmony.

One unintended effect of Aquinas's work was to remove the rational study of subjects such as the natural world, politics and civil law from the arena of theology. So, while it was perfectly proper for the Church to derive its own laws based on the requirements of faith and an understanding of the scriptures, it was also legitimate for secular rulers to derive laws based on rational, not theological, principles. The rational faculties they were using, and the order they were trying to bring about, were both aspects of God's rational plan for the world he had created.

Thomas's attempt to integrate ancient Greek rationalism with Christian theology was resisted by other scholars such as St Bernard, and the philosophers Johannes Duns Scotus and William of Ockham (who were both

Franciscans). Disputes centred on whether faith should ever be supported by reason, and the so-called nominalists' objections to the existence of Plato's forms and Aristotle's essences. Whatever their detailed content, these disputes signalled both the establishment of rationalism in the intellectual life of Europe, and an element of resistance to it. By 1300 there were lively debates among scholars about Aristotle's denial of Plato's ideals, the role of will in determining action, the real meaning of syllogisms, atomism versus substances comprising qualities, and so on. Thomas's work showed how a world of learning might exist quite separately from the Church, thereby opening the way for the development of secular studies of all areas of human life. And though his intellectual opponents disagreed with him, they were using their individual wits to argue their case. Augustinian Christianity could no longer be taken for granted, and the communal mentality of western Christendom began to be transformed into a sea of individual minds, each seeing the world in its own way.

If the rise of national identities, the fallibility of the papacy and the growing importance of the individual mind were long-term, slow-burning tendencies in late medieval Europe, the late fifteenth century saw their realization in a dramatic acceleration of change. The commercial and artistic revolution in northern Italy was accompanied, in about 1450, by the development of a new system of movable type printing by Johannes Gutenberg in Mainz, which made the setting and printing of multiple copies of posters, documents and books a comparatively simple matter.

In 1453 Ottoman armies had finally taken Constantinople and then pushed on across the Balkans, reaching as far as the walls of Vienna – the centre of the eastern church had fallen and the home of the papacy was itself vulnerable. But in 1460 the papacy was unexpectedly enriched when a source of alum, an essential mineral in dyeing textiles, was discovered near Rome. Revenues from alum, as well as from church taxes and land-holdings, made the papacy wealthy and, along with other Italian Renaissance princes, inclined to extravagance. A succession of popes seemed unwilling to choose between secular glory and spiritual leadership; a low point was reached in the reign of Alexander VI, who had numerous mistresses and openly promoted the careers of his many children, including Cesare and Lucrezia Borgia.

The increasing power of the western nations made itself decisively felt when France invaded Italy in 1494, only to be followed by the armies of the empire and Spain. The popes were forced to make political alliances

– and therefore political enemies – while Pope Julius II strapped on armour to lead his armies into battle against the French. The Reformation was not caused solely by hatred of the pope, but their extravagance and military posturing made them, in the eyes of devout Christians, unsympathetic figures. Once again reverence towards the symbol of the papal office was being subtly transformed into judgement of the individual popes.

While Italian popes might provoke hostility, Italy itself was a magnet for scholars, merchants, artists and princes from all over Europe. Dazzled by the sumptuous luxury of Italian courts and by the quality of artistic work, Europeans also caught the Italian fever for all things classical. Refugees from the fall of Constantinople and some determined digging were bringing a flood of texts from ancient Greece and Rome. The narrow concentration on the writings of the Latin church fathers, together with Aristotle and Plato, was swept away under a tide of new discoveries and translations. Scholars began to see the classical world as a boundless treasure chest of philosophies and viewpoints that they could discuss and interpret, rather than a monolithic entity whose dictates they must follow.

The most influential of the post-Renaissance scholars was a Dutchman named Desiderius Erasmus. A truly European citizen, having lived in the Low Countries, Cambrai, Paris, London, Italy, Cambridge, Basle and Louvain, Erasmus became widely known in 1500 with the publication of *Adages*, an entertaining collection of classical proverbs, and became internationally famous when *The Praise of Folly*, a devastating and witty attack on corruption in society and the Church, was published in 1509. In 1516 Erasmus produced the New Testament in its original Greek, with his own Latin translation alongside – even the official Latin scriptures had become open to examination by a trained scholar. Erasmus became famous throughout Europe because his work coincided with the rapid spread of printing, and because literate Europeans used Latin as their lingua franca. His work gives us an idea of the atmosphere of the times, as does the scathing wit of his near-contemporary François Rabelais. Both ridiculed the abuses of priests as Boccaccio had done 200 years before, both were extraordinarily popular (over 100 editions of *Pantagruel and Gargantua* had appeared by 1600), but both remained committed Catholics.

A growing sense of national identity and power; an incipient tendency towards personal devotion; the development of secular learning and classically inspired humanism; the introduction of printing; the growth of an urban commercial culture, together with an embryonic distrust of the institutions of the Church at both local civic and universal papal levels, provide some of the background to the cataclysmic events of the first decades of the sixteenth century. But the crucial episode that brought about the division of western Christianity into rival churches was the provision of a viable alternative to the official Catholic church. None of the Church's critics (with a few minor exceptions) had both advocated and provided an alternative structure within which dissenters could worship. The two men who created the lasting division of western Christianity, Martin Luther and John Calvin, raged against the Catholic church, but they also provided Christians with another institution in which to practise their faith.

The events began in Rome, the centre of western Christendom. In 1506 Pope Julius II made the astonishing decision to demolish St Peter's Basilica, one of the largest and most revered churches in Latin Christendom, sited, according to legend, over the grave of the apostle. Julius's plan was to replace the fourth-century basilica with a building that would embody the classical forms being used to such elevating effect elsewhere in Italy. The new church would sweep away the 1,000-year-old arrangement of the congregation in an oblong nave, facing east towards the altar, in favour of a gigantic square structure with a symmetrical crossing in the centre. The devout concentration of the faithful on the single focus of the high altar would be replaced by a diffusion of loci and an awareness of one's surroundings and of fellow worshippers. This was a deliberate turning-away from the medieval church, both as a building and as the embodiment of the way of being Christian. Julius II also commissioned Michelangelo to paint the ceiling of the Sistine Chapel, while Raphael began work on a series of murals for the papal apartments, including *The School of Athens* with its idealized portraits of the great Greek thinkers such as Plato and Aristotle.

Into this dazzling centre of political power, conspicuous wealth, egotism and cultural patronage came, in 1509, Martin Luther; an Augustinian monk, ordained priest and teacher of theology at the recently established University of Wittenberg in Saxony. The luxuriance of the churches, the affluence and dissipation of the lives of the Vatican officials and the cardinals, the atmosphere of intrigue and backbiting, of politics and personal ambition, offended Luther's sense of Christianity as a deeply spiritual faith. He returned to Saxony determined to continue to develop his own theology, based on piety and close study of the scriptures.

The German-speaking world was then a collection of principalities, duchies, city-states and bishoprics that together comprised the Holy Roman empire. By tradition, the rulers of these states elected one of their number to be emperor, though in practice the imperial crown had become the hereditary possession of the Austrian Habsburg family – Maximilian, emperor from 1493, was to pass the crown to his grandson Charles V in 1519. The relations between the emperor and the states within the empire were never strictly codified, so that the wishes of the emperor were brought about by political persuasion or, in the last resort, by force. This informal arrangement had kept the empire together in a loose confederation for 500 years.

In 1517 Pope Leo X decided to fund his predecessor's plans for the rebuilding of St Peter's through the sale of indulgences. In January the Dominican monk Johann Tetzel was appointed agent in the province of Magdeburg, and in April he reached the borders of Saxony. Martin Luther was infuriated by this method of frightening poor people into giving money to the extravagantly wealthy pope and his cardinals, but Luther also used his theological understanding to question the authority of the pope. He wrote to Cardinal Albrecht von Brandenburg, Archbishop of Mainz, protesting at the false claims being made by Tetzel and others.

Monks and priests, acting with the special authority of the pope, told Christians that buying an indulgence – a kind of written certificate – would help shorten their time in purgatory and lift the burden of their sins. This, from Luther's viewpoint, was both denying the message of Christianity and heretically assuming God-like powers. Augustine had taught that only God had the power to release souls from the burden of sin, that repentance was a continuous and unremitting process, and that sinners, far from buying relief from the just punishment of God, should seek further punishment as a mark of their contrition. Luther said that the pope should sell St Peter's rather than build a new church 'on the flesh and bones of his flock'. In October 1517 Luther posted a copy of his 95 theses, or arguments against indulgences, on the door of the church at Wittenberg, and the following month they were printed and distributed to the public. In December 1517 Cardinal Albrecht forwarded Luther's theses to the authorities in Rome, together with his own denunciation of their content. The stage was set for a little local difficulty, involving a not-very-important theologian, to become the focus of discontent within western Christianity.

Luther was immediately at the centre of a three-way power struggle. In 1518 the pope asked his legate to demand a recantation, or order

Luther to be arrested and brought to Rome. But the pope's confidence in his authority over a citizen of Saxony, even if he was a member of a holy order, was misplaced. Luther had been assiduous in informing, and seeking advice from, Frederick, the ruler of Saxony, who had followed events closely. Frederick declined to arrest Luther or banish him from Saxony. By now the emperor Maximilian had condemned Luther as a heretic, but Frederick held firm – Luther was secure so long as he stayed in Saxony. The most astonishing aspect of this period is the speed with which events followed on from each other, and the rapidity of the spread of Luther's writings and ideas. By now convinced of the evil nature of the papacy, Luther produced a stream of pamphlets, such as *The Babylonish Captivity of the Church* and *To the Christian Nobility of the German Nation*, attacking the pope and calling on the German princes to reform the Church. Luther found eager readers throughout Germany, as he used his passionate German nationalism to turn people against the Italian-dominated church establishment. His freedom to do and write what he pleased made the Church look impotent as well as corrupt and heretical. In October 1520 the new emperor Charles V travelled to Saxony to persuade Frederick to surrender Luther, but Frederick again refused to budge. Pope Leo X immediately sent an edict threatening Luther with excommunication. At nine o'clock on the morning of 10 December 1520 a large crowd of students and teachers from the university made a bonfire, on to which they threw the papal edict. On 3 January 1521 Luther was excommunicated; he was then free of all Roman authority.

By 1521, when the imperial council, or diet, was held at the town of Worms, Luther's fame had spread across Europe. His status was such that the emperor summoned him to the council with a promise of safe passage. But it became clear that Charles V was determined to expel him from the empire, and after his appearance at Worms, Luther's supporters spirited him away to Wartburg castle near Eisenach, where he lived in seclusion for a year, translating the Bible into German. The emperor had held the papal line and endeavoured to impose his authority on the German states but the religious unity of the empire was, in reality, fragmenting before his eyes.

The German states met again at Nuremberg in 1522, by which time the dissenting states had formed a group which pushed through a measure calling for a free Christian council. When they met again at Speyer in 1529 the mood was more strongly in favour of Rome, but a minority of states published a protest (hence the term 'Protestants') that reasserted the unanimous decision of Nuremberg that allowed religious matters to rest between an individual and God. The confusion of edicts and recesses between the Catholic and Protestant parts of the empire was finally resolved in 1555 with the peace of Augsburg. The declaration *cuius regio, eius religio* – 'the religion of the ruler shall be the religion of the people' – averted further splits in the empire. But by then Europe was irredeemably divided between Catholic and Protestant states – with some, like France and Scotland, being a difficult mixture of the two.

What was Luther's message to the people of Germany and the rest of northern Europe? Although fiercely opposed to the extravagant wealth and acquisitiveness of the Roman church, Luther was no progressive. Instead he saw the excesses of the Church in Rome as a despicable modern trend and wanted a return to the simple piety of the past – the early Christian church was his ideal. Luther's anger at the leadership of the Catholic church sprang from a profound disagreement about the nature of humanity's relationship with God. Luther was an Augustinian and held that humanity has no way of knowing or influencing the will of God. His choice of who is to be saved and who is to be damned will not be altered by the feeble attempts of humans to behave better. The task of humans is not to discern a better way but to suffer and live in fear of God. Luther took Augustine's message to mean that while salvation had already been ordained, the devout Christian could take his own utter faith as a sign that he might be saved. Intimations of salvation came not through buying indulgences, or making gifts, or even performing good works or obeying church law, but through faith and faith alone.

The political culture of Germany, together with the development of printing, allowed Lutheranism to flourish; but how did Luther's theology translate into Christian practice, and, politics apart, why was it so attractive to so many German and north European people? Luther was a lightning rod for the spiritual desires of millions of western Christians. His need for a deep relationship with the Christian faith and for hope of salvation echoed the hopes and fears of half a continent. The Catholic church still provided both spiritual experience and a route to salvation for many, but for many others it did not. The community of faith on which the Church had been built had been undermined. But Luther then provided an alternative Church of Christ which offered to fulfil the needs of devout, dissenting Christians. He wrote prayers and hymns for the reformed church, gave orders of service and provided a new administrative and physical structure. The position of the priest, both physically and spiritually, was completely altered, and the meaning of the Mass was changed from the notion of a holy sacrifice conducted by a special person (the priest) to a piece of communication from God to the faithful. The scriptures said simply, 'This is my body . . . this is my blood.' Everyone could partake of this, with the service being conducted by a minister, or servant of the congregation. The high marble altars, half-hidden behind rood screens, were replaced by wooden tables in clear view, and ministers preached from the chancel steps, or from pulpits in the body of the church.

A striking innovation of Luther's church was the use of the German language. Luther's own translation of the Bible became widely available, allowing thousands of literate Germans to read the sacred scriptures for themselves. The delight and wonder experienced by Christians reading Bible stories for the first time drew them to Luther's doctrines, while the service and hymns, also in German, gave the people ownership of their church and forged an alliance between incipient national identity and religious faith. But Luther also related to ordinary Christians by dealing with their age-old concerns about salvation, and their ever-present fears of judgement and damnation. Intensify your faith, he told them, and this will be a sign that you are worthy of salvation. It was a message that many were glad to embrace.

While Luther, aided by new methods of printing, provided the spark and the facility for the division of western Christianity, John Calvin, the other major figure of the Reformation, took a subtly different view of Christian life. Born and educated in France, Calvin became a Protestant in 1533 and was forced to flee to Switzerland. After some toings and froings, he set up a church in the independent city of Geneva that effectively governed the city from 1541 to the end of his life in 1564. Calvin's major work, *The Institutes of Christian Religion,* spoke of the worthlessness of humanity, the universal presence of sinfulness, and predestination: 'For they are not all created with a similar destiny; but eternal life is foreordained for some, and eternal damnation for others. Every man, therefore, being created for one or the other of these ends, we say, he is predestined either to [eternal] life or death.' Those who were to be saved were known (in an echo of Pelagius, see Chapter Four) as the Elect, and, while no one could ever know who the Elect were, believers could look for certain signs that they were deserving of membership, and therefore of salvation. While Luther said that faith alone was a sign of salvation, Calvin believed that the way that you lived your life was evidence of your membership of the Elect.

Calvin's governorship of the city of Geneva enabled him to demonstrate how a Christian life should be lived. The Calvinists wanted nothing from the world and so gave up all entertainment and pleasure; singing, dancing, vivacity, story-books, coloured clothes and alcohol were put away. Instead devotion, work, upright conduct, charity, restraint and thrift were to be the aims of those we have come to know as Puritans. The appearance of sober piety was as important as the actuality – the Elect were to demonstrate to others how life should be lived. Calvinism was a peculiar interpretation of predestination but it gave its members inspiration to live spiritually fulfilled and active lives. It also provided a community of faith in a world of growing individuality.

Unlike Luther, Calvin did not advocate a return to medieval piety; instead he promoted the idea of showing yourself suitable for salvation through work. By the sixteenth century the growing bourgeois class was beginning to dominate many of the cities of the European core. In Italy the mercantile nobility ruled the cities, but in Ulm, Antwerp, Mainz, Utrecht, Lyons and Geneva this did not happen – the power of the nobility was in the countryside and the towns were (within limits) left to their own devices. Educated, literate traders, artisans, lawyers, administrators, clerks, shippers, bankers and teachers did not have wealth to individually control their cities, but collectively they represented the most powerful group. Just as Christianity first flourished among the middle classes of the eastern Mediterranean, Calvinism had its greatest appeal to the bourgeoisie of European cities. Disenchanted with the empty rituals of the Catholic church, suspicious of authority, self-sufficient and rational, the bourgeoisie of Geneva, Amsterdam and Hamburg relished the virtues that Calvin promoted. They were hard-working, pious and undemonstrative people, and they believed in contributing to their communities. Calvinism did not condemn them for making money. If they worked hard and lived by the proper rules, they could become as rich as Croesus and still retain their Christian virtue; indeed, it was their Christian duty to work hard and make money.

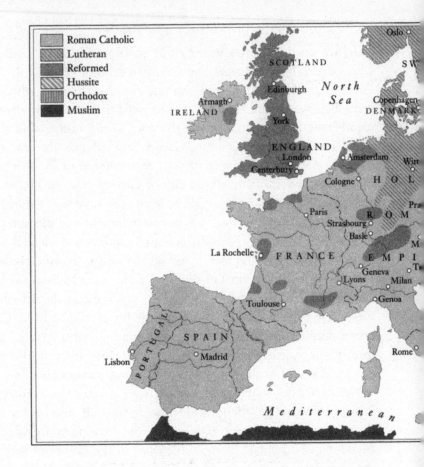

The Reformation is often interpreted as a liberation from the tight grip of the Roman church but in many ways the opposite was true. In the late medieval church, criticism and ridicule were tolerated, as were mystics, magicians, visionaries and all manner of strange self-proclaimed street-corner prophets. But the Church had become too lax and too liberal for many believers and the severe discipline of the Lutherans, Calvinists, Presbyterians and Puritans was a deliberate correction. In Calvin's Geneva, fornication, gluttony and magical practices were punished by imprisonment, while criticism of the Calvinist doctrine was a capital offence.

Like Luther, Calvin was an indefatigable organizer. As well as developing a system of theocratic government in Geneva, and publishing a series of writings that expounded his theology, he set up the Collège de Génève to educate and train priests. The Calvinist systematic doctrine and organization, together with a continual supply of preachers, thereby spread outwards from Geneva across the north of Europe. The Huguenots in France, the northern Dutch United provinces, and parts

The religious divide in Europe
following the Reformation.

of Scotland became, along with Switzerland, the most deeply Calvinist communities. But Calvinism, together with Lutheranism, had a strong influence on the waves of religious dissenters who first settled North America in the seventeenth century – and who set the tone for the religious and political landscape of the future United States.

The historic connection between the spread of Calvinism, along with the more moderate Anglican Protestantism, and the flourishing of capitalism has long been of interest to historians. While the Catholic countries of the south – principally Italy and Spain – went into something of a decline in the seventeenth century, the countries of the Protestant north, in particular England and the Netherlands, began a long period of economic ascendancy based on their embrace of the capitalist system. Eminent historians such as R. W. Tawney and Max Weber have taken Calvin at his word and seen a direct causal link between sanctification and worldly success, and therefore Protestantism and capitalism, with the former giving rise the latter. But it is just as likely that the simple piety of the Lutherans and Calvinists was an emotional response to the growing commercialization of urban life. The intensity of devotion of Protestantism was perhaps not a corollary for money-making and individualism but a corrective to it. We take the co-existence of frugal piety and the Calvinist approval of worldly success to be a rational contradiction, or even hypocrisy; but these apparently opposing ideals provide an emotional balance.

We have returned to the paradoxes set out at the beginning of this chapter, and the historical story may have shown us that we have been making the wrong kinds of connections. Perhaps the key to the Reformation does not lie in our own rationalization of the motives of the principal actors and meanings of the events, but in the emotional lives and spiritual needs of the people of western Christendom. If the Reformation tells us anything, it is that humans live through their emotional needs, not through rational consistency. The Catholic church, rather than offering a spiritual alternative to the commercial materialism, seemed, through its acquisitiveness and love of luxury, to have surrendered to the commercialization of the world. Luther and Calvin made it possible for urban citizens in particular to live spiritual lives in the midst of a world ruled by money.

The Catholic church reacted to the austere piety of Luther and Calvin by following suit. The Counter-Reformation was an attempt by the Church to fight the spread of Protestantism, but it did this by stealing its opponents' clothes. At the Council of Trent, held in 1545–47, 1551–52 and 1562–63, the Catholic church shed its former liberalism and instigated a period of severe discipline. The Inquisition and the order of Jesuits became the controllers of the Catholic faithful, as unorthodox beliefs, visionaries and prophets were persecuted into oblivion and ordinary Catholics lived in real fear of accusations of heresy.

The apparent paradoxes of the Reformation might best be seen as a series of emotional responses, but some paradoxes are contained within Protestantism itself. Luther hated the way that Aristotle had been brought into Christian theology, yet Calvin was a classical scholar, whose first published work was a commentary on Seneca's *De Clementia* ('On Goodness'). Though Luther's Reformation was born out of his distaste for rationalism, and based utterly on faith rather than reason, Protestantism did find ways to accommodate the growing passion for classical scholarship and rational enquiry (see Chapter Ten). The urban origins of the new faith drove this need for an accommodation with rationalism, while also severely weakening Christianity's link with the natural world. Christian theology had always placed humans above the rest of creation, but the Reformation went further and forged a complete separation. Customs of necromancy, alchemy and healing that were tolerated in the old faith became suspect and then positively dangerous – the hunting-out and burning of witches was overwhelmingly a Protestant obsession.

Perhaps the strongest challenge to the old Christian ways came through the growing sense of people existing as individuals, with individual needs, hopes and desires, rather than as elements contributing to a communal society. The Reformation both contributed to and struggled against this tendency – another example of a rational contradiction striking an emotional balance. Luther provided a community of faith, based on small groups of people coming together in humble surroundings – just as he imagined the early Christians had done. Priests were no more touched by the divine than other members of their congregation; they were simply appointed to serve the faith community. But Lutheranism, through his translation of the Bible, and through his theology, put the faithful directly in touch with God. The act of reading, though communal at first, had the potential to give every person entry to a private, personal world, while the absence of priests put the emphasis on the individual mind as the arena for issues of faith. A succession of Protestant sects – Shakers, Mennonites, Bruderhof, Society of Friends (or Quakers), Plymouth Brethren – attempted to preserve or promote communality in a world whose individualism the Reformation had helped to create.

The Protestant community of faith was influential in other ways. In contrast to the Catholic cascade of legitimate authority from on high (beginning ultimately with God), the Calvinist church was organized as a concentric series of elected bodies – consistories, synods, presbyteries and colloquys, leading to regional and national synods. The removal of the intermediary church left the believer face to face with God, but it also brought an alteration in the individual Christian's view of both religious and political authority. The participation of the community in the governance of their church answered an age-old human requirement that would be transferred to the political arena. It is no coincidence that in both the Netherlands and North America Calvinism was intertwined with the desire for political self-determination.

If the Reformation was driven by the need for spirituality in an increasingly commercial world, then what was the response of artists? How would the painters, sculptors and architects, who had been elevated from anonymous artisans to cultural celebrities, adapt to this new world? In Catholic Europe the patronage of the rich and powerful continued, and Italian-style art was employed to glorify its patrons, but without the central artistic impulse of the fifteenth century. The baroque art that began in the seventeenth century appears overblown to our modern eyes – ostentatious and fancy, it seems to show off the skills of the artist without achieving an artistic quality, and in a world where money was the passport to social success, art was used by the wealthy to separate themselves from the common herd. But there are notable exceptions; Caravaggio, Velázquez and others fought against the cloying idealizations of beauty that surrounded them.

The Reformation meant that Protestants had less need of 'art' as a separate entity in their lives; as with medieval Christians, their religion and its associated community of faith answered many of the needs that art attempts to satisfy. In the Protestant lands, church authorities regarded paintings or statues of saints as idolatrous. Painters had to fall back on book illustration and portraits to make a living. Painting as a native craft almost died out in large parts of Germany and England. In the Netherlands, though, painting survived and flourished. The reputation of Flemish painters exceeded even the Italian masters when it came to representations of nature. The exquisite skill of Jan van Eyck, Hugo van der Goes and Rogier van der Weyden in creating surface effects made them famous throughout Europe and was continued by later Flemish painters. When religious paintings were prohibited, painters such as Peter Breughel and Frans Hals specialized in 'natural' scenes and in individual and group portraits. Dutch burghers were particularly keen on depictions of the societies and clubs that underpinned their society, and Hals, and later Rembrandt, were able to depict their combination of individual identity and group purpose – see Hals's *St George Militia Company* and Rembrandt's *Nightwatch*. Other Dutch artists specialized in landscape painting, an art form that arose as a compensation for the separation of urban citizens from the natural world.

Portraiture was a necessary source of income for Flemish artists, but also a sign of individual self-regard. English, German and Dutch merchants joined Italian princes and Spanish kings in commissioning portraits by famous artists. As in fifteenth-century Italy, those that simply served the needs of the patron were unremarkable, but Holbein,

Velázquez, Hals and, on occasion, Rubens brought out the ability of the human figure and face to convey emotional depth, mystery and empathy. But one painter took the art of portraiture to another level. Rembrandt van Rijn (1606–69) was not a fashionable artist and struggled to make a living in Amsterdam. But if others did not commission his skills, Rembrandt looked in another direction – to himself. His series of self-portraits is both an eloquent autobiography and a moving response to an indifferent world. Rembrandt had no need to flatter or beautify his sitter, nor to hurry his task. Instead he sought to convey some sense of the inner world of the mind through the portrayal of its outward manifestation, the human face. As a contemplative and apparently troubled soul, turning away from the world to find both inspiration and subject within itself, Rembrandt was the harbinger of a new kind of western artist.

If painting struggled to find a role outside the Netherlands, literature began to take its place. The impact of printing meant that any well-heeled nobleman could pen a book of poetry or an account of his travels, and circulate copies to his friends, acquaintances and those he wished to influence. In the sixteenth century Europe was awash with books of adventures – a multitude of individuals, each trying to make their voice heard above the crowd. And just as the Flemish artists were producing art which replaced religious subject matter with artistic spirituality and sensibility, so too writers were creating literature without God. Dante, Boccaccio, Chaucer and Rabelais all set their work in a religious world, but Cervantes and Shakespeare most definitely did not – Shakespeare's most peculiar quality is the paucity of religious themes or references in his work – while Michel de Montaigne looked at the world only through his own eyes. Western Europe was still drenched with Christianity, but these were intimations of another world to come. In the Reformation the medieval community gave way to the individual standing before God; before long the central meaning of western civilization would shift once again, as the Christian in intimate relation with God became the rational individual in need of a rational society.

KINGS, ARMIES AND NATIONS

The Rise of the Military State

WHEN, in 1494, King Charles VIII of France crossed the Alps with 30,000 men to claim the Kingdom of Naples, he came as a medieval prince seeking the return of his personal property. But his actions and, just as important, his methods signalled the beginning of the end of the medieval world. By the spring of 1494 Charles's overland advance reached the port of La Spezia where, just shipped in from France, were 40 brand-new cannon. Crude forms of static cannon had been around in Europe for a century or more (the earliest record is a drawing from 1326), but Charles's pieces were mobile, accurate and immensely powerful. The walls of the castle of Firizzano were reduced to rubble, warning against any resistance by towns with apparently secure medieval walls – Florence, for example, surrendered without a fight. Only the Neopolitan fortress of San Giovanni resisted and that was taken in just eight hours, where previously it had withstood a siege for seven years. High walls were not only useless; they made collapse more likely if cannon were fired at the base. Suddenly everyone, Leonardo and Michelangelo included, was interested in the chemistry of gunpowder and the trajectory of cannon balls.

Charles's dominance of Italy was short-lived because others, including Spain and the Austrians, who also had cannon, joined forces against him, and because they could put equally large armies in the field. But the medieval system, where a prince or duke could rule a personal fiefdom based on the loyalty of a few followers and the protection of castle walls, and where towns could exist as impregnable self-contained worlds, was gone. What would be put in its place?

The nations of Europe that began to emerge out of the medieval world had their roots in the past, but were a new type of institution. The medieval prince, king or emperor based his right to rule on his inheritance – of property, land, possessions and, to a degree, the loyalty of his fellow nobles. Kings could survive without being controllers of the territories of their kingdoms – for centuries the French kings had to contend with nobles who were often more powerful and controlled more territory than the monarchs; barons had rights that pre-dated and, in their view, superseded the monarchy. The English kings had an easier time, since the English nobility had been granted lands by the monarch in the aftermath of 1066. Nevertheless, kings and queens of England managed only intermittently to dominate the barons of their courts.

The common culture of the Frankish rulers of late medieval Europe allowed a plethora of intermarriages between ruling families, and these led to a curious patchwork of inheritances, which in turn led to conflicts. Marriages between their offspring were deemed advantageous to the great families, but they gave birth to hereditary disputes. In 1337, for example, Edward III of England claimed the French throne through his mother's inheritance. The result was a series of wars lasting over a century – later called the Hundred Years War. Each camp persuaded the nobility of their realm to lend support but, Shakespeare's accounts notwithstanding, we should not imagine that national honour or even national strategic interest was at stake – the Plantagenet family simply wanted their rightful possessions.

This bloody, futile conflict challenged the medieval idea of war as a chivalrous and honourable undertaking. The Black Prince, the epitome of medieval chivalry, murdered 3,000 of the citizens of Limoges, including women and children who kneeled down before him and begged for mercy. At Agincourt in 1415 the heavily armoured Frankish cavalry that had for 300 years swept all before it was suddenly ineffective as the lowly English yeoman with his longbow cut down the French nobility like grass. After the battle Henry, the English king, ordered his soldiers to murder all their prisoners by cutting their throats, and at the siege of Rouen in 1418–19 he let 12,000 French women and children starve and freeze to death beneath the city walls, trapped by the besieging army. These were his subjects but, for the besieged garrison, they were simply more mouths to feed, so they were left to die.

The Hundred Years War was a typical medieval conflict between two dynasties. And while the slaughter in particular instances was horrific, the war was episodic, localized and indecisive, and remained an internal dispute between groups of knights who were related in culture, blood and, above all, religion. Wars between princes in medieval Europe were moderated by the abilities of the combatants to raise troops, but also by the influence of the universal Church. Medieval popes used their political power to dissuade their spiritual subjects from going to war. The prospect of fellow Christians killing each other in order to gain control over what was, after all, God's earth did not please the universal Church.

Only 40 years separate the end of the Hundred Years War from Charles's invasion of Italy, yet the differences were stark. The destructive power of cannon meant the end of the city-state and, with a few notable exceptions, of the autonomous town. Security for a ruler suddenly meant not high stone walls, but the control of territory. Those princes who could put enough men in the field to protect a given area would survive, those who could not would fall. Another 25 years on from Charles's devastating progress through Italy, and western Christianity was irretrievably divided. The universal Church was no longer a restraint on the ambitions of princes; control of territory, by getting hold of modern artillery and amassing huge numbers of troops, was all that mattered. This new prescription became a self-reinforcing fact that led to the birth of a new kind of state, and a new type of civilization.

In the fifteenth century the cities of Italy had used their extraordinary wealth (both Venice and Florence were wealthier than the kingdoms of England or France) to hire mercenaries or *condottieri*, but the new situation required ever more troops, together with hideously expensive cannon and muskets. To pay for these, the rulers of Milan, Florence, Venice, Rome and Naples had to tax their citizens or subjects more and more heavily. It is in this need for general taxation to pay for military defence, historians argue, that the European state was born. Italian cities were at the vanguard because their small populations and high proportion of taxable citizens put them in a different situation from the feudal kingdoms of the north and west. Italian rulers were able to build up a tax-gathering system that would fund the hiring of mercenaries, because their advanced commercial organization had brought into being a whole class of educated notaries, bookkeepers and clerks – in effect a ready-made state bureaucracy. And once this bureaucracy, and what it represented, became established, its survival became more important to the functioning of the city-state, the dukedom, the principality or the kingdom than the person of the ruler. But the machinery of tax-gathering, administration and disposal, combined with military planning, became more than just the essential spine of the community that it served; the 'state', as it came to be known, became an omnipotent and omnipresent yet somehow indefinable entity that, for good or ill, dominated the lives of its subjects and citizens.

Right from the beginning, different types of states – empires, kingdoms, individual city-states and federations – co-existed in Europe, but from our present viewpoint, it seems that the most successful were those that married changes in the nature of the state to innovations in military technology. Niccolò Machiavelli was one of the first people to see the need for change. The legitimacy of rulers in Italian cities had long been based on a mixture of dynastic claims, popular support, overwhelming wealth and military force. But as the state began to take control of the apparatus of government, the ruler needed a new kind of legitimacy. If he was no longer the father of his people, nor the knight in shining armour leading them into battle, nor the feudal lord, then what was he? Machiavelli's answer, given most persuasively in *The Prince*, was that the ruler must be the servant of the state. This did not mean that the ruler should somehow be subservient, but that, rather than following his personal preferences and instincts, he should at all times consider what was best for the state. *The Prince* became notorious for its amorality – Machiavelli writes, for example, of 'cruelty used well' and 'cruelty used badly' – but his point was that the ruler's choices must depend on political nous, not personal morality, if he was to survive. Kings, princes, emperors and chieftains had used political cunning to grab or maintain power for centuries. The difference in the new state was that the kingdom or principality was no longer the ruler's personal possession. However powerful he might become, his main claim to legitimacy as a ruler was that he served the needs of the state better than anyone else.

The new disembodied state, with its territorial integrity and tax-gathering powers, began life in Italy, but the lessons were soon learned elsewhere. For most of the fifteenth century the English crown had been disputed between different noble families, and before that had made claims on extensive possessions in France. The Tudor dynasty of the sixteenth century achieved an effective administration and, apart from a brief adventure in France, concentrated their efforts on bringing England under their control and dominating the British Isles. Both

Henry VIII and his father were able to enter a virtuous spiral, where more efficient tax-gathering gave them greater resources, which in turn enabled them to pressure their subjects for more revenue. The amounts gathered were still small in modern terms, but the state was not then a provider of services, merely a protector.

The same process was underway in France, where, in the sixteenth century, Louis XII, Francis I and Henri II established a central administration and used the new military technology, together with tax-funded armies, to bring the independent provinces and duchies of Burgundy, Brittany and Gascony under French control. Paradoxically, a series of French defeats in Italy helped the French state to emerge, like the English, as a territorial entity. After the death of Henri II in 1559, France went through a period of dynastic squabbling, but the accession of Henri of Navarre in 1589 confirmed the parameters of the new style of French state. Although the preceding internal conflicts had been fuelled by religious divisions, on his accession Henri, the Protestant leader, converted to Catholicism, made peace with Catholic Spain, and issued the Edict of Nantes guaranteeing freedom of worship to Protestant and Catholic alike. Henri's famous phrase on his conversion, 'Paris is worth a Mass', was, in a fervently religious continent, the ultimate recognition of the new dispensation. For a ruler to gain the throne he must put the requirements of the state before his own personal religious, or any other, concerns.

A similar process had already happened in England, where Henry VIII's legacy was a divided set of offspring. His son Edward was fervently Protestant, and his daughter Mary devoutly Catholic. Their reigns were brief, leaving Elizabeth, whose claim to the throne was at the least contestable, to gain the authority to rule through her understanding of the needs of the English state. Ruthless and determined, Elizabeth was above all pragmatic in adapting herself to the requirements of her nation's situation.

While the French and English states were becoming both territorial and disembodied, the opposite was true of the other principal power in the west – the Habsburg empire. Charles V was born in 1500, inherited the Low Countries on his father's death in 1515, then the throne of Castile and Aragon in 1516, before assuming the throne of Austria and being elected Holy Roman Emperor on the death of his grandfather in 1519; he ruled until 1556, when he abdicated voluntarily, and died in 1558.

For Charles and his son Philip, this vast inheritance, which in earlier times might have been a blessing, proved little short of disastrous. With the sudden need for rulers to be able to protect the territories of their states, such a geographical scattering proved impossible to manage. Charles, who had been brought up in the Netherlands, proved a popular and sympathetic ruler of the semi-autonomous Low Countries, but his continued absence from Spain (and his obvious foreignness) created problems. But it was in the Germanic states that Charles, because of his hostility to Lutheranism, had most difficulties. After wrangling with his supposedly subject states for 30 years, he was finally forced to compromise. The Augsburg agreement of 1555 allowed each elector to choose the religion of his subjects, after which Charles (in notable contrast to Elizabeth and Henri of Navarre) abdicated in despair at his inability to protect the Catholic faith.

Charles divided his realm between the old Holy Roman Empire – direct rule over the Austrian lands and ostensible rule over the German states – and the rest, which included Spain, Naples and the Low Countries. His son Philip took on the latter portion, inheriting many of his father's difficulties. By the time Philip came to the Spanish throne in 1556 the Counter-Reformation was in full flow, and silver from Peru was flooding into the Spanish treasury. Spain suddenly assumed a central role in Europe's affairs as the dominant Catholic power and the wealthiest country, with an almost limitless supply of funds for its army and navy.

Unlike his father, Philip was not regarded with fondness by the Netherlanders. He was in effect a foreign king, who could and should have left them to run their own affairs. But Philip had travelled to the Low Countries in his youth, had become acquainted with the ruling class, and regarded the territories as his dominion. As leader of Catholic Europe, he believed he should not only stamp out Protestantism in his own realm, but bring Catholicism back to countries like England which were temporarily lost to the old faith.

In the 1550s local authorities in the various Netherlands provinces began ignoring their government's orders to persecute the growing numbers of Calvinist and Lutheran heretics. From 1560 some members of the government itself – a collection of nobles, all Catholic, representing the provinces – began to argue for religious tolerance. A deputation led by the Count of Egmont was sent to Spain in 1565 to petition the king to compromise his religious laws. This was the crucial point at which Philip could either impose his personal beliefs on his disparate realm, or decide what was best for the state that he served. Philip dreamt of a Catholic Europe, restored to its medieval unity, instead of a secure

Spain. He refused to compromise and the result was the Dutch Revolt, a bitter, bloody conflict that dragged on for decades.

In the 50 years since French cannon had battered Italy into submission, Dutch engineers had set about building defensive walls that could resist even the most powerful artillery. But Philip had plenty of silver to continue the futile and hideously expensive conflict, and when that ran out he borrowed more – bankrupting the Spanish treasury on three occasions. In 1576 the Spanish army, in protest against lack of pay, went on the rampage in the city of Antwerp, massacring 17,000 of its citizens. The conflict staggered on through Philip's long reign, drawing in troops from France and England. Philip devised a grand strategy to defeat both his Protestant foes by launching a vast Armada that would return England to its Catholic people, who would in turn aid his fight against the Dutch. This all came to nought, and after decades of struggle the Netherlands prevailed because the Spanish were fighting far from home, without allies, and because Spanish wealth was based on imports of Peruvian silver, rather than self-generated prosperity – Philip simply ran out of cash.

The Dutch Revolt showed the weakness of the patchwork Habsburg possessions, ruled by a monarch who placed his personal conscience above the needs of his state. These weaknesses were again devastatingly exposed in the cataclysm of the Thirty Years War (1618–48), which defined the future shape of the continent by acknowledging Europe as a collection of sovereign states. When Lutherans in Bohemia protested against attacks on Protestant churches, and against the assumption of the throne of Bohemia in 1617 by the Catholic Archduke Ferdinand (who became Holy Roman Emperor two years later), the Catholics and Protestants of central Europe lined up on either side. Victory for the Catholic imperial army led to an orgy of revenge in which Bohemia was forcibly made Catholic, while Protestant northern Germany was ravaged by bands of Catholic soldiers and mercenaries, including troops from the Spanish Netherlands, who were forced to live off the people they were terrorizing. In 1625 the Danish king, Christian IV, entered the war on behalf of the Protestants, with financial support from France, the Dutch republic and England. Armies once again crossed central Europe, this time including the Netherlands and the Baltic. After the Danes were forced to withdraw in 1629, the Swedish king Gustavus Adolphus came to the aid of the Lutherans. Swedish forces swept through Germany and, with Vienna under threat, forced the emperor to negotiate. At this point Cardinal Richelieu (ruler of France in Louis XIV's minority) saw an opportunity and promptly invaded Alsace and the Rhineland. While negotiations for peace dragged on, Swedish and French troops (who were Protestant and Catholic respectively) looted the Catholic heartland of Bavaria.

The strategic victor in the war was France, largely due to Richelieu's Machiavellian statecraft, though England and the Netherlands both temporarily benefited from the devastation of the German lands. Richelieu's pragmatic intervention was totally against France's avowedly Catholic stance, but made France, and the French state, the strongest in Europe. Germany's population was reduced from 21 to 13 million, its cities were in ruins; agriculture, manufacturing and trade had ceased under the devastation of nearly half a century of continual warfare, and areas of the country were completely uninhabited.

The destruction of the Thirty Years War was caused in large part by the sheer numbers of troops involved. The introduction of mobile cannon was followed by the musket, making large numbers of infantry the key to military success. But these infantrymen needed to be thoroughly trained, well-disciplined and dedicated in order to hold rank and provide steady fire in the confusion of battle. Mercenaries could not provide the dedication and part-time militias were short of training; only a professional standing army could be relied on. Central authorities had to set up more sophisticated networks for raising money to pay for full-time soldiers, equipment, ships, harbours and modern fortifications. The greater availability of funds, particularly as Europe became more prosperous, led to ever-bigger armies. The Spanish army in 1470 was around 20,000; by the 1630s it numbered 300,000. France in the 1550s had an army of 50,000, by the 1630s it was 150,000 and by 1700 300,000. In 1606 the Dutch republic had 60,000 men in paid military service. By 1644, two years into the civil war, there were 110,000 men under arms in England. In Russia compulsory levies in 1658 rendered 50,000 men to fight against Poland, and in 1667 over 100,000 Russians were conscripted.

The seventeenth century witnessed a growing spiral of centralized bureaucracy, state power, tax-raising and military expenditure. The ultimate centralization came when the monarch achieved enough power within the state to effectively embody the state in his person. But absolute rule, or the divine right of kings, was a difficult and dangerous route for monarchs to take; their right to rule as absolute monarch depended, paradoxically, on the continued consent of the state. When Louis XIV declared '*L'état, c'est moi*' he was boasting of his own supremacy but also acknowledging his place in the scheme of things.

The Stuart kings of England believed in their divine right to rule, though James I understood that this existed within the constitution of the English state. The king and the nobility in parliament could benefit from a centralized state so long as their interests were all served. It was his son Charles I's unwillingness to adapt to the needs of the state that began the long revolution, which ended in 1688 when Charles's second son James II made the same mistake of putting his personal faith above the needs of the state, and was deposed. The three major conflicts in western Europe during the seventeenth century – the Dutch Revolt, the Thirty Years War and the English Revolution – all showed that the modern state, with its territorial integrity and a pragmatic ruler willing to serve its needs, had become more powerful than the medieval conceptions of a princely realm or a disparate empire.

The emergence of the modern state caused a shift in the geopolitics of Europe, with the most adaptive states becoming more dominant; but what did this mean for the people of the continent? The most noticeable effect was the decline of the medieval town and the accompanying rise of the capital city with its national court. The need for a standing army with the ability to control the territory of the state decisively altered the relation between town and countryside. Late medieval prosperity and the power of the guilds had brought high wages and prices to the townsfolk of Europe. Industries were located in towns because of the skilled workforce and the markets, and because the countryside remained insecure. But the control of territory meant that crafts and industries such as textile production and agricultural processing could relocate to rural areas with much lower wages and rents. Rather than being manufacturers themselves, town-dwellers became investors in rural industries. Towns had lived off their tolls and taxes (river tolls were particularly lucrative), but many of these were swept away in the name of national economic efficiency. The disposal of licences for the manufacture or mining or processing of certain materials was assumed by the monarch on behalf of the state, and instead of the traditional regional monopolies being held by local merchants, they were granted nationally for specific products. Monopolies granted for the quarrying and manufacture of materials such as lead, iron ore and alum brought huge sums into national treasuries.

Financial accounting systems had been revolutionized by Florentine and Venetian bankers in the fourteenth century; in the sixteenth century this greater level of organization began to be applied to the creation of national bureaucracies – the state appeared in the form of a vast tax-gathering apparatus. While local tolls and taxes declined, towns became dominated by the agents of the monarch, there to squeeze revenue from the towns' traders. The communal medieval world of towns and villages survived in form but their content was transformed by the centralization of military and political power in capital cities. Power, wealth and status all went hand in hand, and so the nobility, the merchants and the socially ambitious gravitated away from the regional centres and towards the courts. Madrid, Vienna, Paris and London outgrew their provincial rivals by factors of five or ten as the wealth of the kingdoms rubbed up against the political power.

In the late medieval world the power of money had been combined with the intricate and extensive webs of clan and family. The patres-familias of Renaissance Italy used marriage and political cunning to gain wealth and to position themselves as close as possible to the centres of power, which would in turn bring more wealth and status. Money and ambition, as Shakespeare (who set so many of his plays in the gilded cauldron of Renaissance Italy) understood, turn human qualities of association, friendship and mutual support into their opposites. As the town and city-state gave way to the kingdom, power and wealth were concentrated in fewer and fewer hands; and all those who wanted a piece of the action, or a seat at the table, had to connive and manoeuvre ever more ruthlessly to be near to the centre, while the centre was ever further away from everyone else.

The effect on most of the population was a subtle but definite shift of identity, from being a citizen of a town, or an inhabitant of a village or estate, towards being the subject of a monarch. This change took centuries to come about, but the power of all institutions – church, guild, region, town, local militia, county – was gradually integrated into, and made subservient to, the nation state. Most important of all, the state assumed a monopoly of violent force within its borders. As only agents of the state could legitimately use violence against others, private armies, civic defence forces and militias could not exist except as part of a national security force authorized by the state. The people's loyalties were directed to the nation. Despite the religious pragmatism of the likes of Elizabeth I and Richelieu, national self-identity was immeasurably strengthened by the division of western Europe into Catholic and Protestant states, and the consequent founding of national churches. In the Protestant north the Church of England, the Dutch Reformed church and the Lutheran churches of Germany and Scandinavia were bastions of national identity and defence against aggression from Catholic states. Even in Catholic France and Spain, the churches were dominated by the king – the days of domineering popes upbraiding emperors and princes were gone. The European subjects no longer identified with their locality and their universal religion; instead the nation, with its own church, became the community to which one belonged, in a world in which only the state, the family and the individual were deemed legitimate.

The overwhelming purpose of the state was to be a tax-gathering apparatus to fund the increasing costs of war. When we ask why these states went to war, we need to understand that their existence depended on their military function. Their legitimacy came from the need to protect their people from outside invasion and internal rebellion (a function they took over from barons, civic militias and city walls), and continual warfare was the best justification for their existence. This was not just a theoretical matter – people would not stump up taxes unless they thought there was a real emergency. The consequence was that states found it desirable to go to war in order to create the conditions from which they protected their citizens. Wars generally ceased not because of ultimate defeat or victory, but because the antagonists ran out of money and had to be content with small gains, or losses.

A new phenomenon – the peace conference – was devised to cater for this situation. Once upon a time, schoolchildren in western Europe were solemnly told about the treaties of Utrecht, Westphalia, Baden, Paris, Aix-la-Chapelle, Versailles and so on, as if they were transforming events in European history; now they look more like staging posts, or holding operations, in a process of ever-greater militarization. At the peace conferences treaties were worked out in exhaustive detail, allowing all sides to come away with something. The parties then had time to gather money to rebuild their armies in preparation for the next conflict.

While the military foundation of the modern state explains its willingness to go to war, the trigger was often concerned with the playing-out of old dynastic conflicts, which plagued Europe for centuries. Family loyalties and family disputes, the oldest emotional responses in the human psyche, remained central, until the modern state finally drove them out of contention. In the meantime the states of Europe began to align and re-align themselves in a series of alliances. Once the limits of each state's territory had been secured (the first map of Europe showing national boundaries was drawn in 1630), the aim of the state subtly changed from continual aggression and the search for dominance, to protection of its own interests. It became clear that limited wars might continue to promote the legitimate role of the state among its own citizens, but any major conflict might, if lost, end up destroying the state.

By 1700, western Europe had arranged itself into a series of states, with France, England (soon to become Britain through the Act of Union with Scotland) and Austria dominant. (The power of the German states had been gravely reduced by the Thirty Years War, Italy was dominated by outside forces, principally Austria, and Spain had suffered a long decline from its dominance in the sixteenth century.) None of these states wanted war with each other, and so the concept emerged of a 'balance of power' between dominant states. The limitations of the balance of power (which nevertheless persisted for three centuries) were shown immediately by the death of the Spanish king Charles II who, unfortunately, had no children. Leopold I, Holy Roman Emperor, claimed the vacant throne for the Habsburgs, while Louis XIV claimed it for the Bourbons. Both were aware that the other European states would not allow either of them, particularly the Bourbons, to become so dominant, and it has been suggested that each would have been content to let someone else have the throne of Spain, so long as it was not their rival. But there were no other serious claimants, so a conflict which involved every state in western Europe and cost the lives of tens of thousands became inevitable. Neither side came away with their aims achieved, but the balance of power (in reality a restraint on the power of France) was maintained.

While the balance of power failed to head off major conflicts, the presence of a myriad small disputed territories enabled minor wars to continue. These territories gave the opportunity for major states to satisfy the hunger for war, and acted as bargaining chips in the subsequent peace conferences. In the 1660s, for example, Leopold of Austria tried to tempt Louis XIV of France to drop his claim to the throne of Spain by offering him the Spanish Netherlands, Franche-Comté, Naples, Sicily, Navarre and the Philippines as compensation.

States were strengthened and justified by wars, but it was not just the state that apparently benefited from a continual state or threat of war. In the period between 1500 and 1800 most people regarded war as a normal, necessary and even desirable part of life. Because it happened so regularly its causes were hardly ever investigated and it was viewed almost as an act of nature. Wars killed and maimed many people and destroyed property, but it was not clear to most people what the long-term damage was. Shocking as it may seem to us, many thought that peace was an undesirable state of affairs for any nation. Peace made a society weak and lazy, lacking 'moral fibre'; war on the other hand made society energetic, determined and focused and brought out the finer qualities in men.

Many people also saw mass armies as a good method of sweeping up society's undesirables – citizens and subjects were happy to pay a military levy if it meant getting rid of local vagrants and petty criminals. Nor was this just a feature of compulsory conscription; most of those who volunteered for military service were from the margins of society. In poorer parts of Europe, such as Scotland, Castile or Switzerland, the life of a professional soldier was an attractive proposition for a young man. At the height of the Thirty Years War around 25,000 Scots, 10 per cent of the male population of Scotland, went to Germany to fight, while in the seventeenth century almost every army in Europe had a Swiss regiment. People did not complain about wars if they cleansed society and hurt them only in their purse, while the poor and disregarded could find pay, status and purpose in a soldier's uniform.

This new world of the centralized state, with its mass armies, profoundly affected the role of the nobility. The descendants of the Frankish masters of medieval Europe found themselves in a curious limbo between the organs of state – the monarch, council and court – and the common people whose lives their forefathers used to rule. What was the role of the old baronial and ducal families who had once enjoyed almost unfettered rule over their own fiefdoms? Some continued as administrators of the state's control, but the nobility's principal function became military leadership in the new state armies. The new state military reflected both the old Frankish divisions between lords and peasants (which had been reduced in the militias of the medieval towns) and the subtle hierarchies of wealth and status that infected every part of the new commercial-minded Europe. Noble birth or the status of 'gentleman' was still taken to confer a mystical ability in the arts of war. The armies of Europe, facing mass anonymous slaughter by cannon and musket, were still in thrall to the legends of the knights of old, and the descendants of those Frankish knights were held to have military knowledge and prowess that was beyond the efforts or imagination of the common man. An unnamed sixteenth-century observer wrote: 'a nobleman well brought up is able to attain to more knowledge in the art and science military in one year than a private soldier in seven'. The armies were led by lords and manned by peasants; temporarily, at least, war enhanced the status of the socially powerful.

Nevertheless, the new state had taken away the political and military power of the nobility, and so in its place, following the example of the Italian merchant classes, the aristocracy and the gentry sought social and cultural status. Many of our notions of civilization spring from this need of certain sections of society to differentiate themselves from others in a world that had deprived them of their historic role. The nobility were more civilized not because they were wealthier, but because they possessed finer things, had better manners, were better educated and had a finer appreciation of the arts. This was due to their breeding and their nobler character. Many of their ancestors cared little for such things because they distinguished themselves by exercising real power, but this was no longer available, and so gentility and civilized values became the goal of European gentlefolk.

These were the apparent benefits of wars to different parts of the population, but what harm did they do? While wars were acceptable or even desirable for those who were removed from them, soldiering was hard, mortally dangerous work. Improved artillery, close formations and musketry led to huge casualties. The main technique of battle from the sixteenth to the eighteenth century was to use huge numbers of infantry to drive the enemy from the field, despite artillery guns that cut these massed formations of troops to ribbons from a safe distance. During the War of the Spanish Succession, 34,000 French troops were killed or captured at the battle of Blenheim in 1704, while at Malplaquet in 1709 the combined British and Austrian army of 85,000 was victorious but suffered 20,000 dead; the French army lost 12,000 men.

Armies often had to live off the land, causing resentment, fear and hostility from civilian populations. Moreover, the physical destruction caused by, for example, the Thirty Years War led to a massive decrease in trade across the whole of Europe, with huge currency devaluations and market disruptions across an area containing around one third of Europe's population. Foreign trade was drastically affected, while the demand for goods was depressed by falls in population caused by war and disease, by a crisis in agricultural production and earnings, and by the enormous increases in taxation brought in to pay for the conflicts. The war reduced imports of Spanish American silver, reducing the Spanish demand for manufactured goods. Population and production in Spanish manufacturing towns dropped by 50 to 70 per cent from 1620 to 1650; Venice, Milan, Florence, Genoa and Como lost 60 to 80 per cent of textile production from 1620 to 1660; in southern Germany industrial textile towns like Nördlingen, Augsburg and Nuremberg permanently lost their dominance of woollen and cotton manufacture.

The effects of lower wages in most of Europe eventually told on even the Flemish textile industry. In response to the long-term drop in prices, and high urban wages, the Dutch too moved their industries out of towns and became rural industrialists. Europe thereby moved into what historians call its proto-industrial phase as a continent of largely rural cottage industries. The towns became financial, administrative and trading centres, rather than manufactories.

Wars, like plagues, have mixed economic effects. The drastic reductions in population in central and eastern Europe gave opportunities for labourers to press for better rights and wages. In the eastern Germanic provinces, such as Brandenberg and east Saxony, landlords prevented this by forcing labourers to become serfs. Between 1600 and 1650 the practice of tying peasants to their masters' land spread to Poland, the Baltic provinces, Hungary, Bohemia, Moravia and Austria. Governments either colluded with landlords by passing repressive laws, or were too weak to oppose them. In Muscovy in 1649 the state and the landowning aristocracy combined to pass a code of laws that bound the peasants to the land in perpetuity, and forced them to render the landowner any service he required at any time. As well as instituting a life of unremitting toil and loss of liberties for millions of people, the introduction of serfdom ushered in centuries of economic and social stagnation, creating a divergence between eastern and western Europe.

The national and religious wars of the seventeenth century brought catastrophe to central Europe and economic hardship to the whole continent. The period from around 1650 to 1750 allowed a recovery, combined with a change of focus. While Spain had suffered for her part in the Thirty Years War, the other Atlantic powers – France, the Netherlands and, in particular, Britain – saw greater opportunities overseas than in territorial disputes in Europe. The aim of western policy became the preservation of a balance of power in Europe, allowing European nations to exploit the rest of the world. The result was that Britain prospered overseas, while greater tranquillity allowed France to prosper at home. France had long been Europe's most populous territory, with vast resources of rich agricultural land, though the size of the country had made it difficult to control from the centre, and French monarchs had to deal with strong regional power-bases. But between 1589 and 1789 France had just five monarchs, who, along with a succession of adroit finance ministers, brought unity and central control to the country. As a result it became the cultural and economic power of Europe. Louis XIV (who reigned from 1643 to 1715) ruled as an absolute monarch, but it was the skills of his chief Ministers, Cardinal Jules Mazarin (in office 1643–61) and Jean-Baptiste Colbert (served 1665–83), that brought France enough financial stability and resources to be able to afford the king's mistakes. His invasions of the Netherlands, the war for the Spanish crown and his decision to expel all of France's Protestants in 1685 were all immensely harmful to the French state. His successors, overwhelmed by his example, found it impossible to adapt their role to the needs of the state, and France continued as an absolute monarchy, long after other nations had evolved better ways of working.

Although the death of Louis XIV in 1715 brought a period of peace, the weakness of Europe's balance of power was once again exposed, this time by an extreme version of the new centralized state. The aftermath of the Thirty Years War had left the German states within the empire in a reduced state, with Austria, still the base of the emperor, as the only significant power. But in 1701 Frederick I, son of the Elector of Brandenberg, named himself the first king of Prussia and set about building up the military power of this relatively poor north German state. His son Frederick II, later known as Frederick the Great, who ruled from 1740 to 1786, was determined to make Prussia the dominant power in the empire. In two wars, the War of the Austrian Succession in 1740–48 and the Seven Years War of 1756–63, Prussia took on much more powerful states and either won or fought them to a stalemate. In the Seven Years War, the Habsburg empire, France, Russia and Sweden all combined in an attempt to destroy the Prussian forces, but Prussia survived and became a significant European power.

The Prussian example was telling. A smallish state of apparently little consequence had broken into the circle of great nations by sacrificing everything for military power. The balance of power meant little when it excluded such ambitious rulers as Frederick. Prussian methods of drill and organization took military discipline to another level and were copied by other countries – even George Washington's Continental Army had a Prussian inspector-general, Friedrich von Steuben. James Boswell saw Prussian soldiers being drilled until they dropped, the weaklings being whipped and beaten into line. He found it repugnant but commented that the system worked because 'machines are surer instruments than men'. All European soldiers since the eighteenth century have gone through a similar period of dehumanization during their training. Barracks and parade grounds were built to house troops who had normally been billeted in their home towns, and a military career became a separate, self-absorbed and totally involving way of life.

The Prussian model of a militarized state had an influence far beyond the army itself. In Prussia, the Habsburg territories of central Europe, and Russia, not only were uniforms worn at court, the sovereigns themselves began to dress up as high-ranking military officers. The numbers of men in military service in these countries increased dramatically in the eighteenth century: Prussia had an army of 80,000 in 1740, rising to 200,000 in 1782; during the Seven Years War the Prussian army was 260,000 strong, 7 per cent of the total population; the Russian army reached 300,000 by the year 1800. In France, in contrast, the army was reduced from around 380,000 in 1710 to 280,00 by 1760. Western European powers did not grasp the Prussian model of the militarist state with such relish as those in central and eastern Europe. Instead, the eighteenth century saw the great expansion of western navies. In 1714 the British navy, by far the most powerful and expensive in the world, had 247 ships; by 1783, at the end of the American war, this had grown to 468 vessels, including 174 ships of the line; in 1782 France had 81 ships of the line.

While European nation states emerged as defenders of territory and people, in the second half of the eighteenth century, in a growing number of countries, the military became the institution whose needs and demands shaped society. The army had always been used to mop up the undesirable elements of society, but this became more pronounced in the eighteenth century when the question of social control began to concern governments. The population of Europe was recovering from the seventeenth-century crises and the towns and cities had trouble coping. In the 1780s the French minister of war, the Comte de Saint-Germain, said, 'It would undoubtedly be desirable if we could create an army of dependable and specially selected men of the best type. But in order to make an army we must not destroy the nation by depriving it of its best elements. As things are the army must inevitably consist of the scum of the people and all of those for whom society has no use.' The problem of social control also gave the armies another role. There were major civil insurrections in European countries during the later part of the eighteenth century, including the Gordon Riots in London in 1780, which took 12,000 soldiers to quell. The French army's reluctance to intervene in the social disorder in Paris in 1789 was to be the crucial factor that allowed the revolution to proceed.

In Russia and Prussia the army became so powerful that it effectively controlled society; while in the west it became a separate entity within civilian society. This was a cultural as well as a physical phenomenon. The military world was self-sufficient, separate and, so it felt, superior to the civilian world. It had its own laws, codes of conduct and esprit de corps in which loyalty to the regiment meant almost more than loyalty to the country. Soldiers were taken care of by the military 'family'. Awards were given for long service and military funerals were assured.

An altogether new military phenomenon, the general staff, appeared during the eighteenth century. This was a body of military planners brought together to direct the military resources of the nation – planning future campaigns, allocating resources, building fortifications and so on, even during peacetime. The general staff became a major power in European states in the nineteenth century, leading to a dominance of military thinking in foreign policy. The new military demanded highly trained officers. The first English school of any kind financed entirely by the state, and staffed by state-appointed teachers, was a naval academy established in Portsmouth in 1729. Cadet schools for the sons of the wealthy were set up in St Petersburg in 1731, Paris in 1751, Wiener-Neustadt in Austria in 1754, Zamora in Spain in 1790, Prussia in 1717, Saxony in 1725, Bavaria in 1756. In 1776 France opened 12 military schools in the provinces to cater for the poorer nobility that supplied the bulk of the officers.

The growing professionalism and influence of the military, and the military ambitions of certain states, had severe effects on civil society. In the Seven Years War the Prussian army lost around 180,000 men while Prussia itself lost around half a million of its 4.5 million population. The neighbouring state of Pomerania lost 20 per cent of its population and Brandenberg lost 25 per cent. As well as devastation caused by fighting, displacement of peoples and loss of agricultural and manufacturing production, wars brought disease in an age when medicine offered little help. Diseases thrived in the conditions brought by war and were carried to new places by soldiers. In the Russo-Turkish war of 1768–74 soldiers brought plague from the southern Russian steppes to Moscow, where 60,000 people died, and to Kiev, where 14,000 died in 1771. It was not unusual for more soldiers to die from disease than from fighting the enemy. Wars were known to be destructive and expensive, but governments and people still viewed them with optimism.

The growth of national communities may have been built around the demands of almost continual warfare, but how did people see their lives in this new world? In medieval times the drama of the Christian faith and the abundant rules of Catholic theology had provided both a location and a course of guidance for their existence. Were subjects now simply either cannon-fodder or tax-payers? The way was open for a revival of political philosophy, and writers in the sixteenth century, such as Suarez, Hobbes and Grotius, tried to map out ways in which the state, the monarch and the people should relate to each other (see Chapter Twelve). Each raised intriguing questions concerning free will, the right to rule and the obligations of rulers, duties and rights of subjects, the role of the state in protecting the moral rights of citizens, and so on. A century after Luther and Calvin, the basis for understanding the role of humanity had shifted from Christian theology to rationalism. To be sure, people still believed that these two routes to understanding were entirely compatible – humans must use their God-given reason to understand God's will. Nevertheless, while Hobbes, for example, spent much time in showing how the scriptures supported his political views, he also argued against religious laws that might lead to disobedience of state law. The next generation, which included increasing numbers who knew every word of their Bible, was to demonstrate that the scriptures could be used to support every political philosophy, from autocracy to a society of equals. The religious wars of the seventeenth century had proved futile and religion seemed to have lost its power both to explain the world and to guide the construction of society – reason would have to take on the burden.

Historians traditionally tell us about the gradual but inevitable movement from empires and kingdoms (ruled by unaccountable emperors and monarchs) towards nation states, and then on to liberal constitutional government. But much of the 'progress' that took place in the centuries after 1500 showed an increasing amount of control over towns, regions, churches, guilds and individual lives by an increasingly centralized state. The medieval citizen owed allegiance to an array of institutions – feudal lord, village reeve, extended family, local bishop, pope, guild, town, duke or prince – but the state did away with most of these, leaving only itself and the family as the legitimate institutions of the modern world.

Since 1500, western European states have taken different forms, while the form that the state should take has been the principal subject of public discourse and, some would argue, the main cause of military conflict. This has come about because of the mismatch between the lives, thoughts, aspirations and emotions of individuals and the workings of the state. Although the state can only survive with the support of the people it aims to protect, the relation between the two is endlessly complex. As the writer Hanif Kureishi recently pointed out, even a representative government is not the same as the people it represents, and culture – literature, drama, newspapers – arises from the need to continue an 'arduous conversation' with the state. But has the western state succeeded in preserving and enhancing its power (to the point where a small number of states dominate the world) because it offers a moral alibi for its people? States behave in ways that would shame individuals, but they persuade us that they act in 'the national interest' and in the cause of 'national security'. For most of the last five hundred years the people of the west have been content to see every kind of deed committed in their name by an anonymous body in pursuit of an abstract entity.

US AND THEM

Colonization and Slavery

One time the Indians came to meet us, and to receive us with victuals and delicate cheer, and with all entertainment, ten leagues from a great city; and being come at the place they presented us with a great quantity of fish, and of bread, and other meat, together with all that they could do for us to the uttermost. See the Devil incontinent, who put himself into the Spaniards, to put them all to the sword in my presence, without any cause whatsoever, more than three thousand souls, which were set before us, men women and children. I saw there so great cruelties, that never any man living either have or shall see the like . . . The Spaniards with their horses, their spears and lances, began to commit murders, and strange cruelties: they entered into towns, boroughs and villages, sparing neither children nor old men, neither women with childe, neither them that lay in, but that they ripped their bellies, and cut them in pieces, as if they had been opening of lambs shut up in their fold . . . They murdered commonly the lords and nobility in this fashion: They made certain grates of branches laid on pitch-forks, and made a little fire underneath, to the intent that little by little yelling and despairing in these torments, they might give up the ghost.

Bartolomé de las Casas, 1513–20

THE discovery of the New World in 1492 came as an immense shock to Europeans. The clergy, the educated and the common people had all believed that the scriptures, together with the writings of the church fathers and the ancient authorities, contained the sum of all human knowledge. But it was clear to everyone that neither Pliny nor Aristotle nor, in particular, the Bible contained any knowledge of another world across the ocean. God and the church fathers had, it seemed, simply failed to mention the New World. This absence meant that the scriptures and the ancient philosophers provided no guidance on how the New World should be seen – as an earthly paradise, like Eden before the Fall, or a terrifying place inhabited by satanic creatures from which God had protected his flock. And how should Christian Europe deal with a whole continent of pagan people: were these innocent, ignorant souls awaiting baptism into the welcoming arms of the Holy Roman church, or were they dangerous pagans whose impiety put them beyond salvation? Though well used to condemning non-believers and heretics, for the first time in its history the Church had to ask, What is the Christian view of those who have never known Christ's teaching?

The secular philosophers of Europe, using their interpretations of Greek and Roman writers to promote the doctrine of humanism, were similarly thrown into confusion. Were the inhabitants of the Americas the same kind of humans as Europeans; were they just like us but without the benefits of our civilization; were all humans essentially the same, or were some by nature in a lower state of being?

While church authorities and philosophers agonized over these questions, the annexation of the Americas by Europeans was being driven by two stark facts of European life in the sixteenth century – the power of militant nation states, and the spread of the money economy to every part of the continent. Competition between countries and their growing militarization – including the introduction of cannon, muskets, standing armies and ocean-going ships – made the Americas into a battleground between Europeans. At the same time the early conquest of America was fuelled by the desire for gold – as Columbus said, with gold a man could do anything he might wish, while Cortés told the Mexicans that his men had a sickness of the heart that could be cured only by gold. The Europeans came to America with two thoughts united by one desire – to find a sea route to China and India, or to find gold; either way they would be rich men.

By the time Columbus returned from the last of his four voyages in 1504, Portuguese explorers had touched the coast of Brazil and travelled round Africa as far as India; in 1522 Ferdinand Magellan's expedition completed the first circumnavigation of the globe. Nevertheless, until around 1525, Spanish and Portuguese adventurers assumed that Hispaniola and Cuba, and the coasts of Brazil, Yucatán and Florida, were all evidence of islands lying off the coast of Asia; the search for a channel through to the riches of the Orient was still the dream of many.

In the meantime Spaniards came out to the Indies where, they had heard, a man could acquire land and live in the kind of luxury that was beyond their means in Castile. Hernán Cortés was typical; born in 1484 into a family of the lower gentry, he was well educated before becoming, like his father before him and like many other Spaniards of his time, a professional soldier. His aim was to fight as a mercenary in Italy, but at the age of 22 he sailed to the Indies in search of fortune and, perhaps, a little glory. The Caribbean islands offered some kind of living to the incoming Spaniards, but only at the cost of immense devastation. Hispaniola, Cortés's first port of call in 1506, was already half-destroyed and its native population nearly wiped out by disease and slaughter. Cortés went on to Cuba, where he got lucky, finding gold in the east of the island and setting himself up in a hacienda with a large retinue of male and female Indian slaves. There was no restraint on the use of Indians for slavery, sex, forced labour, torture or blood sports, or either murdering them or leaving them to starve – las Casas wrote that, during his four-month stay in Cuba, he witnessed the starvation of 7,000 native people.

While the Caribbean islands encouraged the view that the Americans were simple, primitive people of lower status than Europeans, something quite different existed on the mainland. In 1517 a Spanish expedition landed on the coast of Yucatán (still assumed to be an island) and made contact with the Mayans, a society past its powerful heyday, but still impressive to Europeans. The following year the Spanish governor of Cuba sent his nephew to investigate further. The news Juan de Grijalva brought back was astonishing and electrifying. He first saw Mayan cities with buildings and towers as grand as any in Seville, but then, driven off by suspicious Mayans, he landed further up the coast. There the local Totonacs told him that they, along with all the peoples of this land, were the reluctant subjects of a great empire called Mexico. Grijalva knew, from the huge mountains in the distance, from the size of the rivers and the diversity of human cultures, that this was a vast land, maybe even a continent, and that, far from being an innocent Eden, it was ruled by a sophisticated and immensely powerful empire.

Cortés, by now one of the wealthiest men in Cuba, agreed to fund and lead an expedition from Cuba to the heart of the Mexican empire. At the last minute the Spanish governor, probably sensing that Cortés was intent on personal conquest, withdrew his support, and so Cortés set sail on what was effectively a private mission. Much has been made of the small number – around 400 – of Cortés's Spanish soldiers, and the naivety, gullibility and superstition of the Mexicans. But the fact that the Aztecs had difficulty in understanding the needs, the behaviour and the methods of the Europeans should not surprise us. And once they did understand the threat that Cortés posed, they first expelled him from their city, and then fought with immense courage to hold off his besieging army, which was by then not 400, but over 10,000 strong.

The events of 1519–21 make disturbing reading (though we should not forget that for centuries Cortés was regarded as a European hero). Having scuppered his boats to prevent his plans being reported back to Cuba, Cortés first fought, and then made an alliance with, the powerful Tlaxcalans, who agreed to go with him to the great city of Tenochtitlan, centre of the Aztec empire. After a trek across the high mountain passes, Cortés and his party entered the central valley of Mexico. Nothing could have prepared the Spaniards for the sight of the city. Built in the centre of Lake Texcoco with towns all around the shores, reached by a series of wide causeways and drawbridges, with innumerable houses, palaces, streets and temples, a marketplace used by 70,000 people, and gardens floating on the surface of the lake, it was a dream-like vision. This was not an empty land awaiting occupation, nor a primitive people, but an empire to be conquered – the city alone was probably home to 250,000 people, while the population of Mesoamerica in 1520 has been estimated at 25 million.

The Spaniards were welcomed into the city by Montezuma, leader of the Aztecs, and given food and lodging. Cortés tried the bold strategy of taking Montezuma hostage, but one of his lieutenants made the mistake of massacring worshippers who had gathered in the sacred courtyard of the temple for the Aztec spring festival. Priests and musicians were cut to ribbons by Spanish swords – something that was simply incredible to the Aztecs, whose rules of war and taboos about any violation of the human body were always strictly observed. For them, as for many other cultures, warfare was highly ritualized and even human sacrifice was carried out with great precision and respect for the body. The European warrior culture of finding honour by exposing yourself to danger and attacking with murderous intent was unthinkable. The massacre in the temple brought home the intentions of their guests; the Aztecs stopped feeding them and began to remove the bridges that led out of the city. Cortés fled the city on 1 July 1520, but before he did, he garrotted Montezuma and the other leading Aztecs whom he was holding as hostages. Three quarters of the Spanish were killed in the desperate escape – many drowned as the gold they were carrying dragged them down into the lake. The Aztecs had won the first battle.

Cortés returned six months later with 10,000 Tlaxcalan allies. In the meantime smallpox, brought by the Spanish, had already spread through the Aztec towns and cities, killing vast numbers – it is likely that in the course of the sixteenth century, several tens of millions of Americans died from European pathogens. Despite the superiority of the besiegers' weapons, and the starvation that the siege induced, the Aztecs refused to surrender. Cortés had to destroy the city that he called 'the most beautiful on earth' in order to take it. After 80 days, with only a small portion of the city left to them, the young Aztec king Cuauhtemoc came to Cortés to discuss the terms of surrender, and the tribute that the Aztecs must pay – they still did not understand that the price of defeat was the total destruction of their city, their way of life, their customs and their empire. Cuauhtemoc, whose dignity in defeat impressed the Spanish and their allies, was told by Cortés to order his men to surrender, and then tortured to death in a vain attempt to discover any remaining hordes of gold. The Spaniards and Tlaxcalans looted and destroyed the city, murdering its inhabitants at random, in the search for gold. More than 100,000 Aztecs died in the siege, while the remainder quietly walked away. The Aztecs fought to protect themselves and their city, but they understood that the horrific events that had befallen them were simply meant to be.

A similar series of events was played out, 10 years later and 4,000 kilometres further south, in the heart of the Inca empire. Francisco Pizarro had, like Cortés, made a substantial fortune from gold, this time in the colony of Panama on the Pacific coast. But, again like Cortés, Pizarro wanted a kingdom of his own. In 1527 his expedition travelling south down the west coast of the continent encountered a huge balsa raft carrying an extraordinary cargo of silver, gold, jewellery, embroidery, mirrors, drinking vessels, gemstones and cloth. These, they learned, were being traded by the empire of the Inca, in exchange for corals and other shells. In 1528 Pizarro and a single ship reached the Inca port of Tumbes, where they were welcomed by the governor and the people. The Spanish were amazed that the people were, in their words, 'so rational and so civilized'. The Inca empire stretched as far

as the distance from Seville to Moscow, and was administered and organized with extraordinary efficiency through the use of runners, civil
servants, food storage depots and, when necessary, force. The subject
peoples paid tribute to the empire and in return became part of a trading
system that reached from present-day Ecuador to Chile and south-east
into Argentina.

After his initial contact Pizarro returned to Panama and then to
Europe to raise money for a substantial expedition. In the meantime
the European smallpox pathogen began its relentless devastation of the
Andean peoples – arguably the most momentous tragedy was the death
of the great Inca, Wayna Capac, in May 1528. The resulting civil war
between his sons gave Pizarro his chance to divide and conquer the
empire. While the war raged, Pizarro met Cortés in Toledo and, after
showing King Charles an array of Inca jewellery and artefacts, was
granted royal assent to conquer and rule Peru in the name of the Spanish
crown. But the conquest of the Indies was a commercial as well as a
political venture. Following the example of the Italian merchants and
bankers, Europe was awash with men wanting to put money into
commercial ventures, at a time when money could buy power and influence. News of Cortés's conquests and the gold of the Aztecs and Incas
produced extraordinary excitement, and allowed Pizarro to raise funds
with ease. When he returned to Peru in 1530 he brought 180 men,
including his brothers, men from his home town and other trusted
soldiers. Following Cortés's advice, despite being vastly outnumbered
he seized the Inca leader Atahuallpa and massacred the crowds who
attended him, using gunpowder, horses and unprovoked brutality to
terrify and shock. Atahuallpa tried to appease the Spanish by granting
them access to all parts of the empire, but they were not satisfied. The
sacred sites, full of extraordinary carved gold objects, were stripped –
seven tons of gold and thirteen tons of silver ornaments were shipped
to Pizarro's base, as ransom for Atahuallpa, where they were melted
into ingots. The artistic creations and spiritual core of the Incas were
destroyed, along with their power.

Atahuallpa was killed when he was no further use to Pizarro, while
other nobles and their women were routinely humiliated, raped, tortured
and murdered by the Spanish. Like the Aztecs, the Incas fought back,
inciting a widespread rebellion against the Spanish in 1537. But Pizarro
had time to call in reinforcements from Panama and, like Cortés, he
had taken care to make allies against the Incas among the other peoples

of the region. Peru was subdued and Inca rule ended for ever.

Cortés and Pizarro acted almost as free agents, but the sustained suppression and colonization of the Americas was possible because of the highly developed organization of the Spanish state. Although Charles V and his son Philip II experienced difficulties in maintaining their authority in the rest of Europe, the state they inherited from Ferdinand and Isabella – the monarchs who united Spain and drove the Moors from Andalucia – was a highly effective administrative and military machine. Although individual adventurers and settlers were free to go to the Indies, all trade was highly regulated and controlled by the Spanish state. Seville was granted a monopoly on Atlantic trade and all goods and vessels had to be registered with customs authorities in the city, allowing the Spanish state to dictate the flow of goods and to levy duties on all imports and exports. The setting-up of regulated colonies in the Caribbean was crucial to the conquest of both Mexico and Peru – both carried out by people already settled in the Americas. The gold and silver that Pizarro collected was divided between him and his companions on the one side, and the Spanish crown on the other.

The mutually beneficial relations between the conquistadors and the Spanish government did not last. By the 1540s, reports of atrocities and lawlessness in the Americas were being heard in Spain with ever more frequency and authority. So-called New Laws were passed forbidding the use of natives as slaves and restricting the wilder activities of the conquistadors. Many of the settlers rebelled against these restrictions and, in 1546, Philip was forced to send Pedro de la Gasca to Peru to pacify the rebellion. De la Gasca succeeded in raising an army and defeated the rebel leader Gonzalo, the last of the Pizarro brothers, whom he executed in April 1548.

Philip's measures were the first in a long line of attempts by 'home' authorities – Spanish, British, French, Portuguese – to control their wayward colonial citizens, most of which ultimately ended in failure. In Philip's case he baulked at the first serious obstacle. In 1554, when he was in England preparing to marry Queen Mary, Spanish settlers in Peru petitioned for a concession against the New Laws that would give them the right to use Indian labour in perpetuity. Against the wishes of his own Council of the Indies, Philip granted the concession, and in return the settlers paid him five million gold ducats. Spanish settlers on the island of Hispaniola, who were suffering from an acute shortage of labour, then petitioned the king to allow the seizure of Carib Indians as slaves and for the import of much greater numbers of Africans also to be used as slaves. Philip agreed – both Native Americans and Africans were given the same legal status as beasts of burden.

In 1569 a significant event in the intertwined history of Europe and the Americas took place when Philip II appointed Francisco de Toledo as viceroy of Peru. This was the first time a European state formally created a colonial government to rule over an overseas territory, making Spanish colonization a permanent, consolidated entity. It was historic for another reason: in 1572 Toledo seized and executed the last Inca emperor, Tupac Imaru. This was the symbolic end of a civilization brought about through greed, plunder, ignorance, cruelty, mismanagement and absence of intervention by the Spanish state. The death of Tupac Imaru came just 41 years after the arrival of the Pizarros in Peru. In less than a lifetime an entire human world had been wiped off the earth.

Settlers followed the conquistadors in their thousands as the Spanish crown exerted state control over 'New Spain' (Mexico), Peru and, later, most of the southern continent. Migration both within and from Spain was prodigious. In the sixteenth century, thousands left the market towns and villages of Castile to flood south to the area around Seville and Cadiz, while around 150,000 Spaniards migrated to go to the Indies. Some went in search of gold and silver (by 1800 Mexico produced two thirds of the world's silver); others were encouraged by grants of land, called *encomiendas* or *haciendas*, given by the Spanish crown.

The desire of individual citizens for money strikes us as a natural emotion. But this was only true in a society where customary constraints on the acquisition and use of individual wealth (such as religious sentiment, social status, communal living) had been removed, and where wealth brought status and power. In previous European societies status had been achieved in various ways – through valour, wisdom or spirituality – but in post-Renaissance Europe status and power over others came through money. Visions of personal wealth and luxury had flooded across Europe from Italy in the fifteenth century, together with tales of the ancient worlds of Greece and Rome. History emboldened the adventurers into seeing themselves as modern-day Alexanders and Caesars, bringing civilization to the barbarians at the edge of a sword.

The native peoples of the Americas were unequal to the western Europeans in warfare technology but their subjugation was made even easier because of their different view of conflict. As in most other societies (see Chapters One and Four) warfare among American peoples was limited, involved only particular groups, and was highly ritualistic, consisting of choreographed violence in which as few people as possible were harmed. In contrast European warfare was informed by a moral purpose. Skirmishes and insults and symbolic victories had no place; the central moral ideal was to earn victory by exposing yourself to death and by bringing murderous force to bear on the enemy; any theological discussion of the status of the Indians' souls was overtaken by the brute fact of European soldiers meeting Native Americans face to face.

If the atrocities against the Native Americans had been merely the actions of professional European soldiers, things might not have gone so badly for the non-European world. The scholars of Europe, though, were in no hurry to defend these primitive, backward pagans who had suddenly appeared on their horizons. Those who had studied the history of Europe, of Asia and of those parts of Africa that were known were beginning to conclude that Europeans and European civilization were indeed superior to the peoples and cultures of other continents and that their mastery of these peoples was a 'natural' process. In fact Europeans had little reason to feel superior to outsiders; in 1500 the population of western Europe was under 50 million, while Ming China and Mughal India, both highly sophisticated Asian societies, controlled populations of 200 million and 110 million.

Nevertheless, in 1547 the Spanish theologian Juan Ginés de Sepúlveda wrote: 'with perfect right the Spaniards rule over these barbarians of the New World and the adjacent islands, who, in wisdom, intelligence, virtue and the qualities of civilization are as inferior to Spaniards as infants to adults and women to men. There is as much difference between them as there is between cruel, wild peoples and the most merciful of peoples, between the most monstrously intemperate peoples and those who are temperate and moderate in their pleasures, that is to say, between apes and men.' (Sepúlveda).

When Sepúlveda and others invoked the history of Roman rule over lesser nations as justification for Spanish actions, this was no casual plundering of history but a systematic process that has had profound effects on our view of the past. The rediscovery of the classical world and the falling-away of the great Christian drama of the medieval faith led Europeans to construct a new history. Instead of seeing the world's story framed and punctuated by the Creation, the incarnation of Christ, the Resurrection and the imminent Day of Judgement, scholars saw the connection between themselves and the sages of Greece and Rome as the golden thread in the developing story of humanity. When they looked around they could discern a natural development of human civilization from nomadic hunting tribes, to settled peasant agricultural communities, to sophisticated urban-based societies. Both Athens and Rome had reached this stage and then been destroyed by regressive forces. But European culture had finally recovered and had reached the furthest point so far (with some parts of Asia not far behind). When they saw other peoples, despite their appreciation of Aztec and Inca ornaments, Europeans could not help but marvel at their own achievements. They must, it seems, have been singled out by God as the most worthy of all the peoples of the world.

This was not only a matter of technology. While others remained in ignorant savagery or under the heel of tyrannical monarchs, Europeans were beginning to enjoy freedoms and rights derived from rational argument between the powers of government and the individual. European people were clearly in a higher state of social and political development than the natives of Africa, Asia or America. When European weapons, developed out of this sophisticated, urban, increasingly rationalist and technological culture, scattered the natives of the other continents, all but the most far-sighted rejoiced at their shared triumph.

The writings from the classical world showed Europeans the boundaries between those who were civilized and those who were not. For Romans the boundary was the border of the empire; for western Europeans it was the edge of the old territory of Latin Christendom. The vision of civilization surrounded by barbarity made the civilized feel comfortable in their superiority, but it raised fears about the dangerous forces outside. The New World was the unknown magnified into a whole continent. The landscape was utterly strange and inhabited by a bizarre collection of plants and animals. But the most obvious sign of America being uncivilized was the people themselves. The Native Americans were a stark and unpleasant reminder of the essential, primitive, brutal nature of humans unfettered by civilization's chains. Unclothed, or dressed in peculiar ways; behaving like children, or like curious beasts; stupidly passive or wantonly aggressive – their behaviour was essentially unpredictable and therefore beyond comprehension except as a lower state of humanity. Here St Augustine's doctrine found its vindication – uncivilized humans were prey to the worst desires and basest instincts; they must be civilized or destroyed.

Even if pagan Americans were welcomed into the Christian church, this proved a mixed blessing. Once Catholic missionaries decided to bring them the word of God, the feverish atmosphere of the Counter-Reformation dictated that their religion should be controlled. The Spanish viceroy of Peru banned all native religious practices, and in 1570 an office of the Inquisition was set up in Lima, and then later in other Spanish dominions. Native Americans had little chance of avoiding the culture that had come to take over their continent. Spain established colonies in Mexico, Panama, Peru and later Argentina, the West Indies, Florida and up the east coast of North America as far as the Carolinas, claiming dominion over the whole of the Americas (without knowing how extensive they were) as a warning to other Europeans to keep out. Spain was ideally placed to dominate the Americas throughout the sixteenth century. Her geographical position put her at the natural frontier (Philip annexed Portugal in 1580) and her growing domination of western Europe made other nations fearful of making an enemy of the Spanish king.

However, in the seventeenth century the balance of power in Europe, and thereby in the Americas, changed rapidly. The English, though a marginal military power, emerged as a strong naval force; the French overcame internal turmoil and began a period of stability and increasing power; and the collection of Netherlands states that rebelled against Spain formed the Dutch republic, becoming, for a time, Europe's most important overseas trading nation. England, France and the Netherlands were, despite Spain's declining power, effectively shut out of South America, so all three turned their attention to the north.

In the mid-1600s, following the lead set by Jacques Cartier, French traders travelled down the St Lawrence river, establishing settlements at Quebec, Montreal and Trois Rivières. They then pushed west across the Great Lakes region and south into the Mississippi basin, eventually reaching the Gulf of Mexico in 1682. A settlement at New Orleans was founded in 1718. The territory settled by the French was vast, but they were few in number. French settlement was concentrated along the lower St Lawrence river, where small villages were based on the long-lot pattern, in which each *habitant* had a narrow river frontage and a parcel of land stretching back into the forest; in the Illinois region there were settlements based on medieval communes. Though some tried to make a living from cotton or indigo, most of the French in

America were hunters rather than settlers, living off fur-trapping and trading. In the territories they inhabited, the French were heavily outnumbered by Native Americans from a host of different tribes, but they integrated into the indigenous life far more than the British ever would. In 1750 Louisiana, the name of the vast area claimed by the French crown, was occupied by about 2,000 French and German settlers living among between 200,000 and 300,000 Native Americans, while in Canada marriage between French men and Indian women was encouraged, with the aim of creating a unified nation. But the French never emigrated in significant numbers to dominate either the local population or their European rivals. Their government was concerned about any reduction in the homeland population, and in the seventeenth century France did not suffer the same degree of instability as England and the Netherlands – there was less reason for French people to leave and less support for them to do so.

Dutch and English colonization of North America was intertwined from the beginning. In 1609 Hendrik Hudson, an English explorer employed by the Dutch East India Company, sailed up the river that now bears his name while searching for a sea route to India. Traders from the Netherlands established a settlement at Fort Nassau, the furthest point Hudson had reached, and from around 1624 settled on the islands around the mouth of the Hudson, including Governor's Island and Manhattan. They brought more than 10,000 colonists from Europe, including French Huguenots, Belgians, English, Finns and Swedes, as well as Portuguese Jews from Brazil and Africans. The Dutch retained control of the Hudson only until 1664, when a fleet of English warships appeared and the Dutch settlers accepted British sovereignty.

Despite their short-lived autonomy, the Dutch influence was important. We need to remember that for the merchants and travellers of the pre-industrial age, water was the natural element. People, goods and weapons had always been incomparably easier to move by water than overland by wagon, and the discoveries of America, the East Indies and the sea routes to India and China meant that large parts of the world were accessible only by sea. Before 1776, and even up to the civil war, North America was a series of seaboard colonies, its people living by seaborne trade. The Dutch settlements were part of a worldwide trading network connecting Europe, North America, India, the East Indies, China and South America, and stretching inland along the waterways of the Hudson and Delaware river systems. The Dutch settlement also contributed to the cultural mix of the early colonies, which otherwise would have been almost universally English.

North America 'arrived' at exactly the right time for the English. Historians have long argued over whether England experienced a 'military revolution' in the seventeenth century (see Wheeler), but it is clear that after the civil war of 1642–49, the English realized they could defend their shores most effectively through a powerful navy. State money was put into ships and equipment rather than, as on the continent, a large standing army and heavily fortified castles. The spin-off was dominance of the North Atlantic and thereafter of most of the world's oceans.

Private as well as state money had traditionally been invested in English ships. English gentlemen had, since Elizabethan times, joined together to invest in voyages of exploration, discovery, trade and piracy. The returns were often spectacular: Francis Drake was able to repay his investors many times over from Spanish treasure, but legitimate trade could pay well too. Money from investors was pooled into a company so that risks and profits were shared. In the early seventeenth century, investors who had profited from trading voyages began to ask themselves, why not imitate the Spanish and fund actual settlements?

Though there had been earlier attempts to set up colonies, the only European settlements in North America still in existence in 1600 were Spanish outposts at San Juan in New Mexico and St Augustine in Florida. In the aftermath of the English Revolution of the 1640s Protestant sects outside the approved church were persecuted, while the restoration of the monarchy in 1660 encouraged more dissenters to leave the country. Nonconformist sects, taking Christ's words and life as an example, went overseas in order to create religious communities free from the interference of government or materialism. The New World seemed to offer the chance to build an ideal society. But there were many English settlers who were driven neither by persecution nor idealism but by the need for material gain, or a better life. The English had recent experience of the colonization of Ireland, which had been carved up between the invaders, making soldiers into wealthy landowners. Many hoped the same might happen in North America.

The first permanent English settlement in North America was founded at Jamestown on the Virginia river in 1607. A combination of wealthy chancers, artisans and vagrants hoping for a grant of land once they worked off their indenture, the Virginia colony was a near disaster. Of the 8,000–9,000 people who arrived between 1610 and

1622, no less than 80 per cent had died by the latter date. Plague and malaria (both brought from the Caribbean on their own ships), yellow fever and dysentery killed most of them. The colony was saved by reorganization in 1624, by natural development of disease immunity, and by the discovery of tobacco as a valuable cash crop; by 1643 the population was around 5,000. The nature of the settlement changed as plantation owners bought out their smaller neighbours and land became concentrated in fewer and fewer hands. Once a critical mass of settlers was reached and life became more secure, the Chesapeake Bay area became a magnet for British emigrants.

In 1620 a group of religious dissenters, known later as the Pilgrim Fathers, landed much further north, at Cape Cod in Massachusetts. They too suffered extreme hardship but survived to be joined in the 1630s and 1640s by a large influx of around 18,000 Puritans. The Puritans managed better than others, perhaps through mutual help, and by 1700 there were 100,000 settlers in the Massachusetts area. In 1681 William Penn established a colony for Quakers, a sect that had been persecuted in England, in what became Pennsylvania. This colony, learning from the experience of its predecessors and being luckier with local conditions, was extremely successful, attracting Protestant Nonconformists from Scotland, Germany and Switzerland as well as English Quakers. By 1700 Philadelphia overtook Boston as the biggest city on the Atlantic coast of North America.

The settlers may have brought European habits with them, but the social structures of the new colonies were quite different from European societies. The communities of New England Puritans and Pennsylvanian Quakers were based either in towns or on individual family farmsteads. With no hierarchy of authority, the towns were run largely on communal lines, with the famous town meetings operating as administration council and court. But out in the country, where farmers did their work, there were no European-style villages to act as social, cultural or political centres, and no communities of peasant labourers. A farming family would have a plot of land, in the middle of which they built their house, making long journeys to town for supplies and to sell produce. The isolated settlement remained the template of American rural life for the next 300 years.

Whatever the courage and determination of the early coastal settlers, European settlement of North America was not a benign mixture of adventure and community-building. The three factors that blighted

every colonial adventure – the treatment of the native population, the impact of disputes between Europeans, and slavery – were all evident in the colonization and continuing history of North America. The earliest contacts gave an indication of what was to come, firstly through disease. A Spanish expedition into Texas in 1528 introduced typhus; influenza was brought to the Gulf coast in 1559, smallpox to Florida in 1564, to Carolina in 1615 and Maryland in 1616, and plague to Virginia in 1607 and Maryland and Massachusetts in 1616. Native Americans had no resistance to any of these Eurasian pathogens, and though the numbers were unrecorded, they certainly perished in tens, and probably hundreds, of thousands.

The English colonists began with good intentions to the Native Americans, but once the settlements got a foothold (often with the cooperation of native peoples) their desire for land brought confrontations. The English colonists easily won any military conflict, and settlement, particularly in Virginia, turned into invasion. Unlike many of the

Inhabitants of the southern part of North America before the arrival of the Europeans.

French, who adapted to life alongside the indigenous population, the English were separatist and increasingly hostile to Native Americans. Respectable English settlers despised those who traded with the Indians, viewing them as unpleasant rascals who corrupted the Indian way of life. But it was the respectable farmers, not the disreputable traders, who destroyed the Native American way of life, because they wanted, and could never get enough of, the Indians' land.

In 1763 the British authorities tried, in the first of a long series of measures, to reserve land west of the Appalachians for the Native Americans. But when settlers moved into the reserved area and the subsequent rebellion by the Ottawa Indians was put down, the line of reservation moved a step further west. In 1768 the Iroquois, head of a large confederation of tribes, ceded territory in Ohio in return for a boundary between whites and Indians being drawn at the Ohio river. Within a year British settlers had crossed the river to set up home in Kentucky. By the time of United States independence in 1776 there was irresistible pressure to move westwards, whatever the consequences for the native population.

Once governments started to get involved, the colonization of North America was driven by rivalry between European nations. Spain, England, France and the Netherlands were in a constant flux of alliances and conflicts throughout the seventeenth and the first half of the eighteenth century. Georgia was settled by the British in the 1730s deliberately to protect the Carolina colonies from the Spanish in Florida. War between Britain and France in 1739–48 brought conflict to America, but the decisive blow was the French defeat at the hands of Prussia, aided by Britain, in the Seven Years War (1756–63). The 1763 Treaty of Paris saw France give up its direct dominion over territories in North America, while Spain ceded Florida to Britain and both countries granted all land east of the Mississippi to the British. Britain became undisputed master of the North American colonies. This, though, was really a recognition of inevitability. In 1750 there were over one million British subjects in North America compared to around 70,000 French; Britain dominated North America, and drove out both the French and the Native Americans, through sheer force of numbers. In these conflicts French and British settlers fought on behalf of their home governments (though many were reluctant to do so) and Native Americans were promised grants of land in perpetuity by first one side then the other. It mattered little which European nation 'won' North America – the Native Americans lost their homeland.

The third issue that bedevilled the colonization of the Americas, and North America in particular, was slavery. In the middle decades of the fifteenth century Portuguese navigators had made their way further and further south down the west African coast. Sailors stuck close to the coast of the mainland, but they ventured into the Atlantic as far as the Azores and the island of Madeira. By 1500 they had reached as far south as present-day Sierra Leone, where they set up trading stations and made agreements with local leaders. The Portuguese did not go to Africa in search of slaves but they found that there were slaves to be bought in the same markets where they found goods such as ivory and timber. The crucial change came when Portuguese and Spanish émigrés began to grow sugar cane on the Canary Islands, the Azores, Madeira, Cape Verde and São Tomé and Príncipe. These were ideal plantation sites for the Europeans; mostly uninhabited, they were also free from the dangers and diseases of the west African mainland. Sugar was a luxury crop in Europe, grown in small quantities in the Mediterranean area, but the demand grew rapidly as the supply increased.

It was a relatively simple matter to ship slaves from the coastal markets of mainland Africa to the offshore island plantations. There is some evidence that the Portuguese were initially keen to convert their labourers to Christianity and to treat them as captured workers. But as the profits from sugar escalated, so did the money to be made from slave-trading. The life expectancy of a sugar plantation slave was just seven years, and treating slaves well was a time-consuming and emotionally involving business; traders and growers soon learned that it was better to remain remote and hostile and to regard the slaves as a commodity, rather than as potential congregants in God's church.

After 1492 the Portuguese ventured further afield. Amerigo Vespucci, an Italian merchant in the service of the Portuguese crown, landed on the South American coast around 1500 and claimed the area we know as Brazil for Portugal. By the 1530s north-east Brazil had become a prime location for growing sugar cane. Cutting sugar cane in tropical conditions was brutally hard work. Portuguese planters began by using local Native American labour, but they had little resistance to European diseases and understandably drifted away from European settlement areas. If forced to work, they were able to escape into their own country.

The solution came easily to the Portuguese. In the middle of the sixteenth century, they began to bring African slaves from Madeira and the Azores to Brazil. The Atlantic slave trade was begun as the extension of a system that was already in place, and once it began it made the European colonization of the New World a commercial possibility. By 1600 there were about 16,000 African slaves in Brazil producing 10,000 tons of sugar a year. Thirty years later the sugar output had doubled and the number of slaves had reached 60,000. Portuguese traders were shipping 15,000 Africans a year to Brazil, and finding markets in the American colonies of other European countries.

By the mid-seventeenth century the infamous slave trade triangle was working to the traders' great advantage. The prevailing south-easterly trade winds took their slave-laden ships from the Gulf of Guinea across to the Caribbean; they then sailed back to Europe with cargoes of sugar cane on the Gulf Stream; the triangle was completed by sailing unladen down the west coast of Africa on the Canaries current. Portuguese settlers, seeing the opportunities to be plantation owners, headed for Brazil in increasing numbers. In the short term Portugal thrived on sugar – in the sixteenth century two fifths of Portuguese government income came from sugar duties. But external bonanzas, wealth discovered rather than created, almost always have a devastating effect on domestic economies. Just as silver from the Americas gave Spain its sixteenth century *siglo d'oro*, but destroyed its manufacturing and agricultural economies, so sugar destabilized the Portuguese economy.

The trade in slaves was initially a Portuguese monopoly, but its history followed the rising fortunes of the other European Atlantic powers. By the middle of the seventeenth century the Netherlands was the biggest trading nation in the world, but the Dutch domination of world trade was short-lived and was gradually superseded by the power that would epitomize the Atlantic slave trade and make slavery the engine of the colonization of North America.

The English colonies that succeeded best were not in North America but on Caribbean islands, in particular Barbados. This small island of 430 square kilometres (166 square miles) was made an English colony in 1625, and its subsequent history followed the template of the Portuguese colonies in Brazil and set the pattern for settlements further north. To begin with small-scale settlers arrived in Barbados to grow tobacco and cotton as cash crops. They worked the land themselves and brought indentured labour from England, supplemented by local natives and a small number of Africans. The Africans were treated in much the same way as other indentured labourers – often being granted freedom after seven years. While no island paradise for Africans, this was a racially mixed community with differences in status but no absolute right of European mastery.

In the 1640s all of this changed, as it had done in Brazil, with the advent of sugar. Sugar-growers rapidly outstripped their tobacco- and cotton-growing neighbours, buying out smaller estates and taking over the entire island. They needed slaves, which Dutch traders and the newly founded Royal African Company were only too happy to supply – 134,000 Africans were brought to the island between 1640 and 1700, eventually comprising over 70 per cent of the island's population, which became totally segregated between British slave-owners and African slaves. The situation in which all whites were free and all Africans were slaves was formalized by a new set of laws which provided a model for the rest of the Americas.

By the 1670s, with the English navy in control of the Caribbean and North Atlantic, Barbados had become the wealthiest small island in the world, sending 15,000 tons of sugar per year to England. The sugar boom soon spread – by 1740 there were 10,000 white Europeans controlling 100,000 black African slaves working on 400 sugar plantations on Jamaica, and by the 1770s this had increased to 200,000 slaves working 775 plantations. There were high rewards for the planters, for the shippers and for the merchant investors based in British cities, particularly London, Liverpool and Bristol. In 1730 Bristol overtook London as the major slave port of Britain as Bristol merchants poured over £150,000 per year, together with ships and crews, into the lucrative business of shipping slaves and sugar. Not only were the beautiful streets of Georgian Bristol and Bath built on the slave trade, the British social system was underpinned by the rise of a new class of gentlefolk – small landowners (whose social struggles were later immortalized in the novels of Jane Austen) who became wealthy on the back of sugar and slavery. In early eighteenth-century Britain there were few voices questioning the moral or Christian rightness of slavery – the rewards were too high and the brutality was invisible to polite British society. The British merchant classes were gripped by Caribbean fever; the West Indies were providing endless wealth and little else mattered.

Just like the Spanish and Portuguese further south, the English colonies in North America struggled to establish themselves as viable agricultural economies. Here too Africans worked with Europeans on farms and small plantations with no formal designation of labour by race. But then the struggling colonies discovered another crop for which there was no previous demand in Europe. Tobacco, a plant native to America, had long been cultivated in small quantities, but in the late seventeenth century new tobacco plantations started to spring up, requiring more labour than was readily available in Virginia and the Carolinas. Tobacco-planters turned to the Caribbean islands, where slave-traders were able to supply all their needs. Shirley Plantation in Virginia, for example, was first settled in 1613 and had African workers recorded alongside indentured Europeans in the 1620s. By the 1660s the owner claimed 'headright' or ownership rights over three black workers, and by the late eighteenth century there were 134 slaves living and working at the plantation – half of them under 16 years of age. By that time the nature of the colonies had changed, with the tobacco plantations dominant and the mixing of races ended. The tobacco plantations became highly stratified places where certain races did certain types of work. The lack of a peasant labour force, tied to the land by custom and law, had driven landowners to look elsewhere for workers; the plantation system, bedrock of the American Old South, was the solution.

On the vast sugar plantations of the Caribbean, slaves worked in huge gangs with little contact between the European and African, the black and the white, populations. The tobacco plantations of Virginia were smaller; groups and then families of slaves worked under an owner-master, with women taking up domestic duties. Imports of slaves into the Chesapeake area stopped around 1750, the continuing need for labour being supplied by internal regeneration of the slave community. Africans became African-Americans, with generations of American fore-bears, and continual, if heavily regularized, contact with white European culture. A new culture grew up among the black population of North America – part African and part European but emerging above all out of the uniqueness of their own situation.

Virginia and the Carolinas prospered in the eighteenth century, with great plantation and town houses springing up on the money earned from tobacco, coffee and rice, all worked by slave labour. In 1803 the newly independent United States completed the Louisiana Purchase from France, acquiring rights over a vast territory in the Mississippi basin; the geography of America began to change from a string of coastal colonies to a continent-sized country. European settlers had followed Daniel Boone and other pioneers into Kentucky and then on to Tennessee; after 1803 they flooded into Alabama, Mississippi and Louisiana.

In 1793 Eli Whitney invented a machine that altered the economy of the southern United States. The cotton gin was able to separate cotton fibres from seeds and dirt as fast as 200 pairs of human hands. At just this time, new mills were being built in Lancashire that could process huge quantities of cotton cloth for the burgeoning world market. Settlers soon discovered that cotton was ideally suited to the semi-tropical climate of the Deep South – here was another cash crop that needed vast amounts of labour. There was a ready supply of slaves, and a ready-made labour system in the plantations of Virginia and the Carolinas; and so the methods and the people of the Old South were taken and transported across half a continent and put to work on the new bonanza crop. In 1802 America exported tobacco to the value of $6 million, and $5 million of cotton; by 1830 the figures were $6 million and $30 million, and by 1860 $16 million of tobacco exports and $192 million of cotton; by then the US was producing three quarters of the world's cotton.

Changing attitudes in Britain brought about the abolition of the Atlantic slave trade in 1807 (the United States followed suit in 1808), but this was only the beginning of the biggest movement of slaves within America itself. Between 1810 and 1860 about a million slaves were officially taken across state lines in a forced migration west and south, with many more moved within state boundaries. In this brutal and tragic process, families, friends and lovers who had grown up together over generations in their 'home' plantations were forcibly separated at the whim of slave-owners, sellers, agents, shippers and buyers. In 1846 Elwood Harvey stumbled on an auction of Virginia slaves for the southern market. The master had promised his slaves, born on the estate where the auction was held, that they and their children would not be sold or separated – but they soon saw that they had been betrayed: 'When the horrible truth was revealed to their minds that they were to be sold, and nearest relations and friends parted forever, the effect was indescribably agonising. Women snatched up their babies and ran screaming into the huts. Children hid behind the huts and trees, and the men stood in mute despair . . . During the sale, the quarters resounded with cries and lamentations that made my heart ache.'

The journeys themselves were brutal, demeaning and dangerous, with the slaves transported in chains, without any idea of their eventual fate. Slavery spread across the whole of the south of the United States so that by 1860 there were 380,000 slave-owners. Ordinary people kept slaves for every conceivable task, from cooking to childcare, from building work to hard labour. Owning slaves became a natural and pervasive part of life for southern white settlers.

The slave system underlay the whole of southern society and was kept in place by the use and the threat of violence. Laws were passed that prevented more liberal slave-owners from releasing their slaves or from granting them freedom. Terrible punishments were meted out and casual brutality was a fact of life for most blacks – no white person would ever be punished for mistreating a black slave. In 1846 Samuel Gridley Howe, a leading educationalist, visited a New Orleans prison holding runaway slaves and slaves waiting to be sold. In the courtyard he saw a black girl, tied to a board, being whipped: 'Every stroke brought away a strip of skin, which clung to the lash, or fell quivering on the pavement while the blood followed after it . . . This was in a public and regularly organised prison; the punishment was one recognized and authorized by the law. But you think the poor wretch had committed a heinous offence . . . ? Not at all. She was brought by her master to be whipped by the common executioner, without trial, judge or jury, just at his beck or nod, for some real or supposed offence, or to gratify his own whim or malice. And he may bring her day after day, without cause assigned, and inflict any number of lashes he pleases . . . provided only he pays the fee.'

During the nineteenth century the nature of immigration into North America changed. Immigrants from Scotland, Ireland, Germany, Scandinavia and southern and eastern Europe who came flooding in to the newly independent country were not settlers with an eye on making a fortune out of cash crops or even ranching; they were mostly victims of persecution of one sort or another – the Highland clearances in Scotland, famine in Ireland, religious persecution in Hungary and Russia, poverty in Italy and Greece. Small-time farmers, induced by railroad company adverts promising vast tracts of land, followed in their wake. Improvements in transport – steamboats, canals and navigable rivers – opened the Deep South to exploitation, while the Lake Erie canal made the northern Midwest – Ohio, Michigan, Indiana and Illinois – a natural destination for those arriving in New York. Soon these two cultures – southerners settling in Kentucky, Tennessee and Missouri, and the northerners heading for Ohio, Indiana and Illinois – began to bump into each other. Northern immigrants, often victims of persecution back in Europe, saw gangs of black slaves in chains and manacles being transported by the same steamships that were taking them to the land of liberty. The confrontation of these two cultures – a southern tradition in which slavery had become ingrained, and a northern belief in America as the land of liberty – became central to American society. The civil war, fought in 1861–65, brought about the end of slavery but not, as we shall see in later chapters, the resolution of these traditions.

The story of European annexation of the Americas, the treatment of its native peoples and the forced transportation and enslavement of millions of Africans raises immensely difficult questions about the nature of western society and its people. Perhaps the most disturbing aspect of the conquest of the great civilizations of Mesoamerica is the thought that modern (i.e. post-medieval) western society could not, and cannot, live alongside any other type of culture. We are drawn to wonder whether the western way of thinking and of organizing human affairs makes us incapable of gazing on, and perhaps even learning from, another culture without needing to dominate and destroy it and make it part of the western system. Our subsequent history seems to show that the only non-western societies that have survived have been those that are too physically remote for us to care much about them (the Inuit of northern Canada or the natives of the Amazon basin and the Papua New Guinea highlands), or too militarily strong for us to conquer (China).

But Mesoamerica has another story to tell. The Spanish government, obsessed with the superiority of pure-blood Spaniards, introduced racial categories into Mexico and its other territories. New types sprang up almost immediately – *criollos*, *mestizos*, *castas* were all either of mixed blood or Mexican birth, and were eventually to form the basis of a new national culture. Neither Spanish nor Native American nor African, and composed of a plethora of races mixed together in innumerable combinations, Mexican (and in the same way Brazilian) culture grew into something unique and true to both its origins and its place. In Mexico, it seems, western civilization was subsumed into a greater whole.

The story in North America was different. Sparsely populated in comparison (there were between 6 and 12 million Native Americans in pre-Columbian North America, compared to 20 million in Mexico), with an immense diversity of modes of living, from nomadic hunters to settled fishers and farmers, the Americans of the north lived mainly in village-based societies based on networks of kinship, which were completely swept away by the European incomers. To Europeans, these people seemed either irredeemably primitive and savage, or else wild yet dignified. Either way, beyond a brief Enlightenment flirtation with a confused notion of 'primitive innocence', the amount that Europeans, in half a millennium of living in North America, managed to learn from its inhabitants has been close to zero.

The routine characterization of other civilizations as 'behind' or 'backward' or 'underdeveloped' has remained with us since the sixteenth century. Once the idea of a linear progression in history took hold, it proved impossible to shake off; societies can only be positioned on a straight line that begins in the Stone Age and continues through to the edge of the future in Silicon Valley or Shanghai or Osaka. We have no conceptual apparatus to deal with a society that has developed in ways that do not fit this model, and so we force them to conform.

Slavery made the colonization of America possible; it also provided its most economically successful country, the United States, with an enduring legacy. America is a land of immigrants; people have flocked there from every continent, escaping persecution, seeking opportunity, freedom and prosperity. But Africans came to America in very different circumstances – brought against their will to be enslaved, abused and routinely denigrated. For most Americans, their country's status as the land of opportunity and freedom is part of the history of their families and their people, while for African-Americans the opposite is true. America is a country of continual renewal; waves of immigration, technological innovation and social renewal give the impression of a country that is forever young. But African-Americans, together with Native Americans, are an uncomfortable reminder that the United States, like every other culture, has a past.

Once mass slavery began, white Europeans soon saw that all slaves were Africans; from this they quickly developed the understanding that all black Africans were slaves. They never saw black Africans in any other setting – they did not meet them as tribal leaders or powerful generals or gifted artists or skilful craftspeople, only as helpless human pack animals dependent on white Europeans for work, food and shelter. It was not only the ownership of people (something that was practised in many societies) that was so grave, but the belief that because of their colour they deserved nothing more than to be beasts of burden, combined with unusual cruelty. The Atlantic slave trade was the pretext for brutality on a massive scale, and the victims of such a crime can never be forgiven; they kept on being punished since their very existence was a rebuke to the society that owned them.

History tells us about things that happened but does not offer much guidance for the future – or at least none that we are prepared to accept. The story of the European takeover of the Americas will not stop the same thing happening again. Perhaps all we can learn is that one human civilization, finding itself with a military advantage over another, is quite capable, even if its members believe themselves to be civilized beyond all others, of inflicting unspeakable brutality with the aim of destroying that other civilization. And we know that this is true because it happened.

THE RATIONAL INDIVIDUAL

Theory and Practice in Making Society

WE have long understood the vital role that movable block printing has played in the development of western civilization. The widespread availability of vernacular bibles, as well as the works of classical scholars and contemporary writers such as Erasmus, Luther, Rabelais and Calvin, helped to break down the medieval view of the world, and usher in a different kind of European society. Since then, the ability to reproduce and circulate writings with great rapidity has been a central feature of western culture. What is becoming clearer is the degree to which alphabetic writing and mechanical printing not only influence the circulation of ideas and opinions, but dictate the ways that we think about the world. The birth of abstract thought in ancient Athens has now to be seen in the context of Greek alphabetic writing (see Chapter 3), and some historians argue that it is impossible to separate ideas from the medium in which they are expressed, since ideas are formed with a certain medium in mind.

In the artistic world this is self-evident: Shakespeare wrote for the medium of the stage, Bach for the church organ and the court orchestra, and their works bear the identity of the media for which they were written. The same is true, though less obviously, of other cultural, philosophical and ideological works. The Bible was composed in order to be written down, once the technology of writing arrived in Judea near the beginning of the first millennium BC. Its content, expanded from a set of oral folk tales into a semi-coherent history with an added beginning and an end, was dictated by the requirements of a written document, and the second-century AD development of the codex, with leaves bound together into a book as opposed to a collection of unwieldy scrolls, encouraged the collection of a set of scriptures into a sacred tome.

How then did movable block type change the ways that Europeans thought about the world, and how did these changes affect the development of modern western civilization, and the emergence of a culture of the written word? Johannes Gutenberg did not invent movable type but he developed a fast and precise method of making individual metal letter blocks from moulds. His workshop, founded in the 1450s in Mainz, could turn a new letter out of a cast every few minutes; an individual printing shop could have as many copies of each letter as it wanted, allowing work on different pages or books at the same time. Roman letters found on classical documents (actually a combination of old Roman capitals and lower-case Carolingian minuscules) spread through printing workshops across Europe, so that while there was no common vernacular spoken language, there was a common alphabet. Gutenberg also improved the way printing presses operated and developed better methods of paper-making, so that printing became a craft industry like textiles or pottery.

By 1500 there were presses using movable type in practically every major city in western Europe. Martin Luther wrote: 'The great benefits of book printing cannot be expressed in words. By means of this invention the Holy Scriptures are open to all tongues and languages and can be spread everywhere; all arts and sciences can be preserved, increased and passed on to our descendants.' But the Latin and then the vernacular Bible were only the first of a torrent of mechanically printed works. Plato and Aristotle no longer stood in glorious isolation among classical writers; the works of Plotinus, Proclus, Ptolemy and a host of others rapidly became available in readable, portable editions. Modern scholars could see that ancient authors were as divided in their opinions as their contemporaries. Aristotle, the summarizer and explainer of all Greek knowledge, was shown to be at odds with Plato and with his successors like Plotinus. The medieval project, undertaken by Aquinas and other scholastics, that all knowledge should be unified seemed unattainable and undesirable and the intellectual glue that Aquinas had used in the thirteenth century began to come unstuck in the sixteenth. In 1543 Francesco Vimercati articulated the new attitude: 'I think our faith is much more imperilled when we try to confirm and protect it with the testimonies of Aristotle, Plato, or other outsiders which are inappropriate, unsuitable, and not written by them for that purpose' (quoted in Cameron).

Gentlemen scholars of the sixteenth century, reading the philosophical works of Plato, Aristotle, Cicero and Seneca, but also the poetry of Ovid and Horace, were captivated by their achievements, which they naturally wished to emulate. A continent full of diplomats, soldiers, gentlemen and scholars became eager to inscribe their experiences and thoughts about anything and everything. Educated Englishmen such as Thomas Wyatt, John Donne, Walter Raleigh, William Shakespeare and Philip Sidney were moved to compose books of poems, ruminating exquisitely, in a world infected by money and ambition, on love, friendship and the vagaries of modern life.

The use of classical letters and wisdom as an inspiration and model for contemporary life was taken in another direction by Michel de Montaigne (1533–92), whose *Essais* were published from 1580. The fact that Montaigne, a devout Catholic who knew the works of Augustine, nevertheless felt the need to 'discover a sane and humane way of living' tells us much about the changes in Europeans' view of the world. Augustine had argued for a Christian life based on fear of God, but Montaigne, whose education was dominated by the classics, felt the need to integrate the work of Seneca and Cicero into his view of life. Montaigne was above all a reader, and his way of understanding the world was to see how the works that he read applied to his own life and circumstance. He was not a philosopher trying, like Aquinas, to build a rational system that combined Catholic theology with classical metaphysics, but a man of experience (he had been a soldier and administrator) and an enquirer who distrusted the claims of rationality to be the source of knowledge.

His own experience, combined with his vast reading, led Montaigne to believe that humanity was closer to nature than was widely supposed. Orthodox Christian theology had given humanity dominion over nature; Protestantism placed humanity in direct contact with God without the intermediary of sacred places, animals or objects; and the growing doctrine of rational humanism placed humanity apart from nature because of its unique possession of the faculty of reason. But Montaigne believed the superiority or apartness of humans was an illusion; he believed in a natural theology where evidence of God was to be found in His creation – the natural world – and, arguing against

Christian theology and the advocates of rationality, he asserted that the human body was not a corrupt carcass fit only for the transport of either the soul or the rational mind, but an integral part of every aspect of human existence. Humanity must live *secundum naturam*, according to nature.

Montaigne showed a healthy scepticism towards the faculty of reason, but nevertheless his perpetual question 'What do I know?' focused attention on the thinking individual. In common with a growing number of Europeans, he was able to engage in a dialogue with others through the simple act of sitting in his library and reading. The technology of the printed book turned intellectual debate from a public, communal endeavour into an individual, private pastime. It is little wonder that the private reader was mainly taken up with the impact of his readings on his individual personal life. Although Montaigne was a man of wide experience (something that shows in his writings), his fellow readers had no need to be – everything you needed to know about the world could be found in books. Scholars could be, like their predecessors in Plato's academy, removed from the corruption of the world. (Shakespeare showed Hamlet as the perpetual student, always reading, continually examining his own state of mind and failing to engage with the world around him.) As well as allowing disengagement from the world, the revival of the printed word brought about a division between those with access (physical, financial, educational) to it and those without. There had always been divisions in society, but in medieval times the divide between nobility, clergy and peasantry had still allowed access to spiritual wisdom and salvation to the lowest in society; the revival of a civilization of the written word placed most of the population outside its borders.

Seeing how classical scholars disagreed among themselves, their modern successors were bold enough to question their authority. Access to a greater variety of written and printed material, expressed in more comprehensible form and made more widely available, changed the atmosphere of scholarship from reverence to engagement and criticism. The challenge to accepted authority pervaded all areas of thinking, including studies of the natural world. Nicolas Copernicus' 1543 overthrow of Aristotle's model of the universe came about partly through observation, but also because classical texts, such as Archimedes' report on the heliocentric models of Aristarchus and Pythagoras, became available in Padua and Cracow.

By the late sixteenth century the availability of ancient texts on medicine, cosmology, geometry, architecture and mechanics by Archimedes, Hero of Alexandria, Euclid, Vitruvius, Hippocrates, Galen and others was creating a community of enthusiastic investigators spread across the continent. In universities, while faculties of theology and law continued working within the old Aristotelian–Catholic framework, departments of mathematics and medicine were being infected with new methods. Around 1590 Galileo Galilei (1564–1642), then a professor of mathematics at Pisa University, dropped a number of different weights from the tower at Pisa and found that, in contravention of Aristotle's teachings, they all reached the ground at roughly the same time. Galileo's most important disputes were not with the Catholic church, nor with Aristotle (who, Galileo believed, would have accepted his error with enthusiasm), but with those who would not look at the world: 'Aristotle says that "an iron ball of one hundred pounds falling from a height of one hundred cubits reaches the ground before a one-pound ball has fallen a single cubit." I say that they arrive at the same time. You find, on making the experiment, that the larger outstrips the smaller by two finger-breadths . . . now you surely would not hide behind those two fingers the ninety-nine cubits of Aristotle, nor would you mention my small error and at the same time pass over his very large one.' (*Two New Sciences*, 1638).

At the time of Galileo's experiment Aristotle had been dead for 19 centuries. In all that time no one, so far as we know, had thought to carry out an experiment to test his assertions. But by the time Galileo began performing experiments in the late sixteenth century, Aristotle's authority, while still unchallenged, was being bypassed.

Aristotle had argued that there are two types of knowledge about the natural world, which he called *techne* and *episteme*. *Techne* is the everyday knowledge we acquire through our experience of doing things. Farmers see, for example, that corn grows better on sandy soil, whereas beans do better on clay. We have no need to understand the intricacies of plant physiology in order to make use of this *techne* knowledge, which has existed as an orally transmitted body of wisdom in all societies throughout human history. But *techne* is no use if we want to discover why corn grows better on sandy soil, or why the sun rises every day, or why clouds produce rain; for this we need *episteme*, which comes from the application of reason. Aristotle proposed that everything had a cause, and that the application of reason could uncover these causes of all movement and change in the world. *Techne* was for farmers; *episteme* for scholars. *Techne* was the knowledge of recurring natural patterns; *episteme* was the understanding of causes.

In the Graeco-Roman world the pursuit of *techne* had remained beneath the interest of scholars – they were interested in *episteme*; but in sixteenth-century Italy and in other parts of Europe, this began to change. In their work physicists, engineers and physicians such as Alberti, Baliani, Castelli, Fabricius, Gilbert, Paracelsus, Servetus, Stevin and Vesalius united practice and theory. Faculties of medicine and mathematics began to appear, but many of the most innovative scholars and theorists worked outside the university system – often in practical trades like architecture or civil engineering or medicine. It was these people who began to make *techne* more respectable by making observations of natural phenomena from a practical as well as an intellectual viewpoint. Despite the romantic image of the lone genius, Galileo was not working in isolation. But he understood that the study of the natural world was hampered by Aristotle's search for causes and that investigators should look instead for patterns or laws in nature – in other words unite *episteme* and *techne*. If this sounds a little high-flown, then its practical implications were anything but: if you wanted to know why something happened the way it did, rather than reading about it in Aristotle you went out and had a look for yourself.

Fascinated by the behaviour of falling stones, Galileo was equally intrigued by the swinging chandeliers in Pisa Cathedral, which seemed to take the same time to complete one arc, no matter how wide they swung; and when he dropped more weights he knew that Aristotle was wrong to say that the rate of descent was proportional to the weight of the object. Galileo understood that this was something to do with the increasing speed of the falling objects, so he began rolling balls down inclined slopes and found that they accelerated at the same rate, no matter what their size. All of this was puzzling and interesting but what did it mean? To the Aristotelian professors in the universities it meant nothing. How could the frankly daft practice of throwing objects off towers compare to the cerebral dignity of unlocking the sublime secrets of the great masters through patient, quiet study? But what about Galileo, what did it mean to him? He made it clear that he was not in search of Aristotle's causes: 'The present does not seem to me to be an opportune time to enter into the investigation of the cause of the acceleration of natural motions, concerning which various philosophers have produced various opinions . . . Such fantasies, and others like them, would have to be examined and resolved with little gain.'

So, in effect, Galileo was not really looking *for* anything, he was just looking. Although it seemed irrational, this was an immensely liberating notion. Investigators could experiment freely and speculate endlessly about the natural world without having to search for underlying causes. This was a re-creation of the spirit of Heraclitus and Parmenides, who had, for example, suggested that space 'must have the same geometrical qualities in all places. This was not a provable suggestion but it allowed mathematicians to propose that geometrical relationships that applied in their own experience were, in fact, universal theorems that applied at all places and all times. This meant that a seemingly innocuous and parochial experiment conducted in Pisa or Florence or Ephesus or Alexandria could be of universal significance.

The scarcely believable, the almost incredible, was now within the bounds of human contemplation. Could a sparrow's egg fall to earth at the same speed as a cannon ball? Could the seemingly immovable earth really be spinning through space in daily and yearly cycles? Could we be living on one of a set of planets circling the sun? Instead of dismissing such fantastic ideas, the response from Galileo was, Why not? Anything that did not go against the evidence of the natural world could be proposed.

However, this apparent freedom was not quite what it seemed. Galileo's account, quoted earlier, shows his frustration at those who pointed to the small variations in his experimental results. Objects dropped from the tower at Pisa do not all reach the ground together, but they very nearly do; pendulums of the same length do not swing back and forth at exactly the same time, but they are very close. While claiming to be simply making observations of the world, Galileo convinced himself, and set out to convince others, that he was studying the actual physical world of falling stones and swinging pendulums in order to see beyond them to an underlying truth. His experiments never revealed an absolute obedience to a physical law; he had to use his reason to uncover the laws that underlay natural behaviour.

In effect Galileo was resurrecting Plato's world of Ideal Forms (see Chapter Three) but this time it was a world in which objects fall together and pendulums swing in perfect harmony – in other words a world in which all processes demonstrably follow the laws of nature. For while Galileo had freed investigators from the search for causes, he had set them the task of finding universal laws. There was no need to believe in the actual existence of an ideal world, but the experimenter needed to continually discount local variations in the real world – friction, air resistance and so on – in order to get to the underlying truth in the form of universal physical laws, which must be expressed in the language of mathematics.

Galileo's differences with the Aristotelian professors of Italy's universities brought him into conflict with the Catholic church. His enemies were powerful men, and Aristotle still provided the intellectual underpinning of Catholicism in an era of paranoia about all forms of heresy. At his trial in 1633 Galileo agreed to confess to a minor infringement and was devastated when he was sentenced to indefinite imprisonment. He was able to move to a house adjoining the Franciscan convent at Arcetri where his devoted daughter Maria Celeste was a nun. He lived there until his death in 1642.

The observation of the natural world, particularly the night sky, was as important as experimentation to the discovery of natural laws. In 1601 Johannes Kepler inherited from Tycho Brahe, a Danish astronomer, 40 years of continuous, comprehensive, accurate recordings of planetary, astral and stellar movements. Kepler, who was convinced by Copernicus' theory of the earth orbiting the sun, used Brahe's observations to derive three laws of planetary motion, and by 1610 Galileo had developed the newly invented telescope into an astronomical instrument, opening up a universe that had been beyond Aristotle and the ancient authorities. For centuries Europeans had looked back to the ancients as the source of wisdom, but through technology, they had overleapt their illustrious ancestors.

The telescope and the microscope, invented in 1609, convinced modern scholars that they were right to question the ancient authorities, particularly in the light of the stream of new discoveries being made in America and Asia. Science, or natural philosophy, was engaged in observing the natural world, but its crucial engine was communication through the printed word. Books with 'New' in the title abounded to distinguish them from the outdated ideas of the past. In 1660 the Royal Society was formed in London and began publishing *The Philosophical Transactions*, the prototype of science journals, which began the custom of open exchange of information. Through the medium of print, science became self-selecting, ruling out incidental observations in favour of systematic investigation – working back, in effect, to Galileo's original impulse.

While Galileo was avowedly hostile to philosophical interference in the investigations of the natural world, this did not stop philosophers from weighing in. Montaigne's distrust of rationality and his need to embed humanity in the natural world began to look decidedly quaint once the world was seen to obey laws that could be discerned through objective measurement. Rationality and distance from nature became the keys to the truth.

The English scholar Francis Bacon (1561–1626) argued that instead of looking for abstract causes in the natural world, investigators should accumulate knowledge through observation and then make inductions of underlying truths. 'Matter rather than forms should be the object of our attention, its configurations and changes of configuration, and simple action, and law of action or motion . . .' (*Novum Organum*, 1620). The liberation of knowledge from Aristotelian bonds, as described by Bacon and others, was intoxicating, but it was really the exchange of one kind of knowledge for another. As natural philosophy, then science, became a search for universally applicable laws express-ible in mathematical language, all other kinds of knowledge suffered in comparison. The anecdotal (a word used to denote frivolous irrele-vance), the local, the vernacular, the non-quantifiable were seen as the variations that must be overcome in order to get to the real, incorrupt-ible, invariable and universal truths, and were therefore gradually placed outside the corpus of true knowledge.

This universalism was another reason for human separation from the natural world. In experimental science place is irrelevant because everywhere, as Parmenides said, is the same. As law-seeking principles were applied to the topography of the earth, its different landscapes, its multitude of life forms, the diversity of the local turned out to be simply one result of the playing-out of universal laws. Diversity was a subset of universalism – something to get past to find the real truth. Naturally enough, the spread of reading as an activity added to this sense of disconnection with the diversity of the world – the same book could be read in the same way in Edinburgh, Salamanca or Padua; the myriad communities based on shared physical place – villages, towns, congregations – began to give way to a disembodied community of the mind. While reading silently (as practised by Thomas More, for instance) was regarded as eccentric in the 1500s, by the eighteenth century it was common. The search for universal laws in nature led, eventually, to a similar quest in all areas of human activity. And because this search for abstract universals has always been conducted (in theory at least) by rational means, rational abstraction has become recognized as the route to true knowledge and understanding. A way of thinking devised by Plato 2,000 years earlier came to be the foundation of western scientific culture.

While Francis Bacon was devising a way to account for the new discoveries in natural philosophy, his fellow philosopher René Descartes (1596–1650) was exposing all human knowledge to the rigours of rationalism. Descartes saw that the combined philosophical system of Aquinas and Aristotle did not stand up to proper rational scrutiny, and therefore set out to devise an entirely new structure of thought that would underpin modern Christianity. His famous beginning was to ask the same question as Montaigne, 'What do I know?', and to rationally deduce that since the world could logically be a figment of his imagination, he could know nothing for certain, except that he himself must exist. Because *someone* must be having the thoughts he was experiencing, that person must exist – hence, *cogito ergo sum*, I think therefore I am.

Descartes then employed the method used in the formulation of mathematical equations to show that there must be a world existing independently of our senses, and that this world must be based on mathematical principles. His invention of multidimensional coordinates (the Cartesian axes used on all graphs and charts) allowed the shape and position of any object to be described in mathematical terms, while he predicted that movement was also subject to physical laws that could be mathematically encoded. As well as being able to describe the world mathematically, Descartes's work threw up the astonishing possibility that the future behaviour of the world could be accurately predicted. The vagaries of nature could be overcome and, given enough rational effort, everything could be fitted into a vast clockwork universe. Cause and effect were utterly predictable and completely open to human rational analysis.

In working outwards from his lonely self, who knows only that he exists because he thinks, Descartes placed the individual human mind (which was, incidentally, quite separate from the human body in which it was encased) at the centre of everything. Man, as the only rational being, stood as God's supreme creation, and Montaigne's self-contemplating individual had become, in Descartes's hands, the focus of all human enquiry. There were no dark forces to dictate the course of his existence; human life was a series of actions and consequences that could be predicted and controlled by the rational mind.

It was still possible to say that God had laid down the physical laws that ruled nature, but Descartes's work meant that the workings of the world resembled a gigantically intricate piece of clockwork. This was no accidental metaphor. The clock was a powerful illustration of human ingenuity and superiority over nature – after all, the clock kept accurate time compared to the seasonal vagaries of the sun dial and could be endlessly improved. This kind of mathematical and mechanical thinking fed into other areas of life. Money, for example, was a numerical system by which a man's worth could be calculated, and as the money economy spread across Europe, people began thinking of themselves as producers and spenders, and as economic units rather than spiritual beings. Conversely they began to lose their sense of spiritual affection and empathy with the natural world – how could you feel spiritually connected to a clockwork machine?

Descartes's *Discourse on Method*, published in 1637, tied in with the growing sense, derived from the classical writers, that all areas of human life should be open to rational enquiry. The elements of chance and unpredictability that dogged human existence could surely be removed by the application of reason. The spread of printing and literacy allowed ideas formed in response to Greek, Roman and medieval politics to reach a wider audience. Scholars throughout Europe could read and argue about political developments and ideas from other times and places, and it was a small step to begin to contemplate the application of these ideas to the new challenges presented by the modern state. The sixteenth century had seen tentative stirrings of political philosophy: Machiavelli's writings on the arts of government became known throughout Europe; in 1516 Thomas More wrote about an ideal society called Utopia; and the Spanish Catholic philosopher Francisco Suarez, writing in 1597, debated the right of a king to rule and the right of the people to remove a tyrant.

In the 1640s, theoretical investigations of the principles of the modern state were suddenly given practical urgency by a political crisis in one of Europe's major monarchies. The English Revolution gave the opportunity for political ideas to be aired in public. The assumptions that underlay the foundation of the modern state were laid bare and offered up for scrutiny, and it rapidly became clear that while the state had acquired extraordinary power, the key to its success was in finding a role for the newly assertive, rational, self-regarding individual. The first people to expose this difficulty were not philosophers or scholars but a group of soldiers meeting in a church hall in Putney.

The English Revolution was a protracted and ultimately successful attempt by the English parliament to rid the country of an absolute monarchy, and to quash the latent possibility of a Catholic takeover of England. In all it lasted from the outbreak of civil war in 1642 to the signing of the Bill of Rights in 1689 and the Act of Settlement of 1701. The origins of the conflict have been interpreted in different ways, but at its heart was the refusal of the Stuart kings, and Charles I in particular, to accept the role of the monarch as servant of the state (see Chapter Ten). Both Charles and his father James I acted as absolute monarchs without understanding that this role was only possible if the monarch, paradoxically, agreed to be the personal embodiment of the state.

Charles alienated the Protestant state by promoting proto-Catholics such as William Laud to high positions in the Church of England, by illegally raising tax (known as ship money) without parliamentary approval and by flouting (in the notorious case of the Five Knights) the ancient rights of Englishmen not to be imprisoned without charge or trial. The mutual resentment and suspicion came to a head when Charles, who had attempted to fund his regime through royal monopolies, was forced to recall parliament in order to raise money. There were then two obviously separate and antagonistic loci of power in the country – king and parliament. Printing, as well as bringing the King James Bible into every English parish, brought pamphlets and posters bearing news of Catholic atrocities against Protestants in Bohemia and Saxony. When similar sensationalized and terrifying news came from its own territory in Ireland, the English state was forced to act. But who was the state? Parliament, distrusting his loyalties, refused to allow the king to lead an army against the Catholic Irish. The result was civil war in England.

The most surprising element of the civil war, to modern minds at least, is that it was fought in order to preserve, or to reinstate, ancient traditions. While understanding Athenian democracy as an attempt to hold on to customary ways of dispersing power requires analysis of underlying motives, in the English Revolution no interpretation is necessary; both sides in the civil war explicitly appealed to ancient tradition for justification of their cause. Royalists believed that any challenge to the monarchy destroyed an ancient concept of divine order, while parliamentarians wanted the restoration of their ancient rights established under English common law, which the king and his predecessors had degraded.

Even in the seventeenth century English people spoke and wrote of being under 'the Norman yoke'. This might seem an absurd piece of nostalgia, but the common people knew that the great estates of the English countryside had been given by William I to his supporters after 1066, and believed that before the Norman Conquest the land had belonged to the people. They dated their customary rights to fair trial and protection against oppressive tax to Anglo Saxon times (though they probably reached back much further). The potential conflict between ancient customary rights and the right of the king to make laws was crucial in England and throughout Europe in the seventeenth century. Sir John Davies, a senior law officer, wrote during the reign of James I: 'This customary law is the most perfect and most excellent, and without comparison the best to make and preserve a commonwealth. For the written laws which are made either by the edicts of princes, or by councils of state, are imposed upon the subject before any trial is made . . . But a custom does never become a law to bind the people.' The king's appeal to history was matched by his opponents' secure belief in the primacy of English common law.

The absolutist monarchs of England and France were, in terms of military and economic power, extremely weak. The taxes collected by Charles amounted to an average of seven shillings per person per year, at a time when the average labourer was earning around £9. The courts, militias and poor relief (which were the points of contact between the people and authority) were in the hands of local dignitaries, who were unpaid and largely unsupervised by the centre. But the power of the monarch lay elsewhere.

Everyone, and in particular the nobility, believed that without a unifying monarch the kingdom would disintegrate into chaos. Following Augustine's lead, priests thundered from their pulpits that humans were barbaric animals who, without God's and the king's laws, would descend into uncontrollable sin. The ancient idea of a Great Chain of Being had also survived from classical times, and was now put to work in the service of kingly authority. This universally held notion asserted that in the hierarchy of beings, humanity sat beneath God and the angels but above the beasts. Within humanity kings and princes were nearer to the divine, and commoners further away. As well as being of more divine status, the Stuart kings had the benefit of having survived assassination by Catholics. The exposure of the 1605 Gunpowder Plot meant that anyone who criticized the monarchy risked being branded a Catholic. Nevertheless, Charles managed to throw away all of these levers of authority and leave the English people deeply resentful of his rule.

If the king was distrusted, then the clergy were openly despised, seen by the common people to be on the side of the rich and powerful, determined to curry favour and to line their own pockets. The Reverend Edmund Calamy told the House of Commons in 1642 that 'the people complain of their ministers that they are dumb dogs, greedy dogs, that can never have enough'. The clergy were members of the ruling class and the religion they preached invoked deference to authority and praise of the high-born, but there was a strong tradition of radical religious dissent among the English population, dating back to Elizabethan and earlier times. By the late 1630s altars were being desecrated and statues destroyed, and people called for a new kind of church with itinerant priests living off the charity of their flock, preaching in fields and marketplaces. They wanted the bishops thrown out and their palaces torn down.

The war itself lasted four years. In 1644, after two years of fighting, a group led by Sir Henry Vane and Oliver Cromwell, a country gentleman from Huntingdon, took control of the parliamentary forces and instituted the New Model Army. After defeats at Naseby, Langport and Bristol the king was forced to surrender himself to the uncertain sanctuary of the Scots, who, in January 1647, in return for £20,000 handed him to the English parliamentary commissioners.

Suddenly the world, as Christopher Hill so aptly put it, was turned upside down. The king, the archbishops, the supposed embodiments of authority, were in the hands of the people – the highest were brought low and the lowest raised high. Groups such as the Levellers and Diggers emerged, Bibles in hand, to claim that the world was a treasury to be shared among all God's people, while dissenters like the Quakers advocated abolition of authority and equality for all, including women.

In the wake of victory, parliament's difficulties were twofold – what to do with the king, and what to do with the army. The latter, with arrears of pay outstanding, refused to disband, and sought a statute of indemnity from prosecution – fearing that any settlement that placed the king in power would leave them open to charges of treason. Most important of all, the soldiers sought a voice in government as the reward for their part in the victory of parliament. The majority in parliament was against the army's demands but had no way of ordering them to disband.

The king, under house arrest at Holmby House in Northamptonshire, was able to play the different emergent factions off against one another. Though ostensibly powerless, his approval would be needed for any constitutional settlement, and all sides believed they must retain him as monarch and head of state. In June 1647 the army, fearing that the king was going to be reinstated as a tyrannical monarch, seized Charles and eventually brought him to Hampton Court, while they advanced on London and encamped at Putney. The stage was set for king, parliament and army to resolve their differences. In July 1647 Henry Ireton and John Lambert, two leading army officers, issued an outline of a constitutional settlement, known as the Heads of the Proposals. Though Charles rejected them, they were in any case not democratic enough for many of the soldiers and their representatives, who published a separate document called 'An Agreement of the People'. This was a historic document, the first time that a written constitution had been put forward to establish a representative government and to protect certain inalienable rights. It was 'An Agreement of the People' that was discussed by the Army Council, a body representing all ranks, at the Putney debates.

On 29 October 1647 the debate of the general council of the army was begun at Putney Church. The proceedings were transcribed and stand as a monument to political debate carried out in extraordinary circumstances. The king was under arrest and would not agree to anything, the army was aggrieved and intent on staying put – who was to rule, and who was to say who should rule the country? The tone of the meeting was set on the first morning by Edward Sexby: 'The cause of our misery is upon two things. We sought to satisfy all men, and it was well; but in going about to do it we have dissatisfied all men. We have laboured to please a king, and, I think, except we go about to cut all our throats, we shall not please him; and we have gone to support an house which will prove [made of] rotten studs – I mean Parliament, which consists of a company of rotten members.'

The king's abuse of parliament had rallied many people to its cause. They believed parliament to be a guardian of their rights, but now that men had fought and died for it, they looked closer and found it imperfect. Cromwell and Ireton, who were sympathetic to many of the soldiers' demands, believed they could show that reason was on their side. But the radicals had an equally rational set of arguments. The result was a historically significant articulation of different political philosophies.

Ireton argued that only men of property should have the vote, since they have a stake in the kingdom that others do not. The right to be called an Englishman, and to breathe the air and walk the lands and have use of the laws of the kingdom, is a natural right, but the right to share in the exercise of power is a civil right flowing from the construction of a society. Ireton's main argument for restricting civil rights was that those who have no property, who make up the majority, will pass laws that deprive property-owners of their lands, and that the kingdom will then fall into anarchy and chaos.

Colonel Rainsborough's reply, in the heat of debate, has become famous as a passionate and unprecedented argument for representative government: 'I think that the poorest he that is in England has a life to live as the greatest he; and therefore truly, sir, I think it's clear, that every man that is to live under a government ought first by his own consent to put himself under that government; and I do think that the poorest man in England is not at all bound in a strict sense to that government that he has not had a voice to put himself under . . . I do not find anything in the law of God, that a lord shall choose twenty burgesses, and a gentleman but two, and a poor man shall choose none: I find no such thing in the law of nature or the law of nations.'

Rainsborough had two further arguments against Ireton's concerns about property. Firstly, God's commandment is 'Thou shalt not steal'; this law would continue to exist. Secondly, in sympathy with his countrymen's belief in ancient rights and wrongs, he questioned the status of property in England. 'If it be a property, it is a property by a law . . . and I would fain know what we have fought for . . . that which enslaves the people of England, that they should be bound by laws in which they have no voice at all.'

In this exchange, absolutism, the Great Chain of Being, the unworthiness of the ordinary man in a divinely ordered hierarchy are all forgotten. This is a discussion about the ways in which a state can be made legitimate in the eyes of its members. It seems highly progressive compared to the absolutism of the king, but we need to remember that Rainsborough and Ireton, both soldiers for parliament, were seeking the restoration of ancient rights, albeit in a new setting. Ever since Augustine, priests had used the Bible to convince men of the need for order, but Rainsborough and his contemporaries had no need of others' interpretations. They knew their Bible and they knew that God had not set one man above another. These were indeed ancient rights.

The Putney debates were underpinned not by abstract political philosophy, but by the hard facts of experience. Men who had fought for parliament wanted to know what they had won. Rainsborough and Sexby used the authority of the scriptures to support their case, but their Bible was not an abstract political text; indeed it could be argued that the vernacular Bible was taken up with alacrity by northern Europeans precisely because its sentiments accorded so well with their customary ways of life. Though we are inclined to see custom as regressive and rationalism as progressive, the Putney debates show the dangers of simplistic linear thinking: Rainsborough used the notion of customary rights to argue for universal male suffrage; Ireton used rationality to argue for a limited franchise.

Extreme political circumstance gave birth to the Putney debates, and political events pushed them aside. The king fled Hampton Court to seek refuge at Carisbrooke on the Isle of Wight; but rebellions by royalist forces convinced the army that he must be tried for treason, and on 30 January 1649 the king was executed. Oliver Cromwell (1599–1658) had by then emerged as the skilful manipulator of events and effective manager of the army's grievances. The more radical demands of Rainsborough and Sexby were dropped, and at the end of the long English Revolution, in 1689, it was Ireton's version of reason that won out. A parliament of landowners was made the power in the land (albeit with a strong dose of certain ancient customs), with both kings and commoners placed outside its doors. England had to wait until 1918 for Rainsborough's universal male suffrage to come into being.

The political turmoil that led to the Putney debates continued through the trial and execution of the king, the Commonwealth, Restoration and final removal of James II. Questions of political legitimacy were debated by scholars and soldiers whose writings put their lives at risk. But interesting as these writings were, it is questionable whether they materially affected the political settlement in England. Nevertheless, political philosophy was added to the list of subjects required by the growing community of literate people. Thomas Hobbes's *Leviathan*, an argument for absolutist monarchy on the Augustinian grounds that humanity needed absolute control, was published in 1651 in France, where he was in exile. The restoration of the Stuart monarchy in 1660 might have been justified by reference to Hobbes, but absolutism never took root in England. John Locke's political writings, while in tune with political currents in England, were essentially descriptive of the sentiments of the most powerful group in the English parliament. Hobbes regarded humanity as essentially malign and in need of control, while Locke argued for a benign view of human nature, and the need for a social contract between different members of society, rather than a Hobbesian dictator.

The English Revolution showed that while theoretical writings were growing in volume, their influence on political events was still marginal. People responded to pamphlets calling for action, to the denigration of their customs, and to fear of religious persecution, rather than to theoretical ideas for the construction of new kinds of state. In the course of the next hundred years this situation was to change, and ideas forged in the turmoil of the seventeenth century were put into practice in the eighteenth – the century when rationalism, apparently, triumphed.

The English Revolution gave rise to political debate in speeches, pamphlets and philosophical tracts. And in spite of the turmoil of the revolution, England was becoming a steadily more prosperous country, with a growing class of educated gentlefolk. While the revolution expressed the refusal of this class to be dictated to by an arrogant monarch, the educated English began to make their self-confidence felt in other ways. As well as producing political philosophy based on rational analysis, they developed a community of natural philosophers, including Robert Boyle (1627–91), Robert Hooke (1635–1703) and Isaac Newton (1642–1727), who between them established a new vision of the natural world. It was Newton who provided the greatest vindication of Descartes's austere rationalism, by showing that the universe was, indeed, utterly explainable through mathematical analysis. His

Principia Naturalis Principia Mathematica, published in 1687, demonstrated how the motion of every part of the universe, including the planets, was governed by a simple set of mathematically expressible laws. Even the rates at which different phenomena change could be expressed using a new mathematical device, known as calculus, invented by both Newton and his contemporary Leibniz (1646–1716) specially for the purpose.

Newton's astonishing achievement in showing the physical world to be open to rational analysis was accompanied by a gradual, yet profoundly important, alteration in the mental outlook of western Europeans. During the sixteenth and seventeenth centuries the new interest in rational natural philosophy (what we would call science) had rubbed along with the customary reliance on other forms of knowledge – numerology mingled with mathematics, astrology with astronomy, alchemy with chemistry and so on. But by the late seventeenth century those natural philosophers who, like Isaac Newton, continued to take a serious interest in magic, alchemy and the occult were a small minority: in *The Skeptical Chemist*, published in 1661, Robert Boyle, founder-member of the Royal Society, gently ridiculed 'the generality of alchymists' for their belief that lead could be transformed into gold.

The disapproval of natural philosophers fatally undermined mysticism, alchemy and magic, which had previously held great authority and prestige. But there were other reasons for the decline of European belief in mysticism and magic – a process unique in world history. In England and Holland technical improvements in agriculture gave rural people more faith in the power of human intervention, and although disease remained a threat, the plague, which was surrounded by superstition, did not appear again in England after the 1670s. Printed newspapers and pamphlets brought most towns and villages in contact with rationalist opinion and ideas, even when literacy levels were low.

The beginning of the insurance business around 1700 is an indication of a profound alteration in attitudes. Marine insurance was established in Lloyd's coffee house in London, and following the Great Fire of London of 1666, fire insurance became widespread. Samuel Pepys's famous account of the fire shows him hurrying breathless, from place to place, finding little time to dine or to take ale; but at no time does he enter a church to ask God to intercede. Instead he looks for practical ways to contain the fire and sees others doing the same. Humanity must help itself. By the mid-eighteenth century, there was no need for magic or divine intervention to save your house, you simply called on the parish fire engine, and if it did not arrive in time, you contacted your insurer. People had always helped themselves, but they believed that their fate was part of some greater scheme that was accessible to them only through ancient customs and rituals. The insurance business could, in contrast, use the new mathematical techniques of probability to calculate how long you were likely to live, how many children you might have, and what you might die from. Mathematics, it seemed, was at the heart of everything.

Scientific explanations of the natural world, technical improvements in agriculture, wider circulation of progressive ideas all played their part in the decline of magic, but there were two additional factors. First, the Christian faith offered a vision of a world dominated and controlled by a single all-powerful God. Magic, in contrast, assumes a world full of strange and conflicting forces that are accessible only by arcane methods. Christianity and magic could and did exist alongside each other for a thousand years, but magic was always vulnerable to, rather than aided by, a monotheistic religion. As long as Christianity retained its links to the pagan traditions of the north, the magical element of northern culture survived. But the effect of the Reformation was to sever the links between Christianity and the natural world, which was the source of all customary magic. When Protestantism placed humanity in direct relation with God, without need of ritual or arcane knowledge, magic and mysticism were cast adrift. On top of this, mechanical printing gave more and more people access to a massively impressive body of work that demonstrated how rationality, rather than superstition, could be fruitfully applied to humanity's problems. Here was an apparently irrefutable demonstration of how the fate of humanity lay in its own hands and not buried in the obscurities of mysticism or magic.

At the start of the eighteenth century the British state emerged from a revolution in which the interests of the gentry-in-parliament prevailed over both the king and the common people. The rational individual – the literate, educated gentleman with access to printed works and schol-arly debate, religious but pragmatic – found that this state suited his interests. For the next 200 years or so the British state was able to channel the energies of this self-defining social group more effectively than its rivals, by allowing its members access to power. As other nations followed suit, the tastes, thoughts and prejudices of the gentry (as distinct from both the monarchy and the common people) became the defining motif of western civilization.

Nevertheless, diversity continued to flourish even within the educated classes of Europe. The organization of the different states may have been realized by the ruling classes, but it was still based on customs that varied considerably from one region of Europe to another. The Dutch republic, which emerged from the rebellion against Spain, was, in many ways, the marvel of seventeenth-century Europe – a fact appreciated by the Dutch themselves and many reluctant admirers. In a continent of states ruled by sovereigns, the Dutch were an anomaly, and, as in England, political philosophers were impelled to make rational sense of a situation that arose from the customs of the people. In both countries, the state had to be legitimized in the eyes of both educated people and foreign allies. It may seem curious that while educated Europeans read about the marvels of classical Athens and the Roman republic, they nevertheless believed that a monarchy was the naturally legitimate form of government. But rationality has its limits in human affairs; monarchy properly constrained offered stability in which the educated classes could prosper. The Dutch Revolt against their Spanish king, and the subsequent republic, were legitimized by the Dutch scholar Hugo Grotius (1583–1645), who showed that there had been a continual history of Batavian and Dutch autonomous rule that overrode the claims of the Spanish king. It was, he argued, historically legitimate to be a state without a monarch.

The Dutch republic, even when it adopted a monarchy, thrived because it was able to become a modern state while preserving its ancient customs. Unlike the cities of northern Italy, whose mutual hostility brought their downfall, the Dutch kept the Spanish, French and Austrian empire troops at bay, and so were able to retain the autonomy of their individual provinces within a framework of mutual support. The Netherlanders became renowned for turning their inhospitable land, full of salt marshes and flooding rivers, into a human paradise. New methods of horticulture, reclaiming land and building over water made the Dutch countryside and towns the wonders of Europe. The republic was the only part of Europe where there was no censorship and relative religious tolerance.

The Dutch cities were models of a new type of urban living. In England and France medieval towns were losing their status while the royal capitals were increasing hugely in wealth and power. In the Netherlands the principal cities remained attached to their function as trading and manufacturing centres, while at the same time being designed for pleasant human habitation. Georgian London and Louis XIV Paris contained beautiful squares and houses, but these were planned simply as dwellings for the wealthy, not as working elements of the cities. The Dutch managed, through extraordinary sympathy, to retain the best of the mixed and accidental nature of medieval towns while rigorously planning for the modern commercial world. Amsterdam was laid out as a series of concentric canals, so that each house and workshop had access to a canal and to a canal-side roadway. The canals could be flushed out regularly to take away sewerage, and goods could be brought from the countryside directly into the heart of the city, while a series of canals connected Amsterdam, Leyden and Haarlem. Although some streets were more distinguished than others, there were no palaces in Amsterdam. The millionaire merchants lived in better style but in the same type of houses as their workers. The streets in Dutch towns were paved centuries before other European towns, bringing benefits to merchants, workers and citizens alike. The advantages of the Dutch way of life were not lost on outsiders. A constant stream of English and French exiles fleeing persecution, imprisonment and possible execution sought sanctuary in the Netherlands at various times, including Descartes and Locke. This was the atmosphere in which Dutch painting articulated the opposing strains of commercialism and piety, of individual and community (see Chapter Nine).

The different western states that were emerging needed to cope with the requirements of the literate gentry, well-versed in abstract rationality, aware of concepts such as rights and responsibilities, the balance of state and individual power, and stability versus freedom. Those that were able to meet these requirements most fully, such as Britain and the Dutch republic, retained long-term political stability, while those that ignored them, such as France, created growing, and eventually irresolvable, difficulties.

The new spirit of literate rationalism also spread into relationships between European states. The concept of just war dated back as far as Augustine (and, arguably, to Roman fetial law), but this had been entwined with religious morality. When was it just to go to war against fellow Christians? The Dutch once again led the way. Because many

Dutch burghers were, by religious conviction, against war, Grotius was called on to give a justification for the Dutch East India Company (the commercial arm of the Dutch state) entering into armed conflict, and to show why war was, in some circumstances, lawful. His full response, published as *De Jure Belli ac Pacis* ('On the Law of War and Peace') in 1625, mapped out an international arena in which states were mutually recognized entities whose common interests were served by a network of laws, treaties and individual rights. When a state's rights were grossly abrogated it could justly go to war. Like his fellow political philosophers in England, Grotius was describing the situation that existed in Europe, rather than theorizing about an ideal state, or community of states. But like theirs, his description rationalized the development of the state in terms that appealed to the rulers and their supporters.

The emergence of the omnipotent state that was detailed in Chapter Ten, combined with the spread of printing and literacy, had a profound effect on western citizens and on their sense of their own civilization. The educated individual saw himself as rational, pragmatic and autonomous, part of his community but essentially an individual with free will, rights and duties, and with his destiny in his own hands; while the state in which he lived suppressed any challenges to its authority and adopted a monopoly of violent force within its borders. The combined effect of these two tendencies was to bring about the 'civilizing' of European society.

From the sixteenth century onwards, the rough camaraderie of soldier-knights surrounding a king was replaced by the adoption of courtly etiquette, which spread through the aristocracy and the lower gentry. Bodily functions, including birth and death, were hidden away, while open displays of violence and enjoyment of violent spectacle were both against the interests of the state and, not coincidentally, were increasingly seen as uncivilized. Corridors were introduced into houses so that rooms could be private, and open communal dwelling was restricted to the lower classes. The nobility in many outlying parts of Europe, who were often hereditary clan leaders, were used to sharing their houses and living quarters with their servants, acolytes, musicians and drinking companions, but under the influence of the new civility, this way of living was gradually extinguished. The adoption of good manners among the socially well-to-do seems self-evidently welcome, but it could only come about once all others had surrendered real authority to the state. As early as 1651, Thomas Hobbes pointed out that in return for the removal of unpredictable injury from their lives, the state places its subjects under a permanent threat of violence. The civilizing impulse was eagerly taken up, but its consequences were both profound and unknowable.

During the seventeenth century the spread of mechanical printing, along with the collapse of the medieval world-view, allowed the development of the self-regarding individual and of theoretical writings. These theories were focused on the relationship between the individual human mind and the natural world on the one hand, and the individual and the state on the other. But while human rationalization of the natural world found immediate spectacular fruition in Newton's mechanical universe, political writings were almost exclusively concerned with rationalizing situations that already existed. In the eighteenth century this was to change as the rational, educated individuals of Europe's most powerful country looked to political theory in their attempt to free themselves from despotism, and the focus of political change shifted from England and Holland to France.

ENLIGHTENMENT AND REVOLUTION

Politics and Reason in France and America

THE period from 1770 to 1815 saw immense political, social and economic upheavals in the west. The dislocations caused were so great that many historians see them as not just the beginning of the modern west, but the birth pangs of an entirely new type of society that owes little to any kind of custom or tradition. The formation of a constitutional state in America, the application of revolutionary ideas in France, the agricultural revolution and the rapid growth of industrialization and technology in Britain, the use of total war and the creation of a rational bureaucratic state by Napoleon, the sudden growth of capitalism and world trade and the rise of ethnic nationalism all helped to create the conditions for a new kind of society. The industrialized, technological, capitalist nation state, governed according to a constitution by representative bodies, which is what we mean by western society, came into being in those decades.

The essential change that underlay the events of the late eighteenth century was underway a hundred years earlier, and was itself the real progenitor of the modern world. Once western Europeans began to see themselves as rational autonomous beings, in control of their own destinies, the next requirement was to devise a society in which they could happily exist. This was a truly revolutionary idea, since up until then Europeans had wanted to re-create or retain the rights and restraints that existed in the past, and had done this through their experience of the present. In the late eighteenth century political ideas developed in complete isolation, and often by people with no experience or understanding of the practicalities of governance, were applied in the real world. But the theoretical combination of free individuals living within an orderly society proved much more difficult in practice than anyone could have imagined. In order to understand how the development of ideas affected later political events, we need firstly to look at the intellectual atmosphere created by the French Enlightenment, then at the American and French Revolutions, before finally examining the creation of the modern state in Napoleonic France.

In 1700 the population of England and Wales was around 5.6 million, the Netherlands 1.9 million and Spain 7.5 million, while the population of France was 21.4 million. This huge country, with borders and seaboards facing almost every western European state, had, under the stewardship of Mazarin and Colbert, become economically and militarily, as well as demographically and geographically, the dominant state in western Europe. France's own seventeenth-century revolution, provoked by Mazarin's exclusion of the Paris *parlement* from power, had failed in 1648, leaving France, unlike England and the Netherlands, as a centralized autocracy ruled by an absolute monarch.

France was a paradoxical country. While it was the centre of European cultural and political debate for much of the eighteenth century, and while French was the international language of education, ideas and diplomacy, with French architects, furniture designers, dressmakers and philosophers spreading throughout the rest of Europe, the Bourbon dynasty ruled as autocrats over a country where freedom of speech and expression was severely curtailed. Nevertheless, the death of Louis XIV in 1715 brought a change of atmosphere: the French state was no longer such an aggressive plotter, continually provoking concern and fear in the rest of Europe and among its own citizens. Under the umbrella of a universal French culture, educated Europeans began to think of themselves as part of a brotherhood of humanity. Not only did religious differences begin to seem irrelevant, national boundaries were in danger of dissolving too. Voltaire suggested that Europe was 'a great republic divided between several states', and Rousseau wrote, 'there is no longer a France, a Germany, a Spain, not even English, there are only Europeans. All have the same tastes, the same passions, the same way of life.' Montesquieu believed that he was 'human of necessity' while 'French by accident'. Intellectuals argued that wars were the product of the self-interest of rulers who persuaded and cajoled their hapless and ignorant subjects into inflicting murderous suffering on others, and on themselves. Wars were quarrels between members of dynasties who had no thought of the welfare of their subjects. There were even calls for an international body to be set up to resolve conflicts and to enforce peace and security. If traditional barriers between peoples could be broken down then a peaceful world would emerge. Writers began to argue that the behaviour of a state depended crucially on its form of government – states where power was shared more widely with the people would be more peace-loving and less likely to go to war.

In this optimistic atmosphere French philosophers looked to John Locke's benign view of humanity for a guide to the construction of an ideal society. Locke is best known as the founder of empiricism, the philosophical idea that we can only know anything about the world through the use of our senses, but in his own lifetime it was his political philosophy that made him famous throughout Europe, where he was known as the 'philosopher of freedom'.

Locke's *Civil Government*, published in 1690, recognized two essential components in human society: natural law and the social contract. Natural law dictates that we are all both free and equal by nature and that we combine in society (where we may become unequal and less free) in order to have stability in our lives and in our relations with others. The state of nature does not exist as a historical entity but as the essence of humanity, its essential nature. The social contract we make involves the surrender of some freedom and some equality in order to attain a greater benefit for the individual and society. The people, in their natural freedom, are able to choose how they wish to be governed – by monarchy, oligarchy or democracy. But if the people choose monarchy then the monarch cannot abrogate the natural laws that are the inherent protectors of his subjects' interests. If he did so he would be held to be a tyrant and could be legitimately deposed.

Voltaire and other French *philosophes* (who absorbed the work of Locke with relish) were in a curious situation. Fascinated by the application of reason to politics and society, they were unable to put their knowledge to practical effect. Internally France began to develop two parallel worlds – the machinery of autocratic government based on Versailles, and the ferment of 'enlightenment' based in gentlemen's societies, clubs, libraries and associations across the country. These two worlds overlapped because the nature of the state, in France and elsewhere, was continually developing. Regimes comprising a monarch surrounded by a court of nobles with regional power-bases were being replaced by professional administrations with ministries organized by function rather than region. A specialist French Foreign Office was copied by Spain in 1714, Russia in 1719 and Prussia in 1728. As administrations grew they realized how little they knew about the countries they governed. Gathering statistical information and mapping became functions of the state, with the first official surveys of coastal areas of Britain, for example, begun in 1765. The Austrian equivalent of the British Ordnance Survey produced the remarkable *Josephinische Landesaufnahme* in 1787, a survey-cum-map that showed every house, river, road and wood in the Habsburg empire. The development of state mapping shows the growing political ownership of geographical territory, as well as the changing nature of humanity's relationship with the natural world.

Because the new class of administrators and bureaucrats needed education and training, government service became the main engine of wider literacy and education. Adult male literacy levels in 1600 in England and Wales were roughly 25 per cent, and in France 16 per cent; in 1720 the equivalent figures were 50 per cent for England and Wales, and 29 per cent in France, and by 1800 the respective figures were 65 and 50 per cent. In 1787 the French journalist Sébastien Mercier wrote: 'Ten times more people are reading today than a hundred years ago. Today you can see a maid in a basement or a servant in an anteroom reading a pamphlet. In almost every class of society, people are reading, and so much the better.'

By 1702 London had a single daily newspaper, the *Daily Courant*; by 1760 there were 4 and by 1790 14; in 1727 25 newspapers were being produced in other English cities and stamp duty records from 1753 show seven million copies of newspapers being sold. In 1726 a French visitor declared that 'All Englishmen are great newsmongers. Workmen habitually begin the day by going to the coffee rooms in order to read the latest news.' It is worth noting that education and literacy were highly stratified by social class. Marriage records show that in Toulouse in the mid- to late eighteenth century, 90 to 100 per cent of lower-middle-class men and 70 per cent of their wives could read and write. There was strong resistance among such people to the idea of working-class children being taught how to read and write, since this would enable them to compete for the limited number of clerical jobs. Even liberal thinkers believed that education for the poor

Gods as humans, humans as gods. Images from classical and Hellenistic Greece: Poseidon in bronze (*above left*); the Venus de Milo (*above*); a later marble copy of the Discobulus (*left*).

Humans in action. Classical and
Renaissance depictions of historical
and mythical figures: Pericles as
military leader (*above left*);
Augustus with sceptre and thunderbolt (*above*); Hercules and Cacus
by Baccio Bandinelli (*left*).

Humans in contemplation. Medieval depictions of St Clement (*above*) and St Michael (*above right*) as unworldly ideals; a Renaissance depiction of St Jerome, St Francis and the Madonna and Child as fully embodied figures, by Mirabello Cavalori (*right*).

The medieval world saw Christ and Mary enthroned in heaven awaiting the final act in the great drama of the Christian faith. Detail from *The Last Judgement* by Fra Angelico (*left*); *The Coronation of the Virgin*, attributed to Bicci de Lorenzo (*below left*).

Italian painters of the fifteenth century began to show Christ made flesh, living, suffering and dying as a man. *Calvary* by Giovanni Bellini (*right*); *Lamentation over the Dead Christ*, also by Fra Angelico (*below right*).

Images of twentieth-century civilization, I. Geronimo (*above left*) chief of the Apache, brought into captivity and civilized, appeared at Theodore Roosevelt's 1904 presidential inauguration; in the latter part of the century Native American children (*above right*) remained outsiders in their own country. African-Americans were routinely barred (*below*) while, at the same time, Jesse Owens became a national hero for his performances at the 1936 Berlin Olympics (*right*).

Images of twentieth-century civilization, II. German Jewish women having their heads shaved in November 1938 (*above*); French women, accused of collaboration or fraternizing with Germans, are paraded with heads shaved through the streets of France in 1944, with official police escort (*below*).

Insider-outsiders – Jews, blacks, primitives, homosexuals, convicts – mother-lode of modern western culture. (*Clockwise from top left*) Gustav Mahler; Igor Stravinsky; Pablo Picasso; Bessie Smith; Aretha Franklin; Harold Pinter; Tennessee Williams; Huddie Ledbetter aka Leadbelly.

was worthless; Voltaire wrote that 'as nothing but early habit can render it [hard labour and drudgery] tolerable, therefore to give the meanest of the people beyond that station that providence has assigned to them is doing them a real injury'.

Nothing though could stop the spread of newspapers. By the end of the eighteenth century every substantial town in Germany had its own newspaper, while the provincial press in France, Poland, Russia and the Netherlands expanded rapidly from a standing start after 1770. It became incumbent on an English gentleman of even modest means to possess a library and to send his children – even his daughters – away to be educated. This spread of literacy was part of the transformation of Europe from a largely oral, folk tale culture to an information-based, rational, technological society.

The belief in a rational, universal approach to human problems was reinforced by new discoveries in science. Newton had provided an inspiring example of how rationality could unlock the secrets of the physical world, and chemical and biological investigation by the likes of Lavoisier, von Haller, Cavendish, Scheele, Priestley, Linnaeus, Jenner and Dalton became the great project of eighteenth-century science. Improved microscopes showed that the simplest insect, for example, was in reality an organism of astonishing complexity, while chemists were able to isolate the different components of the air itself. The primacy of ancient authority was finally banished, and natural philosophers saw the world not as a vast system driven by a series of causes, but as a set of behaviours driven by universal laws. The replacement of the search for causes by the search for universal laws was the key development of the seventeenth-century scientific revolution that was carried into the eighteenth-century Enlightenment.

The Enlightenment, a catch-all term to describe the eighteenth-century culture of rationalism, was a self-conscious call for people to use their reason to solve the problems of humanity. Following the example of Newton and his fellow scientists, people believed that if rationality was going to tell them *anything* about the world, it should be able to tell them *everything*. Unfettered rational enquiry would lead to a coherent body of knowledge, driven by underlying universal laws, that would reveal a benevolent pattern in all things. Increasing knowledge of the wonders of the natural world, growing prosperity, relative peace and personal freedom (at least for the gentry) seduced many thinkers into overturning the traditional Christian view that all humanity, save a few lucky souls, was destined to burn in hell for eternity. Instead people began to believe in a providential God who had designed the world for the pleasure and appreciation of humanity. The turning of the seasons, the alternation of night and day, the provision of plants and animals for food and pleasure, the beauty of the natural landscape, all these were surely provided by a good God for the benefit of humanity, His most valued creation.

Enlightenment thinkers believed that humanity was a benevolent force and humans were, by nature, good. There was no conflict between personal gain and the good of the community in moral, social and, as Adam Smith was to argue, economic matters. Men should live well because this benefited everyone, which was what God would surely want. It was better to do this than spend valuable time in prayer and worship. As Dr Johnson said: 'It is our first duty to serve society: and, after we have done that, we may attend wholly to the salvation of our souls.'

The eighteenth century was an age of exploration and colonization. As ships carried them across the world's oceans, Europeans became interested in the cultures of China and India and in particular in the apparent 'natural' state of Polynesian islanders and native North Americans. Adopting the standpoint of an uncivilized yet wise outsider to point up the hypocrisy of European society became a favourite literary conceit (see, for example, Voltaire's *L'Ingénu*). Gentleman naturalists such as Joseph Banks, Louis Bougainville and Alexander Humboldt brought back exotic specimens from all corners of the earth. Europeans like James Cook were not exploring the world just in order to conquer but also to enquire. The impulse of empire-building was no longer simply to suppress and conquer native peoples, but to bring them the benefits of the new developments – scientific, social and cultural – of European society.

The Enlightenment also saw the application of scientific methods to the study of history. Rather than just plundering ideas from the texts of great classical thinkers, historians now set out to gather documentary information. Edward Gibbon's monumental *Decline and Fall of the Roman Empire* (1776–88) told a moral tale in which superstition and religion in the form of Christianity overcame the rational and humanistic principles of the Roman empire. There are two important clues to Enlightenment thinking in Gibbon's work. First, as well as rejecting pagan-based mysticism, people were beginning to question faith in Christianity; and second, historians assumed that humanity was essentially the same at all times and in all places but subject to different forces – the universalism of Plato, which had been revived by Galileo and employed so effectively by Newton, meant that all times as well as all places were essentially the same.

Gibbon garnered facts about the past in the same spirit as the natural philosophers collected every plant and bug they could get their hands on. This spirit even infected literature. The heroes of the novel, the new art form of European literature, were not riven by internal and external forces as in the great stage dramas of the sixteenth and seventeenth centuries, but were out on the road experiencing life in all its forms, being moulded and cajoled and amazed by the world around them. The eponymous heroes of *Moll Flanders* (1721), *Tom Jones* (1749), *Tristram Shandy* (1759–67) and *Candide* (1760) were all ciphers through which the reader viewed an extraordinary kaleidoscope of experiences.

Science, history, literature and philosophy were all aimed at discovering what was essential, natural and universal and differentiating it from the conditional, artificial and local. This unifying spirit culminated in the great project of the French Enlightenment, the *Encyclopédie*, compiled between 1751 and 1772 by Denis Diderot and Jean d'Alembert. This 28-volume work, which became an essential possession of every provincial library and philosophical society in France, and whose contributors included all of France's most famous *philosophes*, demonstrated the interconnectedness and unity of all branches of knowledge. It was the monument of the 'benevolent' Enlightenment.

For many educated people in the eighteenth century, it really did seem that humanity was on the way to establishing a rational unifying basis to all human knowledge and behaviour; a golden age of universal peace, harmony and understanding beckoned. This optimism, though, turned out to be based on an illusion. In reality the mood of the early Enlightenment was founded on the relative peace and prosperity of the times – much of which was based on the exploitation of overseas colonies. People believed that humanity was good and the world was benevolent because they themselves were prospering – rationality and universal human goodness were in fact an intellectual justification for the acquisition of wealth and social status by a growing class of gentry.

This became clear when the fragile balance of power broke down, and Europe once again went to war. The War of the Austrian Succession (1740–48), fought between Habsburg Austria and the small but aggressively militaristic state of Prussia, led to a major European conflict eight years later. In the Seven Years War (1756–63), Austria allied with France, and Britain thereby felt the need to join with Prussia. More than 850,000 troops and 30,000 civilians died as violence, disease, and outright hatred of foreigners welled up throughout Europe. In addition, the war drove Britain, France, Prussia, Austria and Russia near to bankruptcy with profound consequences – the British government's need to raise taxes provoked the American War of Independence, and French military expenditure led directly to the 1789 revolution. As armies and populations were brutalized and impoverished, the optimism of the Enlightenment seemed unsustainable.

Discoveries and events in the natural world further darkened the intellectual climate. Studies of rock formations and fossils seemed to show that ancient volcanoes and creatures no longer found on earth had existed in a past so distant that it preceded any human historical record. Was the world a static creation, or was it an ever-changing entity, of which humans happened to occupy the latest version? The Lisbon earthquake of 1755, which killed more than 30,000 people, could only be described as an act of God, while medical science began to recognize the prognosis of many diseases but remained helpless to prevent or cure them. It began to seem that Newton's work had not revealed a self-sustaining universe designed by God, but a machine without a soul. Not only did science not give any clue to the purpose of God, it was becoming hard to show that there was any purpose for existence at all.

This sounds like high-flown theory, but these issues had real consequences. Adam Smith argued in *The Wealth of Nations* (1776) that personal wealth creation, together with the basic law of supply and demand, was a natural way in which economics worked for the good of everyone. But when food was scarce, prices rose and the poor were in danger of starving. How then should governments behave? Was it wrong for them to intervene in this 'natural' process by taking artificial measures to keep prices down? Or was it a greater wrong to witness the preventable deaths of your fellow citizens? This kind of question undermined the easy self-assurance of the rational Enlightenment.

The optimism of the rationalist scholars and *philosophes* was dealt a further devastating blow by the Scottish philosopher David Hume.

In *A Treatise of Human Nature* (1739), Hume showed that the network of causation that was at the heart of the unifying ideals of his time was an illusion. We make connections between things based on our past experiences of them and we then assume incorrectly that we have made a logical causal link. Hume showed convincingly that no such connections could ever be shown to exist in reality, only as products of our intellect. By following up Locke's sceptical empiricism about the independent existence of the world, Hume demolished the philosophical basis of most of what had followed, and showed that rationalism, taken to its limits, demonstrated precisely nothing about reality. The struggle to understand the world was, it seemed, back to square one. People did not give up on rationalism, of course, but most saw that the immense variety of the natural world and of human experience did not allow a simple unifying analysis. The impulse to unfettered enquiry and the desire for universal principles, the two pillars of Enlightenment thinking, simply could not be reconciled.

While most held on to some kind of belief in rationality, others reacted strongly against its prescriptions. In the late 1700s Jean-Jacques Rousseau argued that rather than being the epitome of human achievement and a natural rational development, European society was in reality a corruption of the natural sublime state of uncivilized humanity; and that the unalloyed emotion and instinct of 'natural' societies were surer guides to truth and wisdom than the sophisticated rationalism of modern Europe. Rousseau's work found a ready audience among philosophers and political agitators, but also among poets, dramatists and artists. The rise of what became known as Romanticism was a sign of the failure of the Enlightenment to unify all human knowledge, and as a consequence European civilization divided into two camps – rationalist versus romantic; scientific versus artistic; deliberation and reason versus passion and instinct.

   Romanticism found its deepest expression in the German states, which after the traumas of the Seven Years War enjoyed a long period of peace, free from the customary interference of the Austrian emperors. Germany, a collection of independent states, began to enjoy the same benefits of diversity within a unified culture shared by the classical Greeks, the cities of the Italian *quattrocento* and the Dutch provinces of the seventeenth century. German artists were faced with articulating human dilemmas in a country undergoing the transformation from a peasant society ruled by princes to a collection of modern states, all under the lowering presence of Frederick the Great's ever-expanding Prussia. And they found ready patrons in the courts and castles of the German world.

German Romanticism is most familiar to us through the overlapping careers of Haydn (1732–1809), Mozart (1759–91), Beethoven (1770–1827) and Schubert (1797–1828). The spiritual legacy of Bach and Handel was transformed into the Viennese classical tradition (dazzling entertainment for the court, intertwined with musical statements of profound passion) by Haydn and Mozart. But it was Beethoven who allowed the emotional content of music to become the basis of its form. Music became the enduring art form of Romanticism, as a vehicle in which intuition and imagination and emotion could be communicated directly without the inhibiting use of language.

At the same time German writers, such as Goethe and Schiller, were inspired by the philosopher Johann Gottfried von Herder's argument that language itself, which is both sensuous and intellectual, is the instrument of understanding. Herder's encouragement of the study and revival of folk songs and stories led Goethe and others to seek a way of thinking that could combine reason and instinct. Goethe even tried to develop a science based on an 'imaginative synthesis' rather than pure reason. Rousseau's *Nouvelle Héloïse* (1761) and Goethe's *Sorrows of Young Werther* (1774) were hugely popular throughout Europe, while the romantically inspired *Lyrical Ballads* (1798) by the young Wordsworth and Coleridge turned English literature from knowing classicism to free-flowing naturalism.

The influence of the late eighteenth-century German 'renaissance' on the future of the west was to be immense. The arguments between rationality and Romanticism, often contained in the work of a single individual, produced a series of different solutions that were in fact a combination of these two apparent opposites. What we might call romantic rationality was an attempt to give meaning to a world that was apparently devoid of spiritual and moral intention. Rationalists needed this because science seemed to show that the natural world had no moral, metaphysical or religious meaning, and Hume had demonstrated that its causal connections were an illusion; what then was the point of studying the world? Romantics reached the same impasse because their focus on the individual provoked the question: Should people abandon society and become introspective idealists or should they engage with the imperfect corrupt world around them; should they go the hills to commune with nature or try to actively tackle society's problems? These two crises or impasses of rationality and Romanticism were answered by a series of German philosophers, including Immanuel Kant (1724–1804), Johann Fichte (1762–1814), Georg Hegel (1770–1813) and Arthur Schopenhauer (1788–1860), and taken forward later by Karl Marx (1818–83). And although there were differences between these philosophers (Schopenhauer's emphasis on irrationality puts him at odds with the others), they were each intent on creating a grand metaphysical structure that would not only encompass the rational and romantic, but would explain every aspect of the individual mind and its relation to the natural world and human society. Some of the results of this ambitious project are discussed in Chapter Sixteen, but we should understand that the impulse for this grand overarching synthesis was based on the urge to repair the intellectual fractures thrown up by the Enlightenment.

The first answer, provided by the philosopher Immanuel Kant, was to make plain the division in human thinking, rather than maintain the illusion of unity. But while Kant's solution was ingenious, it involved dismantling the harmony that had underlain western thought for most of the previous two millennia. Every western scholar had assumed either that the universe was arranged by God in ways that humans could not comprehend, or that some kind of moral order underlay every aspect of the natural world and human existence. It was therefore taken for granted that uncovering information about the natural world, or finding out truths about human behaviour, brought about moral understanding and improvement. Because investigating the secrets of the world would uncover the moral order, the concepts of truth, knowledge and goodness were taken to be synonymous. But by the late eighteenth century this belief was in tatters; what, though, would replace it?

Kant's response was to separate the two concepts of truth and goodness. Acquiring knowledge is the way to discover what is true, while feeling or intuition is the way to understand what is good. Humans could and should study the natural world and gain knowledge about it, free from any sense that it was somehow imbued with a divine or moral harmony. The natural world was simply there, knowledge of it came through our senses, and through the way that we used our innate sense of time and space to understand it, that is, to arrive at the truth about the world.

We should not, therefore, use the natural world to understand how society should operate, or how human beings should make moral choices, or to discover anything about God's will. These all belonged to a separate part of human experience, an inner faculty, that was the moral core of our being and where the mind had an intuitive awareness of itself and its obligations. The route to the good was quite separate from the route to the truth. By dividing human thought into two, Kant managed to accommodate the instinctive romantic with the rationalist. This dualistic way of looking at ourselves, which we now assume to be somehow natural, is an invention of modern western civilization, specifically designed to get round the crisis of rationalism.

But this was only half the problem; the more immediate difficulty facing Europeans was the continuing, and growing, problem of creating societies in which the autonomous individuals of the eighteenth century – both rationalist and romantic – could live. Augustine's brutal beast had been transformed into Aquinas's rational Christian, Calvin's Elect, Locke's empirical rationalist and now Romanticism's free spirit. The best-known work of the French philosopher Jean-Jacques Rousseau (1712–78), the *Social Contract*, begins with the famous line 'Man is born free, and everywhere he is in chains.' This was not so much a call for revolution as a statement of the conditions that prevailed in any society. Rousseau's work demonstrated that the only society in which an individual could live freely was one that matched the individual wills of the people to something called the general will. A natural society must be some sort of binding together of the wills of its individual members. Rousseau's vision was of a 'natural' society so perfect that the needs of its citizens would be secondary to the needs of the society itself.

While Rousseau and his followers sought a natural harmony in society, they did not believe that this harmony existed anywhere in European traditions; instead it must be brought about by *replacing* the existing order. This was a crucial and momentous change from what had gone before. The founding of democracy and republican government in the ancient world, the establishment of the Florentine and Dutch republics, and the English Revolution had all been justified by the call to restore pre-existing traditions. But eighteenth-century rationalism had overturned veneration for the past, while the longevity of the autocratic Versailles regime gave the French *philosophes* a distinct distaste for tradition. Late eighteenth-century political thinkers had no fondness for the past – Thomas Paine asked why he should be dictated to by the conditions and traditions of his forefathers. This was indeed a revolutionary idea; the past was gone and the future could be anything you wanted it to be.

The ideals of the Enlightenment survived, despite its inherent contradiction, and rationality was applied to the creation of a society in the quest for two opposing ideals – universal order and universal freedom. The Enlightenment encouraged the search for liberty and simultaneously gave opportunity for those who wanted perfect order. It introduced the idea that the universe was ever-changing and bequeathed us a science that was the pre-eminent source of knowledge about the natural world – and thereby removed moral and religious meaning from our understanding of nature. The world was enlightened, disenchanted and made rational. There was no turning back. The rationalists and romantics of the late eighteenth century are often thought of as opposing types, but in reality they were two sides of the same coin (with certain exceptions such as Herder and the philosopher of history Giambattista Vico). Both believed that they knew the true nature of humanity that existed everywhere and at all times, and they were both seduced by universal, abstract ideals, whether of a rational or a free world.

So far this chapter has dealt with changes in attitudes and thinking among the growing number of educated, literate people in western Europe. In the seventeenth century, political ideas developed in response to events, with philosophers lagging behind the forces of political change. But in the late eighteenth century political ideas themselves began to influence and inspire political change.

From the end of the medieval period, around 1500, the monarchs and central administrations of western Europe had been locked into a spiral: they needed ever more resources for military expenditure, and developed ever larger bureaucracies to collect and administer their funds. But the nobility and the gentry, who were the principal payers of taxes, were in danger of losing their role as regional powers. So they decided that if they were to pay taxes, they should have a voice in government. The Thirty Years War, the English Revolution and the Dutch Revolt were all fuelled by religion, but they were really challenges to the authority of the monarch over the nobility. At the same time there was an increased sense among the growing numbers of bourgeoisie, the lower orders of 'gentry', that they were being unfairly excluded from power. In Britain, the Netherlands and some German states, where the bourgeoisie was victorious, the result was wider representation in government; in France and Russia, where the monarchy quashed the pretensions to power of the upper and middle orders of society, the result was absolute rule.

It is clear that the American Revolution was part of the same conflict between an increasingly assertive class of educated merchants, landowners, lawyers and farmers on the one hand, and an unsympathetic regime on the other. Unlike the English and Dutch rebellions, the American Revolution was made on a separate continent from its parent regime, apparently free of the restraints of custom and tradition; it also happened at a time when political thinkers were eager to see their ideas put into practice.

War was, once again, the catalyst of crisis. The Seven Years War doubled Britain's national debt and, thanks to the defeat of France, left the British state in control of the eastern part of North America. The American colonies were expensive for Britain to maintain, while the colonists paid virtually no taxes. And so, once the war with France ended, the British government sought to reorganize the administration of North America and to tax its inhabitants. The colonists' fury shows that, while they were subjects of the British crown, they already thought of themselves as autonomous political entities. In Benjamin Franklin's words:

> We have an old mother that peevish is grown;
> She snubs us like children that scarce walk alone;
> She forgets we're grown up and have a sense of our own.

Laws forbidding settlement beyond the Appalachians, and imposing taxes on goods through the infamous Stamp Act, produced boycotts of British goods and tarring and feathering of British customs officials in Boston and other cities. In October 1765 nine of the colonies sent delegates to the first collective political forum of the American colonies, the Stamp Act Congress. Their rallying call was simple, no taxation without representation – while many British subjects had no vote, the colonists included men of substance who expected the privileges of their social class.

The colonists' protests caused a political crisis in London. In 1766

William Pitt was brought back as prime minister and the Stamp Act was repealed. But in Pitt's absence the chancellor of the exchequer, Charles Townshend, imposed taxes on glass, paper, paint and tea to pay the salaries of the colonies' judges and governors. In 1770 the British parliament compromised and repealed all the Townshend taxes except the levy on tea. On 16 December 1773 a group of colonists, disguised as Indians, boarded three ships in Boston Harbour and dumped 342 chests of tea into the water. For George III this was the last straw. He ordered Boston Harbour closed until the damage was paid for, prohibited town meetings, and appointed a British army general as governor of Massachusetts. The route to compromise was closed; the colonists had either to obey or rebel.

The pressure for American independence was rooted in the history of the colonies. Each colony had begun with a single settlement governed by a group chosen by their peers, a pattern that persisted as the colonies grew. Each new town that was founded was forced by necessity to produce some sort of administration, and these town councils were made accountable to their fellow citizens through meetings – regular open forums where grievances could be aired, representatives and committee members elected and decisions taken. Each colony then developed an assembly where representatives from its different towns could meet, debate and pass measures. In the 1770s a network of 300 town meeting committees was in existence in Massachusetts alone.

All of this came about because there was no higher authority to dictate how the colonies' towns and justice systems and schools and militias should be run – the citizens had to do it all for themselves. In its early history, North America was said to be a middle-class society: there was no aristocracy and no peasants; instead there were smallholders, gentleman farmers and artisans. An exaggeration maybe, but the lack of structures of authority gave ample opportunity for citizens' involvement in running their own affairs. The solutions they came up with were, not surprisingly, similar to the structures of communal participation present in most non-hierarchical societies – including the customary societies of western Europe. American democracy is sometimes said to be an ideal creation, devised without the restraint of history and authority. But the 13 colonies themselves had a tradition that had grown out of their situation and the culture of their inhabitants. By the 1770s, the colonists were well used to the infrastructure of constitutional representative government – petitions, votes, public meetings and demonstrations; in the colonies, the spirit of active citizenry was alive and well. This, rather than classical scholarship or abstract reasoning, was the wellspring of American democracy.

In September 1774 representatives and leaders from all the colonies met in Philadelphia. Having shown solidarity with Massachusetts by bringing supplies overland to the isolated colony, they took the profound step of forming themselves into a single, informal union. In the words of Patrick Henry: 'the distinctions between New Englanders and Virginians are no more, I am not a Virginian, but an American'. The meeting, known as the First Continental Congress, voted to boycott all British goods and to press for representation in the British parliament. They also vowed to stick together if any one of them was attacked. The colonists did not have to wait long to fulfil their promise of solidarity. On 19 April 1775 the British commander, General Gage, made a surprise march from Boston to Concord to seize a cache of rebel guns. The rebels were forewarned by Samuel Prescott and Paul Revere and managed to hold off the British at Lexington and Concord, forcing Gage to retreat with 250 dead or wounded. The War of Independence had begun.

The impulse to rebel was rooted in circumstance, but there were plenty of Americans on hand to articulate and rationalize the mood of the people. The colonists' desire to preserve their independence began to be presented as a moral quest for eternal and universal rights. Educated men in America were well aware of the political and social ideas swirling around Paris, Geneva, London and Edinburgh. Benjamin Franklin, Thomas Jefferson and Alexander Hamilton were Enlightenment men, and the opportunity to put political ideas into practice had fallen into their laps.

In 1776 political debate in the colonies was gingered up by the publication of Thomas Paine's pamphlet *Common Sense*, which sold half a million copies in a population of just 2.5 million. Paine, a recent arrival from England, persuaded the colonists that they, along with most Europeans, were living under tyranny; they must either accept the rule of an unelected, unrepresentative monarch or strike a blow for freedom. Paine wanted America to become a free and independent republican state not just for its own sake, but in order to become a beacon to the world and a place of refuge for all the oppressed peoples of the earth. Americans, a set of independent-minded people who resented too much tax and interference, were encouraged to believe they had a mission in the world.

In June 1776 the Continental Congress in Philadelphia appointed a committee of five men – John Adams, Benjamin Franklin, Thomas Jefferson, Robert Livingston and Roger Sherman – to draft a formal Declaration of Independence. Jefferson drafted the document, Franklin made some revisions and the full declaration was presented to the Congress on 28 June. On 2 July it was agreed and on 4 July formally adopted. The 13 United States of America had become an independent country; all they had to do now was defeat the forces of their colonial masters.

Congress chose George Washington, a Virginia farmer, to lead their forces. While no master tactician, Washington turned out to be the inspiring leader needed in a war fought by volunteers against professional soldiers. Washington won early victories and suffered dangerous defeats before capturing 6,000 British troops at Saratoga in October 1777. This was enough to convince the French, whom Benjamin Franklin had been wooing for months, to enter the war. The colonists continued to struggle until they found, in Nathanael Greene, a general who could consistently outthink and outmanoeuvre the British. Greene forced General Cornwallis to withdraw his troops to the garrison town of Yorktown in Virginia, and in 1781 Washington was, for the first time, able to coordinate his own forces with the two French fleets. They surrounded Cornwallis in Yorktown, where, in October 1781, he surrendered with 8,000 troops. The war dragged on as Washington's army cleared out resistance around New York, but after Yorktown the war as a contest was over. A formal peace treaty was signed in February 1783.

The Continental Congress stayed together throughout the war, coordinating the efforts of the 13 colonies and supporting Washington's Continental Army. In 1777 its members drew up the Articles of Confederation, but once the war was won, it was apparent that if the ex-colonies were to form a single nation they would need a clear definition of their individual and collective powers. In May 1787, 55 delegates from the 13 states came together in Philadelphia, and after 17 weeks of secret discussion they came up with a 10-page document that became the United States Constitution.

The Congress records show a heated discussion on two major points: the relation between the individual states and the centre; and the extension of the right to vote. Some delegates preferred that the state assemblies should select their own representatives in both houses. The idea of direct election by the people won, however, because of the same reasons articulated at the Putney debates. Men had fought together for the independence of the colonies as a single body; now they felt they should be able to vote directly for the people who would rule that body.

It was also decided that the president should be elected directly by the people through an electoral college entirely separate from state and federal Congress elections. The president would then hold the executive arm of government and be free to choose his own cabinet and policies; but Congress would be the only body able to pass laws. The vote was given only to those men (women, Indians and slaves were totally excluded) who had 40 shillings taxable freehold property. Just as at Putney, the wealthy representatives argued that property-owners had a particular stake in the country. In any case the colonists had not fought for, and did not seek, democracy; what they wanted was constitutional government.

The constitution laid out the relations between the different arms of the legislature and the executive, and between the federal government and the individual states. It was assumed that everything else would be left to the states themselves. But when the constitution was sent out for ratification it soon became clear that there was something missing. Representatives in the states, led by Massachusetts, wanted the document to include some definition and protection of the rights of individual citizens. This was important because the United States was a new country. Until 1776 all the colonists considered themselves as British, with the full rights under common law, precedent and custom that their ancestors had enjoyed. If they were no longer British, they needed a statement of what their rights were. It was here, rather than in the debates over the powers of federal and state government, or election of a president, that the customs of the people gave American constitutional government its lifeblood.

At the urging of Thomas Jefferson, James Madison drew up a list of amendments to the constitution. Ten of these amendments were adopted and became known collectively as the Bill of Rights. They include rights to freedom of speech and peaceful assembly; to bear arms; to refuse to be a witness against oneself (the much-used Fifth Amendment); and to trial by jury. Having the foresight to see that no set of rules provides unambiguous guidance, the constitutional convention wanted a separate judicial body to settle disputes over constitutional matters and to act as a court of final appeal for citizens of the new country. The Supreme Court was also set up as a guardian of the constitution.

The framework that the constitution and the Bill of Rights put in place has enabled the United States to remain a stable political entity for two centuries, during which the country itself has changed beyond recognition. The constitution, in contrast, has hardly changed at all. The structure drawn up for a nation of 13 coastal states and 2.5 million people, mostly British expatriates living as farmers and small traders, has survived to serve a continent with nearly 300 million citizens drawn from every nation in the world. The United States Constitution contains a careful balance between rights, freedoms and laws. It did not provide its citizens with democracy but it did provide representation and, most importantly, a set of basic laws to protect their interests, and the institutions to enforce these laws on their behalf. Americans were given representational government but they were also given protection from government. The belief in democracy as the ultimate goal of political development often ignores this crucial element of the world's most powerful democracy – the institutions to define and protect the citizen, and to allow dissent, are often more important than democracy. In customary societies they are culturally embedded; in new countries they have to be invented. The United States Constitution is therefore a hybrid. The Bill of Rights, added as an afterthought following consultation with the population, has preserved the customary liberties of societies that are free from oppression, as were the original 13 colonies. But the inviolable and inflexible main body of the document has left American politics at the highest level tied to a rigid set of conditions that does not always serve the interests of the country and its people, while also delivering extraordinary power to a small group.

The last word on representation should go to the man responsible for drafting the Declaration of Independence and for lobbying for a Bill of Rights. Thomas Jefferson understood that a representative government requires an informed and understanding electorate. An old argument (as old as Athens) against enfranchising the people was that they were not educated enough to make informed decisions. The Athenians got round this, as Jefferson well knew, by educating and energizing the citizenry. Jefferson argued for the same in America: 'I know of no depository of the ultimate powers of society but the people themselves; and if we think them not enlightened enough to exercise their control with a wholesome discretion, the remedy is not to take it from them, but to inform their discretion.'

The early decades of the United States were marked by the establishment of a federal finance system, and government by the 'old boys' of the struggle for independence. George Washington was followed in the presidency by John Adams, Thomas Jefferson and James Madison. Adams and Jefferson both worked hard to keep the United States out of the Napoleonic wars, but in 1812 President Madison, under pressure from new members of Congress and from settlers itching to get their hands on Canada, declared war on Britain. The result was the capture of Washington and the burning of the White House by British troops in 1814. The US won an overwhelming victory at New Orleans in January 1815, but by then the war was officially over. Britain and the United States never fought another war and, just as important, America did not get entangled in European conflicts for another century. Freed from its colonial masters, the new country turned away from the Atlantic and faced a different kind of future in the west.

The United States Constitution could not have come out of Venice or London or Edinburgh or Vienna or Madrid; it needed a group of leaders who believed, however inaccurately, that their society had no call on the past, only the principles of the present. They followed Tom Paine's belief that they should not be restricted by the laws of their forefathers. But once the precedent of reinvention had been set by the leaders of the American Revolution, others could follow. Paris in 1789 and St Petersburg in 1917 would not have happened without Philadelphia in 1776.

While the revolution in America had profound consequences, the French Revolution that began just as George Washington was taking office was, at the time, a more cataclysmic political event. France was still, despite its difficulties, the dominant power in western Europe, as well as being the hub of European culture. While for most Europeans American independence was a distant, if interesting, development, France was at the centre of everything.

On 20 August 1786 the French finance minister, Charles-Alexandre de Calonne, presented Louis XVI with a grim picture of the nation's finances. In the previous few years France's national debt had trebled, so that interest payments were absorbing half the regime's revenue, while the next year's projected income was already spent. The basic engine of the state – gathering enough tax to pay for the king's expenditure – was in crisis. Louis was forced to appeal to his nobles for help.

The traditional *parlements* of aristocrats had the theoretical power to raise taxes for the king, but they refused to cooperate without a root-and-branch reorganization of political power. This was not a selfish piece of aristocratic pique – the nobility of France, unlike the king, knew that the nation and the world outside the Palace of Versailles had changed; it was no longer possible for the nobles to impose taxes on a docile population. France had acquired a large middle class which, in effect, ran the administration and wealth-making of the country. Lawyers, merchants, doctors, army officers, government officials, small landowners, manufacturers and bankers comprised a powerful section of society quite outside the traditional power structure of king, nobility and Church. The *parlements* and the recalled finance minister Jacques Necker recognized that the only way to govern France was to bring these people into the power structure, or at least consult with them. In August 1788 Louis agreed to call a meeting of the Estates-General, a traditional and little-used institution comprising representatives of the nobility, the clergy and the bourgeoisie. The last of the three, known as the *Tiers état* or Third Estate, in theory represented the 95 per cent of French people outside the Church and aristocracy; in practice the representatives were educated lawyers, merchants, bureaucrats and doctors.

Louis's financial problems were compounded by bad fortune. Through the 1780s France suffered a series of bad harvests, the worst coming in 1788. By the spring of 1789, following an unusually cold winter, there was insufficient food for the country's huge population of 28 million. There were bread riots in Paris and across France as rumours spread that grain was being withheld by the government. At the end of April a riot in the Faubourg St Antoine in Paris saw 300 people shot by the king's soldiers. Bread riots had happened before, but in 1789 they were combined with political demands. News of the recall of the estates had electrified France, and when the rioters cried '*Vive le tiers!*' it was clear that bread alone would not be enough.

To the members of the Third Estate, arriving in May 1789 from their lawyers' practices and grain merchants' offices, their doctors' surgeries and government agencies in Agen and Briançon and Limoges and Arras, Versailles must have seemed like some kind of fantasy world. Even now the palace is absurdly overblown in scale and sumptuousness; in the eighteenth century it was deliberately otherworldly. Visitors and supplicants were intended to feel that they were entering the domain of a demigod. But if the small landowners of the Third Estate were overwhelmed by Versailles, it did not take long for their awe to turn to irritation; and if Louis hoped to dazzle and intimidate them by trapping them within a gilded cage, he underestimated the determination of his subjects.

The situation of the court in Versailles undoubtedly contributed to the events of 1789 in a different way. Not only was the king isolated from his subjects, Paris was a city without a court. The capital of the most important and wealthiest country, and the largest city in Europe, Paris was without any meaningful purpose as the real seat of government. With no political process or function, the city was, by the late eighteenth century, a broiling mass of discontent, out of love with its distant royalty.

The king wanted the Estates-General to devise a political arrangement that would offer limited representation to the different sections of the French population, in return for acting as a tax-gathering system for the crown. But the three estates had last operated at the beginning of the seventeenth century when France was a semi-feudal society; the same system simply would not work in the France of 1789. The three groups were supposed to meet separately and stick to matters tabled by the king's ministers, but the Third Estate saw that it would be overshadowed by the others while, in reality, it represented the vast majority of the French people. Some members of the nobility and clergy were in sympathy with the Third Estate but there seemed no way of devising a constitutional arrangement that would satisfy all three bodies and the king.

On 10 June 1789 the members of the Third Estate decided to go it alone. They declared themselves to be a single representative assembly and invited deputies from the other estates to join them if they wished. A week later they declared themselves to be the National Assembly of France, effectively disbanding the other estates. On 20 June, still at Versailles, the deputies were barred from entering their meeting hall and had to assemble on the tennis court. Here they took the famous Oath of the Tennis Court, pledging to remain in session until they had drawn up a new constitution for France. In 10 days a group of bourgeoisie had simply assumed that they should be the new sovereign government and constitutional convention of France.

Since the French Revolution was a rebellion by the bourgeoisie, it is worth noting the contemporary meaning of the word. In the nineteenth century 'bourgeoisie' was used to describe those middle-class elements of society who resisted the forces of social change, and who distrusted the romantic endeavours of artists and revolutionaries. But in the eighteenth century a bourgeois was an independent citizen, free from the restrictions of serfdom or vassalage, equal before the law with all other members of the civil society to which he belonged. The aim of the Enlightenment, and of the American and French 'bourgeois' revolutions, was not the promotion of the interests of a section of society, but that *everyone* should be bourgeois. The universal principles of liberty and representation and individual rights should apply to everyone, thereby enabling them to become bourgeois, or independent citizens, too.

The actions of the Third Estate caused panic at Versailles. The king's ministers advised contradictory causes of action, and on 11 July Louis dismissed Jacques Necker, the man who had urged him to call the estates. Necker was popular among the deputies and the public, for whom he was a welcome bringer of change. His dismissal tipped many French people into open defiance of the regime.

While the politicians manoeuvred at Versailles, a dozen miles away in Paris and in other parts of France the common people began to take action against the *ancien régime*, tearing down customs posts and setting up barricades. The crucial element in the rapidly unfolding drama was the behaviour of the army. Would they rally to the king and fire on rebellious civilians – as they had done before – or would they, commoners all, join with their fellow citizens? In the preceding decades the mood, attitude and organization of the French army had significantly changed. Humiliated in the Seven Years War that ended in 1763, the army had begun to remodel itself along the lines of its Prussian adversary. Noble amateurs were eased out, together with seasonal conscription. The French army became a professional organization, billeted in barracks, with an increasing dedication (under the influence of Rousseau and others) to the cause of France, rather than their monarch. French officers and men had served in the American War of Independence, and the impact of fighting alongside colonists trying to free themselves from a tyrannical regime was profoundly felt. Several senior officers, including General Lafayette, hero of the American war, joined the new National Assembly. They were able to persuade the

Paris garrison not to intervene in the riots, thereby bringing the king's reign as an absolute monarch to an end. From then on Louis was forced to do the bidding of the assembly.

On the orders of the assembly Lafayette recruited ex-soldiers and other volunteers into a National Guard loyal to the assembly rather than the king. On 14 July, armed with muskets, a crowd besieged the fortress and prison of the Bastille, symbol of autocratic power. The governor surrendered and the prisoners were released. Throughout France groups of armed peasants raided the houses of the nobility, forcing many of them into exile. The king was impotent, the army either neutral or favourable to reform. All eyes turned to the National Assembly.

In the same way as the Athenians of the fifth century BC, the north Italians of the twelfth century, the English and Dutch of the seventeenth century, and the Americans of the previous decade, the deputies to the French National Assembly found themselves with the sudden unexpected opportunity to shape the political future of their country. In all of these instances citizens were not charged with inventing the idea of dispersing power fairly throughout human society; instead they had to come up with ways in which the ancient, and communally beneficial, human customs of mutual respect, restraint and redress could be adapted to a new situation. In 1789 the new situation was, of course, the French state – by now a vast apparatus attempting to control the lives, and meet the needs, of more than 20 million people inhabiting a diverse territory of more than half a million square kilometres.

The United States and Britain were living examples of constitutional political entities, but there was no shortage of home-grown ideas for French politicians to adopt. Many members of the French bourgeoisie would have been familiar with the work of the Enlightenment philosophers, including Montesquieu, Diderot, Voltaire and Rousseau, and would know how far removed the French regime was from the ideas they expounded. The calling of the Estates-General brought the two parallel worlds of France into direct conflict; the boldness of the assembly saw the educated, enlightened world of the bourgeois finally face down the autocratic regime of the Bourbons.

On 4 August 1789 the assembly abolished all hereditary rights in France and on 26 August published its most significant document, the 'Declaration of the Rights of Man and the Citizen'. In October 1789 an angry crowd of Parisians forcibly removed the king and queen from

Versailles to the capital; the assembly also moved to Paris and continued its work of framing a new constitution. At this stage, although a political revolution had taken place, a peaceful outcome still seemed possible. On 14 July 1790, the first anniversary of the storming of the Bastille, a rally was held at the Champs de Mars at which more than 250,000 people, including the leaders of the assembly, took an oath, drawn up by Charles Maurice Talleyrand, to 'the nation, the law and the King'. A constitutional settlement granting limited powers to the king was still the aim of most French people.

The most significant barrier to a peaceful resolution (apart from the king's possible rejection of any limit to his powers) was the behaviour of French émigrés. Whatever wars they fought over territories and king-ships, the ruling families of Europe were united by blood and by a desire to rule. They had more in common with each other than with their subjects – Marie-Antoinette was, after all, the sister of Emperor Leopold of Austria. Louis's youngest brother, the Comte d'Artois, publicly encouraged other European countries to intervene in France to destroy the revolution and restore Louis to absolute power.

While the National Assembly struggled to devise a constitution, France was becoming politicized in a new way. This, for many histo-rians, was the beginning of the modern western world. Nation states had emerged from the cohesion of regional interests by powerful central-izing monarchs, and in some countries this process had been followed by reforms that allowed a greater voice for men of property in the government of the country. The psychological relation of the people to their country remained a mixture of personal loyalty to the monarch, acknowledgement of the traditional right of monarch and aristocracy to rule, attachment to a national church, identification with an idea of defending one's land, a common language and dislike of foreign enemies. But the events of 1789 completely shattered those connections. Loyalty to king, Church and nobility disappeared, while attachment to country was replaced by loyalty to the revolution, to the political process, and to the French people. If, as the assembly had declared, the only legit-imate source of power was the people, then each deputy, and indeed the whole assembly, depended for authority on the support of the people. The deputies to the National Assembly, their supporters and detractors poured out a continual stream of political pamphlets, notices, posters, declarations and arguments, all designed to win the people to their side.

A new French state came into being and replaced the monarchy as
the centre of the nation's loyalties, and the Church as the centre of
social organization; political life replaced religion at the heart of the
nation's affairs. A constitutional state with a monarchy with limited
powers already existed in Britain and Holland, but the American and
French Revolutions overleapt this compromise. In France, monarchy,
aristocracy and Church had combined to frustrate any political or social
reform for 150 years; so, while people still pledged allegiance to the
king, for many this was merely lip service, as he became an obstacle
to their desires. Unlike in Britain in 1688, the new French state arrived
after 1789 as a kind of semi-mystical ideal, embodied by the figure of
Marianne, and celebrated by the *tricolore* and the cockade. An English
traveller in northern France in 1792 witnessed a new kind of country:
'In every one of the towns between Calais and Paris a full-grown tree
(generally a poplar) has been planted in the marketplace . . . on top of
this tree or pole is a red woollen or cotton night-cap, which is called
the *Cap of Liberty*, with streamers about the pole, or red, blue and
white ribbands. I saw several statues of saints, both within and without
the churches (and in Paris likewise) with similar caps, and several cruci-
fixes with the national cockade tied to the left arm of the image on the
cross . . . All the coats of arms which formerly decorated the gates of
Hôtels are taken away . . . No liveries are worn by servants, that badge
of slavery is likewise abolished' (Twiss).

The very concept of what a nation comprised, and how it should be
run, was altered by this politicization of life. No longer defined by
loyalty to a distant monarch, the French nation became an entity unified
by the participation of the people in its political life. Because the public
were so politically involved, all life became political. The institutions
of the state were able, in the years after the revolution, to spread and
reach into every aspect of French life. Compared to the generally
ramshackle and amateurish administration of traditional monarchies,
the French state became an engine of efficiency and involvement, and
a model for how modern nations should be run. Any sense of vague
allegiance was gone; France was now utterly identifiable by its borders,
its language and its ideals.

Louis might have been able to survive in this politicized atmosphere,
but he was not prepared to take the risk. In June 1791 the king and
queen tried to flee the country, but were arrested at Varennes and
brought back to Paris as prisoners. In September 1791 a new consti-

tution was finally published, enabling elections that reflected the changing mood of the nation. Even so, this might have been the closing chapter of the revolution – the new Legislative Assembly could have run the country with Louis as a puppet monarch. But the commune that governed Paris was not content with the constitutional settlement, believing that the king had given up his right to rule, and demanding a republic. By the summer of 1792 the Jacobins, a radical group in the commune, were threatening to take over the assembly. Events overtook them when the Duke of Brunswick, commander-in-chief of a Prussian army marching towards Paris, sent a manifesto declaring that the Tuileries palace must be inviolate and the king and queen unharmed or he would burn Paris and massacre its inhabitants. The king, now hoping for a rescue, published the Brunswick manifesto and sacked his moderate ministers from the assembly, effectively disabling the new constitution. The effect was incendiary. On 10 August 1792 a Parisian crowd stormed the Tuileries, murdered the guards and took the royal family prisoner. On 22 September France was declared a republic. The Legislative Assembly was immediately dissolved in favour of a Republican National Convention controlled by the Jacobins.

The war against Austria and its allies went badly at first, despite a heroic defensive action at Valmy in September 1792 by a 'citizens' army'. In December the king was brought to trial in front of the convention for plotting treason against France. All 693 deputies voted in favour of a guilty verdict; the death penalty was carried by a small majority. On 21 January 1793 the king was executed in front of a massive crowd of armed citizens.

The following month, with the nation in danger of defeat by foreign armies, an attempt was made at forced conscription. This, together with the execution of the king, provoked the formation of a counter-revolutionary army in the Vendée region of western France. In June 1793 the National Convention set up a Committee of Public Safety as a cabinet and executive. In August 1793, with the Vendée army growing in strength and the Austrians ready to invade through the poorly defended north-east, the committee declared that every citizen of France and every part of their possessions was now conscripted as part of the war effort. This was the famous *levée en masse*, a declaration of the militarization of the entire nation. By involving every citizen in war, the Committee of Public Safety was declaring that not the regime nor the government nor a particular faction but the life of the country itself was at stake. There could therefore be no surrender to an enemy without the total destruction of the nation of France. This was the path to complete victory or total annihilation, in other words total war.

By changing the nature of the nation state, the French Revolution changed the concept of war. The French soldiers were not only fighting for territorial gains and political leverage, they held completely different views from their opponents about the nature of society, the ways that a nation should be governed and the rights of its citizens. Any notion of a polite charade was gone for ever. The French army fought to defend the soil of its now near-mythical state, but also to defend the ideals of the revolution against the tyranny of monarchs, aristocrats and the Church.

The summer of 1792 and the threat of invasion changed the course of the revolution; it became completely tied up with the wars, which were first defensive, then aggressive. The army that emerged from mass conscription might have been hopelessly amateurish and ineffective, but in fact the opposite happened. The new rulers of France wanted an army that reflected and embodied the new France. Reforms brought in the election of officers, the abolition of corporal punishment, increase in pay for common soldiers, rigorous training and, most significantly, promotion on merit, not social status. In 1789 more than 90 per cent of the officers in the French army were noblemen, but by 1794 this was reduced to 3 per cent. Eight of the 26 marshals who were to serve under Napoleon were common soldiers in the pre-revolutionary army. (Marshals Augereau, Lefebvre, Ney and Soult were sergeants; Jourdan, Oudinot and Bernadotte, future king of Sweden, were privates; Victor was a bandsman.) A highly motivated, well-paid, well-trained army, led by experienced professional commanders, was to take on, and nearly defeat, the whole of Europe.

The crisis of the summer of 1793, when French territory was threatened at all points of the compass, while internal rebellion grew alarmingly, was over by the end of the year. The rebel forces in the Vendée, together with rebellious elements in Lyons, Bordeaux, Marseilles, Toulon and other southern cities, were ruthlessly crushed. Brutal methods of repression included burning villages with rebel sympathies; the infamous *noyards*, where around 2,000 victims were imprisoned in barges that were then scuppered on the River Loire; gunning down rows of opponents on the edges of mass graves; and the extension of political repression through revolutionary tribunals.

While the army was making revolutionary France secure, the

members of the Committee of Public Safety, including Georges Danton, who dominated the committee from April to July 1793, and his rival Maximilien Robespierre, who deposed Danton, were reinforcing their political power by eliminating their opponents in a seemingly endless series of executions. The Terror, as it became known, lasted from June 1793 to July 1794. Notorious as the Paris guillotine was, the vast majority of the 35,000 French men and women who died during the period of the Terror were killed in the civil war in the French provinces.

Nevertheless, the Terror was a terrifying glimpse of the dark side of Rousseau's vision that, in order for men to be truly free, the General Will should prevail over the Individual Will. In the Terror, an abstract concern for humanity apparently overrode any concern for human beings. Processions of carts travelled hour after hour, day after day from the revolutionary tribunal to the Place de la Révolution, with another line of carts waiting to take the corpses away. The condemned were led up the steps, strapped to a board and turned horizontal; the board was then run along a track until the victim's head was in position and the knife was dropped. Then, as an observer reported, 'with incredible dexterity and rapidity, two executioners tossed the body into the basket, while another threw the head after it' (Millingen).

The opponents of the revolutionary regime were by no means royalists or reactionaries. For the most part they welcomed many of the reforms that the revolution had brought. Land reforms which freed vast numbers of peasants from the hated feudal or seigneurial system and the distribution of church and feudal property to the people made the Paris regime popular in the countryside. But the closure of churches, the forbidding of public worship and the 'dechristianization' of France alienated many rural supporters. In the cities of the south, Girondin deputies who had lost control of the convention to the Jacobins attempted to organize a rebellion. Despite the presence of a democratic convention, political opposition was only possible through force, and so anyone suspected of opposing the regime was a traitor to France and was executed.

The Terror was a method employed by the Jacobins to retain power, but it was also part of an attempt to bring perfect rational order to an imperfect world and a moral purpose to political activity. The revolutionary regime brought in measures such as progressive taxation, state-funded schools and workshops, pension schemes and famine relief. But while this sense of fairness chimed with customary French society, the desire for total renewal that brought in a new 'rational' calendar (and, incidentally, metric systems of weights and measures) did not. In their need to bring justice and order to society, the Jacobins could not distinguish between the two.

The slaughter was brought to a halt when people understood that the country and the revolution had ceased to be in imminent danger; the war no longer served as an excuse for terrorizing Paris and the rest of France. Robespierre's self-aggrandizement became clear when he organized a Festival of the Supreme Being as the beginning of a new religion for France. On 28 July 1794 members of the National Convention seized the opportunity to arrest Robespierre and 19 others; they were executed the following day. The Terror was over.

The French republic that lasted for the next five years was, in contrast to what came before and after, an unremarkable regime. A new constitution abolished universal suffrage and brought in a property qualification, together with a two-chamber assembly and numerous checks on the power of any executive, which was to be ruled by a five-man directory. Revolutionary tribunals and the National Guard were abolished. But the new republic, which struggled to preserve the ideals of the revolution in a constitutional government, failed because of its very adherence to those ideals. Despite making politics the lifeblood of the nation, the revolutionaries paradoxically always believed themselves to be above politics. The party politics that existed in England (and quickly developed in the United States) was, for them, a betrayal of the central Enlightenment belief that they should be guided only by Nature and by Reason. Dispensing with all recent political precedents, they saw Greece and Rome (which were distant enough to be idealized) as their only inspiration – Cicero and Plutarch were more keenly heeded than even Voltaire and Rousseau.

This idealization of politics left no room for legitimate political opposition, only a succession of regimes each of which must destroy its predecessors and its opponents. The members of the directory began to manipulate and annul any election results that went against them in order to hold on to power. Another coup was engineered in 1797, but politics was by then being guided by the machinations of small groups rather than by the will of the people.

In the meantime France went back to war, which became a matter of political rather than strategic necessity. The *levée en masse* had made France into a military nation with every citizen involved in warfare.

The state then needed continual war simply in order to hold itself together, while the French government had to squeeze as much as it could out of its conquests to feed the citizens of Paris. Whatever their motivation, the French armies continued their success. By 1795 the Prussians, Dutch and Spanish had all come to terms or been defeated – only the British and Austrians were still at war with France. The capture of Italy by its most successful commander, Napoleon Bonaparte, in 1796 made France the master of the whole of western and southern Europe, apart from Britain. Napoleon then launched a daring expedition to Egypt, which ended in the destruction of the French fleet at the battle of the Nile and almost complete military disaster. Nevertheless, the glamorous general was welcomed back to Paris in October 1799 as a hero.

The political situation in France had by then deteriorated. Military defeat in Naples at the hands of a local army showed that the French did not rule western Europe by consent but by military imposition. Any sense of liberating the fellow oppressed in other countries was lost in an upsurge of nationalism. The revolutionary optimism of 1789–94 had given way to nationalistic fervour, with the military seen by all sides as the guardians and champions of the nation. The civilian directory had managed to see off potential rebellions by both Jacobins and royalists, but by late 1799 there were fears, both genuine and deliberately inflated, of a resurgence of the Jacobin faction and a return to the days of the Terror. Abbé Sieyès, a conservative member of the directory, engineered its resignation on 9 November 1799, and its replacement by a three-man consulate. One of the consuls, and the de facto head of state, was the 30-year-old General Napoleon Bonaparte.

In the ten years since the revolution, France had become a nation-in-arms, where the state acted on behalf of all the people, in return for the utter dedication of every citizen to its cause. The people demanded military success from their new leader, and were prepared to sacrifice everything for him. The vast population of France was transformed into a military machine and, as Carl von Clausewitz (a Prussian officer who fought against the French) wrote, 'War suddenly became an affair of the people, and that of a people numbering thirty millions, every one of whom regarded himself as a citizen of the state.'

The Napoleonic wars that followed came in fits and starts but they drew in the whole of Europe, east and west. The opponents of France

– Austria, Prussia and Russia, aided, abetted and sometimes marshalled by Britain – banded together in a series of ever-shifting, ever-distrusting alliances. After a string of French victories, treaties were signed with the continental powers in 1801 and with Britain in 1802. But Napoleon's vision was not of a secure France, but of a French empire. Why should not France, with her citizens' armies and her new vision of a military state, liberate, civilize and rule Europe as Rome had done? In 1802, following in the footsteps of the emperor Augustus, Napoleon made himself First Consul for Life, and in 1804 he was crowned Emperor of the French by a compliant pope.

In 1805–07 French armies defeated the Austrians, Prussians and Russians at Ulm, Austerlitz, Jena, Auerstedt and Friedland. By July 1807 France or, more accurately, Napoleon himself, controlled the whole of continental Europe. His brother Louis was made king of the Netherlands, while brother Jerome was king of the new state of Westphalia, and brother-in-law Joachim Murat Grand Duke of Berg; stepson Eugène de Beauharnais became viceroy of northern Italy, and in 1808 another brother, Joseph, was made king of Spain, having previously been king of Naples, while his sister Élisa was ruler of Tuscany. Napoleon not only created a personal empire, he also introduced the idea of the satellite state. Disaffected generals and aristocrats in the territories that France invaded were placed in government in return for pledging loyalty to the emperor and supplying troops, money and matériel to the Grande Armée. In 1812 the German states supplied 190,000 men for the invasion of Russia.

At home Napoleon continued the revolutionary regime's reconstruction of the French state, giving organizational structure and coherence to the preceding 10 years of reforms. The Code Napoléon brought in a uniform system of civil, commercial, criminal and penal law that replaced both pre-revolutionary measures and the 1,400 laws enacted since 1789. Equality before the law and religious tolerance were enshrined, together with the state's right to manage the industrial and agricultural economy of the nation. The revolution is viewed as a left-wing rebellion, but its abolition of customs dues and other restrictions, as well as its banning of guilds and workers' associations, was an intentional aid to commerce that Napoleon continued. The territory of France was rationalized into communes and departments and districts, run by prefects, sub-prefects and mayors. A national education system, based on local government districts, was established. Napoleon also brought in a Public Audit Office backed by a new and efficient system of tax assessment and collection. In 1802 a national police force came into being, supported by travelling tribunals – while Napoleon was a gifted administrator, the efficiency of the new state allowed him to keep firm control of any political opposition.

Napoleon's first major military setback sprang from his decision in May 1808 to replace the Bourbon king of Spain with his brother Joseph. The Spanish people rebelled against their French masters, and sought help from the British. The Peninsular War became an extended and murderously bloody conflict that showed the limitations of French invulnerability. If the intervention in Spain was a mistake, then the Russian campaign was a disaster. The Russian tsar had made peace at Tilsit in 1807, but was weakening the blockade against Britain. This was a major irritation for France, but was it enough to send an army into the vast unknown territory of Russia? Napoleon undoubtedly believed that with Russia under his control and Britain isolated, there would be no more enemies to trouble him. Driven by the example of Julius Caesar and Augustus, he saw Europe as an extended version of the Roman empire – a peaceful, harmonious territory needing to be defended only at its borders. He may have also learned from the Romans that the way to keep your allies loyal, your captive states under control and your people happy is to keep fighting wars.

The 1812 invasion succeeded in taking Napoleon to Moscow, and then failed to bring his army home. Around 380,000 men were lost through death, capture and desertion. A recent discovery of a mass grave in Lithuania has shown that there were probably 20 nationalities represented in the invasion force, including Portuguese, Italian and Swiss soldiers as well as French. The remnants of the Grande Armée were defeated at Leipzig in October 1813 and the allied forces reached Paris in May 1814 to parade through the Arc de Triomphe that Napoleon had built for his own glorification. He returned from his forced exile in Elba in March 1815, and persuaded the French to take on Europe once again. His final defeat came at Waterloo in June 1815, and Louis XVIII, brother of the executed king, was restored to the French throne. The revolution and the Napoleonic wars were over, and Europe could, for the first time in 25 years, return to peace.

The French Revolution has evoked more passionate responses and provoked more emotional divisions than any event in European history.

This is no distortion of hindsight; when it was in progress the revolution was seen to be an event of world significance. For Europe's most important and fascinating nation to undergo not just the overthrow of a monarch but the replacement of an entire system of government and administration was a monumental event. Add to that the purpose of the revolution – the replacement of a tyrannical, unrepresentative, irrational, hierarchical regime by enlightened, rational, representative, egalitarian government – and this was the fulfilment of the dream of thousands of radical, educated, enlightened people across Europe. But while most assessments of 1789–1815 have focused on the ideological differences of the protagonists, recent historians have highlighted the creation of the modern western state as the theme common to all those involved.

The events in France ushered in a new kind of state, based on a new set of assumptions, loyalties and organizations. By codifying many, though not all, of the revolutionary reforms, Napoleon bequeathed a state that could serve its citizens in every aspect of their lives; in return they gave their loyalty not to a monarch as the symbol of the state, but to the state itself, and allowed it to intervene in every part of their existence. While bringing material benefits, this extension of the state allowed much tighter control of citizens' lives, bringing the possibility of a totalitarian police state. Just as important, the revolutionary era showed that it was possible for a state to bring in laws that would improve the lives of its citizens without recourse to existing tradition. This was recognition of a changing reality, in which ancient customs had to be radically reinterpreted if they were to be of service to the new kind of citizen.

The revolutionary era, as we have already seen, gave politics a moral purpose, but combined this with an idealization that denied the possibility of legitimate opposition. Napoleon continued this belief in a single and uncontestable vision of the perfect state, and set France on course for a long series of coups, restorations and reconstituted republics. However, Great Britain, France's undefeated rival, had developed party politics and loyal opposition, as had the United States. The modern state that emerged in the nineteenth century was to be a combination of French political centralization and citizenship, and the British practice of political difference within an agreed state framework. Nevertheless, in certain quarters, and particularly among philosophers with no experience of political life, the idealization of politics exemplified in the French Revolution shone like a beacon of hope. The ancient belief that there was a rational solution to the problem of building a society, and of reconciling freedom and order, persisted in Europe for most of the next two centuries.

While these political effects were gradually felt over the next century, Napoleon's military adventures had an immediate and long-lasting effect on the ground, permanently altering the geopolitics of Europe. Both Spain and Portugal, militarily and financially exhausted by decades of fighting with and against the French, effectively lost control of their overseas empires as their South and Central American colonies declared themselves independent, while Napoleon's takeover of the whole Italian peninsula inspired the long drive towards national unity by Victor Emmanuel and Giuseppe Garibaldi. But it was in central Europe that Napoleon's geopolitical legacy had the greatest influence. Napoleon dismantled the Holy Roman Empire, forming large parts of it into the more easily manageable Confederation of the Rhine. This was the template for a new state of Germany, which was to become the most powerful and populous nation on the continent of Europe.

As well as paving the way for nationalist movements in Italy and Germany, the French military system, which produced armies that were invincible for nearly 25 years, seemed to show that an enthusiastic nation in arms and a war economy could deliver enormous gains. The lesson learned, by Prussia in particular, was not that these are inevitably defeated, or that their results are illusory and short-lived, but that total war can bring total victory.

For France itself, 23 years of continual war with little opportunity for foreign trade put her well behind in the race to industrialize. While her natural advantages had given pre-eminence in the primarily agricultural economy of the seventeenth century, the lack of coal in France compounded the handicap the wars had given her. In the years from 1789 to 1815 her greatest rival, Great Britain, had forged ahead in technology and productivity. When the trade barriers came down, French industry was swamped by the new industrial giant to the north.

The effects of the revolutionary era on the artistic culture of Europe were profound. Considering it was a political movement built on rational principles, the French Revolution was impossibly romantic – coinciding with, and contributing to, a new mood among European intellectuals and artists. The names of the revolutionaries – Lafayette, Mirabeau, Marat, Danton – echoed around Europe like a roll-call of the gods. Even Napoleon's dictatorship seized the imagination of republicans like

Beethoven, and in *War and Peace*, written more than 50 years later, Tolstoy showed how much the Russian intelligentsia (who spoke French and not Russian to each other) had been besotted with the man who invaded their country in 1812. But perhaps the most convincing artist of the Napoleonic era was the Spanish painter Francisco Goya (1746–1828). Witness to a savage war conducted in his homeland by a foreign power which claimed to speak for reason and order, Goya showed the real cost to humans of grand military strategies. The inscription that is the focus of one of his most important and disturbing sets of images has long been argued over by art historians. But when Goya had seen his country devastated and its people butchered by the forces of an enlightened regime, then we understand his *cri de coeur*, with its bitter echo of Sophocles: The dreams of reason bring forth monsters.

INDUSTRIALIZATION AND NATIONALISM

British Dominance and the Ideology of Freedom

IN the 5,000 years before 1750, the lands and people of Europe had experienced an essentially agricultural civilization. Efficiencies in agriculture, in craft manufacturing and in the organization of commerce had, since the twelfth century, enabled an urban society to emerge. Nevertheless, Europe remained a series of overwhelmingly agricultural societies, with most people working on the land, most wealth and power coming from land ownership, and most economic prosperity and industry dependent on agricultural products. In eighteenth-century western Europe, it was still possible for large numbers of people to starve to death as a result of bad harvests.

Over the following 200 years the face of western Europe changed as the continent became a series of industrialized societies linked by a single commercial system. The change was fitful (as, for example, the Irish famine of the 1840s shows), but by the early twentieth century, western Europe had undergone a remarkable change from a mainly rural, agricultural economy to an overwhelmingly industrial civilization. The effects of this change on the lives of European people have been immense. The most dramatic consequences were the enormous increase in the population of Europe (and, subsequently, the industrialized United States), and the rapid transformation of western people from rural to urban dwellers. These changes brought about the creation of two sets, or classes, of people who had previously barely existed, but whose needs defined the course of subsequent western history. Since the breakdown of the core beliefs of medieval life, Europeans had struggled to construct a society

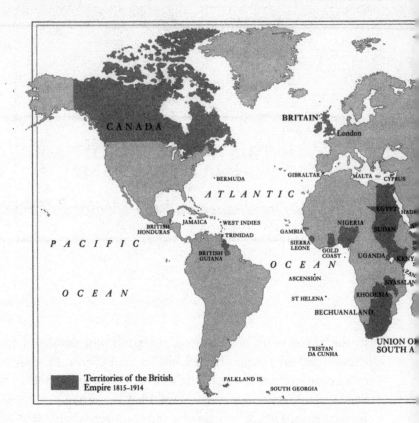

Territories of the British
Empire 1815–1914

in which the new autonomous, rational, educated citizens could be granted the benefits of both freedom and order. In the wake of industrialization the needs of this minority were overtaken by the demands of, firstly, the urban middle class, and then the industrial working class. Most European states found themselves able to construct a civilized political and cultural society that would include the burgeoning middle classes – indeed, this new class began to define western civilization – but this left the industrial workers, the masses who made up an ever-increasing majority of an ever-growing population. The attempts to integrate this majority into society became a dominant motif of western political and cultural life.

While in the late eighteenth century those in search of political ideas and cultural innovation looked to North America and France, after 1815 all eyes turned to Britain. With Germany and Italy each a collection of small states, Austria's power reduced by previous conflicts with Prussia, France suffering the after-effects of Napoleon's defeat, and the United States turning its attention west and south, Britain was uniquely placed to dominate the western world. Britain was also the first country

The British empire, a world-wide network.

to become industrialized, and this, together with her worldwide trading system, sustained by an immensely powerful navy, enabled her to lead the world into a new era.

The Industrial Revolution took such a long time to get going that it scarcely deserves to be called a revolution. The famous iron bridge was built at Coalbrookdale on the Severn in 1779, but this symbol of the beginnings of industrial processes was actually built by the *third* Abraham Darby – his father and grandfather had both been ironmasters (a word used as early as 1674) before him. Cloth fulling, spinning, dyeing and weaving had been a full-blown industry for centuries, as had glass-making, leather-working, and the mining and processing of metals. Nevertheless, a change began to take place in the second half of the eighteenth century that is marked most noticeably not by technology or work practices, but by economic effects. Between 1750 and 1850 the economy of Britain grew at a faster rate than in any previous hundred-year period, and after 1780 annual growth remained at between 2 and 3 per cent per annum for the next hundred years. This level of self-sustained economic growth was such a novel phenomenon in world history that it can only be explained by changes in the economic structure of the country. Economic historians suggest that in late eighteenth-century Britain, there was a decisive break with the universal pattern of economic relations that had existed everywhere through all previous human history, and that the Industrial Revolution can be seen as an economic revolution that enabled industrial production to develop at an unprecedented pace. From this perspective, the few decades from 1750 to 1800 comprise a vastly important watershed in world economic history.

A combination of different effects led to this change. During the seventeenth-century wars with the Netherlands and France, the British government had introduced high tariff barriers to foreign imports and thereby encouraged local production. These tariffs remained in place after the wars ended, protecting home production from overseas competition. In particular this helped to shield the manufacture of textiles from Dutch competition. Britain's social structure also contributed to economic innovation. In the eighteenth century, the British lower gentry enjoyed greater social mobility than any other country's bourgeoisie, and the political structure of the country began to give more voice and power to commercial and professional, as opposed to landed aristocratic, concerns. The British social system was also oddly differentiated. Religious tolerance and diversity meant that groups like Quakers and Calvinists, who played an important role in the Industrial Revolution, flourished in alternative social and economic networks. While powerful politicians did not actively promote structural change, there was no dominant group that worked actively against it. In France, for example, there was really only one 'society', while in Britain there were many.

In the late eighteenth century, land in Britain started to become a commercialized as opposed to a feudal commodity. The enclosure of common land happened in different ways in all European countries, but in Britain it gave access to land ownership for those with capital and served as an encouragement to invest in agriculture. The ownership of land was one element in the formal legalization of rights of property, which became, in theory at least, available to all. Concepts like shares, bills of exchange and patents all helped to extend economic activity by granting ownership to a larger number of people, who made up the expanding merchant class.

Once a large class of people with liquid assets was brought into being, the next requirement was an incentive and route for people to invest in the actual manufacture of goods, rather than in land or in trade of commodities. There were several reasons why this was able to happen in Britain. First, Britain possessed the raw materials for increasing industrial capacity – in particular, fuel and iron ore near to navigable water. Coal from the Durham and Northumberland coalfields could be directly loaded on to coast-going ships and brought into the heart of industrial England via the Tyne, Wear, Tees, Humber, Trent, Thames and Severn river systems, while coalfields in the West Riding of Yorkshire, Lancashire and the Midlands supplied local industries. Coal shipped from Newcastle and Sunderland in 1700 totalled around 500,000 tons per annum; by 1750 this reached 1.2 million tons; by 1800, 2.2 million tons. Iron ore was in plentiful supply from East Cleveland, the Tyne valley, Lincolnshire and elsewhere. The conversion of these resources into a self-sustaining industrial economy required the continuous development of, and investment in, innovative technology. We usually take this to mean new inventions and discoveries, but new ways of organizing work were far more important.

Artisans had produced manufactured goods in their own homes or workshops in every corner of Europe ever since the Bronze Age. In medieval times, urban craft industries had been closely overseen by the guilds, but by the eighteenth century manufacturing had moved out to rural areas, where costs were lower. Home-based artisans as part of a chain of manufacturing presented a low risk for the master, but as demand increased, the domestic system struggled to cope. Improvements in machinery required more skilful workers, while masters were reluctant to put expensive spinning frames and weaving looms in workers' houses. The answer was to bring the workers to the machines.

In 1771 Richard Arkwright and Jedediah Strutt built a water-powered textile factory in Cromford, Derbyshire, and the factory system was born. The investment needed in constructing and equipping huge buildings and the risk of future downturns in the market were outweighed by efficiency savings. Water power had been used since the twelfth century, but in a factory a single water wheel could drive a hundred machines, including ore crushers, riddles, spinning wheels, looms, saws, rollers, and even lifts. From around 1800, thanks to the partnership of James Watt and Matthew Boulton, steam began to replace water as the main source of industrial power; but the principle was the same – power from a single source.

While factories seem to make sense as places of concentrated production, they only do so in the type of economic system that was emerging in Britain. Large-scale investment in buildings and machinery in the expectation of long-term gains could only happen where there was a ready availability of liquid capital, with investors prepared to enter into new types of arrangement. While investment in single voyages or plantations had been happening for centuries, industrial investment needed general confidence in the future, rather than a wish to make a quick return.

The factory system changed the relationships of the workplace, as well as its physical setting. Discipline, time-keeping and application were made conditions of employment rather than self-imposed standards. The workers were still largely paid by piecework but the owners insisted on long hours to raise the productivity of their machines. Many of the factories were hellish places to work, full of dirt, darkness and unbelievable noise. But others stand as architectural marvels, carefully constructed to allow in light and air, and the development of a community of work. Domestic working remained important surprisingly late into the industrialization of Britain; nevertheless, the factory stands as the emblem of industrialization, not as a technical system, nor an economic phenomenon, but as a new way of working and living.

Factories were built where they were most convenient for industrial processing, and the workers were forced to migrate. On coal and iron ore fields, near sources of pottery clay, in Lancashire valleys where water and coal were combined with a damp atmosphere suited to cotton processing, and in places where the growing canal system could reach, industrial villages, towns and cities sprouted like mushrooms.

Maintaining the momentum of industrial growth required ever-larger numbers of workers – Britain's population grew from 10 million in 1800 to 20 million in 1851 and 37 million in 1901. But this could only be sustained by increases in agricultural production. The first phase of the prolonged 'agricultural revolution' – the introduction of new root vegetables such as swedes and turnips and catch crops like clover – allowed greater yields, more animals, and more continual use of land. In the mid eighteenth century the gradual increase in the enclosure of common land, the drainage of marginal land, and increases in the size of farms led to more efficiency and more production. Farming became a profitable industry. Higher demand led to higher prices, which allowed farmers to invest in bought-in fertilizers and artificial animal feeds and encouraged drainage of unproductive claylands. Britain was able to adequately feed itself with an ever-smaller proportion of the workforce being employed in agriculture.

The economic changes that overtook Britain in the second half of the eighteenth century allowed self-sustaining economic growth of a kind that had never been seen before in any country in the world. The conversion of land into a commodity helped investment in industrial processes, and when enterprises showed substantial rewards this encouraged yet more investment; at the same time the disparate social structure and wealth of natural resources provided routes and possibilities for industrial innovation. This was the dynamic economic effect of industrialization, but its effects on the lives of the British working people were, for several decades, dehumanizing. Industrialization subjected millions of people to virtual slave labour in factories and mines. It brought a largely rural population into cities where filth, squalor and disease made their lives miserable and dangerous.

In 1815 an investigation by parliamentary commissioners found that girls started work in flax mills at the age of eight, and worked from 6 a.m. to 7 p.m. at normal times, and from 5 a.m. to 9 p.m. when the mills were busy. The children had 40 minutes' break for lunch at noon, and no other rest. They were beaten if they did not keep up their work of 'doffing' – watching the loom frames to see when they were full, stopping the machinery to remove the bobbins and shuttles and frames, and then loading empty frames and setting the whole thing going again. The commissioners found girls who had become deformed by the work, and it is likely that all were stunted.

While factory conditions were dire, the astonishing and unplanned growth of industrial cities made them into human dumping grounds. Manchester's population increased from 75,000 in 1801 to 252,000 in 1841, with Birmingham, Liverpool and Glasgow following the same pattern. All had reached over 800,000 by the end of the century. Infant mortality in industrial parishes in northern England rose throughout the period 1813–36, reaching 172 per 1,000, while average heights declined in the same period and continued to do so up to the 1860s. The higher wages and better prospect of finding work in urban areas had to be traded off against poorer nutrition and health. Conditions for working-class people in urban districts remained dire throughout the 1830s and 40s, and remained so for decades in many cities.

There was no civic administration available to cater for the vast influx of humanity into industrial towns and cities, which had no organization, no representation, no one to speak for them and their inhabitants in parliament or in government. The administration of Britain was organized on counties and parishes, with parliamentary representation based on a system of boroughs that was open to corruption. These parliamentary constituencies bore little relation to population numbers even before industrialization; afterwards they were a gross distortion.

The customary ways of life that existed in rural Britain were torn apart by the migration to towns and cities, but industrialization was made possible by the changes that were already taking place in the countryside itself. Since agricultural land had been brought into the money economy in the late medieval period, the social structure of rural England had changed. But until the eighteenth century, these changes had more theoretical than practical impact. In the various county surveys made for the Board of Agriculture, the legal ownership of great swathes of the English countryside was in the hands of large-scale landowners, but this legal ownership had little bearing on the customs and traditions that governed rural life and work. Custom and practice dictated that large areas of common land, or common waste, be used by those without access to other means of subsistence. But the Enclosure Acts, which began in 1750 and continued until 1830, permitted landowners to enclose the common land, to confirm their legal ownership, and to employ it for their own use or for rent. One historian has written: 'The appropriation to their own use of practically the whole of the common waste by the legal owners meant that the curtain which separated the growing army of labourers from utter proletarianization was torn down' (Chambers and Mingay). In other words, the appropriators were already the legal owners, but by exercising their rights in this way they destroyed the customary and centuries-old relation of rural labourers to the land, and made them into waged workers. The intricate web of relations, claims, usages and sanctions that had existed since Anglo-Saxon times, and probably long before, was thrown away as land became just another economic commodity, from which those without money were consequently excluded.

Nowhere is the contrast between a literate, individualist, standardizing power and an oral, communal, diverse and local culture more starkly drawn than in the enclosure of common land. Illiterate country people left few records and had little access to formal legal processes;

in contrast the landowners brought the countryside into the world of documents and legal contracts through the assertion of their property rights. Searches of documents, unsurprisingly, seem to show that resistance to the enclosures was remarkably limited. But those documents that do exist indicate a deep and probably widespread resentment. In an anonymous letter sent to the squire of Cheshunt Park, the 'Combin'd of the parish' (i.e. the users of the commons) wrote: '. . . if you intend of inclosing Our Commond fields Lammas Meads Marshes &c Whe Resolve . . . if you proceeded in the aforesaid bloudy act Whe like horse leaches will cry give, give until we have spilt the bloud of every one that wished to rob the inosent unborn' (Anon., 27 February 1799, HO 42.46).

The enclosures produced an unprecedented number of rural people who, with no access to common land, could no longer provide for themselves and their families. From medieval times canon law had required each member of a parish to pay a tithe of one tenth of income to the church, one third of which was set aside for relief of the poor. As church tithes dwindled, the state gradually intervened so that by the sixteenth century, it was a legal requirement for the well-off to give money to provide for the poor; the Poor Law Act of 1601 required each parish to be responsible for the care of its own poor. Some built cottages, or gave employment or relief in money or in kind. By the late eighteenth century, the system was struggling to cope with increasing numbers seeking help. Nevertheless, the tradition of treating the poor as an integral part of a local community persisted until 1834, when the Poor Law Act discarded this localized approach in favour of a standardized, national system.

The British parliament decided that poor relief would be available only to those who submitted themselves to the regime of the workhouse, and that any relief must be below the lowest wage available in the area, regardless of actual need. Workhouses already existed in many towns, but were greatly expanded, and integrated into a formal system, as a result of the 1834 Act. In Blackburn in Lancashire, for example, a new workhouse with a capacity of 650 was built to serve a population of around 60,000. When they entered the workhouse, paupers were stripped, bathed, and all their clothes and possessions put in store. All inmates wore a standard workhouse uniform, often with variations for especially denigrated groups like unmarried mothers.

The law required that inmates be strictly segregated, with husbands, wives and children separated and punished if they tried to speak to one another. If the guardians approved, children under seven could be placed in the female wards. Female occupants worked mainly at laundry and sewing, men at stone-breaking, corn-grinding and, in rural areas, working the land. Despite the hardship, humiliation and inhumanity of workhouse life, the institutions were often unable to cope with the number of applicants. In the mid-Victorian period nearly 10 per cent of the population fell under the provisions of the Poor Law.

There is a belief among some modern historians that the poor conditions of the early industrial period have been overstated, and that statistics show that factory workers were financially better off than both their rural counterparts and their own parents and grandparents. This, though, misses the point. The question that this period raises is not whether more money was earned, but the degree to which a way of life was destroyed, and individual lives degraded, in order to bring an increase in average financial prosperity.

The Enclosure Acts and the Poor Law were part of a growing movement within Britain whose guiding philosophy was that local bylaws, ancient customs, excise duties and tariffs were a grave hindrance to the economic prosperity of the nation. The removal of these obstacles became the central doctrine of the movement for free trade, which was advocated with increasing vigour by merchants, 'progressive' politicians like Richard Cobden, and economic theorists such as David Ricardo, author of the immensely influential *On Principles of Political Economy* (1817). Britain's industrial and agricultural economy had benefited from protectionist measures, and from Napoleon's blockade, but many believed that measures like the 1815 Corn Law (which banned imports of corn until the price reached 80 shillings per quarter) were stifling the free flow of goods, while serving only the interests of the landed aristocrats. After decades of pressure, the Corn Laws were finally repealed in 1846; a measure that signalled the decline of landed interests and the ascendancy of commerce and industry. The measure also confirmed the growing dominance of free trade, as the British state continually intervened to remove restrictions on the flow of goods, money or people. The 400-year-old Statute of Apprentices, for example, was revoked along with controls on wages.

For three decades from the mid-1840s, free trade seemed to work; the British economy prospered as more controls were lifted and income and other taxes were reduced. It seemed that this was the 'natural' way in which an industrial economy should run. But this turned out to be an illusion. It has been convincingly argued (see, for example, Gray) that controlled and regulated markets, with their forest of evolving customary restraints, are the product of 'natural' human society, brought about by the overriding need for social cohesion, while free markets have to be imposed by a strong authoritarian state. The British economy was growing in mid-century because it was the first to industrialize, had held on to its early lead by protecting its markets, and at the same time had control, through its navy, of a worldwide trading network. The most important expansion happened before 1850; 6,000 miles of railways were open, while coal production had risen from 16 million tons in 1815 to 50 million tons in 1848, with iron production up from 250 thousand tons to 2 million tons in the same period. Free trade had more to do with protecting Britain's early lead than creating a sustainable economic system. Once other western countries became industrialized, Britain's advantage was whittled away. Competitors understood that industrialization could only be nurtured by protecting their own industries, rather than trading freely. Bismarck's Germany put up tariff barriers, as did the United States in 1890, specifically to keep out British-manufactured goods – and both flourished as a result.

The human costs of laissez-faire industrialism were, in the meantime, increasingly clear. Britain became, in the eyes of influential commentators such as Benjamin Disraeli (1804–81), Thomas Carlyle (1795–1881) and Matthew Arnold (1822–88), two or even three mutually exclusive and hostile nations. Disraeli coined the term 'two nations' to describe rich and poor in his 1845 novel *Sybil*; Carlyle called them Dandies and Drudges; in *Culture and Anarchy* (1869) Arnold divided his fellow Britons into Barbarians (aristocrats), Philistines (middle classes) and Populace (workers). The middle classes flourished fitfully, but with the constant fear of being sucked into poverty and disgrace (the central theme of Dickens' dark comedy); while the workers lived with the spectre of the workhouse, debtors' prisons or vagrancy. A French visitor to Derby Day in 1861 noticed the numbers of poor beggars dressed in hand-me-down clothes: 'The majority of them have bare feet, all are terribly dirty, and most absurd looking; the reason is that they wear old gentlemen's clothes, worn out fashionable dresses . . . Among us [the French] a peasant, a workman, a labourer, is a different man, not an inferior person; his blouse belongs to him as my coat belongs to me' (Taine). Even allowing for inflated national pride, the difference in attitude is clear: France was still a country of urban bureaucrats and independent peasant farmers, Britain a nation of the rich, those making do, and the destitute.

While industrialization and free trade had immense and traumatic consequences for the working people of Britain, the principal effect on the new urban lower gentry was to propel them to the centre of national, and then western, life. An industrial urban society needed a much more sophisticated administration than a rural economy, and in the second quarter of the nineteenth century the middle classes began to increase as a proportion of a growing population. An army of clerical staff and managers was needed to keep the factories working, while shopkeepers, doctors, solicitors, accountants, small suppliers, civil servants, hoteliers, journalists and engineers appeared in growing numbers. This 'middle' class between the workers and the aristocrats, which numbered around 25 to 30 per cent of the population, began to recognize itself as a particular social group, a process that was to be repeated in all industrializing countries. The middle classes started to develop a strong sense of identity and of self-worth and virtue. They recognized each other and contrasted themselves strongly with both the aristocracy, whom they regarded as corrupt and lazy, and the working class, whom they saw as ignorant, lazy and morally lax. In contrast the middle classes put a premium on the Calvinist ideals of self-help and public virtue.

The provincial town became the prime location of much middle-class activity. Men and women dedicated themselves to voluntary organizations for improving education, promoting temperance and raising money for hospitals and schools. They were proud of and committed to their towns, and they took the leading role in their governance and enhancement. It was the middle classes who pressed parliament for the establishment of Improvement Commissioners who had the power to levy property taxes to fund improvements to sewage and water supplies, paving, lighting and so on.

The nineteenth-century middle classes also began to build what we have come to see as the archetypal home life. Men felt a sense of public duty, but a man needed the support of a wife and family, who displayed the same sense of virtue at home that he showed in public. A new sense of morality took hold; in the eighteenth century magistrates and ministers had been able to live openly with their mistresses with little public opprobrium; in the nineteenth century this was no longer possible. The Victorian middle-class home was a place of refuge from the vast changes overtaking the outside world, but it was also the alter ego of the self-less public citizen. The growing importance of the middle class is not a retrospective notion; it was clearly noted at the time. In 1831 Lord Henry Brougham wrote: 'By the people . . . I mean the middle classes, the wealth and intelligence of the country, the glory of the British name.' An increasing number of writers came from the middle classes, and a cascade of newspapers, journals and books was published for this eager, literate market. Commentators began to write about the middle class as the repository of national virtue, with a history reaching back through the great traditions of the nation.

But despite well-meant acts of public virtue, the divide between the middle and working classes was rigidly retained. The middle classes, being constantly told of their own virtue, saw working-class people as moral failures. Temperance movements and other 'improving' organizations aimed to rectify the failures while avoiding any move towards political rights or real advances in the provision of education or training; indeed, most middle-class people wanted to limit education and literacy in order to restrict access to better jobs. The upper and middle classes believed that extending political rights would mean the rule of the poor and the ignorant over the wealthy and the educated.

The division between different parts of society grew because, in part, successive parliaments and governments were not at all confident or certain of the responsibilities of the British state. Was it the task of the state to promote trade, or raise taxes, or fund the army, or encourage wealth creation, or to protect the workers? A political agenda that built an ideology around the answers to these questions did not emerge in Britain, or anywhere else in the west, until late in the nineteenth century. But there is no doubt too that the increasing power of the middle classes, through representation in parliament and on town councils, and in the bureaucracy of local and national government, did little to help the workers.

While, in many ways, the conditions of towns and cities improved, in other senses they confirmed the industrial landscape as a place of desensitizing anonymity. Captivated by the limitless possibilities of mechanical production, the Victorians built endless streets of houses all made from the same red brick and roofed with the same Welsh slate.

Local diversity counted for nothing, as houses, town halls, railway stations and churches were all designed and built on a national scale. Industrial towns with their smoke-stack chimneys, railway yards and rows of uniform terraces were a reflection of the factory system – an efficient way of housing workers near to the mills and mines.

The Industrial Revolution took place in the country with the longest tradition of representative government. But the British parliament, with no representation from working people, or even from the lower middle class who administered the industries, or from the new urban centres, was ill-equipped to cope. The British political system had been founded on the strength of a parliament of the noble and the worthy, to control the monarch, not administer an industrial state. Nevertheless, the British state flourished because its leading members preferred reform to the prospect of revolution or democracy – but the result was a country divided in two. In a series of measures, beginning with the Reform Act of 1832 (and followed by others in 1867 and 1884), parliament explicitly set out to prevent its takeover by the representatives of the majority. The arguments used by Earl Grey, sponsor of the 1832 Reform Bill, could not have been clearer: 'The principle of my reform is, to prevent the necessity for revolution . . . [there is no one] more dedicated against annual parliaments, universal suffrage, and the ballot [i.e. secret voting] than I am.' The opposition leader, the Duke of Wellington, thought the country had gone over to democracy, whereas Grey believed he had prevented it – but they, along with the rest of parliament, were united in fighting against it. Indeed, the 1832 Act formally disenfranchised some working-class people who had previously had the right to vote, as well as all women. In the run-up to the 1867 Bill, Prime Minister Lord Salisbury said: 'Discontent, insurrection, civil war itself, will, in the long run, produce no worse dangers than absolute or unrestrained democracy . . . The test by which a good Reform Bill may be distinguished from a bad one is that under it the working classes shall not now, or at any proximate period, command a majority in this House.'

Democracy (the word was still anathema to many) meant rule by the majority who were poor over the minority who were well-off. The same argument used in the Putney debates 200 years earlier was redeployed – if the men without property had power, they would surely rob those with more than themselves. When we see eminent Victorians depicted as classical Greek scholars, we should understand that for them, Athenian democracy was an aberration in an otherwise glorious age; they preferred the Roman senate. Neither the Tory conservative nor the Whig liberal tradition had roots in the culture of the common people of Britain, and there was no formal political link to the tradition that had been articulated in the Putney debates.

The Reform Acts and prevailing social attitudes placed the working classes outside social and political society – outside, in effect, British civilization. This self-conscious and deliberate separation was to have a marked effect on the intellectual and political life of Europe and the rest of the world. In 1842 Friedrich Engels was made the Manchester agent for his father's cotton business; within two years he wrote *The Condition of the Working Classes in England* and by 1848 had collaborated with Karl Marx on the *Communist Manifesto*. When Marx moved to London in 1849, the severe English class divide fed his analysis of history and his blueprint for revolution (see Chapter Sixteen). In other parts of Europe, republican and other political movements, together with the retention of customary rights, gave this divide a quite different meaning. Britain valued the stability of its system over the continual upheavals of nineteenth-century France, but French workers always had political routes through which they could make their voices heard. And in both Germany and Italy the nationalist movements that led to unification were based on liberating the people from imperial overlords, and giving them full political rights.

In Britain itself, the improvements in working-class life could be achieved by two routes – help from above, which was largely irrelevant and ultimately counterproductive, and help from within, which eventually succeeded. Help from above came from those improving societies that offered charity and moral instruction, but rejected public education. Traditional histories have made much of the benevolence of the great Victorian reformers, but the Earl of Shaftesbury, who worked to improve the lot of working children, opposed all forms of democracy, while Edwin Chadwick, pioneer of sanitation and public health, was a driving force behind the 1834 Poor Law. While these well-meaning reformers patronized and dictated to the working classes, later intellectuals would, as we shall see, idealize them.

There was an intellectual as well as a political response to the divided society, but once again writers looked for universal solutions through abstract reasoning. In 1859 John Stuart Mill in *On Liberty* asked how individual freedom should be defined within a constitutionally governed society. What restrictions could the state lawfully impose on the citizen and what freedoms could the citizen lawfully and morally expect? Mill's answer, that an individual is free to do anything that does not harm others, was a clever solution, but his belief in the primacy of individual freedom made him, despite being in favour of women's suffrage, suspicious of the tyranny of the majority. Though he was a 'progressive' thinker, Mill failed to cross the divide that separated him from the working people of Britain and Europe.

While their views of what to do with working-class people may have been different, Lords Grey, Shaftesbury and Salisbury shared with each other and with Chadwick, Mill and Marx a disembodied objective viewpoint that saw the workers as a single, undifferentiated mass. This view was reinforced by the enormous growth in population of Britain and other industrialized countries (Europe's population grew from 180 million in 1800 to 460 million in 1914). Many people, including politicians, artists and philosophers, saw the teeming masses of socially inferior people as a kind of plague. This sentiment reached its apogee in the early decades of the twentieth century, as members of the 'civilized' elite reacted with horror to the mass literacy that followed the introduction of universal elementary education across Europe in the 1890s. Far from welcoming education as a way of giving working people the tools to make them responsible citizens, many despaired that there was now little to separate the elite from the masses. Civilization became the preserve of a threatened, sensitive minority.

Those who took the opposite view had little more to offer their social inferiors. Driven by a desire to enlighten the middle classes and to refine, or tame, the workers, philanthropists took art and culture out of the private mansion and back into public view, in galleries and museums. Public authorities soon took over this role and a series of national art galleries and museums was instituted in every western capital, and subsequently in major towns and cities. It was automatically assumed that exposure to great works of art would have a civilizing effect, while appreciation of art was itself a sign of a civilized mind.

In the meantime, working people began to help themselves. An early sign of resistance to laissez-faire economics came in 1834, when six members of an association of agricultural workers at Tolpuddle in Dorset, formed to resist a reduction in wages, were sentenced to transportation. The ensuing mass demonstrations forced the government to pardon the men. The use of open meetings, or even riots, to express popular sentiment was a long tradition, but whereas before 1815 mass gatherings were anti-Catholic or anti-French, after Waterloo they were held to press for political change. Much of the credit Wellington gained at Waterloo was lost four years later when a crowd of over 100,000, gathered to demonstrate for parliamentary reform at St Peter's Fields in Manchester, was scattered by mounted soldiers with sabres. Eleven unarmed people were killed and 400 wounded at what became known as Peterloo.

The exclusion of working people from the 1832 Reform Act, the Poor Law Amendment Act of 1834, the omission of male adults from the 1833 Factory Act and the introduction in 1835 of Britain's first police force gave birth to the first mass working-class organization, the Chartist movement. The six demands of the 1838 People's Charter, drawn up by the founders of the London Working Men's Association, were: the vote for all men; parliamentary elections every year; ballots or secret voting; constituencies containing equal numbers of voters; the removal of property qualifications for MPs; and, finally, payment for MPs. The popularity of the Chartist movement showed that a large element of the population wanted real political rights, but its failure to achieve its goals (the movement faded away after 1848) showed that even in the so-called Age of Reform, argument, popularity and effective propaganda did not bring political change.

The real route to change for working people came through the same industrial processes that had brought them such hardship. The revolution in communications – the building of railways, the spread of the telegraph and the prodigious increase in newspaper sales (up tenfold between 1836 and 1880) – meant greater opportunities for working-class organization. Small-scale unions began to appear in the 1840s – the Miners' Association began in 1841, and in 1851 a host of localized engineering unions combined to form the Amalgamated Society of Engineers, with 11,000 members; by 1868 a meeting of union leaders in Manchester represented over 100,000 members. From the start, and in contrast to other European workers, British unions looked to parliamentary representation to further their aims. Two miners were elected as Liberal MPs in 1874, followed by Henry Broadhurst, secretary of the TUC, in 1880. But despite direction from the centre, local Liberal associations proved reluctant to select working-class candidates. The 1870s saw waves of strikes by unions resisting reductions in wages. In 1886 the Trades Union Congress formed the Labour Electoral Committee and put up Keir Hardie as the first ever Labour candidate. Hardie's poor showing in the 1888 general election convinced him that a full-blown political party, with the same campaigning and organization strength as the Liberals and Conservatives, would be needed if Labour candidates were to win seats.

In 1888 the Scottish Labour Party was formed, and during the early 1890s Independent Labour parties sprang up in towns and cities across Britain. The union movement gained ground and a large degree of sympathy with a series of strikes that gripped the nation's attention. The most remarkable was the 1888 Bryant and May strike at a match factory in east London, where the workers were all women. At the 1892 election Keir Hardie was returned as the first ever Labour MP, and in 1893 a meeting in Bradford, called in support of a firemen's strike, officially inaugurated the national Independent Labour Party. The need for labour representation in parliament was dramatically reinforced in 1901, when the law lords threatened to fine railway unions for the economic damage caused by a strike by its members. The trades unions had to be part of the legislature if they were to prevent this kind of ruling.

While their social betters agonized about granting employment rights, education and votes to British working-class people, the workers – with their unique understanding of their own situation – simply took matters into their own hands. The unions were, in contrast to other public institutions, open and democratic, and their representatives were, on the whole, far-sighted men and women who worked for the good of their members and their communities. But many labouring people wanted more than simply better wages and conditions. They organized themselves and sent people to parliament because they wanted a different kind of society, where social privilege and elevated background did not automatically assume political power. The generations who had grown up in an industrial world were not tied to the old rural hierarchy where the squire always knows best. Just like their seventeenth-century forebears, they wanted a society that recognized and reinstated the dignity of the common man. It was this desire, rather than the writings of political philosophers, that created the doctrine of liberal socialism.

The word socialism has been granted so many meanings that it has lost much of its evocative power. But socialism was, for many of our great-grandparents, a key way of understanding the world and a message of hope for the future. At its simplest, socialism is a state of society in which things are held in common, and it therefore stands in opposition to liberalism, in which private property is a key element in the organization of society. But in the west, socialism has, for the past century, lived within the confines of liberal democracy and so has come to mean something more subtle – something like the distribution and administration of capital, land and the means of production in the interests of all. In contrast to the scientific socialism of Marx, which saw history as a process leading to an ideal workers' state (see Chapter Sixteen), liberal socialism was a working-class response to a real situation, driven by the age-old human need for respect, dignity and communality. Municipal socialism, which took hold in many parts of Europe, was a practical fact not a theory-based system – paving, education, sanitation, parks, libraries, art galleries, museums, trams, hospitals, telegraphs, water and gas supplied by the municipality for the benefit of all citizens of the town. For many western people, socialism replaced the Christian religion as the great source of hope for the world.

This chapter has focused on the British experience of industrialization and political change, but all western industrial countries faced similar processes. However, the various European traditions produced quite different types of industrial and economic structures. The huge disruptions brought to the English countryside by enclosure simply did not happen in France or Germany or Italy or the Low Countries. But one aspect of the industrial economy did infect the whole of Europe. By the mid-nineteenth century it became clear that governments could not stand by and watch the industrial state develop as it might, it must pitch in and shape the economy through political action. While the nation state had been evolving as a tax-gathering and war-making apparatus, industrialization gave it a whole new set of responsibilities and powers. Napoleonic France had shown how the administration of a complex nation state could be effectively organized; industrialization made that organization essential. The central and guiding role of national government became the focus of all western societies. The industrial nation state, with its national economy, became the source of security, pride and prosperity for the politicians and peoples of Europe; and consequently everyone felt the need to belong to a nation. Industrialization and nationalism became inextricably entwined.

The legacy of the French Revolution and the Napoleonic wars was felt much more directly in the rest of Europe than in Britain. Much of Europe had been occupied by French armies and ruled by Napoleonic regimes; the paradoxical result was a surge of interest in the rights of citizens, and a desire for a state that could defend its people against foreign incursion. When the French armies and the puppet regimes were disbanded in 1815, the people of the Confederation of the Rhine, of Savoy, Venice and Naples, as well as France, were not universally over-joyed at the return of their rulers. Napoleon had given them new systems of government and administration – in Italy, for example, he brought in land reforms and representative government – while the printing presses of Europe had flooded the continent with tracts declaring the virtues of liberty and equality and 'The Rights of Man'. The French had also shown the potential power of a state defined by language, culture and the total involvement of all its citizens.

As well as providing an example, the Napoleonic conquests had also simplified the geopolitics of Europe, as the 300-plus political units that existed in 1789 were reduced to just 38 by 1815. But these units were not simply larger than their predecessors; the crucial difference was that the post-Napoleonic states were based on nationalities rather than ancient dynasties. The idea of the ethnic nation state had been born and would, over the next century, become the central ideal of western civilization.

The middle decades of the nineteenth century effectively completed the work that Napoleon had begun, as the client states he had created came together into ethnic nations. The most visible sign of change came in 1848, when open rebellion erupted on the streets of major cities in France, Germany, Austria, Hungary and Italy. The reasons for rebel-lion were by no means uniform – some crowds were demanding polit-ical rights, others national sovereignty, changes of government or just lower food prices. Bad harvests and economic slumps had brought hard-ship to many parts of Europe; the famine in Ireland was by far the worst, but food shortages were felt in cities across Europe. Nevertheless, European dissidents were, once again, inspired by events in Paris, where, in February 1848, King Louis-Philippe was forced to abdicate in favour of a new republic that immediately granted votes to all adult males. Italians, Poles, Germans, Hungarians all wanted similar rights within states controlled by themselves and their fellow citizens.

In the short term much of this came to nothing. An uprising in Paris four months after the February revolution, aimed at securing more rights, was crushed with great bloodshed, and within three years the elected president of the Second Republic (who was Napoleon's nephew) staged a coup and declared himself Emperor Napoleon III. In 1849 the Austrian army defeated a force of Italian nationalists led by Charles Albert. Nevertheless, 1848 brought a change in the attitudes of Europeans. German liberals and conservatives alike began to see a German nation, led by Prussia, as the only route to political and economic progress, and during 1848 France, Prussia and Austria had all granted the vote to all male citizens (even if it was later suspended). Nationalism was born of the need for a central industrial state, but was also a reaction to a series of bewildering changes. In a world where industrialization, urbanization and the sudden arrival of railways and steamships were altering human perceptions beyond recognition, nationalism became a comforting symbol of identity and stability. Politicians began to use nationalism as a persuasive and strategic weapon.

In 1864, Otto von Bismarck, then head of the Prussian government, provoked a series of wars with the aim of uniting the German states around the Prussian cause. War with Denmark over the provinces of Schleswig-Holstein was followed by the defeat of Austria in 1866, effectively excluding the Austrians from any further influence in German affairs. Having humiliated Austria and gained control of the north German states, Bismarck then forced France into war. Before the Franco-Prussian war of 1871, France posed little real threat to any of the German states, but the idea of Prussia defending Germany against the old enemy persuaded the southern German states to combine with their northern co-nationalists. In January 1871, in the palace of Versailles, with the French army defeated, William I, king of Prussia, was pronounced emperor of Germany.

The defeat of Napoleon III saw the withdrawal of the French garrison from Rome, and the final act in the unification of Italy. In 1867 the Austrian empire was converted into a dual monarchy, the Austro-Hungarian empire, in response to Hungarian nationalism. By the 1870s, the numerous duchies, principalities, city-states and empires had been replaced by a clear set of major continental powers – France, Germany, Italy, Austria-Hungary and Russia, with the Ottoman empire still controlling the south-east. Bismarck granted the vote to all German adult males, as did the Third Republic established in France after the defeat of 1871. In Italy and Austria-Hungary political rights were extended.

In the midst of this political change, various regions of Europe were becoming industrialized. Entrepreneurs, politicians, bankers, landowners and technologists were desperate to follow Britain's example, which had shown that investment in industrial processes could pay enormous dividends. Nevertheless, industrial 'take-off' could not be willed into existence by money and desire, it needed particular conditions. Industrialization was therefore a regional rather than a national phenomenon; where there was plentiful coal, iron ore and water transport – such as in Belgium, the Ruhr, north-east France, Bohemia, the north-eastern United States – industrialization followed quickly; other regions took much longer or simply remained as rural economies. And these non-industrial regions fared badly when industrialization drove up urban wages and the prices of manufactured goods. One result was massive emigration from rural areas of Europe to the United States.

The region of Europe that first industrialized was the old Frankish core, from northern Italy through Austria and Bohemia, to the Rhineland and the Ruhr, and to north-east France and the Low Countries; though this was now extended east to Prussia and Silesia and north from south-east England into the industrial Midlands and north of England, south Wales and the Clyde valley. This area, and each of the regions within it, had enough critical mass of resources, transportation and finance to create a self-sustaining industrial economy. In the United States, too, the combination of coal, iron ore, railways and capital ready for investment allowed rapid industrial development in the last decades of the nineteenth century (see Chapter 15). In this process, southern and eastern Europe became more obviously separated from the north and west. Southern Italy, Greece, Spain, Portugal and the Balkans, as well as western France and Ireland and large parts of Scandinavia, remained outside the industrialized zone and served as suppliers of people and food crops to the industrial core.

The regions that came later to industrialization had some distinct advantages. By the late nineteenth century machinery and equipment in British factories was seriously outdated but was kept running, even when others came in with newer, faster and better machines. Many British firms were family businesses in their second or third generations by 1900, and their conservative instincts did not serve them well under pressure from European and American competitors. Germany in particular was able to dominate the new chemical industry that emerged in the 1870s, to the degree that British firms had to hire

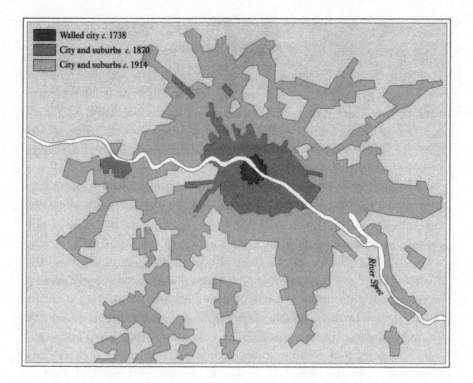

Growth of an industrial capital: Berlin in 1738, 1870 and 1914.

German chemists to run their laboratories and teach their staff. American equipment dominated in areas such as typesetting and electrical goods – the equipment for the electrified London Underground lines was supplied and fitted by American firms. Within two generations the countries of north-western Europe and the United States had caught up and begun to overtake Britain, the world's first industrialized country. Industrialization became ever more competitive as firms fought for market share, rather than simply looking at efficiency of production. The fact that industrial capitalism depended on a continuous process of destruction as well as innovation (first suggested by J. A. Schumpeter in the 1930s) may not have been understood in the late nineteenth century, but its effects were already being felt. Nothing – not family loyalties, cultural traditions, community cohesion or human solidarity – would be allowed to stand in the way of the imperatives of continual renewal.

The lives of the people of western Europe were utterly transformed by the growth of industry and the mass migration from the countryside to towns and cities. The vast increase in population and the emergence of new groups of people – an urban middle class and an industrial working class – made this new society utterly different from what had gone before. How did these changes affect western culture, and if art is a way of recapturing essential human qualities in a changing world, how did artists react to the novelty, the destructiveness and the innovation of industry?

The nineteenth century has proved a difficult period for historians of culture and art. The separation of true art from mere craftsmanship that began in Renaissance Italy was confirmed by the plethora of art academies, connoisseurs and critics in the eighteenth century. Craftsmanship was itself then all but destroyed by industrial machine production. But it is the loss of any recognizable style that condemns nineteenth-century painting, sculpture and, in particular, architecture in the eyes of historians. Dazzled by the available variety of historic styles, architects created Gothic churches, baroque theatres and classical Greek town halls, and some buildings that combine every style available. Critics such as Ernst Gombrich decry the loss of an authentic architectural voice, at the very time when so much building was going on.

But this abundance may be the reason for the loss of cohesion. Seeing so many utilitarian houses and factories, architects and their patrons wanted something distinctive for their churches and libraries and museums. They regarded simplicity as a sign of poverty and lack of imagination, so they made their buildings fussy and heavily decorated. The best nineteenth-century buildings escape this difficulty because they are built for a purpose. Railway stations, viaducts and bridges, steamships and railway engines are the glories of the industrial age and of nineteenth-century visual art.

Painters, meanwhile, no longer felt limited to biblical scenes or frozen enactments of Greek or Roman mythology. Scenes from recent history and the present helped artists compete with the Old Masters for public attention. Jacques-Louis David (1748–1825) depicted the events of the French Revolution (including the murder of Marat, and Napoleon crossing the Alps) almost as soon as they happened; while artists such as William Blake (1757–1827) and Francisco Goya (1746–1828) felt free to display their own visions, unfettered by convention or the requirements of patronage. It was not even necessary to have people in paintings. Landscapes, which had been a minor area of interest, became central to European art.

The work of artists such as Goya, Blake and J. M. W. Turner (1775–1851) demonstrated how the change in subject matter of paintings betrayed a profound alteration in the sense of what art and artists were for. Artists had always painted for clients, and even when the Renaissance made some artists into celebrities, they still painted to fill commissions. Most artists of the nineteenth century, in contrast, were forced to find markets for their work; and so they painted new subjects in order to entice buyers, a process that had immense consequences. The painter needed to produce something pleasing to the buyer *before* the work was bought rather than *after* he was commissioned. The danger of this second-guessing was that art would become formulaic and bland in trying to appeal to the greatest possible number; so then pressure came from the opposite direction. Serious artists felt they would be prostituting their art if they painted for money; instead, following Rembrandt, they saw art as a mode of expression of the inner soul, and so they turned away from popular taste. The artist became a fully fledged romantic; risking poverty and obscurity but staying true to his or her art. This was a complete reversal of the public patronage and adoration that was heaped on Michelangelo, Raphael and Titian, but it is a view of art and artists that has stayed with us.

A truer picture of nineteenth-century culture comes from seeing painting as simply one of a growing number of art forms. In retrospect it seems obvious that different art forms flourish at different times. The paintings of the Italian Renaissance are profoundly affecting because they maintained their connection to the spiritual role of church decoration. But this could not last; paintings became 'art' and were lost to the mass of the population and ceased to embody the culture of their origins. In the nineteenth century the same process happened with a different medium. The oral tradition of European life was transformed over several centuries by the products of thousands of printing presses. Like oil painting before it, fiction exploited the technology and changes of its time – the presses, transport and distribution systems, massive concentrations of people, teeming cities with contrasts of wealth and poverty – while drawing attention back to the human dramas it encompassed and endangered. Dickens, Gaskell, Eliot, Thackeray, Balzac, Hugo, Flaubert, Zola, Turgenev, Tolstoy, Dostoevsky, Hawthorne, Twain, Melville, Hardy and a host of others produced work packed with incident and character, drawn over great scales of distance and time. But they were not self-conscious works of art; they were creations made for an audience, produced mainly for weekly or monthly magazines. The enormous numbers of literate people in Europe and America soaked up novels, along with newspapers and pamphlets, as fast as they could be written.

The nineteenth-century novel appealed to an audience uprooted from an unchanging pattern where succeeding generations had lived in the same house, tilled the same fields and served the same master, to a life of turbulent and dramatic change. The finest novels did not offer comforting certainty but allowed difficult questions to be aired – doubts about religion, the purpose of existence in a brutalized world, general principles of morality versus particular instances of suffering, and so on. In books like Eliot's *Middlemarch*, great questions of life and politics are discussed and decided by 'ordinary' middle-class people, not by kings and generals.

While painters and poets followed the romantic route of separation from ordinary life, novelists reinvented the idea of artists as artisans; like medieval wood-carvers and silversmiths, they were skilled people who were part of society, not apart from it. When we look back at the origins of story-telling (see Chapter 1), we can see how completely and instinctively a writer like Charles Dickens (1812–70) understood his craft. His story lines, in which a well-to-do young man falls into bad company, or brushes with the lower classes, before eventually being rescued and restored to his rightful place in society, are often formulaic. But Dickens knew that the realist story lines (which deftly played on his audience's hopes and fears) were simply a device for drawing his readers into his world; and once there, he treated them to the most bizarre and original comic feast that had ever been put before an audience. Dickens knew the utter importance of the tightrope of genteel respectability; and out of the risks, follies and delusions that people constructed in order to stay aloft, he made a whirling comic dance. How, we might wonder, could any painter compete with the depiction of such a world? No wonder the novel reigned supreme in the hands of such an unselfconscious artist.

Novels reached the literate multitudes of Europe, but they were aimed at the middle classes. And while they drew their vitality from the connection to customs of story-telling, they were not available to the mass of working people. Instead, the customary culture of small rural communities had to be re-created in the monotonous, dehumanized streets and factories of industrial Europe. The result was a working-class culture that, in Europe at least, remained outside the reach and interest of historians, while being despised and denigrated by their contemporary social superiors. Separated from the middle classes, those most disadvantaged by industrialization found an opportunity to build an entirely new communal culture. The urban industrial working class – uprooted, mistreated and thrown into a situation that they all shared in common – were able to build a thriving and distinct culture, precisely because they owed nothing to the culture that controlled them, and wanted nothing from it.

Informal communal groupings and formal institutions sprang naturally from the common situation of working people. Methodist chapels, cooperatives, trade unions, working men's clubs, credit societies, Christmas clubs, football leagues sprang up in industrial cities. Working people with money to spend wanted music, dancing, pubs, magazines, amusement parks and seaside outings. Those from the better classes who were sympathetic to workers' rights and freedoms wanted to sanitize them, rescue them from the cities and take them back to workshops in the countryside. Workers wanted none of it, though; they wanted the city life and were busy building a culture of their own based on mutual support and common interest. Much of their work was drudgery, but many workers took great pride in their strength, knowledge and skills. Nowadays we flock to see working steam engines, water wheels and 'traditional' weaving and printing workshops; the men and women who worked them had to fight for decent employment conditions and for the respect of their employers, but we should not forget the abiding affection that many working people had for the machinery in their charge – for these people work was a source of status, respect and dignity.

By the late nineteenth century the working people of Europe had begun to recover from the trauma of industrialization and urbanization. They began to win material gains, rights in the workplace, elementary education and some degree of social security, and they built a culture based on their shared situation and on their new urban existence. But most Europeans still lived in near-poverty, in houses and streets of dehumanizing drabness and uniformity, while working as physical adjuncts to the machinery of industry. And the gains they made in literacy, in material well-being and education, simply provoked even greater fear and suspicion among their social superiors – the workers were the new barbarians. Europe, and Britain in particular, ended the great century of industrialization with its different classes locked in a relationship of mutual fear, suspicion and ignorance.

Victorian Britain dominated the west in the nineteenth century and bequeathed a legacy that profoundly affected much of the following century. The better-off Victorians believed that they had solved the problems of society, and that with their emphasis on propriety, restraint and gentility they embodied the highest aspirations of civilization. Their belief in progress was driven and sustained by technological change, and by their policy of putting out of sight the effects of poverty (behind the neat walls of the workhouse) and conflict (through wars fought in far-away places against peoples armed with shields and spears). Their confident belief in progress and the idea that enlightened self-interest would bring harmony to the whole world was, in retrospect, an illusion. By the end of the nineteenth century Britain and Europe were heading not to a better society, but towards the catastrophe of mechanized warfare.

FROM RURAL COLONIES TO INDUSTRIAL CONTINENT

The Making of Modern America

IN a little over a hundred years the United States was transformed from a series of coastal settlements with a rural hinterland, dependent on agriculture and fishing, into an industrial continent with an infrastructure of transport and communication that bound it into a single economic and cultural entity. The making of this modern giant involved every aspect of human behaviour – heroism, genocide, violence, idealism, greed and selflessness – magnified on a vast scale. The freeing of millions of immigrant peoples from the restraints of their old European homelands led to both exploitation and opportunity; and while the heroic era of American history is characterized by corruption, genocide and untrammelled greed, the people of this vast, bewildering cauldron of human activity created an entirely new culture that gave a voice to those born into the world of machinery, clocking-on, and the anonymity of city life.

The transformation of America began in 1804 when President Thomas Jefferson negotiated the Louisiana Purchase from France, a deal that would double the size of the United States, and then sent an expedition to explore these new lands. On 21 May Meriweather Lewis and William Clark, with 44 others, pulled out of the frontier town of St Charles with orders to gain information about the territories of the west, and to find a route to the Pacific. They returned three years and 7,000 miles later with news of strange, fertile and almost limitless lands waiting beyond the Appalachians and the Mississippi. The west was to become the new America.

At the time of independence the population of the United States was

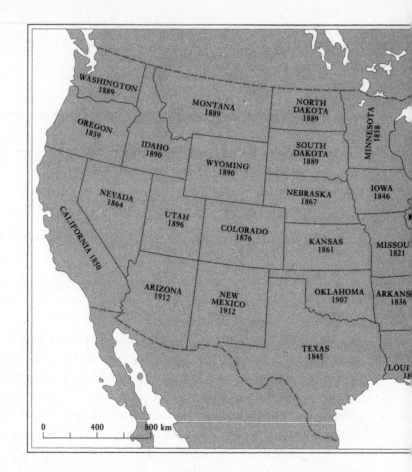

around 2.5 million, by 1810 it was 7.2 million and by 1820 9.6 million – mainly thanks to a constant stream of immigrants from Britain. Settlers moved west in the wake of Lewis and Clark, and south to cash in on the cotton boom. The federal government offered virgin land for sale at $2 an acre for a minimum purchase of 160 acres (later dropped to $1.25 per acre for a minimum of 80 acres), and states were added as fast as people could get to them – another six in the six years after 1815, to bring the total to 24. But people went ever further west beyond the boundaries of the United States territories, effectively migrating to foreign countries – Oregon was a British-owned part of Vancouver province, California and the south-west was owned by Spain, while the 'empty' part in the middle belonged to the plains Indians.

The 1840s were the years of the wagon trains, crossing the Mississippi and following the courses of its western tributaries until they reached the mountains. Maps still show the old roads west from Omaha along

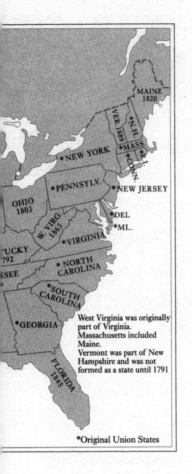

MAINE
1820

VER. 1889

N.H.

MASS.

NEW YORK

CONN

R.I.

PENNSYLV.

NEW JERSEY

OHIO
1803

W. VIRG.
1863

DEL

ML.

VIRGINIA

UCKY
792

NORTH
CAROLINA

SEE

SOUTH
CAROLINA

GEORGIA

West Virginia was originally part of Virginia.
Massachusetts included Maine.
Vermont was part of New Hampshire and was not formed as a state until 1791

FLORIDA
1845

*Original Union States

Westward growth of the United States.

the Platte river, crossing the Rocky Mountain watershed at Laramie and taking the California Trail across the desert towards the Sierra Nevada, or turning north along the Snake river on the Oregon Trail. These were epic journeys into the half-known and a human adventure of historical significance. A curious mixture of farmers and adventurers, the pioneer settlers of the American west created a new nation, but they were also part of a wider phenomenon. In the nineteenth century the numbers of European people grew enormously, sustained by a vast increase in the amount of land subject to human cultivation. As pioneers went west to turn the prairies into farmland, their fellow Europeans were exploring and cultivating the wildernesses of Siberia, Canada, Australia, New Zealand, South America and Africa.

Migration to the American west was steady and unspectacular until, in January 1848, gold was discovered in a creek at Coloma in California. In 1846 the United States, having had their attempt to buy California

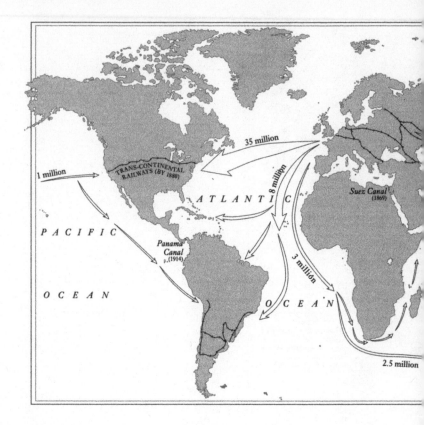

from Mexico refused, had taken it by force. In 1847 Mexico had ceded California and the south-west, and dropped its claim to Texas – the United States had, in the words of New York journalist John L. O'Sullivan, fulfilled its 'manifest destiny to overspread the continent'. In the period 1841–47 around 15,000 people travelled from the east to the western territories; but after gold was found in 1849–50 about 75,000 made the journey, and more than 300,000 by 1854. In 1849 alone more than 500 ships made the long journey round South America to take pioneers to California, with many more sailing direct from Europe. The gold rush changed the nature, as well as the numbers, of people going west. Families and farmers gave way to single men, fugitives and chancers. In 1835 Alexis de Tocqueville wrote that America was characterized by two simultaneous impulses: the sense of community sharing and giving, of mutual interest and support; and the scramble to make as much money as possible. This contrast fed into, and was amply demonstrated by, the birth of the Wild West.

When America turned to the west its people began to appreciate how different their new country was from Europe. Just as a romantic view

The world-wide movement of people in the nineteenth century was dominated by the migration of Europeans to North America.

of nature took hold in Europe in reaction to rationalism and industrialization, so Americans began to look to the natural world around them for a deeper sense of what it meant to be American. Writers like Henry David Thoreau and Walt Whitman were conscious of forming a relationship with the natural world of North America, while Ralph Emerson, Nathaniel Hawthorne, Herman Melville, Emily Dickinson, James Audubon, Mark Twain, and later Willa Cather and others, developed a uniquely American artistic sensibility and culture, based on their very particular physical and social situation. Whitman travelled across America and wrote of his efforts 'to loosen the mind of still-to-be-formed America from the folds, the superstitions and all the long, tenacious and stifling anti-democratic authorities of Asiatic and European past'. America (how much more poetic that sounded than the United States) was to be a new country, turning its back on Europe both figuratively and culturally.

Americans (or, more accurately, European-Americans) were moving into what they regarded as a vacant country with no human history of any importance. Once they had brushed aside the indigenous people,

there was only empty, uninhabited land, in which the disputes and prejudices and hatreds and history of Europe simply melted away. In
America there was no Basque country, no Ulster, no Alsace or Lorraine,
no Schleswig-Holstein, no Kosovo to be claimed or disputed, to kill or
die for. Everyone in America had a stake in all of it.

However, while Americans had solved the problems of European
rivalry, the difficulty of what to do about the indigenous population
and the thorny issue of slavery remained. The mass genocide of the
Native Americans was to take place after the civil war (see later in
this chapter), but the signs of the impending catastrophe were seen
as soon as Europeans settled the west in large numbers. The violence
of the Wild West did not just come from the preponderance of lone
drifters, but from the sense of displacement felt by the new Americans
(and shared by others before and since). First-generation immigrants
from Europe had roots back in the old country, but their children
had little connection with either their place of origin or their new
home. While the immigrants clung to the eastern seaboard, and made
a 'new England' of their country, the strangeness of their situation
was not so troubling, but once European peoples were set adrift in
a vast and unfamiliar landscape, where every town looked the same,
and where they had no roots or cultural customs to call on, then the
sense of displacement became overwhelming. Their response was, on
the one hand, to annihilate with murderous violence those indigenous
peoples whose cultural and social traditions were wedded to the land,
and, on the other, to build communities based around written laws
enforced by severe punishment, and strong Calvinist-inspired
Christian ideals.

The issue of slavery was to prove more damaging to the new country.
The Industrial Revolution in England affected the pattern of settlement
in the United States by opening up a seemingly infinite demand for
American cotton – production doubled every decade from 1820 until,
by 1860, cotton was worth twice all the other American exports
combined. The cotton boom led to a huge increase in the numbers of
slaves, from around 800,000 in 1776 to 1.5 million by 1820, and 4
million by 1860. As well as making good returns from cotton, sugar
and tobacco, southerners made money from buying and selling slaves
– each worth around $1,000 by 1860. Slavery was disappearing else-
where in the western world and political rights were being extended,
but the American south was increasingly inclined to see itself as a place

apart, a separate culture from the north and decidedly against any interference in its internal affairs.

For most of the first half of the nineteenth century there was a formal
legal and political division between the states of the Union. States in
the north had made slavery illegal, while those in the south depended
more and more on the exploitation of slaves. An uneasy stand-off was
maintained for a few decades, but many foresaw either civil war or the
partition of the country. As early as 1820 Thomas Jefferson wrote:
'This momentous question [of slavery], like a fire bell in the night,
awakened me and filled me with terror. I considered it at once as the
knell of the Union.' Three decades later Abraham Lincoln made his
most prophetic speech: 'A house divided against itself cannot stand. I
believe this government cannot endure, permanently half slave and half
free. I do not expect the Union to dissolve – I do not expect the house
to fall – but I do expect it will cease to be divided. It will become all
one thing or all the other.'

Citizens of the north, though generally against slavery, were not in
favour of imposing abolition on the south. The factories of Massachusetts
were doing good business out of taking southern commodities, making
them into clothes and shoes and selling them back again. People in the
north knew that the south would secede rather than give up slavery, and
the notion of fighting a war to preserve the Union had never occurred
to most of them. As Louis Menand has recently pointed out: 'We think
of the Civil War as a war to save the union and to abolish slavery, but
before the fighting began most people regarded these as incompatible
ideals.' This situation changed because of events that happened before
the war but stayed in the minds of all Americans.

In 1857 the case of Dred Scott, a Virginian slave who claimed that
time he had spent in Illinois made him a free man, came before the
Supreme Court. The court's judgement, carried by seven southern
judges, declared that Scott was not regarded as a US citizen and therefore had no right to bring a case to the court; he was a resident of a
slave state and could not claim rights under another state's laws; finally,
he was the property of his master, with the same status as a mule, and
the court had no right to deprive his master of his property. In a ruling
that created deep resentment, the court had therefore decreed that
northern states had no legal right to act as liberators of southern slaves.

The new state of Kansas was north of the agreed line dividing slave
and free states, yet in 1854 Congress passed a measure allowing Kansans

the right to decide the issue of slavery for themselves. The issue gave birth to a new Republican party, and Kansas became a violent stage on which pro- and anti-slavery settlers fought. John Brown, who dedicated his life to keeping pro-slavery settlers out of Kansas, was captured at Harpers Ferry in Virginia in 1859 after killing the mayor and taking over the federal arsenal. Brown was hanged in Virginia – a criminal to the south, and to many northerners a martyr.

By the time of the presidential election in 1860, the Republican party, which was dedicated to preventing the spread of slavery, was seen by many in the south as beyond the pale. When the Republicans chose Abraham Lincoln, a man with an anti-slavery reputation, as their presidential candidate, the south was implacably hostile. The Democratic party split into northern and southern factions, and fielded two candidates. Lincoln thereby won most of the northern and western states but none in the south, making him president, on 40 per cent of the popular vote, of an irreconcilably divided country. On 4 February 1861, a month before Lincoln was formally adopted into office, seven states (later to be joined by four others) seceded from the Union and declared the creation of a new nation, the Confederate States of America, with Jefferson Davis of Mississippi as its president.

In his inaugural address Lincoln did not promise to outlaw slavery; he even offered to make the right to own slaves part of the United States Constitution. But he would not allow the extension of slavery or the secession of any state from the Union. It did not much matter what Lincoln said, though; southerners were giddy with their own daring and the novelty of their situation. They took over federal customs posts and mail offices in the south and excitedly talked up their prospects.

The crisis point was reached in early April 1861, as the nation's eyes turned towards Fort Sumter, a federal outpost in the rebel state of South Carolina. Overlooking Charleston harbour, the fort was the property and instrument of the federal government, and its commander, Major Anderson, refused to surrender his post voluntarily to the confederate authorities. On 12 April 1861 General Beauregard of the Confederate States opened fire on the fort and within three days Lincoln declared his intention of restoring federal authority in the south by force. The border slave states, Virginia, North Carolina, Tennessee and Arkansas, were appalled and promptly joined the confederacy. The battle lines were now drawn.

In response to Lincoln's request for 75,000 volunteers, young men poured into Washington and into recruiting offices across the north. Given their attitudes before the war, we might wonder why so many young men were so keen to join up. The motive of many seems to have been a passionate belief in the need to preserve the United States as a single nation. On the face of it this is a little surprising. The United States was not an ancient nation forged out of indissoluble clan and tribal loyalties, nor a band of subjects united by allegiance to a sovereign. The federal government was a low-key and somewhat ramshackle affair, interfering as little as possible in the business of individual states. Nevertheless, the sober but enthusiastic rush to defend the Union showed a deep and abiding sense of what was at stake. The declaration of secession by the confederacy had been greeted with astonishment in the north, as had the casual denigration of the revered Stars and Stripes. The Union had become the symbolic centre of American life, promoted as passionately by southerners like Andrew Jackson as by northerners, and inculcated into every American child through school classes on the history of their country and the rituals of Thanksgiving and the Fourth of July. Whatever they thought before the conflict, once the war was begun, northerners knew that defeat would mean an incalculable setback for the ideals on which the country had been founded and a betrayal of everything that Americans ought to stand for. America had, even before the civil war, a sense of itself as an ideal creation; a nation made to be, and to do, good.

Lincoln quickly saw that occupying the whole of the south with Union armies would never work; instead, the armies of the south must be brought to battle and soundly defeated. While overoptimistic about the size of the task, Lincoln was clear from the outset that a total military victory was the only option. For much of the war the south had the better military leadership in the shape of Robert E. Lee and his deputy Thomas 'Stonewall' Jackson. In the latter stages, the Union finally found generals – particularly Ulysses S. Grant and William Sherman – who were able to make their numerical and industrial advantages tell. Lee was an audacious general who, rather than waiting on his home territory, struck into the north, calculating that a defeat on home soil would persuade the Union armies to give up the fight. At Antietam in Maryland in September 1862 and Gettysburg in Pennsylvania in July 1863 he narrowly failed to overcome Union armies. In response Grant was able to move down the Mississippi and then across Tennessee in 1863, before wearing down Lee's forces in Virginia in late 1864. This strategy allowed Sherman to march from Tennessee across Georgia to the Atlantic coast, thereby cutting the south in two and isolating its armies. Robert E. Lee bowed to the inevitable, decided not to subject his men to further pointless slaughter, and surrendered to General Grant at Appomattox, Virginia, on 9 April 1865.

The war started as a fight to save the Union, but in late 1862 Lincoln and his cabinet declared slavery to be illegal, and all slaves free. As a legal safeguard he gave until 1 January 1863 for all states to give up the rebellion; if they did not, then the slaves in those states would be forever free. Congress supported the president and the Emancipation Proclamation was passed into law. The Union cause benefited enormously from its embrace of emancipation; slaves in the south deserted their plantations at great personal risk, acted as guides for the advancing armies of the north, and protected Union soldiers isolated behind southern lines. And once they were permitted to, they fought; by the end of the war there were 180,000 black soldiers in 166 Union regiments.

On 19 November 1863, Lincoln attended a ceremony to dedicate part of the Gettysburg battlefield as a cemetery for the fallen Union troops. His short address began with a call to remember history: 'Fourscore and seven years ago our fathers brought forth on this continent, a new nation, conceived in Liberty, and dedicated to the proposition that all men are created equal . . .' and ended with a promise of democracy: '. . . that government of the people, by the people, for the people, shall not perish from the earth'.

The United States Constitution makes no reference to equality, while the country had, for the previous 80 years, tolerated the prodigious growth of slavery. In order to reinforce America's ideals Lincoln had to redefine them by reaching back beyond the constitution to the Declaration of Independence: 'We hold these truths to be self-evident, that all men are created equal . . .' Having ignored those fine words for so long, would the American people, having fought a war to abolish slavery, be prepared to put them into practice?

Lincoln was president at the start of the war and at its end (he was re-elected by a landslide in 1864). Congress and president had worked together to prosecute the war, but they had been able to do more than that. For the first time in 50 years the machinery of Congress was not dominated and hampered by the great divide between north and south.

The south had complained before the war that northern capital, based in New York and Boston, was controlling the whole country; the wartime administration made alliance with that capital to build an infrastructure that would win the war. The government needed railways, guns, steel, clothing, ships, ammunition and equipment, and so industry got to work. Immense profits were made during the war, and at the end of the conflict, returning soldiers put around $70 million dollars' worth of pay and pensions into the economy, fuelling a boom that lasted into the 1870s.

But the war had exerted a terrible price. The scale of loss was simply extraordinary: 359,000 Union and 258,000 Confederate soldiers perished as railways brought vast quantities of men, equipment and artillery to the front line, allowing set-piece battles on an enormous scale. Large areas of the country, particularly in the south, were devastated – towns burned down, crops destroyed, infrastructure dismantled. The war had also flooded the country with small arms. The constitution had allowed the right of every citizen to bear arms, and the war gave them the chance to do just that. Returning soldiers, and anyone else with a mind to, could get their hands on a Springfield rifle and a revolver. The west, in particular, became notorious for the proliferation of guns.

Of more immediate concern were the psychological scars of war, and the plight of the 4.5 million newly liberated African-Americans. Just one week after the surrender at Appomattox, Abraham Lincoln was murdered, leaving his successors with the problem of how to reconcile the civil war enemies and how to organize the lives of the 'freedmen'. Both proved beyond them. The federal government instituted a great programme of southern reconstruction, but this failed from a combination of white southern resentment of the north and a deepening hatred of its own black community. The Fourteenth Amendment to the constitution was passed into law in 1866, giving formal rights of citizenship to all African-Americans, backed up by a civil rights law covering people of 'every race and colour'. In reality this had little effect. As the south became more and more hostile to ex-slaves, and as industry in the north began to expand, African-Americans used the newly built railroads to move to Chicago, Detroit, Cleveland and New York.

By the late 1870s, the failure of reconstruction in the south and the ineffective presidencies of Andrew Johnson (1865–68), Lincoln's

vice-president, and Grant (1868–76), his leading general, led to the
debasement of national politics. The whiff of corruption became a
stench as government officials and elected members creamed off funds
and paybacks from the sale of land in the west, railroad speculation,
gold trading and liquor taxes. The contrast with Lincoln's stern, prin-
cipled determination could hardly have been more stark. America was
getting rich and Washington was cashing in.

The party system began to work against, rather than for, real democracy. The legacy of the war placed almost all states and congressional
districts firmly in one camp or the other, and political campaigning
focused on those few places that might change hands, with all other
representatives effectively chosen by the party machines. In 1877 the
horse-trading of Washington politics reached its lowest ebb. The presidential election seemed to give a substantial victory for the Democrat
Samuel Tilden, but 'reinterpretation' of some electoral college votes
gave the verdict narrowly to the Republican Rutherford Hayes. A subsequent investigating commission voted along party lines in favour of
Hayes. A political crisis was averted when southern Democrats agreed
to back down in return for the withdrawal of federal interference,
including federal troops, from the south. The deal was done and the
freed slaves of the south lost their only protection. The Supreme Court
ruled in 1883 that the federal government had no right to interfere in
segregation by private individuals; in 1896 it asserted the rights of states
to segregate public facilities; and in 1899 the court decided that states
could build schools for whites only, even if there were none for blacks.
The civil war had preserved the Union, but the price was the betrayal
of the imperative that drove the conflict; it seemed that for all Americans
to have, in Daniel Webster's oft-recited speech, 'both Union and Liberty'
was impossible.

The resolution of the civil war allowed the United States, dominated
by the industrialized north-east, to enter a ferocious period of expansion. In the half-century after 1865 mass immigration, the settlement
of the west, and the development of an urban-industrial society brought
about the emergence of the continent-sized country that is modern
America. Changes in transport technology dramatically affected all parts
of the world – between 1869 and 1883 four railway lines were built
east to west across the United States, followed by three across Canada;
by 1900 there was continual railway track from western Europe to

Baku on the Caspian Sea and by 1904 to the Pacific coast at Vladivostock. In 1869 the Suez Canal was completed, followed by the Panama Canal in 1914. By the 1870s steamships ran on all the world's major sea routes, cutting journey times by half and increasing both the reliability and the size of ships. The railways and canals and shipyards employed huge numbers of workers, while at the same time offering easy and relatively cheap methods of migration across great distances.

The rapid industrialization of continental Europe in the 1860s and 1870s gave rural areas the dual problems of price inflation and redundant labour. The result was rural migration to the industrial cities of Europe and across the Atlantic. Further migration was provoked by the racial intolerance that accompanied growing European nationalism. Anti-Jewish pogroms in Russia began in 1882, and persecution in the Austro-Hungarian empire emptied eastern Europe of around one third of its Jewish population, almost all going to America. Polish, Italian and Irish peasants left for America in their millions, driven by economic hardship and the relative ease of migration. Others went simply because, like thousands of Scandinavian and German farmers, they were attracted by the adverts of rail and shipping companies. The steamship companies understood that they got more business if they offered a complete migration package. Shipping lines working out of Liverpool, Bremen, Hamburg and Naples had agents spread throughout Europe, and they teamed up with railway companies in America and Canada who whisked the migrants as far across the continent as they wished, or could afford, to go. In this new world distances did not seem to matter. A Finnish settler in Ontario gave his family directions on how to find him: board the train in Halifax, Nova Scotia, and get off at Timmins, Ontario; he did not bother to mention that it was a three-day ride. Nevertheless they made it, along with around 25 million other Europeans between 1860 and 1920. Migration to America, while still a massive adventure, was no longer a desperate life-or-death gamble.

Following the California gold rush of 1849, gold was found at Pike's Peak, Colorado, and silver in Comstock, Nevada, in 1859, followed by gold and silver in Idaho, Montana, Dakota and Colorado again in the 1870s. Miners, traders and saloon-keepers flooded west in search of wealth, but it was the railroads that pulled settlers to the prairies of the Midwest and to the fruit farms of California. Civil war veterans began new lives as ranchers of cattle on the vast open scrub plains of Texas (finally admitted into the Union in 1845). Hardy breeds brought over by the Spanish proved ideally suited to the arid conditions, but the market for beef was more than a thousand miles away in the cities of the north-east. The solution was to drive the cattle to the nearest railhead at Abilene, Dodge City or Wyoming for onward shipment to the stockyards of Chicago. The cowboy was born; in myth a gunslinger and hard drinker, in reality a solitary type who spent his working life in the saddle, miles from anywhere. Despite his later resurrection in film, the era of the cowboy was short-lived, lasting from the end of the civil war to the extension of the railways and the fencing of the ranges in the early 1890s.

While the rural areas of the Midwest and the far west were settled by ranchers and farmers, the United States was following Europe's example in becoming an urban industrial society. Millions of new immigrants crowded into the industrial cities of the north-east, initially packed together in tenements with little natural light and often no water or sewerage. City administrations, frequently run by the allies of industrialists and landlords, either turned a blind eye to the squalor, or simply failed to cope with the vast expansion of their populations. Within each city a mosaic of ethnic communities attempted to re-create the customs and relations of the immigrants' homelands; Cleveland, Ohio, for example, had more than 15 European ethnic groups, from Finns to Romanians to Bohemians to Italians, living in distinct neighbourhoods in the city centre. Jewish, Russian, Italian and German markets may have been held in every city, just like back in Europe, but life for these immigrants from rural Meath, Macedonia, Belorus and Calabria was very different. Subsistence farming in village communities was exchanged for labouring in giant steel mills, railroad yards and coalmines.

In 1860 the industrial belt was restricted to the north-east coastal strip, taking in the major cities of Baltimore, Philadelphia, New York and Boston, but by 1900 it had spread in an arc west to the great lakes and then south to western Pennsylvania and Ohio. Buffalo, Cleveland, Pittsburgh, Cincinnati and Detroit, Chicago, Milwaukee and St Louis all had over half a million inhabitants by the end of the century. As the overcrowded, congested cities threatened to grind to a halt, and factory-owners saw the need for fit and healthy workers, housing regulations were gradually brought in to give minimum standards of floor area, light, running water and sewerage disposal. American cities competed with each other, and civic pride saw the erection of impressive public buildings, city centre parks, museums and libraries. But the cities just kept growing. When the supply of immigrants from Europe was restricted in the 1920s, internal migration was already answering the needs of another industrial boom.

In 1900, 77 per cent of African-Americans still lived in rural areas of the south, but segregation persuaded many to move north in search of work and freedom from persecution. After 1896 most southern states segregated public buildings, trains, schools and buses and passed laws prohibiting contact between whites and blacks and effectively preventing African-Americans from voting. In the first half of the twentieth century, white and black southerners were born in separate hospitals, educated in separate schools, married in separate churches and buried in separate cemeteries; and every bus, school, diner, boarding house, waiting room, hospital, drinking fountain and prison was either for whites or for blacks but never for both. American public life was to fall into such disrepair that in the 1920s, African-Americans were prohibited from public buildings in the area of Washington DC that contained the memorial to Abraham Lincoln.

Migration from the south was speeded up by the arrival of the boll weevil, which spread across the cotton belt from 1898, destroying the livelihood of hundreds of thousands of African-American families. From 1913 to 1919 around half a million African-Americans went north, to Chicago, St Louis, Detroit, New York, Indianapolis, Cleveland and elsewhere, in a migration that continued until the Second World War. The cities continued to grow because until the 1930s there was still a huge rural population – white and African-American – to draw on. The capacity of the cities to cope was put under strain by every wave of expansion and influx, and they struggled to make life tolerable for their citizens.

The industrial expansion of the United States was as prodigious as the growth of its cities. On the eve of the civil war the value of the country's manufactures was $1.8 billion; by 1899 it was $13 billion and the US had become the biggest manufacturing nation in the world. The railways led the way, employing more than one million people and turning over one billion dollars by 1890. They were also symptomatic of the multiple abuses of the period of 'heroic capitalism' that saw vast fortunes made by dubious methods. The federal government wanted to see the railroads expand, so it made grants of land and money to the railroad companies, which would in turn award themselves government-sponsored contracts to build the railroads, sell off the adjoining land at enormous profit, and bribe politicians with gifts of railroad stock. American capitalism had not yet figured out how to preserve competition by preventing monopolies. Andrew Carnegie, for example, bought up most of the coal and iron ore reserves in America and used them for his own steel mills, blocking anyone else from entering the industry; by 1890 Carnegie was making 70 per cent of the steel in America. In 1901 he sold his business to J. P. Morgan for $450 million. A similar monopoly was created by the Rockefeller family's Standard Oil business. The 1887 Interstate Commerce Act was aimed at breaking the regional monopolies of individual railroad companies, who kept out competition and charged whatever rates they chose, and served as a model for the future regulation of private industry.

The arguments for free trade would not have cut much ice with American industrial capitalists – they prospered while American industries were nurtured and flourished behind a formidable set of trade barriers. At the start of the civil war import tariffs had been introduced to raise funds for military expenses; after the war tariffs were extended and made into full protective measures, and only dismantled when American industry was dominant enough to open its markets to competition.

While American industry was run, owned and exploited by a few 'robber barons', and its cities were centres of corruption and squalor, none of this could suppress the spirit of optimism brought by the millions of immigrants who saw America as the land of opportunity. One immigrant described Ellis Island as 'the nearest earthly likeness we have to the Final Day of Judgment, when we have to prove our fitness to enter Heaven'. In Europe their horizons had been limited by social status, ethnic background and poverty, and by a web of customs and traditions; but in America none of that seemed to matter. The long economic boom encouraged the belief that anyone could do and become anything, and gave birth to a spirit of optimistic endeavour that was captured in the vastly popular books of Horatio Alger, in which young men from poor backgrounds used a combination of hard work and honesty to make their fortune.

At the same time, immigrants from Europe were clustering together in the new industrial cities, re-creating the communities of their homelands in the neighbourhoods of New York, Baltimore, Detroit, Chicago, Pittsburgh and elsewhere. Every American city became a chequerboard of ethnic communities – Italian, Irish, Polish, African-American, Jewish,

Russian, Swedish, German – each preserving and creating traditions that allowed the precious thread of human interaction in a world ruled by machines and money. America became the embodiment of the modern western paradox: a society in pursuit of both individual ambition and social cohesion.

While urban squalor and the promise of a better future were the ingredients of American industrialization, the invisible tragedy of nineteenth-century America was being played out on the plains, hills, deserts and mountains of the west. At the outbreak of the civil war in 1861 there were 300,000 Native Americans living west of the Mississippi. After the war General Carleton decided to clear the south-west for white settlement, and ordered that 'There is to be no council held with the Indians, nor any talks. The men are to be slain whenever and wherever they can be found.' The genocide in the south-west – only the Navajo were eventually allowed to stay on a small patch of land – was a shocking episode but was simply part of a larger disaster.

In late 1862 a Sioux tribe called the Santee, tired of being pushed ever further west, attacked white forts and settlements along the Minnesota river. Inevitably, and as predicted by their leader Little Crow, they lost the conflict and the entire tribe was taken prisoner. Three hundred were sentenced to death, and though this was later restricted to 38 leaders, it was still the largest single legal execution in the history of the United States. The punishment was supposed to teach compliance, but the lesson for many Native Americans was that negotiation or compromise brought defeat; it was better to fight to the death than live in miserable captivity.

In 1865 the United States army was ordered to clear the Great Plains of Indian tribes. The Cheyenne, Arapaho and Sioux banded together under Red Cloud and, through organized resistance, forced the government to guarantee an area of 500,000 square miles exclusively for their people. Almost immediately the authorities changed tack and began the extermination of the plains buffalo, specifically in order to destroy the Native American way of life. As General Sheridan made clear: 'Let them kill, skin and sell until the buffalo is exterminated, as it is the only way to bring about lasting peace and allow civilization to advance.' In 1870 there were around 15 million buffalo on the plains; a decade later there were a few hundred at most, and the Native Americans of the plains soon followed the buffalo into virtual oblivion.

In 1868 a treaty guaranteed the sacred Black Hills of Dakota as the homeland of the Sioux tribes in perpetuity. But in 1874 gold was discovered in the hills, and the United States government ordered the Sioux to sell their land and move on to small reservations in the east. To Sitting Bull and Crazy Horse (as to most non-Europeans) the modern European idea of owning land was incomprehensible, and they had no desire to live like white people on reservations. In the summer of 1876 Sioux and Cheyenne warriors wiped out a column of troopers under the command of Colonel George Custer at Little Big Horn, but by the spring of 1877 most of Sitting Bull's people had surrendered. He fled to Canada but was brought back to live in virtual captivity. Senator John Logan announced to him in public: 'You have no following, no power, no control . . . The government feeds and clothes and educates your children now, and desires to teach you to become farmers, and to civilise you, and make you as white men.'

It was a story as old as western civilization. Like the Arians, pagans, Cathars, English peasants, Incas, Mexicans and Irish Christians before them, the Native Americans were forced either to conform to a strict idea of civilized existence or live as the captives or servants of its exemplars. There was no alternative; western civilization could not contemplate living alongside another kind of social existence on equal terms.

In the late 1880s members of the Sioux and other tribes once again showed signs of rebellion, following a new spiritual leader who advocated resistance based on a ritual known as Ghost Dancing, which would bring an end to white men and their evil. Potential rebel leaders were rounded up and Sitting Bull was shot while being arrested. Other members of his tribe, fearing for their lives, left their reservation and headed out on to the plains. They were apprehended and forced to camp at a place called Wounded Knee Creek in South Dakota. The next day, 29 December 1890, during a search for weapons, a contingent of white cavalrymen systematically murdered 300 of the 350 Sioux. Some were killed by artillery pieces positioned above the camp, others were cut down as they ran for their lives. The massacre at Wounded Knee was the final symbolic act of the destruction of the Native American way of life. For all the wars and crises that were to come, never again would the authority of western civilization to rule America be challenged.

Between 1866 and 1915, 25 million people sailed from Europe to the United States. This was by far the biggest migration in human history and it utterly changed the nature of America. In the two decades from 1890 to 1910 in particular, the tidal wave of immigrants was vast, reaching over 1.2 million in 1907 alone. More than three quarters of these immigrants arrived in New York City, and many of them stayed there; in 1900, 76 per cent of the city's population had been born in Europe. The new immigrants were mostly poor and from a notably different culture to their predecessors. As late as 1882, nearly 90 per cent of new immigrants to America came from north and west Europe, but by 1907 more than 80 per cent were from southern and eastern Europe. In the late nineteenth century America, previously an offshoot of Britain, became a polyglot country. The customs, culture, even the language that had been taken for granted as the bedrock of American life, were replaced by a myriad of traditions and tongues. At the same time an agricultural economy had, in the course of two generations, become an industrial urban society.

The use of steam and then electrical or engine-driven machinery to produce cloth, steel, crockery and machine parts was quickly extended into every kind of production. The challenge of industrialization was to use machines to make everything that humanity required, but also to develop levels of organization that enabled machine technology to be fully exploited. Printing was already a mechanical process, but in the course of the nineteenth and twentieth centuries new technologies vastly increased the speed and volume of printing, brought in the mechanical reproduction of images, introduced photography, telephony, film, radio and television, and devised ways of making these available to the whole population. Although many of these technologies were invented in Europe, they were first exploited in the United States, and it was the enthusiastic adoption and elevation of mass popular culture that was to distinguish America from its European ancestors.

Printing technology developed in stages: in 1828 a double cylinder rotary press was used to print the *Commercial Advertiser* in New York and the *Daily Chronicle* in Philadelphia; in 1861 the use of stereotypes allowed easy duplication of page printing blocks and raised print speeds to between 15,000 and 25,000 sheets per hour; by the 1890s the use of continual reels, or webs, of paper raised speeds to 96,000 eight-page sections per hour, while typesetting machines, typewriters and telephones transformed the editorial side of magazine and newspaper production; the industrialization of paper production led to a threefold increase between 1890 and 1900.

American newspapers enjoyed a growing audience, simply through the growth of population, but they also benefited (unlike their European equivalents) from freedom from both government interference and established prejudice. Newspapers in Europe emerged from the literate culture of the gentry and reflected the governing class's view of society, but American newspapers had a tradition of independence and dissent going right back to Benjamin Franklin's *Philadelphia Gazette*. Joseph Pulitzer, owner of the *St Louis Post-Despatch* and the *New York World*, was a Hungarian immigrant who started out as a reporter, while William Randolph Hearst was the son of a self-made millionaire miner and rancher. Hearst's papers acquired a reputation for sensationalism, but the journalists he employed included Ambrose Bierce, Stephen Crane, Mark Twain and Jack London.

The mass-circulation press acted like social glue, uniting the multi-ethnic country under one language and one culture, using its technologies of communication and transport to produce a distinctly American voice – sceptical, optimistic, romantic, patriotic, full of bluster while drily mocking its own hyperbole – that articulated the opinions and feelings of the ordinary American reader.

Just as newspapers reached the technological level that would sustain them for most of the twentieth century, a new invention arrived in America. In September 1895 the Vitascope, a machine for projecting newly developed flexible film on to a large screen, was demonstrated at a fair in Atlanta. On 23 April 1896 it was first used in a public theatre in New York City, and in 1905 a Pennsylvania store-owner started to show films in a back room, charging a nickel for a ticket. By 1910 there were 10,000 nickelodeons in the US, with an audience of 23 million – 20 per cent of the population – per week. The films were silent – which meant that everyone, from Italians to Ukrainian Jews, could understand and enjoy them. Not that there was much to understand – the movies were such a novelty and so cheap that anything they showed drew crowds. But the companies that made the films realized that better venues would have more appeal and make more money, so around 1913 they began to build custom-made movie houses. By 1926 the United States had 20,000 cinemas with a weekly audience of 100 million – nearly half the population.

The social origins of the audiences were matched by those of the early movie-makers. Since it hardly rated as a cultural activity, there was no social barrier to entering the business – and anyway, this was

America, the land of opportunity. A handful of Jewish immigrants got involved early on and survived the inevitable rationalization. In the first decade of the new century, the industry was centred on New York, but the north-east weather was too unreliable for films that relied on strong natural light, and on top of that, there were legal difficulties. Soon after the Vitascope was invented, a consortium led by Thomas Edison formed a monopoly of the production and distribution of moving pictures. Outsiders ran the risk of being arrested on their own sets or having their equipment smashed. The answer was to move somewhere with good weather and a long way from New York, and with the possibility of skipping across the Mexican border to avoid the authorities. In about 1907 producers and directors started shooting films in and around the southern Californian city of Los Angeles, and in 1911 a company called Nestor built the first permanent studio down a dirt road a few miles north and west of the city. Others followed suit, finding cheap labour, expert technicians and freedom from legal harassment. Within 10 years there were 760 studios in the town and no less than 80 per cent of the world's films were being made in the Los Angeles suburb of Hollywood.

Early European producers made films out of classic literature to cater for an educated, middle-class audience, but Americans, concerned with getting people through the door, put up thrills and spills – westerns, chases, gunfights, cliffhangers – anything with instant appeal. In the second decade of the twentieth century, however, Hollywood studios began to see that films that showed story line and character were more popular and longer-lasting, and paid back the extra investment in production and pre-production planning. They also saw that audiences were greatly attracted to seeing the same actors over and over again – the movie star was born.

The genius of film-makers lay in their ability to take a medium designed for basic entertainment, and use it as a mode of expression for profound and eternal human values. In the same way that Giotto used the humble church fresco, and Dickens the mass-circulation throwaway magazine, so American film-makers used the technology of their time to address the concerns of their audience. The first director fully to exploit the possibilities of film was D. W. Griffith (1875–1948). The son of a famous civil war cavalry leader, Griffith started as a theatre actor before writing story lines for the new movie business in New York. He was taken on by the Biograph studio, and in 1908 directed his first film, *The Adventures of Dolly*, starring his wife Linda Arvidson. Over the next five years Griffith directed an astonishing 450 one-reelers while continually looking for ways to improve communication with the audience. He did not invent techniques such as camera movement, close-ups, long shots, dramatic lighting, changes of angle, parallel action and intercutting, but he used them in a way that made the alliance of technique and story-telling into a seamless whole. In Griffith's hands, and those of his cameraman Billy Bitzer, movies escaped from the static melodrama of taped theatre mixed with wild action, and became a subtle and powerful art form.

Griffith trained his company of actors to use more subtlety and nuance to replace the wild gestures that dominated early productions. He understood that the full-face close-up allowed the actor to portray emotion, uncertainty and reaction with the smallest alterations in facial expression. The use of techniques like close-ups and landscape shots reiterated what revolutionary art forms like the portrait and the novel had done, which was to take areas of experience that have always existed – the variety of expressions of the human face, the effects of changing light on landforms – and make them occupy the complete attention of the audience.

In 1913 Griffith left Biograph to work on the first great epic of American cinema. As well as demonstrating the awesome possibilities of the medium, *Birth of a Nation* was an attempt to construct the mythology of the country, to tell Americans who they were and where they came from. On release in 1915 it was a huge commercial success – people queued around the block to pay the unheard-of price of $2 to see it – and deeply controversial. The depiction of the Ku Klux Klan as the heroic defenders of liberty outraged many Americans (and led Griffith to make *Intolerance* to prove his racially tolerant credentials); nevertheless, the film gave birth to cinema as a commercial art form. While they superficially paid occasional homage to period classics and biblical melodramas, the theme of Hollywood movies became America itself. Beginning with *Birth of a Nation* the movies transformed the westerns and gangster one-reelers of the early days into the founding myths and contemporary histories of their country. Because of the peculiar role of the movie star, American mythology was not just a tale of decent men and women triumphing over hardship in wagon trains or gangster-ridden streets. It was the story of men and women who were just like Lionel Barrymore and Lillian Gish, Clark Gable and Bette Davis, John Wayne and Katharine Hepburn – ordinary, extraordinary heroes.

Cinema allowed twentieth-century American culture to find a unique voice in the complex combination of adventure, restlessness, violence, and the eternal search for individual identity and a spiritual home. The western movie became a morality tale played out against a background of lawlessness, but the best of them became an exploration of the emotional yearnings of their protagonists. John Ford, a second-generation immigrant, depicted the family on the wagon train, the cavalry regiment, the homestead on the prairie, all as fragile attempts to build spiritual homes in a world beset by the violence of the disconnected. It is little wonder that these stories had resonance for Americans crammed into the faceless, often lawless cities of the industrial northeast and Midwest.

While movies found a limitless source of stories in the visceral world of American crime, dime pulp novels and magazines that relentlessly mined the underworld were avidly read across America; by 1922 there were over 20,000 magazine titles in the United States. And once again, certain writers were able to use the apparently workaday genre of the hard-boiled detective story as a vehicle for artistic expression. The crime novels of Dashiell Hammett, Raymond Chandler and James M. Cain conveyed more about the hopes, desires and illusions of American life than the work of almost any other contemporary artist.

The rotary press and the film camera and projector were joined by the phonograph and the radio, which together made possible the mass manufacture and broadcast of recorded music. Once again the content of this new form was as important as the technology. Recorded music in Europe would mean light opera and orchestral suites, but in America something quite different emerged. The segregation of the south gave birth to an African-American culture that stood apart from but physically alongside mainstream white America. African-Americans had no access to the technology with which to create paintings or architecture or literature or films, but they had access to a limited number of musical instruments and to a long tradition of self-made music. In the cities and country districts of the south, itinerant musicians performed a strange style of music called blues, taking traditional European instruments like pianos, cornets and guitars and making them sound entirely new. Because it is so familiar to us, we underestimate the extraordinary innovation that blues music represented. Endless variations within and around its basic form, together with its demand for direct emotional expressiveness on the part of the performer, became dominant elements in twentieth-century music and in all western culture.

In New Orleans jazz was created in a black community with enough to spend on entertainment and musical instruments. The city was always a law unto itself, where musicians, drifters and misfits from all races flourished in a hedonistic atmosphere. In the 1920s jazz was brought out of New Orleans to the cities of the north by Jelly Roll Morton, Louis Armstrong and Bessie Smith and spread far and wide by King Oliver and Fats Waller. There was enough money around in the black community to make stars of Smith and Armstrong. By then, song-writers like Irving Berlin and George Gershwin had begun using blues, jazz and ragtime to create a new style of popular song. Out went the choral, declamatory, European style of the nineteenth century and in came an intimate, expressive, conversational style of music suited to the urban world of the new America.

Meanwhile, out in the country, particularly in Texas and the south, white singers like Jimmy Rogers began to copy the black style of music. Country music was a white version of the blues occasionally mixed in with waltzes and reels. The sentimental love song, whether Tin Pan Alley, country or jazz-oriented swing, became the anthem of America. Expressed in simple, everyday, unpoetic language, sung in a spoken voice rather than declaimed, the personalized love song summed up the belief that in a confusing, shifting, unreceptive world, spiritual sanc-tuary might still be found in love between two people.

The movies, the music, the magazines that swept across America in the 1920s enabled it to become a unified country. Everyone saw the same films, whistled the same tunes and read the same features. A single film would be duplicated and shown all around the country, while songs were recorded and pressed and sent out to every radio station and juke joint. Trains could carry magazines like the *Ladies' Home Journal*, *The Saturday Evening Post* and *McClure's* to every town in America, while telephones and telegraphs ensured that each city paper carried the same national news. And while the country was united by its mass culture, it also shared consumption of the products of mass production.

The magazines, newspapers and radio stations carried adverts for prod-ucts that could be bought anywhere in America. This meant that American industry had to operate on a continental scale, and this became possible through a new kind of capitalism. In the nineteenth and early twentieth centuries individual entrepreneurs had seized on the possibilities that industrialization offered. Often these men were engineers or inventors combining a strong grasp of technical matters with a relish for business. A handful of them built vast industrial empires out of their inventions, their commercial nous and their determination to overcome any competition. The rapidly growing population and laissez-faire, or even corrupt, politics of America allowed these ruthless and determined men to gain monopolies in their fields. Empires built by men like Cornelius Vanderbilt, Henry Ford, John Rockefeller, J. P. Morgan and H. J. Heinz were essentially personal fiefdoms, run by single men or members of their immediate families. The top man was publicly identifiable and took the glory and the blame for his company's operations. The idea of the corporation, where investors put money into a business but took no part in its management, was widely known, but corporate stock trading was restricted to industries such as railways, where the government financed its investments by selling bonds. This changed around the turn of the century when financial capital and manufacturing combined to produce the 'corporate revolution'.

The epitome of this revolution was the formation, in 1900, of the US Steel Corporation. Andrew Carnegie sold his company to a group of bankers headed by J. P. Morgan for $250 million. Morgan got together with other industrialists to form a stock-holding corporation that brought together all the major producers of iron, steel and coke in the US. The power of financial and industrial muscle combined was plain to see, but Morgan was following a trend that already existed. In 1890, the total capital in publicly traded manufacturing companies was $33 million; by 1891 it was $260 million and by 1898 $2 billion. The exponential expansion continued until 1903, when manufacturing stock values reached over $7 billion. By 1904 over half the value of manufacturing in the US was in publicly traded stocks. The total value of stocks then remained around $7 billion until 1914 – this was not a never-ending economic expansion but a transition from one economic system to another.

This change is important to the story of western civilization, because of the pervasive influence held by corporations, both in practice, as dominant forces in the lives of their customers and their staff, and as a model for the organization of all parts of society. After 1900, corporations became active in every aspect of commercial life, and in Europe,

Japan and North America the corporation became the centrepiece of industry, manufacturing and retailing. The production, transportation and disposal of goods in a modern economy required an enormous amount of administration, and so armies of workers became involved in planning, designing, marketing, invoicing, progress-chasing, accounting and bookkeeping, as well as typing, duplicating, telegraphy and telephony. Corporations began with offices adjacent to their factories, but soon the corporate headquarters building assumed an independent life, near to financial services and to the housing and shops that office workers required.

The headquarters office building and its staff, where and by whom the strategies were planned and the destiny of the company decided, became the corporation. For the office staff the corporation was a comforting environment offering a lifetime of material rewards in return for moderately hard work – no one, however badly they performed, would be demoted to digging coal or blasting steel. For the ambitious there were chances of promotion within a large, continually changing organization, and for the gregarious there was the sociability of the office both within and outside work. The corporation, rather than the home, became the great twentieth-century machine for living. White-collar workers took all this for granted; yet it would have been a novelty to their grandparents.

The drawbacks of corporate life are more difficult to specify yet just as pervasive. The need to get on by pleasing others in ways that you don't quite understand, the sense of being watched to see if you are measuring up, the ludicrous yet intense jealousies over cars, furniture and office space and pay, all contributed to a kind of enervating paranoia. In the world of the corporation there was no such thing as simply doing a job well – you must be either rising or falling within the organization. Management of companies was based on fostering low-level fear among staff, the result being a peculiar mixture of individual ambition and corporate conformity – you stayed safe and got on by second-guessing what others wanted, and by adhering to some never-quite-defined corporate code. Adherence to the corporation became a necessary part of workers' psychology, even if they disliked their jobs; conformity became the price of security.

The corporation encouraged loyalty to itself and to one's colleagues, and this could easily confuse relations with the outside world. The managers of any corporation were obliged by law to maximize the value of the shareholders' stocks, removing any obligation (or permission) for the management to act in the wider interests of society. Despite this self-interest, corporations, through their financial power, were seen to be the economic lifeblood of the nation. 'What's good for General Motors is good for America' was held to be self-evidently true. The protection of American corporations became, and remained, a pillar of United States domestic and foreign policy, while the corporate headquarters – a gleaming marble-faced building on Wall Street or Fifth Avenue – became not only the public face of the corporation, but the symbol of the power and prestige of America itself. The Chrysler (1930), Woolworth (1913), Metropolitan Life (1932) and Empire State (1931) buildings in New York are the symbols of the first great age of corporate power.

In the first half of the twentieth century the corporate structure allowed near-limitless expansion of manufacturing organizations. Profitable firms could expand by increasing their share of a growing market or by buying up competitors with cash borrowed from armies of investors. Anti-trust laws, introduced from 1904, outlawed monopolies, but most areas of manufacturing were dominated by two or three corporations. The presence of the same goods in every main street in America helped, along with popular culture, to make the United States into a homogenous society. Their arrival at exactly the same time as the greatest influx of non-British immigrants turned a multitude of different languages and cultures into an identifiable nation. Every family wanted a Ford or Chrysler car, a Singer sewing machine and a Hoover vacuum cleaner.

The cohesion of American life through films, music, magazines, newspapers and consumer products brought huge rewards for American manufacturers and made available to United States citizens great quantities of cheap goods. The corporations gained political power through their wealth and economic importance to the nation, and power over consumers through new styles of advertising. This American phenomenon grew only slowly in Europe, where traditional financial structures and patterns of buying behaviour held sway. Not until after the Second World War was Europe fully exposed to the extraordinary force of the American corporation and American culture.

Modern America arrived with all the contradictions of human society intact, though arranged somewhat differently to the nations of western Europe. Capable of both virtuous idealism and violent persecution, America declared itself free while putting legal and economic shackles on many of its citizens. Fuelled by a long economic expansion that lasted from 1865 to 1929, Americans believed they had solved the problems of modern society by sheer energy, optimism and individual ambition. If they also believed that their country was uniquely created as a force for good, then they were simply following in the footsteps of eminent predecessors in Athens, Rome, Paris and London. It may even be said that they had more reason to create a virtuous myth about their country than their European cousins; the people of the United States were not bound by ties of blood or history, they needed an idea that would unite them, and so their country became an ideal vision – a shining city on the hill.

Alongside this idealism came a much more real response to modern life. Unlike Europe, America embraced the idea of popular culture and developed the technologies that helped to bring it to life. By the early decades of the twentieth century American cities had given birth to an urban culture that communicated and evoked their sense of yearning, of loss, and of a zest for life in the face of the impersonal forces of industry and commerce. Though not everyone, particularly in Europe, would accept it, this was the new civilization of the west.

TOWARDS THE ABYSS

Technology, Ideology, Apocalypse

THE second half of the nineteenth century brought improvements in the lives of many Europeans. Science-based technology began to make life easier, safer and healthier; the spread of industrialization brought more prosperity; political change led to greater rights and freedoms; and intellectual advances seemed to promise an even better future for humanity. Yet in the early decades of the twentieth century all these advances counted for nothing, as millions of Europeans were slaughtered in a catastrophic mechanized war. Any remaining hopes of the inevitability of human progress were then extinguished by the unimaginable truth of the genocide of Europe's Jews.

The outbreak of war in a period of optimistic prosperity seems to defy our understanding of history. Surely wars are fought over scarce resources, or to gain political rights, or in defence of territories. The decades before the First World War show us that none of this is true. Instead it is quite possible for the citizens of prosperous nations to convince themselves that they must go to war with others for almost entirely illusory reasons. The following pages indicate some of those reasons; they also demonstrate that events in history are not bound by universal laws of cause and effect, but simply arise out of unpredictable circumstance. The world wars of the twentieth century had their roots in *everything* that happened before. In this chapter I will trace just some of those roots, beginning with the application of scientific reasoning to all aspects of human society.

* * *

The early phases of industrialization came about through changes in the economic and social organization of society. Continual investment in industrial processes required returns, but also allowed the development of technologies that made these processes more efficient. Machines for spinning and weaving cotton and wool, for firing pottery, and for making steel, and gadgets for transferring power from water wheels to looms, mechanical hammers, drills, elevators and a hundred other uses, all came into use in the late eighteenth and early nineteenth centuries.

At the same time as this practical technical knowledge was increasing, the theoretical investigation of the natural world was moving into new areas. The eighteenth century had seen the spread of Galileo's and Newton's concepts of nature into the composition and behaviour of matter itself. Work by Joseph Black, Claude Louis Berthollet, Anton Lavoisier, Joseph Priestley and others transformed the ancient study of chemistry into a mathematically definable science. Interest in the natural world was given impetus by voyages of discovery and the exotic collections of Joseph Banks, Louis Bougainville and others, while the work of Linnaeus turned the study of plants and animals into a rigorous science of classification. The science of geology began to emerge from separate studies of minerals, fossils and landforms. In 1788, Georges Buffon's *Histoire naturelle* argued that the earth itself had a history, and by 1800 James Hutton had applied Newtonian laws to the formation of the rocks that made up the earth's crust. Around the same time, the English surveyor William Smith devised a system of using fossils to classify rocks, and to uncover predictable patterns in their occurrence. The whole of the natural world was being gathered into a Newtonian system where mathematical formulation and quantitative measurement could be used to reveal underlying patterns of behaviour, and allow the discovery of laws of nature. The intellectual liberation that Kant had provided, by freeing science of any moral meaning, was put to practical effect by men determined to follow Newton's example.

In Europe and North America gentleman amateurs began to form new types of clubs – this time dedicated to special interests. The Linnean Society was founded in London in 1788, followed by the Geological Society (1807), the Chemical Society (1841), and others; in France, for example, the Société Géologique was founded in 1830, with others springing up in Germany and the United States. As well as these national bodies, most cities and towns had philosophical societies, where educated gentlemen could meet in an atmosphere of mutual enthusiasm for natural philosophy. The ethical codes of these gentlemen's clubs were a crucial element in the development of science over the next 180 years, and the foundation of a system in which ideas could be communicated and shared, while priority was acknowledged and trust extended between different scientists, institutions and countries. The customary restraints of society – the disgrace of being found cheating, or of taking unfair advantage – formed the moral code under which science operated, and the division of the natural world into different disciplines – astronomy, physics, chemistry, biology, geology, anatomy – came from the alliances and rivalries between the various clubs.

In the early nineteenth century, the two worlds of technology-driven industry and scientific investigation existed in parallel with little mutual contact. It was their eventual coming-together that was to propel the western world into the modern industrial era, but there were significant obstacles to this combination. In scientific societies gentlemen of independent means presented and published papers in open forums, but in industry trade secrets were closely guarded and techniques improved through trial and error and the application of hard-won skills. The old division of *episteme* and *techne* had in theory broken down, but social barriers prevented the full practical use of this dissolution – tradespeople were working-class artisans, scientists were gentlemen. There were odd exceptions to the separation – alchemy led to gunpowder and distillation, optics to spectacles, astronomical instruments to clocks and aids to navigation – but the synthesis of craft and theory remained patchy until well into the nineteenth century.

An early indication of how science and technology might develop came from the members of the Lunar Society, a group of friends based in Birmingham whose members included Josiah Wedgwood, Erasmus Darwin, Joseph Priestley and Matthew Boulton. In 1775 Boulton, an engineer and factory-owner, formed a partnership with James Watt, who had devised ways of improving the basic steam engine using a steam jacket and a condensing chamber. Boulton encouraged Watt to turn his ideas into practice, partly out of self-interest – he saw that steam power could be used to drive his factory – but also out of a fascination with technology. Watt continued to improve his steam engine by devising a two-cylinder action and a centrifugal governor. Once the limits of water power were reached, steam power spread quickly and the central tool of industrialization became the coal-fuelled steam engine. Railway engines, blast furnaces, rolling mills, textile plants, coal and iron mines all exuded an extraordinary sense of force and dynamism that had somehow been liberated from nature and put into the service of humanity. As the nineteenth century wore on, Europeans could not help but be impressed at their own ability to have brought forth so great a transformation in the world. A plain stone dug from the earth and fired could, with the right skills and knowledge, endlessly power a factory, or send a passenger train hurtling across the land. The energy driving the dynamo of the industrial world had been unlocked by human ingenuity.

Nevertheless Watt was an inventor rather than a scientific investi-gator. The clearest sign of the fusion of science and technology came when gentlemen scientists began to investigate the machinery that was transforming the world, rather than concentrating on the world in its 'natural' state, and to produce mathematical models of industrial processes. In 1824 the French physicist Nicolas Sadi Carnot published his investigations into steam power, outlining the principle of the conser-vation of energy. Carnot's work, which was the foundation of the applied science of thermodynamics, enabled engines to be designed better and more efficiently. In the 1830s Michael Faraday began exper-iments that showed how electricity, magnetism and motion were intri-cately and directly related. Moving a magnet through an electric field induced a current, while passing electricity through a wire within a magnetic field induced the wire to move, allowing both the reliable generation of electricity and the possibility of using electricity to power a motor. Faraday's later experiments showed that light was also part of the electromagnetic system. In 1856 the metallurgist Henry Bessemer invented a system for converting pig iron directly into high-grade steel, oxidizing the impurities by passing air into the converter. The applica-tion of theoretical chemistry produced artificial dyes, new explosives and new methods for manufacturing essential products such as alum. In these and other fields, science began to make a massive contribu-tion to technological development, so that industrial technology soon abandoned its roots in traditional crafts. Industrial firms began to hire scientists to work on improving techniques and processes, while govern-ments began to take account of the need for a science-based education.

By the mid-nineteenth century science was beginning to demonstrate its power to alter the nature of technological change; inventions need no longer be based on trial-and-error improvements but could be founded on sound physical principles. In 1859 science placed itself at the centre of intellectual life, with the publication of Darwin's *On the Origin of Species*. Geologists had already shown how science could alter humanity's view of the world, by proving the biblical history of the earth to be unfeasible. But Darwin's work displaced humanity from its unique place apart from, and above, the animals. The idea that one species might have developed from another had been suggested before, but Darwin outlined the mechanism through which this happened, and how the whole of life on earth had developed through a series of mutations. Biology changed from a project of static classification into the study of dynamic processes as scientists sought to show how all manner of biological phenomena could be explained by the laws of evolution. Everything, including life itself, was subject to universal laws that, given enough ingenuity, could be uncovered.

In the second half of the nineteenth century it seemed that a combination of scientific rationality and science-based technology would be able to solve any problem that humans cared to set. The formation of mountains and oceans, the origins of diseases, the composition of space, the development of life, even the basis of matter; faster trains, bigger steamships, more efficient engines, better sanitation and living conditions, purer metals, better communication, electric light and chemical processes, improved materials and more sophisticated plant and animal breeding all seemed within reach. And if science could be so fruitfully applied to the investigation and improvement of the natural world, then could it not do the same for human society? As scientific thinking spread into more and more disciplines, creating new ones as it went, then what were the limits of this new way of thinking? Were human behaviour, sexuality, history, society, politics, commerce, consciousness and culture similarly governed by 'scientific' laws, and if so, what were those laws? Had Kant merely gone halfway to the truth when he separated knowledge of the world from human behaviour – was not *everything*, in fact, susceptible to rational investigation and, beyond that, devoid of moral meaning?

The increasing physical and intellectual dominance of science and technology brought about a deepening crisis in European Christianity. Belief in supernatural forces and magic had been declining in northern and western Europe since the seventeenth century. When industrialization began to transform society, churches became sources of steadiness and consolation in a rapidly changing world. Nonconformist Protestant movements, such as English Methodism, attracted growing numbers of industrial and agricultural workers. But the official churches burgeoned too, and in Victorian Britain churches were built at a phenomenal rate, particularly in rapidly expanding towns and cities. The Tractarian or Oxford Movement, led by John Henry Newman, emerged in the 1830s as an attempt to recapture the spirituality of the early church fathers and bring about a unity of the Christian congregation. But the revival of Christian spirituality was a temporary reaction to the dehumanization of early industry (though not in America, where Calvinism remained at the root of personal identity); once life began to improve, Europeans began to look to technology to enhance their lives, and to science to provide answers to their most fundamental questions.

In the first half of the nineteenth century the science of geology showed that the age of the earth should be dated in millions, not thousands, of years, and that the creation was not a single series of events taking just six days, but a continual and continuing process. Humans were latecomers in the earth's past and were absent from, and ignorant of, most of its history. It was no longer possible for clergymen simultaneously to promote the truth of the Bible and believe in the truth of science. Darwin's theories compounded the divergence between science and the scriptures, despite the efforts of many theologians to find a path to God that would embrace science.

Important though this intellectual crisis was, wider social developments were crucial in undermining the automatic belief in a Christian God. By the 1860s people began to see that human intervention, often informed by science and engineered by technology, had a direct and immediate improving effect on their lives. They did not rail against God, or deliberately dismiss religion from their lives; it just became irrelevant. While it retained spiritual and emotional meaning for a declining minority, intellectually and practically religion had no hold over most of the people of industrialized Europe.

What, though, would a secular individual and society believe in? Deprived of their place in the great Christian drama of creation, incarnation, apocalypse and eternal resurrection; and removed from a personal connection to salvation through good works; how should modern westerners see their lives? The philosophies of both Augustine and Calvin had combined guidance on the way to live a true Christian life with an overall vision of human history. Or, put the other way round, they answered two essential questions – what is the meaning of human existence; and how, therefore, should I live my life? How could these same questions be answered in a non-Christian world?

The most persuasive single answer to these questions came from the overwhelming belief in progress. While the crisis of the Enlightenment (see Chapter Thirteen) should have put paid to the idea that human existence could keep on improving, an unquestioning belief in progress became essential to nineteenth-century Europeans, and was triumphantly vindicated by their own technological advancement. But what did progress actually mean: was it an endless process, could it be guided in particular ways, or were there underlying forces (similar to Newton's forces of gravitation and momentum) that dictated how humanity had developed and would develop in the future? Was the history of humanity, therefore, another subject that could be illuminated and revolutionized by rational, scientific analysis?

The idea of progress was linked to a view of time that had its roots in the written histories of Herodotus and Thucydides, and in the abstractions of cosmologists dating back to Aristotle and beyond. Mythological and religious time was never quantified – the age of heroes was always just beyond reach, just as the gods were never quite visible; the six days to make the world, and the forty days and forty nights Christ spent in the desert, were poetic evocations, not literal descriptions. But Thucydides counted time, as did Livy and Suetonius. Historical time was seen by their heirs as a line along which humanity moved inexorably. But this way of thinking induced the sense that some parts of humanity had moved along this line rather quicker than others – not only was time a linear phenomenon, so was progress. And if every piece of human history, both past and present, could be seen as a point on a line, then humanity could only go forwards or backwards. This way of looking at the past and present became, and has remained, through education and inculcation, the fundamental and overriding mindset of western people, to the degree that it is almost impossible for us to envisage time in any other way. The other view of time that the nineteenth century bequeathed (but which has fallen out of favour) was cyclic. Taking their cue from the planetary motions that Newton had described, historians began to look for cycles in history that would arise in obedience to the same kind of laws that drove the planets.

The first intellectual to consider history in this way was the German philosopher Georg Hegel (1770–1831). Sciences such as geology and zoology suggested that the history of the earth showed a succession of worlds, each inhabited by different sets of creatures, of which our world was simply the latest example. Hegel suggested that human history was also made up of a succession of phases, in each of which humanity itself was noticeably different. This idea was revolutionary because before Hegel, philosophers and historians had considered the nature of humanity, people's sense of themselves and their world, to be constant through time; after Hegel everyone believed that historical context was an essential element in the analysis of human thought and behaviour.

Hegel suggested that history moved in cycles, marked by significant events or episodes. These episodes came about when individual and collective beliefs, or subjective and objective goals, or, as Hegel put it, desire and reason, were in harmony. This happened in ancient Greece, and the early Christian church, and the Lutheran Reformation (which Hegel saw as the great achievement of the German people), and at each time enabled all human beings to attain spiritual freedom through their own actions, without recourse to authority or outside influence. Hegel believed in cycles of history, but also in progress, so that each cycle brought the world nearer and nearer to perfection. In the perfect state towards which the world was moving, humans would no longer recognize the division between individual and community, or reason and desire, and would enjoy immense spiritual freedom.

This notion of an ideal world seems strange to us, but there were several profound messages in Hegel's work. The first is that all ideas about abstract subjects like morality, objectivity or truth can only be discussed in their historical context. *Everything* changes with time, even our ideas of truth or falsehood, good or evil. Human beings themselves change through time, and in the ideal world that Hegel envisaged, humans would be different again. The second message Hegel gives is that there is an ideal world that can be attained in the final phase of history. He believed in individual freedom but he never reconciled this with what would happen in the ideal world – he simply believed that in the final phase, the individual and society would be as one. In this world there would no longer be any conflict because everything would be brought into harmony. So while Hegel dealt with the meaning of human existence by showing how history was subject to particular forces, his guidance for human individuals was less clear. Humans must strive to make the world so that desire and reason are brought into harmony, but how was this to be brought about? The individual was in danger of being a mere instrument of the disembodied forces of history.

The rational analysis of history was taken on by Karl Marx (1818–83), who applied Hegel's ideas to political and economic change. Marx too felt there was an inevitable development towards an ideal state, but that its arrival would be due to changes in economic or material circumstances, which would in turn alter human behaviour. He saw that the industrialization of Britain and other parts of Europe had transformed the world to such a degree that human society was now best understood through studying its material and economic structures, rather than its political or national or military history. Hegel had suggested that history progressed through a process he called dialectics. Any phase of history was characterized by a certain way of thinking, or *thesis*; but eventually a challenge to this would come in the form of an *antithesis*. These two would then combine to produce another state of being or *synthesis*, which would assume the status of a thesis before itself being challenged, and so on throughout history. Marx applied this analysis to the changing economic conditions of the world in a process that he called dialectical materialism.

Marx believed that industrial capitalism in a society controlled by the bourgeoisie (as in Britain, his adopted home) was a necessary phase of history that would, in time, be superseded by another in which the labouring class would assume control, probably by means of a revolution. This 'dictatorship of the proletariat' is one of those concepts that has, in the light of subsequent history, assumed a sinister connotation; but Marx was really talking about a final phase of history in which conflict between the different social and economic classes would come to an end. Once working people controlled the means of production and distribution, then all need for industrial and economic conflict would disappear. And because Marx believed that political conflict was produced by economic or material conflict, then politics too would be resolved. Indeed, the need for a powerful state to regulate the activities of citizens would gradually disappear, leaving people free to live their lives in harmony. The 'dictatorship of the proletariat' was therefore not intended to be an oppressive totalitarian state, but liberation from the burden of having nothing but your labour to sell.

Marx was a man of his time. In the mid-nineteenth century, machinery was clattering away in every available building in Britain and the industrial regions of Europe, churning out everything that anyone could possibly want. Cloth, crockery, furniture, fireplaces, newspapers, pans, steam engines, carriages, buttons, thimbles, tin trays, bottles, cutlery, medicines, coat hooks, and machine parts for other machines to make yet more things, not to mention coal, iron and other metals, were all being pushed out of factories, mills, mines and kilns at an enormous rate. As fast as houses could be built people were stuffing them with things; the whole world was being filled with objects that machines could turn out at the rate of thousands per day. Limitless demand and limitless production seemed certain to give everyone what they needed and wanted for a decent life, so long as they were shared equitably.

The impact of Hegel, and particularly Marx, came from their combination of logic and romance. Both of them used rational methods to analyse the course of history, and both concluded that humans were on the road to being liberated in a bright and bountiful future. Most dangerously, their shared belief in the possibility of harmony in society led them to the same conclusions, and into the same trap, as the French revolutionaries (see Chapter Thirteen). In the brave new world there would be no need for politics, because everyone would understand that there was only one correct way of organizing and administering society; opposition to the true path of history would be a hindrance to progress and would have to be eliminated.

Hegel and Marx took the idea of progress to its rational limits, but there were plenty of historians and philosophers eager to apply scientific methods to all aspects of society and to search for evidence of progress. In 1848 Thomas Macaulay wrote: 'For the history of our country during the last hundred and sixty years is eminently the history of physical, of moral, and of intellectual improvement.' Henry Buckle combined the Hegelian notion of certain culminating episodes with that of a Great Chain of History. Once Darwin's ideas became common currency, it was natural for these too to be applied to human behaviour and society. The title of Walter Bagehot's 1875 *Physics and Politics: Thoughts on the Application of the Principles of Natural Selection and Inheritance to Political Society* is an indication of the widespread interest in the marriage of science, politics and society; while Herbert Spencer's vast *Programme of a System of Synthetic Philosophy*, begun in 1860, was the grandest attempt to apply evolutionary theory to all fields of human knowledge, including sociology, education and ethics.

For these authors, and almost all nineteenth-century thinkers, belief in progress went hand in hand with the belief in European superiority. If history was a combination of cyclical phases and linear progress, then it was obvious that western Europe had progressed further in the current cycle than any other society. The dual belief in progress and European superiority found its most popular and influential expression in an application (and distortion) of Darwin's evolutionary theories that became known as Social Darwinism. In Darwin's theory, change or mutation happens by accident, and is preserved if it gives the changed individual a better chance of surviving to the age where it can reproduce. But most people who accepted Darwin's theory disliked this rule of accidental mutation. They preferred the earlier theories of Jean-Baptiste Lamarck, who suggested that species acquire certain characteristics because of how they live – his most celebrated example was the giraffe stretching ever higher to reach the leaves of tall trees and gradually extending its neck through successive generations. This doctrine allowed its adherents to attach a definite purpose to evolution, since animals and plants only 'advanced' through their own efforts, or through acts of will. This interpretation of evolution was combined with Darwin's doctrine of 'the survival of the fittest' to produce a social theory in which the strongest were not only naturally intended to dominate the weak, but had attained their positions of strength through the combined will of their forebears and themselves. The economically and physically strong, therefore, had both nature and morality on their side – they had got where they were through their own and their families' efforts. Any attempt to interfere with this situation, for example through the provision of welfare for the poor and the weak, would risk degenerating the whole of society by deflecting it from its natural course. Social Darwinism (which stands in frank contradiction to Darwin's theory) became a doctrine of justification for almost any action, from laissez-faire economics to the enslavement or genocide of 'weaker' races, from the withholding of education from the poor workers to the extermination of smaller countries by larger and more powerful nations. There were naturally degrees of commitment to the dogma of Social Darwinism, but between 1860 and 1939, the rightness of the survival of the fittest and the moral superiority of the strong was a widely held belief in western society.

Although Marxism and Social Darwinism came to be represented by opposite ends of the political spectrum, their common origin was the search for a universal theory that would give an explanation of human existence, and guidance for human behaviour. Inevitably such theories led to abstract ways of thinking about humanity, rather than practical involvement in the improvement of the lives of individual people. Industrialization had created a huge number of working people; these 'masses' were idealized by Marx and denigrated by Social Darwinists, but either way they were seen objectively as an undifferentiated mass, subject to the inevitable forces of history.

All this might not have mattered much; in the late nineteenth century Europeans were enjoying rising standards of living, social reforms and extended political rights. But political ideas were becoming powerful forces. Hegel's belief in historic destiny, the sense among workers' leaders that society should be organized along rational lines, the fear and hatred of the masses among their social superiors, and, above all, the growing attachment to the nation state as a historical, organic, semi-mystical entity, subject to the laws of evolution, including the survival of the fittest, all combined to push an apparently peaceful, prosperous Europe towards military catastrophe. It was a process that seemed to defy the logic of history, and yet it happened.

From Napoleon's defeat at Waterloo on 18 June 1815 to the outbreak of war in August 1914, continental Europe enjoyed a long and prosperous peace. There were international conflicts in the 1860s and 1870s, but the major powers managed to avoid being drawn into a war of continental scale. Continued peace between European nations seemed achievable. But in the decades before 1914, most people in Europe became convinced that a major conflict was not only inevitable but positively desirable. European governments spent the last peaceful decades of the nineteenth century making alliances and building up armaments in the expectation of a major, apocalyptic showdown, and beneath an apparently tranquil surface, militarism and aggressive nationalism infected every area of life. But the change from peaceful co-existence to incipient aggression began much earlier, in the immediate aftermath of the Napoleonic wars.

Nationalism was, along with industrialization, the underlying impulse of nineteenth-century Europe. Following the French Revolution, people in every part of the continent began to promote the idea of a national community and a national will. Nationalists looked to a common history, language, race and culture as the identifiers of their nation, and found, in most cases, that these did not accord with the boundaries of Europe's nation states. The map was full of peculiarities: the German nation was divided into 15 states; Italy was both divided and partly ruled by the Austrian empire; the Slav nation was made up of separate nationalities, some in discrete nation states, others (predominantly Hungarians, Czechs and Slovaks) ruled by Austria; Poland was partitioned between Prussia, Russia and Austria; the Balkans and Greece were part of the Ottoman empire; Norway was forced into a union with Sweden that was dominated by the power of Denmark; Belgium was composed of two peoples, the Flemings and the Walloons; Britain was a peculiar union of four separate historic nations; in contrast, the United States had deliberately invented a single nation out of a multitude of peoples – and fought a civil war to maintain its unity.

The geopolitics of nineteenth-century Europe was, in hindsight, a process of making nations into nation states. The Napoleonic campaigns of 1813–15, in which European armies rolled back the tide of French occupation, were, for many, the beginnings of national liberation. The spirit of nationalism and self-determination that the French had inspired lived on in the hearts of the soldiers and citizens, if not the princes, of Europe. Fifty-five years after the final defeat of Napoleon, Prussia, emboldened by strategic victories over Denmark and Austria, pushed France into war. The pretext was the infamous 1870 Ems telegram,* but the real reason was Bismarck's strategic vision of a united Germany. War against France – regarded as Germany's ancient and aggressive foe – was calculated to bring all the German states into the Prussian fold. The French army, for 200 years the dominant military force on the continent, was defeated in just two months and, in January 1871, in a triumphant vindication of Bismarck's strategy, William I was proclaimed Emperor of Germany in the palace of Versailles. France was forced to sign a treaty ceding Alsace, Metz, Strasbourg and one third of Lorraine, including its coal-fields, to Germany.

Bismarck was the strategic mastermind of German unification, but he had tapped into a deep vein of national consciousness. Hegel had written of 'historic nations', while Heine, Goethe, Schiller, Beethoven, Schumann and Wagner had provided evidence of a deep, historically forged German cultural identity that was matched by the common

---

* A telegram from the Prussian King William I to his prime minister Otto von Bismarck outlining the disagreement between Prussia and France over the throne of Spain. The document was doctored by Bismarck to give the impression that serious insults had passed between France and Prussia, and was then published.

people's growing sense of a national community bonded by language, religion and customs. The German nation was forged in a war against an old enemy and German nationalism was indissolubly linked with militarism – the united German army's defeat of France was a clear lesson that when brought together, the German people were stronger than when apart.

Similar feelings had existed in France since the revolution, and had also developed in Britain, which looked down on others from the commanding heights of its world empire and its industrial dominance. The British people thought themselves special, as did the Germans and the French. But other nations wanted the right to self-determination. Napoleon's legacy gave Italians the desire to live in a united Italy, eventually achieved in 1871; Polish nationalists seized power from Russia in 1863, only to be defeated and rise again in 1905; the 1867 Ausgleich gave Hungarians their own parliament and a dual monarchy with

The German empire in 1871,
showing pre-existing states.

Austria; Greece declared independence from the Ottoman empire in 1825, and won statehood in 1832; in 1830 Belgian nationalists established independence from Dutch rule; other nationalities saw cultural resurgence within states – Czechs in Bohemia, Slovaks in Hungary, Irish and Welsh in Britain, for example. However, it was the events in Germany, France, Italy and the Austrian empire – the old heart of Frankish Europe – that were to have most impact. While German nationalism was boosted by the 1871 victory and the formation of a new state, for the French people the brushing-aside of their army and loss of their eastern provinces had damaged the soul of their nation. For both victor and vanquished, conflict engendered a still greater degree of nationalist fervour.

As well as stoking up mutual hatred, the 1871 conflict brought an increase in the militarization of Europe. The victorious German armies had shown how the rapid deployment of huge numbers – many trained

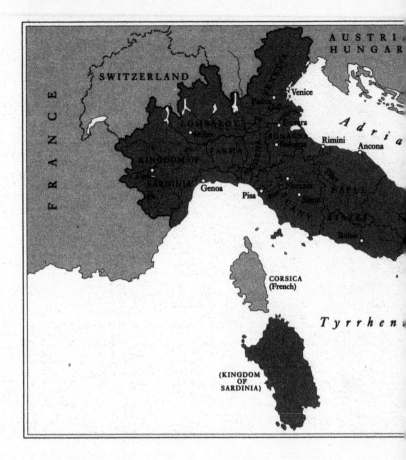

as part of 'national service' arrangements – could bring a swift and decisive victory. All nations felt the need for large numbers of trained recruits, available at short notice. Despite being ostensibly at peace between 1871 and 1914 (the major exceptions were the Russo-Japanese war of 1905, and the British Boer war of 1899–1902), almost every European state adopted compulsory conscription. But the German example and the rise of nationalism did more than simply increase the numbers of people in military service. The use of war as a means of national liberation gave the armies of Europe the status of soul and protector of each nation, while the adoration of the nation can be seen as a partial compensation for the decline of the Christian faith. The military life became an attractive option for many young men. Good food, mechanized transport, decent barracks, high-quality equipment all helped to make the army a civilized place to be and, more importantly, army service became the noblest method of gaining membership of the national community; soldiers were well regarded by their

Bari

Taranto

Reggio

Catania

Syracuse

*Italy after unification (1914 borders),
showing pre-existing states.*

fellow citizens and conscription became a badge of citizenship.

Civilian movements with strong military links and overtones sprang up across Europe. The leaders of organizations like the Pan-German League (Alldeutscher Verband) and the British National Service League, and youth groups such as the Jungdeutschlandbund cadet groups, university officer training corps, the Boys' Brigade, the British Girls' Patriotic League and the Boy Scouts, all advocated military service to instil self-discipline and build character. Robert Baden-Powell, founder of the scouting movement, told his members that the scout motto actually meant 'Be prepared to die for your country.' There was a strong sense in the middle classes that modern urban life had brought about a physical and moral decay among the lower classes. Soldiering promised escape from materialism and aimlessness, mechanization and indecision – as much for middle-class as working-class boys – and war would provide liberation from the stifling world of comfortable bourgeois society and the trashiness of mass culture.

The work of writers like Rudyard Kipling contrasted the hard honest soldier with the dull soft suburbanite; while H. Rider Haggard and dozens of others wrote stirring tales of adventure. War became romanticized in prose and poetry through the use of faux-medieval phrases, in which a horse became a charger, a soldier a warrior, human bodies dust, and blood the sweet wine of youth. But fictional accounts were matched by stories of true-life exploration, daring and heroism – the defence of Rorke's Drift, Livingstone's journeys through Africa, Winston Churchill's exploits against the Boers all made the lives of clerks and shopkeepers seem very dull. Even such non-jingoist artists as Oscar Wilde and Aubrey Beardsley offered, above all, sensation to their otherwise mollycoddled audiences.

The quasi-military groups, with their emphasis on the outdoor life, the countryside and nature, evoked a mythical past when all young men, unpolluted by the gloom and decay of industrial urban life, were pure and strong in mind and body. This was the nostalgic romanticism that so impressed a generation of young German and Austrian nationalists – including those who, 30 years later, led the Third Reich. Many in Europe were tired of peace and longed for the drama, the challenge, the glory and simplicity of war. Helmuth von Moltke, chief of the German general staff from 1871 to 1888, wrote: 'Perpetual peace is a dream, and not even a beautiful dream. War is an element of the divine order of the world. In it are developed the noblest virtues of man: courage and self-denial, fidelity to duty and the spirit of sacrifice: soldiers give their lives. Without war, the world would stagnate and lose itself in materialism.'

While the nations of Europe remained in an increasingly uneasy peace, they used the rest of the world as an outlet for nationalist fervour. During the nineteenth century European armies rarely fought each other on home soil, but they blazed away at each other, and everyone else, in every other part of the world. The loss of French power after 1815 gave Britain an almost free run in building a global empire, but after 1870 other European powers wanted a share of world domination. Industrialization gave France, Belgium, Germany and Italy the military technology to overwhelm any resistance to their overseas ambitions – so long as they avoided conflicts with each other. Any qualms about taking over other parts of the globe were swept aside by the arguments of the Social Darwinists – Europeans were clearly made to rule, and not to do so would be a failure of moral duty. The costs of colonization seemed low and the prestige great.

By 1875 African colonization had remained at roughly the same level for two centuries. European powers had established a few coastal settlements but the interior was a dangerous place with little commercial reward – the only notable export from Africa was palm oil. France and Germany in particular were keen to expand their possessions and interfere with Britain's dominance of world markets; the Belgian king Leopold even took possession of a vast part of the Congo region and made it his personal fiefdom. Others followed, and in 1884 Bismarck held a conference in Berlin to try to regulate the 'scramble for Africa'. The conference declared that occupation of any territory by a European power gave rights of possession, a decision that served to accelerate the colonization of Africa and every other portion of the globe. By 1914 the continent of Africa, along with the remainder of the world, had been carved up between Britain, France, Germany, Russia, the United States, Japan, Spain and Portugal. African kingdoms and peoples, such as the Samori, Bornu, Teke, Lunda, Utetera, Yeke, Kikuyu, Nguni and Shona, were subsumed into states with names like French West Africa, German East Africa or Northern Rhodesia. As well as the takeover of Africa by Britain, France, Germany and Portugal, this period saw the colonization of the west of North America and the Philippines by the United States, European settlement of northern Quebec and the rest of Canada, the annexation of Siberia and central Asia by Russia, the Japanese occupation of Korea, and the French conquest of Indo-China. There were a few independent countries, including Abyssinia and Morocco in Africa, China, and several ex-colonies in South America, but otherwise the whole world was annexed by the industrial powers of Europe, the United States and Japan.

Late nineteenth-century colonization did not merely mean occupation and economic exploitation of indigenous peoples, it brought the whole world into one trading system, whose rules and conditions were dictated by the industrialists and bankers of Europe and the United States. The introduction of rational economic systems, based on open trade and a money economy, had a devastating effect on societies whose trading systems were deeply embedded in their social relations. Customary and highly complex systems of pricing, exchange, withholding, storage and supply were swept away as simplistic laws of profit, supply and demand were implemented across the world. For indigenous peoples, there was terrible hardship. It has been estimated that around 60 million people died of famine in India, China and Brazil between 1876 and 1902, the high point of colonial activity. There were also wars with huge losses, often caused by the approach of famine. The Kanak people of New Caledonia, for example, rebelled against their French masters in 1877, after the land they had been moved on to proved infertile. They were butchered, their leader executed and his head sent back to Paris – the sophisticated Paris of Renoir and Monet and Degas – as a trophy. Other genocides appeared to have no cause beyond savagery and sport. From around 1804 the British began to slaughter, kidnap and enslave the indigenous people of Tasmania, hunting them and using them for target practice; finally, in 1876, after 70 years of unspeakable cruelty, the last native Tasmanian living on the island died (many others had been deported) – and an entire civilization was destroyed.

As trade turned to conquest, the prestige of empire was grasped by small groups of men – military leaders, politicians, journalists, self-promoters – as an antidote to national decline and, subsequently, as part of a new world order. The haphazard trading network of the early empires had, by the mid-nineteenth century, turned into a vision of a new world where everything could be controlled from the cabinet offices and boardrooms of Europe. The doctrine of free trade (see Chapter Fourteen) was combined with an insistence on the rule of law to give ideological justification for the European takeover. But it was not just merchants and politicians who wanted empires. Missionaries claimed the world for Christ, Social Darwinists stressed the manifest destiny of the superior white peoples ruling the inferior brown and black, while explorers romanticized their personal ambition into parables of man pitted against hostile nature. Kipling's 1899 poem 'The White Man's Burden' argued that the foot-soldiers of the empire had a thankless task; serving 'Your new-caught, sullen peoples / Half-devil and half-child' in the cause of making money for someone else: 'To seek another's profit, / And work another's gain.' But Kipling, always on the side of the common soldier, shared the blank incomprehension of non-Europeans that characterized his time. While Europeans, in his sincerely held view, went to Africa and Asia to 'Fill full the mouth of Famine / And bid the sickness cease', they then had to see the natives ruin their best efforts: 'Watch sloth and heathen Folly / Bring all your hopes to nought.' Europeans had the task of bringing civilization to the rest of the world, and carried the burden of seeing their work undone by its lazy heathen recipients.

Politicians in Europe were sometimes tempted to use imperial status to gain popularity, but this was a risky strategy. In the 1870s the British prime minister Benjamin Disraeli set out to make the Tories the party of empire, and to make the empire a symbol of British prestige and greatness and a model of justice and liberty. He bought control of the Suez Canal and annexed Cyprus, but his greatest piece of imperial flummery was a vast ceremony held in Delhi on New Year's Day 1877 to pronounce Queen Victoria Empress of India. Disraeli's cavalier imperialism, however, plunged Britain into wars in Afghanistan and the Zulu Transvaal, and in the 1880 election he was defeated by William Gladstone, who declared the empire to be a tawdry piece of theatre concealing a criminal enterprise, and the wars against the Afghans and the Zulus murderous assaults on innocent people. The British electorate were not, it seems, entirely convinced by the merits of imperialism.

In France, too, politicians found that the empire brought them little credit when it was going well and considerable blame when things went wrong. Napoleon III came to grief over his invasion of Mexico in 1864 – a débâcle that left his country vulnerable to the German invasion of 1870, during which he was captured and sent into exile. The resulting Third French Republic had its fair share of colonial disasters. In 1881 prime minister Jules Ferry lost his job when he ordered the illegal seizure of Tunisia; back in office in 1885, Ferry was ousted again when a French force was defeated with heavy losses in Indo-China. His successor, Henri Brisson, lost office over plans to spend more money on the French army based in Indo-China. In Germany the Reichstag dissolved when, in 1906, the opposition parties refused to vote through a budget in the wake of army atrocities in south-west and east Africa. In Russia, Tsar Nicholas II's dream of an empire in the east led to the disastrous Russo-Japanese war and the 1905 revolution.

Empires were political paradoxes – generally popular among the public, but potentially disastrous for the careless or arrogant politician. The justification for possessing an empire became fatally circular. The need to protect trade and to have a strategic global defence against the ambitions of others meant little, since trade within and between industrialized countries dwarfed any trade with colonies. In fact the colonies were a drain on resources, so spending more and more money to protect their lines of supply and to ward off other countries simply compounded the problem. The populations of Britain and France very probably gained nothing from their empires. A few people profited mightily and a few thousand enjoyed or endured lives of exotic displacement as apparent masters of people who resented their presence. The rest would have been better off without the empire at all.

Nevertheless, imperialist adventures buoyed up many of the folks back home and reinforced the sense of national identity, enthusiasm for the military and distrust of other Europeans. Newspapers were dominated by reports of engagements, troop deployments, regimental movements, military appointments, all happening in places that, while half a world away, became as familiar to the European public as their own backyards. There were heroic deeds to report from Rorke's Drift, Moualok, Little Big Horn and Khartoum, in which European troops had either miraculously defeated, or bravely succumbed to, overwhelming numbers of enemies. The truth was rather different.

On 1 September 1898 General Kitchener, with a force of 20,000 men and 100 guns mounted on boats, faced 50,000 Sudanese forces strung out in a line four miles long. When the Sudanese charged they were mown down. Omdurman was less a battle than a massacre – after just a few hours 10,000 Sudanese lay dead in huge piles on the desert sand. This type of engagement turned warfare into effective genocide. The European armies controlled territory by killing large numbers of inhabitants, and then either displacing or taking command of those that remained. They were better armed, organized and disciplined and they had a totally different idea of warfare from their reluctant enemies. To the indigenous populations of Africa, India and south-east Asia, armed conflict was an undesirable outcome that should involve as little bloodshed as possible; they had no reason to undertake massive and murderous warfare across huge distances. And if their methods were inexplicably brutal, what was it that the Europeans wanted? To them it may have seemed obvious – they wanted to claim a territory as their own – but to the locals this could be bewildering. In some places the Europeans wanted to settle, in others just to trade; sometimes they wanted locals to fight in their regiments, while wanting to annihilate others. Whatever they wanted, they made no reference to the local inhabitants, and set out to ensure that any effective social structure was destroyed so that it could not be used against them. The British, in particular, learned the lesson of the 1857 Indian mutiny and snuffed out any indigenous structures that might allow political or cultural expression in its African colonies.

While imperial adventures served as an outlet for nationalist sentiment, their effect was to increase patriotic fervour. The world became a chessboard-cum-battleground where soldiers and plucky adventurers befriended the 'half-wild, half-child' natives, and pitted themselves against their cunning German, French, British or Italian adversaries. The grouping of Europeans into ethnic states changed the rivalry between nations into a bitter hatred of others, and a denigration of their right to be considered equivalent. A Frenchman would routinely despise a German, not just because of historic rivalry, but because the German people were, *by their nature*, stupid, uncultured, aggressive – sentiments that were repeated back and forth between almost every group of nations. And, in a continent grouped into political units that reflected ethnic identity, there was a real problem for those with no state. In the old ramshackle empires Jews, Romany people, Nonconformists, dissidents, travellers and itinerants of all kinds were relatively untroubled, but in the new Europe of ethnic nationalities, what was the place of these people?

Imperial adventures and the struggles for national liberation vastly increased the prestige of the military. Although, in the late nineteenth century, many democracies elected socially progressive, non-militaristic governments, the generals and military planners strode across the political landscape like giants, while politicians stood in awe of their expertise, their courage and their hold on public esteem. This left the generals free to devise military plans and strategies, unhindered by the constraints of politics – giving the lie, as John Keegan has pointed out, to Clausewitz's dictum that 'war is politics pursued by other means'; in fact war became the negation of politics. In the newly created Germany, the army took 90 per cent of the federal budget, and in 1874 Bismarck secured a sustained level of funding for seven years. He removed military decision-making from the remit of the elected Reichstag and placed it within a separate imperial cabinet headed by the kaiser. By the time the antimilitarist Social Democrats became the largest party in the Reichstag in 1912, the army and navy were reporting direct to the military cabinet and the kaiser, who had made himself into an army officer. In France, the need to prepare for a war of revenge against Germany dominated political-military thinking; the army became the focus of French hopes and was above political interference. In Germany, France, Austria and Russia, foreign policy was dictated by military planning rather than diplomatic considerations. And while conscription prepared millions of young men for mobilization, it also instilled an obedience to military authority.

At the same time, the rapid development of military and civil technology made the militarization of European society potentially catastrophic. The last quarter of the nineteenth century saw technology, the organization of cities and the productivity of industry alter the physical nature of European civil society. The European rail network, reaching from the Atlantic to Russia and the Balkans, was completed, while telegraphy connected the whole continent, and even the Americas – the first transatlantic radio message was sent in 1901. Increasing material prosperity led to a net population increase of 32 per cent (i.e. 100 million), despite 25 million Europeans emigrating to America. Developments in civil technology – the telephone, radio, typesetting machine, typewriter and internal combustion engine all came into daily use – were more than matched by military advances. For the first time high-grade industrial techniques were applied to the manufacture of weapons in private factories run by Armstrong, Krupp, Creusot, Nobel and others. Alfred Nobel's invention of glycerine reduced the size of shells and bullets, doubled their range, and made them far more accurate and lethal. By 1900 all European armies had a bolt-action magazine-loading rifle (Mauzers and Lee Enfields, for example) that could kill a person at a range of 1,400 metres – movement of armies within one kilometre of each other was effectively paralysed. By 1900 all European armies had steel field guns with calibres of 75mm and ranges of 2,500 to 5,000 metres. In 1885, the hand-cranked Gatling gun was replaced by the Maxim, the first true machine gun, which used its own recoil energy to reload up to 250 rounds. No fortress could withstand the new artillery, so a Belgian soldier, General Henri Brialmont, came up with the idea of a 'fortified area' – a labyrinth of trenches and tunnels that linked a series of gun emplacements. The soldiers who defended the guns would live in these trenches along with the artillerymen. Verdun, and other sites on France's vulnerable north-east frontier, were converted into vast fortified entrenchments.

Naval guns and armour also grew prodigiously. From 1860 to 1885 the biggest British naval guns grew from the 68-pounder, weighing less than five tons, to the 16–inch rifled gun, firing shells and weighing

111 tons. Naval armour at the waterline increased from $4^1/_2$ inches to an astounding maximum of 24 inches, and Italy, Germany and the United States all built navies to rival the British and French.

The military planners believed, and convinced everyone else, that the nation in peacetime must be ready for war. There were arms races between Germany, Britain and France in the naval sphere and between France and Germany in munitions technology. The 1894 Dreyfus affair, in which a Jewish French officer was wrongly convicted of supplying military secrets to Germany, betrayed the tensions between military authoritarian paranoia and a socially liberal society. Between 1874 and 1896 the main European powers increased their military spending by 50 per cent, between 1880 and 1914 German arms expenditure rose by 400 per cent, Britain's and Russia's by 200 per cent and France's by almost 100 per cent. Democratic governments felt they had to justify increased spending by continually referring to foreign threats – panics and war scares were common. Civil society was affected by a peculiar febrile energy as, in the first decades of the twentieth century, strikes and political protests across Europe were accompanied by an upsurge in violence (see Dangerfield).

The nation states of Europe, suspicious of others and ambitious for themselves, began to manoeuvre themselves into blocs. Germany was hostile to France and concerned about the threat from Russia; Britain was concerned about Germany's growing naval strength and her ambitions in the Middle East, while France sought allies to protect her from German aggression. In 1882 an alliance was formed between Germany, Austria and Italy, and in 1894 between France and Russia; in 1904 Britain signed an *entente cordiale* with France, and in 1907 with Russia. Europe was by then divided into two opposing armed camps with no bridge between.

Despite the military build-up and the heightened nationalism, at the turn of the twentieth century most Europeans did not think war was inevitable, even if some relished the prospect. The next ten years decisively changed that view. Military experts persuaded their civilian governments that any war would be over quickly, probably in the course of a spring and summer season; so long as they could mobilize a large force of men and equipment, the first push of the campaign should be decisive. Most important of all, the regimes in both Germany and Austria became convinced that there would be a war and that any delay would favour their enemies. They began to look for a pretext to begin a major conflict.

The kaiser's imperial cabinet shared a grand strategic vision of a Germanic empire. Hemmed in by the British navy to the north and west, their eyes had turned towards south-east Europe and the newly discovered oil-fields of the Middle East. An alliance with the Ottoman empire meant that only the Balkans, dominated by Serbia, which was a strong ally of Russia, stood in the way. The Austrian chief of staff, von Hötzendorf, believed that Serbia, backed by Russia, was becoming far too powerful, and should be invaded before the Slav powers dominated the south-east of Europe. Austria and Germany agreed that if Russia came to Serbia's aid, it was better to take them on sooner rather than later.

This left the problem of France, the main ally of Russia. The German regime, well aware of French intentions to take back its territories, decided that they should move against France as soon as Russia defended Serbia. There was no justification for this, except a need to take France out of any war, whether or not she was a participant. The German plan, drawn up by General Schlieffen, was to sweep through neutral Belgium before encircling Paris and the French army in a pincer movement; Schlieffen calculated that any war with France would be over in just six weeks. The Schlieffen plan was never subject to political input or criticism, and the general stated that as a military planner, he could not be bound by international agreements. As the German Imperial Army took control of foreign policy, Theobald von Bethmann-Hollweg, German chancellor in 1914, wrote : 'During my whole term of office there was never any kind of council of war in which politicians intervened in the pros and cons of the military debate' (quoted in Ritter). In the manoeuvrings leading up to the outbreak of war, the German civilian government acted in concert with the army, but the agenda was set by the military timetable. The French army in their turn regarded political and diplomatic means as inadequate for the prize they desired – the restoration of Alsace-Lorraine to France. They had less influence in government than the German army, but their message was taken seriously as it corresponded with the wishes of most French people.

By the summer of 1914 each side (France and Russia vs. Germany and Austria-Hungary) felt itself ready for war, and believed that the other side was about to attack. On 28 July 1914 Austria, encouraged by Berlin (and using the assassination of Archduke Franz Ferdinand in Sarajevo as a pretext), declared war on Serbia and began to bombard

Belgrade. Russia mobilized her troops, and in response Germany declared war on Russia on 1 August. The following day, Germany informed neutral Belgium that it must accept an invasion by German troops in order to prevent a French invasion; on 3 August Germany declared war on France. All of this was exactly as Austria and Germany had planned, but the great unknown was the reaction of Britain, with its relatively small army but enormous and powerful navy. Germany may have calculated that Britain would stay out of the war, but the British government, supported by the majority of its people, felt bound to protect the neutrality of Belgium. By 5 August 1914 all of the major European powers were officially at war.

Once war was declared, all sides were optimistic. Letters, diaries and memoirs record the sense of joy and liberation that at last the phoney sparring was over and the real contest could begin. German military leaders felt their nation was invincible, while the Russians believed they might reach Berlin before the Germans reached Paris. Those on the political left who were in principle against war consoled themselves with the belief that this would be 'the war to end all wars'. In the *Pall Mall Gazette* J. L. Garvin wrote: 'We have to do our part in killing a creed of war. Then at last, after a rain of blood, there may be set the greater rainbow in the Heavens before the vision of the souls of men. And after Armageddon war, indeed, may be no more.' Others, though they were a minority, could hardly believe that Europe had sleep-walked into a war that would involve every major power on the continent.

The widespread sense of joy could not survive the reality of trench warfare, as the illusion of an escape into pastoral manliness or individual heroics was ruthlessly exposed. War became a living nightmare of murderous industrial force inflicting anonymous carnage on millions of human lives. The artillerymen never saw those they killed, the infantrymen never knew who killed them. Despite the losses, the pre-war xenophobia did not allow any kind of negotiated peace, even when the war seemed to grind to a halt.

By late 1914 lines of trenches filled the entire frontier between France and Germany, while a vast area of western Russia became a haphazard combat zone. Advance or retreat were similarly impossible without huge loss of life. Nevertheless, once the first phase was over, the war was re-energized as all the powers diverted their entire industrial sectors into military production – every citizen became involved in the war effort, either as a soldier, or in the production of military material, or as targets of indiscriminate shelling and attacks on shipping. The European powers had paused for breath only in order to be able to blow harder. The destruction that resulted was worse than anyone, even the most pessimistic military thinkers, had predicted; even they had not imagined that the nations of Europe would simply carry on pouring men, machines and money into a catastrophic stalemate.

The prosecution of the war became a matter of national survival and so, in each country, the civilian population and its institutions were made subservient to the war and to the military establishment. In Germany the Social Democrats in the Reichstag abandoned their promise to oppose a capitalist war and backed the conflict. In August 1916 Germany became a virtual military dictatorship run by Generals von Hindenburg and Ludendorff with the kaiser as its honorary head, and with every male between the ages of 17 and 60 conscripted. At the outbreak of war the French parliament adjourned itself indefinitely and handed complete control of the war effort to Marshal Joffre. He persuaded the deputies and the government to leave Paris for their own safety and remain in Bordeaux until it was safe to return; even the French minister for war was barred from visiting the front. In an attempt to unite all the political parties, the British prime minister Herbert Asquith appointed a career soldier, Lord Kitchener, to the traditionally civilian post of secretary of state for war, and thereby placed the military further from the control of the democratic government. In Russia the tsar took personal command of the army, while in Austria-Hungary the declaration of war united the polyglot and recently rebellious elements of the empire behind the emperor. The Austrian Reichsrat dissolved itself in March 1916 for the duration of the conflict, leaving the conduct of the war to the belligerent chief of staff. The political story of the war in all the major powers was of politicians struggling to regain control of the military.

The catastrophic loss of life in 1914–18 is partly explained by military technology and partly by misguided tactics. Most of the generals were used to fighting colonial wars against poorly armed enemies; none had ever fought a war where the only offensive weapon was the infantryman's rifle, while defence was sustained by a vast machinery of artillery, machine guns and wire. The huge rise in population in Europe meant that in 1914 there were millions of men of service age ready to be poured into the murderous conflict. The belief in frontal assaults in which sheer numbers of infantrymen could win the field led to a series of infamous débâcles; on 1 July 1916 British forces on the Somme began a major advance which cost 20,000 dead and 40,000 wounded on the first day; by November they had advanced eight miles at a cost of 400,000 casualties.

By 1916 discontent began to show among the soldiers at the front, and in Germany, Britain, France and Russia politicians voiced opposition to the war. Nevertheless, despite unimaginable losses, army discipline was maintained into 1917. The tempo of the war changed in April 1917 when, believing Germany to be a permanent danger to its shipping, the United States entered the war on the side of Britain and France. In the same month French soldiers mutinied along the whole western front and refused to take part in suicidal assaults. Marshal Pétain restored order but only at the cost of abandoning offensive tactics. In March 1917 Tsar Nicholas II of Russia was forced to abdicate amid huge discontent with the progress of the war, and in November 1917 the Bolshevik party staged a coup which overthrew the constitutional government. In December the new Russian government signed an armistice with Germany.

In early 1917 the United States army was comparatively small, but everyone understood that the immense industrial muscle and manpower available to America would, given time, be decisive. The German command decided they must act. On 21 March 1918 they began a massive offensive that brought them to the Marne, only 80 kilometres from Paris. But this was the high point of their advance. The French and British counterattacked both on the western front and in the southeast. Turkey sued for peace in October 1918, as did Austria-Hungary. In Germany fear of revolution and military crisis at last forced the politicians to act decisively. Ludendorf fled to Sweden, while von Hindenburg insisted on bringing the army back to Germany without further futile casualties. The kaiser was forced to abdicate on 9 November and Friedrich Ebert, a Social Democrat, was appointed chancellor. Two days later, on 11 November 1918, Germany accepted the terms of surrender and the war to end all wars was over.

The 1914–18 war was unlike any previous conflict. Advanced weapons technology, mechanized transport, the availability of millions of fighting men, the vast superiority of defence over offence, the dedication of nations' industrial power to the prosecution of the war and the failures of military strategists all contributed to the killing of around five

million men from the western powers alone in just four years. Despite
the increased populations of Europe, the proportion of deaths was, in
historical terms, extraordinarily high. In most regions, every town and
village suffered loss. A vast area of Europe was also destroyed in the
war – something that had not happened for a hundred years. American
industrial growth was threatening to overtake Europe in any case, but
the First World War brought the United States reluctantly on to the
world stage and provoked the formation of the Soviet Union. This was
the beginning of the end of European, though not western, domination
of world affairs.

In the previous four centuries western Europeans had become used
to the idea of progress. There had been wars, religious schisms, famines
and the dehumanization of early industrialization, but through it all
western Europeans believed they were making the world a better place,
and that they themselves were the evidence of such progress. The First
World War changed all that by providing overwhelming and shattering
evidence that progress was an illusion. Anyone who still believed that
European culture, technology and politics had advanced the cause of
humanity need only look at the battlefields of Flanders and the endless
lists of the war dead. This war was not against, nor provoked by,
'savages' who needed to be taught a lesson, and in whose defeat all
Europeans could rejoice. This had been a war between apparently civilized nations. Industrial capitalism and constitutional government had
failed to prevent war; indeed, the products of industry had hugely
multiplied the numbers of casualties, and the extension of self-
determination had inspired the unstoppable growth of nationalism.
Before the First World War there were no attempts at mutual disarma-
ment or at setting up international organizations to mediate and resolve
conflicts between nations. The glorification of military successes abroad,
rivalry between nations turning to bitter hatred, the desire for revenge
for past humiliations, glamorization of the military life, vast spending
on huge armies and state-of-the-art weapons all contributed to a culture
that saw war as an acceptable activity for nation states to pursue. The
First World War brought an end to the belief in God-given superiority
and effortless progress, it ended the assumed right of European nations
to rule the world, and it gave birth to the long antagonism between
the capitalist and communist systems.

On 10 August 1914, five days after war was declared, Henry
James, in a letter to a friend, expressed his revulsion at the prospect

of war, and articulated the illusion that had preceded it: 'Black and hideous to me is the tragedy that gathers, and I'm sick beyond cure to have lived on to see it. You and I, the ornaments of our generation, should have been spared the wreck of our beliefs that through the long years we had seen civilization grow and the worst become impossible.'

But James and his contemporaries were not spared the wreck of their beliefs; they lived to see that the apparent growth of civilization gave little defence against mass slaughter; and were forced to contemplate the possibility that civilization itself had enabled the needless death or maiming of millions of their fellow Europeans.

THE END OF CIVILIZATION

Depression, Extremism and Genocide in Europe,
America and Asia

THE willing march into the catastrophe of the 1914–18 war defies any rational rules of historical cause and effect. We can map out the burgeoning belief in semi-mystical nationhood, the manoeuvring and alliances, the teetering balance of power, and the growing sense of arrogance and paranoia; but we are left to wonder how a group of nations who believed themselves the most civilized in human history, with a generation of citizens enjoying more political and social rights and better living standards than any in the previous century, could have willingly sent millions of their young men to needless death or maiming. But if the First World War shakes our assumptions of social, political and, above all, moral progress, then the events of the following 30 years were, as Dietrich Bonhoeffer was to write from a Nazi prison, 'utterly bewildering to anyone nurtured in our traditional ethical systems'.

The two world wars have come to be seen as a single conflict, in which the unfinished business of 1918 festered and eventually erupted. This happened against a background of utter disillusionment and anger with the established authorities. A political system and a ruling class that had led Europe into a pointless war, or had, in the minds of German soldiers, betrayed its army by surrendering, could no longer carry the hopes of the people. Either something new, or a return to an older, better society, was needed; and in either case a political ideology that had grown up in the nineteenth century was ready to provide the answer. Growing numbers saw communism, led by the example of the new Soviet Union, as the best hope for Europe, while others saw this as a profound and dangerous threat to civilization and turned instead to a seductive combination of intense nationalism and extreme Social Darwinism.

The twin spectre of communism and fascism came to dominate European political concerns in the 1920s and 1930s. Both were deeply rooted in the ideas and emotions of the previous century, but these were not two sides of the same coin. The nationalism, xenophobia and assumptions of white supremacy that infected late nineteenth-century Europe formed the principles of fascism, but were directly challenged by communism, which promoted internationalism and equality. Before we see how fascism overcame both communism and liberalism in Europe, it is worth looking at events across the Atlantic. The story of America in the 1920s provides an interesting context for the European experience.

Strange as it may seem to us, the underlying concern of American capitalism in the late nineteenth century was the possibility of sufficiency. Just as Marx had envisaged a world where everyone would have enough for a decent life, American capitalists were worried that people would stop buying their goods once they had enough things to live comfortably. There seemed no obvious reason why someone would replace a piece of furniture or a coat or a set of crockery simply because it was old. This problem was solved in large part through the influence of Edward Bernays, a nephew of Sigmund Freud, and principal promoter of his ideas in America. Bernays was intrigued by Freud's view that people are bundles of emotion, passion and desire, and that the real motive for human action is the satisfaction of deep-seated desires rather than rational calculation. Bernays saw that American companies needed to transform the way that people thought about their purchases, so that they would forget about trying to fill their rational needs and instead aim to fulfil their desires. In the 1920s, consumerism, or consumptionism as it was then called, was born. Calvin Coolidge declared that an 'American's importance to his country is not as a citizen but as a consumer'. Rather than selling goods to its customers, the advertising industry began to sell happiness.

But Bernays' influence went beyond advertising. As producers and consumers, the urban masses were driving forward the expansion of industrial America; they were building the railroads, inhabiting the new cities, buying up the increasing variety of goods. But the First World War and the Russian Revolution seemed to show that people acting en masse could be extremely dangerous. The destructive capabilities of the individual and of the masses was a central part of Freud's message.

The presidency of Theodore Roosevelt (1901–08) reinvigorated American democracy and showed that real change could come through politics; it also showed American companies that a powerful reforming president could break up monopolies, regulate child labour and legislate against the adulteration of food products. Bernays, and his clients in American corporations, found themselves in agreement with Freud's view that democracy carried serious risks and should be discouraged. Other commentators such as Walter Lippman, the most influential columnist in America in the 1930s and 1940s, came to agree that democracy was an inappropriate way of governing such a complex country, and that the masses needed an elite to guide them.

Theodore Roosevelt was followed in office by a series of conservative presidents (while Woodrow Wilson was hamstrung by a conservative Congress) keen to restrict social and political rights. The other side of Bernays' message began to work as the consumer boom of the 1920s made the majority of Americans forget about political activity or change. In 1928 President Hoover reinforced Coolidge's sentiment and said that people were 'constantly moving happiness machines'. Just as Freud had suggested that if our selfish desires are satisfied we feel docile and happy, and if they are thwarted we feel aggrieved, Hoover understood that when people are fulfilling their desires they are not inclined to be politically active.

Americans showed that if products were sold to them in the right way, they would buy and buy and that consumerism would make them politically conservative. The old pioneering ethos of America, where hardship was accepted as the price for liberty, gave way to a belief in having things in order to feel good about yourself. Union membership declined and inequality grew; federal tax cuts favoured the wealthy, and when farm incomes fell by half, the government refused to intervene – the free market was allowed to run its course. In the 1920s the Supreme Court struck down laws granting minimum wages for women and children and allowed the development of de facto monopolies. Immigration was severely restricted, while Congress and then the country turned down Woodrow Wilson's attempts to make the US an outward-looking part of the world community. The Jim Crow laws, which segregated much of the country by race, were extended; the Ku Klux Klan, dormant since the 1880s, was revived in 1915 and reached four million members, including many in the industrial north; lynchings and their accompanying picture postcards became common. In 1921 a 'race riot' in Tulsa, Oklahoma (in effect a determined attempt to drive all Negroes out of the city), saw 150 to 200 black people murdered, anti-Semitism was openly proclaimed in newspapers, and there was the first of a series of 'Red Scares' in which 6,000 people were arrested. In 1920, the sale and consumption of alcohol were prohibited, allowing organized crime, in league with corrupt officials, to control the destinies of America's major cities.

What was good for business was good for America, but America had changed. The self-image of the immigrants building communities through mutual help changed to a country in which the opportunities for sheer enjoyment were suddenly everywhere, but where xenophobia, organized crime and corruption flourished. Unbridled capitalism offered new opportunities and was an amazingly efficient way of providing goods and services, but it required the surrender of anything that stood in its way. The cohesion of communities, customary arrangements, family loyalties must all be sacrificed to the continual churning need for better, cheaper, newer goods to be brought to market. All of this kept going because, in the 1920s, American industry found itself in an extremely favourable situation. The more goods it could sell, the more workers it employed and the more consumers it created; and the lower the wages, the higher the company profits. But while the good times lasted for a minority, the low-paid workers began to find their pay packets could no longer bring them the goods they wanted. Despite the slowdown in demand, industry kept on producing until, almost before anyone had noticed, there was massive overcapacity in the economy – shares and stocks were overvalued and warehouses were full of unwanted goods. In October 1929, Wall Street brokers began to sell stocks; the stock market slid down a black hole and took American free-market capitalism with it.

While the United States was becoming an individualist society where politics had virtually disappeared, the politics of Europe became dominated by the struggles of ever-weakening liberal democracies in the face of both communism and fascism. Because these two systems were based on universal political systems, apparently applicable to any society, the role of nationalism and nation states in the rise of communism and fascism is generally underestimated. But it was the Bolsheviks who first showed how the heavily centralized nation state, with its monopoly of force and control of communications, was vulnerable to takeover by a relatively small group. In St Petersburg in the first few hours of 25 October 1917 Bolshevik forces took control of the railway stations, post and telegraph offices, telephone and electricity networks and the state bank, leaving the existing government stranded inside the Winter Palace – which was then occupied. Of course the Bolsheviks needed the support of soldiers and sailors, but their takeover gave most of the instruments of state power to a small group of people; they were then able to use the widespread discontent with the prosecution of the war (a key attraction of Bolshevik policy was the promise, duly delivered, to get Russia out of hostilities) to bring much of the army and navy to their cause.

Russia in the early twentieth century, like France 120 years earlier, was an autocratic society isolated in a world of change. The difference was that the tsar had already been forced to abdicate, in February 1917, and Russia was ruled by an elected *duma*. But prime minister Alexander Kerensky's support for the war gave the Bolsheviks the chance to seize power and suspend all political opposition. Russia, later the Union of Soviet Socialist Republics, became the living embodiment of Marx's final phase of history – the 'dictatorship of the proletariat' had come to pass.

Russia adopted a political system born out of the western Enlightenment, with its principal problem still unresolved – there was, within the intellectual framework of Marxism, no place for political opposition; any opposition to the revolution would of necessity be a reactionary force ranged against the progress of history. Like Plato 2,300 years earlier, the task of the Soviet leaders was to bring about the ideal society that must exist. The rising power of the Soviet Union gave the west an 'east' against which it could contrast itself. But the political ideology of the Soviet Union was an utterly western creation, born out of the belief that universalist abstract reasoning is the route to real truth and wisdom, and to the discovery of those laws that will solve the problems of humanity. The west gave communism to the world and then had to spend decades killing it off.

The Soviet Union established itself as a modern industrialized nation at exactly the time that the west was imploding into economic depression and right-wing extremism. Many western advocates of a socially just society were enthralled to see such a complete alternative to industrial capitalism emerge apparently fully formed. While unemployment and fascism stalked the streets and empty factories of the west, the Soviet Union seemed like a workers' paradise where goods were distributed on the basis of need and services rendered according to ability.

Aside from its purely political impact, socialism became a quasi-spiritual phenomenon (see Chapter Fourteen). In an overwhelmingly secular society, where mechanized war had made people deeply pessimistic about humanity and about the politics of industrial capitalism, belief in socialism became even stronger than before 1914. Socialism stood as an alternative to despair and to Freudian pessimism about human nature; humans were seen by socialists as essentially benign and in need of fairness and respect, rather than malign and in need of containment. As a vehicle for people's desire to do good to others, socialism became, for many people in the west, the repository of hope for the future.

In the 1920s and early 1930s it seemed to many that Soviet society was delivering much of what Marx had promised. State planning enabled food, education, hospitals and industrial goods to be provided in ever-increasing amounts. Newly trained teachers reported rooms full of peasants patiently writing their first sentence over and over: 'We are not slaves. We are not slaves.' Soviet science was led by a generation, including Koltsov, Chetverikov and Vavilov, who dedicated themselves to the new cause and placed the Soviet Union at the forefront of world developments in plant-breeding, population genetics, agricultural science and physics. The emergence of Russian artists, musicians, poets and novelists of world stature – Mayakovsky, Gorky, Sholokhov, Shostakovich, Pasternak, Bulgakov and others – reflected the sense of a new beginning for humanity. Nevertheless, as early as 1918, the German communist leader Rosa Luxemburg saw what the future might hold: 'In place of the representative bodies created by general, popular elections, Lenin and Trotsky have laid down the soviets as the only true representation of the labouring masses . . . Without general elections, without unrestricted freedom of press and assembly, without a free struggle of opinion, life dies out in every public institution . . . Public life gradually falls asleep, a few dozen party leaders of inexhaustible energy and boundless experience direct and rule.'

The hopes of many Russians and western sympathizers lasted through the civil war of the early 1920s and into the 1930s. But by then power was, as Luxemburg had predicted, shared among a small elite. By the late 1920s, though the Soviet Union may have been faring reasonably well, the Communist party was divided and losing direction. The issue that revived its sense of purpose was the most ambitious and most disastrous of its policies, the collectivization of agriculture. Russia was a peasant culture with a highly sophisticated and deeply ingrained sense of community, the intricate social structures of its villages dealing with everything from land allocation to legal disputes. For 10 years after the revolution these were left intact, but from 1928 Stalin used minor fluctuations in grain supplies to argue that wealthy peasants were hoarding grain, and that small family farms were an inefficient way to produce food crops. From 1930 onwards the wealthier peasants or *kulaks* were deported from their villages, collective farms were introduced, and quotas given for the supply of food from each district. The party was once again running the affairs of the country. But the quotas were unreachable, and within two years, the food in the countryside began to run out. By the spring of 1933 millions of peasants in the Ukraine and western Russia – the grain belt of the Soviet Union – were starving to death. One witness wrote later: 'On a battlefield men die quickly, they fight back, they are sustained by fellowship and a sense of duty. Here I saw people dying in solitude by slow degrees, dying hideously, without the excuse of sacrifice for a cause. They had been trapped and left to starve, each in his home, by a political decision made in a far-off capital around conference and banquet tables' (Kravchenko).

The famine was so widespread that officials searching for hidden grain automatically suspected anyone who did not look starved. Out of a Ukrainian farm population of 25 million, about 5 million starved to death.

Using the December 1934 murder of Leningrad party chief Leonid Kirov as a pretext, Stalin had his fellow party leaders arrested, giving him total control over the party and the country. Impressed by Hitler's purge of the Nazi party in June 1934, he set about clearing out any possible resistance. Of the 1,966 delegates to the 1934 party congress, 1,108 were shot; across the country party members and ordinary people were rounded up, given summary trials and either shot or deported to labour camps. These were the years of the Gulag Archipelago, Alexander Solzhenitsyn's term for the network of labour camps: 'For several decades political arrests were distinguished in our country precisely by the fact that people were arrested who were guilty of nothing and therefore unprepared to put up any resistance whatsoever. There was a general feeling of being destined for destruction, of having nowhere to escape from the GPU-NKVD . . . people leaving for work said farewell to their families every day, because they could not be certain they would return at night.'

The lack of resistance to the so-called Great Terror (in which no fewer than 20 million people were shot or died in labour camps) among ordinary people and senior party officials went far beyond a sense of helplessness. The Marxist view of history combined the inevitability of an ideal society with utter faith in human reason. Party members who were arrested believed that they must be enemies of historical progress, and were encouraged to examine themselves and confess to their 'errors'. At party gatherings, speeches by Stalin would be enthusiastically applauded by the audience – and by Stalin himself. Why? Because the applause was not for the leader but for the realization of historical progress – a process of which all present, including Stalin himself, were servants. Prisoners in labour camps would regularly send Stalin birthday congratulations; not through coercion, but because they believed in the common struggle towards the historically prescribed ideal society – in a communist society they were the equal of Stalin but had simply gone astray.

While some in the west regarded communism, or state socialism, as the best hope for humanity, others saw it as a dangerous and potentially catastrophic threat to their way of life. The divergence in these views was most dramatic and extreme in Germany, but the rise of fascism, in part as a reaction to communism, was matched by a general sense of disorientation and foreboding among Europe's population. This was reflected in European culture, where makers of 'high art' – painting, sculpture, architecture, classical music, literature – disillusioned by the horrors of war and the apparent complacency of their predecessors, tried to find a new beginning; while 'mass culture' found itself denigrated by both the socially superior (who considered it a threat to civilization) and left-wing intellectuals (who thought it responsible for a 'false consciousness' of contentment among the masses). Left-wing writers like George Orwell and the Marxist philosophers of the Frankfurt School such as Theodor Adorno and Herbert Marcuse admitted their own dismay at the way the masses were so easily duped and seduced by popular trashy culture (an attitude that never infected America).

Memoirs and autobiographies repeatedly show that middle-class and working-class people had almost no contact with each other; they were occupying different worlds even when they lived in adjacent streets. Middle-class intellectuals who either disdained or idolized the working classes had almost no idea of the real hopes, desires and wishes of the people they spoke for and about. The reading, writing and film-going of working people might have been taken as a reaching-out beyond personal concerns to see and appreciate a wider world, but the opposite view was widespread. The reading matter of the masses was not just contemptible, it was putting the whole enterprise of western civilization in danger. It was feared that somehow the appalling quality of the films and books and magazines that the masses were consuming would pollute the works of art that were constructed out of the same materials. Teaching the masses to read had not been a happy advance for civilization; putting everyone in touch with the ideas and thoughts of the great figures of the past and present had been a disaster that would have dire consequences for the art of the written word.

Taking their lead from a vague belief in Social Darwinism, many believed that education was a waste of time and money since working people were too stupid to learn more than a few basic facts, and could never learn to think for themselves or to gain appreciation of finer things like art, music and literature. The firm belief that intelligence and refinement were passed on in families and could not be induced by education encouraged theories such as eugenics, in which improved offspring could and should be bred from the best people in society. It also stoked fears that the working classes, who had more children, would numerically overwhelm society and produce a race of idiots.

How could European artists respond to political extremism and the continuing divisions in society, and what could European civilization and culture mean after the slaughter in the trenches? The overwhelming sense of the interwar years, reflected in its most notable cultural works, was disorientation. Writers and artists felt the need to break with the catastrophe of the immediate past; but while Freudian ideas pointed them towards their inner selves, the disdain of intellectual artists for their cultural roots left them without a reliable compass. Some writers, such as T. S. Eliot and James Joyce, went back to myth or medieval legend in search of a point of departure, while artists like Marcel Duchamp and George Grosz took the demystification and denigration of current art and society as their starting point. For many artists the shedding of current mores was a liberation. Visual artists were able to open their eyes to the extraordinary beauty of 'primitive' art that had been so patronized by the Enlightenment and so derided by the nineteenth century. Gauguin had already used techniques shown in Polynesian sculptures in his paintings, and Picasso used African masks to render his vision of the human face.

But modernism in most of its guises suffered from its own intellectualism. Its best practitioners were grounded in the real experience of living in societies that nurtured the artists' sense of disorientation. Joyce, Picasso, Miró and Stravinsky came from outside the mainstream of industrial Europe, bearing the unrecognized and astonishing depths of their cultures and the conflicts these cultures presented to artists in the modern world. But for many artists the abandonment of the present meant a search for a past that had no reality, while the denigration of mass culture left them without an emotional wellspring. (Contrast this with the confident creative energies of American cinema in the same period.) Feeling a conflict between the humanity that was the impulse for their art, and the dislike of the actual human beings that confronted them, they responded by creating a distance from the masses, producing art that ordinary people simply would not understand, and which would therefore be safe from their grasp. The negative characteristics of modernist art are its intentional difficulty and its coldness, both springing from a detachment from the culture of European people. We are back, once again, to disorientation.

The uncertainty of depending on the authority of the past was heightened by the astonishing discoveries made in the fields of physics and cosmology. In 1905 and 1916 Albert Einstein showed how time and space, the cornerstones of human perception, were not fixed stable entities, but variables whose inherent properties of distance and duration varied according to the relative situation of the observer. In 1919 Ernest Rutherford split electrons off an atom of oxygen, thereby showing that the basic building block of nature was, in reality, made up of a variety of yet smaller particles. Subsequent work by Niels Bohr, Werner Heisenberg, Erwin Schrödinger and Paul Dirac, among others, revealed that at the sub-atomic level, the objective observation of nature was an illusion – what you saw depended on what you were trying to measure. Light, for example, could appear either as a wave, or a series of particles, while the position and movement of particles could not, according to Heisenberg's Uncertainty Principle, both be measured at any one time.

None of this affected day-to-day reality, but its effect on the intellectual atmosphere of the times was fundamental. At the same time philosophy underwent a serious revolution, brought on by the failure of Bertrand Russell's attempt (in his 1916 *Principia Mathematica*, co-written with Alfred Whitehead) to show that the truths of mathematics are directly derivable from truths of logic. By the time Kurt Gödel demonstrated, in 1931, that no formal system of mathematics was ultimately provable by its own rules, the direction that analytical philosophy had taken ever since Descartes was already seriously in doubt. In Russell's own fiefdom of Cambridge, the Austrian philosopher Ludwig Wittgenstein was arguing that the fundamental belief that language represented reality, and that logical propositions, for example, were descriptions of real situations, was misguided. This sounds intellectually rarefied, but taken together with the work of Einstein, Bohr and Heisenberg, it seriously undermined the belief that we could understand the world by simply observing it and by analysing our observations through an objective use of language. Instead the world was a subjective place where meaning came through situation and context.

In a world where the recent past held no guidance for the future, the politics, culture and very civilization of Europe seemed to many people to be in need of renewal by whoever could seize the moment. Throughout the continent any enthusiasm for communism was matched and over-ridden by a mixture of fear of a communist takeover and a visceral desire to re-create the spirit of a mythical past. Citizens of the ethnic nations of Europe, tired of the pettiness of urban life, and infuriated by the betrayals of the war, felt a need to live more noble lives and to fulfil the destiny of their nations. The new doctrine of fascism sought to answer this need.

The fascist takeover of Europe was astonishingly rapid. In 1920 the whole of Europe, from the border of the Soviet Union to the Atlantic, was ruled by constitutional national governments supported by democratic institutions. One third of the world was under colonial rule, but in those 65 or so states that were independent, all but five held elections between the wars. The catastrophe of the First World War might have made people wary of the idea of progress, but it had not halted the movement towards greater social and political liberalism. There seemed no reason why this near-universal democratization should not endure. Europe seemed to be on the road to a better future where growing prosperity and representative political institutions would deliver a peaceful world.

However, between 1918 and 1939 constitutional liberal government went into a catastrophic collapse. Representative assemblies were dissolved or sidelined in 17 out of 27 European countries before 1939, while another five were negated during the war itself. Only Britain and Finland and the neutral states of Ireland, Sweden and Switzerland maintained democratic institutions through the whole of the period from 1918 to 1945. In other parts of the world, including Japan in 1930–31 and Turkey in the early 1920s, democracies were brushed aside by militarist regimes. In some states communists seized power, but German influence eventually ensured that the regimes that emerged from the collapse of liberalism were from the political right. Inspired by fear of communism and the success of fascism in Italy and Germany, all were militaristic, authoritarian in disallowing dissent, and heavily nationalistic. Some, like King Alexander of Yugoslavia, were old-fashioned conservatives holding back the tide of social reform; others, like Oliveira Salazar in Portugal, wanted to re-create a golden medieval past.

We have seen some of the cultural attitudes that underlay these changes, but in the 1920s and 1930s Europe also saw massive movements of people and rapid developments in working and social arrangements. A political creed and cultural milieu that harked back to a simpler time was attractive to many people. At the same time the European left had split between those Socialist parties that entered into existing democratic politics, and the socialist and communist organizations that sought change through revolutionary means. The Communist International held its first World Congress in 1919, attended by representatives from 26 European countries (as well as the United States, Australia and Japan), all committed to 'proletarian revolution'. In response to the growth of communism and socialism, the lower middle classes, the petit bourgeois, the 'little men' who felt caught between the dominance of big business and the power of organized labour, were attracted to the idealistic promises of fascism. (In Vienna in 1932, of the National Socialists elected as councillors, 56 per cent were white-collar office workers and public employees, 14 per cent blue-collar workers and 18 per cent self-employed.)

Just as important to the growth of fascism was the sense, among citizens of the defeated nations, of the betrayal of a deeply held vision. Many ex-soldiers, returning to lives as factory workers or clerks or shopkeepers, regarded the 1914–18 war as an uplifting experience in which comradeship and the nobility of fighting for a great cause overrode the terror and discomforts of trench warfare. After the epic nature of the struggle, civilian life seemed petty and disappointing – in Italy, more than half of all fascists in the early 1920s were ex-soldiers.

Liberal democracy came under pressure from communism and fascism, but also from the failure of laissez-faire capitalism. The liberal democratic states depended on the consent of all sectors of their populations, and this in turn depended on a degree of prosperity. When

Independent states after World War I

economic depression took their savings and their jobs, people withdrew their consent; to many it seemed that a liberal capitalist democracy was not necessarily the best way to run a country.

All of these factors appeared in their most extreme forms in Germany, the most populous, wealthy and potentially powerful nation in Europe. The 1918 surrender had come without an outright military defeat, leaving large sections of the army feeling betrayed. Their resentment, together with dissatisfaction at the strictures and banalities of modern civilian life, was kept alive in the associations of ex-soldiers, such as the Freikorps. The conditions imposed at the 1919 Versailles peace conference only exacerbated this feeling. France was given back the territory of Alsace-Lorraine, Belgium regained land east of the Maas river; Poland was granted territory in West Prussia, Poznan and Silesia; Lithuania gained land from the now isolated German territory of East

*Europe between the world wars,
showing newly-created states. By
the 1920s every state in Europe
was under democratic government;
by 1940 only four democracies
survived.*

Prussia; the area around the port of Danzig (Gdansk) and the Saar basin were given special status, and the Rhineland was made into a demilitarized buffer zone. In addition Germany was forced to agree to large-scale financial reparations to the victorious allies.

The German imperial borders created in 1871, together with the internal structures of the Austro-Hungarian empire, were dissolving and re-forming. Even before the 1918 armistice, parts of the old Austrian empire, including Czechoslovakia, Hungary and Yugoslavia, had declared themselves independent. In November 1918 Kurt Eisner declared Bavaria to be a 'socialist republic'. Three months later he was assassinated, and the communists who seized power (as they had done in Hungary too) declared the Bavarian Soviet Republic. The proto-fascist Freikorps fought back, engaging in open street battles with communist supporters in Munich and Berlin. In 1919, after an attempted uprising in Berlin, the communist leaders Karl Liebknecht and Rosa Luxemburg were arrested and murdered by a shadowy group of army officers who were probably Freikorps members. In May 1919 the Freikorps, with the support of 30,000 paramilitaries, overthrew the Bavarian Soviet government and put 1,000 men and women to death.

The proto-fascists fought with communists, but reserved their real hatred for liberal parliamentary democracy, which apparently allowed the weak to have power over the strong. With their odd mixture of Social Darwinism and cod mythology, these groups believed that the strong should prevail, and that the compromise of day-to-day politics should be replaced by strong and decisive action. Ernst Röhm, the original leader of the Nazi party storm troopers, said: 'I am an immature and wicked man, war and unrest appeal to me more than good bourgeois order.'

This was the background to the collapse of liberal politics in Germany – civil unrest, with right-wing groups fighting communists on the streets, an ineffective parliament, an autonomous army, and a nationalistic population humiliated and frustrated by their own and their country's position. Political parties began to emerge that articulated these frustrations and the desire for a new Germany. One of the strongest characteristics of these parties was their obsessive hatred of Jews. The elevation of the German nation to a semi-mystical entity involved the idealization of a pure and unsullied racial history. The nineteenth-century building of ethnic nation states in western Europe had put perceived outsiders at risk; after 1918, the same process affected eastern Europe, home to many more Jews than the west. Nevertheless, there were relatively few Jews in Germany and Austria in the early twentieth century – as late as 1933, when the stable German Jewish population had been joined by refugees from Poland and Russia, there were still only 500,000 Jews in Germany (i.e. 0.67 per cent of the population).

In the early twentieth century Jews had entered into mainstream life in Germany and Austria, gaining powerful social and political positions. There was a persistent undercurrent of anti-Semitism among the Austrian and German establishment, but Freud, Einstein, Mahler, Kraus and a host of others had been able to pursue distinguished careers in Berlin and Vienna. Recent research into Hitler's life in Vienna before 1913, for example, has shown that, far from being anti-Semitic, he had many Jewish friends in the men's hostel where he lived (Jews were prominent among the student and bourgeois population, many having come to Vienna for a secular education), and among the art-dealers who bought his paintings. It seems that the 1914–18 war completely altered Hitler's, and many of his countrymen's, outlook on the world, including their attitude to Jews. Heightened nationalism, Jewish refugees from the east, the number of Bolshevik leaders who were Jewish, the need for an easy scapegoat all conspired to inflame anti-Semitism in Germany – a country with a small Jewish population.

In 1921 Adolf Hitler, a disaffected ex-soldier, took control of the Munich-based National Socialist party, and in 1924 tried to rally Bavarian forces for a march on Berlin. His subsequent arrest, trial and brief imprisonment made him a national figure, but taught him that constitutional politics rather than military conflict was the route to power. In the mid- to late 1920s the German economy showed signs of recovery, hyper-inflation was controlled and life for ordinary Germans became easier. Investment flowed in from America – $3.9 billion came from Wall Street to German states and companies between 1923 and 1928 – and the future seemed benign. These were fallow years for extremists – membership of the Nazi party shrank, and in the 1928 national election, when Hitler had been leader of the party for seven years, the Nazis polled just 2.6 per cent of the popular vote. For all his oratorical and organizational skills, Hitler had failed to impress the mass of German people.

The Wall Street Crash of 1929 and the subsequent Depression changed everything. American banks called in their loans and Germany became effectively bankrupt. Economic crisis brought political instability as coalitions of centrist parties formed and collapsed, and elections became more and more frequent. Simplistic solutions began to appeal once more – in the election of 1930 the Nazis received 18.3 per cent of the vote and the Communists 13.1 per cent.

In the early 1930s the atmosphere of danger and violence on the streets and in the bars and meeting halls of Germany increased dramatically. The Nazi party had over 100,000 members in paramilitary uniforms – more than the permitted manpower of the German army. In mid-1932 another coalition collapsed and an election was called for 31 July. This time the Nazis achieved 37.4 per cent of the vote, making them the largest party in the German parliament. The president of the republic, von Hindenburg, nevertheless refused to make Hitler chancellor, fearing a political catastrophe. In the subsequent November 1932 election the Nazi vote shrank to 32 per cent as, once again, the German economy began to improve – this might have been the beginning of the end of the Nazis as a major political force.

However, after the November 1932 election, a group of conservative politicians, officials, industrialists and bankers wrote to President von Hindenburg urging him to appoint Hitler as chancellor. In their eyes the continuing political chaos, with a succession of weak governments, was engendering economic instability and creating the conditions for a communist takeover. The following month the serving chancellor, Franz von Papen, struck a deal with Hitler, in which he agreed to be vice-chancellor (with secret instructions from Hindenburg to restrain the Nazis), with two other Nazis (Göring and Frick), apart from Hitler, in the cabinet. On 30 January 1933 Hitler was made chancellor of Germany. The apparatus of a modern state gave anyone who seized control of its centre immense and, provided they were determined enough, virtually uncontrollable power. Four weeks after taking office, Hitler used a fire in the Reichstag, the German parliament building, as a pretext to suppress all political opposition, to arrest communist sympathizers, and to assume dictatorial powers. Germany's days of democracy were over. When Hindenburg died the following year, Hitler became president as well as chancellor.

The 1930s were a good time for many Germans. Hitler's policy of forcing the unemployed to work building autobahns and other infrastructure had a beneficial effect on the economy. The German people were continually bombarded with anti-Semitic messages, but measures against Jews were welcomed by most; despite the small Jewish population, German people were quite prepared to believe that all bankers, plutocrats and bureaucrats and most lawyers, teachers and doctors were Jewish, and that society would benefit if they were held back. In 1935 the Nuremberg Laws were introduced, restricting Jews to certain occupations and forbidding marriage with gentile Germans. International disapproval was blunted by the Jim Crow laws operating in the south of the United States, which similarly outlawed inter-racial marriage, and by the racially based colonial policies of Britain, France and other European nations. When Hitler explicitly pointed to these examples, this was not a case of twisted logic; Nazism arose in an era in which all white races considered themselves superior. Hitler's prestige with the German people increased through his reoccupation of the Rhineland in 1936, the Berlin Olympics of the same year, and his triumphant entry to a delirious Austria in the spring of 1938. Hitler was giving the German people everything they wanted and if there had to be a little unpleasantness to the Jews along the way, then so be it.

In November 1938 the situation of Germany's Jews, already restricted and denigrated, became much worse. The excuse was the assassination on 7 November of Ernst vom Rath, a German diplomat in Paris. On 9 November Nazi storm troopers destroyed Jewish property and synagogues and beat, arrested and murdered Jews in towns and cities across Germany. Around 400 Jews were killed in what became known as *Kristallnacht*. Many Germans were shocked at the wanton destruction and violence, even at this stage of Nazi rule; but others wanted the Jews to move out of Germany.

Hitler's racial policies were not confined to persecution of the Jews. Germany was an ethnic nation, its people superior to others through the logic of biology. While the Jews were the internal enemy, the great external threat was the Soviet Union. Russia was communist, its revolution had been led by Jews, and its people were Slavs, a race that was inferior to the Germanic Aryans. Russia was also the perfect place for the German people to expand into. The coming war was fuelled, above all, by Hitler's desire to see a historic struggle between Germany and the Soviet Union for the mastery of Europe. Once German forces had pushed their way into Czechoslovakia in 1938, only Poland stood between Germany and the Soviet border. On 31 March 1939 the British and French guaranteed Poland's borders. Hitler did not want to fight on two fronts, and could not invade Poland until he knew how the Soviets would react. In August 1939 Germany signed a non-aggression pact with Stalin (the pay-off for the Soviets was a slice of eastern Poland) and on 1 September 1939 invaded Poland. Within two days Europe was at war.

Hitler was not interested in making Germany a powerful country at the centre of Europe; instead he was consumed by the desire for continual conflict. War, he decided, would be the crucible in which the soul of the German people would be re-forged. While military leaders, even in Germany, were much more cautious about war than they had been in 1914, Europe saw the return of the civilian soldier, the political leader who liked to dress in uniform. Mussolini was the archetype and Hitler followed suit. Hitler's strategy was gradually to reduce the influence of the army's high command until he was controlling every aspect of military warfare and using the generals simply as technical experts. This was a reverse of 1914, when the military had taken control of political foreign policy, but the result was much the same: there were no foreign policy objectives that could be decided in open argument, simply a series of military campaigns that became the reason for their own existence.

Just as developments in artillery and small arms had given birth to the trench system, so new inventions made it obsolete. In the decades since 1918 the internal combustion engine, paved roads, tanks, lorries, aircraft, submarines and radio equipment had all improved beyond recognition, as had methods of manufacturing vehicles, equipment and ammunition. Military planners in Germany devised small, technically trained groups of men working in tanks, submarines, aircraft and mobile artillery batteries, all linked by radio communications. The key to the astonishing success of the *Blitzkrieg* (lightning war) was speed of attack, coordinated through instant communication. The results are well known: the Polish air force was destroyed on the first day, its army was defeated in five weeks; in April 1940 German forces overran Denmark and Norway, allowing Sweden to remain neutral provided it supplied iron ore to the Reich; having bombed Rotterdam to rubble, Germany took over the Low Countries in 18 days; in May 1940 German forces moved out of the Ardennes forest and reached the North Sea at Abbeville on the 19th, cutting off the British and French forces to the north; by 4 June the remnants of the British Expeditionary Force had been evacuated from Dunkirk and the remaining French forces taken out of combat; on 17 June the French government sued for peace and on the 25th agreed an armistice. In three months Hitler had taken over western continental Europe; all he had to do was wait for the British to sue for peace and thereby keep the United States out of the war. When no peace treaty was offered, Hitler began, in September 1940, to bomb London. More than 13,000 Londoners were killed in the Blitz but there was no surrender. In the end the loss of bombers persuaded Hitler that he could not defeat Britain from the air, and he turned his attention to the east.

To the German army and the German people it seemed that Hitler was a miracle-worker. The defeat of France was immensely popular, and everything that Hitler had told them so far had turned out to be true. By the end of 1940 most Germans would have believed anything he said, and followed him anywhere. Hitler's attack on the Soviet Union in June 1941 was intended to be swift and decisive. *Blitzkrieg* worked well in the early part of the Soviet campaign, but the eastern front turned into a different kind of war altogether. The lack of paved roads slowed down the logistical support, so that advanced troops were always in danger of being stranded. More ominously, the German army, which had treated French and British troops with respect, showed little regard for Soviet soldiers or civilians. Soviet soldiers were often shot trying to surrender, and of five million taken prisoner, three million died. This was not a programme carried out by political agents within the military; it was one army's treatment of another. Between 1941 and 1945, 20 million Soviet citizens were to die at the hands of German forces.

We have been brought up with these appalling facts but we do not often register them. War in Europe had become a murderous pursuit in which glory, honour and brutality merged in a lethal combination. Civilized Europeans eased the path of brutality to others by convincing themselves that their enemies were inferior, dangerous and uncivilized. The extermination of such people was their duty to humanity. German soldiers had been told that Russians were barbarians who would gladly murder them at the first chance. They believed it and took pre-emptive revenge.

By preventing Hitler from winning a quick victory, the Soviet Union ensured his final defeat. Soviet industry was rebuilt in the east and began to churn out the tanks, aircraft, ammunition and supplies to equip its numerically superior forces. In 1942 German forces pushed ever deeper into Russia, and towards the oil-fields of the Caspian. In August 1942 the German 6th Army reached the outskirts of the city of Stalingrad on the southern steppe, supported by Romanians and Italians. As Stalingrad held out, Marshal Zhukov edged his forces around the German flanks and then, in November, closed the noose. By February 1943, after three months of fighting street by street and house by house, the German commander was forced to surrender and close to a million soldiers were taken prisoner. The determination of the Soviet troops was decisive as the night-time temperature in Stalingrad in February reached minus 44° C. One million lives were lost, but Stalingrad showed that the Germans were not, after all, invincible. When news of the victory flashed around the world, it was the beginning of the end. Within a year of Stalingrad, Soviet troops were forging west. The Americans and British became desperate to invade France to open a second European front. By early 1944, with Italy out of the conflict, the talk was of shortening the war, rather than working out how to win it. Allied forces invaded France in June 1944 and Soviet soldiers finally reached Berlin in early May 1945.

The Nazis wanted to take over Europe for ideological, not strategic reasons. One strand of their ideology began to be realized during the course of 1941, when the Nazi party and German government developed a firm policy to murder all of Europe's Jews. The policy was codified at a meeting held on 20 January 1942, at a villa on the shores of Lake Wannsee near Berlin. One copy of the minutes of the meeting, known as the Wannsee Protocol, survived and was discovered by United States officials in 1947.

Before 1939 the Nazis had restricted Jewish activity and encouraged Jewish emigration from Germany. But as Germany occupied larger and larger areas of Europe, more Jews came under their control, and with virtually every European country involved in the war, there was nowhere left for the Jews to go. (At one time, the island of Madagascar was cited as a possible destination, but this was ruled out once the British had control of the Suez Canal.) The 'Jewish problem' was demonstrated most clearly in Poland, which became a vast laboratory in which Nazi racial ideas were put into practice. The plan was for all the ethnic Poles to be moved to a sector in the east, while German peoples from Lithuania and Latvia and the Ukraine were moved into the west. This left the problem of what to do with the Polish Jews; the Nazis moved them into particular sectors of Polish cities until a decision was made. But no one did decide, and so the ghettos – in Warsaw, Lodz, Cracow and elsewhere – lived on, becoming ever more crowded with less and less food to go round. While the Polish Jews stayed in their ghettos, the German army pushed on, occupying vast areas of eastern Europe and the Soviet Union with large Jewish populations. And still there was no answer to the 'Jewish problem'.

In *Mein Kampf,* Hitler had described the Jew as a rat, a maggot and a bacillus, and in speeches in the 1930s he mentioned extermination and gassing. We might expect a direct order from Hitler to have begun the mass murder of European Jews, but no such order has ever been found, and despite the importance of anti-Semitism to the Nazi party, no single person or agency was put in charge of the Jewish question; the historian Raul Hilberg compiled a list of 27 different agencies with some involvement. Representatives of many of these agencies met at Wannsee in 1942, but even the minutes of that meeting are unclear about who was actually in charge of implementing the policy.

Historians have wondered whether this vagueness was a deliberate insurance against future incrimination, but recent work by Ian Kershaw has revealed another explanation. After the war every Nazi party official claimed to have been following orders in a system of apparent rigid hierarchy, yet at the pinnacle of the system Hitler himself gave very few orders, did very little instructing and virtually no administrative work. The promulgation, implementation and administration of policy in all areas, including the treatment of Jews, seemed to emerge without policy statements or instructions being handed down from the top. We are used to thinking of a Nazi machine, a totalitarian system of terrifying efficiency – how could this be squared with the evidence?

In his writings Hitler showed a remarkable obsession with applying Darwin's ideas to the problems of human society: 'Men dispossess one another, and one perceives that, at the end of it all, it is always the stronger who triumphs. Is that not the reasonable order of things? If it were otherwise nothing good would ever have existed. If we did not respect the laws of nature, imposing our will by the right of the stronger, a day would come when the wild animals would once again devour us . . .'

Hitler applied, or rather allowed, the doctrine of 'survival of the fittest' to the Nazi party and then to Germany as a whole. Rather than dictating who should occupy which position in the party, he let his subordinates fight among themselves to see who would take control of different functions – the best-suited would, by whatever methods he chose, win out over the others. The structure as well as the personnel of the party would be decided this way too; whoever won positions of power could organize things as they wished. Hitler had the power to limit the ambitions of his inferiors if he chose, but he could do this because he had won the struggle for ultimate power.

Personal and party documents have shown that Nazi officials felt that their role was, as one put it, 'to work towards the Führer'. This meant that their task was to study what the Führer said or wrote and take action according to their own interpretation and circumstances. A 1935 memo from Nazi HQ read: 'Herr Hitler takes the view on principle that it is not the job of the party leadership to "appoint" party leaders . . . the most effective fighter in the National Socialist movement is the man who wins respect for himself as leader through his own achievements. You yourself say in your letter that almost all the members follow you. Then why don't you take over the leadership of the branch?'

The outcome was a confusion of competing interests, and a

widespread desire to please those who had the power to destroy you. Hitler had no need to give a specific order, he only had to allow the correct interpretation to be put on his thoughts – his subordinates would then take the required actions. While further down the hierarchy some officials were issuing direct instructions, many were using their own initiative to bring about the Führer's overall wishes. Almost no one was 'just following orders'; all were interpreting situations for their own benefit.

At this point we return to the most perplexing and important question of twentieth-century western history – how did a civilized country like Germany slide towards not only war, but a genocide of unimaginable scale and cruelty? While the members of the Nazi party followed Hitler's philosophy, what happened to the remainder of the population? How did the small core of the Nazi party make the people of Germany do their bidding? Did they terrorize them into submission, or blind them with propaganda, or appeal to some pre-existing dark instinct? There was certainly an atmosphere of fear and helplessness in the Nazi years in Germany, but the grip of organizations like the Gestapo on the German population was illusory. Of all the 'political crimes' prosecuted by the authorities in Germany between 1933 and 1945, only 10 per cent were actually discovered by the Gestapo, with another 10 per cent passed to them by the police or party officials, leaving 80 per cent reported to the Gestapo by the ordinary civilian population of Germany. Surviving Gestapo files are full of denunciations by members of the public. In one example from Würzburg, a Jewish wine-dealer was denounced for having relations with a German widow, but the Gestapo file shows that nothing was done until the complainants put pressure on the Gestapo and the local party to take action. In August 1933 the SS finally frogmarched the wine-dealer to the local police station with a placard tied around his neck. Amazingly, the placard is still in the Gestapo files. In neat letters it reads, 'This is a Jewish male, Herr Müller. I have been living in sin with a German woman.' Herr Müller was kept in jail despite having broken no law. He left Germany in 1934.

Recent philosophers and historians have argued that the immense evil of the Holocaust, while eventually implemented as a conscious policy, grew out of the thousands of small acts of selfishness committed by German people in the 1930s and 1940s. These acts often sprang from minor decisions based on getting some advantage in life, while being inconsiderate of the effect on others. The denunciations made by people against their fellow citizens undoubtedly gave them a feeling of power, and provided a way of connecting them to the regime, while the sheer number of reports allowed the Nazi officials to believe that the German people would support them in whatever actions they took against social undesirables of any kind – Jews, gypsies, Slavs, the mentally and physically handicapped.

When the German translation of his book *If This Is a Man* was in progress, Primo Levi, an Italian Jew who survived captivity in Auschwitz, felt a desire to understand the German people as a whole: 'Not that handful of high-ranking culprits [tried at Nuremberg], but them, the people, those I had seen from close up, those from among whom the SS militia were recruited, and also those others, those who had believed, who not believing had kept silent, who did not have the frail courage to look into our eyes, throw us a piece of bread, whisper a human word.' This was the source of Levi's greatest perplexity. He understood the difficulties of open rebellion, though he did not excuse the lack of it. But he felt the enormity of the lack of small gestures of kindness and concern. These would not have cost much to confer and each would have built a bridge between the giver and receiver. Without these bridges there was no hope for the Jews.

Photographs of jackbooted thugs and images of Hitler's apparent buffoonery might persuade us that Nazism was a product of the uneducated and the stupid, or a rebellion by the uneducated and marginalized against the clever and sophisticated people who normally run societies. But more recent work has shown how academics, civil servants, town-planners and demographers worked out detailed plans and projections for the murder of Europe's Jewish people. These were not mad, evil fanatics but sober, learned men and women, going about their professions. Most did not join the Nazi party, but they too, like the complainants to the Gestapo, sought status and career advancement. Indeed, the Holocaust itself was carried out by some of the cleverest people in Germany. The 300 or so officials who led the Reich Security Office (RSHA), and had the most influence in devising and implementing the Nazi policies of genocide and persecution, had been part of the student cohort of the 1920s, which was vehement in its rejection of Versailles and the Weimar government. These clever young people had turned away from democracy and kicked Jews out of student bodies long before Hitler came to power. When the time came they were on hand to put Hitler's aspirations into practice and to solve the 'Jewish question'.

*   *   *

Rumours of extermination camps had swirled around Europe from 1942 onwards, but only with the advance of Allied troops was the full horror of the camps exposed. Reporters in the field wrote of the scarcely believable sights they came across. On 15 April 1945 the concentration camp at Belsen was liberated by the British army. Patrick Gordon-Walker broadcast a description of the camp, its 30,000 corpses and 35,000 people on the verge of death, and its children's hut piled high with small bodies, to audiences in the United States. His report ended, 'To you at home, this is one camp. There are many more. This is what you are fighting. None of this is propaganda. This is the plain and simple truth.'

At the war's end Thomas Mann went on German radio to tell the nation what had been found at Auschwitz. Many chose to disbelieve it, but they were soon confronted with the evidence. The Holocaust is generally described as a uniquely evil episode in human history. Its scale and its location in the heart of civilized Europe were certainly unique, but the attempted genocide of Europe's Jews did not emerge from nowhere. For centuries white-skinned European Christians had regarded themselves as superior to other races, and entitled to destroy others in the name of their civilization; in the previous 150 years (and before), people of different colours and customs had been routinely subject to torture, mutilation and mass murder for no other reason than their difference; by the early twentieth century it had become routine to regard others (including the uneducated masses) as not only biologically inferior, but as an insidious threat to the health of European civilization – and to support this view with apparently rational pseudo-scientific theories. Slavery, colonization, legalized segregation were all based on an assumption of racial superiority, and a fear of the oppressed, that pre-dated and has outlasted the uncovering of the Holocaust.

These prevailing assumptions make the achievement of 1930s America, and its leader Franklin Roosevelt, all the more remarkable. A society in danger of losing its generosity of spirit, the United States, like Germany, was hit hard by the Depression. But the country avoided a potential drift into fascism and instead, inspired by Roosevelt's doctrine of mutual support, turned the other way, towards communal endeavour and a revitalized democracy. By the time Japan, a country that modelled itself on the militarized, nationalistic states of Europe, attacked Pearl Harbor in

1941, the United States had already placed itself on the side of the beleaguered liberal democracies. Hundreds of thousands of Americans willingly gave their lives not only to defeat Japan, but to re-establish constitutional government in Europe.

Nevertheless, even Roosevelt could not overcome the ingrained habits of many of his countrymen; segregation by race remained legal in the United States until the 1950s. Nor was America unusual – in 1948 Europeans in South Africa introduced apartheid, based on the classification and separation of races, and within a few years of the closing of Auschwitz, signs reading 'No Blacks or Irish' were commonplace in British boarding-house windows. This kind of petty, unthinking cruelty brings us back, once again, to our central question about the acquiescence of the German people. There is no facile cause-and-effect explanation for this. Historians, psychologists and philosophers struggle to find the key or the grand formula that will enable us to prevent such a thing from happening again. But there is no magic solution, or any easy lessons that we are willing or able to learn. We maintain the same attachment to the nation state that has a monopoly of violence and gives extraordinary power to a few men; we continue to develop technological instruments that are capable of killing thousands if not millions; we still believe that Nazism was a regression to some kind of tribal, bestial behaviour and that human progress will help to prevent its recurrence; and we still regard our civilization as the model that the whole world should follow. But taking our cue from Dietrich Bonhoeffer's comments on page 428, we must consider seriously the possibility that the prevailing beliefs and 'traditional ethical systems' of European civilization, its universal solutions, its conviction that history has some moral meaning, its assumptions of superiority and its promotion of a mystical entity under threat from within and without, all contributed to the German people withdrawing the small acts of kindness and compassion that would have saved the Jewish people from the Nazis. Many German people did reach out the hand of kindness, and did save people from the death camps, but the overwhelming majority, as Primo Levi reminded us, did not. It is the withdrawal of human compassion and kindness in the name of some greater cause that is the real danger that western humanity, with its restless search for significance, continually faces.

THE POST-WAR WORLD

From Social Cohesion to Global Marketplace

THE mere six decades since the end of the Second World War have barely given people who have lived through them time to acquire a historical perspective. Personal memories, day-to-day routine, the small triumphs and disasters of normal existence, interrupted by family tragedies and celebrations, quarrels and reconciliations, all interfere with a dispassionate view of the overarching themes of post-war history. But this of course is how it has always been. The grand strategies of geopolitics, the floods and ebbs of cultural and political change, the renaissances and reformations have always been played out in the messy, emotional journeys of millions of human lives. Written history has enabled us to give structure to the past, but the times in which we have lived should make us aware how life goes on beneath the horizon of history.

Nevertheless, with the benefit of a little hindsight, we can see certain patterns in the story of the western world since 1945. Most obviously this history comprises two settled phases, with a long period of transition in between. In the first phase, lasting roughly from 1945 to 1965, the countries of the west settled into a consensus built around a strong state directing the economic and social needs of its citizens, a network of national economies tied together through fixed exchange rates and controls on movement of capital and goods, and a military alliance dedicated to the restraint of communism. Western European countries, with their state ownership of public utilities and strategic industries, and their occasional socialist sympathies, seemed radically different from their American partners, but in reality the United States federal government put massive indirect support into its key industries, while

Europe was happy to lock itself into an American-led economic system
and military alliance. The institutional politics of this first phase were
largely consensual (this was the celebrated, or notorious, 'post-war
consensus') while the informal opposition was largely limited to radical
socialist, Marxist or communist groups.

The second phase began in roughly 1980 (though the key to its beginning happened in 1973, and its shoots began to show as early as the
mid-1950s) and has continued to the present. In this phase the inherent
value of opening up all aspects of society, and all parts of the world,
to private enterprise and to open competition and free markets has
been taken for granted. The free flow of capital is intended to encourage
efficiency by allowing money to go to wherever in the world it will be
most effectively used. The western military alliance against communism
has been replaced by the concept of 'coalitions of the willing', formed
for specific purposes, while the size and capability of the United States'
armed services dwarfs all others. Institutional politic revolves around
the different ways in which free trade and open markets can be brought
into being and managed, while informal opposition, or compensation,
tends towards promoting the value of non-tangible assets, such as
quality of life, community, environment and religion. The case for open
markets is led by the Anglo-Saxon world, in which the 'Washington
model' has the full backing of the world's most powerful economy and
its military. Other western countries have found it more and more difficult to resist, with those that flourished under the first phase (notably
Japan and Germany) suffering from their reluctance to adapt.

The transition period between these two phases was chaotic and
bitter and yet was the most politically intoxicating and culturally
creative period of the recent past. This might surprise us if we had not
already seen how cultural life is galvanized by, and often in opposition
to, social change. The western world became clearly defined in the first
post-war phase, and in the second it set out to take over the world.
But in the process, the meaning of western civilization was thrown into
doubt. This is the process I will explore in this chapter.

In 1945 the continent of Europe lay in ruins. Its cities were devastated, its industries destroyed, millions of its people homeless and
displaced. The relief that the war was over was tempered by physical and moral devastation. As the full horrors of Nazi-occupied
Europe came to light, the victors and vanquished surveyed a scene of

unparalleled degradation – here in the heart of Europe, apparently the most civilized place on earth, humanity had reached its lowest point. Nevertheless, the urgent need for action overcame the sense of shock at what had gone before. Starvation, disease, homelessness, and the need for the western allies to plan physical, political and social reconstruction were compounded by the resurgence of communism. Soviet armies had driven the Nazis from their own country, and liberated Bulgaria, Romania, Poland, Hungary, Czechoslovakia, Yugoslavia and the eastern part of Germany. There were signs that some countries in the west, particularly Italy, France and Greece, might voluntarily become communist as an alternative to the nationalism, depression and war that capitalism had bequeathed.

The key to the recovery of western Europe lay with the United States. After the 1914–18 war American armies had been disbanded, and the country had maintained trade barriers against its European allies throughout the 1930s; in 1945 it was possible that America would go back into its shell. But while its relative isolation had, in earlier times, benefited American industry, once it became the world's dominant economy, the United States could only benefit from greater engagement with the world. There was another point too – if the sacrifice of United States troops was to mean anything (around 300,000 Americans had died, with another 750,000 injured) then the people of western Europe needed protection from takeover by totalitarian regimes, and that meant making western Europe prosperous as quickly as possible. The situation in Japan was similarly in the hands of the United States, where the atomic bombs dropped on Hiroshima and Nagasaki forced an unconditional surrender and demonstrated the awesome, worldwide power of the American military. While Hiroshima remained a symbol of the human cost of nuclear weapons, the United States showed immense vision in helping its defeated enemy to build a peaceful society.

In 1947 President Truman and his secretary of state George Marshall proposed an aid package of $13 billion to 16 western European countries. A good proportion of the Marshall Plan money was, naturally enough, used to buy American goods, since theirs was the only industrial economy able to fill orders. American goods flooded eastwards and economic ties between western Europe and America became ever stronger. The Marshall Plan was sold to the Republican-dominated Congress as a bulwark against communism, and when Stalin refused the offer of help (and prevented any eastern European countries from accepting it), Europe was formally divided in two. Truman's support for anti-communist regimes in Greece and Turkey was the beginning of the so-called Truman Doctrine, which divided the world and effectively defined the west as 'the free world', with the United States as its leader.

The deterioration in diplomatic relations turned into military confrontation – for 40 years the two blocs, with an ever-increasing amount of armoury on each side, faced each other across the Iron Curtain. The real possibility emerged that humanity might destroy itself when, in 1949, the Soviet Union's explosion of its first hydrogen bomb led to an arms race based on the doctrine of Mutually Assured Destruction (aptly abbreviated to MAD). The fate of humanity rested on the belief that no leader would start a nuclear war that would destroy his own country. This was an extraordinary time in the history of Europe. Western European citizens were able to travel freely almost anywhere in the world, except to the eastern part of their own continent. The post-war generation in the west grew up assuming that countries like Romania and Poland, and cities such as Prague and Dresden, were for ever beyond their reach, locked away behind impenetrable borders. Visits to the east were restricted and supervised by government agents, and so hardly anyone went.

The anti-communism that had helped the Marshall Plan through Congress began to be an ingrained part of western, and in particular American, life. Fear of the Soviet Union fed increasing paranoia about communist subversion from within America itself. In 1947 Republicans in Congress put the House Un-American Activities Committee on a permanent footing, while President Truman, fearful of being outflanked, ordered a 'loyalty review' of all three million federal government employees. In 1948 a former member of the State Department, Alger Hiss, was arrested as a Russian spy, and five years later an apparently innocuous New York couple, Julius and Ethel Rosenberg, were executed for passing atomic secrets to the Soviets. Communist agents were, it seemed, everywhere. In 1950 and 1952 Congress passed bills banning activities that would 'contribute to the establishment of a totalitarian dictatorship' and blocking entry to the United States to anyone who had ever belonged to a 'totalitarian group'. Suspicion and the fear of falling under suspicion infected every soul in the country. In 1952 and 1956 Americans elected the reliable conservative Dwight D. Eisenhower to the presidency and, in Hugh Brogan's memorable phrase, 'A grey

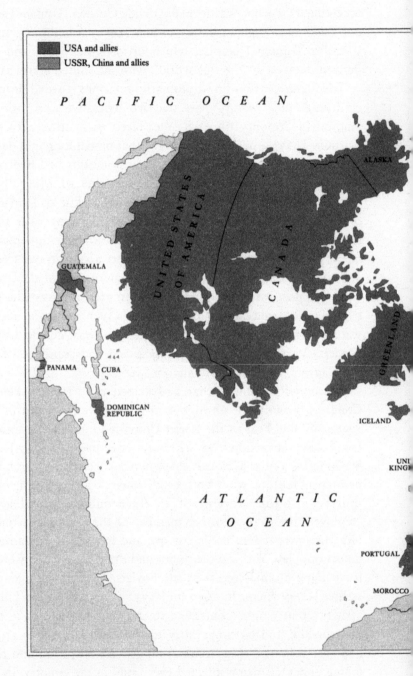

USA and allies
USSR, China and allies

The Cold War.

fog of timid conformity settled over American middle-class life.' In desperately trying to fend off totalitarian communism, the land of the free was allowing itself to be shackled by its own thought police.

In the decades of the Cold War, it became a strategy within American politics to imply that tolerance of diversity, willingness to negotiate, liberalization of social laws, and avoidance of war were somehow non-American. In foreign policy any enemy of communism, no matter how unsavoury, was given American support. The Truman Doctrine allowed America to get involved anywhere in the world, and fatally confused what was good for America with what was good for the world. But the United States was also instrumental in setting up the United Nations and committed itself to supporting and working through multilateral institutions. The balance between exporting American values and working multilaterally became the crucial test of American foreign policy.

Eisenhower managed for the most part to keep the United States out of foreign entanglements – including ending the Korean war in 1953 and coming down hard on the 1956 Suez débâcle. But foreign policy was also driven by the concerns of American corporations; in 1953 the CIA engineered a coup in Guatemala to preserve the national monopoly of the American-owned United Fruit Company, and when in the same year Dr Mossadegh deposed the autocratic Shah of Iran, the CIA and MI6 intervened to bring him back to power in order to preserve American oil interests.

In 1945 Americans had an understandable fear of slipping back into the economic depression of the pre-war years. But the industrial effort that effectively sealed the outcome of the war also secured a lasting economic boom. In the four years of their participation in the war, the United States produced 3 million aircraft, 87,000 ships, 370,000 artillery pieces, 100,000 tanks and armoured vehicles and 2.4 million trucks. The federal government spent $350 billion on the war – double what all previous governments had spent in total since independence. Between 1939 and 1945 the United States Gross National Product doubled, civilian employment increased by 20 per cent, and corporate profits and wages rose significantly. Certain parts of the country did particularly well – aircraft and electrical production was concentrated in the west, particularly in California, which received 10 per cent of federal wartime spending. A region known for its agriculture and movies became an industrial dynamo.

As well as direct military spending, the 1944 GI Bill of Rights gave $13 billion for returning soldiers to enter college, enrol in training programmes or set up in business; while the government eased taxes and most people cashed in their war bonds. There was suddenly an awful lot of money around, and with an industrial sector with huge unfilled capacity, America found itself in a boom economy. The 1950s was a partial repeat of the 1920s. Legislation curtailed workers' rights, while the revival of consumerism engendered political conservatism. In 1952 Eisenhower immediately signalled the return of big business to politics; Secretary of State John Foster Dulles was a corporate lawyer, his deputy was a former head of Quaker Oats, and the Secretary of Defense, Charles Wilson, was formerly head of General Motors, while Edward Bernays reappeared as a government adviser.

In the post-war decades, discoveries and inventions made in the 1920s, 1930s and during the war itself began to be turned into practical innovations that would alter the lives of western people. Antibiotics, television, jet engines, rocket technology, computers, quantum mechanics, nuclear fission, DNA, electronics, materials, metallurgy and plastics were all, in the short and medium term, to feed into a technological revolution of western life. Organizational refinements proved just as influential as technological changes. Mass production of cars had begun in America in the 1920s, but in the war years and after economies of scale, organizational efficiency and improved distribution networks combined with changing technology to make American industry and American corporations the economic powerhouse of the world.

The advertising techniques first introduced in the 1920s, in which consumers were sold happiness rather than goods, came to the fore. The booming economy made people feel that satisfying their own individual desires contributed to national prosperity. The countries that best learned the lessons of American success were Japan and Germany, the defeated nations of 1945. Faced with the urgent need to start anew, they were able to devise distinctive structures in which (in contrast to the United States) their national governments made a priority of strategically guiding investment in manufacturing industry.

The war gave American industry the chance to build a continent-sized infrastructure that pushed it beyond the reach of competition from the devastated continent of Europe. Just as government war spending revitalized American industry in the early 1940s, so federal-funded road schemes gave a huge boost to the automobile, construction and engineering industries in the 1950s and 1960s. By 1950 the United States had 39 per cent of the world's GDP, and built 80 per cent of the world's cars, while the Interstate Highway Act of 1956 committed the federal government to spending $35 billion over 14 years to build a national network of roads. The freeways signalled the end of the domination of rail; after the 1950s goods went by truck and people by car and bus. Car numbers increased vastly, making them ever cheaper to buy, while plentiful gasoline made them absurdly cheap to run. Growing prosperity meant that more homes were being built, but now that everyone (except the poor) had cars there was no need for them to be close to factories or offices or schools or shops. Homes and services spread out along highways. America was, after all, a vast country with enough empty space for everyone to have a decent-sized plot. There was no need for offices or shops to be grouped in one place either, so they began to move out of the old downtown areas and relocate on to highways where they were in easy reach of commuters and shoppers. The geographical size of a city was limited only by the distance a car-driver was willing to travel. The newly expanding cities like Los Angeles, Dallas-Fort Worth and Houston became more extensive than anything previously seen on earth, with vast networks of freeways connecting endless suburbs. American culture was no longer centred on settled towns and cities, but on cars, trucks and freeways, and on endless movement.

The development of motorized technology produced an enormous effect that began almost invisibly but, over the post-war period, brought on the disappearance of a central aspect of western life dating back 5,000 years. By the 1920s and 30s mechanized tractors, harvesters and other machinery were making small farmsteads in the United States redundant. After 1945 the machines got ever bigger, and so the fields and land holdings got bigger too. By the 1950s large machines were being put to work on the agricultural landscape of western Europe, first founded in Neolithic times. Ancient landscape features were routinely destroyed as the need for efficient production over-rode the customary relations of people and land.

At the same time agricultural communities, inheritors and custodians of customs that encouraged and celebrated communal working and living, became irrelevant. As George Evans showed in a series of intimate studies, before mechanization a whole village would turn out for hay-making, or harvesting or stone-picking, but afterwards a single tractor could do the work of 50 men, women and children. Farming became a solitary occupation and the meaning of village life was irrevocably altered.

The countries of western Europe each reacted differently to the victory of 1945, the task of rebuilding and the threat of communism. Nevertheless, democratic politics was universally established, and any surviving monarchies became ceremonial. (Only Spain and Portugal, both of whom had stayed out of the war, remained as quasi-fascist, non-democratic states.) A political consensus emerged, where national governments took a bigger role in the welfare of the population, as well as the running and management of the industrial economy, with essential industries and utilities taken into public ownership. The European state also enlarged its remit, adding the welfare of its people to its duties as a military protector and economic regulator. The mishmash of pre-war social provision was formalized into a 'welfare state'. Steady improvements in prosperity were welcomed by a generation that had known only depression and war and, after a brief flirtation with radical politics, western Europe, like the United States, settled into a period of political, social and cultural conformity. Having defeated an immense threat to the western world and its values, most people were content that civilization should consist of a return to the old ways.

The biggest break with the past was the abandonment of the strident nationalism that had brought catastrophe to the continent of Europe. Both French and German political leaders recognized the cycle of retribution that had marred their countries' relations, and set about building indissoluble ties. In April 1951 the European Coal and Steel Community, comprising France, Italy, West Germany, the Netherlands, Belgium and Luxembourg, was established and, through the work of French politicians Robert Schuman and Jean Monnet, was turned into an economic community covering all areas of trade, formalized in 1957 by the Treaty of Rome. In Britain's voluntary absence France and Germany formed an enduring partnership, building a vision of European integration.

Nationalism was subsumed in the formation of other international bodies, including the United Nations in 1948, and NATO in 1949. Even before the end of the war, the Bretton Woods agreement of 1944 tied the economic destinies of western countries together under an American umbrella. Harry Dexter-White and John Maynard Keynes devised an international system of finance based on the dollar, whose value was fixed against gold and against all the other major currencies.

The agreement, which also set up the International Monetary Fund, World Bank and International Trade Organization, was designed to create stability and growth and open up the world to greater trade. In reality it opened up the world to American capitalism.

Apart from multilateral cooperation and defence against communism, the other great international movement of the immediate post-war years was the retreat from empire. Any possible benefits were now outweighed by the unaffordable costs of policing increasingly assertive local populations, many of whom had fought for their imperial masters during the war. In 1947 India was granted independence from Britain, with Pakistan and Ceylon given status as separate states. Britain managed to extricate itself from the ensuing communal violence but was to become entangled in colonial wars in Malaya, Cyprus, Kenya and Egypt, while avoiding conflict in most of its other African and Caribbean colonies. In retrospect the biggest failure was in the Middle East, where Britain handed the mandate of Palestine to the UN in 1948, after being unable to resolve the claims of European Jews wanting a new homeland with the rights of the indigenous Palestinian population.

By 1946 French troops were already fighting rebellions in Algeria, Syria, Madagascar and Indo-China. After nine years of guerrilla warfare, the French army was lured into a trap at the remote outpost of Dien Bien Phu, and in 1954 France was forced to surrender North Vietnam to its people. An eight-year war of independence in Algeria came close to bringing down the French government, with independence finally granted in 1962.

The world might have hoped that Europeans would, in the light of the Nazi death camps, be reluctant to use violence for political ends. But torture and brutality were routinely used by the British army against the Mau Mau in Kenya, where detention camps were employed, and by French soldiers against the FLN in Algeria. By the 1970s the remainder of France's possessions, along with the Dutch, Belgian and, latterly, Portuguese empires, were liberated. Only a handful of small possessions were left from a set of empires that, only 40 years previously, had covered much of the world.

The western powers may have withdrawn from direct political control of the rest of the world, but their legacy and continuing influence was felt everywhere. Modern Europeans had no concept of governance beyond the centralized nation state; so as they withdrew from their colonies they created a host of new nations. Some were based on ethnic or religious groupings (India and Pakistan; Ireland); others combined different ethnic or religious groups (Hausa, Ibo and Yoruba in Nigeria; Kurds, Sunni and Shia Muslims in Iraq); in many, ethnic groups were divided among different states (Kurds in Iran, Iraq and Turkey); and in some the boundaries between states depended on the colonial powers (west Africa) or on the persuasive skills of local leaders (the division of Kuwait from Iraq). But in all cases the political structures were based on the relatively recent western concept of the nation state. This swept away any vestiges of the customary intricate ways of allowing and restraining authority, and instead handed enormous power to whichever individual or small group could control its centre.

Intimations of change and of challenge to the consensus of the immediate post-war years came first through cultural expression. After 1945 Europe was culturally as well as economically exhausted by the war; many of its artists had fled to America, while its institutions were physically destroyed. The catastrophe of the conflict and the genocidal murder of six million Jews left European artists with little to say. How was it possible to depict the war, and how was it possible to depict anything other than the war? For a decade European culture was lost in reminiscence of an earlier pre-war age, but in America, while conformity deadened mainstream culture, there was room for alternatives to flourish and for outsiders to hone their discordant skills before being 'discovered' by the mainstream. In the years from 1947 to 1960 Tennessee Williams and Arthur Miller produced a series of plays, including *All My Sons*, *Death of a Salesman*, *A Streetcar Named Desire* and *Sweet Bird of Youth,* that exposed the mismatch between the intricacies of personal and community life on the one hand, and the imperatives of social conformity and economic success on the other. At the same time New York filled with European refugee artists, and when Peggy Guggenheim's gallery, Art of This Century, opened in New York in 1942, abstract American painters like Jackson Pollock, Mark Rothko and Robert Motherwell were fêted in their own land. William de Kooning, an immigrant from Europe, living in a city of continually shifting form during a war that disoriented the world, explained that his work, with its slipping planes, visual ambiguities and lack of reference points, was a deliberate analogy of the sense of disorientation of mid-century America and the world. The immigrant's loss of anchorage was once again the touchstone for American cultural expression.

The spirit of the outsider who refuses to conform found expression in the work of Norman Mailer, Jack Kerouac and William Burroughs, all of whom stood in frank opposition to the mainstream values of American society; while intimations of rebellion were seen in movies like *The Wild One* (1953) and *Rebel Without a Cause* (1955). The aspirations of young Americans began to change; instead of wanting to be heroic like Gary Cooper, or sophisticated like Cary Grant, young men wanted to be sullen, inarticulate, authentic and earthy like Marlon Brando, James Dean or Paul Newman. The anti-hero was born.

But the most explosive expression of rebellion against mainstream American life came in popular music. By the mid-1950s the American popular song, based on sentimental love, was becoming stale and formulaic, its artists uninteresting and its infrastructure geared to commercial exploitation. But in African-American communities music was undergoing rapid change. The industrial boom of the 1940s brought more African-Americans to the cities from the rural south, many steeped in the musical culture of so-called country blues, played on acoustic guitars and harmonicas. But in Chicago and Detroit and Cleveland, with jobs in construction and factories, and with a few dollars to spend on a night out, African-Americans did not want to hear how hard life was; they wanted music to drink and dance to. New electric guitars were coupled with the traditional brass instruments of jazz and swing to produce a new kind of sound, while the lyrics became more sexually explicit, wittier and more self-consciously sophisticated. Joe Turner, Muddy Waters, Wynonie Harris, Julia Lee, Fats Domino and Little Richard, among many others, gave their music an extraordinary, unbelievable energy. This was music for adults who wanted a good time, this was rhythm and blues, or jump jive, or 'race music'. Whatever you called it, it was the most instantly intoxicating, joyous, infectious, delirious sound anyone had ever heard.

For African-Americans rhythm and blues was an expression of cultural self-confidence; but for white teenagers, rock and roll, the commercial derivative of rhythm and blues, was an escape from conformity and tedium. In the mid-1950s, the young of white affluent America were frankly bored, and in need of exciting diversion, so long as it stayed within safe bounds. Through Elvis Presley, a white southerner steeped in gospel and race music, black music hit the heart of white America.

Rock and roll music, and the international stardom of Presley, was to form the vanguard for the spread of American culture around the world. Rock and roll made everything European seem dreary and old-fashioned; from the 1950s on, 'modern' meant American. While European culture had become inward-looking and over-literary, American culture had the ability to speak for those who could not speak, and to articulate the life of the inarticulate. It swept the world precisely because it seemed to speak for everyone; the restless questing of the American immigrant suited the disorientation felt by the whole world, and the American landscape, where every town is the same and everyone is just passing through, became the universal backdrop of an increasingly mobile society. America was everywhere and anywhere you wanted it to be. Nevertheless, the commercial instincts of American industry triumphed over the rebellion of rock and roll. By 1960 the untamed beast had been neutered and American popular culture returned, at least temporarily, to bland compliance.

Signs of change in European culture in the 1950s were spurred by the need to confront the past, by the flashes of light coming across the Atlantic, and by impatience with the conformity of post-war society. While much European culture remained tied to traditional forms – novels, poetry and theatre – European cinema began to find a distinctive voice, principally through Italian and French auteur-directors like Rossellini, de Sica, Antonioni, Fellini, Carné, Truffaut and Chabrol, and the Swedish film-maker Ingmar Bergman. British cinema, living on light comedies and remakes of classic literature, was given a new edge and direction by Lindsay Anderson and by Karel Reisz, whose 1959 film *Saturday Night and Sunday Morning* made the lives of working people at a time of impending change a suitable subject for cinematic art.

By the 1960s, citizens of western countries began to shake off their fear of change. The new generation of politicians they elected, such as John Kennedy, Harold Wilson and Willy Brandt, reflected a new optimism; the contrast between the dull but steady Eisenhower and the dynamic, dashing Kennedy, and between the patrician Douglas-Home and the state-educated Wilson could hardly have been greater. Economic recovery in Europe allowed the full spirit of American consumerism to crash into a continent used to thrift and making do. In Britain in particular the social, cultural and commercial energies of American life suddenly exploded into a hierarchical, tight-lipped, authoritarian society. A surge of electricity went through British life, producing an outburst of conflict and creativity and cultural energy. The resulting social changes were so extraordinary that for a few years in the mid-1960s, the country became a goldfish bowl for the world to peer into. Conflicts between the generations, between tradition and modernity and between authority and freedom, made for an intoxicating sense of individual and collective drama that was captured in novels, films, plays, television and popular music.

The music of the Beatles, the Rolling Stones, the Who, the Kinks, and a host of others who all soaked up the music of black America became, in a world of global communications, a global phenomenon, reinvigorating American popular culture in the process. Mass-produced record players and transistor radios spread the message of irreverence, novelty, personal expression and disdain of authority to an eager audience across the world. While much pop music was meaningless and artificial, a small number of musicians managed to make the three-minute single into a sublime form of cultural expression – simultaneously celebrating the cacophony of mass urban life, while yearning for the individual solace of romantic love; conveying the excitement of a new world, while evoking the profound sense of loss at the passing of the old.

This sense of a society undergoing transformation was reinforced by the instigation of one of the most remarkable pieces of popular art ever devised. On 9 December 1960, Granada Television began broadcasting *Coronation Street*, a soap opera of working-class life devised and written by Tony Warren. The programme was revolutionary in its portrayal of the day-to-day lives of ordinary people, and gave its audience a reminder of the drama, humour and sheer vitality of apparently mundane human life, at a time of immense social change.

The social conservatism that followed the war was partially dissolved by the new spirit of optimism, and by the continual revelations of official corruption, incompetence and self-interest. Scepticism towards authority was matched by increasing tolerance; western governments responded by outlawing racial discrimination and legalizing homosexual practices, and while new immigrants to Europe did not see racial prejudice disappear, its most obvious manifestations were made illegal. Educational opportunities were also widened as economic prosperity allowed governments to expand higher education and remove selection procedures based on pre-war beliefs about class. Social mobility increased, though this came about not because the old patricians surrendered their positions, but because the professions and white-collar work increased vastly at the expense of manufacturing.

For Europeans the 1960s are remembered as a time of social liberation, but from 1963 to 1974 the United States, the leading cultural and political force in the west, was in a state of continual crisis. Two issues, civil rights for African-Americans and the Vietnam war, came to dominate American life in the 1960s, and their combination brought the country close to breakdown.

The policy of separate but equal development for whites and blacks in the south had always been a sham; in the 1950s it was exposed to the world. In the age of global communication, photographers and film crews from New York, Los Angeles, London, Paris, Frankfurt or Milan arrived to take pictures of 'Whites Only' or 'Coloreds Only' signs on drinking fountains and railroad waiting rooms in Birmingham, Alabama, or Jackson, Mississippi. Once America went out into the world, its dirty secret was secret no more; segregation became a severe embarrassment to the leader of the so-called free world.

By this time African-Americans, through their wartime experiences and their role in the industrial economy, were more self-confident, beginning to believe that America belonged to them (after all, they had fought and worked for it) as much as anyone else. They began to use a combination of coordinated action and legal challenges to bring equal rights. In 1954 the National Association for the Advancement of Colored People (NAACP) took up the case of Oliver Brown, whose daughter Linda had been refused entry to a nearby whites-only school in the state of Kansas. When the case reached the Supreme Court, segregation of public schools was ruled illegal under the constitution. Chief Justice Earl Warren then overturned the 60-year-old ruling of Plessey vs. Ferguson and outlawed segregation of public facilities. On 1 December 1955, in Montgomery, Alabama, Rosa Parks was arrested after refusing to give her bus seat to a white man. A black boycott of the bus company was led by a local preacher, Martin Luther King, while the Supreme Court told the company to change its rules. The twin tactics of mass action and legal challenge had brought significant results. Nevertheless, by 1963 only 9 per cent of the south's school districts had been desegregated, while violence and intimidation of blacks prevented them exercising their rights to education, voting and public facilities. President Kennedy hoped that getting African-Americans to vote would change the politics of the south, but whites used every means they could think of, including murder, to prevent black voter registration. In 1962 it took 3,000 federal troops to get James Meredith, the first black student to enrol at the University of Mississippi, into the building.

Until 1963, black civil rights remained a southern problem, widely ignored by the rest of the country. The Southern Christian Leadership Conference, led by Martin Luther King, and frustrated by the slow pace of change, decided to mobilize mass protests. Day after day, thousands of African-Americans marched on the city hall in Birmingham, Alabama, demanding equal rights. Television pictures of policemen and dogs attacking defenceless people, including children, stopped America in its tracks and put black civil rights at the top of the national agenda. On 11 June 1963 President Kennedy addressed the nation on television with the words 'We face a moral crisis as a country and a people.' Kennedy sent a civil rights bill to Congress, but even with the prospect of their country disintegrating before their eyes, national politicians refused to act.

On 28 August 1963, the centenary of Lincoln's Declaration of the Emancipation of Slaves, more than 200,000 African-Americans and their white supporters marched through Washington to the Lincoln Memorial. What was then the largest demonstration in Washington's history heard Martin Luther King speak about his dream of a nation where his children 'will not be judged by the color of their skin but by the content of their characters'. The following month four black children were killed when a church in Birmingham, Alabama, was bombed, and two months after that, President Kennedy was assassinated in Dallas. The possibility of a conspiracy to murder the President, open conflict in the south and political immobility in Washington made America seem like a country on the verge of catastrophe. A nation created to promote and embody good was showing itself apparently rotten to the core.

Lyndon Johnson may not have been as charismatic as Kennedy, but he was a smart and seasoned political operator – and a passionate disciple of Franklin Roosevelt to boot. Johnson immediately pushed a strengthened civil rights bill through Congress, giving full legal rights to African-Americans, and setting up bodies to oversee and implement the dismantling of segregation. Civil rights activists and ordinary black residents were still being murdered in Mississippi and Alabama, but more measures were passed in 1965, and under the threat of federal action, the south began to change. Black candidates won seats in state legislatures in the south for the first time in nearly a century.

Subsequent events showed the limitations of legal equality in a society awash with unresolved hatred towards blacks. On 4 April 1968 Martin Luther King was assassinated in Memphis, Tennessee; in the mid- to late sixties there were riots in the Watts area of Los Angeles, in which 34 people died, and in New York, Chicago, Detroit, Atlanta and dozens of other cities. This was the worst and most widespread civil disturbance since the American Revolution. None of these cities practised legal segregation, but the black populations had the worst housing, the worst schools and hospitals, and the least chance of finding work, in cities that were losing their reason for existing.

The riots were a stark reminder of how economic prosperity brings its own problems. The post-war boom meant that by the 1960s nearly every white family owned a car, and so people moved to suburbs where they could have space; large houses with car ports and lawns, and filled with labour-saving and entertainment devices, became the norm for the average American family. The cramped inner cities, with their poor housing and declining amenities, were deserted in this 'white flight' and were filled by incoming African-Americans moving from rural poverty in the south. African-American populations in northern cities increased dramatically between 1950 and 1970, with millions arriving just as the demand for unskilled labour was declining, while the jobs that remained were being moved out to the suburbs. In those two decades the proportion of black citizens in New York increased from 10 to 30 per cent; Chicago from 14 to 33 per cent; Detroit from 16 to 40 per cent; and Washington DC from 35 to 70 per cent. City authorities were hopelessly ineffective at dealing with the social challenge of such massive migration; poor housing schemes were demolished to make way for urban freeways, or business districts, or massive, hideous and inhuman housing 'projects'. In each case, the stores and offices and factories that formed the city's tax base deliberately moved outside the city limits, leaving a small downtown business district surrounded by a sea of social deprivation. The desperation of American cities came to the world's attention when, in 1975, New York, the archetype of the twentieth-century city, declared itself bankrupt and no longer able to function.

The transfer of jobs and housing out of cities was taken a step further by American corporations. The largest companies, such as Ford, General Motors and Hoover, had already built manufacturing plants in Europe to supply customers direct. But from the 1960s, corporations built factories overseas simply in order to take advantage of cheap labour. From 1960 to 1970 the industrial production of major manufacturers in the United States rose by 70 per cent, while their overseas production rose by 500 per cent, and in 1972 the $50 billion worth of goods they exported was dwarfed by the $180 billion worth they produced overseas. The need for unskilled and semi-skilled labour in the United States decreased even further as manufacturing began to give way to a service-based economy.

While the well-educated benefited from a huge expansion in the number of public service jobs – as teachers, college lecturers, public officials, professionals and white-collar workers – the decline of manufacturing was a major blow for African-Americans, working-class whites and other poorly educated groups. Government employment was the largest area of employment expansion in the 1950s and 1960s; this was a boon for professionals, but for the uneducated it meant low-paid work in catering, healthcare or cleaning. In a notable reversal, the white-collar professions became unionized and fought for better pay and conditions, while the working class, fragmented and no longer 'industrial', lost their collective strength. All this would be replicated in Europe a decade or so later.

African-Americans were joined in the inner-city ghettos by Puerto Ricans, Mexicans and Native Americans, all desperate to leave the poverty of their homelands. Citizens of these ghettos often showed their frustration by burning down the shops and tenements that were profiting from their misery; huge areas of major American cities became burned-out wastelands. With little prospect of employment, drugs and violent crime became the only way to make money, or to escape reality as, in the mid-1960s, the American inner city began to descend into a dystopic nightmare. Kennedy and Johnson's dream of a better society built around the modern city, supported by massive federal funding and a blizzard of social measures, came to nothing. By then, the United States had opened up another tear in its social fabric by entering into a catastrophic war.

In Vietnam the two foreign-policy priorities of the west – to fight communism and to give self-rule to colonies – became tragically confused. European empires were being dismantled as all over the world people fought to free themselves from their colonial masters; but American politicians, rather than seeing Vietnam in the same light, viewed it as a communist takeover of a free nation. They believed they could save the country from communism as Truman had failed, in 1949, to save China. The French had withdrawn from the north in 1954, but by 1963 there were 16,000 Americans in South Vietnam acting as special advisers to the puppet regime. North Vietnamese forces and their allies in the south were intent on claiming the south as part of their country, and the Americans were intent on preventing them.

President Johnson gave serious attention to Vietnam only in late 1964, by which time he had few choices open to him. Under Ho Chi Minh, the communist north was pushing towards victory – the United States had to stand and fight or face imminent withdrawal and the disintegration of its anti-communist policy. A small country in south-east Asia became the testing ground for the most powerful nation on earth. No one asked whether the Vietnamese people would ever accept the right of Americans to run their affairs, while the American people were never directly consulted – many people had voted for Johnson in 1964 as the peace candidate.

The first American soldiers, 5,000 marines, arrived in March 1965, followed rapidly by 95,000 more troopers and airmen; by 1968 there were more than half a million. Even without a war, the presence of the American army and air force would have destroyed the country's economic and social infrastructure. By 1965 South Vietnam was a fractured society; occupation by the French, interrupted by Japanese conquest, before giving way to dictatorship by puppets of outside forces, had destroyed its social fabric, leading to divided loyalties and intense faction fighting. The arrival of a fabulously wealthy, technology-based, super-power army in the midst of an already chaotic situation was socially disastrous. Local industry and agriculture were destroyed by the presence of an economic giant shipping in vast quantities of supplies; the local economy was swamped by inflation and effectively disappeared. Middle-class occupations like teaching, medicine and law were abandoned and people fled the dangers and poverty of the countryside, but in Saigon they could only make ends meet by selling goods and services to the Americans, including sex and drugs. The physical fabric of the country was then destroyed as 'free-fire' zones, where everything that moved was annihilated, including the country's agriculture and forests. In fact, the Americans would have found more communists in the towns and cities of the south than in the villages and countryside.

The United States government tried to persuade the world that this was a fight between two different countries – North and South Vietnam – but the Vietnam war quickly became a conflict between outsiders – the Americans – and local people. In war, soldiers are always in a dangerous position, both physically and psychologically; but an occupying army of outsiders, fighting a war in its enemy's own country, cannot easily tell friend from foe or fighter from civilian. The Vietnam war inflicted a terrible price on Vietnam because the Americans, if they were to claim victory, would have had to destroy the country; it inflicted a terrible price on the American army because it destroyed its legitimacy as a force for good. This was revealed to the world when it was reported that on 16 March 1968, American troops under Lieutenant William Calley massacred 109 women and children in the Vietnamese village of My Lai by gunning them down and herding them into huts before lobbing in hand grenades.

The effect of the war back home was further to divide an already fractured nation, and to destroy any consensus on America's role in the world – and, by extension, call into doubt the meaning of western civilization. Many working-class Americans felt it was their patriotic duty to serve their country, while the better-off, and in particular the young middle classes, saw the war as an immoral conflict. In America and in Europe, college students and others used techniques learned from the civil rights movement – mass demonstrations, sit-ins, takeover of institutions – to protest against the war. The movement for civil rights for blacks, the anti-war movement, the disdain of traditional, hypocritical morality and brash materialism came together in an alternative view of western society. The world was divided into those within this charmed circle and those outside – insiders dressing as differently as possible to authority figures, with the smart hair and suits of politicians and businessmen ridiculed and rejected in favour of long hair, beards and colourful clothes.

At first the tactics used by anti-war activists were viewed with distaste and bewilderment by most Americans, but this began to change as the television pictures from Vietnam showed the desperate brutality of the conflict. Americans of all backgrounds began to say that Vietnam was not worth any more American lives. In January 1968 the Tet offensive showed Americans that, far from containing the enemy, their forces had made no headway in three years. In March Lyndon Johnson announced he would not run for president that year, called a halt to the bombing of Vietnam and sought negotiations with Hanoi. Amazingly, it was to take another five years for America to get out of the war.

The following month Martin Luther King was assassinated and the cohesion of black and white liberal interests began to dissolve. King's death was followed in June 1968 by the assassination of Robert Kennedy. While John Kennedy's murder had been greeted with shock and dismay, his younger brother's death was met with sheer disbelief. How could it have happened again? Further outrage came when the Democratic party selected Hubert Humphrey, considered deeply implicated in the escalation of the war, as its candidate for president. The streets around the convention centre in Chicago became a battleground as America, watched on television by the world, seemed to be disintegrating into a murderous, fragmented, frankly ungovernable society.

The alternative vision of society staggered on, but met its nemesis on 6 December 1969 at Altamont, California. Wanting to finish their tour by upstaging the recent Woodstock festival, the Rolling Stones, the world's coolest pop group, put on a hastily arranged outdoor concert at the Altamont race track near San Francisco, with the local Hell's Angels drafted in to provide security. After a day of simmering violence, while the Stones sang their faux-evil song 'Sympathy for the Devil' they were forced to watch in horror as the Hell's Angels beat and stabbed a man to death in front of the low stage. In just a few minutes of mayhem the 'alternative' view of brotherly and sisterly love was exposed to the reality of violence in American society. It was suddenly apparent that living outside the law had its dangers. The alternative society lived on, but after Altamont it became a place of refuge from the world rather than a serious vision of how to organize society. The western world was in transition, but where was it going?

President Richard Nixon, elected in 1968 and 1972, got America out of Vietnam – eventually, and only in his second term. In the meantime he managed to involve Cambodia (which he ordered to be bombed without telling Congress) and Laos in the conflict, leading to their takeover by communist forces and, in Cambodia, a reign of pitiless mass murder by Pol Pot. By the end of the war in 1973, 58,174 Americans had been killed and 304,000 wounded; it is estimated that around one million Vietnamese soldiers and four million civilians lost their lives. But the Vietnam war, as well as helping to shatter the old social and political consensus, propelled the western world into a new phase. By the late 1950s the post-war boom had been running out of steam. In 1960 Kennedy boosted spending on defence in a deliberate attempt to stimulate the economy, and the Vietnam war sucked more and more government money into defence industries. By 1969, 10 per cent of Americans had jobs linked to the defence industries, while two thirds of aircraft companies' and one third of radio and television income was from government; more than 40 per cent of the workforce of Seattle and Los Angeles was dependent on government contracts. Both Johnson and Nixon refused to raise taxes to fund the war, so there was more money around with a smaller civil manufacturing base. The result was rapid inflation and a large trade deficit – something previously unknown in United States history – as Americans sought goods from abroad.

Crucially, inflation jeopardized the value of the one currency, the dollar, that was the bedrock of the Bretton Woods system of global economic governance. How could the dollar remain pegged to the price of gold, and to all the other major currencies, when its value was rapidly falling even in relation to American goods? Something had to give. In 1971, in order to protect the American economy, President Nixon formally ended the western post-war economic consensus. Fixed exchange rates were abolished and the dollar was allowed to float free – currency exchange rates were to be determined by the markets, not by national governments. The subsequent drop in the value of the dollar eased the pressures on the American economy (and helped to get Nixon re-elected in 1972), but it had a serious side effect. Oil, the lifeblood of twentieth-century industry, was and is priced in dollars, and when the value of the dollar fell, oil-producing countries bore the brunt. Their response, in December 1973, was to raise the price of oil by 300 per cent. The industrialized world was immediately plunged into recession. Once again, it was clear that the west was changing, but the direction of change was unclear.

The first oil price shock of 1973–74 was followed by another in 1979, when the Iranian revolutionary government temporarily cut supplies to the west. In 1970 the price of oil had been $2.53 a barrel; by 1980 it was $41. The economies of Europe and America, already suffering from low investment, poor management and a disillusioned workforce, faced abrupt and painful change. Industries such as mining, shipbuilding, printing, steel and car-making were devastated by a combination of outdated equipment and cheaper, and often superior, imports. Thanks to planned investment and a government dedicated to export industries, Japanese firms could make ships, cars, radios, televisions and motorbikes for far less cost than American or European companies. The notable exception was West Germany, where a strategic partnership between government and industry produced manufactured goods of extremely high quality. Elsewhere management and workforces each blamed the other for the state of their industries – lack of foresight and investment, or restrictive practices – and strikes and confrontations became commonplace.

In 1970s Europe the social consequences were similar to the American experience in the 1960s. Old industrial towns and cities became hollowed out as the working population moved to suburbs with new industrial estates and shopping centres, leaving the inner-city housing estates (often system-built creations of the 'brutalist' school of architecture) to the unemployed, the old and the poor. Internal social problems were compounded by the rise of politically motivated terrorism. Groups representing disenfranchised or dispossessed communities in Palestine, Northern Ireland and the Basque country believed they could win political freedoms by staging bombing and kidnappings. Home-grown groups representing some self-justifying political philosophy (the Red Brigades in Italy, Baader-Meinhof in Germany, the Angry Brigade in Britain and a host of smaller fascist groups) brought short-lived terror to the streets of Europe. The world watched on television as Israeli athletes were held hostage, and 11 eventually killed, by Palestinian terrorists at the 1972 Munich Olympics; in 1978 the Red Brigades kidnapped and murdered the Italian prime minister Aldo Moro; and, in the worst atrocity, a bomb planted by a right-wing group at Bologna railway station in August 1980 killed 85 people. Europe, like America, seemed in danger of implosion.

These old-established forms of political opposition, based on left- or right-wing ideologies, were joined in the 1970s by the new kinds of thinking that would form the informal opposition in the new phase of western society. Opportunities for travel, the arrival of immigrants and changes in education gave many of the younger generation a more diverse, tolerant and genuinely interested attitude towards other races and cultures; their disillusion with their own societies encouraging them to look elsewhere for guidance and authenticity. Imported popular music and literature began to show that the Third World was a source of cultural energy, not just poverty and migration. Feminism became a serious intellectual and social force that made everyone, from historians and literary critics to journalists, artists and legislators, reassess their attitudes and their outlook on the world. People also began to see the toll that modern industrial life was taking on the physical world around them. Those who had grown up in villages surrounded by endless fields, or in towns within easy reach of forests and streams, found that their villages were now small towns, the fields now housing estates, the intimate pastures now vast wheatfields. And in towns and cities beautiful buildings and intimate street patterns, some existing since the twelfth century, had been destroyed and replaced by cheap, ugly shopping malls and office blocks, or by urban motorways. The idea of safeguarding the environment and of conserving and adapting buildings and street patterns began to take hold. This was another attempt by western people to hold on to their communal, embedded and unspoken customs in an age of change and destruction.

The cultural response to the upheavals of the 1960s and 1970s was led by the dominant art form of the twentieth century, film. The 1960s had been a fallow period for American cinema. The cultural powerhouse of the mid-century was run by members of a generation who simply did not understand what was happening in their own country. There were exceptions, but American cinema, under threat from television and unable to match the new virtuosity of the Europeans, was in danger of irrelevance. In the late 1960s there were some straws in the wind – in 1967 *Bonnie and Clyde* and *The Graduate* showed that Hollywood could produce films that connected to the changing American psyche. The American auteur-director, immersed in the French new wave, Italian neo-realism and the new German cinema of Fassbinder, Wenders and Herzog, began to replace the old studio system. *Easy Rider* and *Midnight Cowboy* (both 1969) were rapidly followed by *The Last Picture Show* (1971), *The Godfather* (1972), *Mean Streets*, *Badlands* (both 1973) and *Chinatown* (1974). The themes of these films varied, but they fulfilled the eternal requirements of important art, and in the same way as the paintings of Mantegna and the novels of Dickens, they used the technology and techniques of their time – hand-held cameras, jump cuts, cinéma vérité, popular music soundtracks – to produce their effect. American films of the early 1970s showed ordinary people inhabiting a world that was slipping away from them, controlled by forces that they neither understood nor had any influence over. In almost every case their struggle to assert their own relevance is eventually overwhelmed, and in most of the movies cited above, the expected Hollywood happy ending is replaced by violent death or disillusionment.

The beginning of the 1980s saw the start of a new political consensus, arising from the crises of the 1960s and 1970s, while bringing into being different forms of opposition. Both Ronald Reagan in America and Margaret Thatcher in Britain shook off the immediate past by the simple, but effective, strategy of reviving nationalist sentiment. After a decade of self-denigration, it was time for people to feel good about being American, or British, and in an age when people had got used to politicians telling them what they could not do, both preached the doctrine of personal freedom. Their central message was for government to retreat on all fronts and stop interfering in people's lives. But being a nationalist politician while shrinking the power of the state proved more difficult than it seemed.

Both leaders subscribed to a new theory of economics called monetarism, which, in attempting to squeeze inflation through high interest rates, led to a strong dollar. This meant Americans could buy everyone else's goods, while no one could afford theirs. Manufacturing in the United States (and in Britain) crashed as exports slumped and imports soared. Reagan, like Thatcher, used more and more of his budget on welfare payments for the increasing numbers of unemployed. The United States budget deficit climbed to over $200 billion, nearly four times what it had been under his predecessor, and the long-term federal spending on infrastructure, which was crucial to American industry, was all but abandoned. It was like the 1920s all over again. Sure enough, in October 1987 the New York stock market crashed and the world held its breath. There was no great depression this time, only because the United States was not the overwhelmingly dominant economy it had been in 1929. The economy survived Reaganomics because foreign, and particularly Japanese, companies poured money into America. The failure of monetarism to curb government spending gave birth to a new concept – privatization. The British government, in a deliberate attempt to be more like America, sold off its controlling interest in telecommunications, airlines and public housing, and in public utilities like gas, electricity and water, and used the receipts to cover its deficits.

As governments turned public services into market-driven businesses, they also wanted to make the entire world into an international market. The theory was that by deregulating the flow of money, the world economy would be made more efficient, as money would go to where it could make most return, and therefore do most good. Technology made the flow of capital between countries, investment houses, stock markets and currency dealers as simple as pushing a button; in the 1980s the major industrial countries, under pressure from the United States, agreed to allow unlimited flows of capital around the world. Just as in the mid-nineteenth century, politicians sought to portray the liberalization of trade and money as a return to the natural state of economic and social relations. It was only by sweeping away petty restrictions on tariffs, trade unions, building on virgin land, and opening hours that people could be free, economically efficient and prosperous.

The new doctrine was implemented first in the Anglo-Saxon world – in the United States, Britain, New Zealand and Australia – but the commercial and military power of the United States and the deregulation of capital markets have forced other western countries to adopt similar policies, or see their economies suffer. Finance not industry drove the new economies, so that government support for manufacturing was disallowed. In this new atmosphere, business leaders became role models and valued advisers to governments, while the corporation itself became the model organization. Utilities that had been regarded as services were privatized and made into stock-holding companies with a legal duty to maximize their share value. But even those institutions that remained in public ownership were adapted, to varying degrees, to fit the company model. Universities, technical colleges, schools, postal services, health boards, local councils were all restructured and made to think of themselves as businesses. It even became possible for a local health board in Britain, running a series of publicly owned hospitals, to declare itself bankrupt. In 2004, during a debate about tuition fees, Colin Lucas, the vice-chancellor of Oxford University, felt able to declare that 'teaching undergraduates is a loss-making activity'.

Changes in industrial methods, in technology and transportation meant that by the 1980s, the mere production of goods became a cheap and simple affair. The dream of early industrialists had come true – we could produce our basic needs with a fraction of the effort and time available to us. Power shifted away from the producer and towards the consumer as the real challenge came, not in producing basic goods, but in winning customers. The design and quality of goods, and of shops themselves, changed dramatically; supermarkets stayed open later and opened on Sundays, and out-of-town shopping malls and hypermarkets on the American model spread across the western world. For those with money and cars, life became more convenient; while those without either faced being stranded on inner-city housing estates out of reach of shops and services.

The enormous amount of energy and effort put into the service and retail sectors helped to absorb the millions of people no longer required in mines and factories. Miners and machinists became van-drivers and shop assistants or 'consumer advisers' in call centres. For the educated and affluent, brought up with the anti-authoritarian ethos of the 1960s, consumerism had different effects. They demanded an equal relationship with doctors, lawyers, teachers, bank managers and politicians, and the 'doctor knows best' philosophy was dumped by a generation who had learned to be confident of their own rights.

The 1980s focus on the needs and aspirations of the individual accelerated an existing trend. The so-called 'me generation' became not merely interested in personal ambition and material gain, but fascinated by themselves. Though often considered a product of the 1960s, this inward gaze had its origins in the late nineteenth century and the birth of psychology. Once the individual mind became a concern of neurologists on the one hand, and philosophers on the other, it only remained for the rest of us to follow suit. Interest in diet and fashion launched a multitude of magazines to join those that had been around for decades, and these were followed by books and videos on personal fitness, inner well-being and psychological health. Written from a variety of perspectives, this torrent of information and advice was aimed at getting individuals to think about themselves. The way to a better life was to be a better person, and the way to achieve that was through self-examination followed by affirmative action. The western citizen was in full retreat from a publicly active life to one of private self-realization and self-obsession.

Since 1980 the so-called 'Washington Model' of free trade has been imposed on America and, through international agreements and agencies, the rest of the world. Family loyalties, local customs, mutual support, non-economic networks, all of which were embedded in different ways in different societies, have had to be crushed or marginalized in the name of economic efficiency. In the United States the effects have been extraordinary, yet little discussed. From the mid-1970s to the mid-1990s, the real incomes of American workers (adjusted for inflation) fell by around 20 per cent (from $315 to $258 a week), while the take-home pay of chief executives increased by over 60 per cent – an unprecedented growth in inequality. When President Reagan was elected in 1980, around one in a thousand Americans were prisoners; by 1994 the figure was 3.74 per thousand, and by 2004 roughly seven per thousand, representing 1.96 million Americans in jail and over five million under legal restraint. (Approximate imprisonment rates per thousand for other western countries in 2004 were: Britain 1.4; Germany 1.0; France 0.8; Japan 0.5.) African-Americans are seven times more likely to be jailed, with one in seven men having been in prison. In Washington DC in 1992, 40 per cent of the African-American men between the ages of 18 and 35 were either in jail, on probation or parole, or on the run. Despite the massive rate of incarceration, violent crime and drug use are more widespread than in any other developed country. American governments have allowed the disintegration of the restraining influence of family, community, custom and fairness in favour of economic efficiency. As old-established human networks are blown away, a ruthless, and essentially ineffective, system of incarceration has been built to take their place.

The cultural equivalent of this system was a sudden and, in retrospect, quite astonishing revival of the fundamental religious concepts of good and evil. This first came to public attention in the 1980s when United States president Ronald Reagan described the Soviet Union as 'the evil empire'. While the Soviets had long been regarded as the enemy, Reagan's description was quite novel for its time. In reality it was the expression of a deep desire, after the uncertainties of the 1960s and 1970s, to divide the world into moral absolutes. Nowadays, and especially since 11 September 2001, it has become commonplace to describe enemies of the west as terrorists driven only by an evil desire to destroy. This way of thinking has changed the view of crime in a country like Britain, where, in the post-war decades, it was taken for granted that reducing crime meant tackling social deprivation. Nowadays even petty offenders are seen as beyond the pale of decent society, in need of punishment and restraint. Young people are therefore viewed as either impossibly good (particularly when they are victims of crime) or as a dangerous, fearsome evil, hanging around on street corners, waiting to pounce. This view of crime has its ultimate manifestation in the serial killer; unheard-of 30 years ago, this epitome of evil now occupies acres of newsprint and countless novels and films.

As well as portraying serial killers in hugely popular films like *Silence of the Lambs* (1990) and *Seven* (1995), Hollywood had already grasped with relish the new message of a world divided into good and evil. Beginning with *Jaws* (1975) and *Star Wars* (1977), American film turned away from the troubling complexity of the early 1970s in favour of moral certainty coupled with cartoon-style excitement. Even when this tendency was ruthlessly mocked by Quentin Tarantino in *Pulp Fiction* (1994), the same formula was held to.

In Britain the requirement of liberal economics saw the restraint of the power of trade unions, followed by the abolition of local government in London and its emasculation elsewhere, the abolition of wages councils and retail price maintenance, drastic reduction in provision of public housing, and restraint on the power of bodies such as local education authorities. In return, as we have seen, public bodies, from colleges to hospitals to water boards to pension providers, have been made into private or semi-private corporations. The only institution to escape denigration has been, as in earlier times, the family. (The monotonous mantras of all recent politicians in favour of 'hard-working families' or 'faith, flag and family' are revealing – this is the only entity, apart from its own agencies, such as the police and army, that wins the unqualified approval of the modern state.) But here too the new economics have done their work. The requirement for a flexible and mobile workforce has put paid to the old networks of extended families – now spread across nations and continents – while the idealized nuclear family has been forced to reassess the meaning of its existence.

This reassessment, for individuals and family units alike, has been as profound in its way as the attempts by Augustine, Calvin, Rousseau, Smith, Mill, Marx and Freud to understand how, in a world ruled by God, or reason, or self-interest, or passion, or communal endeavour, an individual life should be lived. In the immediate post-war period, the aim of life was collective security within a well-regulated society. But the sudden rise of affluence in the 1960s and 1970s meant that young people were able, and were encouraged, to step outside the restraints of society, including its economic imperatives. Students were supposed to learn for the sake of learning, while any economic gains for themselves or their national economies were secondary, or beneath consideration. Provision for the unemployed and retired, through benefits, pensions and good-quality public rented housing, was taken for granted, so that people could see their lives as social beings, rather than as parts of a relentless industrial machine.

In the new economics, this changed again. As the public provision of housing, pensions and other services has been drastically reduced, the western citizen has been forced to think of himself as an economic unit, and to see his life as an exercise in financial planning. As soon as a middle-class child is born, in Britain or America, its parents must start saving to pay for higher education, which the student will leave with large debts. He or she will then need a high-paid job in order to pay off those debts, and will immediately need to borrow more money to buy a house, as well as saving towards a decent pension. Missing any of these steps, or allowing anything to threaten them, will severely disadvantage the modern citizen. This sounds like financial common sense, but it represents a startling shift in our perception of ourselves, and the world around us.

One of the great paradoxes of the current phase is the way that nation states have used their power to bring about a situation in which, ultimately, their power is reduced. In 1980 France bucked the trend of the Anglo-Saxon world and elected François Mitterand, an old-school socialist, as president. Mitterand immediately implemented a range of policies aimed at turning France into a socialist nation, increasing public spending and taxation, nationalizing industries and so on. But he had not understood the degree to which the world had changed in the previous decade. The deregulation of the movement of capital allowed disgruntled investment houses to sell their holdings in French currency, institutions and companies. Money began to haemorrhage out of the country and the French government was forced to change tack. Governments in France, Germany, Scandinavia and the Low Countries continued to believe in government investment in infrastructure and industry – in a way that Britain and the United States had tried to abandon. But the Mitterand episode brought home a truth that had lain hidden inside the new global economic system. No government could act without the agreement of the financial markets, and the markets (along with the IMF, the World Bank, the OECD, WTO and other international organizations) were most favourable to those national economies that privatized their utilities and cut back on government spending.

The decline of the power of the nation state brought on by deregulated financial markets happened without any public discussion about loss of sovereignty or national identity. The fact that national governments were beholden to groups of people buying and selling currencies and shares, mostly for short-term gain, drew little comment or organized opposition. It just happened. The task of finance ministers was to persuade the markets that they could be trusted to deliver what the markets wanted, while at the same time pursuing their own, heavily restricted, political agenda. In contrast, the combining of European countries into an Economic and Monetary Union (EMU) provoked long and furious debate about precisely those issues of national identity and sovereignty that had been previously passed over.

In the 1990s the economies of the west were joined in the global market by the ex-communist countries of eastern Europe, by countries of the Pacific Rim – Japan (already a major western economy), South Korea, Indonesia, Malaysia and China – as well as newly democratic regimes in Latin America; while major countries like India and Brazil were cajoled into the deregulated global market through a mixture of incentive and threat. The only countries left out were the poverty-stricken ex-colonies of sub-Saharan Africa and the dynastic dictatorships of the Arab world; otherwise the whole world was made part of a single global market. The west, in other words, was becoming the whole world.

The freeing-up of world trade and the extension of patent rights has seen the ubiquity of transnational corporations. Following the omnipresence of Ford, General Motors and Toyota cars, every high street in every moderately affluent town in the world has a McDonald's, Burger King, Starbucks or Disney store, while almost everyone uses Microsoft programs and operating systems. The relentless colonization of the world's high streets brought an enervating sameness to many towns. The building styles, the shops, the goods, have become dismayingly uniform.

Concerns about corporate power and the increasing standardization of life have been brought into focus in the new genetic technology. The human genome has been mapped, intervention in the genetic make-up of organisms has become a standard procedure for competent scientists, and in 1997, Dolly the sheep, the first animal cloned using genetic technology, was born in Edinburgh. While genetic procedures promise the possible elimination of genetic diseases in humans and domestic animals, the possibility of genetically modifying human embryos to produce 'designer' babies, or to eliminate disability, calls into question our understanding of what it means to be a human being.

The new economics needs to have the whole world deregulated, since any resistant part will reduce its theoretical efficiency. This embrace or takeover (depending on how you see it) has been immeasurably aided by the revival of the belief that the west is the most advanced society in the world. The west's hard-won lessons on how to govern a nation, run an economy, structure a judiciary, or build a production line will, it is assumed, be of benefit to all other societies, without exception. The lessons of the catastrophe that the west brought to the world in 1914 and 1939 have been turned inside out, while the idea that other peoples might not want societies like ours is brushed aside. At the commemoration for the sixtieth anniversary of D-Day on 6 June 2004, Tony Blair said of the D-Day operation that 'there was . . . a defining understanding that in the end the values that Britain – and indeed the rest of Europe and America – share were values that should be the guiding light for the future of humankind'. The desire to bring these western values to the rest of humankind, including resistant elements within the west itself, and by force if necessary, has re-emerged.

If this is the overt aim of western society, and the philosophy of those who guide its fortunes, then what has been the reaction of the world, and what is the response of human society? In 1986, 96 countries met in Uruguay to hammer out an agreement that would cut industrial tariffs, reduce agriculture subsidies, enforce intellectual property rights and instigate new rules on investment and services. The so-called Uruguay Round took seven years to complete, ending in 1993 with the setting-up of the World Trade Organization, or WTO. It soon became apparent that the WTO agreements were heavily weighted. Developing countries signed agreements to protect patent rights and opened up their markets and services to First-World countries; in return they were promised a sustained reduction in agricultural subsidies and open access to markets in the industrialized world – a promise that was never fulfilled. The price has been heavy, because intellectual property rights and financial services have become key ingredients in the world economy. Patent and brand image rights mean that a training shoe can be made in Indonesia for a few cents in materials and labour, and sell in New York or Paris for $100, the difference all being made in the west (where the benefits, incidentally, go to executives and shareholders and not western workers).

Local manufacturers in India, Mexico and South Africa are not allowed to make generic copies of drugs for malaria and AIDS where the patents are held by western pharmaceutical companies.

More generally, the second phase of post-war history has been much less generous to poor nations than the first phase. In the early 1960s rich countries spent 0.48 per cent of their combined income on aid; by 2003 the average was 0.23 per cent; and although in 1970 all western countries pledged to increase aid to 0.7 per cent of GDP, none of the G8, the eight richest countries, have yet done so. In 1980 the ratio between the annual production of a western European citizen and a worker in sub-Saharan Africa stood at 15:1; by 1998 it had reached around 70:1. The proximity of extreme wealth and advanced technology destroys the economic and social structures of poorer nations, while the discovery of something that is valuable to the west – oil, diamonds, copper – causes disruption and, in many cases, war.

Reaction against the unfair treatment of developing countries, the ubiquitous and unfettered power of the transnational companies, and the apparent inability of governments to do anything about the environmental degradation of the planet came to a head at the WTO meeting in Seattle in December 1999. Thousands of protestors from across the developing and industrialized worlds brought home to delegates the growing mood of dissatisfaction. But headline-grabbing as the protests were, the meeting was actually halted by a walk-out by African trade ministers, protesting at yet more obfuscation over agriculture subsidies. To the developing world it began to seem that no deal was better than a bad deal.

When the WTO reconvened at Cancun in Mexico in 2003 the world was broadly divided into three groups: the United States and the EU; middle-income countries such as Brazil, Mexico, China, South Africa, India and Indonesia; and those countries, principally in sub-Saharan Africa, with virtually no industrial base, reliant on agriculture or the sale of raw materials and commodities for external income. The surprise at Cancun was the emergence of the middle-income countries as a real and united force. Having witnessed yet more havering over agriculture subsidies from the EU and the United States, they brought the meeting to a halt by the simple expedient of walking out; after Cancun, the west could no longer assume possession of the global market.

The Cancun walk-out was the expression of a broader truth. Newly industrialized countries do not, despite appearances, feel any need to follow western models of capitalism. In China, Russia, India, Brazil and Mexico, traditions of trade are well-established, despite their recent history, and these are quite different from those of America or Britain or Germany or France. There is every sign that each of these countries is finding its own way of becoming an industrial, money-based economy. In this sense, the world is not becoming western; instead, the rest of the world, while using western technology, may be freeing itself of its subservience to the west. It is no coincidence that film, the pre-eminent art form of the last century, is being given new energy in Asia and Latin America.

Citizens of those societies most affected by the new economics, deprived of the emotional foundations of place and custom, have increasingly turned to religion. An ever more mobile society, disconnected from the natural world, has left a spiritual void that has been filled by evangelical faiths. In the United States the mass appeal and political power of evangelical Christianity has markedly increased, and even the traditionally inclusive Anglican church in Britain faces a schism brought on by a rise in fundamental Christianity. As globalization has spread free trade across the world, other cultures have come under pressure. For the people of the Middle East, and for immigrants to Europe from the Muslim world, Islam has assumed a much greater importance. In the 1970s Palestinian political movements were entirely secular; now they are all Islamic; and young Muslims in the west, whose parents were willing to embrace the secularism of their new homes, are once again taking to religion.

Citizens of the west have tried other ways to produce a counterbalance to the logic of the free market. When a major thoroughfare in Copenhagen was closed to traffic for a cultural event in 1973, the initial reluctance of shops, cafés and bars was confounded when business surged. The closure was made permanent, and other towns and cities, their old centres choked by huge increases in car numbers, followed suit. Suddenly town centres, made into pedestrian-only areas, were pleasant places to be, where the old virtues of human interaction, unexpected meetings and accidental pleasures were revived. The western city began to look at itself differently.

To those who chose to look it became clear that, above all else, people valued a sense of continuity and history in their towns. To them, these were not just places to exist, but the physical representations of social fabrics that had been built up in layer upon layer over generations. The affections people held for their cities were a complex combination of memory, pride and belonging. In thousands of towns the public realm had been downgraded in the twentieth century, and made thoughtlessly ugly; public space, the most precious element in a town's physical character, had been ignored. Combining the transformation of the public realm with a revival of cultural life proved a remarkably successful way to regenerate a city's economic and social fortunes, and improve the lives of its citizens.

Baltimore, Glasgow, Milwaukee, Barcelona, Marseilles, Manchester and a host of other cities and towns suffering the familiar spiral of neglect and abandonment managed to revive their fortunes by making themselves into places where people want to live. The rebirth of the western city could only happen when the people of the city were given (or given back) power over its destiny. This has meant an agreed retreat by the central state, a process that in Europe has been helped by the European Union. For decades the needs of provincial cities in much of Europe were neglected by national governments, but in the 1990s they stopped pleading to London or Paris or Madrid for support, and went direct to Brussels. In a clear echo of its medieval, pre-national past, Europe moved ever so slightly towards being a continent of city-states and regions, rather than nation states. National governments, together with metropolitan newspapers, inveighed against this; but for the citizens of Catalonia or Newcastle upon Tyne or Marseilles or Calabria, rule from a national capital holds few advantages over strong regional or civic autonomy supported by a Europe-wide infrastructure. Movements for ecological protection, local food, preservation of buildings, customs and languages are all part of the desire to promote diversity over standardization, and to re-create the special quality of particular places. This change in attitude has come out of economic self-interest too. Globalization is promoted by western leaders, but western citizens see their prosperity, as well as their customs, threatened. The scepticism about progress mentioned in the Prologue comes from a deep fear of a future that appears to be running out of control. For the first time for several generations, the future seems to offer something worse than the present.

There are some signs that western culture has, in the last decade, begun to reflect the tensions between global standardization and local custom. As the mechanically produced, centrally directed culture begins to pall, and as America loses its pre-eminence as *the* cultural arbiter, cultural goods and activities that are tied to the local are slowly becoming more highly valued. The value of a piece of art comes precisely from its inability to be produced mechanically and universally. In this situation, there is a new role for the artist. There is no longer any need to work in isolation, responding only to the urges and promptings of a single mind. Instead artists can respond to commissions and to particular spaces, can work in collaboration, and can immerse themselves in the traditions of a locality. While this has already happened in public sculptures and installations and in live performance, it seems likely to spread to art forms like film, where new technology allows movies to be made at relatively low cost.

Changes in technology have continued to leave much gallery or literature-based art floundering in the wake of popular culture. The continuing social and economic denigration of the black community in the United States has made plain what has been the case for decades – that African-American society is the source of the overwhelming majority of cultural innovations in the west. After decades spent altering black music, dance and speech to make it available to a white audience, unreconstructed music from black urban America is now the soundtrack of young western people's lives. And while educated westerners sit piously in modern art galleries inspecting the work of video artists, astonishingly innovative fusions of sound and vision are being produced, once again, by black American film-makers. But these are pop videos (see, for example, Hype Williams' film of 'I Can't Stand the Rain') and are played to audiences of millions.

There are some signs that, in opposition to their traditional use of abstract analysis to search for universal laws, philosophers are interested in understanding the limits of their discipline. Ludwig Wittgenstein, who gave up teaching during the Second World War to work as a hospital porter, was impatient with his colleagues' fundamental belief that philosophy brought some knowledge about the world that was not available to the rest of humanity. The task of philosophy, Wittgenstein asserted, is the dissolution of philosophical problems. The British philosopher Bernard Williams argued that the thought experiments that are at the root of much moral philosophy (e.g. is it right to kill one person in order to save ten?) are useless, because they completely ignore the lived experience, the intricate complexities of ongoing existence, that each of us brings to any choice we make. These and other philosophers have taken us right back to the beginnings of western thinking (described in Chapter Three) and called into question its fundamental premise.

*　*　*

At the beginning of this chapter, I mentioned that the meaning of western civilization has been thrown into doubt. Perhaps it is more accurate to say that it has been given a new meaning. But what is that new meaning, and does it help us to answer the question 'What is civilization?' that I posed right at the beginning of the book? Indeed, we now need to ask what the history of the west, outlined in the last few hundred pages, tells us about our civilization.

There are two answers to this. First, the history of the last few decades shows us that the leadership of the west has been keen to promote an outlook of moral certainty, where the world is divided into good and evil. It should not surprise us that the concept of civilization has been resurrected and put to use in promoting this outlook. We need (or we are taught) to see the world in a clear and unconfused and unambiguous way; so civilization stands for everything good, and words like chaos, anarchy, terror stand for everything evil. All we need to do is use one to defeat the other.

The second answer is more subtle and takes into account the whole of western history. It is clear that, since its invention in the fifteenth century, and its formal adoption 300 years later, civilization has come to be the story that we tell ourselves in order to secure our place in the world. From the adoption of the Greeks and Romans into the Great Chain of History to the alliance against Nazism, the idea of civilization has served to weld the people of the west together, to give them a common system of beliefs and history. It is also clear that the story of civilization that we are presently being told is simply not credible. There is a profound mismatch between the simplistic rhetoric of good and evil, of the superiority of western values and the historic necessity to bring these to every part of the planet on the one hand, and the real experience, hopes and desires of western people on the other. This is a story that is supposed to bring us comfort and reassurance that whatever the ups and downs, we are heading in the right, inevitable direction – but we no longer believe it.

There remains a belief, particularly among liberal westerners, that this is simply a short-term crisis brought on by the hypocritical piety of certain leaders. There is even an idea that the current situation has been brought about by irrational, religious-based ideas, and that a healthy dose of rationalism will put us back on course. The history of the last 2,500 years, and the last 150 years in particular, shows that this is an illusion. The fundamental western belief that there are rational ways of organizing the world which will bring benefit to all has been at the root of every human-made catastrophe that has overtaken us; yet many of us still believe that we have a bounden duty to bring our simplistic, universalizing, 'progressive' systems of government, economics, education, policing, judiciary and morals to every part of every society on the planet. The uncomfortable truth we need to face is that this belief is as dangerous to humanity as military conquest. Were we to face this honestly, we would have brought real understanding to our search for the meaning of civilization.

The caravan of universal standardization rumbles on, enriching and empowering some, impoverishing and uprooting many others. And in the meantime, the citizens of the west do what they can to accommodate the losses they feel, and to construct lives of real meaning, while making art that reminds them of what it feels like to be truly human. Which then is western civilization – the relentless search for universal significance, the continual emasculation of lives and minds through the machinery of standardization, or the goods produced, and the lives lived, in compensation?

ACKNOWLEDGEMENTS, REFERENCES AND FURTHER READING

W<small>HILE</small> the conception was my sole responsibility, the gestation and birth of this book would not have been possible without the support, encouragement and constructive criticism of my editors Will Sulkin and Jörg Hensgen, whose expertise and experience helped me to steer a path through the potentially overwhelming demands of the subject. This has been a real collaboration.

There are several reasons why I have not attempted a comprehensive bibliography of western civilization. The scope of the subject means that such a bibliography would be both enormous and close to useless. It is now possible for anyone with access to a computer to search, for example, the entire catalogue of the British Library, which gives detailed bibliographical information on virtually every work published in English (as well as many others), allowing readers to track down books with ease. In addition, many of the texts that are relevant to this book are classic works that are available in a variety of editions, including series such as Penguin Classics and Oxford World Classics, all of which carry modern introductions. The cultural products of western civilization can be seen all around us, and it would seem superfluous and selective to list works of literature in a book that includes reference to painting, architecture, film and other art forms. So, while novelists, for example, are referred to in the text, I have not felt it necessary to list their works in this section.

For all these reasons I have simply given, for each chapter, a short list of books that are particularly relevant, or are directly quoted; citing, where appropriate, a modern edition of a classic or contemporary work. In addition I have listed below some recent or recently re-issued books that are mostly available in paperback editions, and that should be of interest to general readers. The first list gives books that bear on every phase of western history, while the second details some outstanding works on particular periods.

General works

Hugh Brogan (1999) *History of the USA*, 2nd edn, Penguin, London
John Carey (ed.) (1987) *Faber Book of Reportage*, Faber, London
Norman Davies (1996) *Europe: A History*, Pimlico, London
Ernst Gombrich (1995) *The Story of Art*, 16th edn, Phaidon, London
John Gray (2002) *Straw Dogs: Thoughts on Humans and Other Animals*, Granta, London
Peter Hall (1998) *Cities in Civilization*, Phoenix, London
Eric Hobsbawm and Terence Ranger (eds.) (1983) *The Invention of Tradition*, Cambridge University Press, Cambridge
John Keegan (1993) *The History of Warfare*, Pimlico, London

Recent books on specific topics, in rough chronological order of period covered

Barry Cunliffe (2001) *Facing the Ocean: The Atlantic and Its Peoples*, Oxford University Press, Oxford
Roberto Calasso (1993) *The Marriage of Cadmus and Harmony*, Jonathan Cape, London
Peter Brown (2003) *The Rise of Western Christendom*, 2nd edn, Blackwell, Oxford
Robert Bartlett (1993) *The Making of Europe: Conquest, Colonization and Cultural Change, 930–1350*, Allen Lane, London
Lauro Martines (2002) *Power and Imagination: City-States in Renaissance Italy*, 2nd edn, Pimlico, London
Diarmaid MacCullough (2003) *Reformation: Europe's House Divided, 1490–1700*, Penguin, London
Michael Bogdanov (2003) *Shakespeare: The Director's Cut, Volume 1*, Capercaille, Edinburgh
John Gray (1998) *False Dawn: The Delusions of Global Capitalism*, Granta, London
John Carey (1992) *The Intellectuals and the Masses*, Faber, London
Lawrence Rees (1997) *The Nazis: A Warning from History*, BBC, London
George Evans (1962, re-issued 1999) *Ask the Fellows Who Cut the Hay*, Faber, London
Nik Cohn (1967) *Awopbopaloobop alopbamboom: Pop from the Beginning*, Paladin; re-issued by Pimlico, London, 2004

Steven Jay Schneider (ed.) (2003) *1001 Movies You Must See Before You Die*, Cassell, London

National Commission on Terrorist Attacks upon the United States (2004) *The 9/11 Commission Report*, Norton, New York

Prologue

Fernand Braudel (1993) *A History of Civilizations*, Penguin, New York and London

Peter Brown (1967) *Augustine of Hippo*, Faber, London

Henry Buckle (1857–61) *History of Civilisation in England*, Parker & Son, London

Jacob Burckhardt (1869) *The Civilization of the Renaissance in Italy*, Phaidon, London

Kenneth Clark (1969) *Civilisation*, BBC; John Murray, London

Norman Davies (1996) *Europe: A History*, Pimlico, London

Jared Diamond (1997) *Guns, Germs and Steel*, Jonathan Cape, London

Richard J. Evans (1997) *In Defence of History*, Granta, London

Felipe Fernández-Armesto (2000) *Civilizations*, Macmillan, London

Orlando Figes (1996) *A People's Tragedy*, Pimlico, London

Sigmund Freud (1930), *Civilization and Its Discontents*, Penguin Freud Library, Volume 12, London, 1985

P. D. James (1990) *The Omnibus P. D. James*, Faber, London

John Keegan (1993) *The History of Warfare*, Pimlico, London

Ian MacDonald (1995) *Revolution in the Head: The Beatles' Songs and the Sixties*, Pimlico, London

Christian Meier (1999) *Athens: A Portrait of the City in Its Golden Age*, Pimlico, London

John Stuart Mill (1859) *On Liberty and Other Essays*, Oxford University Press, Oxford, 1991

W. C. Sellar and R. J. Yeatman (1930) *1066 and All That*, Methuen, London; re-issued by Sutton, Stroud, 1993

Oswald Spengler (1918, 1922; English trans. 1926) *The Decline of the West*, 2 vols., Knopf, New York

Robert Tignor, et al. (2002) *Worlds Together, Worlds Apart*, Norton, New York and London

Arnold Joseph Toynbee (1934–54) *A Study of History*, 10 vols., Oxford University Press, Oxford

Chapter 1: In the Beginning

Françoise Audouze and Olivier Büchsenschütz (1991) *Towns, Villages and Countryside of Celtic Europe*, Batsford, London

Julius Caesar, *The Conquest of Gaul*, Penguin, Harmondsworth, 1951

Kevin Crossley-Holland (1980), *Norse Myths: Gods of the Vikings*, Penguin, London

Barry Cunliffe (1997) 'In Search of the Celts', in Nora Chadwick (1971; paperback edition 1997), *The Celts*, Penguin, London

Barry Cunliffe (2001) *Facing the Ocean: The Atlantic and Its Peoples*, Oxford University Press, Oxford

Daniela Dueck (2000) *Strabo of Amasia: A Greek Man of Letters in Augustan Rome*, Routledge, New York and Rome

Frank Kermode (1967) *The Sense of an Ending: Studies in the Theory of Fiction*, Oxford University Press, New York

Lloyd Laing (1980) *The Origins of Britain*, Routledge, London

The Mabinogion, trans. by Gwyn Jones and Thomas Jones, Everyman, London, 1989; revised 1993

Steven Mithen (2003) *After the Ice: A Global Human History, 20,000–5,000 BC*, Phoenix, London

J. Porter (1995) *Anglo-Saxon Riddles*, Anglo-Saxon Books, Hockwold-cum-Wilton

Richard Rudgley (2002), *Barbarians: Secrets of the Dark Ages*, Channel Four, London

Tacitus, *Germania*, Penguin, Harmondsworth, 1970

Chapter 2: A Torrent of Words

Aeschylus, *Prometheus Bound* and other plays, Penguin London, 1961

A. Andrewes (1977) 'Kleisthenes' Reform Bill', *Classical Quarterly*, 27, 241–8

Aristotle, *The Constitution of Athens* and *The Politics*, Cambridge University Press, Cambridge, 1996

John Boardman (ed.) (1982–91) *The Cambridge Ancient History*, 2nd edn, Cambridge University Press, Cambridge

Roberto Calasso (1993) *The Marriage of Cadmus and Harmony*, Jonathan Cape, London

James Davidson (1997) *Courtesans and Fishcakes: The Consuming Passions of Classical Athens*, HarperCollins, London

Simon Garfield (2001) *Mauve*, Norton, New York

Ernst Gombrich (1995) *The Story of Art*, 16th edn, Phaidon, London

Robert Graves (1960) *The Greek Myths*, Penguin, London

Allan Haley (1995) *Alphabet: The History, Evolution and Design of the Letters We Use Today*, Thames and Hudson, London

B. R. Haydon (1847) *Autobiography and Journals*, quoted in John Carey (ed.), *Faber Book of Reportage*, Faber, London, 1987

Herodotus, *The Histories*, Penguin, London, 1996

Homer, *The Iliad*, Penguin, Harmondsworth, 1950
Homer, *The Odyssey*, Penguin, Harmondsworth, 1946
Robert K. Logan (1986) *The Alphabet Effect*, Morrow, New York
Christian Meier (2000) *Athens: A Portrait of the City in Its Golden Age*, Pimlico, London
Sabine Oswalt (1969), *Greek and Roman Mythology*, Collins, Glasgow and Follett, Chicago
Sophocles, *The Three Theban Plays*, introduction by Bernard Knox, Penguin, London, 1982
W. E. Thompson (1971) 'The deme in Kleisthenes' reforms', *Symbolae Osloenses*, 46, 72–9
Thucydides, *History of the Peloponnesian War*, Penguin, Harmondsworth, 1972
B. Warmington (1960) *Carthage*, Pelican, London

Chapter 3: The Birth of Abstraction

(All of Plato and Aristotle's surviving works are available in modern editions in series such as Penguin Classics or the Loeb Classical Library. Surviving works by earlier Greek philosophers are given in Barnes.)
Jonathan Barnes (1987) *Early Greek Philosophy*, Penguin, London
Paul Cartledge (1999) *Democritus*, Routledge, London
Benjamin Farrington (1944) *Greek Science*, Penguin, Harmondsworth
Michael Grant (1982) *From Alexander to Cleopatra: The Hellenistic World*, Weidenfeld, London
John Gray (2002) *Straw Dogs: Thoughts on Humans and Other Animals*, Granta, London
R. M. Hare (1982) *Plato*, Oxford University Press, Oxford
John Keegan (1993) *The History of Warfare*, Pimlico, London
Karl Popper (1945) *The Open Society and Its Enemies, Volume One: The Spell of Plato*, Routledge, London
Giorgio di Santillana (1961) *The Origins of Scientific Thought*, New American Library, New York
F. W. Walbank (1992) *The Hellenistic World*, 3rd impression, Fontana, London
Xenophon, *A History of My Times (Hellenica)*, Penguin, London, 1979

Chapter 4: The Universal Civilization

Cicero, *Murder Trials*, Penguin, Harmondsworth, 1975
Cicero, *On the Good Life*, Penguin, Harmondsworth, 1971
T. J. Cornell (1995) *The Beginnings of Rome: Italy and Rome from the Bronze Age to the Punic Wars, c.1000–263 BC*, Routledge, London

Edward Gibbon, *The History of the Decline and Fall of the Roman Empire*,
    Penguin, London, 1996
Peter Hall (1998) *Cities in Civilization*, Phoenix, London
Ted Hughes (1997) *Tales from Ovid*, Faber, London
Livy, *The Early History of Rome*, Penguin, London, 2002
Marcus Aurelius, *Meditations*, Penguin, Harmondsworth, 1964
Plutarch, *The Lives of the Noble Greeks and Romans*, Bodley Head, 1864
I. A. Richmond (1963) *Roman Britain*, 2nd edn, Penguin, Harmondsworth
Seneca, *Letters from a Stoic*, Penguin, Harmondsworth, 1969
Tacitus, *The Annals of Imperial Rome*, Penguin, Harmondsworth, 1956
Virgil, *The Aeneid*, Penguin, London, 1990

Chapter 5: Augustine's Vision of Christianity

Peter Brown (1967) *Augustine of Hippo: A Biography*, Faber, London
Peter Brown (1995) *Authority and the Sacred: Aspects of the Christianisation
    of the Roman World*, Cambridge University Press, Cambridge
Robert Carroll and Stephen Prickett (1996) 'Introduction: the Bible as a
    Book', in *The Bible, Authorized King James Version with Apocrypha*,
    Oxford University Press, Oxford
Eusebius, *The Proof of the Gospel (Demonstratio Evangelica)*, London,
    1920
Keith Hopkins (1999) *A World Full of Gods: Pagans, Jews and Christians
    in the Roman Empire*, Phoenix, London
Brian Moynihan (2002) *The Faith: A History of Christianity*, Pimlico, London
Pliny, *Letters of the Younger Pliny*, Penguin, Harmondsworth, 1963
Suetonius, *Lives of the Twelve Caesars*, Wordsworth, Ware, 1997

Chapter 6: Religion as Civilization

Robert Bartlett (1993) *The Making of Europe: Conquest, Colonization and
    Cultural Change, 930–1350*, Allen Lane, London
Bede, *The Ecclesiastical History of the English People*, Oxford University
    Press, Oxford, 1969
Peter Brown (1982) *Society and the Holy in Late Antiquity*, Faber, London
Peter Brown (2003) *The Rise of Western Christendom*, 2nd edn, Blackwell,
    Oxford
The Cloud of Unknowing, Penguin, Harmondsworth, 1961
Barry Cunliffe (2001) *Facing the Ocean: The Atlantic and its Peoples*,
    Oxford University Press, Oxford
H. Daniel-Rops (1959) *The Church in the Dark Ages*, Dent, London
Einhard, quoted in Norman Cantor (ed.) (1963) *The Medieval World*,
    Macmillan, New York

Peregrine Horden and Nicholas Purcell (2005) *The Corrupting Sea: A Study of Mediterranean History*, Blackwell, Oxford

Albert Hourani (1991) *A History of the Arab Peoples*, Faber, London

Emmanuel le Roy Ladurie (1978) *Montaillou: Cathars and Catholics in a French village 1294–1324*, Penguin, London

William Langland, *Piers Plowman: The Vision of a People's Christ*, Dent, London, 1912

Robert Latouche (1967) *The Birth of the Western Economy: Economic Aspects of the Dark Ages*, 2nd edn, Methuen, London

Rosamund McKitterick (ed.) (2001) *The Early Middle Ages: Europe 400–1000*, Oxford University Press, Oxford

Paul E. Sigmund (ed.) (1988) *St Thomas Aquinas on Politics and Ethics*, Norton, New York and London

Preben Sorenson (1997) 'Religions Old and New', in *Oxford Illustrated History of the Vikings*, ed. Peter Sawyer, Oxford University Press, Oxford

Henry Osborn Taylor (1901) *The Classical Heritage of the Middle Ages*, Harper and Row, New York, 1958

Chapter 7: Another Way of Living

John Hutchinson and D. M. Palliser (1980) *York*, Bartholomew, Edinburgh

Maurice Keen (1968) *A History of Medieval Europe*, Routledge, London; Penguin, London, 1991

Michael Middleton (1987) *Man Made the Town*, Bodley Head, London

Lewis Mumford (1938) *The Culture of Cities*, Secker and Warburg, London

Josiah C. Russell (1972) 'Population in Europe', in Carlo M. Cipolla (ed.), *The Fontana Economic History of Europe, Volume I: The Middle Ages*, Fontana, Glasgow

Chapter 8: Art as Civilization

Kenneth R. Bartlett (ed.) (1992) *The Civilization of the Italian Renaissance: A Sourcebook*, Heath, Lexington and Toronto

John Berger (1972) *Ways of Seeing*, BBC and Penguin, Harmondsworth

Giovanni Boccaccio, *The Decameron*, Penguin, Harmondsworth, 1972

Michael Bogdanov (2003) *Shakespeare: The Director's Cut, Volume 1*, Capercaille, Edinburgh

Gene Brucker (1969) *Renaissance Florence*, Wiley, New York and Chichester

Gene Brucker (1977) *The Civic World of Early Renaissance Florence*, Princeton University Press, Princeton

Peter Burke (1987) *The Italian Renaissance: Culture and Society in Italy*, 2nd edn, Polity, Cambridge

Kenneth Clark (1969) *Civilisation*, BBC and John Murray, London
Ernst Gombrich (1950, 1995) *The Story of Art*, 16th edn, Phaidon, London
Lisa Jardine (1996) *Worldly Goods: A New History of the Renaissance*,
   Macmillan, London
Ross King (2000) *Brunelleschi's Dome*, Pimlico, London
Niccolò Machiavelli, *The Prince*, Penguin, London, 1999
Lauro Martines (2002) *Power and Imagination: City-States in Renaissance
   Italy*, 2nd edn, Pimlico, London
Giorgio Vasari, *Lives of the Artists*, Penguin, Harmondsworth, 1965

Chapter 9: The Search for the Christian Life

Norman Cantor (ed.) (1963) *The Medieval World*, Macmillan, New York
David Englander (ed.) (1990) *Culture and Belief in Europe 1450–1600*,
   Open University Press; Blackwell, Oxford
Erasmus, *Praise of Folly*, Penguin, London, 1994
Vivien Green (1998) *The European Reformation*, Sutton, Stroud
Diarmaid MacCullough (2003) *Reformation: Europe's House Divided,
   1490–1700*, Penguin, London
François Rabelais, *Gargantua and Pantagruel*, Penguin, Harmondsworth,
   1955
R. H. Tawney (1926) *Religion and the Rise of Capitalism*, John Murray,
   London: Penguin edition, 1990

Chapter 10: Kings, Armies and Nations

M. S. Anderson (1988) *War and Society in Europe of the Old Regime,
   1618–1789*, Leicester University Press, Leicester
Joseph Bergin (ed.) (2001) *The Seventeenth Century: Europe 1598–1715*,
   Oxford University Press, Oxford
John Brewer (1989) *Sinews of Power: War, Money and the English State
   1688–1763*, Unwin Hyman, London and Knopf, New York
Euan Cameron (ed.) (1999) *Early Modern Europe*, Oxford University Press,
   Oxford
Harif Kureishi (2005) 'The arduous conversation will continue', *Guardian*,
   19 July
Colin Martin and Geoffrey Parker (1999) *The Spanish Armada*, revised
   edn, Mandolin, Manchester
Geoffrey Parker (1985) *The Dutch Revolt*, revised edn, Penguin, London
Geoffrey Parker (1996) *The Military Revolution: Military Innovation and
   the Rise of the West, 1500–1800*, 2nd edn, Cambridge University Press,
   Cambridge
Clifford J. Rogers (ed.) (1995) *The Military Revolution Debate: Readings*

on the Military Transformation of Early Modern Europe, Westview Press, Oxford

Frank Tallett (1992) *War and Society in Early Modern Europe, 1495–1715*, Routledge, London

Philip Bobbitt (2002) *The Shield of Achilles: War, Peace and the Course of History*, Knopf, New York and Penguin, London

Hans Zinsser (1934) *Rats, Lice and History*, Little, Brown, Boston

Chapter 11: Us and Them

Hugh Brogan (1999) *History of the USA*, 2nd edn, Penguin, London

Elwood Harvey (1853) in Harriet Beecher Stowe, *A Key to Uncle Tom's Cabin*, quoted in John Carey (ed.) *Faber Book of Reportage*, Faber, London, 1987

Samuel Gridley Howe (1853) letter to Charles Sumner, quoted in John Carey (ed.) *Faber Book of Reportage*, Faber, London, 1987

Bartolomé de las Casas (*c.* 1542) *Brief Report on the Destruction of the Indians*, quoted in John Carey (ed.), *Faber Book of Reportage*, Faber, London, 1987

John Lynch (1991) *Spain 1516–1598: From Nation State to World Empire*, Blackwell, Oxford

Antony Pagden (1993) *European Encounters with the New World*, Yale University Press, Newhaven and London

Geoffrey Parker (1995) *Philip II*, 3rd edn, Open Court, Chicago

Juan Ginés de Sepúlveda, *Democrates alter de justi belli apud Indos*, quoted in David Englander (ed.) *Culture and Belief in Europe 1450–1600*, Open University Press; Blackwell, Oxford, 1990

Robert Tignor, et al. (2002) *Worlds Together, Worlds Apart*, Norton, New York and London

James Walvin (1992) *Black Ivory: Slavery in the British Empire*, 2nd edn, Blackwell, Malden

James Walvin (1999) *The Slave Trade*, Sutton, Stroud

James Scott Wheeler (1999) *The Making of a World Power: War and the Military Revolution in Seventeenth-Century England*, Sutton, Stroud

Chapter 12: The Rational Individual

Quotations from Sir John Davies, Edward Sexby and Colonel Rainsborough can be found in Wootton; Edmund Calamy is quoted in Hill.

Francis Bacon, *The Major Works*, Oxford University Press, Oxford, 1996

Euan Cameron (ed.) (1999) *Early Modern Europe*, Oxford University Press, Oxford

Stillman Drake and Israel Drabkin (1969) *Mechanics in Sixteenth-Century Italy*, University of Wisconsin Press, Madison

Stillman Drake (1980) *Galileo*, Oxford University Press, Oxford

René Descartes, *Discourse on Method and Other Writings*, Penguin, London, 1968

Galileo Galilei, *Two New Sciences*, Wall and Thompson, Toronto, 1989

Hugo Grotius, *A Grotius Reader*, T. M. C. Asser Instituut, The Hague, 1983

Christopher Hill (1972) *The World Turned Upside Down*, Penguin, London

Thomas Hobbes, *Leviathan*, Penguin, London, 1981

John Locke, *Two Treatises of Government*, Everyman, London, 1993

Michel de Montaigne, *The Complete Essays*, Penguin, London, 1993

Thomas More, *Utopia*, Penguin, London, 1965

Steven Shapin (1996) *The Scientific Revolution*, University of Chicago Press, Chicago and London

Keith Thomas (1971) *Religion and the Decline of Magic*, Penguin, London

David Wootton (ed.) (1986) *Divine Right and Democracy: An Anthology of Political Writing in Stuart England*, Penguin, London

Chapter 13: Enlightenment and Revolution

Quotations from Voltaire, Rousseau, Montesquieu and Dr Johnson can be found in Hampson; Patrick Henry and Thomas Jefferson are quoted in Brogan.

Hugh Brogan (1999) *History of the USA*, 2nd edn, Penguin, London

Carl von Clausewitz, *On War*, Penguin, London, 1982

Bernard Crick (2002) *Democracy*, Oxford University Press, Oxford

Robert Darnton (1984) *The Great Cat Massacre and Other Episodes in French Cultural History*, Basic Books, New York

Benjamin Franklin, *The Autobiography and Other Writings*, Penguin, New York, 1986

Johann Wolfgang von Goethe, *The Sorrows of Young Werther*, Penguin, London, 1989

Norman Hampson (1968) *The Enlightenment: An Evaluation of Its Assumptions and Values*, Penguin, London

Colin Jones (2002) *The Great Nation: France from Louis XV to Napoleon*, Allen Lane, London

Sebastian Mercier, quoted in Peter Martland (ed.) (2002) *The Future of the Past*, Pimlico, London

J. G. Millingen (*c.* 1793) quoted in John Thompson (1938), *English Witnesses of the French Revolution*, Oxford, Blackwell

Thomas Paine, *Rights of Man*, Wordsworth, Ware, 1996

Roy Porter (2000) *Enlightenment: Britain and the Creation of the Modern World*, Penguin, London

Jean-Jacques Rousseau, *The Social Contract*, Wordsworth, Ware, 1998

Laurence Sterne, *The Life and Opinions of Tristram Shandy, Gentleman*, Penguin, London, 2003

Laurence Sterne, *A Sentimental Journey*, Penguin, London, 2001

Lawrence Stone (1969) 'Literacy and Education in England 1640–1900', *Past and Present*, 42

J. M. Thompson (1952) *Napoleon Bonaparte*, Blackwell, Oxford

Richard Twiss (1792) *A Trip to Paris*, quoted in John Carey (ed.), *Faber Book of Reportage*, Faber, London, 1987

Giambattista Vico, *New Science*, Penguin, London, 1999

Voltaire, *Philosophical Dictionary*, Penguin, London, 1972

Voltaire, *Candide and Other Stories*, Oxford University Press, Oxford, 1990

Max Weber, *The Protestant Ethic and the Spirit of Capitalism*, Roxbury, Los Angeles and Blackwell, Oxford, 2002

William Wordsworth and Samuel Taylor Coleridge, *Lyrical Ballads*, Penguin, London, 1999

Chapter 14: Industrialization and Nationalism

Quotations from Earl Grey and Lord Salisbury can be found in Cunningham.

Anon., quoted in E. P. Thompson (1963) *The Making of the English Working Class*, Penguin, London

Lord Henry Brougham (1838) *Spectator*, 7 October

John Carey (1973) *The Violent Effigy: A Study of Dickens' Imagination*, Faber, London

J. D. Chambers and G. E. Mingay (1966) *The Agricultural Revolution, 1750–1880*, Batsford, London

Hugh Cunningham (2001) *The Challenge of Democracy, Britain 1832–1918*, Pearson, Harlow

John Gray (1998) *False Dawn: The Delusions of Global Capitalism*, Granta, London

Peter Mathias (1983) *The First Industrial Nation: The Economic History of Britain, 1700–1914*, 2nd edn, Routledge, London

Hippolyte Taine (1872) *Notes on England*, quoted in John Carey (ed.) *Faber Book of Reportage*, Faber, London, 1987

E. P. Thompson (1963) *The Making of the English Working Class*, Penguin, London

David Thomson (1950) *England in the Nineteenth Century*, Penguin, London

Ian Watt (1957) *The Rise of the Novel*, Chatto, London

Igor Webb (1981) *From Custom to Capital: the English Novel and the Industrial Revolution*, Cornell University Press, Ithaca and London

Chapter 15: From Rural Colonies to Industrial Continent

Quotations from Thomas Jefferson, Generals Carleton and Sheridan, and John Logan can be found in Carroll and Noble; quotes from Lincoln's speeches are taken from van Doren Stern.

Edward L. Ayers (1992) *The Promise of the New South: Life after Reconstruction*, Oxford University Press, New York

Hugh Brogan (1999) *History of the USA*, 2nd edn, Penguin, London

Dee Brown (1970) *Bury My Heart at Wounded Knee: An Indian History of the American West*, Holt, Rinehart and Winston, New York

Peter N. Carroll and David W. Noble (1988) *The Free and the Unfree: A New History of the United States*, 2nd edn, Penguin, New York

Henry Luce (1941) 'The American Century', *Life*, 17 February

Louis Menand (2001) *The Metaphysical Club*, Farrar, Strauss and Giroux, New York

William G. Roy (1997) *Socializing Capital: The Rise of the Large Industrial Corporation in America*, Princeton University Press, New York

Philip van Doren Stern (ed.) (1940) *The Life and Writings of Abraham Lincoln*, Random House, New York; Modern Library, 2000

Helen Hornbeck Tanner (1995) *The Settling of North America*, Macmillan, New York

Richard S. Tedlow (1991) *The Rise of the American Business Corporation*, Harwood, New York

Henry David Thoreau, *Walden* and *Civil Disobedience*, Penguin, New York, 1983

Alexis de Tocqueville, *Democracy in America*, Wordsworth, Ware, 1998

Walt Whitman, *Leaves of Grass and Other Writings*, Norton, New York and London, 2002

Chapter 16: Towards the Abyss

Quotations from Thomas Macaulay and J. L. Garvin are from Thomson; Helmuth von Moltke is quoted in Bond.

Brian Bond (1983) *War and Society in Europe, 1870–1970*, Leicester University Press, Leicester

Carl von Clausewitz (1832) *On War*, Routledge, London, 1968

George Dangerfield (1936) *The Strange Death of Liberal England*, Constable, London

Mike Davis (2000) *Late Victorian Holocausts*, Verso, London

Paul Fussell (1975) *The Great War and Modern Memory*, Oxford University Press, Oxford

Henry James (1914) letter to Rhoda Broughton, quoted in Frank Kermode and Anita Kermode (1995) *The Oxford Book of Letters*, Oxford University Press, Oxford

John Keegan (1993) *The History of Warfare*, Pimlico, London

John Stuart Mill, *On Liberty and Other Essays*, Oxford University Press, Oxford, 1998

Karl Polanyi (1944) *The Great Transformation: The Political and Economic Origins of Our Time*, Farrar and Rinehart, New York

Douglas Porch (2000) *Wars of Empire*, Cassell, London

Gerhard Ritter (1969–73) *The Sword and the Scepter*, 4 vols., Allen Lane, London

David Thomson (1950) *England in the Nineteenth Century*, Penguin, Harmondsworth

Chapter 17: The End of Civilization

Quotations from Calvin Coolidge and Herbert Hoover are from Curtis; Ernst Röhm is quoted in Rees, Adolf Hitler in Kershaw.

Götz Aly and Susanne Heim (2002) *Architects of Annihilation: Auschwitz and the Logic of Destruction*, Weidenfeld, London

Dietrich Bonhoeffer, *Letters and Papers from Prison*, published posthumously by SCM Press, 1953

John Carey (1992) *The Intellectuals and the Masses*, Faber, London

E. H. Carr (1979) *The Russian Revolution: From Lenin to Stalin (1917–1929)*, Macmillan, London

Robert Conquest (1968, 1990) *The Great Terror: A Reassessment*, Pimlico, London

Robert Conquest (1986, 2002) *Harvest of Sorrow: Soviet Collectivisation and the Terror-famine*, Pimlico, London

Adam Curtis (2002) 'The Century of the Self', television series, broadcast on BBC2 beginning 17 March 2002

Orlando Figes (1996) *A People's Tragedy*, Pimlico, London

M. I. Finley (1975) *The Use and Abuse of History*, Pimlico, London

Sigmund Freud (1930) *Civilization and Its Discontents*, Penguin Freud Library, Volume 12, London, 1985

Patrick Gordon-Walker quoted in John Carey (ed.), *The Faber Book of Reportage*, Faber, London, 1987

Brigitte Hamann (1999) *Hitler's Vienna: A Dictator's Apprenticeship*, Oxford University Press, New York and Oxford

Eric Hobsbawm (1994) *The Age of Extremes: The Short Twentieth Century, 1914–1991*, Michael Joseph, London

Ian Kershaw (1998, 2000) *Hitler*, 2 vols., Allen Lane, London

Victor Kravchenko (1946) *I Chose Freedom: The Personal and Political*

Life of a Soviet Official, Scribner, New York

Primo Levi (1960) *If This Is a Man*, Orion, London

Primo Levi (1988) *The Drowned and the Saved*, Sphere, London

Rosa Luxemburg (1961), *The Russian Revolution*, University of Michigan, Ann Arbor, 1961

Susan Neiman (2002) *Evil in Modern Thought: An Alternative History of Philosophy*, Princeton University Press, Princeton

Lawrence Rees (1997) *The Nazis: A Warning from History*, BBC, London

Gerhard Ritter (1969–73) *The Sword and the Scepter*, 4 vols., Allen Lane, London

Mark Roseman (2002) *The Villa, the Lake, the Meeting: Wannsee and the Final Solution*, Allen Lane, London

Aleksandr Solzhenitsyn (1973–76) *The Gulag Archipelago: 1918–1956*, Harper and Row, New York

Frank J. Sulloway (1979) *Freud, Biologist of the Mind*, Basic Books, New York

Slavoj Zizek (2005) 'The Two Totalitarianisms', *London Review of Books*, 27, 6, 17 March

Chapter 18: The Post-War World

David Anderson (2005) *Histories of the Hanged: Britain's Dirty War in Kenya and the End of Empire*, Weidenfeld, London

Tony Blair (2004) quoted in *Observer*, 6 June

Hugh Brogan (1999) *History of the USA*, 2nd edn, Penguin, London

Peter N. Carroll and David W. Noble (1988) *The Free and the Unfree: A New History of the United States*, 2nd edn, Penguin, New York

Nik Cohn (1967) *Awopbopaloobop alopbamboom: Pop from the Beginning*, Paladin, London; re-issued by Pimlico, London, 2004

George Evans (1962) *Ask the Fellows Who Cut the Hay*, Faber, London

Ian MacDonald (1995) *Revolution in the Head: The Beatles' Songs and the Sixties*, Pimlico, London

Ray Monk (1990) *Ludwig Wittgenstein: The Duty of Genius*, Jonathan Cape, London

Wayne Northcutt (ed.) (1992) *Historical Dictionary of French 4th and 5th Republics 1946–1991*, Greenwood Press, New York and London

Oxfam (2004) *Paying the Price*, Oxfam Campaign Report, Oxford

Douglas Porch (2000) *Wars of Empire*, Cassell, London

Barbara Rose (1970) *American Painting: The Twentieth Century*, 2nd edn, Macmillan, London

Steven Jay Schneider (ed.) (2003) *1001 Movies You Must See Before You Die*, Cassell, London

INDEX